Digital

Complete **Digital** Experience

Allow your students to save by purchasing a stand-alone MyEconLab directly from Pearson at **www.myeconlab.com**. Pearson's industry-leading learning solution features a **full Pearson eText** and course management functionality. Most importantly, MyEconLab helps you hold students accountable for class preparation and supports more active learning styles. Visit **www.myeconlab.com** to find out more.

Students can purchase a three-hole-punched, full-color version of the text via myeconlab.com at a **significant discount delivered right to their door**.

Instant eText Access

The **CourseSmart eBookstore** provides instant, online access to the textbook and course materials students need at a lower price. CourseSmart's eTextbooks are fully searchable and offer the same paging and appearance as the printed texts. You can preview eTextbooks online anytime at **www.coursesmart.com**.

Homework and Tutorial Only

Same great assessment technology without the **Pearson eText**.

Students can purchase a three-hole-punched, full-color version of the text via myeconlab.com at a **significant discount delivered right to their door**.

Digital + Print

Great Content + Great **Value**

Package our premium bound textbook with a MyEconLab access code for the most enduring student experience. Find out more at **www.myeconlab.com**.

Great Content + Great **Price**

Save your students money and promote an active learning environment by offering a Student Value Edition—a three-hole-punched, full-color version of the premium textbook that's available at a 35% discount—packaged with a MyEconLab access code at your bookstore.

Custom

Customized Solutions

Customize your textbook to match your syllabus. Trim your text to include just the chapters you need or add chapters from multiple books. With no unused material or unnecessary expense, Pearson Custom Solutions provides the right content you need for a course that's entirely your own. **www.pearsoncustom.com**

Contact your **Pearson representative** for more information on Pearson Choices.

Students learn best when they attend lectures and keep up with their reading and assignments... but learning shouldn't end when class is over.

MyEconLab *Picks Up Where Lectures and Office Hours Leave Off*

Instructors choose MyEconLab:

"MyEconLab offers them a way to practice every week. They receive immediate feedback and a feeling of personal attention. As a result, my teaching has become more targeted and efficient."

—**Kelly Blanchard, Purdue University**

"Students tell me that offering them MyEconLab is almost like offering them individual tutors."

—**Jefferson Edwards, Cypress Fairbanks College**

"Chapter quizzes offset student procrastination by ensuring they keep on task. If a student is having a problem, MyEconLab indicates exactly what they need to study."

—**Diana Fortier, Waubonsee Community College**

Students choose MyEconLab:

In a recent study, 87 percent of students who used MyEconLab regularly felt it improved their grade.

"It was very useful because it had EVERYTHING, from practice exams to exercises to reading. Very helpful."

—**student, Northern Illinois University**

"It was very helpful to get instant feedback. Sometimes I would get lost reading the book, and these individual problems would help me focus and see if I understood the concepts."

—**student, Temple University**

"I would recommend taking the quizzes on MyEconLab because they give you a true account of whether or not you understand the material."

—**student, Montana Tech**

Macroeconomics

PRINCIPLES, APPLICATIONS, AND TOOLS

SEVENTH EDITION

Arthur O'Sullivan
Lewis and Clark College

Steven M. Sheffrin
Tulane University

Stephen J. Perez
California State University, Sacramento

Prentice Hall

Boston   Columbus   Indianapolis   New York   San Francisco   Upper Saddle River
Amsterdam   Cape Town   Dubai   London   Madrid   Milan Munich   Paris   Montréal   Toronto
Delhi   Mexico City   São Paulo   Sydney   Hong Kong   Seoul   Singapore   Taipei   Tokyo

The Pearson Series in Economics

Abel/Bernanke/Croushore
*Macroeconomics**

Bade/Parkin
*Foundations of Economics**

Berck/Helfand
The Economics of the Environment

Bierman/Fernandez
Game Theory with Economic Applications

Blanchard
*Macroeconomics**

Blau/Ferber/Winkler
The Economics of Women, Men and Work

Boardman/Greenberg/Vining/Weimer
Cost-Benefit Analysis

Boyer
Principles of Transportation Economics

Branson
Macroeconomic Theory and Policy

Brock/Adams
The Structure of American Industry

Bruce
Public Finance and the American Economy

Carlton/Perloff
Modern Industrial Organization

Case/Fair/Oster
*Principles of Economics**

Caves/Frankel/Jones
World Trade and Payments: An Introduction

Chapman
Environmental Economics: Theory, Application, and Policy

Cooter/Ulen
Law & Economics

Downs
An Economic Theory of Democracy

Ehrenberg/Smith
Modern Labor Economics

Ekelund/Ressler/Tollison
*Economics**

Farnham
Economics for Managers

Folland/Goodman/Stano
The Economics of Health and Health Care

Fort
Sports Economics

Froyen
Macroeconomics

Fusfeld
The Age of the Economist

Gerber
*International Economics**

Gordon
*Macroeconomics**

Greene
Econometric Analysis

Gregory
Essentials of Economics

Gregory/Stuart
Russian and Soviet Economic Performance and Structure

Hartwick/Olewiler
The Economics of Natural Resource Use

Heilbroner/Milberg
The Making of the Economic Society

Heyne/Boettke/Prychitko
The Economic Way of Thinking

Hoffman/Averett
Women and the Economy: Family, Work, and Pay

Holt
Markets, Games and Strategic Behavior

Hubbard/O'Brien
*Economics**
*Money, Banking, and the Financial System**

Hughes/Cain
American Economic History

Husted/Melvin
International Economics

Jehle/Reny
Advanced Microeconomic Theory

Johnson-Lans
A Health Economics Primer

Keat/Young
Managerial Economics

Klein
Mathematical Methods for Economics

Krugman/Obstfeld/Melitz
*International Economics: Theory & Policy**

Laidler
The Demand for Money

Leeds/von Allmen
The Economics of Sports

Leeds/von Allmen/Schiming
*Economics**

Lipsey/Ragan/Storer
*Economics**

Lynn
Economic Development: Theory and Practice for a Divided World

Miller
*Economics Today**
Understanding Modern Economics

Miller/Benjamin
The Economics of Macro Issues

Miller/Benjamin/North
The Economics of Public Issues

Mills/Hamilton
Urban Economics

Mishkin
*The Economics of Money, Banking, and Financial Markets**
*The Economics of Money, Banking, and Financial Markets, Business School Edition**
*Macroeconomics: Policy and Practice**

Murray
Econometrics: A Modern Introduction

Nafziger
The Economics of Developing Countries

O'Sullivan/Sheffrin/Perez
*Economics: Principles, Applications and Tools**

Parkin
*Economics**

Perloff
*Microeconomics**
*Microeconomics: Theory and Applications with Calculus**

Perman/Common/McGilvray/Ma
Natural Resources and Environmental Economics

Phelps
Health Economics

Pindyck/Rubinfeld
*Microeconomics**

Riddell/Shackelford/Stamos/Schneider
Economics: A Tool for Critically Understanding Society

Ritter/Silber/Udell
*Principles of Money, Banking & Financial Markets**

Roberts
The Choice: A Fable of Free Trade and Protection

Rohlf
Introduction to Economic Reasoning

Ruffin/Gregory
Principles of Economics

Sargent
Rational Expectations and Inflation

Sawyer/Sprinkle
International Economics

Scherer
Industry Structure, Strategy, and Public Policy

Schiller
The Economics of Poverty and Discrimination

Sherman
Market Regulation

Silberberg
Principles of Microeconomics

Stock/Watson
Introduction to Econometrics
Introduction to Econometrics, Brief Edition

Studenmund
Using Econometrics: A Practical Guide

Tietenberg/Lewis
Environmental and Natural Resource Economics
Environmental Economics and Policy

Todaro/Smith
Economic Development

Waldman
Microeconomics

Waldman/Jensen
Industrial Organization: Theory and Practice

Weil
Economic Growth

Williamson
Macroeconomics

About the Authors

ARTHUR O'SULLIVAN

is a professor of economics at Lewis and Clark College in Portland, Oregon. After receiving his B.S. in economics at the University of Oregon, he spent two years in the Peace Corps, working with city planners in the Philippines. He received his Ph.D. in economics from Princeton University in 1981 and has taught at the University of California, Davis, and Oregon State University, winning teaching awards at both schools. He is the author of the best-selling textbook *Urban Economics*, currently in its seventh edition.

Professor O'Sullivan's research explores economic issues concerning urban land use, environmental protection, and public policy. His articles have appeared in many economics journals, including the *Journal of Urban Economics*, *Journal of Environmental Economics and Management*, *National Tax Journal*, *Journal of Public Economics*, and *Journal of Law and Economics*.

Professor O'Sullivan lives with his family in Portland, Oregon. For recreation, he enjoys hiking, kiteboarding, and squash.

STEVEN M. SHEFFRIN

is professor of economics and executive director of the Murphy Institute at Tulane University. Prior to joining Tulane in 2010, he was a faculty member at the University of California, Davis, and served as department chairman of economics and dean of social sciences. He has been a visiting professor at Princeton University, Oxford University, London School of Economics, and Nanyang Technological University, and he has served as a financial economist with the Office of Tax Analysis of the United States Department of the Treasury. He received his B.A. from Wesleyan University and his Ph.D. in economics from the Massachusetts Institute of Technology.

Professor Sheffrin is the author of 10 other books and monographs and over 100 articles in the fields of macroeconomics, public finance, and international economics. His most recent books include *Rational Expectations* (second edition) and *Property Taxes and Tax Revolts: The Legacy of Proposition 13* (with Arthur O'Sullivan and Terri Sexton).

Professor Sheffrin has taught macroeconomics and public finance at all levels, from general introduction to principles classes (enrollments of 400) to graduate classes for doctoral students. He is the recipient of the Thomas Mayer Distinguished Teaching Award in economics.

He lives with his wife Anjali (also an economist) in New Orleans, Louisiana, and has two daughters who have studied economics. In addition to a passion for current affairs and travel, he plays a tough game of tennis.

STEPHEN J. PEREZ

is a professor of economics and NCAA faculty athletics representative at California State University, Sacramento. After receiving his B.A. in economics at the University of California, San Diego, he was awarded his Ph.D. in economics from the University of California, Davis, in 1994. He taught economics at Virginia Commonwealth University and Washington State University before coming to California State University, Sacramento, in 2001. He teaches macroeconomics at all levels as well as econometrics, sports economics, labor economics, and mathematics for economists.

Professor Perez's research explores most macroeconomic topics. In particular, he is interested in evaluating the ability of econometric techniques to discover the truth, issues of causality in macroeconomics, and sports economics. His articles have appeared in many economics journals, including the *Journal of Monetary Economics*; *Econometrics Journal*; *Economics Letters*; *Journal of Economic Methodology*; *Public Finance and Management*; *Journal of Economics and Business*; *Oxford Bulletin of Economics and Statistics*; *Journal of Money, Credit, and Banking*; *Applied Economics*; and *Journal of Macroeconomics*.

TO OUR CHILDREN
CONOR, MAURA, MEERA, KIRAN, DAVIS, AND TATE

Editorial Director: Sally Yagan
Editor in Chief: Donna Battista
Acquisitions Editor: Noel Seibert
Editorial Project Manager: Carolyn Terbush
Managing Editor: Nancy H. Fenton
Senior Production Project Manager: Meredith Gertz
Supplements Production Project Manager: Alison Eusden
Director of Marketing: Kate Valentine
Executive Marketing Manager: Lori DeShazo
Marketing Assistant: Kim Lovato
Art Director/Cover Designer: Anthony Gemmellaro
Text Designer: Liz Harasymczuk Design
Illustration (Interior): GEX Publishing Services
Manager, Rights and Permissions, Text: Michael Joyce

Image Manager/Image Asset Services: Rachel Youdelman
Photo Researcher: Caroline Commins
Cover Illustration: Russell Lipp
Media Director: Susan Schoenberg
Senior Media Producer: Melissa Honig
Content Lead, MyEconLab: Noel Lotz
Full-Service Project Management: GEX Publishing Services
Composition: GEX Publishing Services
Printer/Binder: Courier Kendallville
Cover Printer: Lehigh, Phoenix/Hagerstown
Text Font: 10/12 Janson Text
Senior Manufacturing Buyer: Carol Melville

Credits and acknowledgments borrowed from other sources and reproduced, with permission, in this textbook appear on appropriate page within text (or on page 418).

Microsoft® and Windows® are registered trademarks of the Microsoft Corporation in the U.S.A. and other countries. Screen shots and icons reprinted with permission from the Microsoft Corporation. This book is not sponsored or endorsed by or affiliated with the Microsoft Corporation.

Many of the designations by manufacturers and seller to distinguish their products are claimed as trademarks. Where those designations appear in this book, and the publisher was aware of a trademark claim, the designations have been printed in initial caps or all caps.

Library of Congress Cataloging-in-Publication Data
O'Sullivan, Arthur.
  Macroeconomics: principles, applications, and tools / Arthur O'Sullivan, Steven M. Sheffrin, Stephen J. Perez. -- 7th ed.
     p. cm.
  Includes index.
  ISBN 978-0-13-255549-4 (pbk.)
  1. Macroeconomics. I. Sheffrin, Steven M. II. Perez, Stephen J. III. Title.

  HB172.5.O85 2012
  339--dc22

                    2010048072

10 9 8 7 6 5 4 3 2 1

Brief Contents

Contents

► APPLYING THE CONCEPTS

This is an Applications-driven textbook. We carefully selected over 120 real-world Applications that help students develop and master essential economic concepts. Here is an example of our approach from Chapter 4, "Demand, Supply, and Market Equilibrium."

APPLYING THE CONCEPTS

1 How do changes in demand affect prices?
   Hurricane Katrina and Baton Rouge Housing Prices

2 How do changes in supply in one market affect other markets?
   Honeybees and the Price of Ice Cream

3 How do simultaneous changes in supply and demand affect the equilibrium price?
   The Supply and Demand for Cruise Ship Berths

4 How do changes in supply affect prices?
   The Bouncing Price of Vanilla Beans

5 How do producers respond to higher prices?
   Drought in Australia and the Price of Rice

We start each chapter with three to five thought-provoking Applying the Concepts questions that convey important economic concepts.

Once we present the economic logic behind a concept, we illustrate its use with a real-world Application.

---

strawberries, raspberries, and almonds, leading to higher prices for these ingredients for ice cream. The higher prices for berries and nuts have increased the cost of producing food products, such as ice cream, increasing their prices as well.

Figure 4.15 shows the effects of the decline of the bee population on the market for ice cream. Increases in the prices of ingredients (berries and nuts) increase the cost of producing ice cream, shifting the supply curve upward. As a result, the equilibrium price of ice cream increases.

The collapsing of bee colonies is a mystery. The ice cream maker Häagen-Dazs donated money to Pennsylvania State University and the University of California, Davis to support research exploring the causes of CCD and possible solutions. To increase consumer awareness of the problem, Häagen Dazs launched a new flavor, Vanilla Honey Bee. **Related to Exercises 7.2 and 7.7.**

SOURCE: Based on Parija Kavilanz, "Disappearing Bees Threaten Ice Cream Sellers," *CNNMoney.com*, February 20, 2008.

► FIGURE 4.15
Honeybees and the Price of Ice Cream
A decrease in pollination by bees decreases the output of fruit and nuts, increasing the prices of some ingredients for ice cream. The resulting increase in the cost of producing ice cream shifts the supply curve upward, increasing the equilibrium price and decreasing the equilibrium quantity.

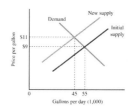

APPLICATION 3

THE SUPPLY AND DEMAND FOR CRUISE SHIP BERTHS

APPLYING THE CONCEPT #3: How do simultaneous changes in supply and demand affect the equilibrium price?

What happens when an increase in supply is combined with a decrease in demand? In 2009 the cruise industry invested $4.7 billion on 14 new ships, and in 2010 the industry launched 12 additional new ships. While the supply of cruise berths increased, the demand for cruises decreased, a result of a recession and lower real income. As shown in Figure 4.16, the simultaneous increase in supply and decrease in demand decreased the equilibrium price. To entice consumers, some cruise lines cut prices by as much as 40 percent. Although consumers responded by purchasing more cruises (about 3 percent more in 2009 than in 2008), the cruise lines' revenues decreased. For Carnival Corporation, the world's largest cruise line, total revenue decreased by 10 percent. **Related to Exercises 7.3 and 7.8.**

SOURCE: Based on "Dam the Torpedoes: Cruise Lines in the Recession," *Economist*, February 13, 2010, 67.

6.10 Zero Price for Used Newspapers. In 1987 you could sell a ton of used newspaper for $60. Five years later, you couldn't sell them at any price. In other words, the price of used newspapers dropped from $60 to zero in just five years. Over this period, the quantity of used newspapers bought and sold increased. What caused the drop in price? Illustrate your answer with a complete graph.

6.11 Decrease in the Price of Heroin. Between 1990 and 2003, the price of heroin decreased from $235 per gram to $76. Over the same period, the quantity of heroin consumed increased from 376 metric tons to 482 metric tons. Use a demand and supply graph to explain these changes in price and quantity.

4.7 Applications of Demand and Supply

7.1 Arrow up or down: Hurricane Katrina _____ the demand for housing in Baton Rouge, so the price of housing _____ and the quantity of housing _____. (Related to Application 1 on page 87.)

7.2 Arrows up or down: The decrease in the number of bee colonies _____ the supply of fruits and berries, _____ the cost of producing ice cream, and _____ the equilibrium price of ice cream. (Related to Application 2 on pages 87–88.)

7.3 Between 2008 and 2009, the equilibrium price of cruises _____ because _____ and demand _____. (Related to Application 3 on pages 88–89.)

7.4 Arrow up or down: The development of a sun-tolerant variety of the vanilla plant _____ the supply of vanilla and its price. (Related to Application 4 on pages 89–90.)

7.5 Arrow up or down: The drought in Australia _____ the supply of rice and _____ its price. (Related to Application 5 on page 90.)

7.6 **Katrina Victims Move Back.** Suppose that five [years] after Hurricane Katrina, half the people who ha[d relo]cated to Baton Rouge move back to a rebui[lt New] Orleans. Use a demand and supply graph of th[e Baton] Rouge housing market to show the market ef[fect of] the return of people to New Orleans. (Rel[ated to] Application 1 on page 87.)

7.7 **Honeybees and Ice Cream.** Suppose the de[cline in] bee colonies increases the prices of some ingr[edients] used to produce ice cream. Consider two flavor[s: choco]cream, strawberry and vanilla. The cost of pr[oducing] strawberry ice cream increases by 20 percent [and] the cost of producing vanilla ice cream incre[ases by] only 5 percent. Use a supply–demand graph t[o show] the implications for the equilibrium prices and [quanti]ties of the two flavors of ice cream. (Rel[ated to] Application 2 on pages 87–88.)

7.8 **Cruise Ships Berths.** Consider the change in th[e equi]librium quantity shown in Figure 4.16. Draw [a supply] graph (with a decrease in demand and an incr[ease in] supply) such that the equilibrium quantity (the [number] of passengers) decreases. What is the fundament[al dif]ference between your graph and Figure 4.16? (R[elated] to Application 3 on pages 88–89.)

7.9 **Artificial versus Natural Vanilla.** An artificia[l alter]native to natural vanilla is cheaper to produ[ce, but] doesn't taste as good. Suppose the makers of a[rtificial] vanilla discover a new recipe that improves it[s taste.] Use a demand and supply graph to show the eff[ect on] the equilibrium price and quantity of natural [vanilla.] (Related to Application 4 on pages 89–90.)

7.10 **Drought and Rice Prices.** Consider the mar[ket for] rice. Use a demand and supply graph to illust[rate the] following statement: "The drought was a major [factor] in a near doubling of rice prices." (Rel[ated to] Application 5 on page 90.)

ECONOMIC EXPERIMENT

Market Equilibrium

This simple experiment takes about 20 minutes. We start by dividing the class into two equal groups: consumers and producers.

• The instructor provides each consumer with a number indicating the maximum amount he or she is willing to pay (WTP) for a bushel of apples: The WTP is a number between $1 and $100. Each consumer has the opportunity to buy one bushel of apples per trading period. The consumer's score for a single trading period equals the gap between the WTP and the price actually paid for

apples. For example, if the consumer's WTP is $80 and he or she pays only $30 for apples, the consumer's score is $50. Each consumer has the option of not buying apples. This will be sensible if the best price the consumer can get exceeds the WTP. If the consumer does not buy apples, his or her score will be zero.

• The instructor provides each producer with a number indicating the cost of producing a bushel of apples (a number between $1 and $100). Each producer has the opportunity to sell one bushel per trading period. The producer's score for a single trading period equals the gap between the selling prices and the cost of producing

---

For each Application and Applying the Concept question, we provide exercises that test students' understanding of the concepts. In addition, some chapters contain an Economic Experiment section that gives them the opportunity to do their own economic analysis.

▶ WHY FIVE KEY PRINCIPLES?

In Chapter 2, "The Key Principles of Economics," we introduce the following five key principles and then apply them throughout the book:

1. **The Principle of Opportunity Cost.** The opportunity cost of something is what you sacrifice to get it.

2. **The Marginal Principle.** Increase the level of an activity as long as its marginal benefit exceeds its marginal cost. Choose the level at which the marginal benefit equals the marginal cost.

3. **The Principle of Voluntary Exchange.** A voluntary exchange between two people makes both people better off.

4. **The Principle of Diminishing Returns.** If we increase one input while holding the other inputs fixed, output will increase, but at a decreasing rate.

5. **The Real-Nominal Principle.** What matters to people is the real value of money or income—its purchasing power—not the face value of money or income.

This approach of repeating five key principles gives students the big picture—the framework of economic reasoning. We make the key concepts unforgettable by using them repeatedly, illustrating them with intriguing examples, and giving students many opportunities to practice what they've learned. Throughout the text, economic concepts are connected to the five key principles when the following callout is provided for each principle:

MARGINAL PRINCIPLE

Increase the level of an activity as long as its marginal benefit exceeds its marginal cost. Choose the level at which the marginal benefit equals the marginal cost.

▶ HOW IS THE BOOK ORGANIZED?

Chapter 1, "Introduction: What Is Economics?" uses three current policy issues—traffic congestion, poverty in Africa, and Japan's prolonged recession—to explain the economic way of thinking. Chapter 2, "The Key Principles of Economics," introduces the five principles we return to throughout the book. Chapter 3, "Exchange and Markets," is devoted entirely to exchange and trade. We discuss the fundamental rationale for exchange and introduce some of the institutions modern societies developed to facilitate trade.

Students need to have a solid understanding of demand and supply to be successful in the course. Many students have difficulty understanding movement along a curve versus shifts of a curve. To address this difficulty, we developed an innovative way to organize topics in Chapter 4, "Demand, Supply, and Market Equilibrium." We examine the law of demand and changes in quantity demanded, the law of supply and changes in quantity supplied, and then the notion of market equilibrium. After students have a firm grasp of equilibrium concepts,

we explore the effects of changes in demand and supply on equilibrium prices and quantities. For organization options, please see the alternative course sequence chart on page xiii.

Summary of the Macroeconomics Chapters

Part 2, "The Basic Concepts of Macroeconomics" (Chapters 5 and 6), introduces students to the key concepts—GDP, inflation, unemployment—that are used throughout the text and in everyday economic discussion. The two chapters in this section provide the building blocks for the rest of the book. Part 3, "The Economy in the Long Run" (Chapters 7 and 8), analyzes how the economy operates at full employment and explores the causes and consequences of economic growth.

Next we turn to the short run. We begin the discussion of business cycles, economic fluctuations, and the role of government in Part 4, "Economic Fluctuations and Fiscal Policy" (Chapters 9 through 12). We devote an entire chapter to the structure of government spending and revenues and the role of fiscal policy. In Part 5, "Money, Banking, and Monetary Policy" (Chapters 13 and 14), we introduce the key elements of both monetary theory and policy into our economic models. Part 6, "Inflation, Unemployment, and Economic Policy" (Chapters 15 through 17), brings the important questions of the dynamics of inflation and unemployment into our analysis. Finally, the last two chapters in Part 7, "The International Economy" (Chapters 18 and 19), provide an in-depth analysis of both international trade and finance.

A Few Features of Our Macroeconomics Chapters

The following are a few features of our macroeconomics chapters:

- **Flexibility.** A key dilemma confronting economics professors has always been how much time to devote to long-run topics, such as growth and production, versus short-run topics, such as economic fluctuations and business cycles. Our book is designed to let professors choose. It works like this: To pursue a long-run approach, professors should initially concentrate on Chapters 1 through 4, followed by Chapters 5 through 8.

- To focus on economic fluctuations, start with Chapters 1 through 4, present Chapter 5, "Measuring a Nation's Production and Income," and Chapter 6, "Unemployment and Inflation," and then turn to Chapter 9, "Aggregate Demand and Aggregate Supply."

- Chapter 11, "The Income-Expenditure Model," is self-contained, so instructors can either skip it completely or cover it as a foundation for aggregate demand.

- **Long Run.** Throughout most of the 1990s, the U.S. economy performed very well—low inflation, low unemployment, and rapid economic growth. This robust performance led to economists' increasing interest in trying to understand the processes of economic growth. Our discussion of economic growth in Chapter 8, "Why Do Economies Grow?" addresses the fundamental question of how long-term living standards are determined and why some countries prosper while others do not. This is the essence of economic growth. As Nobel Laureate Robert E. Lucas, Jr., once wrote, "Once you start thinking about growth, it is hard to think of anything else."

- **Short Run.** The great economic expansion of the 1990s came to an end in 2001, as the economy started to contract. The recession beginning in 2007 was the worst downturn since World War II. Difficult economic times remind us that macroeconomics is also concerned with understanding the causes and consequences of economic fluctuations. Why do economies experience recessions and depressions, and what steps can policymakers take to stabilize the economy and ease the devastation people suffer from them? This has been a constant theme of macroeconomics throughout its entire history and is covered extensively in the text.

- **Policy.** Macroeconomics is a policy-oriented subject, and we treat economic policy in virtually every chapter. We discuss both important historical and more recent macroeconomic events in conjunction with the theory. In addition, we devote Chapter 17, "Macroeconomic Policy Debates," to three important policy topics that recur frequently in macroeconomic debates: the role of government deficits, whether the Federal Reserve should target inflation or other objectives, and whether income or consumption should be taxed.

▶ MYECONLAB

myeconlab Both the text and supplement package provide ways for instructors and students to assess their knowledge and progress through the course. MyEconLab, the new standard in personalized online learning, is a key part of O'Sullivan, Sheffrin, and Perez's integrated learning package for the seventh edition.

For the Instructor

MyEconLab is an online course management, testing, and tutorial resource. Instructors can choose how much or how little time to spend setting up and using MyEconLab. Each chapter contains two Sample Tests, Study Plan Exercises, and Tutorial Resources. Student use of these materials requires no initial set-up by the instructor. The online Gradebook records each student's performance and time spent on the Tests and Study Plan and generates reports by student or by chapter. Instructors can assign tests, quizzes, and homework in MyEconLab using four resources:

- Preloaded Sample Test questions
- Problems similar to the end-of-chapter exercises
- Test Item File questions
- Self-authored questions using the Econ Exercise Builder

Exercises use multiple-choice, graph drawing, and free-response items, many of which are generated algorithmically so that each time a student works them, a different variation is presented. MyEconLab grades each of these problem types, even those with graphs. When working homework exercises, students receive immediate feedback with links to additional learning tools.

Customization and Communication MyEconLab in CourseCompass™ provides additional optional customization and communication tools. Instructors who teach distance learning courses or very large lecture sections find the CourseCompass format useful because they can upload course documents and assignments, customize the order of chapters, and use communication features such as Digital Drop Box and Discussion Board.

Experiments in MyEconLab Experiments are a fun and engaging way to promote active learning and mastery of important economic concepts. Pearson's experiments program is flexible and easy for instructors and students to use.

- Single-player experiments allow students to play an experiment against virtual players from anywhere at anytime with an Internet connection.
- Multiplayer experiments allow instructors to assign and manage a real-time experiment with their class.

In both cases, pre-and post-questions for each experiment are available for assignment in MyEconLab.

For the Student

MyEconLab puts students in control of their learning through a collection of tests, practice, and study tools tied to the online, interactive version of the textbook, and other media resources. Within MyEconLab's structured environment, students practice what they learn, test their understanding, and pursue a personalized Study Plan generated from their performance on Sample Tests and tests set by their instructors. At the core of MyEconLab are the following features:

- Sample Tests, two per chapter
- Personal Study Plan
- Tutorial Instruction
- Graphing Tool

Sample Tests Two Sample Tests for each chapter are preloaded in MyEconLab, enabling students to practice what they have learned, test their understanding, and identify areas in which they need further work. Students can study on their own, or they can complete assignments created by their instructor.

Personal Study Plan Based on a student's performance on tests, MyEconLab generates a personal Study Plan that shows where the student needs further study. The Study Plan consists of a series of additional practice exercises with detailed feedback and guided solutions that are keyed to other tutorial resources.

Tutorial Instruction Launched from many of the exercises in the Study Plan, MyEconLab provides tutorial instruction in the form of step-by-step solutions and other media-based explanations.

Graphing Tool A graphing tool is integrated into the Tests and Study Plan exercises to enable students to make and manipulate graphs. This feature helps students understand how concepts, numbers, and graphs connect.

Additional MyEconLab Tools MyEconLab includes the following additional features:

1. **Weekly News Update**—This feature provides weekly updates during the school year of news items with links to sources for further reading and discussion questions.
2. **eText**—While students are working in the Study Plan or completing homework assignments, part of the tutorial resources available is a direct link to the relevant page of the text so that students can review the appropriate material to help them complete the exercise.
3. **Glossary Flashcards**—Every key term is available as a flashcard, allowing students to quiz themselves on vocabulary from one or more chapters at a time.

MyEconLab content has been created over the years through the efforts of Charles Baum, Middle Tennessee State University; Peggy Dalton, Frostburg State University; Sarah Ghosh, University of Scranton; Russell Kellogg, University of Colorado, Denver; Bert G. Wheeler, Cedarville University; and Douglas A. Ruby, Noel Lotz, and Courtney Kamauf, Pearson Education.

▶ WHAT INSTRUCTOR'S SUPPLEMENTS DID WE DEVELOP?

A fully integrated teaching and learning package is necessary for today's classroom. Our supplement package helps you provide new and interesting real-world Applications and assess student understanding of economics. The supplements are coordinated with the main text through the numbering system of the headings in each section. The major sections of the chapters are numbered (1.1, 1.2, 1.3, and so on), and that numbering system is used consistently in the supplements to make it convenient and flexible for instructors to develop assignments.

Two Test Item Files

There are two test item files for *Macroeconomics*. Each test item file offers multiple-choice, true/false, and short-answer questions. The questions are referenced by topic and are presented in sequential order. Each question is keyed by degree of difficulty, with questions ranging on a scale of one to three. Easy questions involve straightforward recall of information in the text. Moderate questions require some

analysis on the student's part. Difficult questions usually entail more complex analysis and may require the student to go one step further than the material presented in the text. Questions are also classified as *fact*, *definition*, *conceptual*, and *analytical*. Fact questions test the student's knowledge of factual information presented in the text. Definition questions ask the student to define an economic concept. Conceptual questions test the student's understanding of a concept. Analytical questions require the student to apply an analytical procedure to answer the question.

The test item files include tables and a series of questions asking students to solve for numeric values, such as profit or equilibrium output. There are also numerous questions based on graphs: Several questions ask students to interpret data presented in a graph, draw a graph on their own, and answer related questions.

In each chapter there are several questions that support the Applications in the main book. Each test item file chapter also includes an additional Application based on a newspaper, journal, or online news story. There are also new questions to support the updated and new content in the main book.

The Association to Advance Collegiate Schools of Business (AACSB) The authors of the test item files have connected questions to the general knowledge and skill guidelines found in the AACSB assurance of learning standards.

What Is the AACSB? AACSB is a not-for-profit corporation of educational institutions, corporations, and other organizations devoted to the promotion and improvement of higher education in business administration and accounting. A collegiate institution offering degrees in business administration or accounting may volunteer for AACSB accreditation review. The AACSB makes initial accreditation decisions and conducts periodic reviews to promote continuous quality improvement in management education. Pearson Education is a proud member of the AACSB and is pleased to provide advice to help you apply AACSB assurance of learning standards.

What Are AACSB Assurance of Learning Standards?
One of the criteria for AACSB accreditation is quality of the curricula. Although no specific courses are required, the AACSB expects a curriculum to include learning experiences in the following areas:

- Communication
- Ethical Reasoning
- Analytic Skills
- Use of Information Technology
- Multiculturalism and Diversity
- Reflective Thinking

Questions that test skills relevant to these guidelines are appropriately tagged. For example, a question testing the moral questions associated with externalities would receive the Ethical Reasoning tag.

How Can Instructors Use the AACSB Tags? Tagged questions help you measure whether students are grasping the course content that aligns with the AACSB guidelines noted. In addition, the tagged questions may help instructors identify potential applications of these skills. This in turn may suggest enrichment activities or other educational experiences to help students achieve these skills.

For Macroeconomics . . . Test Item File 1, prepared by Randy Methenitis of Richland College, includes approximately 3,000 multiple-choice, true/false, short-answer, and graphing questions. Test Item File 2, prepared by Brian Rosario of California State University, Sacramento, contains over 3,000 multiple-choice, true/false, and short-answer questions. Both test item files are available in a computerized format using TestGen, test-generating software.

TestGen

Macroeconomics test item files 1 and 2 appear in print and as computer files that may be used with TestGen test-generating software. This test-generating program permits instructors to edit, add, or delete questions from the test bank; analyze test results; and organize a database of tests and student results. This software allows for flexibility and ease of use. It provides many options for organizing and displaying tests, along with a search and sort feature.

Instructor's Manual

The instructor's manual, revised by Jeff Phillips of Colby-Sawyer College, follows the textbook's organization, incorporating extra Applications questions. The manual also provides detailed outlines (suitable for use as lecture notes) and solutions to all questions in the textbook. The instructor's manual is also designed to help the instructor incorporate applicable elements of the supplement package. The instructor's manual contains the following for each chapter:

- Summary: a bulleted list of key topics in the chapter
- Approaching the Material: student-friendly examples to introduce the chapter
- Chapter Outline: summary of definitions and concepts
- Teaching Tips on how to encourage class participation
- Summary and discussion points for the Applications in the main text
- New Applications and discussion questions
- Solutions to all end-of-chapter exercises

The instructor's manual is also available for download from the Instructor's Resource Center.

PowerPoint® Presentations

Three sets of PowerPoint® slides are available for download from the Instructor's Resource Center at **www.pearsonhighered.com/irc**.

1. A comprehensive set of PowerPoint® slides that can be used by instructors for class presentations. These Powerpoints, prepared by Brock Williams of Metropolitan Community College, includes all the graphs, tables, and equations in the textbook, as well as lecture notes that outline the chapter.
2. A comprehensive set of PowerPoint® slides with Classroom Response Systems (CRS) questions built in so that instructors can incorporate CRS "clickers" into their classroom lectures. This presentation is also prepared by Brock Williams of Metropolitan Community College. For more information on Pearson's partnership with CRS, see the following description. Instructors may download these PowerPoint® presentations from the Instructor's Resource Center (**www.pearsonhighered.com/irc**).
3. A PDF version of the PowerPoint® slides is also available as PDF files from the Instructor's Resource Center. This version of the PowerPoint slides can be printed and used in class.

Instructor's Resource Center on CD-ROM

The test item files, TestGen files, instructor's manuals, and PowerPoint® slides are also available on this CD-ROM. Faculty can pick and choose from the various supplements and export them to their hard drive.

CourseSmart

The CourseSmart eTextbook for the text is available through **www.coursesmart.com**. CourseSmart goes beyond traditional expectations, providing instant, online access to the textbooks and course materials you need at a lower cost to students. And, even as students save money, you can save time and hassle with a digital textbook that allows you to search the most relevant content at the very moment you need it. Whether it's evaluating textbooks or creating lecture notes to help students with difficult concepts, CourseSmart can make life a little easier. See how when you visit **www.coursesmart.com/instructors**.

Instructor's Resource Center Online

This password-protected site is accessible from **www.pearsonhighered.com/irc** and hosts all of the resources previously listed: test item files, TestGen files, instructor's manuals, and PowerPoint® slides. Instructors can click on the "Help downloading Instructor Resources" link for easy-to-follow instructions on getting access or contact their sales representative for further information.

Classroom Response Systems

Classroom Response Systems (CRS) is an exciting new wireless polling technology that makes large and small classrooms even more interactive because it enables instructors to pose questions to their students, record results, and display those results instantly. Students can answer questions easily using compact remote-control transmitters. Pearson has partnerships with leading CRS providers and can show you everything you need to know about setting up and using a CRS system. We'll provide the classroom hardware, text-specific PowerPoint® slides, software, and support, and we'll also show you how your students can benefit! Learn more at **www.pearsonhighered.com/elearning**.

▶ WHAT STUDENT SUPPLEMENTS DID WE DEVELOP?

To accommodate different learning styles and busy student lifestyles, we provide a variety of print and online supplements.

Study Guide

The study guide, created by David Eaton of Murray State University, reinforces economic concepts and Applications from the main book and helps students assess their learning. Each chapter of the study guide includes the following features:

- Chapter Summary: Provides a summary of the chapter, key term definitions, and review of the Applications from the main book.
- Study Tip: Provides students with tips on understanding key concepts.
- Key equations: Alerts students to equations they are likely to see throughout the class.
- Caution!: Alerts students to potential pitfalls and key figures or tables that deserve special attention.
- Activity: Encourages students to think creatively about an economic problem. An answer is provided so students can check their work.
- Practice Test: Includes approximately 25 multiple-choice and short-answer questions that help students test their knowledge. Select questions include a graph or table for students to analyze. Some of these questions support the Applications in the main book.
- Solutions to the practice test.

▶ REVIEWERS

A long road exists between the initial vision of an innovative principles text and the final product. Along our journey we participated in a structured process to reach our goal. We wish to acknowledge the assistance of the many people who participated in this process.

▶ REVIEWERS OF THE CURRENT EDITION

The guidance and recommendations from the following professors helped us develop the revision plans for this new edition:

Alabama

JIM PAYNE, *Calhoun Community College*
JAMES SWOFFORD, *University of South Alabama*

Florida

BARBARA MOORE, *University of Central Florida*

Georgia

SCOTT BEAULIER, *Mercer College*

Massachusetts

HANS DESPAIN, *Nichols College*

Nebraska

BROCK WILLIAMS, *Metropolitan Community College*

New Hampshire

JEFF PHILLIPS, *Colby Sawyer College*

New York

EZGI UZEL, *SUNY-Maritime*

Ohio

ERWIN EHRARDT, *University of Cincinnati*
KEN FAH, *Ohio Dominican University*
DANDAN LIU, *Kent State University*

South Carolina

GARY STONE, *Winthrop University*

Texas

STEVE SCHWIFF, *Texas A&M University, Commerce*

▶ REVIEWERS OF PREVIOUS EDITIONS

We benefited from the assistance of many dedicated professors who reviewed all or parts of previous editions in various stages of development:

Alabama

JAMES SWOFFORD, *University of South Alabama*

Alaska

Paul Johnson, *University of Alaska, Anchorage*

Arizona

Pete Mavrokordatos, *Tarrant County College/University of Phoenix*
Evan Tanner, *Thunderbird, The American Graduate School of International Management*
Donald Wells, *University of Arizona*

California

Antonio Avalos, *California State University, Fresno*
Collette Barr, *Santa Barbara Community College*
T. J. Bettner, *Orange Coast College*
Peter Boelman-Lopez, *Riverside Community College*
Matthew Brown, *Santa Clara University*
Jim Cobb, *Orange Coast College*
John Constantine, *Sacramento City College*
Peggy Crane, *San Diego State University*
Albert B. Culver, *California State University, Chico*
Jose L. Esteban, *Palomar College*
Gilbert Fernandez, *Santa Rosa Junior College*
E. B. Gendel, *Woodbury University*
Charles W. Haase, *San Francisco State University*
John Henry, *California State University, Sacramento*
George Jensen, *California State University, Los Angeles*
Janis Kea, *West Valley College*
Rose Kilburn, *Modesto Junior College*
Philip King, *San Francisco State University*
Anthony Lima, *California State University, Hayward*
Bret McMurran, *Chaffey College*
Jon J. Nadenichek, *California State University, Northridge*
Alex Obiya, *San Diego City College*
Jack W. Osman, *San Francisco State University*
Jay Patyk, *Foothill College*
Stephen Perez, *California State University, Sacramento*
Ratha Ramoo, *Diablo Valley College*
Greg Rose, *Sacramento City College*
Kurt Schwabe, *University of California, Riverside*
Terri Sexton, *California State University, Sacramento*
David Simon, *Santa Rosa Junior College*
Xiaochuan Song, *San Diego Mesa College*
Ed Sorensen, *San Francisco State University*
Susan Spencer, *Santa Rosa Junior College*
Linda Stoh, *Sacramento City College*
Rodney Swanson, *University of California, Los Angeles*
Daniel Villegas, *California Polytechnic State University*

Colorado

Steve Call, *Metropolitan State College of Denver*

Connecticut

John A. Jascot, *Capital Community Technical College*

Delaware

Lawrence Stelmach, *Delaware Valley College*

Florida

Irma de Alonso, *Florida International University*
Jay Bhattacharya, *Okaloosa-Walton Community College*
Edward Bierhanzl, *Florida A&M University*
Eric P. Chiang, *Florida Atlantic University*
Martine Duchatelet, *Barry University*
George Greenlee, *St. Petersburg College, Clearwater*
Martin Markovich, *Florida A&M University*
Thomas McCaleb, *Florida State University*
Stephen Morrell, *Barry University*
Carl Schmertmann, *Florida State University*
Garvin Smith, *Daytona Beach Community College*
Noel Smith, *Palm Beach Community College*
Michael Vierk, *Florida International University*
Joseph Ward, *Broward Community College, Central*
Virginia York, *Gulf Coast Community College*
Andrea Zanter, *Hillsborough Community College*

Georgia

Ashley Harmon, *Southeastern Technical College*
Steven F. Koch, *Georgia Southern University*
L. Wayne Plumly, Jr., *Valdosta State University*
Greg Trandel, *University of Georgia*

Hawaii

Barbara Ross-Pfeiffer, *Kapiolani Community College*

Idaho

Charles Scott Benson, Jr., *Idaho State University*
Tesa Stegner, *Idaho State University*

Illinois

Diane Anstine, *North Central College*
Rosa Lea Danielson, *College of DuPage*
Sel Dibooglu, *Southern Illinois University*
Linda Ghent, *Eastern Illinois University*
Gary Langer, *Roosevelt University*
Nampeang Pingkarawat, *Chicago State University*
Dennis Shannon, *Belleville Area College*
Chuck Sicotte, *Rock Valley College*

Indiana

John L. Conant, *Indiana State University*

MOUSUMI DUTTARAY, *Indiana State University*
JAMES T. KYLE, *Indiana State University*
VIRGINIA SHINGLETON, *Valparaiso University*

Iowa

DALE BORMAN, *Kirkwood Community College*
JONATHAN O. IKOBA, *Scott Community College*
SAUL MEKIES, *Kirkwood Community College, Iowa City*

Kansas

CARL PARKER, *Fort Hays State University*
JAMES RAGAN, *Kansas State University*
TRACY M. TURNER, *Kansas State University*

Kentucky

DAVID EATON, *Murray State University*
JOHN ROBERTSON, *University of Kentucky*

Louisiana

JOHN PAYNE BIGELOW, *Louisiana State University*
SANG LEE, *Southeastern Louisiana University*
RICHARD STAHL, *Louisiana State University*

Maine

GEORGE SCHATZ, *Maine Maritime Academy*

Maryland

CAREY BORKOSKI, *Anne Arundel Community College*
GRETCHEN MESTER, *Anne Arundel Community College*
IRVIN WEINTRAUB, *Towson State University*

Massachusetts

BRIAN DEURIARTE, *Middlesex Community College*
DAN GEORGIANNA, *University of Massachusetts, Dartmouth*
JAMES E. HARTLEY, *Mount Holyoke College*
MARLENE KIM, *University of Massachusetts, Boston*
MARK SIEGLER, *Williams College*
GILBERT WOLFE, *Middlesex Community College*

Michigan

CHRISTINE AMSLER, *Michigan State University*
BHARATI BASU, *Central Michigan University*
NORMAN CURE, *Macomb Community College*
SUSAN LINZ, *Michigan State University*
SCANLON ROMER, *Delta College*
ROBERT TANSKY, *St. Clair County Community College*
WENDY WYSOCKI, *Monroe Community College*

Minnesota

MIKE MCILHON, *Augsburg College*
RICHARD MILANI, *Hibbing Community College*

Mississippi

ARLENA SULLIVAN, *Jones County Junior College*

Missouri

DUANE EBERHARDT, *Missouri Southern State College*
DAVID GILLETTE, *Truman State University*
BRAD HOPPES, *Southwest Missouri State University*
DENISE KUMMER, *St. Louis Community College*
STEVEN M. SCHAMBER, *St. Louis Community College, Meramec*
ELIAS SHUKRALLA, *St. Louis Community College, Meramec*
KEITH ULRICH, *Valencia Community College*
GEORGE WASSON, *St. Louis Community College, Meramec*

Nebraska

THEODORE LARSEN, *University of Nebraska, Kearney*
TIMOTHY R. MITTAN, *Southeast Community College*
STANLEY J. PETERS, *Southeast Community College*
BROCK WILLIAMS, *Metropolitan Community College*

Nevada

STEPHEN MILLER, *University of Nevada, Las Vegas*
CHARLES OKEKE, *College of Southern Nevada*

New Jersey

LEN ANYANWU, *Union County College*
RICHARD COMERFORD, *Bergen Community College*
JOHN GRAHAM, *Rutgers University*
PAUL C. HARRIS, JR., *Camden County College*
CALVIN HOY, *County College of Morris*
TAGHI RAMIN, *William Paterson University*
BRIAN DE URIARTE, *Middlesex County College*

New Mexico

CARL ENOMOTO, *New Mexico State University*

New York

FARHAD AMEEN, *State University of New York, Westchester County Community College*
KARIJIT K. ARORA, *Le Moyne College*
ALEX AZARCHS, *Pace University*
KATHLEEN K. BROMLEY, *Monroe Community College*
BARBARA CONNELLY, *Westchester Community College*
GEORGE FROST, *Suffolk County Community College*
SUSAN GLANZ, *St. John's University*
SERGE S. GRUSHCHIN, *ASA College of Advanced Technology*
ROBERT HERMAN, *Nassau Community College*
CHRISTOPHER INYA, *Monroe Community College*
MARIE KRATOCHVIL, *Nassau Community College*
MARIANNE LOWERY, *Erie Community College*
JEANNETTE MITCHELL, *Rochester Institute of Technology*
TED MUZIO, *St. John's University*
GRAY ORPHEE, *Rockland County Community College*

CRAIG ROGERS, *Canisius College*
FRED TYLER, *Fordham University*
MICHAEL VARDANYAN, *Binghamton University*

North Carolina

KATIE CANTY, *Cape Fear Community College*
LEE CRAIG, *North Carolina State University*
HOSSEIN GHOLAMI, *Fayetteville Technical Community College*
MICHAEL G. GOODE, *Central Piedmont Community College*
CHARLES M. OLDHAM, JR., *Fayetteville Technical Community College*
RANDALL PARKER, *East Carolina University*
DIANE TYNDALL, *Craven Community College*
CHESTER WATERS, *Durham Technical Community College*
JAMES WHEELER, *North Carolina State University*

North Dakota

SCOTT BLOOM, *North Dakota State University*

Ohio

FATMA ABDEL-RAOUF, *Cleveland State University*
JEFF ANKROM, *Wittenberg University*
TAGHI T. KERMANI, *Youngstown State University*

Oklahoma

JEFF HOLT, *Tulsa Community College*
MARTY LUDLUM, *Oklahoma City Community College*
DAN RICKMAN, *Oklahoma State University*

Oregon

TOM CARROLL, *Central Oregon Community College*
JIM EDEN, *Portland Community College*
JOHN FARRELL, *Oregon State University*
DAVID FIGLIO, *University of Oregon*
RANDY R. GRANT, *Linfield College*
LARRY SINGELL, *University of Oregon*

Pennsylvania

KEVIN A. BAIRD, *Montgomery County Community College*
CHARLES BEEM, *Bucks County Community College*
ED COULSON, *Pennsylvania State University*
TAHANY NAGGAR, *West Chester University*
ABDULWAHAB SRAIHEEN, *Kutztown University*

South Carolina

DONALD BALCH, *University of South Carolina*
CALVIN BLACKWELL, *College of Charleston*
JANICE BOUCHER BREUER, *University of South Carolina*
BILL CLIFFORD, *Trident Technical College*
FRANK GARLAND, *Tri-County Technical College*
CHARLOTTE DENISE HIXSON, *Midlands Technical College*
WOODROW W. HUGHES, JR., *Converse College*

MIREN IVANKOVIC, *Southern Wesleyan University*
CHIRINJEV PETERSON, *Greenville Technical College*
DENISE TURNAGE, *Midlands Technical College*
CHAD TURNER, *Clemson University*

South Dakota

JOSEPH SANTOS, *South Dakota State University*

Tennessee

CINDY ALEXANDER, *Pellissippi State University*
NIRMALENDU DEBNATH, *Lane College*
QUENTON PULLIAM, *Nashville State Technical College*
ROSE RUBIN, *University of Memphis*
THURSTON SCHRADER, *Southwest Tennessee Community College*

Texas

RASHID AL-HMOUD, *Texas Technical University*
MAHAMUDU BAWUMIA, *Baylor University*
STEVEN BECKHAM, *Amarillo College*
OMAR BELAZI, *Midland College*
JACK BUCCO, *Austin Community College*
CINDY CANNON, *North Harris College*
DAVID L. COBERLY, *Southwest Texas State University*
ED COHN, *Del Mar College*
DEAN DRAINEY, *St. Phillips College*
MICHAEL I. DUKE, *Blinn College*
GHAZI DUWAJI, *University of Texas, Arlington*
HARRY ELLIS, *University of North Texas*
S. AUN HASSAN, *Texas Tech University*
THOMAS JEITSCHKO, *Texas A&M University*
DELORES LINTON, *Tarrant County Community College, Northwest*
JESSICA MCCRAW, *University of Texas, Arlington*
RANDY METHENITIS, *Richland College*
WILLIAM NEILSON, *Texas A&M University*
MICHAEL NELSON, *Texas A&M University*
RHEY NOLAN, *Tyler Junior College*
PAUL OKELLO, *University of Texas, Arlington*
JOSHUA PICKRELL, *South Plains College*
JOHN PISCIOTTA, *Baylor University*
JOHN RYKOWSKI, *Kalamazoo Valley Community College*
DAVE SHORROW, *Richland College*
JAMES R. VANBEEK, *Blinn College*
INSKE ZANDVLIET, *Brookhaven College*

Utah

REED GOOCH, *Utah Valley University*
ALI HEKMAT, *College of Eastern Utah*
GLENN LOWELL, *Utah Valley University*

Virginia

JAMES BRUMBAUGH, *Lord Fairfax Community College, Middleton Campus*

BRUCE BRUNTON, *James Madison University*
MICHAEL G. HESLOP, *North Virginia Community College*
GEORGE HOFFER, *Virginia Commonwealth University*
MELANIE MARKS, *Longwood College*
THOMAS J. MEEKS, *Virginia State University*
JOHN MIN, *Northern Virginia Community College, Alexandria*
SHANNON K. MITCHELL, *Virginia Commonwealth University*
BILL REESE, *Tidewater Community College, Virginia Beach*

Washington

WILLIAM HALLAGAN, *Washington State University*
MARK WYLIE, *Spokane Falls Community College*

Australia

HAK YOUN KIM, *Monash University*

▶ CLASS TESTERS

A special acknowledgment goes to the instructors who were willing to class-test drafts of early editions in different stages of development. They provided us with instant feedback on parts that worked and parts that needed changes:

SHERYL BALL, *Virginia Polytechnic Institute and State University*
JOHN CONSTANTINE, *University of California, Davis*
JOHN FARRELL, *Oregon State University*
JAMES HARTLEY, *Mt. Holyoke College*
KAILASH KHANDKE, *Furman College*
PETER LINDERT, *University of California, Davis*
LOUIS MAKOWSKI, *University of California, Davis*
BARBARA ROSS-PFEIFFER, *Kapiolani Community College*

▶ FOCUS GROUPS

We want to thank the participants who took part in the focus groups for the first and second editions; they helped us see the manuscript from a fresh perspective:

CARLOS AQUILAR, *El Paso Community College*
JIM BRADLEY, *University of South Carolina*
THOMAS COLLUM, *Northeastern Illinois University*
DAVID CRAIG, *Westark College*
JEFF HOLT, *Tulsa Junior College*
THOMAS JEITSCHKO, *Texas A&M University*
GARY LANGER, *Roosevelt University*
MARK MCCLEOD, *Virginia Polytechnic Institute and State University*
TOM MCKINNON, *University of Arkansas*
AMY MEYERS, *Parkland Community College*

HASSAN MOHAMMADI, *Illinois State University*
JOHN MORGAN, *College of Charleston*
NORM PAUL, *San Jacinto Community College*
NAMPEANG PINGKARATWAT, *Chicago State University*
SCANLAN ROMER, *Delta Community College*
BARBARA ROSS-PFEIFFER, *Kapiolani Community College*
ZAHRA SADERION, *Houston Community College*
VIRGINIA SHINGLETON, *Valparaiso University*
JIM SWOFFORD, *University of South Alabama*
JANET WEST, *University of Nebraska, Omaha*
LINDA WILSON, *University of Texas, Arlington*
MICHAEL YOUNGBLOOD, *Rock Valley Community College*

▶ A WORLD OF THANKS . . .

We would also like to acknowledge the team of dedicated authors who contributed to the various ancillaries that accompany this book: Jeff Phillips of Colby-Sawyer College; David Eaton of Murray State University; Randy Methenitis of Richland College; Robert L. Shoffner III of Central Piedmont Community College; Brian Rosario of California State University, Sacramento; and Brock Williams of Metropolitan Community College.

For the seventh edition, Meredith Gertz was the production project manager who worked with Kelly Morrison at GEX Publishing Services to turn our manuscript pages into a beautiful published book. Noel Seibert, acquisitions editor; Carolyn Terbush, assistant editor; and Alison Eusden, supplements production project manager, guided the project and coordinated the schedules for the book and the extensive supplement package that accompanies the book.

From the start, Pearson provided us with first-class support and advice. Over the first six editions, many people contributed to the project, including Leah Jewell, Rod Banister, P. J. Boardman, Marie McHale, Gladys Soto, Lisa Amato, Victoria Anderson, Cynthia Regan, Kathleen McLellan, Sharon Koch, David Theisen, Steve Deitmer, Christopher Bath, Ben Paris, Elisa Adams, Jodi Bolognese, David Alexander, Virginia Guariglia, and Lynne Breitfeller.

Last but not least, we must thank our families, who have seen us disappear, sometimes physically and other times mentally, to spend hours wrapped up in our own world of principles of economics. A project of this magnitude is very absorbing, and our families have been particularly supportive in this endeavor.

ARTHUR O'SULLIVAN
STEVEN SHEFFRIN
STEPHEN PEREZ

Introduction: What Is Economics?

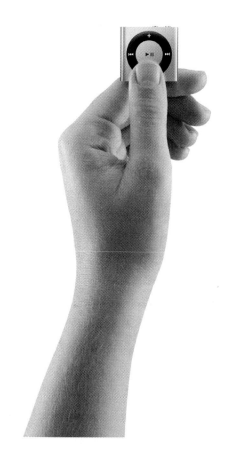

Economics is the science of choice, exploring the choices made by individuals and organizations. Over the last few centuries, these choices have led to substantial gains in the standard of living around the globe. In the United States, the typical person today has roughly seven times the income and purchasing power of a person 100 years ago. Our prosperity is the result of choices made by all sorts of people, including inventors, workers, entrepreneurs, and the people who saved money and loaned it to others to invest in machines and other tools of production. One reason we have prospered is greater efficiency: We have discovered better ways to use our resources—raw materials, time, and energy—to produce the goods and services we value.

As an illustration of changes in the standard of living and our growing prosperity, let's compare the way people listened to music in 1891 with how we listen today. You can buy an iPod shuffle® for $49 and fill it with 500 songs at $0.99 each. If you earn a wage of $15 per hour, it would take you about 36 hours of work to purchase and then fill an iPod. Back in 1891, the latest technological marvel was Thomas Edison's cylinder phonograph, which played music recorded on 4-inch cylinders. Imagine that you lived back then and wanted to get just as much music as you could fit on an iPod. Given the wages and prices in 1891, it would take you roughly 800 hours of work to earn enough money to buy the phonograph and all the cylinders. And if you wanted to keep your music with you, you would need 14 backpacks to carry the cylinders.

Although prosperity and efficiency are widespread, they are not universal. In some parts of the world, many people live in poverty. For example, in sub-Saharan Africa 388 million people—about half the population—live on less than $1.25 per day. And in all nations of the world, inefficiencies still exist, with valuable resources being wasted. For example, each year the typical urban commuter in the United States wastes more than 47 hours and $84 worth of gasoline trapped in rush hour traffic.

APPLYING THE CONCEPTS

1 Do people respond to incentives?
Responding to Production Rewards

2 What is the role of prices in allocating resources?
The Economic Solution to Spam

3 How do we compute percentage changes?
The Perils of Percentages

Economics provides a framework to diagnose all sorts of problems faced by society and then helps create and evaluate various proposals to solve them. Economics can help us develop strategies to replace poverty with prosperity, and to replace waste with efficiency. In this chapter, we explain what economics is and how we all can use economic analysis to think about practical problems and solutions.

1.1 WHAT IS ECONOMICS?

Economists use the word **scarcity** to convey the idea that resources—the things we use to produce goods and services—are limited, while human wants are unlimited. Therefore, we cannot produce everything that everyone wants. As the old saying goes, you can't always get what you want. **Economics** studies the choices we make when there is scarcity; it is all about trade-offs. Here are some examples of scarcity and the trade-offs associated with making choices:

- You have a limited amount of time. If you take a part-time job, each hour on the job means one less hour for study or play.
- A city has a limited amount of land. If the city uses an acre of land for a park, it has one less acre for housing, retailers, or industry.
- You have limited income this year. If you spend $17 on a music CD, that's $17 less you have to spend on other products or to save.

People produce goods (music CDs, houses, and parks) and services (the advice of physicians and lawyers) by using one or more of the following five **factors of production**, also called *production inputs* or simply *resources*:

- **Natural resources** are provided by nature. Some examples are fertile land, mineral deposits, oil and gas deposits, and water. Some economists refer to all types of natural resources as *land*.
- **Labor** is the physical and mental effort people use to produce goods and services.
- **Physical capital** is the stock of equipment, machines, structures, and infrastructure that is used to produce goods and services. Some examples are forklifts, machine tools, computers, factories, airports, roads, and fiber-optic cables.
- **Human capital** is the knowledge and skills acquired by a worker through education and experience. Every job requires some human capital: To be a surgeon, you must learn anatomy and acquire surgical skills. To be an accountant, you must learn the rules of accounting and acquire computer skills. To be a musician, you must learn to play an instrument.
- **Entrepreneurship** is the effort used to coordinate the factors of production—natural resources, labor, physical capital, and human capital—to produce and sell products. An entrepreneur comes up with an idea for a product, decides how to produce it, and raises the funds to bring it to the market. Some examples of entrepreneurs are Bill Gates of Microsoft, Steve Jobs of Apple Computer, Howard Schultz of Starbucks, and Ray Kroc of McDonald's.

Given our limited resources, we make our choices in a variety of ways. Sometimes we make our decisions as individuals, and other times we participate in collective decision making, allowing the government and other organizations to choose for us. Many of our choices happen within *markets*, institutions or arrangements that enable us to buy and sell things. For example, most of us participate in the labor market, exchanging our time for money, and we all participate in consumer markets, exchanging money for food and clothing. But we make other choices outside markets—from our personal decisions about everyday life to our political choices about matters that concern society

---

scarcity
The resources we use to produce goods and services are limited.

economics
The study of choices when there is scarcity.

factors of production
The resources used to produce goods and services; also known as *production inputs* or *resources*.

natural resources
Resources provided by nature and used to produce goods and services.

labor
Human effort, including both physical and mental effort, used to produce goods and services.

physical capital
The stock of equipment, machines, structures, and infrastructure that is used to produce goods and services.

human capital
The knowledge and skills acquired by a worker through education and experience and used to produce goods and services.

entrepreneurship
The effort used to coordinate the factors of production—natural resources, labor, physical capital, and human capital—to produce and sell products.

as a whole. What unites all these decisions is the notion of scarcity: We can't have it all; there are trade-offs.

Economists are always reminding us that there is scarcity—there are trade-offs in everything we do. Suppose that in a conversation with your economics instructor you share your enthusiasm about an upcoming launch of the space shuttle. The economist may tell you that the resources used for the shuttle could have been used instead for an unmanned mission to Mars.

By introducing the notion of scarcity into your conversation, your instructor is simply reminding you that there are trade-offs, that one thing (a Mars mission) is sacrificed for another (a shuttle mission). Talking about alternatives is the first step in a process that can help us make better choices about how to use our resources. For example, we could compare the scientific benefits of a shuttle mission to the benefits of a Mars mission and choose the mission with the greater benefit.

Positive versus Normative Analysis

Economics doesn't tell us what to choose—shuttle mission or Mars mission—but simply helps us to understand the trade-offs. President Harry S. Truman once remarked,

> All my economists say, "On the one hand, . . . ; On the other hand, ..." Give me a one-handed economist!

An economist might say, "On the one hand, we could use a shuttle mission to do more experiments in the gravity-free environment of Earth's orbit; on the other hand, we could use a Mars mission to explore the possibility of life on other planets." In using both hands, the economist is not being evasive, but simply doing economics, discussing the alternative uses of our resources. The ultimate decision about how to use our resources—shuttle mission or Mars exploration—is the responsibility of citizens or their elected officials.

Most modern economics is based on **positive analysis**, which predicts the consequences of alternative actions by answering the question "What *is*?" or "What *will be*?" A second type of economic reasoning is normative in nature. **Normative analysis** answers the question "What *ought to be*?"

In Table 1.1, we compare positive questions to normative questions. Normative questions lie at the heart of policy debates. Economists contribute to policy debates by conducting positive analyses of the consequences of alternative actions. For example, an economist could predict the effects of an increase in the minimum wage on the number of people employed nationwide, the income of families with minimum-wage workers, and consumer prices. Armed with the conclusions of the economist's positive analysis, citizens and policymakers could then make a normative decision

positive analysis
Answers the question "What *is*?" or "What *will be*?"

normative analysis
Answers the question "What *ought to be*?"

TABLE 1.1 COMPARING POSITIVE AND NORMATIVE QUESTIONS	
Positive Questions	**Normative Questions**
• If the government increases the minimum wage, how many workers will lose their jobs?	• Should the government increase the minimum wage?
• If two office-supply firms merge, will the price of office supplies increase?	• Should the government block the merger of two office-supply firms?
• How does a college education affect a person's productivity and earnings?	• Should the government subsidize a college education?
• How do consumers respond to a cut in income taxes?	• Should the government cut taxes to stimulate the economy?
• If a nation restricts shoe imports, who benefits and who bears the cost?	• Should the government restrict imports?

about whether to increase the minimum wage. Similarly, an economist could study the projects that could be funded with $1 billion in foreign aid, predicting the effects of each project on the income per person in an African country. Armed with this positive analysis, policymakers could then decide which projects to support.

Economists don't always reach the same conclusions in their positive analyses. The disagreements often concern the magnitude of a particular effect. For example, most economists agree that an increase in the minimum wage will cause unemployment, but disagree about how many people would lose their jobs. Similarly, economists agree that spending money to improve the education system in Africa will increase productivity and income, but disagree about the size of the increase in income.

The Three Key Economic Questions: What, How, and Who?

We make economic decisions at every level in society. Individuals decide what products to buy, what occupations to pursue, and how much money to save. Firms decide what goods and services to produce and how to produce them. Governments decide what projects and programs to complete and how to pay for them. The choices of individuals, firms, and governments answer three questions:

1 *What products do we produce?*   Trade-offs exist: If a hospital uses its resources to perform more heart transplants, it has fewer resources to care for premature infants.

2 *How do we produce the products?*   Alternative means of production are available: Power companies can produce electricity with coal, natural gas, or wind power. Professors can teach in large lecture halls or small classrooms.

3 *Who consumes the products?*   We must decide how to distribute the products of society. If some people earn more money than others, should they consume more goods? How much money should the government take from the rich and give to the poor?

As we'll see later in the book, most of these decisions are made in markets, where prices play a key role in determining what products we produce, how we produce them, and who gets the products. In Chapter 3, we'll examine the role of markets in modern economies and the role of government in market-based economies.

Economic Models

Economists use *economic models* to explore the choices people make and the consequences of those choices. An economic model is a simplified representation of an economic environment, with all but the essential features of the environment eliminated. An **economic model** is an abstraction from reality that enables us to focus our attention on what really matters. As we'll see throughout the book, most economic models use graphs to represent the economic environment.

economic model

A simplified representation of an economic environment, often employing a graph.

To see the rationale for economic modeling, consider an architectural model. An architect builds a scale model of a new building and uses the model to show how the building will fit on a plot of land and blend with nearby buildings. The model shows the exterior features of the building, but not the interior features. We can ignore the interior features because they are unimportant for the task at hand—seeing how the building will fit into the local environment.

Economists build models to explore decision making by individuals, firms, and other organizations. For example, we can use a model of a profit-maximizing firm to predict how a firm will respond to increased competition. If a new car stereo store opens up in your town, will the old firms be passive and simply accept smaller market shares, or will they aggressively cut their prices to try to drive the new rival out of business? The model of the firm includes the monetary benefits and costs of doing business, and assumes that firms want to make as much money as possible. Although there may be other motives in the business world—to have fun or to help the world—the economic model ignores these other motives. The model focuses our attention on the profit motive and how it affects a firm's response to increased competition.

1.2 ECONOMIC ANALYSIS AND MODERN PROBLEMS

Economic analysis provides important insights into real-world problems. To explain how we can use economic analysis in problem solving, we provide three examples. You'll see these examples again in more detail later in the book.

Economic View of Traffic Congestion

Consider first the problem of traffic congestion. According to the Texas Transportation Institute, the typical U.S. commuter wastes about 47 hours per year because of traffic congestion.[1] In some cities, the time wasted is much greater: 93 hours in Los Angeles, 72 hours in San Francisco, and 63 hours in Houston. In addition to time lost, we also waste 2.3 billion gallons of gasoline and diesel fuel each year.

To an economist, the diagnosis of the congestion problem is straightforward. When you drive onto a busy highway during rush hour, your car takes up space and decreases the distance between the vehicles on the highway. A driver's normal reaction to a shorter distance between moving cars is to slow down. So when you enter the highway, you force other commuters to slow down and thus spend more time on the highway. If each of your 900 fellow commuters spends just two extra seconds on the highway, you will increase the total travel time by 30 minutes. In deciding whether to use the highway, you will presumably ignore these costs you impose on others. Similarly, your fellow commuters ignore the cost they impose on you and others when they enter the highway. Because no single commuter pays the full cost (30 minutes), too many people use the highway, and everyone wastes time.

One possible solution to the congestion problem is to force people to pay for using the road, just as they pay for gasoline and tires. The government could impose a congestion tax of $8 per trip on rush-hour commuters and use a debit card system to collect the tax: Every time a car passes a checkpoint, a transponder would charge the commuter's card. Traffic volume during rush hours would then decrease as travelers (a) shift their travel to off-peak times, (b) switch to ride sharing and mass transit, and (c) shift their travel to less congested routes. The job for the economist is to compute the appropriate congestion tax and predict the consequences of imposing it.

Economic View of Poverty in Africa

Consider next the issue of poverty in Africa. In the final two decades of the twentieth century, the world economy grew rapidly, and the average per capita income (income per person) increased by about 35 percent. In contrast, the economies of poverty-stricken sub-Saharan Africa shrank, and per capita income *decreased* by about 6 percent. Africa is the world's second-largest continent in both area and population and accounts for more than 12 percent of the world's human population. Figure 1.1 shows a map of Africa. The countries of sub-Saharan Africa are highlighted in yellow.

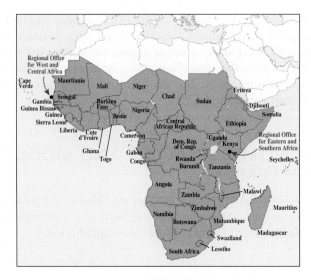

▲ **FIGURE 1.1**
Map of Africa
Africa is the world's second-largest continent in both area and population, and accounts for more than 12 percent of the world's human population. The countries of sub-Saharan Africa are high-lighted in orange.
SOURCE: web.worldbank.org/WBSITE/EXTERNAL/COUNTRIES/AFRICA

Economists have found that as a nation's economy grows, its poorest households share in the general prosperity.[2] Therefore, one way to reduce poverty in sub-Saharan Africa is to increase economic growth. Economic growth occurs when a country expands its production facilities (machinery and factories), improves its public infrastructure (highways and water systems), widens educational opportunities, and adopts new technology.

The recent experience of sub-Saharan Africa is somewhat puzzling because in the last few decades the region has expanded educational opportunities and received large amounts of foreign aid. Some recent work by economists on the sources of growth suggests that institutions such as the legal system and the regulatory environment also play key roles in economic growth.[3] In sub-Saharan Africa, a simple legal dispute about a small debt takes about 30 months to resolve, compared to 5 months in the United States. In Mozambique, it takes 174 days to complete the procedures required to set up a business, compared to just 2 days in Canada. In many cases, institutions impede rather than encourage the sort of investment and risk taking—called entrepreneurship—that causes economic growth and reduces poverty. As a consequence, economists and policymakers are exploring ways to reform the region's institutions. They are also challenged with choosing among development projects that will generate the biggest economic boost per dollar spent—the biggest bang per buck.

Economic View of the Current World Recession

Over the last several decades, the U.S. economy has performed well and has raised our standard of living. The general consensus was that our policymakers had learned to manage the economy effectively. Although the economy faltered at times, policymakers seemed to know how to restore growth and prosperity.

That is why the financial crisis and the recession that began in late 2007 has so shaken the confidence of people in the United States and around the world. The problems started innocently enough, with a booming market for homes that was fueled by easy credit from financial institutions. But we later discovered that many purchasers of homes and properties could not really afford them, and when many homeowners had trouble making their mortgage payments, the trouble spread to banks and other financial institutions. As a result, businesses found it increasingly difficult to borrow money for everyday use and investment, and economic activity around the world began to contract.

The major countries of the world have implemented aggressive policies to try to halt this downturn. Policymakers want to avoid the catastrophes that hit the global economy in the 1930s. Fortunately, they can draw on many years of experience in economic policy to guide the economy during this difficult time.

1.3 THE ECONOMIC WAY OF THINKING

How do economists think about problems and decision making? The economic way of thinking is best summarized by British economist John Maynard Keynes (1883–1946):[4]

> The theory of economics does not furnish a body of settled conclusions immediately applicable to policy. It is a method rather than a doctrine, an apparatus of the mind, a technique of thinking which helps its possessor draw correct conclusions.

Let's look at the four elements of the economic way of thinking.

Use Assumptions to Simplify

Economists use assumptions to make things simpler and focus attention on what really matters. If you use a road map to plan a car trip from Seattle to San Francisco, you make two unrealistic assumptions to simplify your planning:

- The earth is flat: The flat road map doesn't show the curvature of the earth.
- The roads are flat: The standard road map doesn't show hills and valleys.

Instead of a map, you could use a globe that shows all the topographical features between Seattle and San Francisco, but you don't need those details to plan your trip. A map, with its unrealistic assumptions, will suffice because the curvature of the earth and the topography of the highways are irrelevant to your trip. Although your analysis is based on two unrealistic assumptions, that does not mean your analysis is invalid. Similarly, if economic analysis is based on unrealistic assumptions, that doesn't mean the analysis is faulty.

What if you decide to travel by bike instead of by automobile? Now the assumption of flat roads really matters, unless of course you are eager to pedal up and down mountains. If you use a standard map, and thus assume there are no mountains between the two cities, you may inadvertently pick a mountainous route instead of a flat one. In this case, the simplifying assumption makes a difference. The lesson is that we must think carefully about whether a simplifying assumption is truly harmless.

Isolate Variables—Ceteris Paribus

Economic analysis often involves *variables* and how they affect one another. A **variable** is a measure of something that can take on different values, for example, your grade point average. Economists are interested in exploring relationships between two variables—like the relationship between the price of apples and the quantity of apples consumers purchase. Of course, the quantity of apples purchased depends on many other variables, including the consumer's income. To explore the relationship between the quantity and price of apples, we must assume that the consumer's income—and

variable

A measure of something that can take on different values.

anything else that influences apple purchases—doesn't change during the time period we're considering.

Alfred Marshall (1842–1924) was a British economist who refined the economic model of supply and demand and provided a label for this process.[5] He picked one variable that affected apple purchases (price) and threw the other variable (income) into what he called the "pound" (in Marshall's time, the "pound" was an enclosure for holding stray cattle; nowadays, a pound is for stray dogs). That variable waited in the pound while Marshall examined the influence of the first variable. Marshall labeled the pound *ceteris paribus*, the Latin expression meaning that other variables are held fixed:

> . . . the existence of other tendencies is not denied, but their disturbing effect is neglected for a time. The more the issue is narrowed, the more exactly can it be handled.

This book contains many statements about the relationship between two variables. For example, the quantity of computers produced by Dell depends on the price of computers, the wage of computer workers, and the cost of microchips. When we say, "An increase in the price of computers increases the quantity of computers produced," we are assuming that the other two variables—the wage and the cost of microchips—do not change. That is, we apply the *ceteris paribus* assumption.

ceteris paribus
The Latin expression meaning that other variables are held fixed.

Think at the Margin

Economists often consider how a small change in one variable affects another variable and what impact that has on people's decision making. In other words, if circumstances change only slightly, how will people respond? A small, one-unit change in value is called a **marginal change**. The key feature of marginal change is that the first variable changes by only one unit. For example, you might ask, "If I study just one more hour, by how much will my exam score increase?" Economists call this process "thinking at the margin." Thinking at the margin is like thinking on the edge. You will encounter marginal thinking throughout this book. Here are some other marginal questions:

marginal change
A small, one-unit change in value.

- If I keep my barbershop open one more hour, by how much will my revenue increase?
- If I stay in school and earn another degree, by how much will my lifetime earnings increase?
- If a car dealer hires one more sales associate, how many more cars will the dealer sell?

As we'll see in the next chapter, economists use the answer to a marginal question as a first step in deciding whether to do more or less of something, for example, whether to keep your barbershop open one more hour.

Rational People Respond to Incentives

A key assumption of most economic analysis is that people act rationally, meaning they act in their own self-interest. Scottish philosopher Adam Smith (1723–1790), who is also considered the founder of economics, wrote that he discovered within humankind[6]

> a desire of bettering our condition, a desire which, though generally calm and dispassionate, comes with us from the womb, and never leaves us until we go to the grave.

APPLICATION 1

RESPONDING TO PRODUCTION REWARDS

APPLYING THE CONCEPTS #1: Do people respond to incentives?

To illustrate the notion that people are rational and respond to incentives, consider an experiment conducted by the managers of a Chinese factory that produces electronic products such as GPS navigation devices and notebook computers. Workers were divided into three groups: Workers in the control group were simply paid their regular wages, while workers in the second and third groups (treatment groups) were promised a bonus of about $12 if their weekly output exceeded a production target. For the two treatment groups, the language of the bonus was slightly different. Workers in the "reward" group were simply told that if they met the target they would get the bonus. Workers in the "punishment" group were told that they had tentatively been awarded the bonus, but that they would "lose" the bonus if their output fell short of the production target.

The results of this experiment revealed the power—and the subtleties—of incentives. Compared to the control group, the output of workers in the treatment groups was on average 7 percent higher. In other words, the possibility of a bonus increased productivity by 7 percent. Among the workers in the two treatment groups, productivity was on average 1 percent higher for workers in the "punishment" group. This suggests that the fear of a loss provides a greater incentive than prospect of a gain.   **Related to Exercise 3.4.**

SOURCE: Based on Tanjum Hossain and John A. List, "The Behavioralist Visits the Factory: Increasing Productivity Using Simple Framing Manipulators," NBER Working Papers 15623, December 2009.

Smith didn't say people are motivated exclusively by self-interest, but rather that self-interest is more powerful than kindness or altruism. In this book, we will assume that people act in their own self-interest. Rational people respond to incentives. When the payoff, or benefit, from doing something changes, people change their behavior to get the benefit.

Example: London Addresses its Congestion Problem

To illustrate the economic way of thinking, let's consider again how an economist would approach the problem of traffic congestion. Recall that each driver on the highway slows down other drivers but ignores these time costs when deciding whether to use the highway. If the government imposes a congestion tax to reduce traffic during rush hour, the economist is faced with a question: How high should the tax be?

To determine the appropriate congestion tax, an economist would assume that people respond to incentives and use the three other elements of the economic way of thinking:

- **Use assumptions to simplify.** To simplify the problem, we would assume that every car has the same effect on the travel time of other cars. Of course, this is unrealistic because people drive cars of different sizes in different ways. But the alternative—looking at the effects of each car on travel speeds—would needlessly complicate the analysis.

APPLICATION 2

THE ECONOMIC SOLUTION TO SPAM

APPLYING THE CONCEPTS #2: What is the role of prices in allocating resources?

Spam—unwanted commercial e-mail—torments people around the world, interrupting their work and congesting their computer networks. What's more, spam is spreading to cell phones, with annoying beeps to announce its arrival and sometimes a $0.20 charge to the recipient. A spammer pays nothing to send a million e-mail messages, but earns a profit if just a few people buy an advertised product. The first response to the spam problem was a system of e-mail filters to separate spam from legitimate e-mail. When that didn't work, many states passed laws that made spam illegal. Despite these efforts, the spam problem persists.

The economic approach to spam is to establish a price for commercial e-mail. One idea is to follow the lead of snail mail and require a $0.01 electronic stamp for each commercial e-mail message. A bundle of one million e-mails would cost $10,000, so if a spammer expects just a few people to buy an advertised product, spamming won't be profitable. A second approach is to charge senders a penalty of $1 for each e-mail that is declared "unwanted" by a recipient. If each e-mail account has a credit limit of $200, the sender's internet service provider (ISP) would shut down an account once it receives 200 complaints. This actually solves the problem of viral spam because if a virus turns your grandmother's computer into a spam machine, her account will be shut down—and the spreading of the virus will stop—after 200 complaints. Of course, the ISP must be clever enough to quickly realize that grandma is not a spammer, and then reconnect her.   **Related to Exercise 3.5**

SOURCES: Based on "Make 'em Pay: The Fight Against Spam," *Economist*, February 14, 2004, 58; Laura M. Holson, "Spam Moves to Cellphones and Gets More Invasive," *New York Times*, May 10, 2008.

- **Isolate variables—use *ceteris paribus*.** To focus attention on the effects of a congestion tax on the number of cars using the highway, we would make the *ceteris paribus* assumption that everything else that affects travel behavior—the price of gasoline, bus fares, and consumer income—remains fixed.

- **Think at the margin.** To think at the margin, we would estimate the effects of adding one more car to the highway. Now consider the marginal question: If we add one more car to the highway, by how much does the total travel time for commuters increase? Once we answer this question, we can determine the cost imposed by the marginal driver. If the marginal driver forces each of the 900 commuters to spend two extra seconds on the highway, total travel time increases by 30 minutes. If the value of time is, say, $16 per hour, the appropriate congestion tax would be $8 (equal to $16 × 1/2 hour).

If the idea of charging people for using roads seems odd, consider the city of London, which for decades had experienced the worst congestion in Europe. In February 2003, the city imposed an $8 tax per day to drive in the city between 7:00 A.M. and 6:30 P.M. The tax reduced traffic volume and cut travel times for cars and buses in half. Because the tax reduced the waste and inefficiency of congestion, the city's economy thrived. Given the success of London's ongoing congestion tax, other cities, including Toronto, Singapore, and San Diego, have implemented congestion pricing.

1.4 PREVIEW OF COMING ATTRACTIONS: MACROECONOMICS

The field of economics is divided into two categories: macroeconomics and micro-economics. **Macroeconomics** is the study of the nation's economy as a whole; it focuses on the issues of inflation (a general rise in prices), unemployment, and economic growth. These issues are regularly discussed on Web sites, in newspapers, and on television. Macroeconomics explains why economies grow and change and why economic growth is sometimes interrupted. Let's look at three ways we can use macroeconomics.

macroeconomics
The study of the nation's economy as a whole; focuses on the issues of inflation, unemployment, and economic growth.

Using Macroeconomics to Understand Why Economies Grow

As we discussed earlier in the chapter, the world economy has been growing in recent decades, with per capita income increasing by about 1.5 percent per year. Increases in income translate into a higher standard of living for consumers—better cars, houses, and clothing and more options for food, entertainment, and travel. People in a growing economy can consume more of all goods and services because the economy has more of the resources needed to produce these products. Macroeconomics explains why resources increase over time and the consequences for our standard of living. Let's look at a practical question about economic growth.

Why do some countries grow much faster than others? Between 1960 and 2001, the economic growth rate was 2.2 percent per year in the United States, compared to 2.3 percent in Mexico and 2.7 percent in France. But in some countries, the economy actually shrunk, and per capita income dropped. Among the countries with declining income were Sierra Leone and Haiti. In the fastest-growing countries, citizens save a large fraction of the money they earn. Firms can then borrow the funds saved to purchase machinery and equipment that make their workers more productive. The fastest-growing countries also have well-educated workforces, allowing firms to quickly adopt new technologies that increase worker productivity.

Using Macroeconomics to Understand Economic Fluctuations

All economies, including those that experience a general trend of rising per capita income, are subject to economic fluctuations, including periods when the economy temporarily shrinks. During an economic downturn, some of the economy's resources—natural resources, labor, physical capital, human capital, and entrepreneurship—are idle. Some workers are unemployed, and some factories and stores are closed. By contrast, sometimes the economy grows too rapidly, causing prices to rise. Macroeconomics helps us understand why these fluctuations occur—why the economy sometimes cools and sometimes overheats—and what the government can do to moderate the fluctuations. Let's look at a practical question about economic fluctuations.

Should Congress and the president do something to reduce the unemployment rate? For example, should the government cut taxes to free up income to spend on consumer goods, thus encouraging firms to hire more workers to produce more output? If unemployment is very high, the government may want to reduce it. However, it is important not to reduce the unemployment rate too much, because, as we'll see later in the book, a low unemployment rate will cause inflation.

Using Macroeconomics to Make Informed Business Decisions

A third reason for studying macroeconomics is to make informed business decisions. As we'll see later in the book, the government uses various policies to influence interest rates (the price of borrowing money) and the inflation rate. A manager who intends to borrow money for a new factory or store could use knowledge of macroeconomics to predict the effects of current public policies on interest rates and then decide whether to borrow the money now or later. Similarly, a manager must keep an eye on the inflation rate to help decide how much to charge for the firm's products and how much to pay workers. A manager who studies macroeconomics will be better equipped to understand the complexities of interest rates and inflation and how they affect the firm.

1.5 PREVIEW OF COMING ATTRACTIONS: MICROECONOMICS

microeconomics

The study of the choices made by households, firms, and government and how these choices affect the markets for goods and services.

Microeconomics is the study of the choices made by households (an individual or a group of people living together), firms, and government and how these choices affect the markets for goods and services. Let's look at three ways we can use microeconomic analysis.

Using Microeconomics to Understand Markets and Predict Changes

One reason for studying microeconomics is to better understand how markets work and to predict how various events affect the prices and quantities of products in markets. In this book, we answer many practical questions about markets and how they operate. Let's look at a practical question that can be answered with some simple economic analysis.

How would a tax on beer affect the number of highway deaths among young adults? Research has shown that the number of highway fatalities among young adults is roughly proportional to the total amount of beer consumed by that group. A tax on beer would make the product more expensive, and young adults, like other beer drinkers, would therefore consume less of it. Consequently, a tax that decreases beer consumption by 10 percent will decrease highway deaths among young adults by about 10 percent, too.

Using Microeconomics to Make Personal and Managerial Decisions

On the personal level, we use economic analysis to decide how to spend our time, what career to pursue, and how to spend and save the money we earn. Managers use economic analysis to decide how to produce goods and services, how much to produce, and how much to charge for them. Let's use some economic analysis to look at a practical question confronting someone considering starting a business.

If the existing coffee shops in your city are profitable and you have enough money to start your own shop, should you do it? If you enter this market, the competition among the shops for consumers will heat up, causing some coffee shops to drop their prices. In addition, your costs may be higher than the costs of the stores that are already established. It would be sensible to enter the market only if you expect a small drop in price and a small difference in costs. Indeed, entering what appears to be a lucrative market may turn out to be a financial disaster.

Using Microeconomics to Evaluate Public Policies

Although modern societies use markets to make most of the decisions about production and consumption, the government does fulfill several important roles. We can use economic analysis to determine how well the government performs its roles in the market economy. We can also explore the trade-offs associated with various public policies. Let's look at a practical question about public policy.

Like other innovations, prescription drugs are protected by government patents, giving the developer the exclusive right to sell a new drug for a fixed period of time. Once the patent expires, other pharmaceutical companies can legally produce and sell generic versions of the drug, which causes its price to drop. Should drug patents be shorter? Shortening the patent has trade-offs. The good news is that generic versions of the drug will be available sooner, so prices will drop sooner and more people will use the drug to improve their health. The bad news is that the financial payoff from developing new drugs will be smaller, so pharmaceutical companies won't develop as many new drugs. The question is whether the benefit of shorter patents (lower prices) exceeds the cost (fewer drugs developed).

SUMMARY

Economics is about making choices when options are limited. Options in an economy are limited because the factors of production are limited. We can use economic analysis to understand the consequences of our choices as individuals, organizations, and society as a whole. Here are the main points of the chapter:

1 Most of modern economics is based on *positive analysis*, which answers the question "What *is*?" or "What *will be*?" Economists contribute to policy debates by conducting positive analyses about the consequences of alternative actions.

2 *Normative analysis* answers the question "What *ought to be*?"

3 The choices made by individuals, firms, and governments answer three questions: What products do we produce? How do we produce the products? Who consumes the products?

4 To think like an economist, we (a) use assumptions to simplify, (b) use the notion of *ceteris paribus* to focus on the relationship between two variables, (c) think in marginal terms, and (d) assume that rational people respond to incentives.

5 We use *macroeconomics* to understand why economies grow, to understand economic fluctuations, and to make informed business decisions.

6 We use *microeconomics* to understand how markets work, to make personal and managerial decisions, and to evaluate the merits of public policies.

KEY TERMS

ceteris paribus, p. 8

economic model, p. 4

economics, p. 2

entrepreneurship, p. 2

factors of production, p. 2

human capital, p. 2

labor, p. 2

macroeconomics, p. 11

marginal change, p. 8

microeconomics, p. 12

natural resources, p. 2

normative analysis, p. 3

physical capital, p. 2

positive analysis, p. 3

scarcity, p. 2

variable, p. 7

EXERCISES

Visit www.myeconlab.com to complete these exercises online and get instant feedback.

1.1 What Is Economics?

1.1 The three basic economic questions a society must answer are _____ products do we produce? _____ do we produce the products? _____ consumes the products?

1.2 List the five factors of production.

1.3 Which of the following statements is true?

    a. Positive statements answer questions like "What will happen if …?" Normative economic statements answer questions like "What ought to happen to …?"

b. Normative statements answer questions like "What will happen if . . .?" Positive economic statements answer questions like "What ought to happen to . . .?"

c. Most modern economics is based on normative analysis.

1.4 Indicate whether each of the following questions is normative or positive.

a. Should your city build levees strong enough to protect the city from Category Five hurricanes?

b. How did Hurricane Katrina affect housing prices in New Orleans and Baton Rouge?

c. Who should pay for a new skate park?

d. Should a school district increase teachers' salaries by 20 percent?

e. Would an increase in teachers' salaries improve the average quality of teachers?

1.2 Economic Analysis and Modern Problems

2.1 What is the economist's solution to the congestion problem?

a. Require people to carpool.

b. Charge a toll during rush hour.

c. Require people to move closer to their jobs.

d. No economist would suggest any of the above.

2.2 Some recent work by economists on the sources of growth suggests that institutions such as the _____ and the _____ play key roles in economic growth.

1.3 The Economic Way of Thinking

3.1 A road map incorporates two unrealistic assumptions: (1) _____ and (2) _____.

3.2 The four elements of the economic way of thinking are (1) use _____ to simplify the analysis, (2) explore the relationship between two variables by _____, (3) think at the _____, and (4) rational people respond to _____.

3.3 Which of the following is the Latin expression meaning *other things being held fixed*?

a. *setiferous proboscis*

b. *ceteris paribus*

c. *e pluribus unum*

d. *tres grand fromage*

3.4 The experiment in the Chinese factory suggests that the fear of a loss provides a _____ incentive than the prospect of a gain. (Related to Application 1 on page 9.)

3.5 The economic approach to spam is to follow the lead of _____ and establish a _____ for e-mail. (Related to Application 2 on page 10.)

3.6 True or False: Adam Smith suggested that people are motivated solely by self interest.

APPENDIX A
USING GRAPHS AND PERCENTAGES

Economists use several types of graphs to present data, represent relationships between variables, and explain concepts. In this appendix, we review the mechanics of graphing variables. We'll also review the basics of computing percentage changes and using percentages to compute changes in variables.

1A.1 USING GRAPHS

A quick flip through the book will reveal the importance of graphs in economics. Every chapter has at least several graphs, and many chapters have more. Although it is possible to do economics without graphs, it's a lot easier with them in your toolbox.

Graphing Single Variables

As we saw earlier in Chapter 1, a *variable* is a measure of something that can take on different values. Figure 1A.1 shows two types of graphs, each presenting data on a single variable. Panel A uses a pie graph to show the breakdown of U.S. music sales by type of music. The greater the sales of a type of music, the larger the pie slice. For example, the most popular type is rock music, comprising 24 percent of the market. The next largest type is country, followed by rap/hip-hop, R&B/urban, and so on. Panel B of Figure 1A.1 uses a bar graph to show the revenue from foreign sales (exports) of selected U.S. industries. The larger the revenue, the taller the bar. For example, the bar for computer software, with export sales of about $60 billion, is over three times taller than the bar for motion pictures, TV, and video, with export sales of $17 billion.

▼ FIGURE 1A.1
Graphs of Single Variables

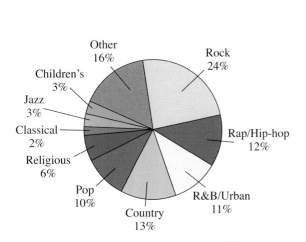

(A) Pie Graph for Types of Recorded Music Sold in the United States

SOURCE: Author's calculations based on Recording Industry Association of America, "2004 Consumer Profile."

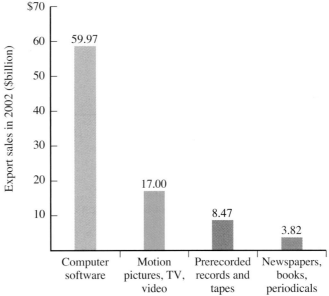

(B) Bar Graph for U.S. Export Sales of Copyrighted Products

SOURCE: Author's calculations based on International Intellectual Property Alliance, "Copyright Industries in the U.S. Economy, 2004 Report."

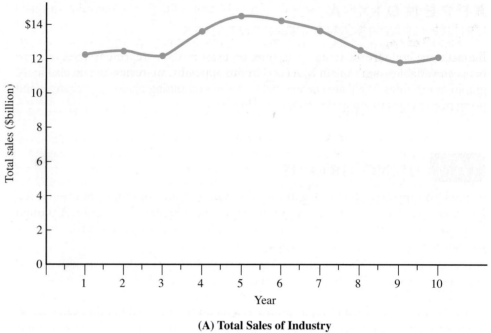

(A) Total Sales of Industry

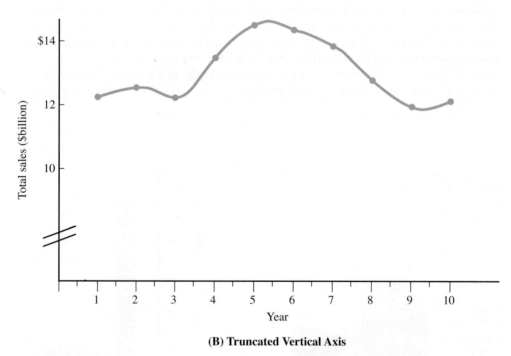

(B) Truncated Vertical Axis

▲ **FIGURE 1A.2**
Time-Series Graph

A third type of single-variable graph shows how the value of a variable changes over time. Panel A of Figure 1A.2 shows a time-series graph, with the total dollar value of a hypothetical industry for years 1 through 10. Time is measured on the horizontal axis, and sales are measured on the vertical axis. The height of the line in a particular year shows the value in that year. For example, in Year 1 the value was

$12.32 billion. After reaching a peak of $14.59 billion in Year 5, the value dropped over the next several years.

Panel B of Figure 1A.2 shows a truncated version of the graph in Panel A. The double hash marks in the lower part of the vertical axis indicate that the axis doesn't start from zero. This truncation of the vertical axis exaggerates the fluctuations in total sales.

Graphing Two Variables

We can also use a graph to show the relationship between two variables. Figure 1A.3 shows the basic elements of a two-variable graph. One variable is measured along the horizontal, or x, axis, while the other variable is measured along the vertical, or y, axis. The *origin* is the intersection of the two axes, where the values of both variables are zero. Dashed lines show the values of the two variables at a particular point. For example, for point a, the value of the horizontal, or x, variable is 10, and the value of the vertical, or y, variable is 13.

To see how to draw a two-variable graph, suppose that you have a part-time job and you are interested in the relationship between the number of hours you work and your weekly income. The relevant variables are the hours of work per week and your weekly income. In Figure 1A.4, the table shows the relationship between the hours worked and income. Let's assume that your weekly allowance from your parents is $40 and your part-time job pays $8 per hour. If you work 10 hours per week, for example, your weekly income is $120 ($40 from your parents and $80 from your job). The more you work, the higher your weekly income: If you work 20 hours, your weekly income is $200; if you work 30 hours, it is $280.

Although a table with numbers is helpful in showing the relationship between work hours and income, a graph makes it easier to see the relationship. We can use data in a table to draw a graph. To do so, we perform five simple steps:

1. Draw a horizontal line to represent the first variable. In Figure 1A.4, we measure hours worked along the horizontal axis. As we move to the right along the horizontal axis, the number of hours worked increases, from 0 to 30 hours.

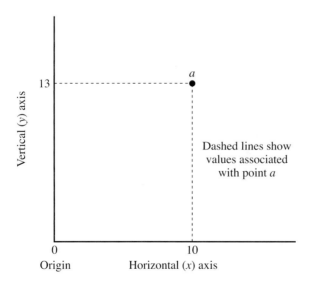

▲ FIGURE 1A.3

Basic Elements of a Two-Variable Graph

One variable is measured along the horizontal, or x, axis, while the other variable is measured along the vertical, or y, axis. The origin is defined as the intersection of the two axes, where the values of both variables are zero. The dashed lines show the values of the two variables at a particular point.

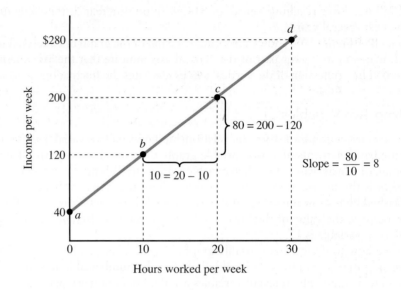

Hours Worked per Week	Income per Week	Point on the Graph
0	$ 40	a
10	120	b
20	200	c
30	280	d

▲ FIGURE 1A.4
Relationship between Hours Worked and Income
There is a positive relationship between work hours and income, so the income curve is positively sloped. The slope of the curve is $8: Each additional hour of work increases income by $8.

2 Draw a vertical line intersecting the first line to represent the second variable. In Figure 1A.4, we measure income along the vertical axis. As we move up along the vertical axis, income increases from $0 to $280.

3 Start with the first row of numbers in the table, which shows that with 0 hours worked, income is $40. The value of the variable on the horizontal axis is 0, and the value of the variable on the vertical axis is $40, so we plot point *a* on the graph. This is the *vertical intercept*—the point where the curve cuts or intersects the vertical axis.

4 Pick a combination with a positive number for hours worked. For example, in the second row of numbers, if you work 10 hours, your income is $120.

4.1 Find the point on the horizontal axis with that number of hours worked—10 hours—and draw a dashed line vertically straight up from that point.

4.2 Find the point on the vertical axis with the income corresponding to those hours worked—$120—and draw a dashed line horizontally straight to the right from that point.

4.3 The intersection of the dashed lines shows the combination of hours worked and income. Point b shows the combination of 10 hours worked and $120 in income.

5 Repeat step 4 for different combinations of work time and income shown in the table. Once we have a series of points on the graph (*a*, *b*, *c*, and *d*), we can connect them to draw a curve that shows the relationship between hours worked and income.

There is a **positive relationship** between two variables if they move in the same direction. As you increase your work time, your income increases, so there is a positive relationship between the two variables. In Figure 1A.4, as the number of hours worked increases, you move upward along the curve to higher income levels. Some people refer to a positive relationship as a *direct relationship*.

There is a **negative relationship** between two variables if they move in opposite directions. For example, there is a negative relationship between the amount of time you work and the time you have available for other activities such as recreation, study, and sleep. Some people refer to a negative relationship as an *inverse relationship*.

positive relationship

A relationship in which two variables move in the same direction.

negative relationship

A relationship in which two variables move in opposite directions.

Computing the Slope

How sensitive is one variable to changes in the other variable? We can use the slope of the curve to measure this sensitivity. To compute the **slope of a curve**, we pick two points and divide the vertical difference between the two points (the *rise*) by the horizontal difference (the *run*):

slope of a curve

The vertical difference between two points (the *rise*) divided by the horizontal difference (the *run*).

$$\text{Slope} = \frac{\text{Vertical difference between two points}}{\text{Horizontal difference between two points}} = \frac{\text{rise}}{\text{run}}$$

To compute the slope of a curve, we take four steps:

1. Pick two points on the curve, for example, points b and c in Figure 1A.4.
2. Compute the vertical difference between the two points (the rise). For points b and c, the vertical difference between the points is $80 ($200 – $120).
3. Compute the horizontal distance between the same two points (the run). For points b and c, the horizontal distance between the points is 10 hours (20 hours – 10 hours).
4. Divide the vertical distance by the horizontal distance to get the slope. The slope between points b and c is $8 per hour:

$$\text{Slope} = \frac{\text{Vertical difference}}{\text{Horizontal difference}} = \frac{\$200 - 120}{20 - 10} = \frac{\$80}{10} = \$8$$

In this case, a 10-hour increase in time worked increases income by $80, so the increase in income per hour of work is $8, which makes sense because this is the hourly wage. Because the curve is a straight line, the slope is the same at all points along the curve. You can check this yourself by computing the slope between points c and d.

We can use some shorthand to refer to the slope of a curve. The mathematical symbol Δ (delta) represents the change in a variable. So we can write the slope of the curve in Figure 1A.4 as

$$\text{Slope} = \frac{\Delta \text{ Income}}{\Delta \text{ Work hours}}$$

In general, if the variable on the vertical axis is y and the variable on the horizontal axis is x, we can express the slope as

$$\text{Slope} = \frac{\Delta y}{\Delta x}$$

Moving Along the Curve versus Shifting the Curve

Up to this point, we've explored the effect of changes in variables that cause movement along a given curve. In Figure 1A.4, we see the relationship between hours of work (on the horizontal axis) and income (on the vertical axis). Because the total income also depends on the allowance and the wage, we can make two observations about the curve in Figure 1A.4:

1 To draw this curve, we must specify the weekly allowance ($40) and the hourly wage ($8).

2 The curve shows that an increase in time worked increases the student's income, *ceteris paribus*. In this case, we are assuming that the allowance and the wage are both fixed.

A change in the weekly allowance will shift the curve showing the relationship between work time and income. In Figure 1A.5, when the allowance increases from $40 to $90 the curve shifts upward by $50: For a given number of work hours, income increases by $50. For example, the income associated with 10 hours of work is $170 (point *f*), compared to $120 with the original allowance (point *b*). The upward shift also means that to reach a given amount of income, fewer work hours are required. In other words, the curve shifts upward and to the left.

We can distinguish between movement along a curve and a shift of the entire curve. In Figure 1A.5, an increase in the hours worked causes movement along a single income curve. For example, if the allowance is $40, we are operating on the lower of the two curves, and if the hours worked increases from 10 to 20, we move from point *b* to point *c*. In contrast, if something other than the hours worked changes, we shift the entire curve, as we've seen with an increase in the allowance.

This book uses dozens of two-dimensional curves, each of which shows the relationship between *only two* variables. A common error is to forget that a single curve tells only part of the story. In Figure 1A.5, we needed two curves to explore the effects

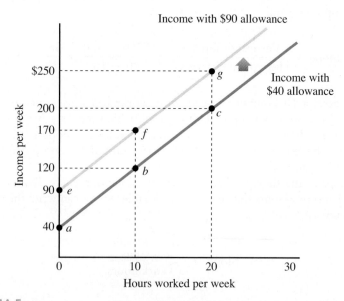

▲ FIGURE 1A.5

Movement Along a Curve versus Shifting the Curve

To draw a curve showing the relationship between hours worked and income, we fix the weekly allowance ($40) and the wage ($8 per hour). A change in the hours worked causes movement along the curve, for example, from point *b* to point *c*. A change in any other variable shifts the entire curve. For example, a $50 increase in the allowance (to $90) shifts the entire curve upward by $50.

of changes in three variables. Here are some simple rules to keep in mind when you use two-dimensional graphs:

- A change in one of the variables shown on the graph causes movement along the curve. In Figure 1A.5, an increase in work time causes movement along the curve from point *a* to point *b*, to point *c*, and so on.
- A change in one of the variables that is not shown on the graph—one of the variables held fixed in drawing the curve—shifts the entire curve. In Figure 1A.5, an increase in the allowance shifts the entire curve upward.

Graphing Negative Relationships

We can use a graph to show a negative relationship between two variables. Consider a consumer who has an annual budget of $360 to spend on CDs at a price of $12 per CD and downloaded music at a price of $1 per song. The table in Figure 1A.6 shows the relationship between the number of CDs and downloaded songs. A consumer who doesn't buy any CDs has $360 to spend on downloaded songs and can get 360 of them at a price of $1 each. A consumer who buys 10 CDs at $12 each has $240 left to spend on downloaded songs (point *b*). Moving down

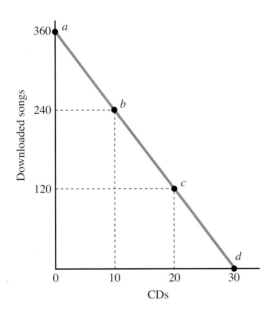

Number of CDs Purchased	Number of Songs Downloaded	Point on the Graph
0	360	a
10	240	b
20	120	c
30	0	a

▲ FIGURE 1A.6

Negative Relationship between CD Purchases and Downloaded Songs

There is a negative relationship between the number of CDs and downloaded songs that a consumer can afford with a budget of $360. The slope of the curve is –$12: Each additional CD (at a price of $12 each) decreases the number of downloadable songs (at $1 each) by 12 songs.

through the table, as the number of CDs increases, the number of downloaded songs decreases.

The graph in Figure 1A.6 shows the negative relationship between the number of CDs and the number of downloaded songs. The vertical intercept (point *a*) shows that a consumer who doesn't buy any CDs can afford 360 downloaded songs. There is a negative relationship between the number of CDs and downloaded songs, so the curve is negatively sloped. We can use points *b* and *c* to compute the slope of the curve:

$$\text{Slope} = \frac{\text{Vertical difference}}{\text{Horizontal difference}} = \frac{120 - 240}{20 - 10} = \frac{-120}{10} = -12$$

The slope is 12 downloaded songs per CD: For each additional CD, the consumer sacrifices 12 downloaded songs.

Graphing Nonlinear Relationships

We can also use a graph to show a nonlinear relationship between two variables. Panel A of Figure 1A.7 shows the relationship between hours spent studying for an exam and the grade on the exam. As study time increases, the grade increases,

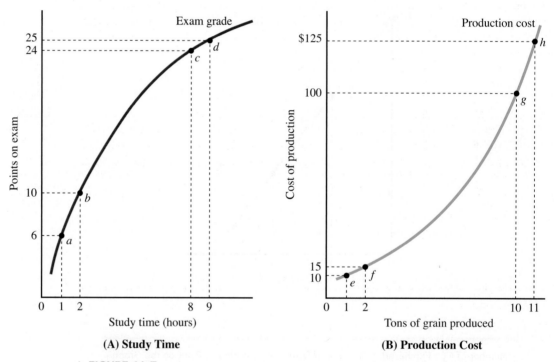

▲ FIGURE 1A.7
Nonlinear Relationships

(A) Study time There is a positive and nonlinear relationship between study time and the grade on an exam. As study time increases, the exam grade increases at a decreasing rate. For example, the second hour of study increased the grade by 4 points (from 6 points to 10 points), but the ninth hour of study increases the grade by only 1 point (from 24 points to 25 points).

(B) Production cost There is a positive and nonlinear relationship between the quantity of grain produced and total production cost. As the quantity increases, the total cost increases at an increasing rate. For example, to increase production from 1 ton to 2 tons, production cost increases by $5 (from $10 to $15) but to increase the production from 10 to 11 tons, total cost increases by $25 (from $100 to $125).

but at a decreasing rate. In other words, each additional hour increases the exam grade by a smaller and smaller amount. For example, the second hour of study increases the grade by 4 points—from 6 to 10 points—but the ninth hour of study increases the grade by only 1 point—from 24 points to 25 points. This is a non-linear relationship: The slope of the curve changes as we move along the curve. In Figure 1A.7, the slope decreases as we move to the right along the curve: The slope is 4 points per hour between points a and b but only 1 point per hour between points c and d.

Another possibility for a nonlinear curve is that the slope increases as we move to the right along the curve. Panel B of Figure 1A.7 shows the relationship between the amount of grain produced on the horizontal axis and the total cost of production on the vertical axis. The slope of the curve increases as the amount of grain increases, meaning that production cost increases at an increasing rate. On the lower part of the curve, increasing output from 1 ton to 2 tons increases production cost by $5, from $10 to $15. On the upper part of the curve, increasing output from 10 to 11 tons increases production cost by $25, from $100 to $125.

1A.2 COMPUTING PERCENTAGE CHANGES AND USING EQUATIONS

Economists often express changes in variables in terms of percentage changes. This part of the appendix provides a brief review of the mechanics of computing percentage changes. It also reviews some simple rules for solving equations to find missing values.

Computing Percentage Changes

In many cases, the equations that economists use involve percentage changes. In this book, we use a simple approach to computing percentage changes: We divide the change in the variable by the initial value of the variable and then multiply by 100:

$$\text{Percentage change} = \frac{\text{New value} - \text{initial value}}{\text{Initial value}} \times 100$$

For example, if the price of a book increases from $20 to $22, the percentage change is 10 percent:

$$\text{Percentage change} = \frac{22 - 20}{20} \times 100 = \frac{2}{20} \times 100 = 10\%$$

Going in the other direction, suppose the price decreases from $20 to $19. In this case, the percentage change is –5 percent:

$$\text{Percentage change} = \frac{19 - 20}{20} \times 100 = -\frac{1}{20} \times 100 = -5\%$$

The alternative to this simple approach is to base the percentage change on the average value, or the midpoint, of the variable:

$$\text{Percentage change} = \frac{\text{New value} - \text{initial value}}{\text{Average value}} \times 100$$

For example, if the price of a book increases from $20 to $22, the computed percentage change under the midpoint approach is 9.52 percent:

$$\text{Percentage change} = \frac{22 - 20}{(20 + 22) \div 2} \times 100 = \frac{2}{42 \div 2} \times 100$$

$$= \frac{2}{21} \times 100 = 9.52\%$$

If the change in the variable is relatively small, the extra precision associated with the midpoint approach is usually not worth the extra effort. The simple approach allows us to spend less time doing tedious arithmetic and more time doing economic analysis. In this book, we use the simple approach to compute percentage changes: If the price increases from $20 to $22, the price has increased by 10 percent.

If we know a percentage change, we can translate it into an absolute change. For example, if a price has increased by 10 percent and the initial price is $20, then we add 10 percent of the initial price ($2 is 10 percent of $20) to the initial price ($20), for a new price of $22. If the price decreases by 5 percent, we subtract 5 percent of

APPLICATION 3

THE PERILS OF PERCENTAGES

APPLYING THE CONCEPTS #3: How do we compute percentage changes?

In the 1970s the government of Mexico City repainted the highway lane lines on the *Viaducto* to transform a four-lane highway into a six-lane highway. The government announced that the highway capacity had increased by 50 percent (equal to 2 divided by 4). Unfortunately, the number of collisions and traffic fatalities increased, and one year later, the government restored the four-lane highway and announced that the capacity had decreased by 33 percent (equal to 2 divided by 6). The government announced that the net effect of the two changes was an increase in the highway capacity by 17 percent (equal to 50 percent minus 33 percent).

This anecdote reveals a potential problem with using the simple approach to compute percentage changes. Because the initial value (the denominator) changes, the computation of percentage increases and decreases are not symmetric. In contrast, if the government had used the midpoint method, the percentage increase in capacity would be 40 percent (equal to 2 divided by 5), the same as the percentage decrease. In that case, we get the more sensible result that the net effect of the two changes is zero. **Related to Exercise A8.**

SOURCE: Based on "The Perils of Percentages," *Economist*, April 18, 1998, 70.

the initial price ($1 is 5 percent of $20) from the initial price ($20), for a new price of $19.

Using Equations to Compute Missing Values

It will often be useful to compute the value of the numerator or the denominator of an equation. To do so, we use simple algebra to rearrange the equation to put the missing variable on the left side of the equation. For example, consider the relationship between time worked and income. The equation for the slope is

$$\text{Slope} = \frac{\Delta \text{ Income}}{\Delta \text{ Work hours}}$$

Suppose you want to compute how much income you'll earn by working more hours. We can rearrange the slope equation by multiplying both sides of the equation by the change in work hours:

$$\text{Work hours} \times \text{Slope} = \Delta \text{ Income}$$

By swapping sides of the equation, we get

$$\Delta \text{ Income} = \Delta \text{ Work hours} \times \text{Slope}$$

For example, if you work seven extra hours and the slope is $8, your income will increase by $56:

$$\Delta \text{ Income} = \Delta \text{ Work hours} \times \text{Slope} = \$7 \times \$8 = 56$$

We can use the same process to compute the difference in work time required to achieve a target change in income. In this case, we multiply both sides of the slope equation by the change in work time and then divide both sides by the slope. The result is

$$\Delta \text{Work hours} = \frac{\Delta \text{ Income}}{\text{Slope}}$$

For example, to increase your income by $56, you need to work seven hours:

$$\Delta \text{Work hours} = \frac{\Delta \text{Income}}{\text{Slope}} = \frac{\$56}{\$8} = 7$$

KEY TERMS

negative relationship, p. 19   positive relationship, p. 19   slope of a curve, p. 19

Visit www.myeconlab.com to complete these exercises online and get instant feedback.

A.1 Suppose you belong to a tennis club that has a monthly fee of $100 and a charge of $5 per hour to play tennis.

a. Using Figure 1A.4 on page 18 as a model, prepare a table and draw a curve to show the relationship between the hours of tennis (on the horizontal axis) and the monthly club bill (on the vertical axis). For the table and graph, use 5, 10, 15, and 20 hours of tennis.

b. The slope of the curve is _____ per _____.

c. Suppose you start with 10 hours of tennis and then decide to increase your tennis time by 3 hours. On your curve, show the initial point and the new point. By how much will your monthly bill increase?

d. Suppose you start with 10 hours and then decide to spend an additional $30 on tennis. On your curve, show the initial point and the new point. How many additional hours can you get?

A.2 The following graph shows the relationship between the number of Frisbees produced and the cost of production. The vertical intercept is $_____, and the slope of the curve is $_____ per Frisbee. Point *b* shows that the cost of producing _____ Frisbees is $_____. The cost of producing 15 Frisbees is $_____.

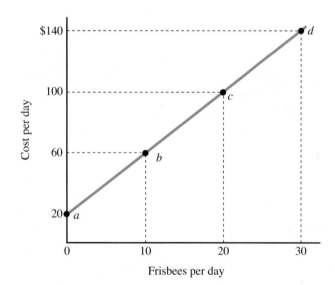

A.3 Suppose you have $120 to spend on CDs and movies. The price of a CD is $12, and the price of a movie is $6.

a. Using Figure 1A.6 on page 21 as a model, prepare a table and draw a curve to show the relationship

between the number of CDs (on the horizontal axis) and movies (on the vertical axis) you can afford to buy.

b. The slope of the curve is _____ per _____.

A.4 You manage Gofer Delivery Service. You rent a truck for $50 per day, and each delivery takes an hour of labor time. The hourly wage is $8.

a. Draw a curve showing the relationship between the number of deliveries (on the horizontal axis) and your total cost (on the vertical axis). Draw the curve for between 0 and 20 deliveries.

b. The slope of the cost curve is _____ per _____.

c. To draw the curve, what variables are held fixed?

d. A change in _____ would cause a movement upward along the curve.

e. Changes in _____ would cause the entire curve to shift upward.

A.5 A change in a variable measured on an axis of a graph causes movement _____ a curve, while a change in a relevant variable that is not measured on an axis _____ the curve.

A.6 Compute the percentage changes for the following:

Initial Value	New Value	Percentage Change
10	11	
100	98	
50	53	

A.7 Compute the new values for the following changes:

Initial Value	Percentage Change	New Value
100	12%	
50	8	
20	15	

A.8 Suppose the price of an mp3 player decreases from $60 to $40. Using the midpoint approach, the percentage change in price is _____. Using the initial-value approach, the percentage change in price is _____. (Related to Application 3 on page 24.)

NOTES

1. Texas Transportation Institute, *2005 Urban Mobility Study*, http://mobility.tamu.edu/ums/

2. William Easterly, *The Elusive Quest for Growth* (Cambridge, MA: MIT Press, 2001), Chapter 1.

3. William Easterly, *The Elusive Quest for Growth* (Cambridge, MA: MIT Press, 2001); World Bank, *World Development Report 2000/2001: Attacking Poverty* (New York: Oxford University Press, 2000).

4. John Maynard Keynes, *The Collected Writings of John Maynard Keynes, Volume 7*, ed. Donald Moggridge (London: Macmillan, 1973), 856. Reproduced with permission of the publisher.

5. Alfred Marshall, *Principles of Economics*, 9th ed., ed. C.W. Guillebaud (1920; repr., London: Macmillan, 1961), 366. Reproduced with permission of the publisher.

6. Adam Smith, *An Inquiry into the Nature and Causes of the Wealth of Nations* (1776); Book 2, Chapter 3.

2

The Key Principles of Economics

What do we sacrifice by preserving tropical rainforests rather than mining or logging the land? Recent experiences in Guyana and other tropical countries suggest that in some places, the answer is "not much"—only $1 per hectare per year ($0.40 per acre per year).[1] Conservation groups have a new strategy for conserving rain forests—bidding against loggers and miners for the use of the land. When the payoff from developing tropical forest land is relatively low, conservation groups can outbid developers at a price as low as $1 per hectare. When we add the cost of hiring locals to manage the ecosystems, the total cost of preservation is as low as $2 per hectare per year. A conservation group based in Amherst, New Hampshire, started by leasing 81,000 hectares of pristine forest in Guyana, and since then has leased land in Peru, Sierra Leone, Papua New Guinea, Fiji, and Mexico.

(APPLYING THE CONCEPTS)

1 **What is the opportunity cost of running a business?**
   Don't Forget the Costs of Time and Invested Funds

2 **How do people think at the margin?**
   Why Not Walk up an Escalator?

3 **What is the rationale for specialization and exchange?**
   Jasper Johns and Housepainting

4 **Do farmers experience diminishing returns?**
   Fertilizer and Crop Yields

5 **How does inflation affect the real minimum wage?**
   The Declining Real Minimum Wage

6 **How does inflation affect lenders and borrowers?**
   Repaying Student Loans

In this chapter, we introduce five key principles that provide a foundation for economic analysis. A *principle* is a self-evident truth that most people readily understand and accept. For example, most people readily accept the principle of gravity. As you read through the book, you will see the five key principles of economics again and again as you do your own economic analysis.

2.1 THE PRINCIPLE OF OPPORTUNITY COST

Economics is all about making choices, and to make good choices we must compare the benefit of something to its cost. **Opportunity cost** incorporates the notion of scarcity: No matter what we do, there is always a trade-off. We must trade off one thing for another because resources are limited and can be used in different ways. By acquiring something, we use up resources that could have been used to acquire something else. The notion of opportunity cost allows us to measure this trade-off.

opportunity cost

What you sacrifice to get something.

PRINCIPLE OF OPPORTUNITY COST

The opportunity cost of something is what you sacrifice to get it.

In most decisions we choose from several alternatives. For example, if you spend an hour studying for an economics exam, you have one less hour to pursue other activities. To determine the opportunity cost of an activity, we look at what you consider the best of these "other" activities. For example, suppose the alternatives to studying economics are studying for a history exam or working in a job that pays $10 per hour. If you consider studying for history a better use of your time than working, then the opportunity cost of studying economics is the four extra points you could have received on a history exam if you studied history instead of economics. Alternatively, if working is the best alternative, the opportunity cost of studying economics is the $10 you could have earned instead.

We can also apply the principle of opportunity cost to decisions about how to spend money from a fixed budget. For example, suppose that you have a fixed budget to spend on music. You can buy your music either at a local music store for $15 per CD or online for $1 per song. The opportunity cost of 1 CD is 15 one-dollar online songs. A hospital with a fixed salary budget can increase the number of doctors only at the expense of nurses or physician's assistants. If a doctor costs five times as much as a nurse, the opportunity cost of a doctor is five nurses.

In some cases, a product that appears to be free actually has a cost. That's why economists are fond of saying, "There's no such thing as a free lunch." Suppose someone offers to buy you lunch if you agree to listen to a sales pitch for a time-share condominium. Although you don't pay any money for the lunch, there is an opportunity cost because you could spend that time in another way—such as studying for your economics or history exam. The lunch isn't free because you sacrifice an hour of your time to get it.

The Cost of College

What is the opportunity cost of a college degree? Consider a student who spends a total of $40,000 for tuition and books. Instead of going to college, the student could have spent this money on a wide variety of goods, including housing, electronic devices, and world travel. Part of the opportunity cost of college is the $40,000 worth of other goods the student sacrifices to pay for tuition and books. Also, instead of going to college, the student could have worked as a bank clerk for $20,000 per year and earned $80,000 over four years. That makes the total opportunity cost of this student's college degree $120,000:

Opportunity cost of money spent on tuition and books	$ 40,000
Opportunity cost of college time (four years working for $20,000 per year)	80,000
Economic cost or total opportunity cost	$120,000

We haven't included the costs of food or housing in our computations of opportunity cost. That's because a student must eat and live somewhere even if he or she doesn't go to college. But if housing and food are more expensive in college, then we would include the extra costs of housing and food in our calculations.

There are other things to consider in a person's decision to attend college. As we'll see later, a college degree can increase a person's earning power, so there are benefits from a college degree. In addition, college offers the thrill of learning and the pleasure of meeting new people. To make an informed decision about whether to attend college, we must compare the benefits to the opportunity costs.

The Cost of Military Spending

We can use the principle of opportunity cost to explore the cost of military spending.[2] In 1992, Malaysia bought two warships. For the price of the warships, the country could have built a system to provide safe drinking water for 5 million citizens who lacked it. In other words, the opportunity cost of the warships was safe drinking water for 5 million people. The policy question is whether the benefits of the warships exceed their opportunity cost.

In the United States, economists have estimated that the cost of the war in Iraq will be at least $1 trillion. The economists' calculations go beyond the simple budgetary costs and quantify the opportunity cost of the war. For example, the resources used in the war could have been used in various government programs for children—to enroll more children in preschool programs, to hire more science and math teachers to reduce class sizes, or to immunize more children in poor countries. For example, each $100 billion spent on the war could instead support one of the following programs:

- Enroll 13 million preschool children in the Head Start program for one year.
- Hire 1.8 million additional teachers for one year.
- Immunize all the children in less-developed countries for the next 33 years.

The fact that the war has a large opportunity cost does not necessarily mean that it is unwise. The policy question is whether the benefits from the war exceed its opportunity cost. Taking another perspective, we can measure the opportunity cost of war in terms of its implications for domestic security. The resources used in the war in Iraq could have been used to improve domestic security by securing ports and cargo facilities, hiring more police officers, improving the screening of airline passengers and baggage, improving fire departments and other first responders, upgrading the Coast Guard fleet, and securing our railroad and highway systems. The cost of implementing the domestic-security recommendations of various government commissions would be about $31 billion, a small fraction of the cost of the war. The question for policymakers is whether money spent on domestic security would be more beneficial than money spent on the war.

Opportunity Cost and the Production Possibilities Curve

Just as individuals face limits, so do entire economies. As we saw in Chapter 1, the ability of an economy to produce goods and services is determined by its factors of production, including labor, natural resources, physical capital, human capital, and entrepreneurship.

Figure 2.1 shows a production possibilities graph for an economy that produces wheat and steel. The horizontal axis shows the quantity of wheat produced by the economy, and the vertical axis shows the quantity of steel produced. The shaded area shows all the possible combinations of the two goods the economy can produce. At point *a*, for example, the economy can produce 700 tons of steel and 10 tons of wheat. In contrast, at point *e*, the economy can produce 300 tons of steel and 20 tons of wheat. The set of points on the border between the shaded and unshaded area is called the **production possibilities curve** (or *production possibilities frontier*) because it separates the combinations that are attainable from those that are not. The attainable combinations are shown by the shaded area within the curve and the curve itself. The unattainable combinations are shown by the unshaded area outside the curve. The points on the curve show the combinations that are possible if the economy's resources are fully employed.

The production possibilities curve illustrates the notion of opportunity cost. If an economy is fully utilizing its resources, it can produce more of one product only if it produces less of another product. For example, to produce more wheat, we must take resources away from steel. As we move resources out of steel, the quantity of steel produced will decrease. For example, if we move from point *a* to point *b* along the

production possibilities curve

A curve that shows the possible combinations of products that an economy can produce, given that its productive resources are fully employed and efficiently used.

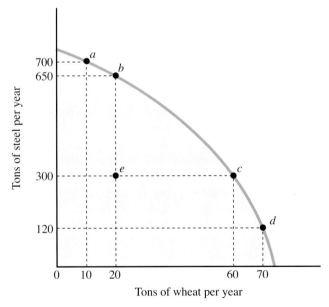

▲ FIGURE 2.1
Scarcity and the Production Possibilities Curve
The production possibilities curve illustrates the principle of opportunity cost for an entire economy. An economy has a fixed amount of resources. If these resources are fully employed, an increase in the production of wheat comes at the expense of steel.

APPLICATION 1

DON'T FORGET THE COSTS OF TIME AND INVESTED FUNDS

APPLYING THE CONCEPTS #1: What is the opportunity cost of running a business?

Betty has a degree in fine arts, and makes a unique product—decorative bottle-cap pins. She paints recycled bottle caps with attractive images, and attaches a pin so the bottle caps can be displayed on sweaters or jackets. She has asked you to compute the annual cost of her business. She uses machines and tools that have a current market value of $10,000. The annual cost of her raw materials (bottle caps, paint, pins) is $2,000. She could be earning $30,000 in another job.

We can use the principle of opportunity cost to compute Betty's costs. In addition to the $2,000 cost of raw materials, we must include two other sorts of costs:

- **Opportunity cost of funds invested.** Betty could have invested the $10,000 in a bank account. If the interest rate on a bank account is 8 percent, the annual cost of her capital (machines and tools) is the $800 she could have earned in a bank account during the year.

- **Opportunity cost of her time.** The opportunity cost of Betty's time is the $30,000 salary she sacrifices by being her own boss.

Adding the $800 cost of funds and the $30,000 cost of her time to the $2,000 materials cost, we find Betty's cost of doing business is $32,800 per year. **Related to Exercise 1.7.**

---

production possibilities curve in Figure 2.1, we sacrifice 50 tons of steel (700 tons – 650 tons) to get 10 more tons of wheat (20 tons – 10 tons). Further down the curve, if we move from point *c* to point *d*, we sacrifice 180 tons of steel to get the same 10-ton increase in wheat.

Why is the production possibilities curve bowed outward, with the opportunity cost of wheat increasing as we move down the curve? The reason is that resources are not perfectly adaptable for the production of both goods. Some resources are more suitable for steel production, while others are more suitable for wheat production. Starting at point *a*, the economy uses its most fertile land to produce wheat. A 10-ton increase in wheat reduces the quantity of steel by only 50 tons, because plenty of fertile land is available for conversion to wheat farming. As the economy moves downward along the production possibilities curve, farmers will be forced to use land that is progressively less fertile, so to increase wheat output by 10 tons, more and more resources must be diverted from steel production. In the move from point *c* to point *d*, the land converted to farming is so poor that increasing wheat output by 10 tons decreases steel output by 180 tons.

The production possibilities curve shows the production options for a given set of resources. As shown in Figure 2.2, an increase in the amount of resources available to the economy shifts the production possibilities outward. For example, if we start at point *f*, and the economy's resources increase, we can produce more steel (point *g*), more wheat (point *h*), or more of both goods (points between *g* and *h*). The curve will also shift outward as a result of technological innovations that enable us to produce more output with a given quantity of resources.

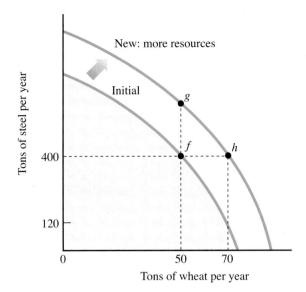

▲ **FIGURE 2.2**

Shifting the Production Possibilities Curve

An increase in the quantity of resources or technological innovation in an economy shifts the production possibilities curve outward. Starting from point *f*, a nation could produce more steel (point *g*), more wheat (point *h*), or more of both goods (points between *g* and *h*).

2.2 THE MARGINAL PRINCIPLE

Economics is about making choices, and we rarely make all-or-nothing choices. For example, if you sit down to read a book, you don't read the entire book in a single sitting, but instead decide how many pages or chapters to read. Economists think in marginal terms, considering how a one-unit change in one variable affects the value of another variable and people's decisions. When we say *marginal*, we're looking at the effect of a small, or incremental, change.

The marginal principle is based on a comparison of the marginal benefits and marginal costs of a particular activity. The **marginal benefit** of an activity is the additional benefit resulting from a small increase in the activity. For example, the marginal benefit of keeping a bookstore open for one more hour equals the additional revenue from book sales. Similarly, the **marginal cost** is the additional cost resulting from a small increase in the activity. For example, the marginal cost of keeping a bookstore open for one more hour equals the additional expenses for workers and utilities for that hour. Applying the marginal principle, the bookstore should stay open for one more hour if the marginal benefit (the additional revenue) is at least as large as the marginal cost (the additional cost). For example, if the marginal benefit is $80 of additional revenue and the marginal cost is $30 of additional expense for workers and utilities, staying open for the additional hour increases the bookstore's profit by $50.

marginal benefit

The additional benefit resulting from a small increase in some activity.

marginal cost

The additional cost resulting from a small increase in some activity.

MARGINAL PRINCIPLE

Increase the level of an activity as long as its marginal benefit exceeds its marginal cost. Choose the level at which the marginal benefit equals the marginal cost.

Thinking at the margin enables us to fine-tune our decisions. We can use the marginal principle to determine whether a one-unit increase in a variable would make us better off. Just as a bookstore owner could decide whether to stay open for one more hour, you could decide whether to study one more hour for a psychology midterm. When we reach the level where the marginal benefit equals the marginal cost, we cannot do any better, and the fine-tuning is done.

How Many Movie Sequels?

To illustrate the marginal principle, let's consider movie sequels. When a movie is successful, its producer naturally thinks about doing another movie, continuing the story line with the same set of characters. If the first sequel is successful too, the producer thinks about producing a second sequel, then a third, and so on. We can use the marginal principle to explore the decision of how many movies to produce.

Figure 2.3 shows the marginal benefits and marginal costs for movies. On the benefit side, a movie sequel typically generates about 30 percent less revenue than the original movie, and revenue continues to drop for additional movies. In the second column of the table, the first movie generates $300 million in revenue, the second generates $210 million, and the third generates $135 million. This is shown in the graph as a negatively sloped marginal-benefit curve, with the

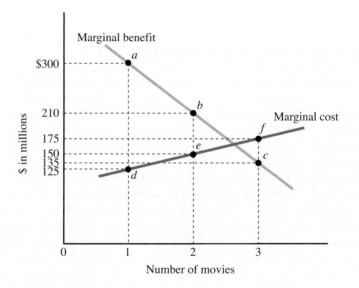

Number of Movies	Marginal Benefit ($ millions)	Marginal Cost ($ millions)
1	$300	$125
2	210	150
3	135	175

▲ **FIGURE 2.3**

The Marginal Principle and Movie Sequels

The marginal benefit of movies in a series decreases because revenue falls off with each additional movie, while the marginal cost increases because actors demand higher salaries. The marginal benefit exceeds the marginal cost for the first two movies, so it is sensible to produce two, but not three, movies.

marginal benefit decreasing from $300 for the first movie (point *a*), to $210 (point *b*), and then to $135 (point *c*). On the cost side, the typical movie in the United States costs about $50 million to produce and about $75 million to promote.[3] In the third column of the table, the cost of the first movie (the original) is $125 million. In the graph, this is shown as point *d* on the marginal-cost curve. The marginal cost increases with the number of movies because film stars typically demand higher salaries to appear in sequels. In the table and the graph, the marginal cost increases to $150 million for the second movie (point *e*) and to $175 million for the third (point *f*).

In this example, the first two movies are profitable, but the third is not. For the original movie, the marginal benefit ($300 million at point *a*) exceeds the marginal cost ($125 million at point *d*), generating a profit of $175 million. Although the second movie has a higher cost and a lower benefit, it is profitable because the marginal benefit still exceeds the marginal cost, so the profit on the second movie is $60 million ($210 million – $150 million). In contrast, the marginal cost of the third movie of $175 million exceeds its marginal benefit of only $135 million, so the third movie *loses* $40 million. In this example, the movie producer should stop after the second movie.

Although this example shows that only two movies are profitable, other outcomes are possible. If the revenue for the third movie were larger, making the marginal benefit greater than the marginal cost, it would be sensible to produce the third movie. Similarly, if the marginal cost of the third movie were lower—if the actors didn't demand such high salaries—the third movie could be profitable. Many movies have had multiple sequels, such as *Harry Potter and the Sorcerer's Stone* and *Star Wars*. Conversely, many profitable movies, such as *Wedding Crashers* and *Groundhog Day*, didn't result in any sequels. In these cases, the expected drop-off in revenues and run-up in costs for the second movie were large enough to make a sequel unprofitable.

Renting College Facilities

Suppose that your student film society is looking for an auditorium to use for an all-day Hitchcock film program and is willing to pay up to $200. Your college has a new auditorium that has a daily rent of $450, an amount that includes $300 to help pay for the cost of building the auditorium, $50 to help pay for insurance, and $100 to cover the extra costs of electricity and janitorial services for a one-day event. If your film society offers to pay $150 for using the auditorium, should the college accept the offer? The college could use the marginal principle to make the decision.

To decide whether to accept your group's offer, the college should determine the marginal cost of renting out the auditorium. The marginal cost equals the extra costs the college incurs by allowing the student group to use an otherwise vacant auditorium. In our example, the extra cost is $100 for additional electricity and janitorial services. It would be sensible for the college to rent the auditorium, because the marginal benefit ($150 offered by the student group) exceeds the marginal cost ($100). In fact, the college should be willing to rent the facility for any amount greater than $100. If the students and the college split the difference between the $200 the students are willing to pay and the $100 marginal cost, they would agree on a price of $150, leaving both parties better off by $50.

Most colleges do not use this sort of logic. Instead, they use complex formulas to compute the perceived cost of renting out a facility. In most cases, the perceived cost includes some costs that the university bears even if it doesn't rent out the facility for the day. In our example, the facility manager included $300 worth of construction costs and $50 worth of insurance, for a total cost of $450 instead of just $100. Because many colleges include costs that aren't affected by the use of a facility, they overestimate the actual cost of renting out their facilities, missing opportunities to serve student groups and make some money at the same time.

Automobile Emissions Standards

We can use the marginal principle to analyze emissions standards for automobiles. The U.S. government specifies how much carbon monoxide a new car is allowed to emit per mile. The marginal question is "Should the standard be stricter, with fewer units of carbon monoxide allowed?" On the benefit side, a stricter standard reduces health-care costs resulting from pollution: If the air is cleaner, people with respiratory ailments will make fewer visits to doctors and hospitals, have lower medication costs, and lose fewer work days. On the cost side, a stricter standard requires more expensive control equipment on cars and may also reduce fuel efficiency. Using the marginal principle, the government should make the emissions standard stricter as long as the marginal benefit (savings in health-care costs and work time lost) exceeds the marginal cost (the cost of additional equipment and extra fuel used).

(APPLICATION 2)

WHY NOT WALK UP AN ESCALATOR?

APPLYING THE CONCEPTS #2: How do people think at the margin?

Why do people walk up stairs, but do not walk up escalators? The rationale for walking up stairs is obvious—if you just stand still, you won't get anywhere. If the benefit of getting to the top of the stairs exceeds the cost (the walking effort), you'll walk up the stairs. So why do most people stand still on escalators? This is a bit of a puzzle because the cost of walking is the same whether you're on a staircase or an escalator, and in both cases, walking allows you to arrive sooner and spend more time at your destination.

We can use the marginal principle to solve this puzzle. Suppose you're on the way to listen to a free concert, and you'd be willing to pay $10 to hear the music. Suppose your cost of walking up a long staircase is $3—that's how much you'd be willing to pay to avoid the staircase. Walking the staircase generates a net benefit of $7 = $10 – $3, so climbing the stairs is sensible. Suppose that the following week you have the same music opportunity, but there is an escalator instead of a staircase. If you stand still on the escalator, you'll get the $10 benefit without any walking cost, so your net benefit would be $10. If you walk up the escalator, you will arrive at your destination sooner and get to listen to more music, but there would be a $3 walking cost. Should you walk or stand still? It depends on the *marginal* benefit of the extra music you will hear if you walk up the escalator instead of standing still, compared to the $3 *marginal* cost. If arriving sooner generates an extra benefit less than $3, it will be sensible for you to stand still, like most people. **Related to Exercises 2.4.**

SOURCE: Based on Steven E. Landsburg, "One Small Step for Man . . . And One Giant Leap for Economists: How We Figured Out Why People Walk Up Stairs but Not Up Escalators, *Slate.com*, August 28, 2002.

Driving Speed and Safety

Consider the decision about how fast to drive on a highway. The marginal benefit of going one mile per hour faster is the travel time you'll save. On the cost side, an increase in speed increases your chances of colliding with another car, and also increases the severity of injuries suffered in a collision. A rational person will pick the speed at which the marginal benefit of speed equals the marginal cost.

In the 1960s and 1970s, the federal government required automakers to include a number of safety features, including seat belts and collapsible steering columns. These new regulations had two puzzling effects. Although deaths from automobile collisions decreased, the reduction was much lower than expected. In addition, more bicyclists were hit by cars and injured or killed.

We can use the marginal principle to explain why seat belts and other safety features made bicycling more hazardous. The mandated safety features decreased the marginal cost of speed: People who wear seat belts suffer less severe injuries in a collision, so every additional unit of speed is less costly. Drivers felt more secure because they were better insulated from harm in the event of a collision, and so they drove faster. As a result, the number of collisions between cars and bicycles increased, meaning that the safer environment for drivers led to a more hazardous environment for bicyclists.

2.3 THE PRINCIPLE OF VOLUNTARY EXCHANGE

The principle of voluntary exchange is based on the notion that people act in their own self-interest. Self-interested people won't exchange one thing for another unless the trade makes them better off.

PRINCIPLE OF VOLUNTARY EXCHANGE

A voluntary exchange between two people makes both people better off.

Here are some examples.

- If you voluntarily exchange money for a college education, you must expect you'll be better off with a college education. The college voluntarily provides an education in exchange for your money, so the college must be better off, too.

- If you have a job, you voluntarily exchange your time for money, and your employer exchanges money for your labor services. Both you and your employer are better off as a result.

Exchange and Markets

Adam Smith stressed the importance of voluntary exchange as a distinctly human trait. He noticed[4]

> a propensity in human nature . . . to truck, barter, and exchange one thing for another . . . It is common to all men, and to be found in no other . . . animals . . . Nobody ever saw a dog make a fair and deliberate exchange of one bone for another with another dog.

As we saw in Chapter 1, a market is an institution or arrangement that enables people to exchange goods and services. If participation in a market is voluntary and

APPLICATION 3

JASPER JOHNS AND HOUSEPAINTING

APPLYING THE CONCEPTS #3: What is the rationale for specialization and exchange?

Jasper Johns is a contemporary American artist whose painting *False Start* sold for $80 million, the largest sum paid for a painting of a living artist. According to Skate's Art Market Research, Mr. Johns is among the top 30 artists in terms of the monetary value of art produced. Mr. Johns appears as a guest star in a 1999 episode of *The Simpsons* in which Homer uses a mangled barbeque to launch a career as a contemporary artist.

Mr. Johns is a very productive painter, and his painting skills presumably translate into house painting. If Mr. Johns is ten times more productive at house painting than a professional house painter, should he paint his own house? For example, suppose Mr. Johns can paint his house in one day, compared to 10 days for a professional. Should he take a day to paint his house, or hire someone who will take 10 days to complete the same task?

We can use the principle of voluntary exchange to explain why Mr. Johns should hire the less productive house painter to paint his house. If Mr. Johns can earn $5,000 per day painting works of art, the opportunity cost of house painting is $5,000—the income he sacrifices by spending a day painting the house rather than producing works of art. If the housepainter charges $150 per day, Mr. Johns could hire him to paint the house for only $1,500. By switching one day from house painting to art production, Mr. Johns earns $5,000 and incurs a cost of only $1,500, so he is better off by $3,500. Mr. Johns specializes in what he does best, and then buys goods and services from other people.   **Related to Exercise 3.5.**

---

people are well informed, both people in a transaction—buyer and seller—will be better off. The next time you see a market transaction, listen to what people say after money changes hands. If both people say "thank you," that's the principle of voluntary exchange in action: The double "thank you" reveals that both people are better off.

The alternative to exchange is *self-sufficiency*: Each of us could produce everything for him- or herself. As we'll see in the next chapter, it is more sensible to specialize, doing what we do best and then buying products from other people, who in turn are doing what they do best. For example, if you are good with numbers but an awful carpenter, you could specialize in accounting and buy furniture from Woody, who could specialize in making furniture and pay someone to do his bookkeeping. In general, exchange allows us to take advantage of differences in people's talents and skills.

Online Games and Market Exchange

As another illustration of the power of exchange, consider the virtual world of online games. Role-playing games such as *World of Warcraft* and *EverQuest* allow thousands of people to interact online, moving their characters through a landscape of survival challenges. Each player constructs a character—called an *avatar*—by choosing some initial traits for it. The player then navigates the avatar through the game's challenges, where it acquires skills and accumulates assets, including clothing, weapons, armor, and even magic spells.

The curious part about these role-playing games is that players use real-life auction sites, including eBay and Yahoo! Auctions, to buy products normally acquired in the game.[5] Byron, who wants a piece of armor for his avatar (say, a Rubicite girdle), can use eBay to buy one for $50 from Selma. The two players then enter the online game, and Selma's avatar transfers the armor to Byron's avatar. It is even possible to buy another player's avatar, with all its skills and assets. Given the time required to acquire various objects such as Rubicite girdles in the game and the prices paid for them on eBay, the implicit wage earned by the typical online player auctioning them off is $3.42 per hour: That's how much the player could earn by first taking the time to acquire the assets in the game and then selling them on eBay.

2.4 THE PRINCIPLE OF DIMINISHING RETURNS

Xena has a small copy shop, with one copying machine and one worker. When the backlog of orders piled up, she decided to hire a second worker, expecting that doubling her workforce would double the output of her copy shop from 500 pages per

---

APPLICATION 4

FERTILIZER AND CROP YIELDS

APPLYING THE CONCEPTS #4: Do farmers experience diminishing returns?

The notion of diminishing returns applies to all inputs to the production process. For example, one of the inputs in the production of corn is nitrogen fertilizer. Suppose a farmer has a fixed amount of land (an acre) and must decide how much fertilizer to apply. The first 50-pound bag of fertilizer will increase the crop yield by a relatively large amount, but the second bag is likely to increase the yield by a smaller amount, and the third bag is likely to have an even smaller effect. Because the farmer is changing just one of the inputs, the output will increase, but at a decreasing rate. Eventually, additional fertilizer will actually decrease output as the other nutrients in the soil are overwhelmed by the fertilizer.

Table 2.1 shows the relationship between the amount of fertilizer and the corn output. The first 50-pound bag of fertilizer increases the crop yield from 85 to 120 bushels per acre, a gain of 35 bushels. The next bag of fertilizer increases the yield by only 15 bushels (from 120 to 135), followed by a gain of 9 bushels (from 135 to 144) and then a gain of only 3 bushels (from 144 to 147). The farmer experienced diminishing returns because the other inputs to the production process are fixed.   **Related to Exercises 4.5 and 4.6.**

TABLE 2.1 FERTILIZER AND CORN YIELD	
Bags of Nitrogen Fertilizer	Bushels of Corn Per Acre
0	85
1	120
2	135
3	144
4	147

hour to 1,000. Xena was surprised when output increased to only 800 pages per hour. If she had known about the principle of diminishing returns, she would not have been surprised.

PRINCIPLE OF DIMINISHING RETURNS

Suppose output is produced with two or more inputs, and we increase one input while holding the other input or inputs fixed. Beyond some point—called the *point of diminishing returns*—output will increase at a decreasing rate.

Xena added a worker (one input) while holding the number of copying machines (the other input) fixed. Because the two workers must share a single copying machine, each worker spent some time waiting for the machine to be available. As a result, adding the second worker increased the number of copies, but did not double the output. With a single worker and a single copy machine, Xena has already reached the point of diminishing returns: As she increases the number of workers, output increases, but at a decreasing rate. The first worker increases output by 500 pages (from 0 to 500), but the second worker increases output by only 300 pages (from 500 to 800).

Diminishing Returns from Sharing a Production Facility

This principle of diminishing returns is relevant when we try to produce more output in an existing production facility (a factory, a store, an office, or a farm) by increasing the number of workers sharing the facility. When we add a worker to the facility, each worker becomes less productive because he or she works with a smaller piece of the facility: More workers share the same machinery, equipment, and factory space. As we pack more and more workers into the factory, total output increases, but at a decreasing rate.

It's important to emphasize that diminishing returns occurs because one of the inputs to the production process is fixed. When a firm can vary all its inputs, including the size of the production facility, the principle of diminishing returns is not relevant. For example, if a firm doubled all its inputs, building a second factory and hiring a second workforce, we would expect the total output of the firm to at least double. The principle of diminishing returns does not apply when a firm is flexible in choosing all its inputs.

2.5 THE REAL-NOMINAL PRINCIPLE

One of the key ideas in economics is that people are interested not just in the amount of money they have but also in how much their money will buy.

REAL-NOMINAL PRINCIPLE

What matters to people is the real value of money or income—its purchasing power—not its "face" value.

APPLICATION 5

THE DECLINING REAL MINIMUM WAGE

APPLYING THE CONCEPTS #5: How does inflation affect the real minimum wage?

Between 1974 and 2007, the federal minimum wage increased from $2.00 to $5.85. Was the typical minimum-wage worker better or worse off in 2007? We can apply the real-nominal principle to see what's happened over time to the real value of the federal minimum wage.

As shown in the first row of Table 2.2, the minimum wage was $2.00 per hour in 1974, and by 2007 it had risen to $5.85. These are nominal figures, indicating the face value of the minimum wage. By working 40 hours per week, a minimum-wage worker could earn $80 in 1974 and $234 in 2007. The third row of Table 2.2 shows the cost of a standard basket of consumer goods, which includes a standard mix of housing, food, clothing, and transportation. In 1974, consumer prices were relatively low, and the cost of buying all the goods in the standard basket was only $47. Between 1974 and 2007, consumer prices increased, and the cost of this standard basket of goods increased to $202.

The last row in Table 2.2 shows the purchasing power of the minimum wage in 1974 and 2007. In 1974, the $80 in weekly income could buy 1.70 standard baskets of goods. Between 1974 and 2007, the weekly income nearly tripled, but the cost of the standard basket of goods more than quadrupled, from $47 to $202. As a result, the weekly income of $234 in 2007 could buy only 1.16 baskets of goods. Because prices increased faster than the nominal wage, the real value of the minimum wage actually decreased over this period.

The minimum wage increased to $6.55 in July 2008 and $7.25 one year later. These wage hikes are not large enough to restore the 1974 purchasing power of the minimum wage. For that to happen, the minimum wage in July of 2008 would have to be about $8.84.   **Related to Exercises 5.5 and 5.7.**

TABLE 2.2 THE REAL VALUE OF THE MINIMUM WAGE, 1974–2007		
	1974	2007
Minimum wage per hour	$ 2.00	$ 5.85
Weekly income from minimum wage	80.00	234.00
Cost of a standard basket of goods	47.00	202.00
Number of baskets per week	1.70	1.16

To illustrate this principle, suppose you work in your college bookstore to earn extra money for movies and snacks. If your take-home pay is $10 per hour, is this a high wage or a low wage? The answer depends on the prices of the goods you buy. If a movie costs $4 and a snack costs $1, with one hour of work you could afford to see two movies and buy two snacks. The wage may seem high enough for you. But if a movie costs $8 and a snack costs $2, an hour of work would buy only one movie and one snack, and the same $10 wage doesn't seem so high. This is the real-nominal principle in action: What matters is not how many dollars you earn, but what those dollars will purchase.

APPLICATION 6

REPAYING STUDENT LOANS

APPLYING THE CONCEPTS #6: How does inflation affect lenders and borrowers?

Suppose you finish college with $20,000 in student loans and start a job that pays a salary of $40,000 in the first year. In 10 years, you must repay your college loans. Which would you prefer: stable prices, rising prices, or falling prices?

We can use the real-nominal principle to compute the real cost of repaying your loans. The first row of Table 2.3 shows the cost of the loan when all prices in the economy are stable—including the price of labor, your salary. In this case, your nominal salary in 10 years is $40,000, and the real cost of repaying your loan is the half year of work you must do to earn the $20,000 you owe. However, if all prices double over the 10-year period, your nominal salary will double to $80,000, and, as shown in the second row of Table 2.3, it will take you only a quarter of a year to earn $20,000 to repay the loan. In other words, a general increase in prices lowers the real cost of your loan. In contrast, if all prices decrease and your annual salary drops to $20,000, it will take you a full year to earn the money to repay the loan. In general, people who owe money prefer inflation (a general rise in prices) to deflation (a general drop in prices). **Related to Exercises 5.6 and 5.9.**

TABLE 2.3 EFFECT OF INFLATION AND DEFLATION ON LOAN REPAYMENT		
Change in Prices and Wages	Annual Salary	Years of Work to Repay $20,000 Loan
Stable	$40,000	1/2 year
Inflation: Salary doubles	80,000	1/4 year
Deflation: Salary cut in half	20,000	1 year

Economists use special terms to express the ideas behind the real-nominal principle:

nominal value
The face value of an amount of money.

- The **nominal value** of an amount of money is simply its face value. For example, the nominal wage paid by the bookstore is $10 per hour.

real value
The value of an amount of money in terms of what it can buy.

- The **real value** of an amount of money is measured in terms of the quantity of goods the money can buy. For example, the real value of your bookstore wage would fall as the prices of movies and snacks increase, even though your nominal wage stayed the same.

The real-nominal principle can explain how people choose the amount of money to carry around with them. Suppose you typically withdraw $40 per week from an ATM to cover your normal expenses. If the prices of all the goods you purchase during the week double, you would have to withdraw $80 per week to make the same purchases. The amount of money people carry around depends on the prices of the goods and services they buy.

Government officials use the real-nominal principle when they design public programs. For example, Social Security payments are increased each year to ensure that the checks received by the elderly and other recipients will purchase the same amount of goods and services, even if prices have increased. The government also uses this principle when it publishes statistics about the economy. For example, its reports about changes in "real wages" in the economy over time take into account the prices of the goods workers purchase. Therefore, the real wage is stated in terms of its buying power, rather than its face value or nominal value.

SUMMARY

This chapter covers five key principles of economics, the simple, self-evident truths that most people readily accept. If you understand these principles, you are ready to read the rest of the book, which will show you how to do your own economic analysis.

1 Principle of opportunity cost. The opportunity cost of something is what you sacrifice to get it.

2 Marginal principle. Increase the level of an activity as long as its marginal benefit exceeds its marginal cost. Choose the level at which the marginal benefit equals the marginal cost.

3 Principle of voluntary exchange. A voluntary exchange between two people makes both people better off.

4 Principle of diminishing returns. Suppose that output is produced with two or more inputs, and we increase one input while holding the other inputs fixed. Beyond some point—called the *point of diminishing returns*—output will increase at a decreasing rate.

5 Real-nominal principle. What matters to people is the real value of money or income—its purchasing power—not the face value of money or income.

KEY TERMS

marginal benefit, p. 33

marginal cost, p. 33

nominal value, p. 42

opportunity cost, p. 29

production possibilities curve, p. 31

real value, p. 42

EXERCISES

Visit www.myeconlab.com to complete these exercises online and get instant feedback.

2.1 The Principle of Opportunity Cost

1.1 Consider Figure 2.1 on page 31. Between points *c* and *d*, the opportunity cost of _____ tons of wheat is _____ tons of steel.

1.2 Arrow up or down: An increase in the wage for high-school graduates _____ the opportunity cost of college.

1.3 Arrow up or down: An increase in the market interest rate _____ the economic cost of holding a $500 collectible for a year.

1.4 You just inherited a house with a market value of $300,000, and do not expect the market value to change. Each year, you will pay $1,000 for utilities and $3,000 in taxes. You can earn 6 percent interest on money in a bank account. Your cost of living in the house for a year is $_____.

1.5 What is the cost of a pair of warships purchased by Malaysia?

1.6 Conservationists have a new strategy for preserving rainforests: _____ loggers and other developers for the land, paying as little as $_____ per hectare per year.

1.7 **The Cost of a Flower Business.** Jen left a job paying $40,000 per year to start her own florist shop in a building she owns. The market value of the building is $200,000. She pays $30,000 per year for flowers and other supplies, and has a bank account that pays 8 percent interest. The annual economic cost of Jen's business is _____. (Related to Application 1 on page 32.)

1.8 **The Opportunity Cost of a Mission to Mars.** The United States has plans to spend billions of dollars on a mission to Mars. List some of the possible opportunity costs of the mission. What resources will be used to execute the mission, and what do we sacrifice by using these resources in a mission to Mars?

1.9 **Interest Rates and ATM Trips.** Carlos, who lives in a country where interest rates are very high, goes to an ATM every day to get $10 of spending money. Art, who lives in a country with relatively low interest rates, goes to the ATM once a month to get $300 of spending money. Why does Carlos use the ATM more frequently?

1.10 **Correct the Cost Statements.** Consider the following statements about cost. For each incorrect statement, provide a correct statement about the relevant cost.

   a. One year ago, I loaned a friend $100, and she just paid me back the whole $100. The loan didn't cost me anything.

   b. An oil refinery bought a million barrels of oil a month ago, when the price was only $75 per barrel, compared to $120 today. The cost of using a barrel of oil to produce gasoline is $75.

   c. Our new football stadium was built on land donated to the university by a wealthy alum. The cost of the stadium equals the $50 million construction cost.

   d. If a commuter rides a bus to work and the bus fare is $2, the cost of commuting by bus is $2.

1.11 **Production Possibilities Curve.** Consider a nation that produces baseball mitts and soccer balls. The following table shows the possible combinations of the two products.

Baseball mitts (millions)	0	2	4	6	8
Soccer balls (millions)	30	24	18	10	0

   a. Draw a production possibilities curve with mitts on the horizontal axis and balls on the vertical axis.

   b. Suppose the technology for producing mitts improves, meaning that fewer resources are needed for each mitt. In contrast, the technology for producing soccer balls does not change. Draw a new production possibilities curve.

   c. The opportunity cost of the first two million mitts is _____ million soccer balls and the opportunity cost of the last two million mitts is _____ million soccer balls.

1.12 **Cost of Antique Furniture.** Colleen owns antique furniture that she bought for $5,000 ten years ago.

Your job is to compute Colleen's cost of owning the furniture for the next year. To compute the cost, you need two bits of information: _____ and _____.

2.2 The Marginal Principle

2.1 A taxi company currently has nine cabs in its fleet, and its total daily cost is $4,000. If the company added a tenth cab, its daily total cost would be $4,200, or $420 per cab. Adding the tenth cab will increase the daily total revenue by $300. Should the company add the tenth cab? _____ (Yes/No)

2.2 In Figure 2.3 on page 34, suppose the marginal cost of movies is constant at $125 million. Is it sensible to produce the third movie? _____ (Yes/No)

2.3 Suppose that stricter emissions standards would reduce health-care costs by $50 million but increase the costs of fuel and emissions equipment by $30 million. Is it sensible to tighten the emissions standards? _____ (Yes/No)

2.4 Arrows up or down: The decision about whether to walk up an escalator is based on the _____ benefit and the _____ cost. (Related to Application 2 on page 36.)

2.5 **How Fast to Drive?** Suppose Duke is driving to a nearby town to attend a dance party, and must decide how fast to drive. The marginal benefit of speed is the extra dance time he will get by driving faster, and the marginal cost is the additional risk of a collision. The marginal-benefit curve is negatively sloped, and the marginal-cost curve is positively sloped.

   a. Draw a pair of curves that suggest Duke will drive 40 mph.

   b. Suppose the normal country band is replaced by Adam Smith and the Invisible Hands, Duke's favorite punk band. Duke's utility from slam dancing is twice his utility from the two-step. Use your curves to show how Duke's chosen speed will change.

   c. Suppose Duke's favorite dance partner, Daisy, is grounded for makeup violations. Use your curves to show how Duke's chosen speed will change.

   d. Suppose the legal speed limit is set at 35 mph, and there is a 50 percent chance that Duke will be caught if he speeds. Use your curves to show how Duke's chosen speed will change.

2.6 **Continental Airlines Goes Marginal.** In the 1960s, Continental Airlines puzzled observers of the airline industry and dismayed its stockholders by running flights with up to half the seats empty. The average cost of running a flight was $4,000, a figure that includes fixed costs such as airport fees and the cost of running the reservation system. A half-full aircraft generated only $3,100 of revenue.

   a. Use the marginal principle to explain why Continental ran half-empty flights.

   b. It will be sensible to run a half-empty flight if the marginal _____ of flight is _____ than $_____.

2.7 Marginal Airlines. Marginal Airlines runs 10 flights per day at a total cost of $50,000, including $30,000 in fixed costs for airport fees and the reservation system and $20,000 for flight crews and food service.

   a. If an 11th flight would have 25 passengers, each paying $100, would it be sensible to run the flight?

   b. If the 11th flight would have only 15 passengers, would it be sensible to run the flight?

2.8 How Many Police Officers? In your city, each police officer has a budgetary cost of $40,000 per year. The property loss from each burglary is $4,000. The first officer hired will reduce crime by 40 burglaries, and each additional officer will reduce crime by half as much as the previous one. How many officers should the city hire? Illustrate with a graph with a marginal-benefit curve and a marginal-cost curve.

2.9 How Many Hours at the Barber Shop? The opportunity cost of your time spent cutting hair at your barbershop is $20 per hour. Electricity costs $6 per hour, and your weekly rent is $250. You normally stay open nine hours per day.

   a. What is the marginal cost of staying open for one more hour?

   b. If you expect to give two haircuts in the 10th hour and you charge $15 per haircut, is it sensible to stay open for the extra hour?

2.10 How Many Pints of Blackberries? The pleasure you get from each pint of freshly picked blackberries is $2.00. It takes you 12 minutes to pick the first pint, and each additional pint takes an additional 2 minutes (14 minutes for the second pint, 16 minutes for the third pint, and so on). The opportunity cost of your time is $0.10 per minute.

   a. How many pints of blackberries should you pick? Illustrate with a complete graph.

   b. How would your answer to (a) change if your pleasure decreased by $0.20 for each additional pint ($1.80 for the second, $1.60 for the third, and so on)? Illustrate with a complete graph.

2.3 The Principle of Voluntary Exchange

3.1 When two people involved in an exchange say "thank you" afterwards, they are merely being polite. _____ (True/False)

3.2 Consider a transaction in which a consumer buys a book for $15. The value of the book to the buyer is at least $_____, and the cost of producing the book is no more than $_____.

3.3 Arrow up or down: Andy buys and eats one apple per day, and smacks his lips in appreciation as he eats it. The greater his satisfaction with the exchange of money for an apple, the larger the number of smacks. If the price of apples decreases, the number of smacks per apple will _____.

3.4 Sally sells one apple per day to Andy, and says "ca-ching" to show her satisfaction with the transaction. The greater her satisfaction with the exchange, the louder her "ca-ching." If the price of apples decreases, her "ca-ching" will become _____(louder/softer).

3.5 Should a Heart Surgeon Do Her Own Plumbing? A heart surgeon is skillful at unplugging arteries and rerouting the flow of blood, and these skills also make her a very skillful plumber. She can clear a clogged drain in six minutes, about 10 times faster than the most skillful plumber in town. (Related to Application 3 on page 38.)

   a. Should the surgeon clear her own clogged drains? Explain.

   b. Suppose the surgeon earns $20 per minute in heart surgery, and the best plumber in town charges $50 per hour. How much does the surgeon gain by hiring the plumber to clear a clogged drain?

3.6 Fishing versus Boat Building. Half the members of a fishing tribe catch two fish per day and half catch eight fish per day. A group of 10 members could build a boat for another tribe in one day and receive a payment of 40 fish for the boat.

   a. Suppose the boat builders are drawn at random from the tribe. From the tribe's perspective, what is the expected cost of building the boat?

   b. How could the tribe decrease the cost of building the boat, thus making it worthwhile?

3.7 Solving a Tree Cutting Problem. Consider a hilly neighborhood where large trees provide shade but also block views. When a resident announces plans to cut down several trees to improve her view, her neighbors object and announce plans to block the tree cutting. One week later, the trees are gone, but everyone is happy. Use the principle of voluntary exchange to explain what happened.

2.4 The Principle of Diminishing Returns

4.1 Consider the example of Xena's copy shop. Adding a second worker increased output by 300 pages. If she added a third worker, her output would increase by fewer than _____ pages.

4.2 If a firm is subject to diminishing marginal returns, an increase in the number of workers decreases the quantity produced. _____ (True/False)

4.3 Fill in the blanks with "at least" or "less than": If a firm doubles one input but holds the other inputs fixed, we normally expect output to _____ double; if a firm doubles all inputs, we expect output to _____ double.

4.4 Fill in the blanks with "flexible" or "inflexible": Diminishing returns is applicable when a firm is _____ in choosing inputs, but does not apply when a firm is _____ in choosing its inputs.

4.5 Arrows up or down: As a farmer adds more and more fertilizer to the soil, the crop yield _____, but at a _____ rate. (Related to Application 4 on page 39.)

4.6 **Feeding the World from a Flowerpot?** Comment on the following statement: "If agriculture did not experience diminishing returns, we could feed the world using the soil from a small flowerpot." (Related to Application 4 on page 39.)

4.7 **When to Use the Principle of Diminishing Returns?** You are the manager of a firm that produces memory chips for mobile phones.

 a. In your decision about how much output to produce this week, would you use the principle of diminishing returns? Explain.

 b. In your decision about how much output to produce two years from now, would you use the principle of diminishing returns? Explain.

4.8 **Diminishing Returns in Microbrewing?** Your microbrewery produces craft beer, using a single vat, various ingredients, and workers.

 a. If you double the number of workers and ingredients, but don't add a second vat, would you expect your output (gallons per hour) to double? Explain.

 b. If you double the number of workers and ingredients and add a second vat, would you expect your output (gallons per hour) to double? Explain.

4.9 **Diminishing Returns and the Marginal Principle.** Molly's Espresso Shop has become busy, and the more hours Ted works, the more espressos Molly can sell.

The price of espressos is $2 and Ted's hourly wage is $11. Complete the following table:

Hours for Ted	Espressos Sold	Marginal Benefit from Additional Hour	Marginal Cost from Additional Hour
0	100	—	—
1	130	$60 = $2 × 30 additional espressos	$11 = hourly wage
2	154		
3	172		
4	184		
5	190		
6	193		

If Molly applies the marginal principle, how many hours should Ted work?

2.5 The Real-Nominal Principle

5.1 Your savings account pays 4 percent per year: Each $100 in the bank grows to $104 over a one-year period. If prices increase by 3 percent per year, by keeping $100 in the bank for a year you actually gain $_____.

5.2 You earn 5 percent interest on funds in your money-market account. If consumer prices increase by 7 percent per year, your earnings on $1,000 in the money-market account is $_____ per year.

5.3 Suppose that over a one-year period, the nominal wage increases by 2 percent and consumer prices increase by 5 percent. Fill in the blanks: The real wage _____ by _____ percent.

5.4 Suppose you currently live and work in Cleveland, earning a salary of $60,000 per year and spending $10,000 for housing. You just heard that you will be transferred to a city in California where housing is 50 percent more expensive. In negotiating a new salary, your objective is to keep your real income constant. Your new target salary is $_____.

5.5 Between 1974 and 2005, the federal minimum wage increased from $2.00 to $5.15. Was the typical minimum-wage worker better off in 2005? _____ (Yes/No) (Related to Application 5 on page 41.)

5.6 Suppose you graduate with $20,000 in student loans and repay the loans 10 years later. Which is better for you, inflation (rising prices) or deflation (falling prices)? _____ (Related to Application 6 on page 42.)

5.7 Changes in Welfare Payments. Between 1970 and 1988, the average monthly welfare payment to single mothers increased from $160 to $360. Over the same period, the cost of a standard basket of consumer goods (a standard bundle of food, housing, and other goods and services) increased from $39 to $118. Fill the blanks in the following table. Did the real value of welfare payments increase or decrease over this period? (Related to Application 5 on page 41.)

	1970	1988
Monthly welfare payment	$160	$360
Cost of a standard basket of goods	39	118
Number of baskets per week		

5.8 Changes in Wages and Consumer Prices. The following table shows for 1980 and 2004 the cost of a standard basket of consumer goods (a standard bundle of food, housing, and other goods and services) and the nominal average wage (hourly earnings) for workers in several sectors of the economy.

Year	Cost of Consumer Basket	Nominal Wage: Manufacturing	Nominal Wage: Professional Services	Nominal Wage: Leisure and Hospitality	Nominal Wage: Information
1980	$ 82	$ 7.52	$ 7.48	$4.05	$ 9.83
2004	189	16.34	17.69	9.01	21.70
Percent change from 1980 to 2004					

a. Complete the table by computing the percentage changes of the cost of the basket of consumer goods and the nominal wages.

b. How do the percentage changes in nominal wages compare to the percentage change in the cost of consumer goods?

c. Which sectors experienced an increase in real wages, and which sectors experienced a decrease in real wages?

5.9 Repaying a Car Loan. Suppose you borrow money to buy a car and must repay $20,000 in interest and principal in five years. Your current monthly salary is $4,000. (Related to Application 6 on page 42.)

a. Complete the following table.

b. Which environment has the lowest real cost of repaying the loan?

Change in Prices and Wages	Monthly Salary	Months of Work to Repay $20,000 Loan
Stable	$4,000	
Inflation: Prices rise by 25%		
Deflation: Prices drop by 50%		

5.10 Inflation and Interest Rates. Len buys MP3 music at $1 per tune, and prefers music now to music later. He is willing to sacrifice 10 tunes today as long as he gets at least 11 tunes in a year. When Len loans $50 to Barb for a one-year period, he cuts back his music purchases by 50 tunes.

a. To make Len indifferent about making the loan, Barb must repay him _____ tunes or $_____. The implied interest rate is _____ percent.

b. Suppose that over the one-year period of the loan, all prices (including the price of MP3 tunes) increase by 20 percent, and Len and Barb anticipate the price changes. To make Len indifferent about making the loan, Barb must repay him _____ tunes or $_____. The implied interest rate is _____ percent.

ECONOMIC EXPERIMENT

Producing Fold-Its

Here is a simple economic experiment that takes about 15 minutes to run. The instructor places a stapler and a stack of paper on a table. Students produce "fold-its" by folding a page of paper in thirds and stapling both ends of the folded page. One student is assigned to inspect each fold-it to be sure that it is produced correctly. The experiment starts with a single student, or worker, who has one minute to produce as many fold-its as possible. After the instructor records the number of fold-its produced, the process is repeated with two students, three students, four students, and so on. How does the number of fold-its change as the number of workers increases?

 For additional economic experiments, please visit *www.myeconlab.com.*

NOTES

1. "Rent a Tree," *The Economist*, March 3, 2008.

2. United Nations Development Program, *Human Development Report 1994* (New York: Oxford University Press, 1994); Linda Blimes and Joseph Stiglitz, "The Economic Costs of the Iraq War: An Appraisal Three Years After the Beginning of the Conflict," *Faculty Research Working Papers*, Harvard University, January 2006; Center for American Progress, "The Opportunity Costs of the Iraq War," August 25, 2004; Scott Wallsten and Katrina Kosec, "The Economic Costs of the War in Iraq," AEI-Brookings Joint Center for Regulatory Studies, September 2005; Joseph Stiglitz and Linda Bilmes, *The Three Trillion Dollar War* (New York: WW Norton, 2008).

3. Colin Kennedy, "Lord of the Screens," in *Economist: The World in 2003* (London, 2003), 29.

4. Adam Smith, *An Inquiry into the Nature and Causes of the Wealth of Nations* (1776), Book 1, Chapter 2.

5. Edward Castronova, *Synthetic Worlds: The Business and Culture of Online Games* (Chicago: University of Chicago Press, 2005).

Exchange and Markets

Mattel's Barbie, the most profitable doll in history, is sold in 140 countries around the world at a rate of two dolls per second. Annual sales are $1.6 billion.[1] Most people think the doll symbolizes U.S. culture, but Barbie is really an international product. Saudi Arabia provides the oil used in Taiwanese factories to produce the vinyl plastic pellets that become Barbie's body. Japan supplies Barbie's nylon hair, and China provides her cotton clothes. The machinery used in Barbie factories in China, Indonesia, and Malaysia comes from Japan, Europe, and the United States. The United States provides the designs, the molds used to form the dolls, and the pigments and oils used to paint them. Barbie dolls come in a box labeled "Made in China," but only about $0.33 of the $10 retail price goes to the factories in China that assemble the dolls. The rest goes to input suppliers around the world and to Mattel, which collects a $1 profit on each Barbie doll sold.

APPLYING THE CONCEPTS

1 Does the protection of one domestic industry harm another?
   Candy Cane Makers Move to Mexico for Cheap Sugar

2 What is the role of opportunity cost in the development of markets?
   Gold Farming for World of Warcraft

3 Why do markets develop?
   The Shakers and the Market for Garden Seeds

In Chapter 1, we saw that a society makes three types of economic decisions: what products to produce, how to produce them, and who gets them. In modern economies, most of these decisions are made in markets. Most of us participate in the labor market and are paid for jobs in which we produce goods and services for others. We participate in consumer markets, spending our incomes on food, clothing, housing, and other products. In this chapter, we explain why markets exist and then explore the virtues and the shortcomings of markets. We also examine the role of government in a market-based economy.

3.1 COMPARATIVE ADVANTAGE AND EXCHANGE

As we saw earlier in the book, a market is an institution or arrangement that enables people to buy and sell things. An alternative to buying and selling in markets is to be self-sufficient, with each of us producing everything we need for ourselves. Rather than going it alone, most of us specialize: We produce one or two products for others and then exchange the money we earn for the products we want to consume.

Specialization and the Gains from Trade

We can explain how people can benefit from specialization and trade with a simple example of two people and two products. Suppose that the crew of the television show *Survivor* finishes filming a season of episodes on a remote tropical island, and when the crew returns to the mainland two people miss the boat and are left behind. The two real survivors produce and consume two goods, coconuts and fish. The first row of Table 3.1 shows their production possibilities. Each day Fred can either gather 2 coconuts or catch 6 fish, while Kate can either gather 1 coconut or catch 1 fish.

We'll show that the two survivors will be better off if each person specializes in one product and then exchanges with the other person. We can use one of the key principles of economics to explore the rationale for specialization.

 ## PRINCIPLE OF OPPORTUNITY COST

The opportunity cost of something is what you sacrifice to get it.

Fred's opportunity cost of 1 coconut is 3 fish—that's how many fish he could catch in the time required to gather 1 coconut. Similarly, his opportunity cost of a fish is 1/3 coconut, the number of coconuts he could gather in the time required to catch 1 fish. For Kate, the opportunity cost of 1 coconut is 1 fish, and the opportunity cost of 1 fish is 1 coconut.

To demonstrate the benefits of exchange, let's imagine that both people are initially self-sufficient, with each producing enough of both goods to satisfy their own desires. Suppose they devote six days per week to finding food. If Fred initially devotes two days per week to gathering coconuts and four days per week to catching fish, he

TABLE 3.1 PRODUCTIVITY AND OPPORTUNITY COSTS				
	Fred		Kate	
	Coconuts	*Fish*	*Coconuts*	*Fish*
Output per day	2	6	1	1
Opportunity cost	3 fish	1/3 coconut	1 fish	1 coconut

will produce and consume 4 coconuts (2 per day times two days) and 24 fish (6 per day times four days) per week. This is shown in the first column of Figure 3.1. If Kate initially devotes one day per week to coconuts and five days per week to fish, she will produce and consume 1 coconut and 5 fish per week.

Specialization will increase the total output of our little survivor economy. It is sensible for each person to specialize in the good for which he or she has a lower opportunity cost. We say that a person has a **comparative advantage** in producing a particular product if he or she has a lower opportunity cost than another person:

comparative advantage
The ability of one person or nation to produce a good at a lower opportunity cost than another person or nation.

- Fred has a comparative advantage in producing fish because his opportunity cost of fish is 1/3 coconut per fish, compared to 1 coconut per fish for Kate.

- Kate has a comparative advantage in harvesting coconuts because her opportunity cost of coconuts is 1 fish per coconut, compared to 3 fish per coconut for Fred.

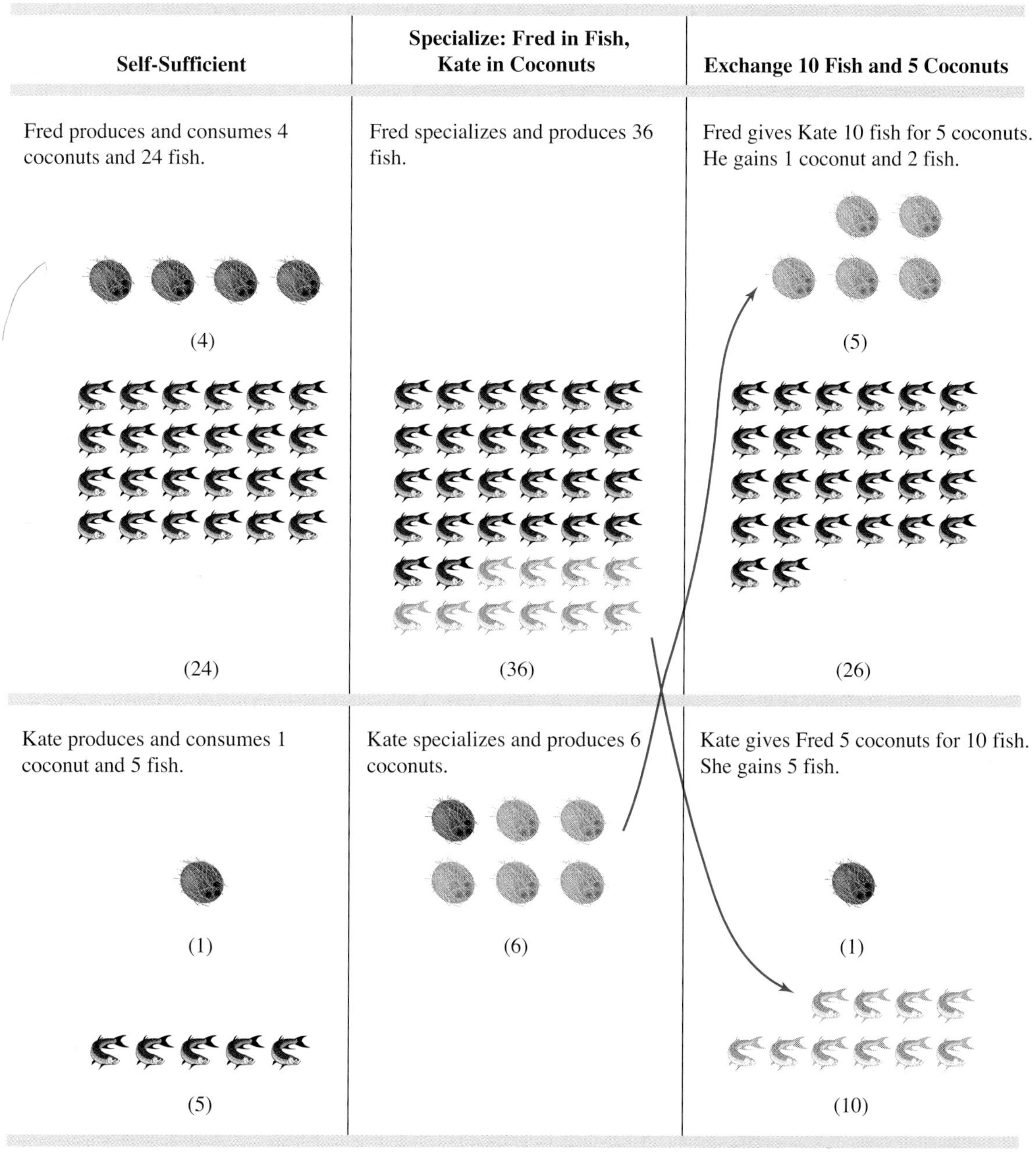

Self-Sufficient	Specialize: Fred in Fish, Kate in Coconuts	Exchange 10 Fish and 5 Coconuts
Fred produces and consumes 4 coconuts and 24 fish.	Fred specializes and produces 36 fish.	Fred gives Kate 10 fish for 5 coconuts. He gains 1 coconut and 2 fish.
(4)		(5)
(24)	(36)	(26)
Kate produces and consumes 1 coconut and 5 fish.	Kate specializes and produces 6 coconuts.	Kate gives Fred 5 coconuts for 10 fish. She gains 5 fish.
(1)	(6)	(1)
(5)		(10)

▲ FIGURE 3.1
Specialization and the Gains from Trade

The second column of Figure 3.1 shows what happens to production when the two people specialize: Fred produces 36 fish and Kate produces 6 coconuts. The total output of both goods increases: The number of coconuts increases from 5 to 6, and the number of fish increases from 29 to 36. Specialization increases the output of both goods because both people are focusing on what they do best.

If specialization is followed by exchange, both people will be better off. Suppose Fred and Kate agree to exchange 2 fish per coconut. Fred could give up 10 fish to get 5 coconuts. As shown in the third column of Figure 3.1, that leaves him with 5 coconuts and 26 fish. Compared to the self-sufficient outcome, he has more of both goods—1 more coconut and 2 more fish. If Kate gives up 5 coconuts to get 10 fish, that leaves her with 1 coconut and 10 fish, which is better than her self-sufficient outcome of 1 coconut and 5 fish. Specialization and exchange make both people better off, illustrating one of the key principles of economics:

PRINCIPLE OF VOLUNTARY EXCHANGE

A voluntary exchange between two people makes both people better off.

Comparative Advantage versus Absolute Advantage

We've seen that it is beneficial for each person to specialize in the product for which he or she has a comparative advantage—a lower opportunity cost. You may have noticed that Fred is more productive than Kate in producing both goods. Fred requires a smaller quantity of resources (in this case less labor time) to produce both goods, so he has an **absolute advantage** in producing both goods. Despite his absolute advantage, Fred gains from specialization and trade because he has a comparative advantage in fish. Fred is twice as productive as Kate in producing coconuts, but six times as productive in producing fish. By relying on Kate to produce coconuts, Fred frees up time to spend producing fish, the good for which he has the larger productivity advantage over Kate. The lesson is that specialization and exchange result from comparative advantage, not absolute advantage.

absolute advantage
The ability of one person or nation to produce a product at a lower resource cost than another person or nation.

The Division of Labor and Exchange

So far we've seen that specialization and trade exploit differences in productivity across workers and make everyone better off. We've assumed that the differences in productivity are innate, not acquired. In his 1776 book *An Inquiry into the Nature and Causes of the Wealth of Nations*, Adam Smith noted that specialization actually increased productivity through the division of labor. He used the example of the pin factory to illustrate how the division of labor increased output:[2]

> A workman . . . could scarce, perhaps with his utmost industry, make one pin a day, and certainly could not make twenty. But the way in which this business is now carried on . . . one man draws out the wire, another straightens it, a third cuts it, a fourth points it, a fifth grinds the top for receiving the head; to make the head requires two or three distinct operations . . . . The . . . making of a pin is, in this manner, divided into about eighteen distinct operations . . . . I have seen a small manufactory of this kind where ten men . . . make among them . . . upward of forty eight thousand pins in a day.

Smith listed three reasons for productivity to increase with specialization, with each worker performing a single production task:

1 *Repetition.* The more times a worker performs a particular task, the more proficient the worker becomes at that task.

2 *Continuity.* A specialized worker doesn't spend time switching from one task to another. This is especially important if switching tasks requires a change in tools or location.

3 *Innovation.* A specialized worker gains insights into a particular task that lead to better production methods. Smith believed that workers were innovators:[3]

> A great part of the machines made use of in those manufactures in which labour is most subdivided, were originally the inventions of common workmen, who, being each of them employed in some simple operation, naturally turned their thoughts toward finding out easier and readier methods of performing it.

To summarize, specialization and exchange result from differences in productivity that lead to comparative advantage. Differences in productivity result from differences in innate skills and the benefits associated with the division of labor. Adam Smith wrote that "every man thus lives by exchanging, or becomes in some measure a merchant, and the society itself grows to be what is properly a commercial society."[4]

3.2 COMPARATIVE ADVANTAGE AND INTERNATIONAL TRADE

The lessons of comparative advantage and specialization apply to trade between nations. Each nation could be self-sufficient, producing all the goods it consumes, or it could specialize in products for which it has a comparative advantage. Even if one nation is more productive than a second nation in producing all goods, trade will be beneficial if the first nation has a bigger productivity advantage in one product—that is, if one nation has a comparative advantage in some product. An **import** is a product produced in a foreign country and purchased by residents of the home country. An **export** is a product produced in the home country and sold in another country.

Many people are skeptical about the idea that international trade can make everyone better off. President Abraham Lincoln expressed his discomfort with importing goods:[5]

> I know if I buy a coat in America, I have a coat and America has the money—If I buy a coat in England, I have the coat and England has the money.

What President Lincoln didn't understand is that when he buys a coat in England, he sends dollars to England, but the dollars don't just sit there. Eventually they are sent back to the United States to buy goods produced by U.S. workers. In the words of economist Todd Buchholz, the author of *New Ideas from Dead Economists,*[6]

> Money may not make the world go round, but money certainly goes around the world. To stop it prevents goods from traveling from where they are produced most inexpensively to where they are desired most deeply.

Outsourcing

When a domestic firm shifts part of its production to a different country, we say the firm is *outsourcing* or *offshoring*. The chapter opener on Mattel's Barbie relates a classic example of outsourcing, with production occurring in Saudi Arabia, Taiwan, Japan, China, Indonesia, Malaysia, Europe, and the United States. In the modern global

import

A good or service produced in a foreign country and purchased by residents of the home country (for example, the United States).

export

A good or service produced in the home country (for example, the United States) and sold in another country.

APPLICATION 1

CANDY CANE MAKERS MOVE TO MEXICO FOR CHEAP SUGAR

APPLYING THE CONCEPTS #1: Does the protection of one domestic industry harm another?

About 90 percent of the world's candy canes are consumed in the United States, and until recently most were produced domestically. Domestic producers were closer to consumers, so they had lower transportation costs and lower prices than their foreign competitors. Domestic firms used their superior access to consumers to dominate the market.

In recent years, the domestic production of candy canes has decreased. In 2003, Spangler Candy Company of Bryan, Ohio, shifted half its production to a plant in Juarez, Mexico. The company opened the Mexico plant because the cost of sugar, the key ingredient in candy, is only $0.06 per pound in Mexico, compared to $0.21 in the United States. The shift to Mexico saves the firm about $2.7 million per year on sugar costs. The high price of sugar has caused other candy manufacturers to shift their operations overseas. Since 1998, the Chicago area, the center of the U.S. confection industry, has lost about 3,000 candy-production jobs.

Why is the price of sugar in the United States so high? The government protects the domestic sugar industry from foreign competition by restricting sugar imports. As a result, the supply of sugar in the United States is artificially low and the price is artificially high. In this case, the protection of jobs in one domestic industry reduces jobs in another domestic industry.　**Related to Exercises 2.4 and 2.6.**

SOURCES: Based on "Sugar Costs Give Candy Cane Makers a Bitter Aftertaste," *Chicago Tribune*, December 25, 2003, 14; Melina Kroll, "Spangler Candy Company: Ramping up for Another 100 Years," *Universal Advisor* 2007, no. 2.

---

economy, transportation and communication costs are relatively low, so firms can spread production across many countries. By taking advantage of the comparative advantages of different countries, a firm can produce its product at a lower cost, charge a lower price, and sell more output.

Firms shift functions such as customer service, telemarketing, document management, and medical transcription overseas to reduce production costs, allowing them to sell their products at lower prices. Some recent studies of outsourcing have reached a number of conclusions:[7]

1 The loss of domestic jobs resulting from outsourcing is a normal part of a healthy economy because technology and consumer preferences change over time. The number of jobs lost to outsourcing is a small fraction of the normal job loss experienced by a healthy economy. For example, in the first three months of 2004, a total of 239,361 workers were laid off, with 9,985 jobs moving to another location within the United States, 4,633 outsourced to another country, and the rest simply lost to the economy. This means that roughly 2 percent of reported layoffs were caused by outsourcing.

2 The jobs lost to outsourcing are at least partly offset by jobs gained through *insourcing*, jobs that are shifted from overseas to the United States.

3 The cost savings from outsourcing are substantial, leading to lower prices for consumers and more output for firms. The jobs gained from increased output at least partly offset the jobs lost to outsourcing.

3.3 MARKETS

Earlier in the chapter, we used a simple example of direct exchange to show the benefits of specialization and exchange. In a modern economy, people don't directly exchange goods like fish and coconuts, but instead rely on all sorts of markets to exchange goods and services, trading what they have for what they want. In a **market economy**, most people specialize in one productive activity by picking an occupation, and use their incomes to buy most of the goods they consume. In addition to the labor and consumer markets, many of us participate in the market for financial capital: We earn interest from savings accounts and money-market accounts and pay interest on mortgages, car loans, and student loans. Friedrich Hayek, a famous twentieth-century economist, suggested that if the market system hadn't arisen naturally, it would have been proclaimed the greatest invention in human history.[8]

market economy
An economy in which people specialize and exchange goods and services in markets.

Although it appears that markets arose naturally, a number of social and government inventions have made them work better:

- **Contracts specify the terms of exchange, facilitating exchange between strangers.** If you have a cell phone provider, you expect to have reliable phone service as long as you pay your bill. If you operate a bookstore, you expect book wholesalers to deliver the books you've purchased. In both cases, a contract specifies the terms of exchange.

- **Insurance reduces the risk entrepreneurs face.** If you operate a bagel shop, fire insurance reduces your losses in the event of a fire.

- **Patents increase the profitability of inventions, encouraging firms to develop new products and production processes.** Pharmaceutical companies such as Bayer Pharmaceutical and Merck spend billions of dollars to create, test, and bring new products to the market. A patent prevents other companies from copying a new product, making it more likely that the revenue from a new product will be large enough to cover research and development costs.

- **Accounting rules provide potential investors with reliable information about the financial performance of a firm.** If you are thinking about investing in Apple Inc., you can use publicly available information to examine the company's financial history.

Virtues of Markets

To assess the virtues of the market system, imagine an alternative—a **centrally planned economy** in which a planning authority decides what products to produce, how to produce them, and who gets them. To make these decisions, a planner must first collect a huge amount of widely dispersed information about consumption desires (what products each individual wants), production techniques (what resources are required to produce each product), and the availability of factors of production (labor, human capital, physical capital, and natural resources). Then the planner must decide how to allocate the productive resources among the alternative products. Finally, the planner must divide the output among the economy's citizens. Clearly, a central planner has a formidable task.

centrally planned economy
An economy in which a government bureaucracy decides how much of each good to produce, how to produce the good, and who gets the good.

Under a market system, decisions are made by the millions of people who already have information about consumers' desires, production technology, and resources. These decisions are guided by prices of inputs and outputs. To illustrate, suppose you buy a wool coat. The dozens of people who contributed to the production of the coat—including the farmers who manage the sheep, the workers who transform raw wool into cloth and the cloth into a coat, the truckers who transport the inputs and the actual coat, and the merchant who sold the coat—didn't know *you* wanted a coat:

- The farmer knew that the price of wool was high enough to justify raising and shearing sheep.
- The workers knew that wages were high enough to make their efforts worthwhile.
- The merchant knew that the retail price of the coat was high enough to make it worthwhile to acquire the coat in anticipation of selling it.

In a market system, prices provide individuals the information they need to make decisions.

Prices provide signals about the relative scarcity of a product and help an economy respond to scarcity. For example, suppose wool becomes scarcer, either because a new use for wool is discovered or an old source of wool disappears. The greater scarcity will increase the price of wool, and producers and consumers will respond in ways that diminish scarcity:

- The higher price encourages fabric producers to use the available wool more efficiently and encourages farmers to produce more of it.
- The higher price also encourages consumers to switch to coats made from alternative fabrics.

These two responses help the economy accommodate an increase in scarcity. Consumers and producers don't need to know why wool is scarcer for these mechanisms to kick in—they only need to know that the price is higher.

The decisions made in markets result from the interactions of millions of people, each motivated by his or her own interest. Adam Smith used the metaphor of the "invisible hand" to explain that people acting in self-interest may actually promote the interest of society as a whole:[9]

> It is not from the benevolence of the butcher, the brewer, or the baker that we expect our dinner, but from their regard to their own interest. We address ourselves, not to their humanity but to their self-love, and never talk to them of our own necessities but of their advantages . . . . [Man is] led by an invisible hand to promote an end which was no part of this intention . . . . By pursuing his own interest he frequently promotes that of the society more effectually than when he really intends to promote it . . . . Nobody but a beggar chooses to depend chiefly upon the benevolence of his fellow citizens.

The market system works by getting each person, motivated by self-interest, to produce products for other people.

The Role of Entrepreneurs

Entrepreneurs play a key role in a market economy. Prices and profits provide signals to entrepreneurs about what to produce. If a product suddenly becomes popular, competition among consumers to obtain it will increase its price and increase the profits earned by firms producing it. Entrepreneurs will enter the market and increase production to meet the higher demand, switching resources from the production of other products. As entrepreneurs enter the market, they compete for customers, driving the price back down to the level that generates just enough profit for them to remain in business. In contrast, if a product becomes less popular, the process is reversed. Producers will cut prices in order to be sure of selling the product to the smaller number of customers who want it. Entrepreneurs will leave the

(**APPLICATION 2**)

GOLD FARMING FOR *WORLD OF WARCRAFT*

APPLYING THE CONCEPTS #2: What is the role of opportunity cost in the development of markets?

As an example of a market that results from comparative advantage, consider the market for virtual currency. Firms in China pay workers (called gold farmers) to play the online game *World of Warcraft* (*WoW*). In the game, workers earn virtual currency in the form of gold coins by killing monsters. In the real world, firms pay the workers a piece rate of about $0.0125 per coin, which translates into a wage of about $0.30 per hour. The firm sells the coins to an online retailer for about $0.03 per coin, and the retailer then sells the coins to consumers for about $0.20 per coin. The consumers in this market are *WoW* gamers in the United States, who are willing to pay cash for game shortcuts—they use the purchased coins to buy the equipment and magic spells required to battle virtual monsters and move to the next level of the game.

Let's look at this exchange in terms of opportunity cost. Suppose a gamer in the United States is roughly half as productive as a gold farmer in earning gold in the game, getting 12 coins per hour. The gamer can either spend an hour to earn 12 coins or take a shortcut by paying $0.20 per coin, or $2.40. If the gamer's opportunity cost is greater than $2.40 per hour, buying the coins is sensible.

The use of gold farmers in *WoW* is controversial. Many gamers believe that buying gold coins rather than earning them by battling virtual monsters is unethical. In 2006, the company that runs *WoW* banned 50,000 *WoW* accounts belonging to gold farmers, and the company eventually eliminated millions of gold farmers. The decrease in the supply of virtual currency increased the price of *WoW* gold from $0.06 cents per coin to $0.35.   **Related to Exercises 3.2 and 3.6.**

SOURCE: Based on Julian Dibbel, "The Life of the Chinese Gold Farmer," *New York Times Magazine*, June 17, 2007.

---

unprofitable market, finding other products to produce, and the price will eventually rise back to the level where profits are high enough for the remaining producers to justify staying in business.

Example of the Emergence of Markets: POW Camps

To illustrate the pervasiveness of exchange, consider the emergence of markets in prisoner of war (POW) camps during World War II.[10] During World War II, the International Red Cross gave each Allied prisoner a weekly parcel with the same mix of products—tinned milk, jam, butter, biscuits, corned beef, chocolate, sugar, and cigarettes. In addition, many prisoners received private parcels from family and friends. The prisoners used barter to exchange one good for another, and cigarettes emerged as the medium of exchange. Prisoners wandered through the camp calling out their offers of goods. For example, "cheese for seven" meant that the prisoner was willing to sell a cheese ration for 7 cigarettes. In addition to food, the prisoners bought and sold clothing (80 cigarettes per shirt), laundry services (2 cigarettes per garment), and hot cups of coffee (2 cigarettes per cup).

The prices of products reflected their scarcity. The tea-drinking British prisoners demanded little coffee. Because the British were confined to their compound,

> ## APPLICATION 3

THE SHAKERS AND THE MARKET FOR GARDEN SEEDS

APPLYING THE CONCEPTS #3: Why do markets develop?

In 1802, a new market developed in the United States—garden seeds sold in small packets. The new market was developed by the Shakers, a religious group whose members took a vow of celibacy and lived in communes ranging in size from 10 to about 100 believers. The Shakers were committed to common property and communal distribution of the output of their many agricultural enterprises.

The Shakers packaged seeds for peas, beets, onions, and lettuce, and distributed the packets throughout the United States. The Shakers dominated the market, and although they tried to coordinate the marketing of seeds from different Shaker villages by establishing sales territories, there was often spirited competition between the Shaker villages. In 1836, the agents from one village complained that their brethren had gone up "every river and bayou" on the Mississippi and left "no hole" for them. They wrote, "It makes us think that the first and great commandment was almost given in vain."

Why were the Shakers able to dominate the garden-seed market? Although the reasons for their domination remain a mystery, it appears that two factors gave them a comparative advantage. First, they were committed to work as an expression of their religious beliefs: In the words of their founder Mother Ann Lee, "Put your hands to work and your hearts to God." Second, their agricultural operations were much larger than traditional farms: In 1850, the average Shaker operation had five times as much land and capital. The Shaker seed business was disrupted by the Civil War and was discontinued in 1870.   **Related to Exercise 3.3.**

SOURCE: Based on Stephen J. Stein, *The Shaker Experience in America* (New Haven: Yale University Press, 1992); Metin M. Cosgel and John Murray, "Productivity of a Commune: The Shakers 1850–1880,".*The Journal of Economic History* 50, no. 2 (1998).

---

packets of coffee beans sold for just a few cigarettes. Enterprising British prisoners bribed prison guards to permit them to travel to the French compound, where they could sell coffee for dozens of cigarettes. Religious groups such as the Sikhs didn't eat beef, and the excess supply of beef in the Sikh compound led to low beef prices. One prisoner who knew the Sikh language bought beef at a low price in the Sikh compound and sold it at a higher price in other compounds. Eventually, other people entered the Sikh beef trade, and beef prices across compounds became roughly equal.

3.4 MARKET FAILURE AND THE ROLE OF GOVERNMENT

Although markets often operate efficiently on their own, sometimes they do not. *Market failure* happens when a market doesn't generate the most efficient outcome. Later in the book, we'll explore several sources of market failure and discuss possible responses by government. Here is a preview of the topics:

- **Pollution.** For markets to work efficiently, the people making the decisions about production and consumption must bear the full costs of their decisions. In some cases, however, other people bear some of the costs. For example, people living downwind from a paper mill breathe dirty air. The people who decide how much paper to produce will ignore these other costs, so their decisions about how much paper produce will be inefficient from the social perspective. Similarly, people with asthma suffer from the emissions of cars and SUVs. Drivers ignore these other costs, so their decisions about how much to drive will be inefficient from the social perspective. The role of government is to ensure that polluters bear the full cost of their production and consumption decisions.

- **Public goods.** A public good is available for everyone to utilize, regardless of who pays and who doesn't. Another requirement for market efficiency is that decision makers must reap the full benefits from their decisions. In the case of a public good such as a levee, the benefits go to everyone in the area protected from flooding, not just the person who builds the levee. The role of government is to facilitate the collective decision making for public goods such as levees, national defense, parks, and space exploration.

- **Imperfect information.** For markets to operate efficiently, people must have enough information to make informed decisions about how much to produce or consume. When they don't, the role of government is to disseminate information and promote informed choices.

- **Imperfect competition.** Some markets are dominated by a few large firms, and the lack of competition leads to high prices and small quantities. For example, DeBeers dominates the diamond market. The role of government is to foster competition, which leads to lower prices and more choices.

What are the other roles of government in a market-based economy? The government enforces property rights by protecting the property and possessions of individuals and firms from theft. The government uses the legal system—police, courts, and prisons—to enforce those rights. The protection of private property guarantees that people will keep the fruits of their labor, encouraging production and exchange. The government has two additional roles to play in a market economy:

- Establishing rules for market exchange and using its police power to enforce the rules.
- Reducing economic uncertainty and providing for people who have lost a job, have poor health, or experience other unforeseen difficulties and accidents.

Government Enforces the Rules of Exchange

The market system is based on exchanges between strangers. These exchanges are covered by implicit and explicit contracts that establish the terms of trade. For example, real-estate transactions and other business dealings are sealed with explicit contracts that specify who pays what, and when. To facilitate exchange, the government helps to enforce contracts by maintaining a legal system that punishes people who violate them. This system allows people to trade with the confidence that the terms of the contracts they enter will be met.

In the case of consumer goods, the implicit contract is that the product is safe to use. The government enforces this implicit contract through product liability or tort law. If a consumer is harmed by using a particular product, the consumer can file a lawsuit against the manufacturer and seek compensation. For example, consumers who are injured in defective automobiles may be awarded settlements to cover the cost of medical care, lost work time, and pain and suffering.

The government also disseminates information about consumer products. The government requires firms to provide information about the features of their products, including warnings about potentially harmful uses of the product. For example, cigarettes have warning labels like "Quitting Smoking Now Greatly Reduces Serious

Risks to Your Health." Some cold medications warn consumers to avoid driving while taking the medication.

We've already seen one of the virtues of a market system—competition among producers tends to keep prices low. As we'll see later, the government uses antitrust policy to foster competition by (a) breaking up monopolies (a single seller of a product), (b) preventing firms from colluding to fix prices, and (c) preventing firms that produce competing products from merging into a single firm. In some markets, the emergence of a single firm—a monopolist—is inevitable because the entry of a second firm would make both firms unprofitable. Some examples are cable television providers and electricity producers. Governments regulate these firms, controlling the price of the products they produce.

Government Can Reduce Economic Uncertainty

A market economy provides plenty of opportunities to people, but it has risks. Your level of success in a market economy—how much income you earn and how much wealth you accumulate—will depend on your innate intelligence as well as your efforts. But there is also an element of luck: Your fate is affected by where you were born, what occupation you choose, and your genetic makeup and health. Chance events, such as natural disasters and human accidents, also can affect your prosperity. Finally, some people lose their jobs when the national economy is in a slump and firms lay off workers. Given the uncertainty of market economies, most governments fund a "social safety net" that provides for citizens who fare poorly in markets. The safety net includes programs that redistribute income from rich to poor, from the employed to the unemployed. The idea behind having a social safety net is to guarantee a minimum income to people who suffer from job losses, poor health, or bad luck.

Of course, there are private responses to economic uncertainty. For example, we can buy our own insurance to cover losses from fire and theft, to cover our medical expenses, and to provide death benefits to our survivors in the event of an accident or disaster. Private insurance works because only a fraction of the people who buy insurance eventually file claims and receive reimbursements from insurance companies. In other words, the payments, or premiums, of many are used to pay the claims of a few. Private insurance works when enough low-risk people purchase insurance to cover the costs of reimbursing the high-risk people.

Some types of insurance are unavailable in the private insurance market. As a result, the government steps in to fill the void. For example, unemployment insurance (UI) is a government program that provides 26 weeks of compensation for people who lose their jobs. The insurance is financed by mandatory contributions from employers. Because all employers contribute to the system, the cost of the insurance stays low.

SUMMARY

This chapter explored specialization and exchange and the virtues and shortcomings of markets. We also discussed the role of government in a market economy. Here are the main points of the chapter:

1 It is sensible for a person to produce the product for which he or she has a *comparative advantage*, that is, a lower opportunity cost than another person.

2 *Specialization* increases productivity through the division of labor, a result of the benefits of repetition, continuity, and innovation.

3 A system of international specialization and trade is sensible because nations have different opportunity costs of producing goods, giving rise to comparative advantages.

4 Under a *market system*, self-interested people, guided by prices, make the decisions about what products to produce, how to produce them, and who gets them.

5 Government roles in a market economy include establishing the rules for exchange, reducing economic uncertainty, and responding to market failures.

KEY TERMS

absolute advantage, p. 52

centrally planned economy, p. 55

comparative advantage, p. 51

export, p. 53

import, p. 53

market economy, p. 55

EXERCISES  Visit www.myeconlab.com to complete these exercises online and get instant feedback.

3.1 Comparative Advantage and Exchange

1.1 Consider an accounting firm with two accountants.
  a. Fill in the blanks in the following table.

	Quigley		Slokum	
	Financial Statements	Tax Returns	Financial Statements	Tax Returns
Output per hour	2	8	1	1
Opportunity cost				

  b. Quigley has a comparative advantage in _____, while Slokum has a comparative advantage in _____.

1.2 Mike, the manager of a car wash, is more productive at washing cars than any potential workers he could hire. Should he wash all the cars himself? _____ (Yes/No)

1.3 Pat and Terry run a landscaping firm that cuts lawns and prunes trees. Pat is more productive than Terry at both tasks. Pat should cut lawns and Terry should prune trees if Pat has a _____ in cutting lawns.

1.4 Adam Smith listed three reasons for specialization to increase productivity: (1) _____; (2) _____; and (3) _____.

1.5 President Lincoln's discomfort with imports resulted from his failure to recognize that money sent to England eventually _____.

1.6 **Exchange in an Island Economy.** Robin and Terry are stranded on a deserted island and consume two products, coconuts and fish. In a day, Robin can catch 2 fish or gather 8 coconuts, and Terry can catch 1 fish or gather 1 coconut.
  a. Use these numbers to prepare a table like Table 3.1 on page 50. Which person has a comparative advantage in fishing? Which person has a comparative advantage in gathering coconuts?
  b. Suppose that each person is initially self-sufficient. In a six-day week, Robin produces and consumes 32 coconuts and 4 fish, and Terry produces and consumes 3 coconuts and 3 fish. Show that specialization and exchange (at a rate of 3 coconuts per fish) allows Robin to consume more coconuts and the same number of fish and allows Terry to consume more coconuts and the same number o fish. Illustrate your answer with a graph like Figure 3.1 on page 51.

1.7 **Technological Innovation and Exchange.** Recall the example of Fred and Kate shown in Table 3.1 on page 50. Suppose a technological innovation, such as a rope ladder, increases the coconut productivity of both people: Fred can now produce three coconuts per day, while Kate can now produce two coconuts per day. Their productivity for fish has not changed. Suppose they agree to trade one coconut for each fish. Will both people gain from specialization and trade?

1.8 **Comparative Advantage in Selling.** Selma is a better salesperson than Mark in both city A and city B.

	Selma	Mark
Sales per day in city A	48	24
Sales per day in city B	40	10

  a. If each person handles one city and the objective is to maximize total sales, which city should each person handle?
  b. Is your answer to (a) consistent with the notion of exploiting comparative advantage?

3.2 Comparative Advantage and International Trade

2.1 Arrows up or down: Outsourcing _____ production costs and _____ consumer prices.

2.2 In the first three months of 2004, the number of jobs moving to another state was _____ (larger/smaller) than the number of jobs moving to another country.

2.3 Approximately what percentage of job losses in the first three months of 2004 were caused by outsourcing—2, 10, or 25 percent?

2.4 Candy cane manufacturers are shutting down plants in the United States and moving to Mexico because import restrictions have caused higher _____ prices in the United States. (Related to Application 1 on page 54.)

2.5 Consider a bicycle producer that initially employs 200 production workers and 10 customer-service workers. When the firm outsources its customer-service operation to India, the 10 customer-service workers lose their jobs.
   a. Explain why the net effect from outsourcing could be a loss of fewer than 10 jobs in the firm.
   b. Under what circumstances will there be a net gain in jobs in the firm?

2.6 **The Steel Industry versus the Appliance Industry.** Suppose the United States limits the imports of steel to protect its domestic steel industry. Explain the implications of the import restrictions on industries such as appliance manufacturers who use steel as an input. (Related to Application 1 on page 54.)

2.7 **Data on Exports and Imports.** Access the *Statistical Abstract of the United States* on the Internet and download the tables in the section entitled "Foreign Commerce and Aid." One of the tables lists U.S. exports and imports by selected Standard Industrial Trade Classification (SITC) commodity. Fill in the blanks in the following table for the most recent year listed in the table.

Commodity	Export Value ($ millions)	Import Value ($ millions)	Net Exports = Exports − Imports ($ millions)
Coffee			
Corn			
Soybeans			
Airplanes			
Footwear			
Vehicles			
Crude oil			

2.8 **Trade Balances by Country.** Access the *Statistical Abstract of the United States* on the Internet and download the tables in the section entitled "Foreign Commerce and Aid." One of the tables lists U.S. exports and imports and merchandise trade balance by country. Fill in the blanks in the following table for the most recent year listed in the table.

Country	Exports ($ millions)	General Imports ($ millions)	Merchandise Trade Balance ($ millions)
Australia			
China			
Italy			
Japan			
Mexico			
Netherlands			
Saudi Arabia			
Singapore			

3.3 Markets

3.1 Four social inventions that support markets are (1) _____, which specify the terms of exchange; (2) _____, which reduce the risk of entrepreneurs; (3) _____, which increases the profitability of inventions; and (4) _____ rules, which provide potential investors with reliable information about the financial performance of firms.

3.2 Gold farmers earn a wage of roughly _____ ($0.30, $2.00, $10.00) per hour. It will be sensible for a gamer to buy gold coins rather than earning them in the game if the gamer's _____ is relatively _____. (Related to Application 2 on page 57.)

3.3 One possible source of comparative advantage of the Shaker garden-seed enterprise is that the Shaker farms were roughly _____ times _____ (larger/smaller) than traditional farms. (Related to Application 3 on page 58.)

3.4 Arrow up or down: Trade between different POW compounds _____ the difference in the price of beef across the compounds.

3.5 To explain the virtues of markets, Adam Smith used the metaphor of the invisible pancreas. _____ (True/False)

3.6 **Responding to Higher Prices.** Consider the gold-farm application. Suppose that the elimination of some gold farmers increases the price of gold coins to $0.50. In addition, suppose the typical gamer can acquire 10 gold coins per hour.

a. A gamer will be indifferent between playing for gold coins and buying them if his or her opportunity cost of *WoW* time is _____ .

b. As the price of gold coins increases, the number of gamers buying the coins will _____ (increase, decrease). Explain. (Related to Application 2 on page 57.)

3.7 **Coffee and Cheese Exchange in a POW Camp.** Suppose that in the British compound of a POW camp, the price of cheese is 6 cigarettes per cheese ration and the price of coffee beans is 3 cigarettes per coffee ration. In the French compound, the price of coffee beans is 24 cigarettes per ration.

a. Is there an opportunity for beneficial exchange?

b. A British prisoner could exchange his cheese ration for _____ cigarettes, then exchange the extra cigarettes for _____ coffee rations in the British compound. If he travels to the French compound, he could exchange the extra coffee for _____ cigarettes. When he returns to the British compound, he can exchange the extra cigarettes for _____ cheese rations. In other words, his net gain from trade is _____ cheese rations.

3.8 **Extending Trade outside the Camp.** Late in World War II, a German guard exchanged bread and chocolate at the rate of one loaf for one chocolate bar. Inside the Allied POW camp, the price of chocolate was 15 cigarettes per bar, and the price of bread was 40 cigarettes per loaf.

a. Is there an opportunity for beneficial exchange?

b. With the guard, a POW could exchange three chocolate bars for _____ loaves of bread. In the camp, the POW could exchange the extra loaves for _____ cigarettes, and then exchange the extra cigarettes for _____ chocolate bars. In other words, the POW's net gain from trade is _____ chocolate bars.

3.4 Market Failure and the Role of Government

4.1 For markets to operate efficiently, the people making consumption and production decisions must bear the full _____ and reap the full _____ from their decisions.

4.2 Pollution from a paper mill is an example of market failure because people living downwind of the mill bear part of _____ of production.

4.3 Some markets are dominated by a few large firms, leading to high _____ and small _____ .

4.4 By promoting competition, the government generates _____ product prices.

4.5 **Pirating Textbooks?** The government protects intellectual property rights by enforcing copyright rules on textbooks. Suppose an organization scans the pages of this and other introductory economics textbooks and makes them available for downloading at no charge.

a. As a current textbook consumer, would you be better off or worse off?

b. What are the implications for the next generation of economics students?

4.6 **Unemployment Insurance.** Each worker employed by Risky Business has a 20 percent chance of losing his or her job in the next year. Each worker employed by Safe Business has a 2 percent chance of losing his or her job in the next year. You manage an insurance company that provides a lump sum of $10,000 to each unemployed worker.

a. What is the minimum amount you would charge Risky Business for each employee covered by the unemployment policy?

b. What is the minimum amount you would charge Safe Business for each employee covered by the unemployment policy?

c. Suppose you charge the same premium to both businesses. The companies have the same number of workers and are required to purchase unemployment insurance. What is the minimum amount you would charge?

NOTES

1. Rone Tempest, "Barbie and the World Economy," *Los Angeles Times*, September 22, 1996, A1; Eric Sinrod, "Perspective: Barbie Comes out Swinging," *cnetNews.com*, August 29, 2007.

2. Adam Smith, *An Inquiry into the Nature and Causes of the Wealth of Nations* (1776), Book 1, Chapter 1.

3. Ibid.

4. Adam Smith, *An Inquiry into the Nature and Causes of the Wealth of Nations* (1776), Book 4, Chapter 2.

5. Todd G. Buchholz, New Ideas from Dead Economists: *An Introduction to Modern Economic Thought* (New York: Penguin, 2007), 76.

6. Todd G. Buchholz, New Ideas from Dead Economists: *An Introduction to Modern Economic Thought* (New York: Penguin, 2007), 76–77.

7. U.S. Bureau of Labor Statistics, "Extended Mass Layoffs Associated with Domestic and Overseas Relocations, First Quarter 2004," June 2004.

8. Todd G. Buchholz, New Ideas from Dead Economists: *An Introduction to Modern Economic Thought* (New York: Penguin, 2007), 21.

9. Adam Smith, *An Inquiry into the Nature and Causes of the Wealth of Nations* (1776), Book 4, Chapter 2.

10. R. A. Radford, "The Economic Organization of a P.O.W. Camp," *Economica*, November 1945, 189–201.

Demand, Supply, and Market Equilibrium

Earthquake and the Price of Paper. A powerful earthquake in February 2010 damaged many of Chile's wood-pulp mills and the infrastructure (roads, water systems, and ports) required to produce and export wood pulp to the United States, Europe, and China. Chile is responsible for 8 percent of the world supply of wood pulp, and the decrease in the supply of pulp increased the world price by $40 per ton, to $950. Pulp producers in Canada and the United States responded to the higher price by increasing their output, hiring more workers and earning more profit in the process.

The decrease in the supply of wood pulp affected the market for paper. Wood pulp is the main raw material for paper, and the increase in the pulp price increased the cost of producing paper and its price. In other words, part of the cost of the earthquake was borne by paper consumers.

APPLYING THE CONCEPTS

1 How do changes in demand affect prices?
Hurricane Katrina and Baton Rouge Housing Prices

2 How do changes in supply in one market affect other markets?
Honeybees and the Price of Ice Cream

3 How do simultaneous changes in supply and demand affect the equilibrium price?
The Supply and Demand for Cruise Ship Berths

4 How do changes in supply affect prices?
The Bouncing Price of Vanilla Beans

5 How do producers respond to higher prices?
Drought in Australia and the Price of Rice

O ur discussion of the virtues of exchange and markets in Chapter 3 has set the stage for this chapter, where we explore the mechanics of markets. We use the model of demand and supply—the most important tool of economic analysis—to see how markets work. We'll see how the prices of goods and services are affected by all sorts of changes in the economy, including bad weather, higher income, technological innovation, bad publicity, and changes in consumer preferences. This chapter will prepare you for the applications of demand and supply you'll see in the rest of the book.

The model of demand and supply explains how a perfectly competitive market operates. A **perfectly competitive market** has many buyers and sellers of a product, so no single buyer or seller can affect the market price. The classic example of a perfectly competitive firm is a wheat farmer who produces a tiny fraction of the total supply of wheat. No matter how much wheat an individual farmer produces, the farmer can't change the market price of wheat.

perfectly competitive market

A market with many sellers and buyers of a homogeneous product and no barriers to entry.

4.1 THE DEMAND CURVE

On the demand side of a market, consumers buy products from firms. We have one main question about this side of the market: How much of a particular product are consumers willing to buy during a particular period? Notice that we define *demand* for a particular period, for example, a day, a month, or a year.

We'll start our discussion of demand with the individual consumer. A consumer who is willing to buy a particular product is willing to sacrifice enough money to purchase it. The consumer doesn't merely have a desire to buy the good, but is also willing and able to sacrifice something to get it. How much of a product is an individual willing to buy? It depends on a number of variables. Here is a list of the variables that affect an individual consumer's decision, using the pizza market as an example:

- The price of the product (for example, the price of a pizza)
- The consumer's income
- The price of substitute goods (for example, the prices of tacos or sandwiches or other goods that can be consumed instead of pizza)
- The price of complementary goods (for example, the price of lemonade or other goods consumed with pizza)
- The consumer's preferences or tastes and advertising that may influence preferences
- The consumer's expectations about future prices

Together, these variables determine how much of a particular product an individual consumer is willing and able to buy, the **quantity demanded**. We'll start our discussion of demand with the relationship between price and quantity demanded, a relationship we represented graphically by the demand curve. Later in the chapter, we will discuss the other variables that affect the individual consumer's decision about how much of a product to buy.

quantity demanded

The amount of a product that consumers are willing and able to buy.

The Individual Demand Curve and the Law of Demand

demand schedule

A table that shows the relationship between the price of a product and the quantity demanded, *ceteris paribus*.

The starting point f or a discussion of individual demand is a **demand schedule**, which is a table of numbers showing the relationship between the price of a particular product and the quantity that an individual consumer is willing to buy. The demand schedule shows how the quantity demanded by an individual changes with the price, *ceteris paribus* (everything else held fixed). The variables that are held fixed in the demand schedule are the consumer's income, the prices of substitutes and complements, the consumer's tastes, and the consumer's expectations about future prices.

The table in Figure 4.1 shows Al's demand schedule for pizza. At a price of $2, Al buys 13 pizzas per month. As the price rises, he buys fewer pizzas: 10 pizzas at a price of $4, 7 pizzas at a price of $6, and so on, down to only 1 pizza at a price of $10. Remember that in a demand schedule, any change in quantity results from a change in price alone.

The **individual demand curve** is a graphical representation of the demand schedule. By plotting the numbers in Al's demand schedule—various combinations of price and quantity—we can draw his demand curve for pizza. The demand curve shows the relationship between the price and the quantity demanded by an individual consumer, *ceteris paribus*. To get the data for a single demand curve, we change only the price of pizza and observe how a consumer responds to the price change. In Figure 4.1, Al's demand curve shows the quantity of pizzas he is willing to buy at each price.

Notice that Al's demand curve is negatively sloped, reflecting the **law of demand**. This law applies to all consumers:

There is a negative relationship between price and quantity demanded, *ceteris paribus*.

The words *ceteris paribus* remind us that in order to isolate the relationship between price and quantity demanded, we *must* assume that income, the prices of related goods

individual demand curve

A curve that shows the relationship between the price of a good and quantity demanded by an individual consumer, *ceteris paribus*.

law of demand

There is a negative relationship between price and quantity demanded, *ceteris paribus*.

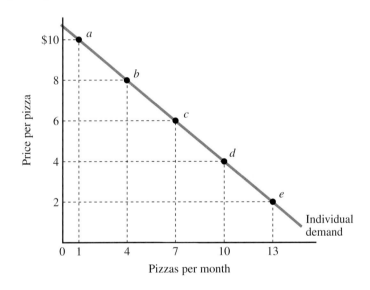

AL'S DEMAND SCHEDULE FOR PIZZAS		
Point	Price	Quantity of Pizzas per Month
a	$10	1
b	8	4
c	6	7
d	4	10
e	2	13

▲ FIGURE 4.1

The Individual Demand Curve

According to the law of demand, the higher the price, the smaller the quantity demanded, everything else being equal. Therefore, the demand curve is negatively sloped: When the price increases from $6 to $8, the quantity demanded decreases from seven pizzas per month (point *c*) to four pizzas per month (point *b*).

change in quantity demanded

A change in the quantity consumers are willing and able to buy when the price changes; represented graphically by movement along the demand curve.

market demand curve

A curve showing the relationship between price and quantity demanded by all consumers, *ceteris paribus*.

such as substitutes and complements, and tastes are unchanged. As the price of pizza increases and nothing else changes, Al moves upward along his demand curve and buys a smaller quantity of pizza. For example, if the price increases from $8 to $10, Al moves upward along his demand curve from point *b* to point *a*, and buys only one pizza per month, down from four pizzas at the lower price. A movement along a single demand curve is called a **change in quantity demanded**, a change in the quantity a consumer is willing to buy when the price changes.

From Individual Demand to Market Demand

The **market demand curve** shows the relationship between the price of the good and the quantity demanded by *all* consumers, *ceteris paribus*. As in the case of the individual demand curve, when we draw the market demand curve we assume that the other variables that affect individual demand (income, the prices of substitute and complementary goods, tastes, and price expectations) are fixed. In addition, we assume the number of consumers is fixed.

Figure 4.2 shows how to derive the market demand curve when there are only two consumers. Panel A shows Al's demand curve for pizza, and Panel B shows Bea's demand curve. At a price of $8, Al will buy 4 pizzas (point *a*) and Bea will buy 2 pizzas (point *b*), so the total quantity demanded at this price is 6 pizzas. In Panel C, point *c* shows the point on the market demand curve associated with a price of $8. At this price, the market quantity demanded is 6 pizzas. If the price drops to $4, Al will buy

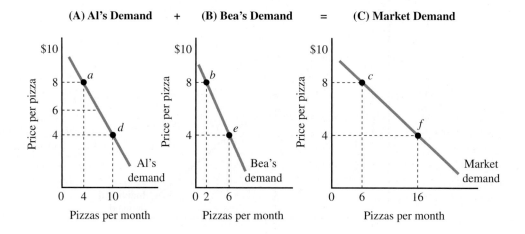

QUANTITY OF PIZZA DEMANDED			
Price	Al +	Bea =	Market Demand
$8	4	2	6
6	7	4	11
4	10	6	16
2	13	8	21

▲ FIGURE 4.2

From Individual to Market Demand

The market demand equals the sum of the demands of all consumers. In this case, there are only two consumers, so at each price the market quantity demanded equals the quantity demanded by Al plus the quantity demanded by Bea. At a price of $8, Al's quantity is four pizzas (point *a*) and Bea's quantity is two pizzas (point *b*), so the market quantity demanded is six pizzas (point *c*). Each consumer obeys the law of demand, so the market demand curve is negatively sloped.

10 pizzas (point *d*) and Bea will buy 6 pizzas (point *e*), for a total of 16 pizzas (shown by point *f* on the market demand curve). The market demand curve is the horizontal sum of the individual demand curves.

The market demand is negatively sloped, reflecting the law of demand. This is sensible, because if each consumer obeys the law of demand, consumers as a group will too. When the price increases from $4 to $8, there is a change in quantity demanded as we move along the demand curve from point *f* to point *c*. The movement along the demand curve occurs if the price of pizza is the only variable that has changed.

4.2   THE SUPPLY CURVE

On the supply side of a market, firms sell their products to consumers. Suppose you ask the manager of a firm, "How much of your product are you willing to produce and sell?" The answer is likely to be "it depends." The manager's decision about how much to produce depends on many variables, including the following, using pizza as an example:

- The price of the product (for example, the price per pizza)
- The wage paid to workers
- The price of materials (for example, the price of dough and cheese)
- The cost of capital (for example, the cost of a pizza oven)
- The state of production technology (for example, the knowledge used in making pizza)
- Producers' expectations about future prices
- Taxes paid to the government or *subsidies* (payments from the government to firms to produce a product)

Together, these variables determine how much of a product firms are willing to produce and sell, the **quantity supplied**. We'll start our discussion of market supply with the relationship between the price of a good and the quantity of that good supplied, a relationship we represent graphically by the supply curve. Later in the chapter we will discuss the other variables that affect the individual firm's decision about how much of a product to produce and sell.

quantity supplied
The amount of a product that firms are willing and able to sell.

The Individual Supply Curve and the Law of Supply

Consider the decision of an individual producer. The starting point for a discussion of individual supply is a **supply schedule**, a table that shows the relationship between the price of a particular product and the quantity that an individual producer is willing to sell. The supply schedule shows how the quantity supplied by an individual producer changes with the price, *ceteris paribus*. The variables we hold fixed in the supply schedule are input costs, technology, price expectations, and government taxes or subsidies.

The table in Figure 4.3 shows the supply schedule for pizza at Lola's Pizza Shop. At a price of $2, Lola doesn't produce any pizzas, indicating that a $2 price is not high enough to cover her cost of producing a pizza. In contrast, at a price of $4 she supplies 100 pizzas. In this example, each $2 increase in price increases the quantity supplied by 100 pizzas to 200 at a price of $6, 300 at a price of $8, and so on. Remember that in a supply schedule, a change in quantity results from a change in price alone.

supply schedule
A table that shows the relationship between the price of a product and quantity supplied, *ceteris paribus*.

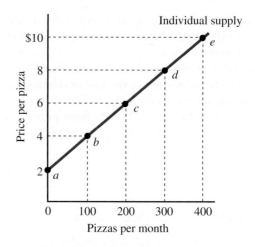

INDIVIDUAL SUPPLY SCHEDULE FOR PIZZA		
Point	Price	Quantity of Pizzas per Month
a	$ 2	0
b	4	100
c	6	200
d	8	300
e	10	400

▲ **FIGURE 4.3**

The Individual Supply Curve

The supply curve of an individual supplier is positively sloped, reflecting the law of supply. As shown by point a, the quantity supplied is zero at a price of $2, indicating that the minimum supply price is just above $2. An increase in price increases the quantity supplied to 100 pizzas at a price of $4, 200 pizzas at a price of $6, and so on.

individual supply curve

A curve showing the relationship between price and quantity supplied by a single firm, *ceteris paribus*.

The **individual supply curve** is a graphical representation of the supply schedule. By plotting the numbers in Lola's supply schedule—different combinations of price and quantity—we can draw her supply curve for pizza. The individual supply curve shows the relationship between the price of a product and the quantity supplied by a single firm, *ceteris paribus*. To get the data for a supply curve, we change only the price of pizza and observe how a producer responds to the price change.

Figure 4.3 shows Lola's supply curve for pizza, which shows the quantity of pizzas she is willing to sell at each price. The individual supply curve is positively sloped, reflecting the **law of supply**, a pattern of behavior that we observe in producers:

law of supply

There is a positive relationship between price and quantity supplied, *ceteris paribus*.

There is a positive relationship between price and quantity supplied, *ceteris paribus*.

The words *ceteris paribus* remind us that to isolate the relationship between price and quantity supplied we assume the other factors that influence producers are unchanged. As the price of pizza increases and nothing else changes, Lola moves upward along her individual supply curve and produces a larger quantity of pizza. For example, if the price increases from $6 to $8, Lola moves upward along her supply curve from point c to point d, and the quantity supplied increases from 200 to 300. A movement along a single supply curve is called a **change in quantity supplied**, a change in the quantity a producer is willing and able to sell when the price changes.

change in quantity supplied

A change in the quantity firms are willing and able to sell when the price changes; represented graphically by movement along the supply curve.

The **minimum supply price** is the lowest price at which a product is supplied. A firm won't produce a product unless the price is high enough to cover the marginal cost of producing it. As shown in Figure 4.3, a price of $2 is not high enough to cover the cost of producing the first pizza, so Lola's quantity supplied is zero (point *a*). But when the price rises above $2, she produces some pizzas, indicating that her minimum supply price is just above $2.

minimum supply price

The lowest price at which a product will be supplied.

Why Is the Individual Supply Curve Positively Sloped?

The individual supply curve is positively sloped, consistent with the law of supply. To explain the positive slope, consider how Lola responds to an increase in price. A higher price encourages a firm to increase its output by purchasing more materials and hiring more workers. To increase her workforce, Lola might be forced to pay overtime or hire workers who are more costly or less productive than the original workers. But the higher price of pizza makes it worthwhile to incur these higher costs.

The supply curve shows the marginal cost of production for different quantities produced. We can use the marginal principle to explain this.

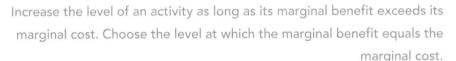

MARGINAL PRINCIPLE

Increase the level of an activity as long as its marginal benefit exceeds its marginal cost. Choose the level at which the marginal benefit equals the marginal cost.

For Lola, the marginal benefit of producing a pizza is the price she gets for it. When the price is only $2.00, she doesn't produce any pizza, which tells us that the marginal cost of the first pizza must be greater than $2.00; otherwise, she would have produced it. But when the price rises to $2.01, she produces the first pizza because now the marginal benefit (the $2.01 price) exceeds the marginal cost. This tells us that the marginal cost of the first pizza is less than $2.01; otherwise, she wouldn't produce it at a price of $2.01. To summarize, the marginal cost of the first pizza is between $2.00 and $2.01, or just over $2.00. Similarly, point *b* on the supply curve in Figure 4.3 shows that Lola won't produce her 100th pizza at a price of $3.99, but will produce at a price of $4.00, indicating that her marginal cost of producing that pizza is between $3.99 and $4.00, or just under $4.00. In general, the supply curve shows the marginal cost of production.

From Individual Supply to Market Supply

The **market supply curve** for a particular good shows the relationship between the price of the good and the quantity that all producers together are willing to sell, *ceteris paribus*. To draw the market supply curve, we assume the other variables that affect individual supply are fixed. The market quantity supplied is simply the sum of the quantities supplied by all the firms in the market. To show how to draw the market supply curve, we'll assume there are only two firms in the market. Of course, a perfectly competitive market has a large number of firms, but the lessons from the two-firm case generalize to a case of many firms.

Figure 4.4 shows how to derive a market supply curve from individual supply curves. In Panel A, Lola has relatively low production costs, as reflected in her relatively low minimum supply price ($2 at point *a*). In Panel B, Hiram has higher production costs, so he has a higher minimum price ($6 at point *f*). As a result, his supply curve lies above Lola's. To draw the market supply curve, we add the

market supply curve

A curve showing the relationship between the market price and quantity supplied by all firms, *ceteris paribus*.

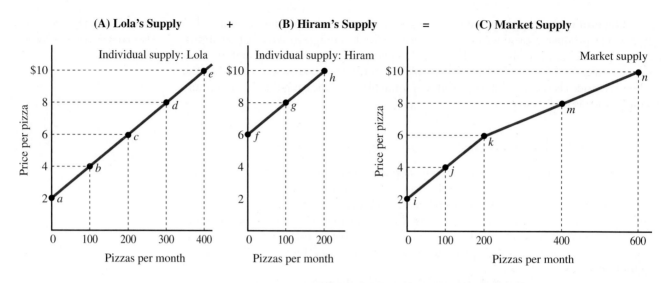

QUANTITY OF PIZZA SUPPLIED			
Price	Lola +	Hiram =	Market Supply
2	0	0	0
4	100	0	100
6	200	0	200
8	300	100	400
10	400	200	600

▲ FIGURE 4.4

From Individual to Market Supply

The market supply is the sum of the supplies of all firms. In Panel A, Lola is a low-cost producer who produces the first pizza once the price rises above $2 (shown by point *a*). In Panel B, Hiram is a high-cost producer who doesn't produce pizza until the price rises above $6 (shown by point *f*). To draw the market supply curve, we sum the individual supply curves horizontally. At a price of $8, market supply is 400 pizzas (point *m*), equal to 300 from Lola (point *d*) plus 100 from Hiram (point *g*).

individual supply curves horizontally. This gives us two segments for the market supply curve:

- **Prices between $2 and $6:** Segment connecting points *i* and *k*. Hiram's high-cost firm doesn't supply any output, so the market supply is the same as the individual supply from Lola. For example, at a price of $4 Lola supplies 100 pizzas (point *b*) and Hiram does not produce any, so the market supply is 100 pizzas (point *j*).

- **Prices above $6:** Segment above point *k*. At higher prices, the high-cost firm produces some output, and the market supply is the sum of the quantities supplied by the two firms. For example, at a price of $8 Lola produces 300 pizzas (point *d*) and Hiram produces 100 pizzas (point *g*), so the market quantity supplied is 400 pizzas (point *m*).

A perfectly competitive market has hundreds of firms rather than just two, but the process of going from individual supply curves to the market supply curve is the same. We add the individual supply curves horizontally by picking a price and adding up the quantities supplied by all the firms in the market. In the more realistic case of many firms, the supply curve will be smooth rather than kinked. This smooth line is shown in Figure 4.5. In this case, we assume that there are 100 firms identical to Lola's firm.

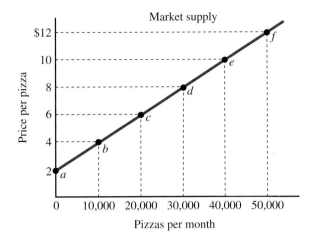

▲ FIGURE 4.5
The Market Supply Curve with Many Firms
The market supply is the sum of the supplies of all firms. The minimum supply price is $2 (point a), and the quantity supplied increases by 10,000 for each $2 increase in price to 10,000 at a price of $4 (point b), 20,000 at a price of $6 (point c), and so on.

The minimum supply price is $2, and for each $2 increase in price, the quantity supplied increases by 10,000 pizzas.

Why Is the Market Supply Curve Positively Sloped?

The market supply curve is positively sloped, consistent with the law of supply. To explain the positive slope, consider the two responses by firms to an increase in price:

- **Individual firm.** As we saw earlier, a higher price encourages a firm to increase its output by purchasing more materials and hiring more workers.

- **New firms.** In the long run, new firms can enter the market and existing firms can expand their production facilities to produce more output. The new firms may have higher production costs than the original firms, but the higher output price makes it worthwhile to enter the market, even with higher costs.

Like the individual supply curve, the market supply curve shows the marginal cost of production for different quantities produced. In Figure 4.5, the marginal cost of the first pizza is the minimum supply price for the firm with the lowest cost (just over $2.00). Similarly, point d on the supply curve shows that the 30,000th pizza won't be produced at a price of $7.99, but will be produced at a price of $8.00. This indicates that the marginal cost of producing the 30,000th pizza is just under $8.00. Like the individual supply curve, the market supply curve shows the marginal cost of production.

4.3 MARKET EQUILIBRIUM: BRINGING DEMAND AND SUPPLY TOGETHER

In Chapter 3 we saw that a market is an arrangement that brings buyers and sellers together. So far in this chapter we've seen how the two sides of a market—demand and supply—work. Now we bring the two sides of the market together to show how prices and quantities are determined.

market equilibrium

A situation in which the quantity demanded equals the quantity supplied at the prevailing market price.

When the quantity of a product demanded equals the quantity supplied at the prevailing market price, we have reached a **market equilibrium**. When a market reaches an equilibrium, there is no pressure to change the price. If pizza firms produce exactly the quantity of pizza that consumers are willing to buy, each consumer will get a pizza at the prevailing price, and each producer will sell all its pizza. In Figure 4.6, the equilibrium price is shown by the intersection of the demand and supply curves. At a price of $8, the supply curve shows that firms will produce 30,000 pizzas, which is exactly the quantity that consumers are willing to buy at that price.

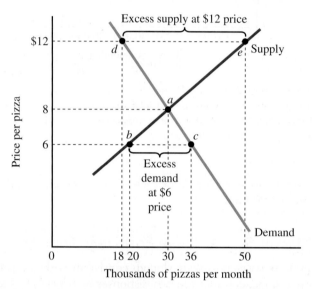

▲ **FIGURE 4.6**

Market Equilibrium

At the market equilibrium (point *a*, with price = $8 and quantity = 30,000), the quantity supplied equals the quantity demanded. At a price below the equilibrium price ($6), there is excess demand—the quantity demanded at point *c* exceeds the quantity supplied at point *b*. At a price above the equilibrium price ($12), there is excess supply—the quantity supplied at point *e* exceeds the quantity demanded at point *d*.

Excess Demand Causes the Price to Rise

excess demand

A situation in which, at the prevailing price, the quantity demanded exceeds the quantity supplied.

If the price is below the equilibrium price, there will be excess demand for the product. **Excess demand** (sometimes called a *shortage*) occurs when, at the prevailing market price, the quantity demanded exceeds the quantity supplied, meaning that consumers are willing to buy more than producers are willing to sell. In Figure 4.6, at a price of $6, there is an excess demand equal to 16,000 pizzas: Consumers are willing to buy 36,000 pizzas (point *c*), but producers are willing to sell only 20,000 pizzas (point *b*) because the price is less than the marginal cost of producing pizza number 20,001 and beyond. This mismatch between demand and supply will cause the price of pizza to rise. Firms will increase the price they charge for their limited supply of pizza, and anxious consumers will pay the higher price to get one of the few pizzas available.

An increase in price eliminates excess demand by changing both the quantity demanded and quantity supplied. As the price increases, the excess demand shrinks for two reasons:

- The market moves upward along the demand curve (from point *c* toward point *a*), decreasing the quantity demanded.
- The market moves upward along the supply curve (from point *b* toward point *a*), increasing the quantity supplied.

Because the quantity demanded decreases while the quantity supplied increases, the gap between the quantity demanded and the quantity supplied narrows. The price will continue to rise until excess demand is eliminated. In Figure 4.6, at a price of $8 the quantity supplied equals the quantity demanded, as shown by point *a*.

In some cases, government creates an excess demand for a good by setting a maximum price (sometimes called a *price ceiling*). If the government sets a maximum price that is less than the equilibrium price, the result is a permanent excess demand for the good. Later in the book we will explore the market effects of such policies.

Excess Supply Causes the Price to Drop

What happens if the price is *above* the equilibrium price? **Excess supply** (sometimes called a *surplus*) occurs when the quantity supplied exceeds the quantity demanded, meaning that producers are willing to sell more than consumers are willing to buy. This is shown by points *d* and *e* in Figure 4.6. At a price of $12, the excess supply is 32,000 pizzas: Producers are willing to sell 50,000 pizzas (point *e*), but consumers are willing to buy only 18,000 (point *d*). This mismatch will cause the price of pizzas to fall as firms cut the price to sell them. As the price drops, the excess supply will shrink for two reasons:

> **excess supply**
> A situation in which the quantity supplied exceeds the quantity demanded at the prevailing price.

- The market moves downward along the demand curve from point *d* toward point *a*, increasing the quantity demanded.
- The market moves downward along the supply curve from point *e* toward point *a*, decreasing the quantity supplied.

Because the quantity demanded increases while the quantity supplied decreases, the gap between the quantity supplied and the quantity demanded narrows. The price will continue to drop until excess supply is eliminated. In Figure 4.6, at a price of $8, the quantity supplied equals the quantity demanded, as shown by point *a*.

The government sometimes creates an excess supply of a good by setting a minimum price (sometimes called a *price floor*). If the government sets a minimum price that is greater than the equilibrium price, the result is a permanent excess supply. We'll discuss the market effects of minimum prices later in the book.

4.4   MARKET EFFECTS OF CHANGES IN DEMAND

We've seen that market equilibrium occurs when the quantity supplied equals the quantity demanded, shown graphically by the intersection of the supply curve and the demand curve. In this part of the chapter, we'll see how changes on the demand side of the market affect the equilibrium price and equilibrium quantity.

Change in Quantity Demanded versus Change in Demand

Earlier in the chapter we listed the variables that determine how much of a particular product consumers are willing to buy. The first variable is the price of the product. The demand curve shows the negative relationship between price and quantity demanded, *ceteris paribus*. In Panel A of Figure 4.7, when the price decreases from $8 to $6, we move downward along the demand curve from point *a* to point *b*, and the quantity demanded increases. As noted earlier in the chapter, this is called a *change in quantity demanded*. Now we're ready to take a closer look at the other variables that affect demand besides price—income, the prices of related goods, tastes, advertising, and the number of consumers—and see how changes in these variables affect the demand for the product and the market equilibrium.

If any of these other variables change, the relationship between the product's price and quantity—shown numerically in the demand schedule and graphically in the

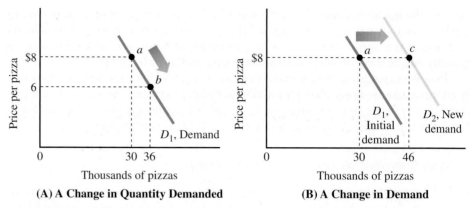

▲ FIGURE 4.7
Change in Quantity Demanded versus Change in Demand
(**A**) A change in price causes a change in quantity demanded, a movement along a single demand curve. For example, a decrease in price causes a move from point *b* to point *b*, increasing the quantity demanded.
(**B**) A change in demand caused by changes in a variable other than the price of the good shifts the entire demand curve. For example, an increase in demand shifts the demand curve from D_1 to D_2.

demand curve—will change. That means we will have an entirely different demand schedule and an entirely different demand curve. In Panel B of Figure 4.7, we show this result as a *shift* of the entire demand curve from D_1 to D_2. This particular shift means that at any price consumers are willing to buy a larger quantity of the product. For example, at a price of $8 consumers are willing to buy 46,000 pizzas (point *c*), up from 30,000 with the initial demand curve. To convey the idea that changes in these other variables change the demand schedule and the demand curve, we say that a change in any of these variables causes a **change in demand**.

Increases in Demand Shift the Demand Curve

What types of changes will increase the demand and shift the demand curve to the right, as shown in Figure 4.7? An increase in demand like the one represented in Figure 4.7 can occur for several reasons, listed in Table 4.1:

- **Increase in income.** Consumers use their income to buy products, and the more money they have, the more money they spend. For a **normal good**, there is a positive relationship between consumer income and the quantity consumed. When income increases, a consumer buys a larger quantity of a normal good. Most goods fall into this category—including new clothes, movies, and pizza.

change in demand
A shift of the demand curve caused by a change in a variable other than the price of the product.

normal good
A good for which an increase in income increases demand.

TABLE 4.1 INCREASES IN DEMAND SHIFT THE DEMAND CURVE TO THE RIGHT		
When this variable...	increases or decreases...	the demand curve shifts in this direction...
Income, with normal good	↑	
Income, with inferior good	↓	
Price of a substitute good	↑	
Price of complementary good	↓	
Population	↑	
Consumer preferences for good	↑	
Expected future price	↑	

- **Decrease in income.** An **inferior good** is the opposite of a normal good. Consumers buy larger quantities of inferior goods when their income *decreases*. For example, if you lose your job you might make your own coffee instead of buying it in a coffee shop, rent DVDs instead of going to the theater, and eat more macaroni and cheese. In this case, homemade coffee, DVDs, and macaroni and cheese are examples of inferior goods.

- **Increase in price of a substitute good.** When two goods are **substitutes**, an increase in the price of the first good causes some consumers to switch to the second good. Tacos and pizzas are substitutes, so an increase in the price of tacos increases the demand for pizzas as some consumers substitute pizza for tacos, which are now more expensive relative to pizza.

- **Decrease in price of a complementary good.** When two goods are **complements**, they are consumed together as a package, and a decrease in the price of one good decreases the cost of the entire package. As a result, consumers buy more of both goods. Pizza and lemonade are complementary goods, so a decrease in the price of lemonade decreases the total cost of a lemonade-and-pizza meal, increasing the demand for pizza.

- **Increase in population.** An increase in the number of people means there are more potential pizza consumers—more individual demand curves to add up to get the market demand curve—so market demand increases.

- **Shift in consumer preferences.** Consumers' preferences or tastes can change over time. If consumers' preferences shift in favor of pizza, the demand for pizza increases. One purpose of advertising is to change consumers' preferences, and a successful pizza advertising campaign will increase demand.

- **Expectations of higher future prices.** If consumers think next month's pizza price will be higher than they had initially expected, they may buy a larger quantity today and a smaller quantity next month. That means the demand for pizza today will increase.

We can use Figure 4.8 to show how an increase in demand affects the equilibrium price and equilibrium quantity. An increase in the demand for pizza resulting from

inferior good
A good for which an increase in income decreases demand.

substitutes
Two goods for which an increase in the price of one good increases the demand for the other good.

complements
Two goods for which a decrease in the price of one good increases the demand for the other good.

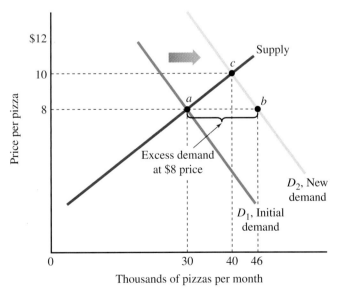

▲ **FIGURE 4.8**
An Increase in Demand Increases the Equilibrium Price
An increase in demand shifts the demand curve to the right: At each price, the quantity demanded increases. At the initial price ($8), there is excess demand, with the quantity demanded (point *b*) exceeding the quantity supplied (point *a*). The excess demand causes the price to rise, and equilibrium is restored at point *c*. To summarize, the increase in demand increases the equilibrium price to $10 and increases the equilibrium quantity to 40,000 pizzas.

one or more of the factors listed in Table 4.1 shifts the demand curve to the right, from D_1 to D_2. At the initial price of $8, there will be excess demand, as indicated by points *a* and *b*: Consumers are willing to buy 46,000 pizzas (point *b*), but producers are willing to sell only 30,000 (point *a*). Consumers want to buy 16,000 more pizzas than producers are willing to supply, and the excess demand causes upward pressure on the price. As the price rises, the excess demand shrinks because the quantity demanded decreases while the quantity supplied increases. The supply curve intersects the new demand curve at point *c*, so the new equilibrium price is $10 (up from $8), and the new equilibrium quantity is 40,000 pizzas (up from 30,000).

Decreases in Demand Shift the Demand Curve

What types of changes in the pizza market will decrease the demand for pizza? A decrease in demand means that at each price consumers are willing to buy a smaller quantity. In Figure 4.9, a decrease in demand shifts the market demand curve from D_1 to D_0. At the initial price of $8, the quantity demanded decreases from 30,000 pizzas (point *a*) to 14,000 pizzas (point *b*). A decrease in demand like the one represented in Figure 4.9 can occur for several reasons, listed in Table 4.2:

- **Decrease in income.** A decrease in income means that consumers have less to spend, so they buy a smaller quantity of each normal good.
- **Increase in income.** Consumers buy smaller quantities of an inferior good when their income increases.
- **Decrease in the price of a substitute good.** A decrease in the price of a substitute good such as tacos makes pizza more expensive relative to tacos, causing consumers to demand less pizza.
- **Increase in the price of a complementary good.** An increase in the price of a complementary good such as lemonade increases the cost of a lemonade-and-pizza meal, decreasing the demand for pizza.

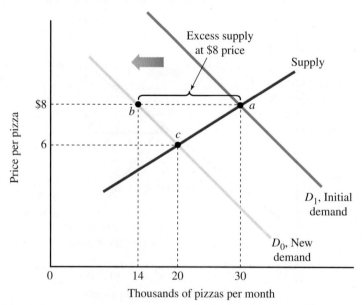

▲ **FIGURE 4.9**
A Decrease in Demand Decreases the Equilibrium Price
A decrease in demand shifts the demand curve to the left: At each price, the quantity demanded decreases. At the initial price ($8), there is excess supply, with the quantity supplied (point *a*) exceeding the quantity demanded (point *b*). The excess supply causes the price to drop, and equilibrium is restored at point *c*. To summarize, the decrease in demand decreases the equilibrium price to $6 and decreases the equilibrium quantity to 20,000 pizzas.

TABLE 4.2 DECREASES IN DEMAND SHIFT THE DEMAND CURVE TO THE LEFT

When this variable...	increases or decreases...	the demand curve shifts in this direction...
Income, with normal good	↓	
Income, with inferior good	↑	
Price of a substitute good	↓	
Price of complementary good	↑	
Population	↓	
Consumer preferences for good	↓	
Expected future price	↓	

- **Decrease in population.** A decrease in the number of people means that there are fewer pizza consumers, so the market demand for pizza decreases.
- **Shift in consumer tastes.** When consumers' preferences shift away from pizza in favor of other products, the demand for pizza decreases.
- **Expectations of lower future prices.** If consumers think next month's pizza price will be lower than they had initially expected, they may buy a smaller quantity today, meaning the demand for pizza today will decrease.

A Decrease in Demand Decreases the Equilibrium Price

We can use Figure 4.9 to show how a decrease in demand affects the equilibrium price and equilibrium quantity. The decrease in the demand for pizza shifts the demand curve to the left, from D_1 to D_0. At the initial price of $8, there will be an excess supply, as indicated by points *a* and *b*: Producers are willing to sell 30,000 pizzas (point *a*), but given the lower demand consumers are willing to buy only 14,000 pizzas (point *b*). Producers want to sell 16,000 more pizzas than consumers are willing to buy, and the excess supply causes downward pressure on the price. As the price falls, the excess supply shrinks because the quantity demanded increases while the quantity supplied decreases. The supply curve intersects the new demand curve at point *c*, so the new equilibrium price is $6 (down from $8), and the new equilibrium quantity is 20,000 pizzas (down from 30,000).

4.5   MARKET EFFECTS OF CHANGES IN SUPPLY

We've seen that changes in demand shift the demand curve and change the equilibrium price and quantity. In this part of the chapter, we'll see how changes on the supply side of the market affect the equilibrium price and equilibrium quantity.

Change in Quantity Supplied versus Change in Supply

Earlier in the chapter we listed the variables that determine how much of a product firms are willing to sell. Of course, one of these variables is the price of the product. The supply curve shows the positive relationship between price and quantity, *ceteris paribus*. In Panel A of Figure 4.10, when the price increases from $6 to $8 we move along the supply curve from point *a* to point *b*, and the quantity of the product supplied increases. As noted earlier in the chapter, this is called a *change in quantity supplied*. Now we're ready to take a closer look at the other variables that

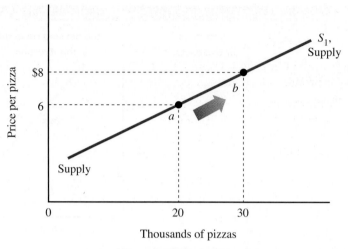

(A) Change in Quantity Supplied

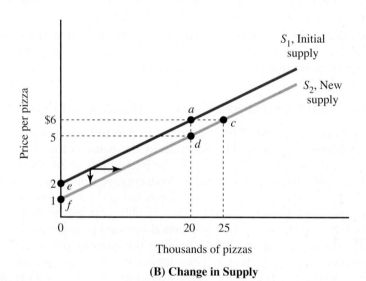

(B) Change in Supply

▲ **FIGURE 4.10**

Change in Quantity Supplied versus Change in Supply

(**A**) A change in price causes a change in quantity supplied, a movement along a single supply curve. For example, an increase in price causes a move from point *a* to point *b*.

(**B**) A change in supply (caused by a change in something other than the price of the product) shifts the entire supply curve. For example, an increase in supply shifts the supply curve from S_1 to S_2. For any given price (for example, $6), a larger quantity is supplied (25,000 pizzas at point *c* instead of 20,000 at point *a*). The price required to generate any given quantity decreases. For example, the price required to generate 20,000 pizzas drops from $6 (point *a*) to $5 (point *d*).

affect supply—including wages, material prices, and technology—and see how changes in these variables affect the supply curve and the market equilibrium.

If any of these other variables change, the relationship between price and quantity—shown numerically in the supply schedule and graphically in the supply curve—will change. That means that we will have an entirely different supply schedule and a different supply curve. In Panel B of Figure 4.10, this is shown as a shift of the entire supply curve from S_1 to S_2. In this case, the supply curve shifts downward and to the right:

- The shift to the right means that at any given price (for example, $6), a larger quantity is produced (25,000 pizzas at point *c*, up from 20,000 at point *a*).
- The shift downward means that the price required to generate a particular quantity of output is lower. For example, the new minimum supply price is just over $1 (point *f*), down from just over $2 (point *e*). Similarly, the price required to generate 20,000 pizzas is $5 (point *d*), down from $6 (point *a*).

To convey the idea that changes in these other variables change the supply curve, we say that a change in any of these variables causes a **change in supply**.

change in supply
A shift of the supply curve caused by a change in a variable other than the price of the product.

Increases in Supply Shift the Supply Curve

What types of changes increase the supply of a product, shifting the supply curve downward and to the right? Consider first the effect of a decrease in the wage paid to pizza workers. A decrease in the wage will decrease the cost of producing pizza and shift the supply curve:

- **Downward shift.** When the cost of production decreases, the price required to generate any given quantity of pizza will decrease. In general, a lower wage means a lower marginal cost of production, so each firm needs a lower price to cover its production cost. In other words, the supply curve shifts downward.
- **Rightward shift.** The decrease in production costs makes pizza production more profitable at a given price, so producers will supply more at each price. In other words, the supply curve shifts to the right.

A decrease in the wage is just one example of a decrease in production costs that shifts the supply curve downward and to the right. These supply shifters are listed in Table 4.3. A reduction in the costs of materials (dough, cheese) or capital (pizza oven) decreases production costs, decreasing the price required to generate any particular quantity (downward shift) and increasing the quantity supplied at any particular price (rightward shift). An improvement in technology that allows the firm to economize on labor or material inputs cuts production costs and shifts the supply curve in a similar fashion. The technological improvement could be a new machine or a new way of doing business—a new layout for a factory or store, or a more efficient system of ordering inputs and distributing output. Finally, if a government subsidizes production by paying the firm some amount for each unit produced, the net cost to the firm is lowered by the amount of the subsidy, and the supply curve shifts downward and to the right.

Two other possible sources of increases in supply are listed in Table 4.3. First, if firms believe that next month's price will be lower than they had initially expected, they may try to sell more output now at this month's relatively high price, increasing supply this month. Second, because the market supply is the sum of the quantities supplied by all producers, an increase in the number of producers will increase market supply.

As summarized in Table 4.3, the language of shifting supply is a bit tricky. An increase in supply is represented graphically by a shift to the right (a larger quantity supplied at each price) and down (a lower price required to generate a particular quantity). The best way to remember this is to recognize that the *increase* in "increase in supply" refers to the increase in quantity supplied at a particular price—the horizontal shift of the supply curve to the right.

TABLE 4.3 CHANGES IN SUPPLY SHIFT THE SUPPLY CURVE DOWNWARD AND TO THE RIGHT		
When this variable...	increases or decreases...	the supply curve shifts in this direction...
Wage	↓	
Price of materials or capital	↓	
Technological advance	↑	
Government subsidy	↑	
Expected future price	↓	
Number of producers	↑	

An Increase in Supply Decreases the Equilibrium Price

We can use Figure 4.11 to show the effects of an increase in supply on the equilibrium price and equilibrium quantity. An increase in the supply of pizza shifts the supply curve to the right, from S_1 to S_2. At the initial price of $8, the quantity supplied increases from 30,000 pizzas (point *a*) to 46,000 (point *b*).

The shift of the supply curve causes excess supply that eventually decreases the equilibrium price. At the initial price of $8 (the equilibrium price with the initial supply curve), there will be an excess supply, as indicated by points *a* and *b*: Producers are

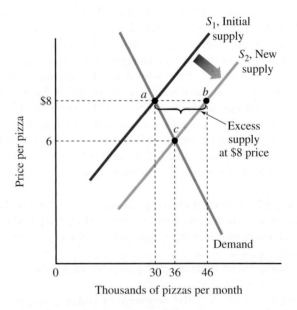

▲ FIGURE 4.11

An Increase in Supply Decreases the Equilibrium Price

An increase in supply shifts the supply curve to the right: At each price, the quantity supplied increases. At the initial price ($8), there is excess supply, with the quantity supplied (point *b*) exceeding the quantity demanded (point *a*). The excess supply causes the price to drop, and equilibrium is restored at point *c*. To summarize, the increase in supply decreases the equilibrium price to $6 and increases the equilibrium quantity to 36,000 pizzas.

willing to sell 46,000 pizzas (point *b*), but consumers are willing to buy only 30,000 (point *a*). Producers want to sell 16,000 more pizzas than consumers are willing to buy, and the excess supply causes pressure to decrease the price. As the price decreases, the excess supply shrinks, because the quantity supplied decreases while the quantity demanded increases. The new supply curve intersects the demand curve at point *c*, so the new equilibrium price is $6 (down from $8) and the new equilibrium quantity is 36,000 pizzas (up from 30,000).

Decreases in Supply Shift the Supply Curve

Consider next the changes that cause a decrease in supply. As shown in Table 4.4, anything that increases a firm's production costs will decrease supply. An increase in production cost increases the price required to generate a particular quantity (an upward shift of the supply curve) and decreases the quantity supplied at each price (a leftward shift). Production costs will increase as a result of an increase in the wage, an increase in the price of materials or capital, or a tax on each unit produced. As we saw earlier, the language linking changes in supply and the shifts of the supply curve is tricky. In the case of a decrease in supply, the *decrease* refers to the change in quantity at a particular price—the horizontal shift of the supply curve to the left.

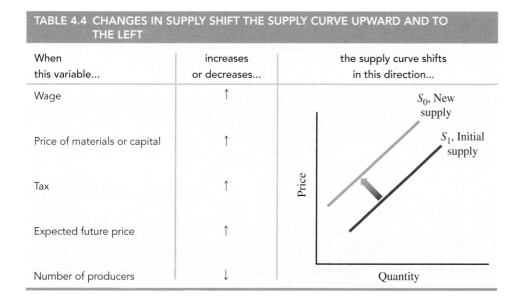

TABLE 4.4 CHANGES IN SUPPLY SHIFT THE SUPPLY CURVE UPWARD AND TO THE LEFT

When this variable...	increases or decreases...	the supply curve shifts in this direction...
Wage	↑	
Price of materials or capital	↑	
Tax	↑	
Expected future price	↑	
Number of producers	↓	

A decrease in supply could occur for two other reasons. First, if firms believe next month's pizza price will be higher than they had initially expected, they may be willing to sell a smaller quantity today and a larger quantity next month. That means that the supply of pizza today will decrease. Second, because the market supply is the sum of the quantities supplied by all producers, a decrease in the number of producers will decrease market supply, shifting the supply curve to the left.

A Decrease in Supply Increases the Equilibrium Price

We can use Figure 4.12 to show the effects of a decrease in supply on the equilibrium price and equilibrium quantity. A decrease in the supply of pizza shifts the supply curve to the left, from S_1 to S_0. At the initial price of $8 (the equilibrium price with the initial supply curve), there will be an excess demand, as indicated by

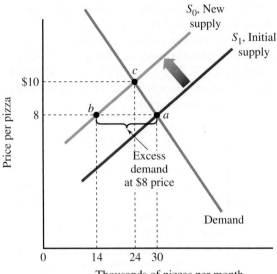

▲ **FIGURE 4.12**

A Decrease in Supply Increases the Equilibrium Price

A decrease in supply shifts the supply curve to the left. At each price, the quantity supplied decreases. At the initial price ($8), there is excess demand, with the quantity demanded (point a) exceeding the quantity supplied (point b). The excess demand causes the price to rise, and equilibrium is restored at point c. To summarize, the decrease in supply increases the equilibrium price to $10 and decreases the equilibrium quantity to 24,000 pizzas.

points *a* and *b*: Consumers are willing to buy 30,000 pizzas (point *a*), but producers are willing to sell only 14,000 pizzas (point *b*). Consumers want to buy 16,000 more pizzas than producers are willing to sell, and the excess demand causes upward pressure on the price. As the price increases, the excess demand shrinks because the quantity demanded decreases while the quantity supplied increases. The new supply curve intersects the demand curve at point *c*, so the new equilibrium price is $10 (up from $8), and the new equilibrium quantity is 24,000 pizzas (down from 30,000).

Simultaneous Changes in Demand and Supply

What happens to the equilibrium price and quantity when both demand and supply increase? It depends on which change is larger. In Panel A of Figure 4.13, the increase in demand is larger than the increase in supply, meaning the demand curve shifts by a larger amount than the supply curve. The market equilibrium moves from point *a* to point *b*, and the equilibrium price increases from $8 to $9. This is sensible because an increase in demand tends to pull the price up, while an increase in supply tends to push the price down. If demand increases by a larger amount, the upward pull will be stronger than the downward push, and the price will rise.

We can be certain that when demand and supply both increase, the equilibrium quantity will increase. That's because both changes tend to increase the equilibrium quantity. In Panel A of Figure 4.13, the equilibrium quantity increases from 30,000 to 44,000 pizzas.

Panel B of Figure 4.13 shows what happens when the increase in supply is larger than the increase in demand. The equilibrium moves from point *a* to point *c*, meaning that the price falls from $8 to $7. This is sensible because the downward pull on the price resulting from the increase in supply is stronger than the upward pull from

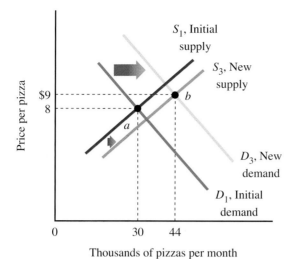

(A) Larger Increase in Demand

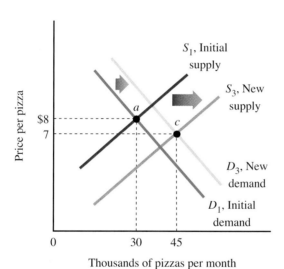

(B) Larger Increase in Supply

▲ FIGURE 4.13

Market Effects of Simultaneous Changes in Demand and Supply

(A) Larger increase in demand. If the increase in demand is larger than the increase in supply (if the shift of the demand curve is larger than the shift of the supply curve), both the equilibrium price and the equilibrium quantity will increase.

(B) Larger increase in supply. If the increase in supply is larger than the increase in demand (if the shift of the supply curve is larger than the shift of the demand curve), the equilibrium price will decrease and the equilibrium quantity will increase.

the increase in demand. As expected, the equilibrium quantity rises from 30,000 to 45,000 pizzas.

What about simultaneous *decreases* in demand and supply? In this case, the equilibrium quantity will certainly fall because both changes tend to decrease the equilibrium quantity. The effect on the equilibrium price depends on which change is larger, the decrease in demand, which pushes the price downward, or the decrease in supply, which pulls the price upward. If the decrease in demand is larger, the price will fall because the force pushing the price down will be stronger than the force pulling it up. In contrast, if the decrease in supply is larger, the price will rise because the force pulling the price up will be stronger than the force pushing it down.

4.6 PREDICTING AND EXPLAINING MARKET CHANGES

We've used the model of demand and supply to show how equilibrium prices are determined and how changes in demand and supply affect equilibrium prices and quantities. Table 4.5 summarizes what we've learned about how changes in demand and supply affect equilibrium prices and quantities:

- When demand changes and the demand curve shifts, price and quantity change in the *same* direction: When demand increases, both price and quantity increase; when demand decreases, both price and quantity decrease.
- When supply changes and the supply curve shifts, price and quantity change in *opposite* directions: When supply increases, the price decreases but the quantity increases; when supply decreases, the price increases but the quantity decreases.

TABLE 4.5 MARKET EFFECTS OF CHANGES IN DEMAND OR SUPPLY

Change in Demand Supply	How does the equilibrium price change?	How does the equilibrium quantity change?
Increase in demand	↑	↑
Decrease in demand	↓	↓
Increase in supply	↓	↑
Decrease in supply	↑	↓

We can use these lessons about demand and supply to predict the effects of various events on the equilibrium price and equilibrium quantity of a product.

We can also use the lessons listed in Table 4.5 to explain the reasons for changes in prices or quantities. Suppose we observe changes in the equilibrium price and quantity of a particular good, but we don't know what caused these changes. Perhaps it was a change in demand, or maybe it was a change in supply. We can use the information in Table 4.5 to work backward, using what we've observed about changes in prices and quantities to determine which side of the market—demand or supply—caused the changes:

- If the equilibrium price and quantity move in the same direction, the changes were caused by a change in demand.
- If the equilibrium price and quantity move in opposite directions, the changes were caused by a change in supply.

4.7 APPLICATIONS OF DEMAND AND SUPPLY

We can apply what we've learned about demand and supply to real markets. We can use the model of demand and supply to *predict* the effects of various events on equilibrium prices and quantities. We can also *explain* some observed changes in equilibrium prices and quantities.

APPLICATION 1

HURRICANE KATRINA AND BATON ROUGE HOUSING PRICES

APPLYING THE CONCEPTS #1: How do changes in demand affect prices?

In the late summer of 2005, Hurricane Katrina caused a storm surge and levee breaks that flooded much of New Orleans and destroyed a large fraction of the city's housing. Hundreds of thousands of residents were displaced, and about 250,000 relocated to nearby Baton Rouge. The increase in population was so large that Baton Rouge became the largest city in the state, and many people started calling the city "New Baton Rouge."

Figure 4.14 shows the effects of Hurricane Katrina on the housing market in Baton Rouge. Before Katrina, the average price of a single-family home was $130,000, as shown by point *a*. The increase in the city's population shifted the demand curve to the right, causing excess demand for housing at the original price. Just before the hurricane, there were 3,600 homes listed for sale in the city, but a week after the storm, there were only 500. The excess demand caused fierce competition among buyers for the limited supply of homes, increasing the price. Six months later, the average price had risen to $156,000 as shown by point *b*.   **Related to Exercises 7.1 and 7.6.**

SOURCE: Based on Federal Deposit Insurance Corporation, *Louisiana State Profile—Fall 2005.*

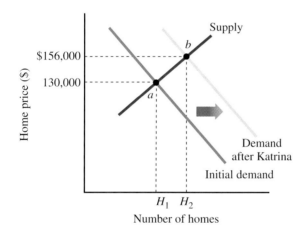

▲ **FIGURE 4.14**
Hurricane Katrina and Housing in Baton Rouge
An increase in the population of Baton Rouge increases the demand for housing, shifting the demand curve to right. The equilibrium price increases from $130,000 (point *a*) to $156,000 (point *b*).

APPLICATION 2

HONEYBEES AND THE PRICE OF ICE CREAM

APPLYING THE CONCEPTS #2: How do changes in supply in one market affect other markets?

In the last few years thousands of honeybee colonies have vanished, a result of bee colony collapse disorder (CCD). Roughly one-third of the U.S. food supply—including a wide variety of fruits, vegetables, and nuts—depends on pollination from bees. The decline of honeybees threatens $15 billion worth of crops in the United States. The decrease in pollination by bees has decreased the supply of strawberries, raspberries, and almonds, leading to higher prices for these ingredients for ice cream. The higher prices for berries and nuts have increased the cost of producing food products, such as ice cream, increasing their prices as well.

Figure 4.15 shows the effects of the decline of the bee population on the market for ice cream. Increases in the prices of ingredients (berries and nuts) increase the cost of producing ice cream, shifting the supply curve upward. As a result, the equilibrium price of ice cream increases.

The collapsing of bee colonies is a mystery. The ice cream maker Häagen-Dazs donated money to Pennsylvania State University and the University of California, Davis to support research exploring the causes of CCD and possible solutions. To increase consumer awareness of the problem, Häagen Dazs launched a new flavor, Vanilla Honey Bee.   **Related to Exercises 7.2 and 7.7.**

SOURCE: Based on Parija Kavilanz, "Disappearing Bees Threaten Ice Cream Sellers," *CNNMoney.com*, February 20, 2008.

▶ **FIGURE 4.15**

Honeybees and the Price of Ice Cream

A decrease in pollination by bees decreases the output of fruit and nuts, increasing the prices of some ingredients for ice cream. The resulting increase in the cost of producing ice cream shifts the supply curve upward, increasing the equilibrium price and decreasing the equilibrium quantity.

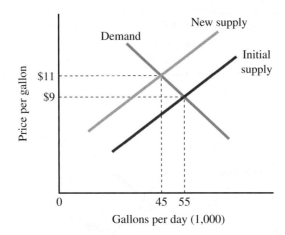

(**APPLICATION 3**)

THE SUPPLY AND DEMAND FOR CRUISE SHIP BERTHS

APPLYING THE CONCEPT #3: How do simultaneous changes in supply and demand affect the equilibrium price?

What happens when an increase in supply is combined with a decrease in demand? In 2009 the cruise industry invested $4.7 billion on 14 new ships, and in 2010 the industry launched 12 additional new ships. While the supply of cruise berths increased, the demand for cruises decreased, a result of a recession and lower real income. As shown in Figure 4.16, the simultaneous increase in supply and decrease in demand decreased the equilibrium price. To entice consumers, some cruise lines cut prices by as much as 40 percent. Although consumers responded by purchasing more cruises (about 3 percent more in 2009 than in 2008), the cruise lines' revenues decreased. For Carnival Corporation, the world's largest cruise line, total revenue decreased by 10 percent. **Related to Exercises 7.3 and 7.8.**

SOURCE: Based on "Dam the Torpedoes: Cruise Lines in the Recession," *Economist*, February 13, 2010, 67.

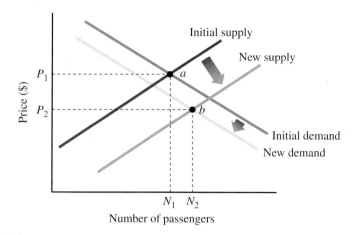

▲ **FIGURE 4.16**

Increase in Supply and Decrease in Demand for Cruise Ship Berths

An increase in the number of cruise ships increases the supply of berths on cruise ships, while a decrease in income reduces the demand for berths. The increase in supply and decrease in demand combine to decrease the equilibrium price (from P_1 to P_2) and increase the equilibrium quantity (from N_1 to N_2).

APPLICATION 4

THE BOUNCING PRICE OF VANILLA BEANS

APPLYING THE CONCEPTS #4: How do changes in supply affect prices?

The price of vanilla beans has been bouncing around a lot. The price was $50 per kilogram (2.2 pounds) in 2000, then rose to $500 in 2003, then dropped to $25 in 2006. We can use the model of demand and supply to explain the bouncing price.

Figure 4.17 shows the changes in the vanilla market in recent years. Point *a* shows the initial equilibrium in 2000, with a price of $50 per kilogram. The 2000 cyclone that hit Madagascar, the world's leading vanilla producer, destroyed that year's crop and a large share of the vines that produce vanilla beans. Although the vines were replanted, new plants don't bear usable beans for three to five years, so the supply effects of the cyclone lasted several years. In Figure 4.17, the cyclone shifted the supply curve upward and to the left, generating a new equilibrium at point *b*, with a higher price and a smaller quantity.

In Figure 4.17, the changes between 2003 and 2006 are shown by a shift of the supply curve downward and to the right. In 2006, the vines replanted in Madagascar in 2001 started to produce vanilla beans. In addition, other countries, including India, Papua New Guinea, Uganda, and Costa Rica, entered the vanilla market. The vines planted in these other countries started to produce beans in 2006, so the world supply curve for 2006 lies below and to the right of the original supply curve (in 2000). Given the larger supply of vanilla beans in 2006, the price dropped to about half of its 2000 level, to $25 per kilogram. The increase in supply from other countries was facilitated by the development of a sun-tolerant variety of the vanilla plant that allows it to be grown as a plantation crop. The new variety is an example of technological progress. **Related to Exercises 7.4 and 7.9.**

SOURCES: Based on Rhett Butler, "Collapsing Vanilla Prices Will Affect Madagascar," *mongabay.com*, May 9, 2005; Noel Paul, "Vanilla Sky High," *Christian Science Monitor*, August 11, 2003, http://www.csmonitor.com; G.K. Nair, "Vanilla Prices Fall on Undercutting," *Hindu Business Line*, April 3, 2006, http://www.thehindubusinessline.com.

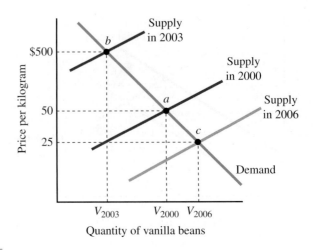

▲ **FIGURE 4.17**
The Bouncing Price of Vanilla Beans
A cyclone destroyed much of Madagascar's crop in 2000, shifting the supply curve upward and to the left. The equilibrium price increased from $50 per kilogram (point *a*) to $500 per kilogram (point *b*). By 2005, the vines replanted in Madagascar—along with new vines planted in other countries—started producing vanilla beans, and the supply curve shifted downward and to the right, beyond the supply curve for 2000. The price dropped to $25 per kilogram (point *c*), half the price that prevailed in 2000. (To represent the large changes in price and quantity, the graph is not drawn to scale.)

APPLICATION 5

DROUGHT IN AUSTRALIA AND THE PRICE OF RICE

APPLYING THE CONCEPTS #5: How do producers respond to higher prices?

In 2008, the continuation of a six-year drought in Australia reduced the amount of water available to irrigate Australia's rice crop. Farmers responded by reducing the amount of land devoted to rice. The drought was a major factor in a near doubling of rice prices, which led to violent protests in Cameroon, Egypt, Ethiopia, Haiti, Indonesia, Italy, the Ivory Coast, Mauritania, and the Philippines.

The increase in the price of rice generated a number of responses that could eventually increase the quantity of rice produced. Farmers in Australia are experimenting with different varieties and growing techniques that require less water. The more costly techniques do not make economic sense when the price of rice is low, but are sensible when the price is high. In Thailand, farmers are investing in generators to irrigate their fields, allowing a second harvest each year. If the price of rice stays high, the farmers will reap a large profit, but if the price falls, the costs of adding a second crop will exceed the benefits, and farmers will lose money. **Related to Exercises 7.5 and 7.10.**

SOURCES: Based on David Streitfeld and Keith Bradsher, "Worries Mount as Farmers Push for Big Harvest," *New York Times*, June 10, 2008; Keith Bradsher, "A Drought in Australia, a Global Shortage of Rice," *New York Times*, April 17, 2008.

SUMMARY

In this chapter, we've seen how demand and supply determine prices. We also learned how to predict the effects of changes in demand or supply on prices and quantities. Here are the main points of the chapter:

1 A *market demand curve* shows the relationship between the quantity demanded and price, *ceteris paribus.*

2 A *market supply curve* shows the relationship between the quantity supplied and price, *ceteris paribus.*

3 *Equilibrium* in a market is shown by the intersection of the demand curve and the supply curve. When a market reaches equilibrium, there is no pressure to change the price.

4 A *change in demand* changes price and quantity in the same direction: An increase in demand increases the equilibrium price and quantity; a decrease in demand decreases the equilibrium price and quantity.

5 A *change in supply* changes price and quantity in opposite directions: An increase in supply decreases price and increases quantity; a decrease in supply increases price and decreases quantity.

KEY TERMS

change in demand, p. 76

change in quantity demanded, p. 68

change in quantity supplied, p. 70

change in supply, p. 81

complements, p. 77

demand schedule, p. 66

excess demand (shortage), p. 74

excess supply (surplus), p. 75

individual demand curve, p. 67

individual supply curve, p. 70

inferior good, p. 77

law of demand, p. 67

law of supply, p. 70

market demand curve, p. 68

market equilibrium, p. 74

market supply curve, p. 71

minimum supply price, p. 71

normal good, p. 76

perfectly competitive market, p. 66

quantity demanded, p. 66

quantity supplied, p. 69

substitutes, p. 77

supply schedule, p. 69

EXERCISES 

Visit www.myeconlab.com to complete these exercises online and get instant feedback.

4.1 The Demand Curve

1.1 Arrow up or down: According to the law of demand, an increase in price _____ the quantity demanded.

1.2 From the following list, choose the variables that are held fixed in drawing a market demand curve:
- The price of the product
- Consumer income
- The price of other related goods
- Consumer expectations about future prices
- The quantity of the product purchased

1.3 From the following list, choose the variables that change as we draw a market demand curve:
- The price of the product
- Consumer income
- The price of other related goods
- Consumer expectations about future prices
- The quantity of the product purchased

1.4 The market demand curve is the _____ (horizontal/vertical) sum of the individual demand curves.

1.5 A change in price causes movement along a demand curve and a change in _____.

1.6 **Draw a Demand Curve.** Your state has decided to offer its citizens vanity license plates for their cars and wants to predict how many vanity plates it will sell at different prices. The price of the state's regular license plates is $20 per year, and the state's per-capita income is $30,000. A recent survey of other states with approximately the same population (3 million people) generated the following data on incomes, prices, and vanity plates:

State	B	C	D	E
Price of vanity plate	$ 60	$ 55	$ 50	$ 40
Price of regular plates	20	20	35	20
Income	30,000	25,000	30,000	30,000
Quantity of vanity plates	6,000	6,000	16,000	16,000

a. Use the available data to identify some points on the demand curve for vanity plates and connect the points to draw a demand curve. Don't forget *ceteris paribus*.

b. Suppose the demand curve is linear. If your state set a price of $50, how many vanity plates would be purchased?

4.2 The Supply Curve

2.1 Arrow up or down: According to the law of supply, an increase in price _____ the quantity supplied.

2.2 From the following list, choose the variables that are held fixed when drawing a market supply curve:
- The price of the product
- Wages paid to workers
- The price of materials used in production
- Taxes paid by producers
- The quantity of the product purchased

2.3 The minimum supply price is the _____ price at which a product is supplied.

2.4 The market supply curve is the _____ (horizontal/vertical) sum of the individual supply curves.

2.5 A change in price causes movement along a supply curve and a change in _____.

2.6 **Marginal Cost of Housing.** When the price of a standard three-bedroom house increases from $150,000 to $160,000, a building company increases its output from 20 houses per year to 21 houses per year. What does the increase in the quantity of housing reveal about the cost of producing housing?

2.7 **Imports and Market Supply.** Two nations supply sugar to the world market. Lowland has a minimum supply price of 10 cents per pound, while Highland has a minimum supply price of 24 cents per pound. For each nation, the slope of the supply curve is 1 cent per million pounds.

a. Draw the individual supply curves and the market supply curve. At what price and quantity is the supply curve kinked?

b. The market quantity supplied at a price of 15 cents is _____ million pounds. The market quantity supplied at a price of 30 cents is _____ million pounds.

2.8 **Responses to Higher Soybean Prices.** Suppose that in initial equilibrium in the soybean market, each of the 1,000 farmers produces 50 units, for a total of 50,000 units of soybeans. Suppose the price of soybeans increases, and everyone expects the price to stay at the higher level for many years.

a. Arrows up or down: Over a period of several years, we expect the quantity of soybeans supplied to _____ as the number of soybean farmers _____ and the output per farmer _____.

b. A farmer who enters the market is likely to have a _____ (higher/lower) marginal cost of production than an original firm.

4.3 Market Equilibrium: Bringing Demand and Supply Together

3.1 The market equilibrium is shown by the intersection of the _____ curve and the _____ curve.

3.2 Excess demand occurs when the price is (less/greater) than the equilibrium price; excess supply occurs when the price is _____ (less/greater) than the equilibrium price.

3.3 Arrow up or down: An excess demand for a product will cause the price to _____. As a consequence of the price change, the quantity demanded will _____ and the quantity supplied will _____.

3.4 Arrow up or down: An excess supply of a product will cause the price to _____. As a consequence of the price change, the quantity demanded will _____, and the quantity supplied will _____.

3.5 **Interpreting the Graph.** The following graph shows the demand and supply curves for CD players. Complete the following statements.

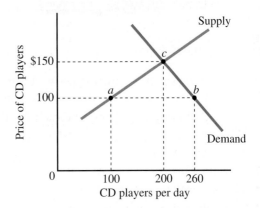

a. At the market equilibrium (shown by point _____), the price of CD players is _____ and the quantity of CD players is _____.

b. At a price of $100, there would be excess _____, so we would expect the price to _____.

c. At a price exceeding the equilibrium price, there would be excess _____, so we would expect the price to _____.

3.6 **Draw and Find the Equilibrium.** The following table shows the quantities of corn supplied and demanded at different prices.

Price per Ton	Quantity Supplied	Quantity Demanded
$ 80	600	1,200
90	800	1,100
100	1,000	1,000
110	1,200	900

a. Draw the demand curve and the supply curve.

b. The equilibrium price of corn is _____, and the equilibrium quantity is _____.

c. At a price of $110, there is excess _____ (supply/demand) equal to _____.

4.4 Market Effects of Changes in Demand

4.1 A change in demand causes a _____ (movement along/shift of) the demand curve. A change in quantity demanded causes a _____ (movement along/shift of) the demand curve.

4.2 Circle the variables that change as we move along the demand curve for pencils and cross out those that are assumed to be fixed.

- Quantity of pencils demanded
- Number of consumers
- Price of pencils
- Price of pens
- Consumer income

4.3 **Online Movies.** Consider the effects of online distribution of movies. A decrease in the price of online movies shifts the demand for DVD movies to the _____ (left, right). A decrease in downloading time shifts the demand for DVD movies to the _____ (left, right).

4.4 Arrow up or down: The market demand curve for a product will shift to the right when the price of a substitute good _____, the price of a complementary good _____, consumer income _____, and the population _____.

4.5 Arrow up or down: An increase in demand for a product _____ the equilibrium price and _____ the equilibrium quantity.

4.6 **Market Effects of Increased Income.** Consider the market for restaurant meals. Use a demand and supply graph to predict the market effects of an increase in consumer income. Arrow up or down: The equilibrium price of restaurant meals will _____, and the equilibrium quantity of restaurant meals will _____.

4.7 **Public versus Private Colleges.** Consider the market for private college education. Use a demand and supply graph to predict the market effects of an increase in the tuition charged by public colleges.

Arrow up or down: The equilibrium price of a private college education will _____, and the equilibrium quantity will _____.

4.8 **Gas Prices and New Gas Guzzlers.** Use a demand and supply graph to predict the implications for the market for new full-size SUVs. Arrow up or down: The equilibrium price of a full-size SUV will _____, and the equilibrium quantity will _____.

4.5 Market Effects of Changes in Supply

5.1 A change in supply causes a _____ (movement along/shift of) the supply curve. A change in quantity supplied causes a _____ (movement along/shift of) the supply curve.

5.2 Circle the variables that change as we move along the supply curve for pencils and cross out those that are assumed to be fixed:

- Quantity of pencils supplied
- Price of wood
- Price of pencils
- Production technology

5.3 Arrow up or down: An increase in the price of wood shifts the supply curve for pencils _____; an improvement in pencil-production technology shifts the supply curve for pencils _____; a tax on pencil production shifts the supply curve for pencils _____.

5.4 Arrow up or down: An increase in the supply of a product _____ the equilibrium price and _____ the equilibrium quantity.

5.5 If both demand and supply increase simultaneously, the equilibrium price will increase if the change in _____ is relatively large.

5.6 Arrow up or down: If supply increases while demand decreases, the equilibrium price will _____.

5.7 If supply increases while demand decreases, the equilibrium quantity will decrease if the change in _____ (supply/demand) is relatively large.

5.8 **Effect of Weather on Prices.** Suppose a freeze in Florida wipes out 20 percent of the orange crop. How will this affect the equilibrium price and quantity of Florida oranges? Illustrate your answer with a graph.

5.9 **Immigration Control and Prices.** Consider the market for raspberries. Suppose a new law outlaws the use of foreign farm workers on raspberry farms, and the wages paid to farm workers increase as a result. Use a demand and supply graph to predict the effects of the higher wage on the equilibrium price and quantity of raspberries. Arrow up or down: The equilibrium price of raspberries will _____, and the equilibrium quantity of raspberries will _____ .

5.10 Market Effects of Import Ban. Consider the market for shoes in a nation that initially imports half the shoes it consumes. Use a demand and supply graph to predict the market effect of a ban on shoe imports. Arrow up or down: The equilibrium price will _____ , and the equilibrium quantity will _____ .

5.11 Market Effects of a Tax. Consider the market for fish. Use a demand and supply graph to predict the effect of a tax paid by fish producers of $1 per pound of fish. Use a demand and supply graph to predict the market effect of the tax. Arrow up or down: The equilibrium price will _____, and the equilibrium quantity will _____ .

5.12 Innovation and the Price of Mobile Phones. Suppose that the initial price of a mobile phone is $100 and that the initial quantity demanded is 500 phones per day. Use a graph to show the effects of a technological innovation that decreases the cost of producing mobile phones. Label the starting point with "*a*" and the new equilibrium with "*b*."

5.13 Used Cars: Gas Guzzlers versus Gas Sippers. Consider the market for used cars. In 2008, the price of gas rose while the price of used full-size SUVs dropped and the price of used compact cars increased.
  a. Use a supply–demand graph to show the effects of a higher gasoline price on the market for used full-size SUVs.
  b. Use a supply–demand graph to show the effects of a higher gasoline price on the market for used compact cars.

4.6 Predicting and Explaining Market Changes

6.1 Fill in the blanks in the following table. Note that the ordering of the first column has been scrambled.

Change in Demand or Supply	How does the equilibrium price change?	How does the equilibrium quantity change?
Increase in supply		
Decrease in demand		
Decrease in supply		
Increase in demand		

6.2 When _____ (supply/demand) changes, the equilibrium price and the equilibrium quantity change in the same direction. When _____ (supply/demand) changes, the equilibrium price and the equilibrium quantity change in opposite directions.

6.3 Suppose the equilibrium price of accordions recently increased while the equilibrium quantity decreased. These changes were caused by a(n) _____ (increase/decrease) in _____ (supply/demand).

6.4 Suppose the equilibrium price of housing recently increased, and the equilibrium quantity increased as well. These changes were caused by a(n) _____ (increase/decrease) in _____ (supply/demand).

6.5 What Caused the Higher Gasoline Price? In the last month, the price of gasoline increased by 20 percent. Your job is to determine what caused the increase in price: a change in demand or a change in supply. Ms. Info has all the numbers associated with the gasoline market, and she can answer a single factual question. (She cannot answer the question "Was the higher price caused by a change in demand or a change in supply?")
  a. What single question would you ask?
  b. Provide an answer to your question that implies that the higher price was caused by a change in demand. Illustrate with a complete graph.
  c. Provide an answer to your question that implies that the higher price was caused by a change in supply. Illustrate with a complete graph.

6.6 Rising Price of Milk. In 2007, the price of milk increased by roughly 10 percent while the quantity consumed decreased. Use a supply–demand graph to explain the changes in price and quantity.

6.7 Rising Price of Used Organs. Over the last few years, the price of transplantable human organs (livers, kidneys, hearts) has increased dramatically. Why? What additional information about the market for used organs would allow you to prove that your explanation is the correct one?

6.8 The Price of Summer Cabins. As summer approaches, the equilibrium price of rental cabins increases and the equilibrium quantity of cabins rented increases. Draw a demand and supply graph that explains these changes.

6.9 Simplest Possible Graph. Consider the market for juice oranges. Draw the simplest possible demand and supply graph consistent with the following observations. You should be able to draw a graph with no more than four curves. Label each of your curves as "supply" or "demand" and indicate the year (1, 2, or 3).

Year	1	2	3
Price	$5	$7	$4
Quantity	100	80	110

6.10 Zero Price for Used Newspapers. In 1987 you could sell a ton of used newspaper for $60. Five years later, you couldn't sell them at any price. In other words, the price of used newspapers dropped from $60 to zero in just five years. Over this period, the quantity of used newspapers bought and sold increased. What caused the drop in price? Illustrate your answer with a complete graph.

6.11 Decrease in the Price of Heroin. Between 1990 and 2003, the price of heroin decreased from $235 per gram to $76. Over the same period, the quantity of heroin consumed increased from 376 metric tons to 482 metric tons. Use a demand and supply graph to explain these changes in price and quantity.

4.7 Applications of Demand and Supply

7.1 Arrow up or down: Hurricane Katrina _____ the demand for housing in Baton Rouge, so the price of housing _____ and the quantity of housing _____. (Related to Application 1 on page 87.)

7.2 Arrows up or down: The decrease in the number of bee colonies _____ the supply of fruits and berries, _____ the cost of producing ice cream, and _____ the equilibrium price of ice cream. (Related to Application 2 on pages 87–88.)

7.3 Between 2008 and 2009, the equilibrium price of cruises _____ because _____ and demand _____. (Related to Application 3 on pages 88–89.)

7.4 Arrow up or down: The development of a sun-tolerant variety of the vanilla plant _____ the supply of vanilla and its price. (Related to Application 4 on pages 89–90.)

7.5 Arrow up or down: The drought in Australia _____ the supply of rice and _____ its price. (Related to Application 5 on page 90.)

7.6 Katrina Victims Move Back. Suppose that five years after Hurricane Katrina, half the people who had relocated to Baton Rouge move back to a rebuilt New Orleans. Use a demand and supply graph of the Baton Rouge housing market to show the market effects of the return of people to New Orleans. (Related to Application 1 on page 87.)

7.7 Honeybees and Ice Cream. Suppose the decline of bee colonies increases the prices of some ingredients used to produce ice cream. Consider two flavors of ice cream, strawberry and vanilla. The cost of producing strawberry ice cream increases by 20 percent, while the cost of producing vanilla ice cream increases by only 5 percent. Use a supply–demand graph to show the implications for the equilibrium prices and quantities of the two flavors of ice cream. (Related to Application 2 on pages 87–88.)

7.8 Cruise Ship Berths. Consider the change in the equilibrium quantity shown in Figure 4.16. Draw a new graph (with a decrease in demand and an increase in supply) such that the equilibrium quantity (the number of passengers) decreases. What is the fundamental difference between your graph and Figure 4.16? (Related to Application 3 on pages 88–89.)

7.9 Artificial versus Natural Vanilla. An artificial alternative to natural vanilla is cheaper to produce but doesn't taste as good. Suppose the makers of artificial vanilla discover a new recipe that improves its taste. Use a demand and supply graph to show the effects on the equilibrium price and quantity of natural vanilla. (Related to Application 4 on pages 89–90.)

7.10 Drought and Rice Prices. Consider the market for rice. Use a demand and supply graph to illustrate the following statement: "The drought was a major factor in a near doubling of rice prices." (Related to Application 5 on page 90.)

ECONOMIC EXPERIMENT

Market Equilibrium

This simple experiment takes about 20 minutes. We start by dividing the class into two equal groups: consumers and producers.

- The instructor provides each consumer with a number indicating the maximum amount he or she is willing to pay (WTP) for a bushel of apples: The WTP is a number between $1 and $100. Each consumer has the opportunity to buy one bushel of apples per trading period. The consumer's score for a single trading period equals the gap between the WTP and the price actually paid for

apples. For example, if the consumer's WTP is $80 and he or she pays only $30 for apples, the consumer's score is $50. Each consumer has the option of not buying apples. This will be sensible if the best price the consumer can get exceeds the WTP. If the consumer does not buy apples, his or her score will be zero.

- The instructor provides each producer with a number indicating the cost of producing a bushel of apples (a number between $1 and $100). Each producer has the opportunity to sell one bushel per trading period. The producer's score for a single trading period equals the gap between the selling prices and the cost of producing apples. So if a producer sells apples for $20, and the cost is only $15, the producer's score is $5. Producers have the option of not selling apples, which is sensible if the best price the producer can get is less than the cost. If the producer does not sell apples, his or her score is zero.

Once everyone understands the rules, consumers and producers meet in a trading area to arrange transactions. A consumer may announce how much he or she is willing to pay for apples and wait for a producer to agree to sell apples at that price. Alternatively, a producer may announce how much he or she is willing accept for apples and wait for a consumer to agree to buy apples at that price. Once a transaction has been arranged, the consumer and producer inform the instructor of the trade, record the transaction, and leave the trading area.

Several trading periods are conducted, each of which lasts a few minutes. After the end of each trading period, the instructor lists the prices at which apples sold during the period. Then another trading period starts, providing consumers and producers another opportunity to buy or sell apples. After all the trading periods have been completed, each participant computes his or her score by adding the scores from the trading periods.

 For additional economic experiments, please visit *www.myeconlab.com*.

Measuring a Nation's Production and Income

During the deep economic downturn in 2009 and 2010, economists, business writers, and politicians anxiously awaited the news from the government about the latest economic developments. They pored over the data to determine if the economy was beginning to recover from its doldrums and when more robust economic activity would resume.

At the same time, a distinguished group of economists, led by Nobel Laureates Joseph Stiglitz and Amartya Sen and French economist Jean-Paul Fitoussi, issued a report calling for major revision in the way we measure economic performance. They suggested that our government statisticians focus more on how much we consume and how much leisure we enjoy, and not solely on what we produce. They also suggested that we should be more concerned about whether our current activities are sustainable over the long run, perhaps recognizing environmental constraints.

But perhaps their most radical suggestion was that we switch our focus away from economic production to measuring people's economic well-being. This could include examining the diets and living conditions of the poorest people. For residents of developed countries, this might involve analyzing surveys of people's reported happiness with their own lives.

These changes, however, may be far in the future. Economists and businesses will still rely for some time on the traditional measures of economic activity that we study in this chapter.

─────────(**APPLYING THE CONCEPTS**)─────────

1 How can we use economic analysis to compare the size of a major corporation to the size of a country?
   Using Value Added to Measure the True Size of Wal-Mart

2 How severe was the most recent recession for the United States?
   Comparing the Severity of Recessions

3 Do increases in gross domestic product necessarily translate into improvements in the welfare of citizens?
   The Links between Self-Reported Happiness and GDP

macroeconomics

The study of the nation's economy as a whole; focuses on the issues of inflation, unemployment, and economic growth.

This chapter begins your study of **macroeconomics**: the branch of economics that deals with a nation's economy as a whole. Macroeconomics focuses on the economic issues—unemployment, inflation, growth, trade, and the gross domestic product—that are most often discussed in newspapers, on the radio and television, and on the Internet.

Macroeconomic issues lie at the heart of political debates. In fact, all presidential candidates learn a quick lesson in macroeconomics. Namely, their prospects for reelection will depend on how well the economy performs during their term in office. If voters believe the economy has performed well, the president will be reelected. Democrat Jimmy Carter as well as Republican George H. W. Bush failed in their bids for reelection in 1980 and 1992, respectively, partly because of voters' macroeconomic concerns. Both Republican Ronald Reagan in 1984 and Democrat Bill Clinton in 1996 won reelection easily because voters believed the economy was performing well in their first terms. Public opinion polling shows that presidential popularity rises and falls with the performance of the economy.

Macroeconomic events profoundly affect our everyday lives. For example, if the economy fails to create enough jobs, workers will become unemployed throughout the country, and millions of lives will be disrupted. Similarly, slow economic growth means that living standards will not increase rapidly. If prices for goods begin rising rapidly, some people will find it difficult to maintain their lifestyles.

This chapter and the next will introduce you to the concepts you need to understand what macroeconomics is all about. In this chapter, we'll focus on a nation's production and income. We'll learn how economists measure the income and production for an entire country and how they use these measures. In the next chapter, we'll look carefully at unemployment and inflation. Both chapters will explain the terms the media often uses when reporting economic information.

Macroeconomics focuses on two basic issues: long-run economic growth and economic fluctuations. We need to understand what happens during the long run to understand the factors behind the rise in living standards in modern economies. Today, living standards are much higher in the United States than they were for our grandparents. Living standards are also much higher than those of millions of people throughout the globe. Although living standards have improved over time, the economy has not always grown smoothly. Economic performance has fluctuated over time. During periods of slow economic growth, not enough jobs are created, and large numbers of workers become unemployed. Both the public and policymakers become concerned about the lack of jobs and the increase in unemployment.

inflation

Sustained increases in the average prices of all goods and services.

At other times, unemployment may not be a problem, but we become concerned that the prices of everything that we buy seem to increase rapidly. Sustained increases in prices are called **inflation**. We'll explore inflation in the next chapter.

5.1 THE "FLIP" SIDES OF MACROECONOMIC ACTIVITY: PRODUCTION AND INCOME

Before we can study growth and fluctuations, we need to have a basic vocabulary and understanding of some key concepts. We begin with the terms *production* and *income* because these are the "flip" sides of the macroeconomic "coin," so to speak. Every day, men and women go off to work, where they produce or sell merchandise or provide services. At the end of the week or month, they return home with their paychecks or "income." They spend some of that money on other products and services, which are produced by other people. In other words, production leads to income, and income leads to production.

But this chapter really isn't about production and income of individuals in markets. That's what a microeconomist studies. On the contrary, this chapter is about the production and income of the economy *as a whole*. From a "big picture" perspective, we will look at certain measures that will tell us how much the economy is producing and how well it is growing. We will also be able to measure the total income generated in the economy and how this income flows back to workers and investors. These two measures—a country's production and income—are critical to a nation's economic health. Macroeconomists collect and analyze production and income data to understand how many people will find jobs and whether their living standards are rising or falling. Government officials use the data and analysis to develop economic policies.

The Circular Flow of Production and Income

Let's begin with a simple diagram known as the *circular flow*, shown in Figure 5.1. We'll start with a very simple economy that does not have a government or a foreign sector. Households and firms make transactions in two markets known as *factor markets* and *product markets*. In factor, or input, markets, households supply labor to firms. Households are also the ultimate owners of firms, as well as of all the resources firms use in their production, which we call *capital*. Consequently, we can think of households as providing capital to firms—land, buildings, and equipment—to produce output. Product, or output, markets are markets in which firms sell goods and services to consumers.

The point of the circular flow diagram is simple and fundamental: Production generates income. In factor markets, when households supply labor and capital to firms they are compensated by the firms. They earn wages for their work, and they earn interest, dividends, and rents on the capital they supply to the firms. The households then use their income to purchase goods and services in the product markets. The firm uses the revenues it receives from the sale of its products to pay for the factors of production (land, labor, and capital).

When goods and services are produced, income flows throughout the economy. For example, consider a manufacturer of computers. At the same time the computer manufacturer produces and sells new computers, it also generates income through its production. The computer manufacturer pays wages to workers, perhaps pays rent on offices and factory buildings, and pays interest on money it borrowed from a bank. Whatever is left over after paying for the cost of production is the firm's profit, which is income to the owners of the firm. Wages, rents, interest, and profits are all different forms of income.

In an example with a government, your taxes pay for a school district to hire principals, teachers, and other staff to provide educational services to the students in your community. These educational services are an important part of production in our modern economy that produces both goods and services. At the same time, the principals, teachers, and staff all earn income through their employment with the school district. The school district may also rent buildings where classes are held and pay interest on borrowed funds.

Our goal is to understand both sides of this macroeconomic "coin"—the production in the economy and the generation of income in the economy. In the United

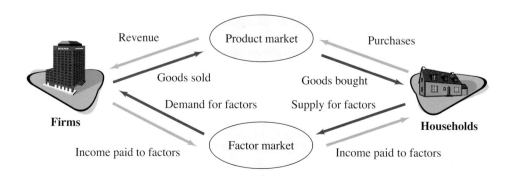

◄ **FIGURE 5.1**
The Circular Flow of Production and Income
The circular flow shows how the production of goods and services generates income for households and how households purchase goods and services produced by firms.

States, the national income and product accounts, published by the Department of Commerce, are the source for the key data on production and income in the economy. As we will see, we can measure the value of output produced in the economy by looking at either the production or income side of the economy. Let's begin by learning how to measure the production for the entire economy.

5.2 THE PRODUCTION APPROACH: MEASURING A NATION'S MACROECONOMIC ACTIVITY USING GROSS DOMESTIC PRODUCT

To measure the production of the entire economy, we need to combine an enormous array of goods and services—everything from new computers to NBA and WNBA basketball games. We can actually add computers to basketball games, as we could add apples and oranges if we were trying to determine the total monetary value of a fruit harvest. Our goal is to summarize the total production of an entire economy into a single number, which we call the **gross domestic product (GDP)**. Gross domestic product is the total market value of all the final goods and services produced within an economy in a given year. GDP is also the most common measure of an economy's total output. All the words in the GDP definition are important, so let's analyze them.

"Total market value" means we take the quantity of goods produced, multiply them by their respective prices, and then add up the totals. If an economy produced two cars at $25,000 per car and three computers at $2,000 per computer, the total value of these goods will be

$$2 \text{ cars} \times \$25,000 \text{ per car} = \$50,000$$

$$+$$

$$3 \text{ computers} \times \$2,000 \text{ per computer} = \$6,000$$

$$= \$56,000$$

The reason we multiply the goods by their prices is that we cannot simply add together the number of cars and the number of computers. Using prices allows us to express the value of everything in a common unit of measurement—in this case, dollars. (In countries other than the United States, we express the value in terms of the local currency.) We add apples and oranges together by finding out the value of both the apples and the oranges, as measured by what you would pay for them, and adding them up in terms of their prices.

"Final goods and services" in the definition of GDP means those goods and services that are sold to ultimate, or final, purchasers. For example, the two cars that were produced would be final goods if they were sold to households or to a business. However, to produce the cars the automobile manufacturer bought steel that went into the body of the cars, and we do not count this steel as a final good or service in GDP. Steel is an example of an **intermediate good**, one that is used in the production process. An intermediate good is not considered a final good or service.

The reason we do not count intermediate goods as final goods is to avoid double-counting. The price of the car already reflects the price of the steel contained in it. We do not want to count the steel twice. Similarly, the large volumes of paper a commercial printing firm uses also are intermediate goods, because the paper becomes part of the final product delivered by the printing firm to its clients.

The final words in our definition of GDP are "in a given year." GDP is expressed as a rate of production, that is, as "X" amount of dollars per year. In 2008, for example, GDP in the United States was $14,196 billion. Goods produced in prior years, such as cars or houses, are not included in GDP for a given year, even if

gross domestic product (GDP)
The total market value of final goods and services produced within an economy in a given year.

intermediate goods
Goods used in the production process that are not final goods and services.

one consumer sells a house or car to another in that year. Only *newly produced* products are included in GDP.

Because we measure GDP using the current prices for goods and services, GDP will increase if prices increase, even if the physical amount of goods that are produced remains the same. Suppose that next year the economy again produces two cars and three computers, but all the prices in the economy double: The price of cars is $50,000, and the price of computers is $4,000. GDP will also be twice as high, or $112,000, even though the quantity produced is the same as during the prior year:

$$2 \text{ cars} \times \$50,000 \text{ per car} = \$100,000$$

$$+$$

$$3 \text{ computers} \times \$4,000 \text{ per computer} = \$ 12,000$$

$$= \$112,000$$

But to say that GDP has doubled would be misleading, because exactly the same goods were produced. To avoid this problem, let's apply the real-nominal principle, one of our five basic principles of economics.

REAL-NOMINAL PRINCIPLE

What matters to people is the real value of money or income—its purchasing power—not the face value of money or income.

What we need is another measure of total output that doesn't increase just because prices increase. For this reason, economists have developed the concept of **real GDP**, a measure that controls for changes in prices. Later in this chapter, we explain how real GDP is calculated. The basic idea is simple. When we use current prices to measure GDP, we are using **nominal GDP**. Nominal GDP can increase for one of two reasons: Either the production of goods and services has increased, or the prices of those goods and services have increased.

To explain the concept of real GDP, we first need to look at a simple example. Suppose an economy produces a single good: computers. In year 1, 10 computers were produced, and each sold for $2,000. In year 2, 12 computers were produced, and each sold for $2,100. Nominal GDP is $20,000 in year 1 and $25,200 in year 2; it has increased by a factor of 1.26 or 26 percent. However, we can also measure real GDP by using year 1 prices as a measure of what was produced in year 1 *and* what was produced in year 2. In year 1, real GDP is

$$10 \text{ computers} \times \$2,000 \text{ per computer} = \$20,000$$

In year 2, real GDP (in year 1 terms) is

$$12 \text{ computers} \times \$2,000 \text{ per computer} = \$24,000$$

Real GDP in year 2 is still greater than real GDP in year 1, now by a factor of 1.2, or 20 percent. The key idea is that we construct a measure using the same prices for both years and thereby take price changes into account.

Figure 5.2 plots real GDP for the U.S. economy for the years 1930 through 2009. The graph shows that real GDP has grown substantially over this period. This is what economists call **economic growth**—sustained increases in the real GDP of an economy over a long period of time. In Chapter 8, we'll study economic growth in detail. Later in this chapter, we'll look carefully at the behavior of real GDP over shorter periods, during which time it can rise and fall. Decreases in real GDP disrupt the economy greatly and lead to unemployment.

real GDP
A measure of GDP that controls for changes in prices.

nominal GDP
The value of GDP in current dollars.

economic growth
Sustained increases in the real GDP of an economy over a long period of time.

▲ FIGURE 5.2

U.S. Real GDP, 1930–2009

During the Great Depression in the 1930s, GDP initially fell and then was relatively flat. The economy was not growing much. However, the economy began growing rapidly in the 1940s during Word War II and has grown substantially since then.

SOURCE: U.S. Department of Commerce.

The Components of GDP

Economists divide GDP into four broad categories, each corresponding to different types of purchases represented in GDP:

1 *Consumption expenditures:* purchases by consumers

2 *Private investment expenditures:* purchases by firms

3 *Government purchases:* purchases by federal, state, and local governments

4 *Net exports:* net purchases by the foreign sector (domestic exports minus domestic imports)

Before discussing these categories, let's look at some data for the U.S. economy to get a sense of the size of each of these four components. Table 5.1 shows the figures for GDP for the fourth quarter of 2009. (A quarter is a three-month period; the first quarter runs from January through March, while the fourth quarter runs from October through December. Quarterly GDP expressed at annual rates is GDP for a year if the entire year were the same as the measured quarter.) In the fourth quarter of 2009, GDP was $14,461 billion, or approximately $14.4 trillion. To get a sense of the magnitude, consider that the U.S. population is approximately 300 million people, making GDP per person

TABLE 5.1 COMPOSITION OF U.S. GDP, FOURTH QUARTER 2009 (BILLIONS OF DOLLARS EXPRESSED AT ANNUAL RATES)				
GDP	Consumption Expenditures	Private Investment Expenditures	Government Purchases	Net Exports
$14,461	$10,234	$1,716	$2,960	–$449

SOURCE: U.S. Department of Commerce.

approximately $48,203. (This does not mean every man, woman, and child actually spends $48,203, but it is a useful indicator of the productive strength of the economy.)

CONSUMPTION EXPENDITURES   **Consumption expenditures** are purchases by consumers of currently produced goods and services, either domestic or foreign. These purchases include flat-screen TVs, smart phones, automobiles, clothing, hair-styling services, jewelry, movie or basketball tickets, food, and all other consumer items. We can break down consumption into durable goods, nondurable goods, and services. *Durable goods*, such as automobiles or refrigerators, last for a long time. *Nondurable goods*, such as food, last for a short time. *Services* are work in which people play a prominent role in delivery (such as a dentist filling a cavity). They range from haircutting to health care and are the fastest-growing component of consumption in the United States. Overall, consumption spending is the most important component of GDP, constituting about 70 percent of total purchases.

consumption expenditures
Purchases of newly produced goods and services by households.

PRIVATE INVESTMENT EXPENDITURES   **Private investment expenditures** in GDP consist of three components:

1 First, there is spending on new plants and equipment during the year. If a firm builds a new factory or purchases a new machine, the new factory or new machine is included in the year's GDP. Purchasing an existing building or buying a used machine does not count in GDP, because the goods were not produced during the current year.

2 Second, newly produced housing is included in investment spending. The sale of an existing home to a new owner is not counted, because the house was not built in the current year.

3 Finally, if firms add to their stock of inventories, the increase in inventories during the current year is included in GDP. If a hardware store had $1,000 worth of nuts and bolts on its shelves at the beginning of the year and $1,100 at the year's end, its inventory investment is $100 ($1,100 – $1,000). This $100 increase in inventory investment is included in GDP.

private investment expenditures
Purchases of newly produced goods and services by firms.

We call the total of new investment expenditures **gross investment**. During the year, some of the existing plant, equipment, and housing will deteriorate or wear out. This wear and tear is called **depreciation**, or sometimes a *capital consumption allowance*. If we subtract depreciation from gross investment, we obtain net investment. **Net investment** is the true addition to the stock of plant, equipment, and housing in a given year.

Make sure you understand this distinction between gross investment and net investment. Consider the $1,716 billion in total investment spending for the fourth quarter of 2009, a period in which there was $1,525 billion in depreciation in the private sector. That means there was only $191 billion ($1,716 – $1,525) in net investment by firms in that year; 88 percent of gross investment went to make up for depreciation of existing capital.

gross investment
Total new investment expenditures.

depreciation
Reduction in the value of capital goods over a one-year period due to physical wear and tear and also to obsolescence; also called *capital consumption allowance*.

net investment
Gross investment minus depreciation.

Warning: When we discuss measuring production in the GDP accounts, we use *investment* in a different way than that with which you may be accustomed. For an economist, investment in the GDP accounts means purchases of new final goods and services by firms. In everyday conversation, we may talk about investing in the stock market or investing in gold. Buying stock for $1,800 on the stock market is a purchase of an existing financial asset; it is not the purchase of new goods and services by firms. Therefore, that $1,800 does not appear anywhere in GDP. The same is true of purchasing a gold bar. In GDP accounting, *investment* denotes the purchase of new capital. Be careful not to confuse the common usage of *investment* with the definition of *investment* as we use it in the GDP accounts.

GOVERNMENT PURCHASES   **Government purchases** are the purchases of newly produced goods and services by federal, state, and local governments. They include any goods that the government purchases plus the wages and benefits of all

government purchases
Purchases of newly produced goods and services by local, state, and federal governments.

government workers (paid when the government purchases their services as employees). Investment spending by government is also included. The majority of spending in this category comes from state and local governments: $1,790 billion of the total $2,960 billion in 2009. Government purchases affect our lives very directly. For example, all salaries of U.S. postal employees and federal airport security personnel are counted as government purchases.

transfer payments

Payments from governments to individuals that do not correspond to the production of goods and services.

This category does not include all spending by governments. It excludes **transfer payments**, payments to individuals that are not associated with the production of goods and services. For example, payments for Social Security, welfare, and interest on government debt are all considered transfer payments and thus are not included in government purchases in GDP. Nothing is being produced by the recipients in return for money being paid, or "transferred," to them. But wage payments to the police, postal workers, and the staff of the Internal Revenue Service are all included, because they do correspond to services these workers are currently producing.

Because transfer payments are excluded from GDP, a vast portion of the budget of the federal government is not part of GDP. In 2008, the federal government spent approximately $3,454 billion, of which only $1,170 billion (about 33 percent) was counted as federal government purchases. Transfer payments are important, however, because they affect both the income of individuals and their consumption and savings behavior. Transfer payments also affect the size of the federal budget deficit, which we will study in a later chapter. At this point, keep in mind the distinction between government purchases—which are included in GDP—and total government spending or expenditure—which may *not* be included.

import

A good or service produced in a foreign country and purchased by residents of the home country (for example, the United States).

export

A good or service produced in the home country (for example, the United States) and sold in another country.

net exports

Exports minus imports.

NET EXPORTS   To understand the role of the foreign sector, we first need to define three terms. **Imports** are goods and services we buy from other countries. **Exports** are goods and services made here and sold to other countries. **Net exports** are total exports minus total imports. In Table 5.1, we see that net exports in the first quarter of 2009 were –$449 billion. Net exports were negative because our imports exceeded our exports.

Consumption, investment, and government purchases include all purchases by consumers, firms, and the government, whether or not the goods were produced in the United States. However, GDP is supposed to measure the goods produced in the United States. Consequently, we subtract purchases of foreign goods by consumers, firms, or the government when we calculate GDP, because these goods were not produced in the United States. At the same time, we add to GDP any goods produced here and sold abroad, for example, airplanes made in the United States and sold in Europe. By including net exports as a component of GDP, we correctly measure U.S. production by adding exports and subtracting imports.

Suppose someone in the United States buys a $25,000 car made in Japan. If we look at final purchases, we will see that consumption spending rose by $25,000 because a consumer made a purchase of a consumption good. Net exports fell by $25,000, however, because we subtracted the value of the import (the car) from total exports. Notice that total GDP did not change with the purchase of the car. This is exactly what we want in this case, because the car wasn't produced in the United States.

Now suppose the United States sells a car for $22,000 to a resident of Spain. In this case, net exports increase by $22,000 because the car was a U.S. export. GDP will also be a corresponding $22,000 higher because this sale represents U.S. production.

trade deficit

The excess of imports over exports.

trade surplus

The excess of exports over imports.

Recall that for the United States in the fourth quarter of 2009 net exports were –$449 billion dollars. In other words, in that quarter the United States bought $449 billion more goods from abroad than it sold abroad. When we buy more goods from abroad than we sell, we have a **trade deficit**. A **trade surplus** occurs when our exports exceed our imports. Figure 5.3 shows the U.S. trade surplus as a share of GDP from 1960 to 2009. Although at times the United States has had a small trade surplus, it has generally run a trade deficit. In recent years, the trade deficit has increased and has fluctuated between 3 and 6 percent of GDP. In later chapters, we study how trade deficits can affect a country's GDP.

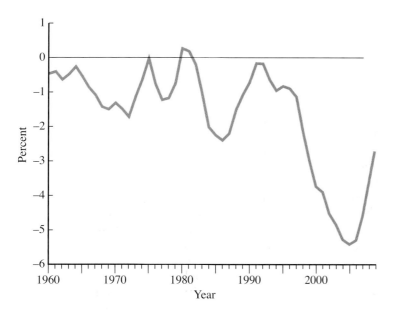

Putting It All Together: The GDP Equation

We can summarize our discussion of who purchases GDP with a simple equation that combines the four components of GDP:

$$Y = C + I + G + NX$$

where

$$Y = \text{GDP}$$
$$C = \text{Consumption}$$
$$I = \text{Investment}$$
$$G = \text{Government purchases}$$
$$NX = \text{Net exports}$$

In other words,

GDP = consumption + investment + government purchases + net exports

This equation is an *identity*, which means it is always true no matter what the values of the variables are. In any economy, GDP consists of the sum of its four components.

5.3 THE INCOME APPROACH: MEASURING A NATION'S MACROECONOMIC ACTIVITY USING NATIONAL INCOME

Recall from the circular flow that one person's production ends up being another person's income. Income is the flip side of our macroeconomic "coin." As a result, in addition to measuring a nation's activity by measuring production, we can also gauge it by measuring a nation's income. The total income earned by U.S. residents working in the United States and abroad is called **national income**.

Measuring National Income

To measure national income, economists first make two primary adjustments to GDP.

First, we add to GDP the net income earned by U.S. firms and residents abroad. To make this calculation, we add to GDP any income earned abroad by U.S. firms or residents and subtract any income earned in the United States by foreign firms or

national income

The total income earned by a nation's residents both domestically and abroad in the production of goods and services.

residents. For example, we add the profits earned by U.S. multinational corporations that are sent back to the United States but subtract the profits from multinational corporations operating in the United States that are sent back to their home countries. The profits Wal-Mart sends back to the United States from its stores in Mexico are added to GDP. The profits Toyota earns in the United States that it sends back to Japan are subtracted from GDP. The result of these adjustments is the total income earned worldwide by U.S. firms and residents. This is the **gross national product (GNP)**.

gross national product
GDP plus net income earned abroad.

The distinction between what they produce within their borders, GDP, and what their citizens earn, GNP, is not that important to most countries. For the United States, the difference between GDP and GNP is typically just 1 percent. In some countries, however, the differences are much larger. The country of Kuwait, for example, earned vast amounts of income from its oil riches, which it invested abroad in stocks, bonds, and other types of investments. These earnings comprised approximately 9 percent of Kuwait's 2006 GNP. Foreigners have traditionally made large investments in Australia. As they sent their profits back to their home countries, Australia's net income from abroad was negative in 2006, and Australian GDP in that year exceeded Australian GNP by 4.1 percent.

The second adjustment we make when calculating national income is to subtract depreciation from GNP. Recall that depreciation is the wear and tear on plant and equipment that occurred during the year. In a sense, our income is reduced because our buildings and machines are wearing out. When we subtract depreciation from GNP, we reach *net national product (NNP)*, where *net* means "after depreciation."

After making these adjustments and taking into account statistical discrepancies, we reach *national income*. (Statistical discrepancies arise when government statisticians make their calculations using different sources of the same data.) Table 5.2 shows the effects of these adjustments for the fourth quarter of 2009.

TABLE 5.2 FROM GDP TO NATIONAL INCOME, FOURTH QUARTER 2009 (BILLIONS OF DOLLARS)	
Gross domestic product	$14,242
Gross national product	14,363
Net national product	12,513
National income	12,259

In turn, national income is divided among six basic categories: compensation of employees (wages and benefits), corporate profits, rental income, proprietors' income (income of unincorporated business), net interest (interest payments received by households from business and from abroad), and other items. Approximately 65 percent of all national income goes to workers in the form of wages and benefits. For most of the countries in the world, wages and benefits are the largest part of national income.

personal income
Income, including transfer payments, received by households.

In addition to national income, which measures the income earned in a given year by the entire private sector, we are sometimes interested in determining the total payments that flow directly into households, a concept known as **personal income**. To calculate personal income, we begin with national income and subtract any corporate profits that are retained by the corporation and not paid out as dividends to households. We also subtract all taxes on production and imports and social insurance taxes, which are payments for Social Security and Medicare. We then add any personal interest income received from the government and consumers and all transfer payments. The result is the total income available to households, or personal income.

personal disposable income
Personal income that households retain after paying income taxes.

The amount of personal income that households retain after paying income taxes is called **personal disposable income**.

Measuring National Income through Value Added

Another way to measure national income is to look at the **value added** of each firm in the economy. For a firm, we can measure its value added by the dollar value of the firm's sales minus the dollar value of the goods and services purchased from other firms. What remains is the sum of all the income—wages, profits, rents, and interest—that the firm generates. By adding up the value added for all the firms in the economy (plus nonprofit and governmental organizations), we can calculate national income. Let's consider a simple example illustrated in Table 5.3.

value added

The sum of all the income—wages, interest, profits, and rent—generated by an organization. For a firm, we can measure value added by the dollar value of the firm's sales minus the dollar value of the goods and services purchased from other firms.

TABLE 5.3 CALCULATING VALUE ADDED IN A SIMPLE ECONOMY

	Automobile Firm	Steel Firm	Total Economy
Total sales	$16,000	$6,000	$22,000
Less purchases from other firms	6,000	0	6,000
Equals value added: the sum of all wages, interest, profits, and rents	10,000	6,000	16,000

Suppose an economy consists of two firms: an automobile firm that sells its cars to consumers and a steel firm that sells only to the automobile firm. If the automobile company sells a car for $16,000 to consumers and purchases $6,000 worth of steel from the steel firm, the auto firm has $10,000 remaining—its value added—which it can then distribute as wages, rents, interest, and profits. If the steel firm sells $6,000 worth of steel but does not purchase any inputs from other firms, its value added is $6,000, which it pays out in the form of wages, rents, interest, and profits. Total value added in the economy from both firms is $16,000 ($10,000 + $6,000), which is the sum of wages, rents, interest, and profits for the entire economy (consisting of these two firms).

As this example illustrates, we measure the value added for a typical firm by starting with the value of its total sales and subtracting the value of any inputs it purchases from other firms. The amount of income that remains is the firm's value added, which is then distributed as wages, rents, interest, and profits. In calculating national income, we need to include all the firms in the economy, even the firms that produce intermediate goods.

APPLICATION 1

USING VALUE ADDED TO MEASURE THE TRUE SIZE OF WAL-MART

APPLYING THE CONCEPTS #1: How can we use economic analysis to compare the size of a major corporation to the size of a country?

During 2008, Wal-Mart's sales were approximately $374 billion, nearly 2.6 percent of U.S. GDP. Some social commentators might want to measure the impact of Wal-Mart just through its sales. But to produce those sales, Wal-Mart had to buy goods from many other companies. Wal-Mart's value added was substantially less than its total sales. Based on Wal-Mart's annual reports, its cost of sales was $286 billion, leaving approximately $88 billion in value added. This is a very large number, as might be expected from the world's largest retailer, but it is much smaller than its total sales. If we used Wal-Mart's sales to compare it to a country, it would have a GDP similar to that of Belgium, which is ranked 28th in the world. However, using the more appropriate measure of value added, Wal-Mart's size is closer to Bulgaria, ranked 56th in the world.   **Related to Exercise 3.9.**

SOURCE: Based on Wal-Mart Annual Report, 2008, http://walmartstores.com/sites/AnnualReport/2008/docs/finrep_00.pdf (accessed July, 2008).

An Expanded Circular Flow

Now that we have examined both production and income, including both the government and the foreign sector, let's take another look at a slightly more realistic circular flow. Figure 5.4 depicts a circular flow that includes both the government and the foreign sector. Both households and firms pay taxes to the government. The government, in turn, supplies goods and services in the product market and also purchases inputs—labor and capital—in the factor markets, just like private-sector firms do. Net exports, which can be positive or negative, are shown entering or leaving the product market.

In summary, we can look at GDP from two sides: We can ask who buys the output that is produced, or we can ask how the income that is created through the production process is divided between workers and investors. From the spending side, we saw that nearly 70 percent of GDP consists of consumer expenditures. From the income side, we saw that nearly 65 percent of national income is paid in wages and benefits. Macroeconomists may use data based either on the production that occurs in the economy or on its flip side, the income that is generated, depending on whether they are more focused on current production or on current income.

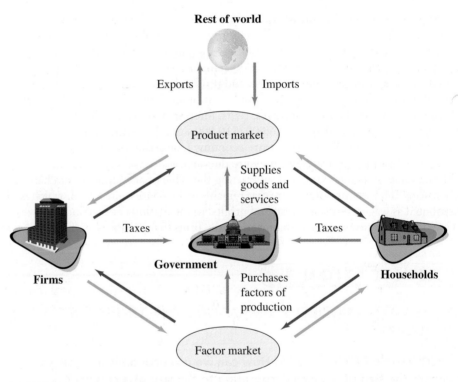

▲ **FIGURE 5.4**

The Circular Flow with Government and the Foreign Sector

The new linkages (in blue) demonstrate the roles that the government and the foreign sector (imports and exports) play in the circular flow.

5.4 A CLOSER EXAMINATION OF NOMINAL AND REAL GDP

We have discussed different ways to measure the production of an economy, looking at both who purchases goods and services and the income it generates. Of all the measures we have discussed, GDP is the one most commonly used both by the public and by economists. Let's take a closer look at it.

Measuring Real versus Nominal GDP

Output in the economy can increase from one year to the next. And prices can rise from one year to the next. Recall that we defined nominal GDP as GDP measured in current prices, and we defined real GDP as GDP adjusted for price changes.

Now we take a closer look at how real GDP is measured in modern economies. Let's start with a simple economy in which there are only two goods—cars and computers—produced in the years 2011 and 2012. The data for this economy—the prices and quantities produced for each year—are shown in Table 5.4. The production of cars and the production of computers increased, but the production of computers increased more rapidly. The price of cars rose, while the price of computers remained the same.

TABLE 5.4 GDP DATA FOR A SIMPLE ECONOMY

Year	Quantity Produced		Price	
	Cars	Computers	Cars	Computers
2011	4	1	$10,000	$5,000
2012	5	3	12,000	5,000

Let's first calculate nominal GDP for this economy in each year. Nominal GDP is the total market value of goods and services produced in each year. Using the data in the table, we can see that nominal GDP for the year 2011 is

$$(4 \text{ cars} \times \$10,000) + (1 \text{ computer} \times \$5,000) = \$45,000$$

Similarly, nominal GDP for the year 2012 is

$$(5 \text{ cars} \times \$12,000) + (3 \text{ computers} \times \$5,000) = \$75,000$$

Now we'll find real GDP. To compute real GDP, we calculate GDP using constant prices. What prices should we use? For the moment, let's use the prices for the year 2011. Because we are using 2011 prices, real GDP and nominal GDP for 2011 are both equal to $45,000. But for 2012, they are different. In 2012, real GDP is

$$(5 \text{ cars} \times \$10,000) + (3 \text{ computers} \times \$5,000) = \$65,000$$

Note that real GDP for 2012, which is $65,000, is less than nominal GDP for 2012, which is $75,000. The reason real GDP is less than nominal GDP here is that prices of cars rose by $2,000 between 2011 and 2012, and we are measuring GDP using 2011 prices. We can measure real GDP for any other year simply by calculating GDP using constant prices.

We now calculate the growth in real GDP for this economy between 2011 and 2012. Because real GDP was $45,000 in 2011 and $65,000 in 2012, real GDP grew by $20,000. In percentage terms, this is a $20,000 increase from the initial level of $45,000 or

$$\text{Percentage growth in real GDP} = \frac{\$20,000}{\$45,000} = .444$$

which equals 44.4 percent. This percentage is an average of the growth rates for both goods—cars and computers.

Figure 5.5 depicts real and nominal GDP for the United States from 1950 to 2009. Real GDP is measured in 2000 dollars, so the curves cross in 2000. Before 2000, nominal GDP is less than real GDP because prices in earlier years were lower than they were in 2000. After 2000, nominal GDP exceeds real GDP because prices in later years were higher than they were in 2000.

▶ **FIGURE 5.5**
U.S. Nominal and Real GDP, 1950–2009
This figure plots both real and nominal GDP for the United States in billions of dollars. Real GDP is measured in 2000 dollars.

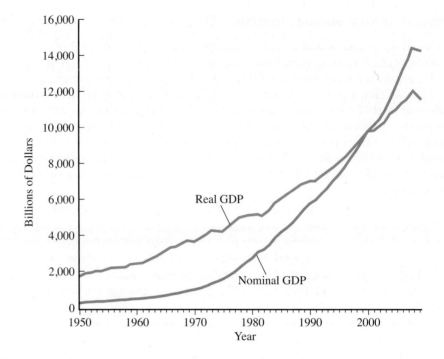

How to Use the GDP Deflator

We can also use the data in Table 5.4 to measure the changes in prices for this economy of cars and computers. The basic idea is that the differences between nominal GDP and real GDP for any year arise only because of changes in prices. So by comparing real GDP and nominal GDP, we can measure the changes in prices for the economy. In practice, we do this by creating an index, called the **GDP deflator**, that measures how prices of goods and services change over time. Because we are calculating real GDP using year 2011 prices, we will set the value of this index equal to 100 in the year 2011, which we call the base year. To find the value of the GDP deflator for the year 2012 (or other years), we use the following formula:

GDP deflator
An index that measures how the prices of goods and services included in GDP change over time.

$$\text{GDP Deflator} = \frac{\text{Nominal GDP}}{\text{Real GDP}} \times 100$$

Using this formula, we find that the value of the GDP deflator for 2012 is

$$\frac{\$75,000}{\$65,000} \times 100 = 1.15 \times 100 = 115$$

Because the value of the GDP deflator is 115 in 2012 and was 100 in the base year of 2011, this means prices rose by 15 percent between the two years:

$$\frac{115 - 100}{100} = \frac{15}{100} = 0.15$$

Note that this 15 percent is a weighted average of the price changes for the two goods—cars and computers.

Until 1996, the Commerce Department, which produces the GDP figures, used these formulas to calculate real GDP and measure changes in prices. Economists at the department chose a base year and measured real GDP by using the prices in that base year. They also calculated the GDP deflator, just as we did, by taking the ratio of nominal GDP to real GDP. Today, the Commerce Department calculates real GDP and the price index for real GDP using a more complicated method. In our example, we measured real GDP using 2011 prices. But we could have also measured real GDP using prices from 2012. If we did, we would have come up with slightly different numbers both for the increase in prices between the two years and for the increase in real GDP. To avoid this problem, the Commerce Department now uses a **chain-weighted index**, which is a method for calculating price changes that takes an average of price changes using base years from consecutive years (that is, 2011 and 2012 in our example). If you look online or at the data produced by the Commerce Department, you will see real GDP measured in chained dollars and a chain-type price index for GDP.

chain-weighted index

A method for calculating changes in prices that uses an average of base years from neighboring years.

5.5 FLUCTUATIONS IN GDP

As we have discussed, real GDP does not always grow smoothly—sometimes it collapses suddenly, and the result is an economic downturn. We call such fluctuations *business cycles*. Let's look at an example of a business cycle from the late 1980s and early 1990s. Figure 5.6 plots real GDP for the United States from 1988 to 1992. Notice that in mid-1990, real GDP begins to fall. A **recession** is a period when real GDP falls for six or more consecutive months. Economists talk more in terms of quarters of the year—consecutive three-month periods—than in terms of months. So they would say that a recession occurs when real GDP falls for two consecutive quarters. The date at which the recession starts—that is, when output starts to decline—is called the **peak**. The date at which it ends—that is, when output starts to increase again—is called the **trough**. In Figure 5.6, we see the peak and trough of the recession. After a trough, the economy enters a recovery period, or period of **expansion**.

From World War II through 2010, the United States experienced 11 recessions. Table 5.5 contains the dates of the peaks and troughs of each recession, the percent decline in real GDP from each peak to each trough, and the length of the recessions in months. Complete information is not yet available for the most recent recession, which began in December 2007. Aside from the most recent recession, which was very severe, the sharpest decline in output occurred during the recession from 1973 to 1975, which started as a result of a sharp rise in world oil prices. This was also one of the longest recessions, although the most recent recession will most likely be the longest.

In the last three decades, there have been four recessions, three of them starting near the beginning of each of the decades: 1981, 1990, and 2001. In the 2001 recession, employment began to fall in March 2001, before the terrorist attack on the United States on September 11, 2001. The attack further disrupted economic activity and damaged producer and consumer confidence, and the economy tumbled through a recession. The recession that began in December 2007 followed a sharp decline in the housing sector and the financial difficulties associated with this decline. It deepened during the financial crisis that hit in September and October of 2008. As credit

recession

Commonly defined as six consecutive months of declining real GDP.

peak

The date at which a recession starts.

trough

The date at which output stops falling in a recession.

expansion

The period after a trough in the business cycle during which the economy recovers.

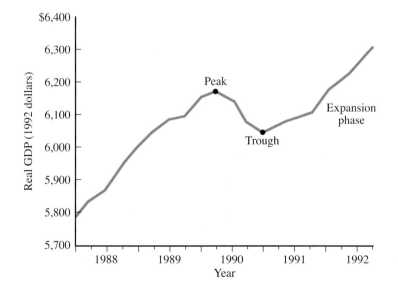

◀ **FIGURE 5.6**
The 1990 Recession
Recessions can be illustrated by peaks, troughs, and an expansion phase. The date at which the recession starts and output begins to fall is called the peak. The date at which the recession ends and output begins to rise is called the trough. The expansion phase begins after the trough.
SOURCE: U.S. Department of Commerce.

TABLE 5.5 ELEVEN POSTWAR RECESSIONS			
Peak	Trough	Percent Decline in Real GDP	Length of Recession (months)
November 1948	October 1949	−1.5	11
July 1953	May 1954	−3.2	10
August 1957	April 1958	−3.3	8
April 1960	February 1961	−1.2	10
December 1969	November 1970	−1.0	11
November 1973	March 1975	−4.1	16
January 1980	July 1980	−2.5	6
July 1981	November 1982	−3.0	16
July 1990	March 1991	−1.4	8
March 2001	November 2001	−0.6	8
December 2007	June 2009	−4.1	18

SOURCE: National Bureau of Economic Research, "Business Cycle Expansions and Contractions," http://wwwdev.nber.org/cycles/cyclesmain.html.

became less available to both businesses and consumers, the effects of the financial crisis began to show up in reduced consumer spending for durable goods such as automobiles and reduced business investment.

Throughout the broader sweep of U.S. history, other downturns have occurred—20 of them from 1860 up to World War II. Not all were particularly severe, and in some unemployment hardly changed. However, some economic downturns, such as those in 1893 and 1929, were severe.

Although we used the common definition of a recession as a period when real GDP falls for six months, in practice, a committee of economists at the National Bureau of Economics Research (NBER), a private research group in Cambridge,

APPLICATION 2

COMPARING THE SEVERITY OF RECESSIONS

APPLYING THE CONCEPTS #2: How severe was the most recent recession for the United States?

Was the most recent recession the most severe economic downturn since the Great Depression? With the data now in, it appears that the recession starting in December 2007 will rival the recession starting in November 1973, which was caused by a sharp and unexpected rise in oil prices. From Table 5.5, we see that the fall in output from peak to trough was 4.1 percent. A similar calculation based on available quarterly data for the recent recession from the fourth quarter of 2007 to the second quarter of 2009 reveals a fall of approximately 4.1%. On this measure, the 2007 recession was equally severe as measured by the decline in GDP.

However, along other important dimensions, the 2007 recession was more damaging to the economy. The 1973 recession lasted 16 months, while the 2007 recession lasted 18 months, the longest in the postwar era. Additionally, the toll on workers appears greater in the most recent recession. Unemployment rose from 4.9 percent to 8.5 percent in the earlier recession as compared to 4.6 percent to 10.0 percent in the most recent recession.

Of course, governments can offset some of these effects on individuals through social programs such as payments to those individuals who become unemployed or welfare payments. For a complete analysis, we would want to look at the incomes of those who lost their jobs as well as those who kept their jobs.   **Related to Exercises 5.6 and 5.7.**

Massachusetts, of primarily academic economists, officially proclaims the beginning and end of recessions in the United States using a broader set of criteria than just GDP. The NBER's formal definition is "a significant decline in economic activity, spread across the economy, lasting more than a few months, normally visible in production, employment, real income, and other indicators." As you can see, it uses a wide variety of indicators to determine whether a recession has occurred and its length.

Depression is the common term for a severe recession. In the United States, the Great Depression refers to the years 1929 through 1933, the period when real GDP fell by over 33 percent. This drop in GDP created the most severe disruptions to ordinary economic life in the United States during the twentieth century. Throughout the country and in much of the world, banks closed, businesses failed, and many people lost their jobs and their life savings. Unemployment rose sharply. In 1933, over 25 percent of people who were looking for work failed to find jobs.

depression
The common name for a severe recession.

Although the United States has not experienced a depression since that time, other countries have. In the last 20 years, several Asian countries (for example, Thailand) and Latin American countries (for example, Argentina) suffered severe economic disruptions that were true depressions.

5.6 GDP AS A MEASURE OF WELFARE

GDP is our best measure of the value of output produced by an economy. As we have seen, we can use GDP and related indicators to measure economic growth within a country. In a later chapter, we will use GDP to compare the value of output across countries as well. Economists use GDP and related measures to determine if an economy has fallen into a recession or has entered into a depression. But while GDP is a very valuable measure of the health of an economy, it is not a perfect measure.

Shortcomings of GDP as a Measure of Welfare

There are several recognized flaws in the construction of GDP. We should thus be cautious in interpreting GDP as a measure of our economic well-being, because it does not take into account housework and childcare, leisure, the underground economy, or pollution.

HOUSEWORK AND CHILDCARE   First, GDP ignores transactions that do not take place in organized markets. The most important example is services, such as cleaning, cooking, and providing free childcare, that people do for themselves in their own homes. Because these services are not transferred through markets, GDP statisticians cannot measure them. If we included household production in GDP, measured GDP would be considerably higher than currently reported.

LEISURE   Second, leisure time is not included in GDP because GDP is designed to be a measure of the production that occurs in the economy. To the extent that households value leisure, increases in leisure time will lead to higher social welfare, but not to higher GDP.

UNDERGROUND ECONOMY   Third, GDP ignores the underground economy, where transactions are not reported to official authorities. These transactions can be legal, but people don't report the income they have generated because they want to avoid paying taxes on it. For example, wait staff may not report all their tips and owners of flea markets may make under-the-table cash transactions with their customers. Illegal transactions, such as profits from the illegal drug trade, also result in unreported income. In the United States in 2005, the Internal Revenue Service estimated (based on tax returns from 2001) that about $310 billion in federal income taxes from the underground economy was not collected each year. If the federal income tax rate that applies to income evaded from taxes was about 20 percent, approximately $1.5 trillion ($310 billion ÷ 0.20) in income from the underground economy escaped the GDP accountants that year, or about 15 percent of GDP at the time.

APPLICATION 3

THE LINKS BETWEEN SELF-REPORTED HAPPINESS AND GDP

APPLYING THE CONCEPTS #3: Do increases in gross domestic product necessarily translate into improvements in the welfare of citizens?

Two economists, David Blanchflower of Dartmouth College and Andrew Oswald of Warwick University in the United Kingdom, have systematically analyzed surveys over a nearly 30-year period that ask individuals to describe themselves as "happy, pretty happy, or not too happy." The results of their work are provocative. Over the last 30 years, reported levels of happiness have declined slightly in the United States and remained relatively flat in the United Kingdom despite very large increases in per capita income in both countries. Could it be the increased stress of everyday life has taken its toll on our happiness despite the increase in income?

At any point in time, however, money does appear to buy happiness. Holding other factors constant, individuals with higher incomes do report higher levels of personal satisfaction. But these "other factors" are quite important. Unemployment and divorce lead to sharply lower levels of satisfaction. Blanchflower and Oswald calculate that a stable marriage is worth $100,000 per year in terms of equivalent reported satisfaction.

Perhaps most interesting are their findings about trends in the relative happiness of different groups in our society. While whites report higher levels of happiness than African Americans, the gap has decreased over the last 30 years, as the happiness of African Americans has risen faster than that of whites. Men's happiness has risen relative to that of women over the last 30 years.

Finally, in recent work Blanchflower and Oswald looked at how happiness varies over the life cycle. Controlling for income, education, and other personal factors, they found that in the United States, happiness among men and women reaches a minimum at the ages of 49 and 45, respectively. Since these are also the years in which earnings are usually the highest, it does suggest that work takes its toll on happiness. **Related to Exercises 6.2 and 6.9.**

SOURCE: David Blanchflower and Andrew Oswald, "Well-Being Over Time in Britain and the USA," (working paper 7847, National Bureau of Economic Research, January 2000) and "Is Well-being U-Shaped over the Life Cycle," (working paper 12935, February 2007).

Economists have used a variety of methods to estimate the extent of the underground economy throughout the world. They typically find that the size of the underground economy is much larger in developing countries than in developed countries. For example, in the highly developed countries, estimates of the underground economy are between 15 and 20 percent of reported or official GDP. However, in developing countries, estimates are closer to 40 percent of reported GDP. Table 5.6 contains

TABLE 5.6 THE WORLD UNDERGROUND ECONOMY, 2002–2003	
Region of the World	Underground Economy as Percent of Reported GDP
Africa	41%
Central and South America	41
Asia	30
Transition Economies	38
Europe, United States, and Japan	17
Unweighted Average over 145 Countries	35

SOURCE: Based on estimates by Friedrich Schneider in "The Size of Shadow Economies in 145 Countries from 1999 to 2003," unpublished paper, 2005.

estimates of the underground economy as a percent of reported GDP for different regions of the world.

POLLUTION   Fourth, GDP does not value changes in the environment that occur in the production of output. Suppose a factory produces $1,000 of output but pollutes a river and lowers its value by $2,000. Instead of recording a loss to society of $1,000, GDP will show a $1,000 increase. This is an important limitation of GDP accounting as a measure of our economic well-being, because changes in the environment affect our daily lives. Previous attempts by the Commerce Department to measure the effects of changes in environment by adding positive or subtracting negative changes to the environment from national income did not yield major results. But they were limited and looked only at a very select part of the environment. Has our environment improved or deteriorated as we experienced economic growth? Finding the answer to this question will pose a real challenge for the next generation of economic statisticians.

Most of us would prefer to live in a country with a high standard of living, and few of us would want to experience poverty up close. But does a higher level of GDP really lead to more satisfaction?

SUMMARY

In this chapter, we learned how economists and government statisticians measure the income and production for an entire country and what these measures are used for. Developing meaningful statistics for an entire economy is difficult. As we have seen, statistics can convey useful information—if they are used with care. Here are some of the main points to remember in this chapter:

1 The circular flow diagram shows how the production of goods and services generates income for households and how households purchase goods and services by firms. The expanded circular flow diagram includes government and the foreign sector.

2 *Gross domestic product* (GDP) is the market value of all final goods and services produced in a given year.

3 GDP consists of four components: consumption, investment, government purchases, and net exports. The following equation combines these components:

$$Y = C + I + G + NX$$

The *GDP deflator* is an index that measures how the prices of goods and services included in GDP change over time. The following equation helps us find the GDP deflator:

$$\text{GDP Deflator} = \frac{\text{Nominal GDP}}{\text{Real GDP}} \times 100$$

4 *National income* is obtained from GDP by adding the net income U.S. individuals and firms earn from abroad, then subtracting depreciation.

5 *Real GDP* is calculated by using constant prices. The Commerce Department now uses methods that take an average using base years from neighboring years.

6 *A recession* is commonly defined as a six-month consecutive period of negative growth. However, in the United States, the National Bureau of Economic Research uses a broader definition.

7 GDP does not include nonmarket transactions, leisure time, the underground economy, or changes to the environment.

KEY TERMS

private investment expenditures, p. 103

real GDP, p. 101

recession, p. 111

trade deficit, p. 104

trade surplus, p. 104

transfer payments, p. 104

trough, p. 111

value added, p. 107

EXERCISES  Visit www.myeconlab.com to complete these exercises online and get instant feedback.

5.1 The "Flip" Sides of Macroeconomic Activity: Production and Income

1.1 The circular flow describes the process by which GDP generates _____, which is spent on goods and services.

1.2 Labor and capital are exchanged in _____ markets.

1.3 Which government department produces the National Income and Product Accounts?
a. The Department of Education
b. The Department of Commerce
c. The Congressional Budget Office
d. The Council of Economic Advisors

1.4 The provision of educational services is not counted as output in modern economies. _____ (True/False)

1.5 **Understanding the Circular Flow Diagram.** In the circular flow diagram, why do the arrows corresponding to the flow of dollars and the arrows corresponding to the flow of goods go in the opposite direction?

1.6 **Types of Income.** Sometimes economists distinguish between wages on the one hand, and rents, interest, and profits on the other. What is the basis of that distinction?

5.2 The Production Approach: Measuring a Nation's Macroeconomic Activity Using Gross Domestic Product

2.1 Which of the following is not a component of GDP?
a. Consumption
b. Investment
c. Producer Price Index
d. Government purchases
e. Net exports

2.2 What part of government spending is excluded from GDP because it does not correspond to goods and services currently being produced?
a. National defense
b. Transfer payments
c. Education
d. Purchases of police cars

2.3 If depreciation exceeds gross investment, net investment will be _____.

2.4 A trade deficit occurs when _____ exceeds _____.

2.5 **GDP Statistics and Unemployed Workers.** In Economy A, the government puts workers on the payroll who cannot find jobs for long periods, but these "employees" do no work. In Economy B, the government does not hire any long-term unemployed workers but gives them cash grants. Comparing the GDP statistics between the two otherwise identical economies, what can you determine about measured GDP and the actual level of output in each economy?

2.6 **Health Care Subsidies.** If the federal government provides subsidies for individuals to buy health-care insurance, is this included in the federal budget? Is it included in GDP?

2.7 **The Upside and Downside of Trade Deficits.** A student once said, "Trade deficits are bad because we are buying goods from abroad and not making them here." What is an upside to trade deficits?

2.8 **Depreciation and Consumer Durables.** Consumer durables depreciate just like investment goods. Suppose you purchase a refrigerator for $1000 and, at the same time, four new designer dresses worth $1,000. After one year, has the refrigerator or the designer dresses depreciated more? Why?

2.9 **Investment Spending versus Intermediate Goods.** A publisher buys paper, ink, and computers to produce textbooks. Which of these purchases is included in investment spending? Which are intermediate goods?

5.3 The Income Approach: Measuring a Nation's Macroeconomic Activity Using National Income

3.1 What do we add to GDP to reach GNP?
a. Net income earned abroad by U.S. households
b. Personal income
c. Depreciation
d. Net exports

3.2 What is the largest component of national income?

    a. Compensation of employees (wages and benefits)

    b. Corporate profits

    c. Rental income

    d. Proprietors' income (income of unincorporated business)

    e. Net interest

3.3 Personal income and personal disposable income refer to payments ultimately flowing to _____ (households/firms).

3.4 The difference between gross national product and net national product is _____.

3.5 **Measuring Value Added for a Charity.** The United Way is a nonprofit charity and does not sell products. Explain one way you could measure its value added.

3.6 **Understanding Why GNP and GDP May Differ.** If a country discovered vast amounts of oil, sold it abroad, and invested the proceeds throughout the world, how would its GDP and GNP compare?

3.7 **Transfer Payments, National Income, and Personal Income.** Taking into account the role of transfer payments, explain why national income could fall more than personal income during a recession.

3.8 **Philippine Immigrants Abroad.** Every year, the Philippines sends many workers abroad including nurses, health professionals, and oil workers. How do you think GNP and GDP in the Philippines compare?

3.9 **Sales versus Value Added.** Explain carefully why value added may be a better measure than total sales in comparing a country to a corporation. Hint: If we measured total sales in a country, would this exceed GDP? (Related to Application 1 on page 107.)

5.4 A Closer Examination of Nominal and Real GDP

4.1 The GDP deflator is calculated for any given year by dividing nominal GDP by _____ GDP and multiplying by 100.

4.2 If the base year is 2010, then real and nominal GDP in 2010 will be equal. _____ (True/False)

4.3 Measured price changes do not depend on the particular base year chosen when calculating

    a. the traditional GDP deflator.

    b. the chain-weighted GDP deflator.

    c. real GDP.

4.4 To compute nominal GDP, it is important to use an accurate price index. _____ (True/False)

4.5 **Calculating Real GDP, Price Indices, and Inflation.** Using data from the following table, answer the following questions:

    a. Calculate real GDP using prices from 2011. By what percent did real GDP grow?

    b. Calculate the value of the price index for GDP for 2012 using 2011 as the base year. By what percent did prices increase?

	Quantities Produced		Prices	
	CDs	Tennis Rackets	Price per CD	Price per Tennis Racket
2011	100	200	$20	$110
2012	120	210	22	120

4.6 **Using a New Base Year to Calculate Real GDP and Inflation.** Repeat Exercise 4.5 but use prices from 2012.

4.7 **Understanding the Relationship between Real and Nominal GDP in a Figure.** In Figure 5.5 the base year is 2000. Explain why the line for nominal GDP lies below the line for real GDP in the years prior to 2000. If the base year was 2005, where would the two lines cross?

4.8 **Using U.S. Economic Data to Measure the Economy.** Go to the Web site for the Federal Reserve Bank of St. Louis (www.research.stlouisfed.org/fred2). Find the data for nominal GDP, real GDP in chained dollars, and the chain price index for GDP.

    a. Calculate the percentage growth for nominal GDP since 2000 until the most recent year.

    b. Calculate the percentage growth in real GDP since 2000 until the most recent year.

    c. Finally, calculate the percentage growth in the chain price index for GDP over this same period and compare it to the difference between your answers to (a) and (b).

5.5 Fluctuations in GDP

5.1 The date that a recession begins is called the _____.

5.2 Since World War II, the United States has experienced seven recessions. _____ (True/False)

5.3 The _____ marks the date that ends a recession and output starts to increase again.

5.4 The organization that officially dates recessions in the United States is the

    a. Congressional Budget Office.
    b. Department of Commerce.
    c. National Bureau of Economic Research.
    d. Council of Economic Advisors.

5.5 **Counting Recessions.** Consider the data for the fictitious economy of Euronet:

Year and Quarter	2003: 1	2003: 2	2003: 3	2003: 4	2004: 1	2004: 2	2004: 3
Real GDP	195	193	195	196	195	194	198

How many recessions occurred in the economy over the time indicated?

5.6 **Alternative Methods of Measuring Recessions.** To compare how deeply recessions affected the economies of two different countries, we might use the following measures:

    a. The number of recessions
    b. The proportion of time each economy was in a recession
    c. The magnitude of the worst recession

Here are data from three hypothetical economies. According to each of the measures listed, which economy was affected most deeply by recessions? (Related to Application 2 on page 112.)

Year and Quarter	Country 1	Country 2	Country 3
2010.1	100.0	100.0	100.0
2010.2	103.0	103.0	103.0
2010.3	100.9	106.1	106.1
2010.4	95.9	102.9	109.3
2011.1	91.1	99.8	87.4
2011.2	86.5	96.8	69.9
2011.3	90.9	93.9	72.0
2011.4	95.4	91.1	74.2
2012.1	100.2	88.4	76.4
2012.2	105.2	85.7	78.7
2012.3	99.9	83.1	81.1
2012.4	94.9	85.6	83.5
2013.1	90.2	88.2	86.0
2013.2	85.7	90.9	88.6
2013.3	90.0	93.6	91.2
2013.4	94.5	96.4	94.0

5.7 **Most Severe Recession?** Using the data in Table 5.5, identify the two most severe recessions since World War II. What other information might you want to know about these and other recessionary periods to judge their severity? (Related to Application 2 on page 112.)

5.6 GDP as a Measure of Welfare

6.1 Which of the following are not included in GDP?

    a. Leisure time
    b. Sales of new cars
    c. Strawberries sold in a grocery store
    d. Economics textbooks sold in the bookstore

6.2 Men's reported happiness has increased relative to women's reported happiness in the last several decades. _____ (True/False) (Related to Application 3 on page 114.)

6.3 The approximate percentage of GDP in the United States that goes unreported because of the underground economy is _____.

6.4 Illegal activities are not computed as part of measured GDP because they are not

    a. legal.
    b. production.
    c. reported.
    d. big enough to worry about.

6.5 **Does Spending Measure Welfare?** Suppose a community spends $1 million on salaries and equipment for its police department. Because it believes that citizens are now more law abiding, the community decides to cut back on the number of police it employs. As a result, the community now spends $800,000 less on the police officers. The crime rate remains the same.

    a. What happens to measured GDP?
    b. Does GDP accurately reflect welfare in this case? Discuss the underlying issue that this example poses.

6.6 **Disappearing Trees and National Income.** Suppose you were worried that national income does not adequately take into account the extraction of trees that provide shade and help stem global warming. How would you advise the Commerce Department to include this factor in its calculations?

6.7 **Air Quality and Measured GDP.** Air quality in Los Angeles deteriorated in the 1950s through the 1970s and then improved in the 1980s and 1990s. Can a change in air quality such as this be incorporated into our measures of national income? Discuss.

6.8 **Comparing Welfare across Countries.** Suppose Country A and Country B have exactly the same measured real GDP, but in Country A, the average worker spends more time at home, either doing housework or on vacation. Which country has a higher level of welfare and why?

6.9 **Does Money Buy Happiness?** Although people with high incomes appear to be happier than those with low incomes, people in the United States in general have become less happy over the last 30 years even though real GDP has risen. What are some of the reasons why the increase in real GDP does not always imply greater happiness? (Related to Application 3 on page 114.)

6.10 **Measuring Happiness across States.** Suppose statisticians find from survey data that the residents of California and Louisiana report that they are equally happy. However, incomes in California are higher, on average, than those in Louisiana. Could you make a case that living in Louisiana actually makes you happier than living in California?

6 Unemployment and Inflation

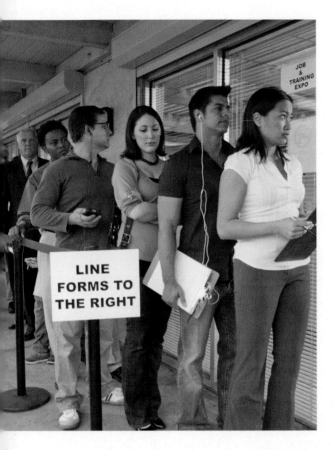

LINE FORMS TO THE RIGHT

For February 2010, the Bureau of Labor Statistics (BLS) reported that the unemployment rate was 9.7 percent. The unemployed were those who did not have jobs, but were actively looking for work.

However, the official unemployment statistics did not include the following individuals:

- A steelworker in Ohio who was laid off two years ago. He stopped looking for work because there were no steel mills remaining in his town, and he believed no jobs were available.
- A young woman living in the far suburbs of a city. She wanted to work and had worked in the past, but she had no transportation to the places where jobs were available.
- A young computer programmer who was working 25 hours a week. He wanted to work 40 hours a week, but his employer did not have enough work for him, because most of the company's programming work had been contracted to India. Nor could he easily find another job.

The BLS publishes an alternative measure of unemployment that includes these cases. In February 2010 the unemployment rate by that measure was 16.8 percent. Which unemployment measure gives a more accurate picture of the labor market?

(APPLYING THE CONCEPTS)

1 What do the recent data show about trends in the percentage of women who are working?
After Growing Sharply, Women's Labor Force Participation Has Leveled Off

2 Does more liberal disability insurance decrease measured unemployment?
More Disability, Less Unemployment?

3 Are you less upset from being unemployed if unemployment is common in your peer group?
Social Norms, Unemployment, and Perceived Happiness

4 How large is the bias in the CPI due to not immediately incorporating new goods?
The Introduction of Cell Phones and the Bias in the CPI

In this chapter, we look at unemployment and inflation, two key phenomena in macroeconomics. Losing a job is one of the most stressful experiences a person can suffer. For the elderly, the fear that the purchasing power of their wealth will evaporate with inflation is also a source of deep concern.

We will examine how economists define unemployment and inflation and the problems in measuring them. We also will explore the various costs that unemployment and inflation impose on society. Once we have a basic understanding of what unemployment and inflation are, we will be able to investigate their causes further.

6.1   EXAMINING UNEMPLOYMENT

When an economy performs poorly, it imposes costs on individuals and society. Recall from Chapter 5 that one of the key issues for macroeconomics is understanding fluctuations—the ups and downs of the economy. During periods of poor economic performance and slow economic growth, unemployment rises sharply and becomes a cause of public concern. During times of good economic performance and rapid economic growth, unemployment falls, but does not disappear. Our first task is to understand how economists and government statisticians measure unemployment and then learn to interpret what they measure.

How Is Unemployment Defined and Measured?

Let's begin with some definitions. The *unemployed* are those individuals who do not currently have a job but who are actively looking for work. The phrase *actively looking* is critical. Individuals who looked for work in the past but who are not looking currently are not counted as unemployed. The *employed* are individuals who currently have jobs. Together, the unemployed and employed comprise the **labor force**:

Discouraged

$$\text{labor force} = \text{employed} + \text{unemployed}$$

The **unemployment rate** is the number of unemployed divided by the total labor force. This rate represents the percentage of the labor force unemployed and looking for work:

$$\text{unemployment rate} = \frac{\text{unemployed}}{\text{labor force}} \times 100$$

Finally, we need to understand what is meant by the **labor force participation rate**, which is the labor force divided by the population 16 years of age and older. This rate represents the percentage of the population 16 years of age and older that is in the labor force:

$$\text{labor force participation rate} = \frac{\text{labor force}}{\text{population 16 years and older}} \times 100$$

To illustrate these concepts, suppose an economy consists of 200,000 individuals 16 years of age and older. Of all these people, 122,000 are employed and 8,000 are unemployed. This means that 130,000 (122,000 + 8,000) people are in the labor force. The labor force participation rate is 0.65, or 65 percent (130,000/200,000), and the unemployment rate is 0.0615, or 6.15 percent (8,000/130,000).

Figure 6.1 helps to put these measurements into perspective for the U.S. economy. The total civilian population 16 years of age and older in February 2010 was 236,998,000 individuals. We divide this population into two groups: those in the labor force (the employed plus the unemployed, totaling 153,512,000) and those outside the labor force 83,487,000. For this year, the labor force participation rate was 65 percent (153,512,000/236,998,000). As you can see, approximately two thirds of the U.S. population participates in the labor force. Within the labor force,

labor force
The total number of workers, both the employed and the unemployed.

unemployment rate
The percentage of the labor force that is unemployed.

labor force participation rate
The percentage of the population over 16 years of age that is in the labor force.

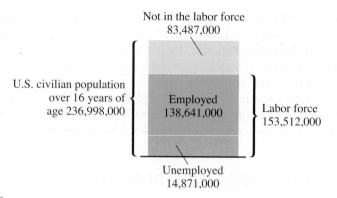

▲ **FIGURE 6.1**

Unemployment Data, February 2010

Approximately 65 percent of the civilian population is in the labor force. The unemployment rate in February 2010 was 9.7 percent.

SOURCE: Bureau of Labor Statistics, U.S. Department of Labor, 2010.

138,641,000 were employed and 14,871,000 were unemployed. The unemployment rate was 9.7 percent (14,871,000/153,512,000). Military personnel are excluded from these measures.

One of the most important trends in the last 50 years has been the increase in the participation of women in the labor force. But, as the next Application indicates, it appears that increase has come to an end.

Figure 6.2 contains international data on unemployment for 2010 for developed countries. Despite the fact these countries all have modern, industrial economies, notice the sharp differences in unemployment. For example, Belgium had a 12.1 percent unemployment rate, whereas Japan had an unemployment rate of 4.9 percent. These sharp differences reflect a number of factors, including how much government support is provided to unemployed workers. In countries in which support is the most generous, there is less incentive to work and unemployment will tend to be higher.

▶ **FIGURE 6.2**

Unemployment Rates in Developed Countries

Among the developed countries, unemployment rates vary substantially.

SOURCE: The Economist, March 20–26, 2010.

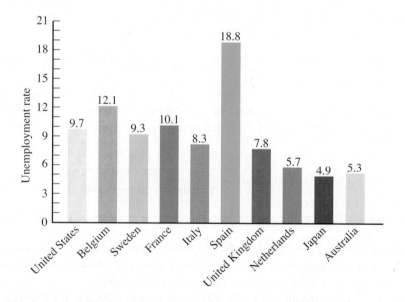

Alternative Measures of Unemployment and Why They Are Important

We defined the unemployed as those people who are looking for work but who do not currently have jobs. With that in mind, let's take a closer look at our measures of unemployment.

It is relatively straightforward in principle to determine who is employed: Just count the people who are working. What is more difficult is to distinguish between those who are unemployed and those who are not in the labor force. How are these two groups distinguished? The BLS, which is part of the Department of Labor, interviews a large sample of households each month. The BLS asks about the employment situation of all household members 16 years of age and older. If someone in a household is not working, the interviewer asks whether the person is actively looking for work. If the answer is "yes," he or she is classified as unemployed. If the answer is "no"—he or she is not actively looking for work—that person is classified as not being in the labor force.

The BLS measure of unemployment, however, does not capture all the employment experiences individuals face. In the chapter opener, we highlighted the cases of three individuals who wanted full-time jobs but did not have them: a steelworker who stopped looking for work because he felt there were no jobs, a young woman who did not seek work because she had no transportation, and a computer programmer who worked only part-time but sought full-time employment. None of them would be counted as unemployed in the official statistics—the first two were not in the labor force and the third was employed. Because of these limitations, in 1994 the BLS began to publish alternative statistics that reflect these circumstances.

Individuals who want to work and have searched for work in the prior year, but are not currently looking for work because they believe they won't be able to find a job are called **discouraged workers**. Note that these individuals are not included in the official statistics because they are not currently looking for work.

discouraged workers
Workers who left the labor force because they could not find jobs.

In addition to discouraged workers, there are individuals who would like to work and have searched for work in the recent past, but have stopped looking for work for a variety of reasons. These individuals are known as *marginally attached workers*. Marginally attached workers consist of two groups: discouraged workers (who left the

(APPLICATION 1)

AFTER GROWING SHARPLY, WOMEN'S LABOR FORCE PARTICIPATION HAS LEVELED OFF

APPLYING THE CONCEPTS #1: What do the recent data show about trends in the percentage of women who are working?

In 1948, the labor force participation rate for women 20 years and older was 32 percent. By 1970, it had grown to 43 percent, and by 1997 it had reached 60 percent. This trend reflected remarkable changes in our economy and society as women dramatically increased their presence in the workforce. But since 1997, the figure has remained virtually constant at 60 percent. It appears that women's labor force participation has reached a peak in the United States, somewhat short of the men's labor force participation rate of approximately 76 percent.

One explanation for this trend is that women may simply have run out of available time. From 1948 to the mid-1990s, women were able to increase their hours of work by cutting back on the time that they spent on housework and other home duties. With the advent of new technologies such as washing machines, dishwashers, and other labor-saving devices, women could increase their labor force participation yet still take primary care of their households. But even with new technology, housework and childcare do take time. Because women provide more household services than men, it is understandable why their labor force participation may have reached a peak. **Related to Exercise 1.8.**

SOURCE: Based on Bureau of Labor Statistics, 2010.

labor force because they could not find jobs) and workers who are not looking for jobs for other reasons, including lack of transportation or childcare.

Finally, there are those workers who would like to be employed full-time but hold part-time jobs. These individuals are counted as employed in the BLS statistics because they have a job. However, they would like to be working more hours. They are known as *individuals working part time for economic reasons*. We do not include in this category individuals who prefer part-time employment.

How important are these alternative measures? Figure 6.3 puts them into perspective. In February 2010, 14.87 million individuals were officially classified as unemployed. The number of discouraged workers was 1.20 million. Including the discouraged workers, there were 2.52 million marginally attached workers. If we add the marginally attached individuals to those who were involuntarily working part time, the total is 11.31 million. Thus, depending on the statistic you want to emphasize, there were anywhere between 14.87 million unemployed (the official number) and 26.18 million unemployed (the official number plus all those seeking full-time employment who did not have it). If we count those 26.18 million as unemployed, the unemployment rate in 2010 would be 16.8 percent—substantially higher than the official rate of 9.7 percent. As we have seen, the official statistics for unemployment do not include the full range of individuals who would like to participate fully in the labor market.

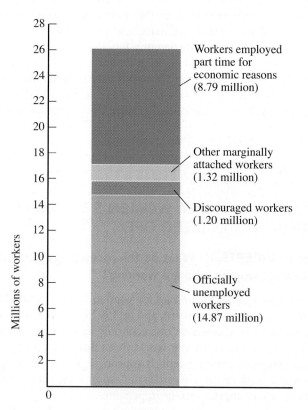

▲ FIGURE 6.3
Alternative Measures of Unemployment, February 2010
Including discouraged workers, marginally attached workers, and individuals working part time for economic reasons substantially increases measured unemployment in 2010 from 14.87 million to 26.18 million.
SOURCE: Bureau of Labor Statistics, U.S. Department of Labor, 2010.

Who Are the Unemployed?

Another fact about unemployment is that different groups of people suffer more unemployment than others. Figure 6.4 contains some unemployment statistics for selected groups for February 2010. Adults have substantially lower unemployment rates than

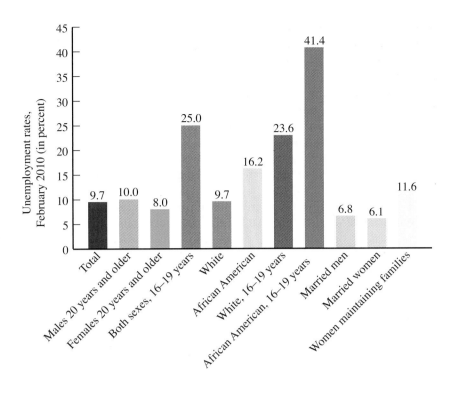

◄ **FIGURE 6.4**
Selected U.S. Unemployment
Statistics, Unemployment Rates
for February 2010
The incidence of unemployment differs
sharply among demographic groups.
*SOURCE: Bureau of Labor Statistics, U.S.
Department of Labor, 2010.*

teenagers. Minorities have higher unemployment rates. African-American teenagers have extremely high unemployment rates. On average, men and women have similar unemployment rates, but the unemployment rates for married men and married women are lower than unemployment rates of women who maintain families alone.

These differentials do vary somewhat as GDP rises and falls. Teenage and minority unemployment rates often rise very sharply during poor economic times, as was

APPLICATION **2**

MORE DISABILITY, LESS UNEMPLOYMENT?

APPLYING THE CONCEPTS #2: Does more liberal disability insurance decrease measured unemployment?

The federal Disability Insurance program provides income to nonelderly workers who are deemed unable to engage in substantial employment. It also provides health care to these individuals. After 1984, the guidelines were changed to make it easier for individuals to enter the program. From 1984 to 2001, the number of nonelderly adults receiving payments from this program rose by 60 percent to 5.3 million.

Economists David Autor and Mark Duggan studied the impact of this program on labor force participation. They found that the changes in the rules administering the program, the increased generosity of the benefits of the program for low-skilled workers, and the increase in the value of health-care services all contributed to an increase in participation in this program. They estimated that the combination of these factors led to a decrease in the labor force participation for high school dropouts and other low-skilled workers. Since these workers, a portion of whom would have been unemployed, were no longer in the labor force, the economists estimated that the effect of the Disability Insurance program was to lower the measured unemployment rate by 0.5 percent, a very large effect.   **Related to Exercises 1.4 and 1.9.**

SOURCE: Based on David H. Autor and Mark G. Duggan, "The Rise in Disability Rolls and the Decline in Unemployment," *Quarterly Journal of Economics* (February 2003): 157–206.

the case in the most recent recession. In better times, a reduction of unemployment for all groups typically occurs. Nonetheless, teenage and minority unemployment remains relatively high at all times.

Many economic time series, including employment and unemployment, are substantially influenced by seasonal factors. These are recurring calendar-related effects caused by, for example, the weather, holidays, the opening and closing of schools, and related factors. Unemployment due to recurring calendar effects is called **seasonal unemployment**. Examples of seasonal unemployment include higher rates of unemployment for farm workers and construction workers in the winter and higher unemployment rates for teenagers in the early summer as they look for summer jobs.

The BLS uses statistical procedures to remove these seasonal factors—that is, it seasonally adjusts the statistics—so that users of the data can more accurately interpret underlying trends in the economy. The seasonally adjusted unemployment rates control for these predictable patterns, so those patterns aren't reflected in the overall unemployment numbers.

seasonal unemployment
The component of unemployment attributed to seasonal factors.

6.2 CATEGORIES OF UNEMPLOYMENT

To better understand the labor market, economists have found it very useful to break unemployment into a variety of categories. As we shall see, it is valuable to distinguish among the several different types of unemployment.

Types of Unemployment: Cyclical, Frictional, and Structural

After seasonally adjusting the unemployment statistics, we can divide unemployment into three other basic types: cyclical, frictional, and structural. By studying each type separately, we can gain insight into some of the causes of each type of unemployment.

The unemployment rate is closely tied to the overall fortunes of the economy. Unemployment rises sharply during periods when real GDP falls and decreases when real GDP grows rapidly. During periods of falling GDP, firms will not want to employ as many workers as they do in good times because they are not producing as many goods and services. Firms will lay off or fire some current workers and will be more reluctant to add new workers to their payrolls. The result will be fewer workers with jobs and rising unemployment. Economists call the unemployment that occurs during fluctuations in real GDP **cyclical unemployment**. Cyclical unemployment rises during periods when real GDP falls or grows at a slower-than-normal rate and decreases when the economy improves.

However, unemployment still exists even when the economy is growing. For example, the unemployment rate in the United States has not fallen below 3.9 percent of the labor force since 1970. Unemployment that is not associated with economic fluctuations is either frictional unemployment or structural unemployment.

Frictional unemployment is the unemployment that occurs naturally during the normal workings of an economy. It occurs because it simply takes time for people to find the right jobs and for employers to find the right people to hire. This happens when people change jobs, move across the country, get laid off from their current jobs and search for new opportunities, or take their time after they enter the labor force to find an appropriate job. Suppose that when you graduate from college, you take six months to find a job you like. During the six months in which you are looking for a good job, you are among those unemployed who make up frictional unemployment. Searching for a job, however, makes good sense. It would not be wise to take the first job you were offered if it had low wages, poor benefits, and no future. Likewise, employers are wise to interview multiple applicants for jobs to find the best employees, even if it takes some time.

cyclical unemployment
Unemployment that occurs during fluctuations in real GDP.

frictional unemployment
Unemployment that occurs with the normal workings of the economy, such as workers taking time to search for suitable jobs and firms taking time to search for qualified employees.

Could we eliminate unemployment by posting all job vacancies on the Internet along with the résumés of job seekers and automatically match them up with one another? It's possible that such an automated system could shorten the duration of frictional unemployment, but it wouldn't eliminate it entirely. Some workers, for example, would prefer to continue searching for jobs in their own area rather than moving across the country to take the jobs they had been automatically matched with. Firms would also still want to scrutinize employees very carefully, because hiring and training a worker is costly.

Structural unemployment occurs when the economy evolves. It occurs when different sectors give way to other sectors or certain jobs are eliminated while new types of jobs are created. For example, when the vinyl record industry gave way to the CD music industry in the 1980s, some workers found themselves structurally unemployed, which meant they had to take the time to train themselves for jobs in different industries. Structural unemployment is more of a "permanent condition" than frictional unemployment.

The line between frictional unemployment and structural unemployment is sometimes hard to draw. Suppose a highly skilled software engineer is laid off because his company shuts down its headquarters in his area and moves his job overseas. The worker would like to find a comparable job, but only lower-wage work is available in his immediate geographic location. Jobs are available, but not his kind of job, and this high-tech company will never return to the area. Is this person's unemployment frictional or structural? There really is no correct answer. You might think of the software engineer as experiencing either frictional or structural unemployment. For all practical purposes, however, it does not matter which it is. The former software engineer is still unemployed.

The Natural Rate of Unemployment

Total unemployment in an economy is composed of all three types of unemployment: cyclical, frictional, and structural. The level of unemployment at which there is no cyclical unemployment is called the **natural rate of unemployment**. The natural rate of unemployment consists of only frictional unemployment and structural unemployment. The natural rate of unemployment is the economist's notion of what the rate of unemployment should be when there is **full employment**. It may seem strange to think that workers can be unemployed when the economy is at full employment. However, the economy actually needs some frictional unemployment to operate efficiently: Frictional unemployment exists so that workers and firms find the right employment matches. An economy that lacks frictional unemployment will become stagnant.

In the United States today, economists estimate that the natural rate of unemployment is between 5.0 and 6.5 percent. The natural rate of unemployment varies over time and differs across countries. In Europe, for example, estimates of the natural rate of unemployment place it between 7 and 10 percent. In a later chapter, we explore why the natural rate of unemployment is higher in Europe than in the United States and why the natural rate of unemployment can vary over time in the same country.

The actual unemployment rate can be higher or lower than the natural rate of unemployment. During a period in which the real GDP fails to grow at its normal rate, there will be positive cyclical unemployment, and actual unemployment can far exceed the natural rate of unemployment. For example, in the United States in 2010 unemployment was about 10 percent of the labor force. As we pointed out in the previous chapter, a more extreme example occurred in 1933 during the Great Depression, when the unemployment rate reached 25 percent. When the economy grows very rapidly for a long period, actual unemployment can fall below the natural rate of unemployment. With sustained rapid economic growth, employers will be aggressive in hiring workers. During the late 1960s, unemployment rates fell below

structural unemployment
Unemployment that occurs when there is a mismatch of skills and jobs.

natural rate of unemployment
The level of unemployment at which there is no cyclical unemployment. It consists of only frictional and structural unemployment.

full employment
The level of unemployment that occurs when the unemployment rate is at the natural rate.

4 percent, and the natural rate of unemployment was estimated to be over 5 percent. In this case, cyclical unemployment was negative.

Unemployment also fell to 4 percent in 2000. In this case, many economists believed that the natural rate of unemployment had fallen to close to 5 percent, so that cyclical unemployment in that year was negative.

Just as a car will overheat if the engine is overworked, so will the economy overheat if economic growth is too rapid. At low unemployment rates, firms will find it difficult to recruit workers, and competition among firms will lead to increases in wages. As wages increase, increases in prices soon follow. The sign of this overheating will be a general rise in prices for the entire economy, which we commonly call *inflation*. As we discuss in later chapters, when the actual unemployment rate falls below the natural rate of unemployment, inflation will increase.

6.3   THE COSTS OF UNEMPLOYMENT

When there is excess unemployment—actual unemployment above the natural rate of unemployment—both society and individuals suffer economic loss. From a social point of view, excess unemployment means that the economy is no longer producing at its potential. The resulting loss of output can be very large. For example, in 1983, when the unemployment rate averaged 9.6 percent, typical estimates of the shortfall of GDP from potential were near 6 percent. Simply put, this meant that society was wasting 6 percent of the total resources at its disposal.

unemployment insurance

Payments unemployed people receive from the government.

To families with fixed obligations such as mortgage payments, the loss in income can bring immediate hardships. **Unemployment insurance**, payments received from the government upon becoming unemployed, can cushion the blow to some degree, but unemployment insurance is typically only temporary and does not replace a worker's full earnings.

The effects of unemployment can also linger into the future. Workers who suffer from a prolonged period of unemployment are likely to lose some of their skills. For example, an unemployed stockbroker might be unaware of the latest developments and trends in financial markets. This lack of knowledge will make it more difficult for that person to find a job in the future. Economists who have studied the high rates of unemployment among young people in Europe point to the loss of both skills and good work habits (such as coming to work on time) as key factors leading to long-term unemployment.

The costs of unemployment are not simply financial. In our society, a person's status and position are largely associated with the type of job the person holds. Losing a job can impose severe psychological costs. Some studies have found, for example, that increased crime, divorce, and suicide rates are associated with increased unemployment.

Not all unemployment lasts a long period of time for individuals. Some unemployment is very short term. Table 6.1 shows the percent of unemployed by the duration or length of unemployment. In February 2010, approximately 18.3 percent of unemployed workers had been out of work less than 5 weeks. At the other end, 40.9 percent were unemployed more than 27 weeks. During better economic times with lower overall

TABLE 6.1 THE DURATION OF UNEMPLOYMENT, FEBRUARY 2010

Weeks of Unemployment	Percent of the Unemployed
Fewer than 5 weeks	18.3
5 to 14 weeks	22.8
15 to 26 weeks	18.0
Greater than 27 weeks	40.9

SOURCE: Bureau of Labor Statistics, U.S. Department of Labor, 2010.

APPLICATION 3

SOCIAL NORMS, UNEMPLOYMENT, AND PERCEIVED HAPPINESS

APPLYING THE CONCEPTS #3: Are you less upset from being unemployed if unemployment is common in your peer group?

We know that individuals do not like to become unemployed. But how do feelings about becoming unemployed depend on the experiences of those around one? Economist Andrew E. Clark carefully examined the perceptions and the behavior of the unemployed in Great Britain over a seven-year period. He looked at the responses to survey questions by those individuals who became unemployed and constructed an index of their general happiness or well-being.

He found, as expected, that people's perceived well-being declined as they became unemployed, and also that employed people become less happy if others around them became unemployed. But his interesting and somewhat surprising finding was that, for men, becoming unemployed caused *less* of a decrease in perceived well-being if those in their peer group—family, household, or region—were also unemployed. In other words, misery loved company. It was better (or less worse) to be unemployed if others in their peer group were also unemployed.

Why did this matter? Clark also found that the more unhappy an individual was, the more aggressive he or she would be to try to find a new job. So, if your peer group is also unemployed, you may not be as aggressive in searching for work. Unemployment, therefore, may last longer for individuals in these circumstances.
Related to Exercise 3.5.

SOURCE: Based on Andrew E, Clark, "Unemployment as a Social Norm: Psychological Evidence from Panel Data," *Journal of Labor Economics* 21, no. 2 (2003): 323–351.

---

unemployment, the percentage of short-term spells of unemployment increases and percentage of long-term spells decrease. In the United States, unemployment is a mixture of both short- and long-term unemployment.

Although unemployment insurance can temporarily offset some of the financial costs of job loss, the presence of unemployment insurance also tends to increase the length of time that unemployed workers remain unemployed. The extra financial cushion that unemployment insurance provides allows workers to remain unemployed a bit longer before obtaining another job. In other words, unemployment insurance actually leads to additional time spent unemployed.

6.4 THE CONSUMER PRICE INDEX AND THE COST OF LIVING

Suppose you were reading a book written in 1964 in which the main character received a starting salary of $5,000. Was that a high or low salary back then? To answer that, we need to know what $5,000 could purchase. Or, to put it another way, we need to know the *value* of the dollar—what a dollar would actually buy—in 1964. Only then could we begin to know whether this was a high or low salary.

Or take another example. In 1976, a new starting professor in economics received a salary of $15,000. In 2010, at the same university, a new starting professor received $90,000. Prices, of course, had risen in these 30 years along with salaries. Which starting professor had the better deal?

These examples are illustrations of one of our five principles of economics, the real-nominal principle.

REAL-NOMINAL PRINCIPLE

What matters to people is the real value of money or income—its purchasing power—not the face value of money or income.

Consumer Price Index

A price index that measures the cost of a fixed basket of goods chosen to represent the consumption pattern of a typical consumer.

Economists have developed a number of different measures to track the cost of living over time. The best known of these measures is the **Consumer Price Index (CPI)**.

The CPI is widely used to measure changes in the prices consumers face. It measures changes in prices of a fixed *basket of goods*—a collection of items chosen to represent the purchasing pattern of a typical consumer. We first find out how much this basket of goods costs in a given year. This is called the *base year* (it serves a similar purpose as the base year we designated for the GDP deflator). We then ask how much it costs in other years and measure changes in the cost of living relative to this base year. The CPI index for a given year, say year *K*, is defined as

$$\text{CPI in year } K = \frac{\text{cost of basket in year } K}{\text{cost of basket in base year}} \times 100$$

Suppose a basket of goods costs $200 in 1992, which we'll define as the base year. In 2004, the same basket of goods is $250. First, the value for the CPI in 1992 (the base year) is

$$\text{CPI in 1992} = \frac{200}{200} \times 100 = 100$$

That is, the CPI for 1992 is 100. Note that the base year for the CPI will always equal 100. Now let's calculate the value of the CPI for 2004:

$$\text{CPI in 2004} = \frac{250}{200} \times 100 = 125$$

The CPI in 2004 is 125. The CPI rose from 100 in 1992 to 125 in 2004 in this example, a 25 percent increase in average prices over this 12-year period.

Here is how you would use this information. Suppose you had $300 in 1992. How much money would you need to be able to have the same standard of living in 2004? Find the answer by multiplying the $300 by the ratio of the CPI in 2004 to the CPI in 1992:

$$\$300 \times \frac{125}{100} = \$375$$

You need $375 in 2004 just to maintain what was your standard of living in 1992. This is the type of calculation that economists do to evaluate changes in living standards over time.

How do we actually calculate the CPI in practice? Each month, the BLS sends its employees out to sample prices for over 90,000 specific items around the entire country. This is how they construct their representative basket of goods. Figure 6.5 shows the broad categories the BLS uses in the CPI and the importance of each category in household budgets. Rent and food and beverages account for 44 percent of total spending by households.

The CPI versus the Chain Index for GDP

In Chapter 5, we discussed measuring nominal GDP and real GDP. We also mentioned that since 1996 the Commerce Department has used a chain-weighted index (replacing the GDP deflator) to measure changes in prices for goods and services included in GDP. The chain-weighted index for GDP and the CPI are both measures of average prices for the economy, yet they differ in several ways.

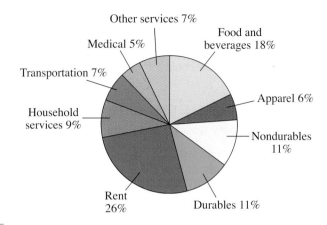

▲ **FIGURE 6.5**

Components of the Consumer Price Index (CPI)

Rent and food and beverages make up 44 percent of the CPI basket. The remainder consists of other goods and services.

SOURCE: Bureau of Labor Statistics, U.S. Department of Labor, 2006.

First, the CPI measures the costs of a typical basket of goods for consumers. It includes goods produced in prior years (such as older cars) as well as imported goods. The chain-weighted price index for GDP does not measure price changes from either used goods or imports. The reason is that it is based on the calculation of GDP, which, as we've seen, measures only goods and services produced in the United States in the current year.

Second, unlike the chain-weighted price index for GDP, the CPI asks how much a *fixed* basket of goods costs in the current year compared to the cost of those same goods in a base year. Because consumers tend to buy less of goods whose prices rise, the CPI will tend to overstate true changes in the cost of living. For example, if the price of steak rises, consumers may switch to chicken and spend less on steak. But if the current basket of goods and services in the CPI includes steak, the CPI thinks the amount of higher-priced steak in the basket is the same as the amount of steak before its price increase. It does not allow the amount of steak in the index to decrease. Another measurement problem occurs when new products are introduced into the marketplace, again because the CPI measures a fixed basket of goods. The BLS will eventually adjust its "basket" to account for successful new products, but it takes some time.

Problems in Measuring Changes in Prices

Most economists believe that in reality all the indexes, including the chain-weighted index for GDP and the CPI, overstate actual changes in prices. In other words, the increase in prices is probably less than the reported indexes tell us. The principal reason for this overstatement is that we have a difficult time measuring quality improvements. Suppose the new computers sold to consumers become more powerful and more efficient each year. Suppose further that the dollar price of a new computer remains the same each year. Even though the price remains the same, the computers in later years are of much higher quality. If we looked simply at the price and did not take into account the change in quality, we would say there was no price change for computers. But in later years we are getting more computer power for the same price. If we failed to take the quality change into account, we would not see that the price of computer power has fallen.

Government statisticians do try to adjust for quality when they can. But quality changes are so common in our economy and products evolve so rapidly that it is impossible to keep up with all that is occurring. As a result, most economists believe we overestimate the inflation rate by between 0.5 and 1.5 percent each year. This overstatement has important consequences. Some government programs, such as

(**APPLICATION 4**)

THE INTRODUCTION OF CELL PHONES AND THE BIAS IN THE CPI

APPLYING THE CONCEPTS #4: How large is the bias in the CPI due to not immediately incorporating new goods?

Today, it is hard to imagine a world without cell phones. Every college student and most high school students carry them everywhere. But cell phones were not introduced to the public until 1983, and it took 15 years, until 1998, before the Bureau of Labor Statistics included them in calculating the CPI!

Economist Jerry Hausman of MIT estimated the bias in the CPI caused by the failure to include cell phones in a timely manner. He calculated that because of this delay, the telecommunication component of the price index was biased upwards by between 0.8 and 1.9 percent per year. In other words, instead of rising by 1.1 percent per year, telecommunication prices should have been falling by 0.8 percent per year. This is a significant bias.

But cell phones are not the only examples of the slow introduction of goods into the CPI. The BLS also took 15 years to recognize room air conditioners in the CPI. Since new products are constantly invented and introduced, the bias in the CPI can be large.   **Related to Exercise 4.9.**

SOURCE: Based on Jerry Hausman, "Cellular Telephone, New Products, and the CPI," *Journal of Business & Economic Statistics* 17, no. 2 (1999): 186–194.

---

cost-of-living adjustments (COLAs)
Automatic increases in wages or other payments that are tied to the CPI.

Social Security, automatically increase payments when the CPI goes up. Some union contracts also have **cost-of-living adjustments (COLAs)**, automatic wage changes based on the CPI. If the CPI overstates increases in the cost of living, the government and employers might be overpaying Social Security recipients and workers for changes in the cost of living.

6.5 INFLATION

We have now looked at two different price indexes: the chain-weighted price index used for calculating real GDP and the Consumer Price Index. Using either price index, we can calculate the percentage rate of change of the index. The percentage rate of change of a price index is the **inflation rate**:

inflation rate
The percentage rate of change in the price level.

inflation rate = percentage rate of change of a price index

Here is an example. Suppose a price index in a country was 200 in 1998 and 210 in 1999. Then the inflation rate between 1998 and 1999 was

$$\text{inflation rate} = \frac{210 - 200}{200} = 0.05 = 5\%$$

In other words, the country experienced a 5 percent inflation rate.

It is important to distinguish between the price level and the inflation rate. In everyday language, people sometimes confuse the level of prices with inflation. You might hear someone say inflation is high in San Francisco because rents for apartments are high, but this is not a correct use of the term *inflation*. Inflation refers not to the level of prices, whether they are high or low, but to their *percentage change*. If rents were high in San Francisco but remained constant over two years, there would be no inflation in rents there during that time.

Historical U.S. Inflation Rates

To gain some historical perspective, Figure 6.6 plots a price index for GDP from 1875 to 2009 for the United States. As you can see from the figure, from 1875 to the period just before World War I, there was virtually no change in the price level. The price level rose during World War I, fell after the war ended, and also fell sharply during the early 1930s. However, the most pronounced feature of the figure is the sustained rise in prices beginning around the 1940s. Unlike the earlier periods, in which the price level did not have a trend, after 1940 the price level increased sharply. By 2010, the price level had increased by a factor of 14 over its value in 1940. Table 6.2 contains the prices of a few selected goods from the 1940s and in 2010. Wouldn't you like to buy a postage stamp today for $0.03?

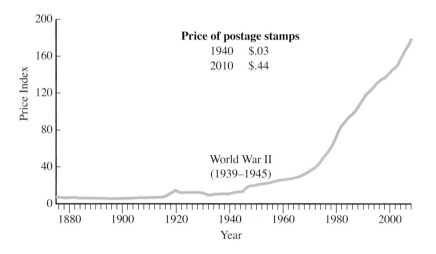

◄ **FIGURE 6.6**
Price Index for U.S. GDP, 1875–2009
After remaining relatively flat for 60 years, the price level began to steadily increase after World War II. The price of a postage stamp in 1940 and 2009 illustrates the change in the overall price level that occurred.
SOURCES: R. J. Gordon, Macroeconomics (New York: Harper Collins, 1993) and U.S. Department of Commerce, 2010.

TABLE 6.2 PRICES OF SELECTED GOODS, 1940S AND 2010

Item	1940s Price	2010 Price
Gallon of gasoline	$0.18	$3.10
Loaf of bread	0.08	3.59
Gallon of milk	0.34	3.49
Postage stamp	0.03	0.44
House	6,550	350,000
Car	800	22,000
Haircut in New York City	0.50	50
Movie tickets in New York City	0.25	11.00
Men's tweed sports jacket in New York City	15	189
Snake tattoo on arm	0.25	60.00

SOURCES: Scott Derks, The Value of a Dollar 1860–1989 (Farmington Hills, MI: Gale Group, 1993) and author's research and estimates.

Taking a closer look at the period following World War II, Figure 6.7 plots the inflation rate, the percentage change in the price index, from 1950 to 2009. In the 1950s and 1960s, the inflation rate was frequently less than 2 percent a year. The inflation rate was a lot higher in the 1970s, reaching nearly 10 percent per year. In those years, the economy suffered from several increases in the world price of oil. In recent years, the inflation rate has subsided and has been between 2 and 3 percent.

The Perils of Deflation

Prices rarely fall today, but they have actually fallen at times in world history. You might think it would be great if prices fell and we had what economists term a **deflation**. It may surprise you, however, that we think you should hope deflation never occurs.

deflation
Negative inflation or falling prices of goods and services.

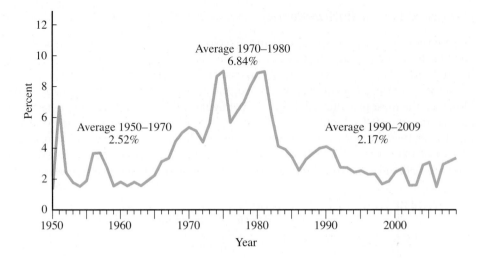

During the Great Depression, the United States underwent a severe deflation. Prices fell 33 percent on average, and wages fell along with prices. The biggest problem caused by a deflation is that people cannot repay their debts. Imagine you owe $40,000 for your education and expect to be able to pay it off over several years if you earn $27,000 a year. If a massive deflation caused your wages to fall to $18,000, you might not be able to pay your $40,000 debt, which does not fall with deflation. You would be forced to default on your loan, as millions of people did during the Great Depression.

In the 1990s, Japan experienced a deflation, although much milder than the Great Depression in the United States—only about 1 percent per year. Nonetheless, banks in Japan faced rocky economic times as borrowers, including large corporations, defaulted on their loans. With its banks in difficult shape, Japan's economy has suffered. Its experience in the 1990s mirrored the experience of other countries throughout the world in the 1930s during the period of deflation.

6.6 THE COSTS OF INFLATION

Economists typically separate the costs of inflation into two categories. One includes costs associated with fully expected or **anticipated inflation**. The other includes the costs associated with unexpected or **unanticipated inflation**. Although inflation causes both types of costs, it is convenient to discuss each case separately.

Anticipated Inflation

Let's consider the costs of anticipated inflation first. Suppose the economy had been experiencing 5 percent annual inflation for many years and everyone was fully adjusted to it.

Even in this case, inflation still has some costs. First, there are the actual physical costs of changing prices, which economists call **menu costs**. Restaurant owners, catalog producers, and any other business that must post prices will have to incur costs to physically change their prices because of inflation. For example, they will need to pay to reprint their menus or billboards. Economists believe these costs are relatively small for the economy.

Second, inflation will erode the value of the cash people hold. They will respond by holding less cash at any one time. If they hold less cash, they must visit the bank or their ATM more frequently because they will run out of cash sooner. Economists use the term **shoe-leather costs** to refer to the additional costs people incur to hold less cash. Economists who have estimated these costs find that they can be large, as much as 1 percent of GDP.

In practice, our tax and financial systems do not fully adjust even to anticipated inflation. It is difficult for the government and businesses to change their normal rules

anticipated inflation
Inflation that is expected.

unanticipated inflation
Inflation that is not expected.

menu costs
The costs associated with changing prices and printing new price lists when there is inflation.

shoe-leather costs
Costs of inflation that arise from trying to reduce holdings of cash.

of operation every time inflation changes. As an example, consider the tax system. Our tax system is typically based on nominal income, not real income. Suppose you own a stock in a corporation and its value increases by 5 percent during the year. If the inflation rate is also 5 percent a year, your stock did not increase in real terms—it just kept up with inflation. Nonetheless, if you sold your stock at the end of the year, you would be taxed on the full 5 percent gain, despite the fact that the real value of your stock did not increase. Inflation distorts the operation of our tax and financial system.

Unanticipated Inflation

What if inflation is unexpected? The cost of unexpected inflation is arbitrary redistributions of income. Suppose you expected the inflation rate would be 5 percent and you negotiated a salary based on that expectation. On the one hand, if you miscalculate and the inflation rate turns out to be higher, the purchasing power of your wages will be less than you anticipated. Your employer will have gained at your expense. On the other hand, if the inflation rate turned out to be less than 5 percent, the purchasing power of your wage would be higher than you had anticipated. In this case, you would gain at the expense of the company. As long as the inflation rate differs from what is expected, there will be winners and losers.

These redistributions eventually impose real costs on the economy. Consider an analogy. Suppose you live in a very safe neighborhood where no one locks the doors. If a rash of burglaries (transfers between you and crooks) starts to occur, people will invest in locks, alarms, and more police. You and your community will incur real costs to prevent these arbitrary redistributions.

The same is true for unanticipated inflation. If a society experiences unanticipated inflation, individuals and institutions will change their behavior. For example, potential homeowners will not be able to borrow from banks at fixed rates of interest, but will be required to accept loans whose rates can be adjusted as inflation rates change. Banks do not want to lend money at a fixed interest rate if there is a strong likelihood that inflation will erode the real value of the income stream they expected. However, if banks become reluctant to make loans with fixed interest rates, this imposes more risk on homeowners.

What about the loans made prior to the unanticipated inflation? In this case, debtors will gain at the expense of creditors. Creditors, on the one hand, will lose because inflation will erode the amount of money they planned to earn on the loans. But since the loans have already been made, there's nothing they can do about it. Debtors, on the other hand, will get a deal. It will be easier for them to repay their loans with inflated dollars.

If unanticipated inflation becomes extreme, individuals will spend more of their time trying to profit from inflation rather than working at productive jobs. As inflation became more volatile in the late 1970s in the United States, many people devoted their time to speculation in real estate and commodity markets to try to beat inflation, and the economy became less efficient. Latin American countries that have experienced high and variable inflation rates know all too well these costs from inflation. Indeed, when inflation rates exceed 50 percent per month, we have what is called **hyperinflation**. Think about what an inflation rate of 50 percent a month means: If a can of soda costs $1.25 at the beginning of the year, it would cost $162.00 at the end of year! In a later chapter, we'll study the causes of hyperinflation, but you can readily see that inflation of this magnitude would seriously disrupt normal commerce.

Even in less extreme cases, the costs of inflation are compounded as inflation rises. At high inflation rates, these costs grow rapidly, and at some point policymakers are forced to take actions to reduce inflation. As we mentioned earlier, when unemployment falls below the natural rate, inflation increases. Similarly, in later chapters we'll see that stopping inflation may require unemployment to exceed its natural rate and even plunge an economy into a recession. Although unemployment and recessions are quite costly to society, they sometimes become necessary in the face of high inflation.

hyperinflation
An inflation rate exceeding 50 percent per month.

SUMMARY

In this chapter, we continued our introduction to the basic concepts of macroeconomics and explored the nature of both unemployment and inflation. We also looked at the complex issues involved in measuring unemployment and inflation as well as the costs of both to society. Here are the key points to remember:

1 The unemployed are individuals who do not have jobs but who are actively seeking employment. The *labor force* comprises both the employed and the unemployed. The *unemployment rate* is the percentage of the labor force that is unemployed:

$$\text{unemployment rate} = \frac{\text{unemployed}}{\text{labor force}} \times 100$$

2 Economists distinguish among different types of unemployment. Seasonal patterns of economic activity lead to *seasonal unemployment*. There are three other types of unemployment. *Frictional unemployment* occurs through the normal dynamics of the economy as workers change jobs and industries expand and contract. *Structural unemployment* arises because of a mismatch of workers' skills with job opportunities. *Cyclical unemployment* occurs with the fluctuations in economic activity.

3 Unemployment rates vary across demographic groups. Alternative measures of unemployment take into account individuals who would like to work full time, but who are no longer in the labor force or are holding part-time jobs.

4 Economists measure changes in the cost of living through the *Consumer Price Index (CPI)*, which is based on the cost of purchasing a standard basket of goods and services. The CPI is used to measure changes in average prices over different periods of time. The CPI index for a given year, say year *K*, is defined as

$$\text{CPI in year } K = \frac{\text{cost of basket in year } K}{\text{cost of basket in base year}} \times 100$$

5 We measure *inflation* as the percentage change in the price level.

6 Economists believe that most price indexes, including the CPI and the chain-weighted index for GDP, overstate true inflation because they fail to capture quality improvements in goods and services.

7 Unemployment imposes both financial and psychological costs on workers.

8 Both *anticipated* and *unanticipated* inflation impose costs on society.

KEY TERMS

anticipated inflation, p. 134

Consumer Price Index (CPI), p. 130

cost-of-living adjustments (COLAs), p. 132

cyclical unemployment, p. 126

deflation, p. 133

discouraged workers, p. 123

frictional unemployment, p. 126

full employment, p. 127

hyperinflation, p. 135

inflation rate, p. 132

labor force, p. 121

labor force participation rate, p. 121

menu costs, p. 134

natural rate of unemployment, p. 127

seasonal unemployment, p. 126

shoe-leather costs, p. 134

structural unemployment, p. 127

unanticipated inflation, p. 134

unemployment insurance, p. 128

unemployment rate, p. 121

EXERCISES

Visit www.myeconlab.com to complete these exercises online and get instant feedback.

6.1 Examining Unemployment

1.1 Which of the following is not included in the labor force?
   a. People who are employed.
   b. People who do not have a job, but who are actively searching for one.
   c. People who do not have jobs and do not want one.
   d. The entire population is included in the labor force.

1.2 Individuals who have stopped looking for work because they became discouraged are not counted as unemployed in the traditional unemployment statistics. _____ (True/False)

1.3 The labor force participation rate shows the percentage of the
   a. labor force that has a job.
   b. labor force that is unemployed.
   c. relevant population that is employed.
   d. relevant population that is in the labor force.

1.4 What would happen to the measured unemployment rate if unemployed individuals left the labor force to enter a disability program? (Related to Application 2 on page 125.)

1.5 **New Government Employment and True Unemployment.** Suppose the U.S. government hires workers who are currently unemployed but does not give them any work to do. What will happen to the measured U.S. unemployment rate? Under these circumstances, do changes in the measured U.S. unemployment rate accurately reflect changes in the underlying economic situation and production?

1.6 **Part Time Work.** Paul supports his wife and child through employment. He has decided to work as a blogger for an entertainment Web site. He would like to work 40 hours a week but is only offered 20 hours of work a week by his employer. Is Paul unemployed? Would he be counted as working part time for economic reasons?

1.7 **Calculating Data for the U.S. Economy.** Here are some data for the U.S. economy in January 2010:

236.8 million individuals 16 years of age and older

138.3 million employed

14.8 million unemployed

Calculate the labor force, the labor force participation rate, and the unemployment rate for the U.S. economy.

1.8 **Women and Labor Force Participation.** What factors might limit women's labor force participation relative to men? Are these factors that could change as social customs change? (Related to Application 1 on page 123.)

1.9 **Disability and Low-Skilled Workers.** Disability payments replace a higher fraction of the wages of low-wage workers than of high-wage workers. Overall, average disability payments rise with the average wage. Suppose wages of low-skilled workers fell sharply relative to high-wage workers. How would this affect the incentives to enter disability for low-wage workers? (Related to Application 2 on page 125.)

1.10 **Unemployment Rates in June.** Raw, unadjusted data show virtually every year that the number of unemployed rise in June. Why? Would this show up in seasonally adjusted data?

1.11 **Alternative Unemployment Measures.** An economy has 100,000,000 people employed, 8,000,000 unemployed, and 4,000,000 marginally attached workers. What is the conventional measure of the unemployment rate? What would be the best alternative measure that takes into account marginally attached workers?

1.12 **Discouraged Workers in Japan and the United States.** Japan was concerned about a group of workers called "NEETs," which meant "not in education, employment, or training." In the United States, we also have young, discouraged workers. Discuss the types of young, discouraged workers you would most likely find in the United States.

6.2 Categories of Unemployment

2.1 The three key types of unemployment are cyclical, structural, and _____.

2.2 The natural rate of unemployment consists solely of _____ and _____ unemployment.

2.3 When the economy is at full employment, there is only cyclical unemployment. _____ (True/ False)

2.4 When iPods and MP3 players came on to the scene, replacing CDs, what type or types of unemployment were created?
  a. Structural and frictional
  b. Structural and cyclical
  c. Frictional and cyclical
  d. Discouraged and cyclical

2.5 **Understanding Unemployment Differences across Countries.** A student looking at Figure 6.2 on page 122 argues that Spain must have very high cyclical unemployment compared to Japan because the Spanish unemployment rate is so high. Explain why the student may be wrong.

2.6 **Apartment Vacancies and Unemployment.** In a major city, the vacancy rate for apartments was approximately 5 percent, yet substantial numbers of individuals were searching for new apartments. Explain why this occurs. Relate this phenomenon to unemployment.

2.7 **Unemployment Rates in Large African Cities.** In many African countries, the government and international corporations pay high wages for jobs in the major cities, and many people migrate to the cities from farms where earnings are low. Unemployment rates in the city, therefore, are large. Can this be explained in terms of frictional unemployment? Why or why not?

2.8 **Falling Oil Prices and Frictional Unemployment.** Explain how falling oil prices, which benefit some industries more than others, can affect frictional unemployment.

6.3 The Costs of Unemployment

3.1 Virtually all unemployment has a duration of less than five weeks. _____ (True/False)

3.2 Most states do not replace the entire wages of individuals on unemployment insurance; instead, they replace about _____ percent.

3.3 The effects of unemployment today may carry over into the future because
  a. discouraged workers are not measured in the unemployment rate.

b. those that experience prolonged unemployment lose job skills that are difficult to recover.

c. a person must be actively seeking work to be counted as unemployed.

d. None of the above

3.4 In 2010, approximately 40 percent of the unemployed had been unemployed more than _____ weeks.

3.5 **Understanding Peer Effects of Unemployment.** You might think it would be worse if other people are unemployed at the same time as you were because it would be harder to find a job. But the psychological evidence shows the opposite. Give a few reasons why unemployment may seem less painful to individuals if their peers are also unemployed. (Related to Application 3 on page 129.)

3.6 **Long-Term Effects of Unemployment.** Why might you expect individuals who were unemployed in their 20s to have lower wages at the age of 40 than individuals with identical educational backgrounds but who were not unemployed?

3.7 **Recessions and the Duration of Unemployment.** During a recession, what do you think happens to the fraction of workers with spells of unemployment less than five weeks? Can you find data to support your theory?

6.4 The Consumer Price Index and the Cost of Living

4.1 The value of a price index in the base year is equal to _____.

4.2 Economists believe that the CPI tends to overestimate the increase in the cost of living over time. _____ (True/False)

4.3 Unlike the CPI, the chain-weighted price index for GDP does not include used goods or _____ goods.

4.4 The single largest component of the basket of goods that comprises the CPI is the category for _____.

4.5 **Which Professor Is Better Off?** The starting salary for a new assistant economics professor was $15,000 in 1976 and $90,000 in 2010. The value of the CPI for 2010 was 216.3, compared to 56.9 in 1976. In which year did a newly hired professor earn more in real terms?

4.6 **What Are Comparable Real Salaries?** A job paid $53,000 in 2002. The CPI in 1960 was 29.6, compared to 179.9 in 2002. In 1960, what salary would be comparable to 2002's $53,000 in real terms?

4.7 **High Prices and Inflation.** Critically evaluate the following statement: "Tokyo is an expensive place to live. There must be a high inflation rate in Japan."

4.8 **What Does It Cost?** The Bureau of Labor Statistics now makes price data available on its Web site at http://data.bls.gov/PDQ/outside.jsp?survey=ap. Use this search engine to see how the prices of a few commodities you are interested in have increased over time.

4.9 **New Goods and the CPI Bias.** Many "cell phones" today are more than cell phones—they are mini-computers on which you check your e-mail and surf the Web. Suppose the BLS treated them as old-fashioned cell phones. How would this cause a bias in the CPI? (Related to Application 4 on page 132.)

6.5 Inflation

5.1 If a price index is 50 in 1998 and 60 in 1999, the rate of inflation between the two years is _____.

5.2 Inflation in the United States was higher from 1990 to 2009 than it was from 1970 to 1980. _____ (True/False)

5.3 Which of the following countries experienced a deflation in the 1990s?

a. United States

b. Japan

c. Canada

5.4 If the price of gasoline in 1940 was $0.18 a gallon and $3.00 a gallon in 2009, the percentage rate of change for gasoline over this period was _____ percent.

5.5 **Calculating an Inflation Rate.** A country reports a price index of 55 in 2005 and 60 in 2006. What is the inflation rate between 2005 and 2006?

5.6 **Price Indexes for the Elderly.** Use the Web to find articles that discuss price indexes that are most appropriate for elderly Americans. Why might the inflation rate for the elderly differ from the nonelderly? How would a finding that the elderly face a different inflation rate affect the debates on Social Security?

6.6 The Costs of Inflation

6.1 Inflation that is not expected is known as _____ inflation.

6.2 Shoe-leather costs typically increase with rate of inflation. _____ (True/False)

6.3 Creditors gain from unanticipated inflation. _____ (True/False)

6.4 Hyperinflation occurs when the inflation rate exceeds _____ percent per month.

6.5 **Online Shopping and Menu Costs.** How do you think the Internet and online shopping would affect the menu costs of inflation?

6.6 **Taxes on Stocks and Inflation.** Explain why the real tax burden on buying and then selling stocks tends to increase with inflation.

6.7 **Inflation and ATM Withdrawals.** As the inflation rate increases, would you take more or less money out per each ATM visit? If you walked to the ATM, would that increase or decrease the wear and tear on your shoes?

The Economy at Full Employment

While immigration is a big issue in the United States, emigration—the outflow of people—is a major issue in other countries. Take the case of the Philippines. With a population of 92 million, the estimate of overseas Philippine workers is about 11 million, or 10 percent, of the population. About half of these workers are only temporarily abroad—still that accounts for 5 percent of the total population and an even higher percentage of the potential workforce.

These workers range in skills and occupations. In Hong Kong many families have live-in Philippine domestic help. But skilled Philippine workers play a major role in construction and operations in the Middle East oil industries, and the Philippines is recognized as a major source of skilled nurses all over the globe.

These workers all sought higher wages and better opportunities abroad. But what would happen to GDP and wages in the Philippines if they returned? How does emigration affect these two crucial macroeconomic variables?

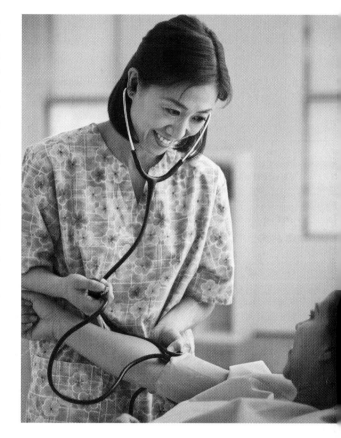

APPLYING THE CONCEPTS

1 How can changes in the supply of labor affect real wages?
   The Black Death and Living Standards in Old England

2 Do differences in taxes and government benefits explain why Europeans work substantially fewer hours per year than do U.S. workers or the Japanese?
   A Nobel Laureate Explains Why Europeans Work Less Than U.S. Workers or the Japanese

3 Can real business cycle models explain the origin and persistence of the Great Depression?
   Can Labor Market Policies Account for the Great Depression?

In this chapter we will explain how the amount of capital and labor helps determine GDP when the economy is operating at full employment. Although the economy experiences booms and busts, in the long run it returns to full employment. This makes full employment an important benchmark, or barometer, of real GDP.

We will see how full employment is determined at any point in time when wages and prices adjust freely and quickly to changes in demand and supply. It is this flexibility in wages and prices that allows the economy to operate at full employment. In the next chapter we will study economic growth when the amount of capital and technology evolves over time.

We will develop the model of full employment and use it to examine important macroeconomic issues and debates, such as the extent to which taxes may depress economic activity and lower the level of GDP. We will also learn about real business cycle theory, a relatively recent school of thought that can help us understand why booms and busts occur.

7.1 WAGE AND PRICE FLEXIBILITY AND FULL EMPLOYMENT

classical models

Economic models that assume wages and prices adjust freely to changes in demand and supply.

The economic model of the economy at full employment that we develop in this chapter assumes wages and prices adjust freely and quickly to changes in demand and supply. Models that make this assumption are called **classical models**. The term *classical* refers to a school of economics that believed that over a relatively short period of time wages and prices would adjust quickly and naturally to bring the economy back to full employment. The classical school of thought dominated economics until about the mid-1930s.

Following the Great Depression in the 1930s, though, economists began to change their minds about the classical school. During the Great Depression, unemployment was rampant—nearly 25 percent of the labor force was unemployed—and economists began to develop models that explained persistent unemployment. In these models, wages and prices don't always adjust quickly to changes in demand and supply—which is why booms and busts occur.

Economists today, however, believe that even though wages and prices may be slow to adjust in the short run, they will respond eventually and restore the economy to full employment. That's why it is important to study the full-employment model. We can use this model to analyze the long-term issues we address in this chapter, such as the role taxes play in determining the level of GDP and how immigration affects wages and GDP.

An economy at full employment doesn't mean that there are no unemployed workers. Recall the distinctions among frictional, structural, and cyclical unemployment. Frictional unemployment occurs naturally in the labor market as workers search for jobs. Structural unemployment arises from a mismatch of skills and jobs. Cyclical unemployment is the part of unemployment that rises and falls with economic fluctuations. Cyclical unemployment can be positive, when unemployment exceeds the natural rate during a recession, or negative, when unemployment is less than the natural rate during a boom. Full employment means an economy has frictional and structural unemployment but no cyclical unemployment. In other words, at full employment the economy is experiencing neither a boom nor a bust.

7.2 THE PRODUCTION FUNCTION

Recall that a critical part of the circular flow of economic activity is the production of total goods and services from the factors of production. The factors of production include the labor, natural resources, physical capital, human capital, and entrepreneurship that are the inputs to a technologically based production process. We'll discuss more of these aspects in the next chapter. In this chapter, however, we develop the idea of a **production function** to study how this production actually occurs. The production function explains how the total level of output or GDP in the economy is generated from the factors of production.

To simplify our discussion of the economy's production function, let's first assume there are only two factors of production: capital and labor. The **stock of capital** is all the machines, equipment, and buildings in the entire economy. **Labor** consists of the efforts, both physical and mental, of all the workers in the economy used to produce goods and services. The production function is written as follows:

$$Y = F(K, L)$$

where Y is total output, or GDP; K is the stock of capital; and L is the labor force. (F represents the relationship between the factors of production and output.) What the math says in words is that we produce total output from both capital and labor. The production function, $F(K, L)$, is a model that tells us how much output we produce from the inputs to production, K and L: More inputs of either capital or labor in an economy lead to increased output.

The stock of capital a society has at any point in time is determined by investments it has made in new buildings, machines, and equipment in the past. Investments made today will have little or no immediate effect on the total stock of buildings, machines, and equipment used in production today, because today's level of investment is typically just a small fraction of all past investments. Therefore, it takes time for investment to change the stock of capital. In this chapter, we will assume for most of our discussion that the stock of capital is fixed at a constant level, which we call K. But we will stray from that assumption a few times to consider what happens when the stock of capital changes. (We promise to let you know where we are straying from the assumption of fixed capital.)

With the stock of capital fixed at the constant level K, only variations in the amount of labor can change the level of output in the economy. Figure 7.1 plots the relationship between the amount of labor used in an economy and the total level of output with a fixed stock of capital. Although the stock of capital is fixed, we do vary the amount of labor employed in production.

Figure 7.1 shows that as we increase labor from L_1 to L_2, output increases sharply from Y_1 to Y_2. However, as more labor is put into production to get us to L_3 and Y_3, output does not rise as sharply. With capital fixed, the relationship between output and labor shown here reflects the principle of diminishing returns.

production function
The relationship between the level of output of a good and the factors of production that are inputs to production.

stock of capital
The total of all machines, equipment, and buildings in an entire economy.

labor
Human effort, including both physical and mental effort, used to produce goods and services.

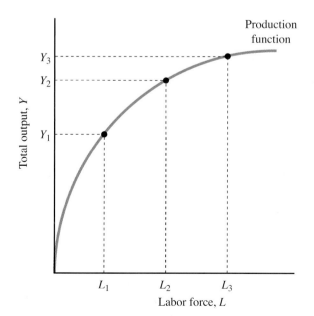

◄ FIGURE 7.1
The Relationship between Labor and Output with Fixed Capital
With capital fixed, output increases with labor input, but at a decreasing rate.

PRINCIPLE OF DIMINISHING RETURNS

Suppose we produce output with two or more inputs and we increase one input while holding the other inputs fixed. Beyond some point—called the *point of diminishing returns*—output will increase at a decreasing rate.

To explain what diminishing marginal returns means, look at the data in Table 7.1 from a typical production function. The table shows the amount of output we can produce from different amounts of labor inputs while we hold the stock of capital constant at some amount. (We don't care what amount, as long as it is constant.) First, notice that as the amount of labor increases, so does the amount of output we produce. Second, as output increases, it increases at a diminishing rate. For example, as labor input increases from 300 to 400 labor units, output increases by 500 output units—from 1,000 to 1,500 output units. But as labor input increases from 400 to 500 labor units, output increases by only 400 output units—from 1,500 to 1,900 output units. The rate of output dropped from 500 output units per additional unit of labor to 400 output units per additional unit of labor input. That's diminishing returns at work.

TABLE 7.1 OUTPUT AND LABOR INPUT	
Y (Output)	*L* (Labor Input)
1,000	300
1,500	400
1,900	500
2,200	600

What happens if the stock of capital increases, say, from K_1 to K_2? Figure 7.2 shows that when the stock of capital increases, the entire short-run production function shifts upward. At any level of labor input, we can produce more output than before we increased the stock of capital. As we add more capital, workers become more productive and can produce more output. That's why the production function curve is higher for more capital. For example, suppose an office has five staff members

▶ **FIGURE 7.2**

An Increase in the Stock of Capital
When the capital increases from K_1 to K_2, the production function shifts up. At any level of labor input, the level of output increases.

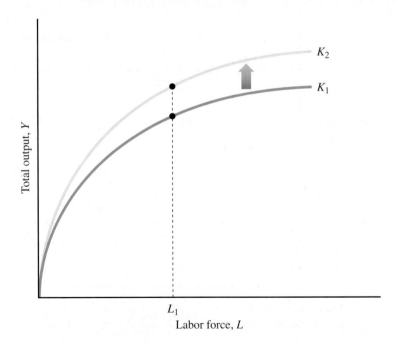

who must share one copier. They will inevitably waste some time waiting to use it. Adding a copier will enable the staff to be more productive.

Capital is one of the key factors of production. As we have seen, the benefits of additional capital are a higher level of output from any level of labor input. Throughout the world, countries have increased their level of output by adding to their stock of capital.

7.3 WAGES AND THE DEMAND AND SUPPLY FOR LABOR

We've just learned from the production function that with the amount of capital fixed, the level of output in the economy will be determined exclusively by the amount of labor employed. Now we'll see how the amount of employment in an economy is determined by the demand and supply for labor.

On the basis of what you already know about demand and supply from Chapter 4, you should be able to see what Figure 7.3 represents when it comes to wages and the demand and supply for labor for the entire economy. The amount of labor firms in the economy will hire depends on the **real wage**: the wage rate paid to employees adjusted for changes in the price level. The real wage tells us what goods and services workers are able to purchase from their labor and also what it costs, in real terms, for employers to pay their workers for their services.

real wage
The wage rate paid to employees adjusted for changes in the price level.

As the real-wage rate falls, firms will hire more labor. That is, consistent with the law of demand, the labor demand curve in Figure 7.3 is downward sloping. In Panel A we see that as the real wage falls from $20 to $10 per hour, the firm will increase the amount of its labor from 5,000 to 10,000 workers.

While the labor-demand curve is based on the decisions by firms, the labor-supply curve is based on the decisions of workers. They must decide how many hours they want to work and how much leisure they want to enjoy. Although many complex factors enter into the decision to supply labor, in this chapter we will typically assume an increase in the real wage will lead to an increase in the quantity of labor supplied in the market. In Panel B of Figure 7.3 we see that 5,000 people would like to work at $10 per hour, but $20 per hour motivates 10,000 people to want to work.

Labor Market Equilibrium

Panel C of Figure 7.3 puts the demand and supply curves together. At a wage of $15 per hour, the amount of labor firms want to hire—7,500 workers—will be equal to the number of people who want to work—7,500 workers. This is the labor market equilibrium: The quantity demanded for labor equals the quantity supplied. Together, the demand and supply curves determine the level of employment in the economy and

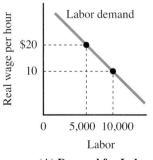
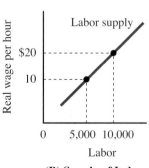
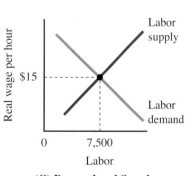

(A) Demand for Labor   **(B) Supply of Labor**   **(C) Demand and Supply**

▲ **FIGURE 7.3**
The Demand and Supply of Labor
Together, the demand and supply for labor determine the level of employment and the real wage.

the level of real wages. Now that we have a model of labor market equilibrium, we can analyze changes in demand and supply for labor.

Changes in Demand and Supply

In deciding how many workers to hire, a firm will compare the marginal benefit from hiring a worker to the marginal cost. This is an example of the marginal principle.

MARGINAL PRINCIPLE

Increase the level of an activity as long as its marginal benefit exceeds its marginal cost. Choose the level at which the marginal benefit equals the marginal cost.

Now let's apply this principle to understanding how a change in the capital stock affects the demand for labor. When firms increase their capital stock, they find that each worker becomes more productive with the additional capital. For example, suppose the marginal benefit to the firm of an additional hour of work is initially $15, and the wage rate is also $15. An increase in the supply of capital raises the marginal benefit to the firm to $20. Firms will want to hire additional workers at the existing wage of $15 until the marginal benefit again equals the marginal cost.

Because the demand for labor increases at any real wage, the labor-demand curve shifts to the right. Panel A of Figure 7.4 shows the effects of an increase in labor demand. The new market equilibrium moves from *a* to *b*. Real wages increase, and the amount of labor employed in the economy increases as well. Having more capital in the economy is beneficial for workers.

We also can analyze the effect of an increase in the supply of labor that might come, for example, from immigration. If the population increases, we would expect more people would want to work at any given wage. This means the labor-supply curve would shift to the right. Panel B of Figure 7.4 shows that with an increase in the supply of labor, the labor market equilibrium moves from *a* to *b*. Real wages have fallen, and the amount of labor employed has increased. Workers who were employed before the increase in labor supply suffer because real wages have fallen—all wages, including theirs.

Our demand and supply of labor model helps us see why currently employed workers might be reluctant to favor increased immigration—their wages fall.

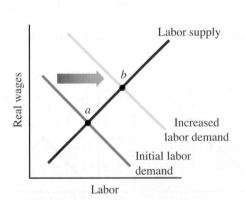

(A) If the demand for labor increases, real wages rise and the amount of labor employed increases.

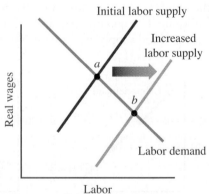

(B) If the supply of labor increases, real wages fall and the amount of labor employed increases.

▲ **FIGURE 7.4**
Shifts in Labor Demand and Supply
Shifts to demand and supply will change both real wages and employment.

APPLICATION 1

THE BLACK DEATH AND LIVING STANDARDS IN OLD ENGLAND

APPLYING THE CONCEPTS #1: How can changes in the supply of labor affect real wages?

According to the research of Professor Gregory Clark of the University of California, Davis, the level of real wages for laborers in England was nearly the same in 1200 as it was in 1800. Yet, during the period from 1350 to 1550, wages were considerably higher—nearly 75 percent higher in 1450, for instance, than they were in 1200. Why were real wages temporarily so high during this period?

The simple answer was the bubonic plague—also known as the Black Death—that arrived from Asia in 1348 and caused a long decline in total population through the 1450s. With fewer workers, there was less labor supplied to the market. The result was higher real wages, although less total output.

In the era before consistent and rapid technological advance, changes in population was the primary factor controlling living standards. As the economist Thomas Malthus (1766–1834) observed, social maladies such as the Black Death would temporarily raise living standards until higher living standards led to increased population.   **Related to Exercises 3.8 and 3.9.**

SOURCE: Based on Gregory Clark, *A Farewell to Alms* (Princeton University Press, 2007).

However, there's a flip side to this. Wages are an input price that firms use in determining the price of the goods and services they produce. Lower input prices—such as wages—eventually lead to lower prices for the products workers buy. In other words, there are trade-offs from immigration for society. Our model also explains why workers would like to see increases in the supply of machines and equipment as long as full employment can be maintained. The increased supply of capital (which increases labor productivity) increases labor demand and leads to higher real wages.

Demand and supply for labor can often change at the same time, but by looking at wages and employment we can determine which effect dominates. Here is an example: Suppose you were told that in a small European country both wages and employment increased substantially over a five-year period. As you try to determine what happened, would you look primarily at factors that increased labor demand or that increased labor supply?

To answer this question, we would want to examine some factors, such as the increase in the stock of capital or a change in technology, that would increase labor demand and both wages and employment. These factors could account for why wages and employment increased in the small European country. Increases in the supply of labor (more people in the workforce) would account for the increase in employment, but not for the increase in wages.

7.4 LABOR MARKET EQUILIBRIUM AND FULL EMPLOYMENT

We can now join the production function and the demand and supply for labor. Together, they will give us a model that helps us determine how much output the economy can produce when it is operating at full employment and also help us understand how taxes on employers affect the level of output.

Figure 7.5 brings the model of the labor market together with the short-run production function. Panel B depicts equilibrium in the labor market, which we saw in

▶ **FIGURE 7.5**
Determining Full-Employment Output
Panel B determines the equilibrium level of employment at *L* and the real wage rate of *W*. Full-employment output in Panel A is *Y*.

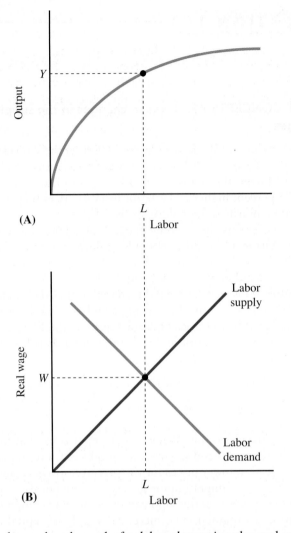

(A)

(B)

Figure 7.3. The demand and supply for labor determine the real-wage rate *W* and identify the level of employment *L*. Panel A plots the short-run production function. With the level of employment determined at *L* in Panel B, we move upward to Panel A and use that level of employment to determine that the level of production is *Y*. **Full-employment output** is the level of output produced when the labor market is in equilibrium and the economy is producing at full employment. It is also known as *potential output*.

Note that full-employment output is based on the idea that the labor market is in equilibrium, with the quantity of labor supplied equal to the quantity of labor demanded at the equilibrium wage. Potential output is not the absolute maximum level of output an economy can produce—an economy could produce more with higher levels of labor input—but potential output reflects the level of labor input that workers wish to supply.

How do economists typically measure the level of full-employment output, or potential output? They start with an estimate of what the unemployment rate would be if cyclical unemployment were zero—that is, if the only unemployment were due to frictional or structural factors. In the United States, estimates of the natural rate in recent years have varied between 5.0 and 6.5 percent. Economists then estimate how many workers will be employed and use the production function to determine potential output.

Let's look at some real numbers. In 1996, the unemployment rate was 5.6 percent, very close to the natural rate of unemployment. The labor force in that year was approximately 133.9 million, and 126.7 million individuals were employed. Real GDP in that year was $7.8 trillion, measured in 1996 dollars. This level of GDP was produced with

full-employment output

The level of output that results when the labor market is in equilibrium and the economy is producing at full employment.

the labor of the 126.7 million employed workers and the existing stock of capital and technology. Because the unemployment rate in 1996 was close to the natural rate, the level of real GDP was also very close to the level of potential output in that year.

The level of potential output in an economy increases as the supply of labor increases or the stock of capital increases. An increase in the supply of labor, perhaps from more liberal immigration, would shift the labor-supply curve to the right and lead to a higher level of employment in the economy. With a higher level of employment, the level of full-employment output will increase. An increase in the stock of capital will increase the demand for labor. As labor demand increases, the result will be higher wages and increased employment. Higher employment will again raise the level of full-employment output.

Potential output depends on both capital and labor. Consequently, differences in the quantity of labor supplied to the market will affect the level of potential output in a country. Countries do differ in the amount of labor their workers supply to the market. Apart from national holidays, workers in the United States take an average of 12 days of vacation, compared to 28 days in the United Kingdom, 35 days in Germany, and an amazing 42 days (over eight work weeks) in Italy. These differences in labor supply are important. Per capita output is higher in the United States than in Germany but, other things being equal, this difference would disappear if German workers toiled as much as their U.S. counterparts.

7.5 USING THE FULL-EMPLOYMENT MODEL

We use the full-employment model extensively in macroeconomics to analyze a wide range of issues. For example, many politicians and economists have argued that high tax rates have hurt the U.S. economy and reduced the level of output and production. We can use the full-employment model to explore the logic of these claims. We will also see how to use the model to explain booms and recessions—fluctuations in output. This will allow us to understand the fundamental idea of an influential school of economic thought known as real business cycle theory.

Taxes and Potential Output

We use the full-employment model in Figure 7.6 to study the effects of taxes employers pay for hiring labor, such as the taxes they pay for their portion of workers' Social Security. (Economists use similar arguments to study a variety of taxes, including personal and corporate income taxes.) A tax on labor will make labor more expensive and raise the marginal cost of hiring workers. For example, let's say there is no tax on labor and suddenly a tax of 10 percent is imposed. An employer who had been paying $10 an hour for workers will now find that labor costs $11 an hour. Because the marginal cost of hiring workers has gone up but the marginal benefit to the firm has not changed, employers will respond by hiring fewer workers at any given wage. In Panel A of Figure 7.6, the labor-demand curve shifts to the left, reflecting the change in demand due to the tax. As the demand curve shifts to the left, the market equilibrium moves from *a* to *b*. The result is lower real wages and lower employment.

As we have just seen, higher taxes lead to less employment. With reduced employment, potential output in the economy will be reduced as the economy moves to a lower level of output on the short-run production function. Higher taxes therefore lead to lower output. The size of the reduction in output depends critically on the slope of the labor-supply curve. The slope of the labor-supply curve indicates how sensitive labor supply is to changes in real wages.

Panel B in Figure 7.6 shows the effect of the same tax with a vertical labor-supply curve. A vertical labor-supply curve means workers will supply the same amount of labor regardless of the wage. For example, a single parent might work a full 40 hours a week regardless of the wage, so the supply curve will be vertical. If, say, other workers in the economy also put in the same hours regardless of the wage, the supply curve

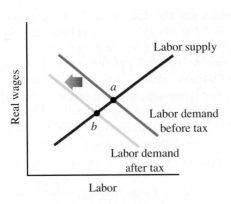

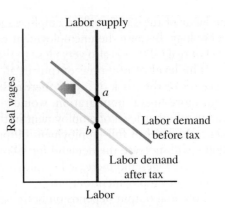

(A) **A tax on labor shifts the labor demand curve to the left and leads to lower wages and reduced employment.**

(B) **If the supply curve for labor is vertical, wages fall but employment does not change.**

▲ **FIGURE 7.6**
How Employment Taxes Affect Labor Demand and Supply
In Panel A, a tax burden on labor shifts the labor demand curve to the left and leads to lower wages and reduced employment. In Panel B, the supply curve for labor is vertical, which means that wages fall but employment does not change.

for labor in the entire economy will be vertical. In Panel B, we see that with a vertical supply curve, the change in demand will move the market equilibrium from *a* to *b*. The tax will reduce wages but have no effect on employment and therefore no effect on output.

This example illustrates that taxes can affect wages and output. In both cases, either output or wages were lowered when the tax was imposed. However, the extent of the decline in output depends on the slope of the labor-supply curve. To understand the effects of taxes on output, we need information about the slope of the labor-supply curve.

Labor supply has been the focus of many studies. The evidence is strong that part-time workers or second earners in a family are very sensitive to changes in wages and do vary their labor supply when wages change. There is less of a consensus about the behavior of primary earners in the family. For many years, economists believed their labor supply was not very sensitive to changes in compensation. However, recent research has shown that taxes do matter, even for primary earners.

The entire area of taxation and economics is an active branch of economics research. Economists such as Martin Feldstein of Harvard University have studied how many different types of taxes affect employment, saving, and production. Economists use models to try to measure these effects, just as we did for the employment tax.

Real Business Cycle Theory

Fluctuations in economic activity can result from a variety of causes. Here are some examples: A developing country that is highly dependent on agriculture can lose its cash crop because of a prolonged drought. According to economic historian Stanley Lebergott, the nineteenth-century U.S. agricultural-based economy was devastated by grasshopper invasions in North Dakota from 1874 to 1876 and by the boll-weevil migration from Mexico to Texas in 1892.[1] Sharp increases in the price of oil can hurt economies that use oil in production, as was the case throughout the world in both 1973 and 1979. Wars can devastate entire regions of the world, and natural disasters, such as earthquakes or floods, can cause sharp reductions in GDP.

Major shifts in technology, which we'll discuss more in the next chapter, can also cause economic fluctuations. Consider some economic developments, starting with

APPLICATION 2

A NOBEL LAUREATE EXPLAINS WHY EUROPEANS WORK LESS THAN U.S. WORKERS OR THE JAPANESE

APPLYING THE CONCEPTS #2: Do differences in taxes and government benefits explain why Europeans work substantially fewer hours per year than do U.S. workers or the Japanese?

On average today, the French (and other Europeans) work one-third fewer hours than do U.S. workers. You might be tempted to attribute this difference to Europeans' taste for leisure or vacations. However, in the early 1970s Europeans actually worked slightly more hours than did U.S. workers. What explains this dramatic turnaround in the space of just 20 years?

Nobel Laureate Edward Prescott, professor at Arizona State University and a senior advisor of the Federal Reserve Bank of Minneapolis, has compared the experiences of the United States and Europe. Prescott attributes the decreases in hours of work in Europe to increases in the tax burden that ultimately falls on workers. Government spending and transfers play a larger role in European economies than in the United States. For example, workers in these countries pay higher taxes, but they also receive more benefits, such as health care. Transfers in European countries increased from the 1970s to the 1990s, along with tax burdens during this period. Taking into account all taxes, Prescott calculated that the effective rate of tax on labor was 40 percent in the United States, 59 percent in Germany and France, and 64 percent in Italy. Japan's tax burden was similar to the United States, and its hours of work were also similar.

Prescott notes that as our society ages and the burdens of Social Security and Medicare increase, the United States may be tempted to increase its tax rates to European levels. Indeed, to maintain the current benefits promised by these programs, the United States will need to increase tax rates substantially. If we do not make changes in the underlying programs and allow tax rates to increase, Prescott warns that we will also see sharp declines in labor supply—and potential output—in the United States in the future. Living standards would fall as a result.   **Related to Exercises 5.4 and 5.5.**

SOURCE: Based on Edward Prescott, "Why Do Americans Work So Much More Than Europeans," *Federal Reserve Bank of Minneapolis Quarterly Review* (July 2004): 2–13.

---

the early nineteenth century. There were large investments in textile mills and steam power. The birth of the steel industry and railroads dominated the last half of the century. At the end of the nineteenth century, new industries arose that were based on chemical manufacturing, electricity, and the automobile. It is inconceivable that the vast changes in technology that led to the creation of these new industries would not have profound effects on the economy. For example, the invention of the automobile sounded the death knell for makers of horse-drawn buggies, buggy whips, and a host of other industries.

Economic fluctuations can also occur because a number of small shocks all hit the economy at the same time. For example, a case of mad cow disease could cause consumer preferences to change from beef to pork. Or a series of small improvements in breeding technology could cause output to rise among worldwide producers of cattle.

One school of economic thought, known as **real business cycle theory**, emphasizes that shocks to technology can be a major cause of economic fluctuations. Led by Nobel Laureate economist Edward Prescott, real business cycle economists have developed newer models that integrate shocks to technology into the full-employment model we have been discussing.

real business cycle theory
The economic theory that emphasizes how shocks to technology can cause fluctuations in economic activity.

The idea behind real business cycle theory is simple: Changes in technology will usually change the level of full employment or potential output. A significant technological improvement will enable the economy to increase the level of both actual and potential output. For example, the advances in technology that allowed computer users to transfer data-intensive images easily across the Internet created many new opportunities for businesses to grow and flourish. Adverse technological developments (or adverse shocks to the economy) will cause output and potential output to fall. For example, the Internet crashing would bring business communication systems and ordering systems to a halt.

Figure 7.7 gives a simple example of how the real business cycle theory works. Suppose an adverse technological shock occurred, decreasing the demand for labor. The demand curve for labor would shift to the left, and the labor market equilibrium would move from *a* to *b*. The result would be a lower level of employment and lower real wages. Total GDP would fall because employment is low and because the economy is less productive than before.

Conversely, a positive technological shock would increase labor demand and result in both higher wages and higher employment. Total GDP would rise because employment is high and because the economy is more productive than before.

An economy buffeted by positive and negative technological shocks would experience economic fluctuations even though it would always be at full-employment output. The key lesson from real business cycle theory is that potential output itself will vary over time.

The real business cycle school of thought has been influential with some academic economists, but in its most extreme form it has been viewed as controversial. Critics find it difficult to understand how many of the post–World War II recessions can be explained by adverse changes in technology. In addition, the real business cycle model does not provide an explanation of unemployment. In the model the labor market is in equilibrium, and the quantity demanded for labor equals the quantity supplied. At the equilibrium wage, the quantity of labor demanded equals the quantity of labor supplied, and everyone who seeks employment finds employment.

Proponents of the real business cycle model counter that other types of economic models can explain unemployment and that the real business cycle can still explain fluctuations in employment. Real business cycle theory is an active area of research, and both its methods and approach, grounded in firm economic reasoning, have had a major influence on professional research today. Scholars working in this tradition have

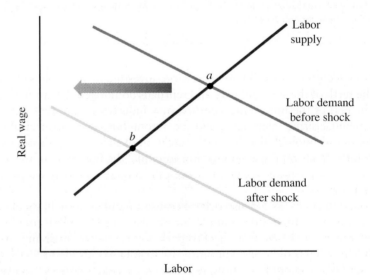

▲ **FIGURE 7.7**
How an Adverse Technology Shock Affects Labor Demand and Supply
An adverse shock to technology will decrease the demand for labor. As a result, both real wages and employment fall as the market equilibrium moves from *a* to *b*.

> (**APPLICATION 3**)

CAN LABOR MARKET POLICIES ACCOUNT FOR THE GREAT DEPRESSION?

APPLYING THE CONCEPTS #3: Can real business cycle models explain the origin and persistence of the Great Depression?

Early critics of real business cycle models claimed that these models could not explain major events like the Great Depression, and, indeed, there appears to be a puzzle about the Great Depression. If negative technology shocks were responsible for the origin and decade-long persistence of the Great Depression, we would expect that the fall in output would be accompanied by a decline in the real wage, just as in Figure 7.7. However, real wages actually rose substantially during the 1930s.

Economists Harold L. Cole and Lee E. Ohanian of the University of California, Los Angeles, extended the standard real business cycle model to include other important factors, in particular government interventions that affected the labor market. For example, President Franklin Roosevelt's New Deal featured the National Industrial Recovery Act, which allowed firms to collude with one another and avoid competition as long as they recognized unions and raised wages. Prior to the onset of the Great Depression, President Herbert Hoover also promoted policies that led firms to raise wages. Ohanian and Cole show that incorporating these factors into a standard real business cycle model can explain both the origin and severity of the Great Depression.

Of course, as we will see in later chapters, many other factors could have added to the severity of the Great Depression. Banks failed both in the United States and worldwide and international trade—which had been very vibrant in the 1930s—ground to a halt. Nonetheless, the work of Ohanian and Cole demonstrates that a modified version of real business cycle models can add to our understanding of this important episode.   **Related to Exercise 5.8.**

SOURCE: Based on Harold L. Cole and Lee E. Ohanian, "New Deal Policies and the Persistence of the Great Depression: A General Equilibrium Analysis," *Journal of Political Economy* 112, no.4 (2004): 779–816 and Lee E. Ohanian, "What—or Who—Started the Great Depression," *Journal of Economic Theory* 144 (2009): 2310–2335.

begun to offer modifications of the basic model that can potentially explain major economic events.

7.6 DIVIDING OUTPUT AMONG COMPETING DEMANDS FOR GDP AT FULL EMPLOYMENT

Our model of full employment is based entirely on the supply of factors of production and the state of technology. The demand for and supply of labor determine the real wage and total employment in the economy. Together, labor and the supply of capital determine the level of output through the production function. And that means that in a full-employment economy, total GDP is determined by the supply of factors of production.

Because society faces scarce resources, it must divide full-employment GDP among competing demands. From Chapters 5 and 6, you know that GDP is composed of consumption, investment, government purchases, and net exports, which we denote as $C + I + G + NX$. In this section, we see how societies divide total spending among these four components. Because governments, for many different reasons, increase their level of spending, we would like to know how increased government spending affects private spending. We will see how increases in government spending must reduce other types of expenditures when the economy is operating at full employment.

International Comparisons

Countries divide GDP among its four components in very different ways. Table 7.2 presents data on the percent of GDP in alternative uses for five countries in 2008. Recall that consumption (*C*), investment (*I*), and government purchases (*G*) refer to total spending by residents of that country. Net exports (*NX*) is the difference between exports (sales of goods to foreign residents) and imports (purchases of goods abroad). If a country has positive net exports—for example, Hong Kong, France, China, and Germany—it is selling more goods in other countries than it is buying from other countries. If a country has negative net exports—such as the United States—it is buying more goods than it is selling to other countries.

Let's make one more point: These data are from the International Financial Statistics, which is published by the International Monetary Fund. In these statistics, government purchases include only government consumption, such as military spending or wages for government employees. Government investment, such as spending on bridges or roads, is included in the investment category (*I*).

Table 7.2 reveals considerable diversity among countries. The United States consumes 70 percent of its GDP, a higher fraction than all the other countries. As far as investment goes, Germany and the United States invest a smaller share of GDP than the other countries in the table. China invests the most by far—44 percent. Countries also differ greatly when it comes to government consumption. France has the highest rate of government consumption, while Hong Kong has the lowest. Finally, the countries also differ in the size of net exports relative to GDP.

This wide diversity challenges economists to explain these differences. Some economists have suggested that China's high savings rate (low share of consumption) can be explained by its one-child-per-family policy. They argue that this leads workers to save more for retirement because they cannot depend on their children to support them. Other economists attribute the high savings rate to the fact that China provides very little government-sponsored retirement benefits. In general, differences across countries are hard to explain. For example, there are no obvious, purely economic reasons why the United States, France, and Germany should exhibit such different behavior.

Crowding Out in a Closed Economy

We know government spending is part of GDP. Let's say GDP is fixed and the government increases its spending. What happens in a country that increases its government purchases within a fixed GDP? Because the level of full-employment output is given by the supply of factors in the economy, an increase in government spending must come at the expense of other uses of GDP. Or, stated another way, increased government spending crowds out other demands for GDP. This is called **crowding out**. Crowding out illustrates the principle of opportunity cost:

crowding out

The reduction in investment (or other component of GDP) caused by an increase in government spending.

 ## PRINCIPLE OF OPPORTUNITY COST

The opportunity cost of something is what you sacrifice to get it.

TABLE 7.2 SHARES OF SPENDING IN GDP, ASSORTED COUNTRIES, 2008				
	C	I	G	NX
Hong Kong	60	20	9	11
United States	70	19	16	−5
France	56	21	23	1
China	36	44	13	8
Germany	56	19	18	6

SOURCE: International Monetary Statistics, International Monetary Fund, 2010.

At full employment, the opportunity cost of increased government spending is some other component of GDP.

To understand crowding out, let's first consider what will happen when government spending increases in an economy without international trade, called a **closed economy**. In a closed economy, full-employment output is divided among just three different demands: consumption, investment, and government purchases. We can write this as

closed economy
An economy without international trade.

$$\text{output} = \text{consumption} + \text{investment} + \text{government purchases}$$
$$Y = C + I + G$$

Because we are considering an economy at full employment, the supply of output (Y) is fixed. Increases in government spending must reduce—that is, crowd out—either consumption or investment. In general, both are affected. On the investment side, the government will be in increased competition with businesses trying to borrow funds from the public to finance its investment plans. This increased competition from the government will make it more difficult and costly for businesses to make those investments. As a result, business investment spending will decrease. In other words, government crowds out investment.

Crowding out occurred in the United States during World War II as the share of government spending as a part of GDP rose sharply. Figures 7.8 and 7.9 show that at the same time the share of government spending increased, the shares of consumption and investment spending in GDP decreased.

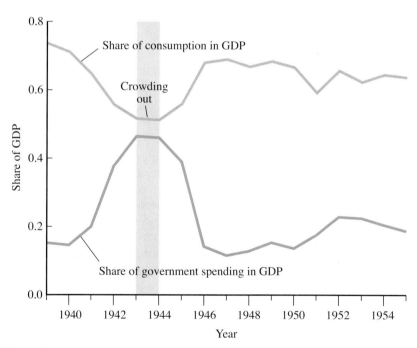

▲ FIGURE 7.8
U.S. Consumption and Government Spending during World War II
Increased government spending crowds out consumption by consumers. The vertical bar highlights the time period during which crowding out occurred.
SOURCE: U.S. Department of Commerce.

Crowding Out in an Open Economy

An economy with international trade is called an **open economy**. In an open economy, full-employment output is divided among four uses: consumption, investment, government purchases, and net exports (exports – imports):

open economy
An economy with international trade.

$$Y = C + I + G + NX$$

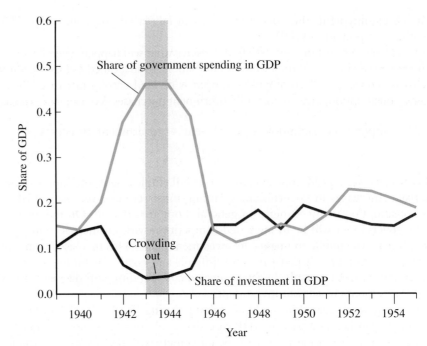

▲ FIGURE 7.9

U.S. Investment and Government Spending during World War II
Increased government spending also crowds out private investment spending. The vertical bar highlights the time period during which crowding out occurred.
SOURCE: U.S. Department of Commerce.

Increased government spending need not crowd out either consumption or investment. It could lead to reduced exports and increased imports. Therefore, what could get crowded out instead is net exports.

Here is how this crowding out might happen: Suppose the U.S. government began buying domestic goods—for example, computer paper—to use for its offices. Let's say consumers would have purchased this paper but now cannot. If consumers want to maintain their same consumption of computer paper despite the fact that the government now has it, they could purchase domestic computer paper previously sold abroad (exports) or purchase paper sold by foreign countries (imports). The result would be a decrease in the amount of paper exported and an increase in imported paper, that is, a decrease in total net exports. In practice, increases in government spending in an open economy would crowd out consumption, investment, and net exports.

Crowding in

Governments do not always increase spending. Sometimes they decrease it. When the government cuts spending and the level of output is fixed, some other type of spending will increase. We call this **crowding in**. In a closed economy, consumption or investment, or both, could increase. In an open economy, net exports could increase as well. As an example, after a war we might see increases in consumption, investment spending, or net exports as they replace military spending.

The nature of changes in government spending will have some effect on the type of spending that is crowded in (or crowded out). If the government spent less on mail service—leading to longer delays in the mail—businesses and households would most likely want to spend more on private mail or delivery services. If the government built more public swimming pools, households would most likely cut back their own spending on backyard pools.

crowding in

The increase of investment (or other component of GDP) caused by a decrease in government spending.

SUMMARY

In this chapter, we studied the economy at full employment. In the model we developed, the level of GDP is determined by the supply of the factors of production—labor, natural resources, physical capital, human capital, and entrepreneurship. We focused on how the economy operates when it is at full employment. In later chapters, we consider economic fluctuations. Here are the main points from this chapter:

1 Models that assume wages and prices adjust freely to changes in demand and supply are called *classical models.* They are useful to understand how the economy operates at full employment.

2 *Full-employment output*, or potential output, is the level of GDP produced from a given supply of capital when the labor market is in equilibrium. Potential output is fully determined by the supply of factors of production in the economy.

3 Increases in the *stock of capital* raise the level of full-employment output and real wages.

4 Increases in the supply of labor will raise the level of full-employment output but lower the level of real wages.

5 The full-employment model has many applications. Many economists use it to study the effects of taxes on potential output. Others have found the model useful in understanding economic fluctuations in models of *real business cycles.*

6 At full employment, increases in government spending must come at the expense of other components of GDP. In a closed economy, either consumption or investment must be crowded out. In an open economy, net exports can be crowded out as well. Decreases in government spending will crowd in other types of spending.

KEY TERMS

classical models, p. 140

closed economy, p. 153

crowding in, p. 154

crowding out, p. 152

full-employment output, p. 146

labor, p. 141

open economy, p. 153

production function, p. 141

real business cycle theory, p. 149

real wage, p. 143

stock of capital, p. 141

EXERCISES

Visit www.myeconlab.com to complete these exercises online and get instant feedback.

7.1 Wage and Price Flexibility and Full Employment

1.1 Economic models that assume that wages and prices adjust freely to changes in demand and supply are known as _____ models.

1.2 At full employment, there are only frictional and _____ unemployment.

1.3 The classical school of thought came to its fruition during the Great Depression. _____ (True/False)

1.4 There is no _____ unemployment at full employment.

7.2 The Production Function

2.1 The production function illustrates the relationship between _____ and _____.

2.2 With the stock of capital fixed, output increases with labor input, but at a rate that _____ (increases/decreases).

2.3 A decrease in the stock of capital shifts the production function _____ (upward/downward). Show this with a graph.

2.4 Increasing returns occur when we increase both labor and capital. _____ (True/False)

2.5 **The Production Function and the Effects of War on the Stock of Capital.** During World War II, France lost 30 percent of its capital stock. Draw a graph that illustrates how the production function shifted.

2.6 **The Production Function and the Effects of War on the Labor Force.** France lost 550,000 people of 42 million in World War II. Show how this affected output using the graph from Exercise 2.5.

2.7 **Diminishing Returns?** An economy increased employment first from 10,000 to 20,000 and then from 20,000 to 30,000. The corresponding increases in output were 15,000 and 20,000, respectively. Nothing else changed during this period. Did this economy exhibit diminishing returns?

7.3 Wages and the Demand and Supply for Labor

3.1 Labor market equilibrium occurs at a real wage at which the quantity demanded for labor equals the quantity _____ of labor.

3.2 An increase in the amount of capital in the economy will shift the demand for labor curve to the _____ (right/left), leading to higher real wages and employment.

3.3 Increased immigration is likely to lead to a shift in the labor-supply curve to the _____ (right/left).

3.4 If wages and employment both rise, this is likely caused by an increase in the demand for labor. _____ (True/False)

3.5 **Historical Immigration Patterns and Real Wages.** Between 1870 and 1910, 60 million Europeans left Europe to go to the United States, Canada, Australia, and Argentina. This immigration sharply increased the labor force in these countries, but decreased it in Europe.
   a. Draw demand and supply graphs to show what happened to wages in Europe.
   b. Draw demand and supply graphs to show what happened to wages in other countries.

3.6 **Immigration and the Wage Gap between High-School Graduates and College Graduates.** Some economists have argued that while immigration does not have a major effect on the overall level of wages, it does increase the wage gap between high-school graduates and college graduates. Can you explain this effect of immigration on the wage gap?

3.7 **Philippines and Emigration.** Suppose overseas Philippine workers returned to their home country. Using Figure 7.4 on page 144, illustrate the effects of this reverse flow of people on wages and employment.

3.8 **Malthus and Subsistence Wages.** Thomas Malthus wrote that if wages exceeded subsistence levels the population would increase, which, in turn would drive real wages back down to subsistence. Suppose there were an increase in the demand for labor, which raised real wages. Under Malthus's theory, show how the supply curve for labor would shift. (Related to Application 1 on page 145.)

3.9 **Malthus, Population Size, and Technology.** Malthus believed the population would always adjust to bring real wages back to a fixed subsistence level. Using a demand and supply for labor diagram, show that an improvement in technology will lead to a higher level of population. (Related to Application 1 on page 145.)

7.4 Labor Market Equilibrium and Full Employment

4.1 Suppose the supply of labor increases. Draw a graph to show how potential output and wages change.

4.2 Draw a graph to show how potential output and wages change when the stock of capital decreases.

4.3 The typical European works more hours per year than the typical U.S. worker. _____ (True/False)

4.4 Another term for potential output is _____.

4.5 **Estimates of the Natural Rate and Full Employment.** Two economists differ on their estimates of the natural rate. One economist believes it is 6 percent, while the other believes it is 5 percent. All else being equal, which economist will estimate a higher value for potential output?

4.6 **Germany and the United States.** Per-capita output is higher in the United States than in Germany. According to recent studies, what is the main cause of this difference?

4.7 **A Bad Analogy.** People without economic training sometimes think of full employment as the maximum possible level of employment—reaching it is like hitting a barrier. Explain carefully why this analogy is wrong.

7.5 Using the Full-Employment Model

5.1 On a graph of the labor market, show the effects of an increase in the payroll tax.

5.2 On a graph of the labor market, show the effects of a negative shock to technology on wages and employment.

5.3 Two examples of major technological innovations that could have caused major economic fluctuations are _____ and _____.

5.4 Edward Prescott believes that Europeans work fewer hours than U.S. workers because _____ are higher in Europe. (Related to Application 2 on page 149.)

5.5 **Payroll Tax for a Health Program.** To finance a universal health-care program, the government decides to place a 10-percent payroll tax on all labor hired. (Related to Application 2 on page 149.)
   a. Draw a graph to show how this shifts the demand for labor.
   b. If the labor-supply curve is vertical, what are the effects on real wages, output, and employment? Explain why economists say labor bears the full burden of the tax in this case.
   c. If the labor-supply curve were horizontal, what would be the effects on wages, output, and employment?
   d. Can your answer to part (c) explain Edward Prescott's claim about the causes of the changes in hours of work in Europe compared to Japan and the United States?

5.6 **Analyzing the Effects of Tax Rate Changes for Families with Different Incomes.** The Tax Reform Act of 1986 cut the tax rates sharply for high-income earners. Consider the families in the top 1 percent of all families ranked in terms of income. Before the law was passed, a woman in this group faced a marginal tax rate (the tax rate applied to the last dollar she earned) of 52 percent on average. After the law was passed, the rate fell to 38 percent. The decreases in tax rates were much less, however, for families with lower levels of income. According to a study by Professor Nada Eissa,[2] after the decrease in taxes took effect, the labor supply of women in the highest income group increased more than that of women in other income groups. Use a labor demand and supply model to illustrate the differences between the high-income group and the other groups.

5.7 **Tax Revenue and Labor Supply.** Tax revenue collected from a payroll tax equals the tax rate times the earnings of individuals subject to the payroll tax. Let's say the labor-supply curve is close to vertical. Explain why, in this case, raising payroll tax rates will increase the total revenue the government receives from the payroll tax.

5.8 **Explaining a Depression Using Real Business Cycle Theory.** Real business cycle theorists look at economic fluctuations in a particular way.

   a. Draw a graph to show how a real business cycle economist would explain an economic depression.

   b. According to real business cycle theory, how do real wages behave during depressions?

   c. How did actual real wags behave during the Great Depression?

   d. According to Professor Ohanian, what other factors may have caused wages to behave this way? (Related to Application 3 on page 151.)

5.9 **Taxes on Capital Gains and Tax Revenue.** The U.S. government currently taxes increases in the value of stocks when they are sold. This is called the capital gains tax. Explain why, if the government reduced the tax rate on capital gains, it could actually receive more total revenue. In your answer, carefully distinguish between the tax rate and tax revenues.

5.10 **Researching Studies on Taxation, Economic Behavior, and Revenue Collection.** Go to the Web site for the Congressional Budget Office (www.cbo.gov) and find a study that explores the effects of taxation on economic behavior and on total tax revenue. Draw a graph that shows how an increase in tax rates can increase tax revenue.

7.6 Dividing Output among Competing Demands for GDP at Full Employment

6.1 When the economy operates at full employment, an increase in government spending must crowd out consumption. _____ (True/False)

6.2 A(n) _____ economy is open to trade, whereas a closed economy is not.

6.3 In an open economy, increases in government spending can crowd out consumption, investment, or _____.

6.4 Compared to other countries, China has a relatively _____ share of consumption spending in GDP.

6.5 **An Investment Boom in an Open Economy.** Suppose the government provides additional incentives for investment in new plant and equipment and investment spending increases. Consumption and government purchases remain the same. In an open economy, what must happen to allow this investment increase?

6.6 **Consumption or Investment Crowding Out?** Suppose local governments in suburban communities around the country started building large community swimming pools. Explain what type of spending this might crowd out. Compare this to the effect of government spending on exploration of Mars.

6.7 **Marital Gifts and Savings.** In Japan, it is a custom for the bride's family to give a gift having very large monetary value to the family of the groom. How might this affect the savings rate in Japan?

NOTES

1. Stanley Lebergott, *The Americans* (W.W. Norton: New York and London, 1984), chap. 30.

2. Nada Eissa, "Taxation and the Labor Supply of Married Women: The Tax Reform Act of 1986 as a Natural Experiment," (working paper 5023, National Bureau of Economic Research, 1995).

8 Why Do Economies Grow?

For many people, the thought of poverty conjures up poor, African children. Indeed, Africa is a poor continent, but as economists Xavier Sali-i-Martin and Maxim Pinkovskiy have recently shown, prospects are improving.

Since 1995, poverty rates in Africa have been falling steadily. Indeed, if this trend continues, the rate of poverty could meet ambitious goals set by the United Nations for poverty reduction by 2015. Economic growth in Africa has not come at the expense of the poor. The current income distribution in Africa is less unequal than it was in 1995, indicating that the growth of income has been shared across the population. The decline in poverty has been widespread across the continent. It has fallen in landlocked as well as coastal countries, mineral-rich and mineral-poor countries, and in countries with varying degrees of agriculture.

Their results even apply to countries that were particularly disadvantaged by slavery. The message of these economists is optimistic: Even countries hindered by geography or history can still reduce poverty through economic growth.[1]

APPLYING THE CONCEPTS

1 How may global warming affect economic growth?
Global Warming, Rich Countries, and Poor Countries

2 Does economic growth necessarily cause more inequality?
Growth Need Not Cause Increased Inequality

3 How can we use economic analysis to understand the sources of growth in different countries?
Sources of Growth in China and India

4 How much did the information revolution contribute to U.S. productivity growth?
Growth Accounting and Information Technology

5 How do varying political institutions affect economic growth?
The Role of Political Factors in Economic Growth

6 Did culture or evolution spark the Industrial Revolution?
Culture, Evolution, and Economic Growth

7 Why are clear property rights important for economic growth in developing countries?
Lack of Property Rights Hinders Growth in Peru

Our living standards are dramatically different today because of the remarkable growth in GDP per person. Growth in GDP is perhaps the most critical aspect of a country's economic performance. Over long periods, it is the only way to raise the standard of living in an economy.

This chapter begins by looking at some data from both rich and poor countries over the last several decades. We will see how GDP per capita (meaning per person—every man, woman, and child) compares over this period. We'll then look at how growth occurs. Economists believe two basic mechanisms increase GDP per capita over the long term. One is **capital deepening**, or increases in an economy's stock of capital (such as buildings and equipment) relative to its workforce. **Technological progress** is the other; to economists this means an economy operates more efficiently, producing more output, but without using any more inputs such as capital or labor. We'll examine different theories of the origins of technological progress and discuss how to measure its overall importance for the economy. We'll also discuss in detail the role of education, experience, and investments in human beings, which are called **human capital**.

The appendix to this chapter contains a simple model of capital deepening known as the Solow model. It shows how increases in capital per worker lead to economic growth. The model will also allow us to better understand the role of technological progress in sustaining economic growth.

capital deepening

Increases in the stock of capital per worker.

technological progress

More efficient ways of organizing economic affairs that allow an economy to increase output without increasing inputs.

human capital

The knowledge and skills acquired by a worker through education and experience and used to produce goods and services.

8.1   ECONOMIC GROWTH RATES

Throughout the world there are vast differences in standards of living and in rates of economic growth. To understand these differences, we first need to look at the concepts and the tools economists use to study economic growth.

But before we learn how to measure growth, let's take a broad overview of what we mean by *economic growth*. We can understand economic growth by using one of the tools we developed in Chapter 2: the production possibilities curve. The production possibilities curve shows the set of feasible production options for an economy at a given point of time. In Figure 8.1 we show an economy's trade-off when it comes to producing consumer goods versus military goods. As the economy grows, the entire production possibilities curve shifts outward. This means the economy can produce

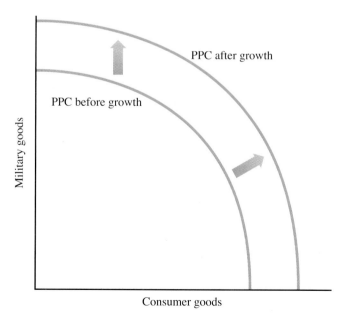

▲ **FIGURE 8.1**

What Is Economic Growth?

Economic growth means an expanded production possibilities curve (PPC).

more of both goods—that is what we mean by economic growth. Growth also expands the amount of goods available for people to consume. Just think about your own family. A typical family 40 years ago had only one car, whereas today many families have two or three. As our chapter-opening story highlights, the economic growth we take for granted is recent and does not apply evenly across all societies.

Measuring Economic Growth

From earlier chapters we know that real gross domestic product (GDP) measures in constant prices the total value of final goods and services in a country. Because countries differ in the size of their populations, we want to know a country's real GDP per person, or its **real GDP per capita**.

real GDP per capita

Gross domestic product per person adjusted for changes in prices. It is the usual measure of living standards across time and among countries.

Real GDP per capita typically grows over time. A convenient way to describe the changes in real GDP per capita is with growth rates. The **growth rate** of a variable is the percentage change in that variable from one period to another. For example, to calculate the growth rate of real GDP from year 1 to year 2, suppose real GDP was 100 in year 1 and 104 in year 2. In this case, the growth rate of real GDP is

growth rate

The percentage rate of change of a variable from one period to another.

$$\text{growth rate} = \frac{(\text{GDP in year 2} - \text{GDP in year 1})}{(\text{GDP in year 1})}$$

$$= \frac{(104 - 100)}{100}$$

$$= \frac{4}{100}$$

$$= 4\% \text{ per year}$$

In other words, real GDP grew by 4 percent from year 1 to year 2. This also means that GDP in year 2 was $(1 + 0.04)$ times GDP in the year 1.

Economies can grow at different rates from one year to the next. But it often is useful to consider what happens when an economy grows at a constant rate, say g, for a number of years. Let's start simply. Suppose real GDP for an economy was 100 and the economy grew at a rate g for two years. How large would the real GDP be two years later? After one year, GDP would be $(1+g)$ 100. In the second year, it would grow by $(1+g)$ again, or

$$\text{GDP [2 years later]} = (1 + g)^2 (100)$$

We can generalize this to consider the case where the economy grows a constant rate g for n years. How large would GDP be after n years? A simple formula gives the answer:

$$\text{GDP [n years later]} = (1 + g)^n (100)$$

Example: If the economy starts at 100 and grows at a rate of 4 percent a year for 10 years, output (after 10 years) will be

$$\text{GDP [10 year later]} = (1 + 0.04)^{10} (100) = (1.48)(100) = 148$$

which is nearly 50 percent higher than in the first year.

Here's a rule of thumb to help you understand the power of growth rates. Suppose you know the growth rate of real GDP, and it is constant, but you want to know how many years it will take until the level of real GDP doubles. The answer is given by the **rule of 70**:

rule of 70

A rule of thumb that says output will double in 70/x years, where x is the percentage rate of growth.

$$\text{years to double} = \frac{70}{(\text{percentage growth rate})}$$

Example: For an economy that grew at 5 percent a year, it would take

$$\frac{70}{5} = 14 \text{ years}$$

for real GDP to double. (In case you are curious, the rule of 70 is derived by using the mathematics of logarithms.)

Comparing the Growth Rates of Various Countries

Making comparisons of real GDP or GNP across countries is difficult. Not only do countries have their own currencies, but patterns of consumption and prices can differ sharply among countries. Two examples can illustrate this point. First, because land is scarce in Japan, people live in smaller spaces than do residents of the United States, so the price of housing is higher (relative to other goods) than in the United States. Second, developing countries (such as India or Pakistan) have very different price structures than developed countries. In particular, in developing countries goods that are not traded—such as household services or land—are relatively cheaper than goods that are traded in world markets. In other words, while all residents of the world may pay the same price for gold jewelry, hiring a cook or household helper is considerably less expensive in India or Pakistan than in the United States.

It is important to take these differences into account. Fortunately, a team of economists led by Robert Summers and Alan Heston of the University of Pennsylvania has devoted decades to developing methods for measuring real GNP across countries. The team's procedures are based on gathering extensive data on prices of comparable goods in each country and making adjustments for differences in relative prices and consumption patterns. These methods are now used by the World Bank and the International Monetary Fund, two prominent international organizations.

According to these methods, the country with the highest level of income in 2008 was Luxembourg; its real income per capita was $64,320. Norway, with its oil wealth, was at $58,500 while the United States was at $46,970.

Table 8.1 lists real Gross National Income (GNI) per capita for 2004 and the average annual growth rate of GNI per capita between 1960 and 2008 for 11 countries. (Gross National Income is most commonly used in international comparisons, while 2008 is the most recent year for which fully consistent data back to 1960 is available.) The United Kingdom, with a GNI per capita of $36,130, follows the United States. Not far behind are Japan, France, and Italy. More representative of typical

TABLE 8.1 GROSS NATIONAL INCOME PER CAPITA AND ECONOMIC GROWTH

Country	Gross National Income Per Capita in 2008 Dollars	Per Capita Growth Rate 1960–2008
United States	$46,970	2.38%
United Kingdom	36,130	2.54
Japan	35,220	4.09
France	34,400	2.91
Italy	30,250	2.92
Mexico	14,270	2.95
Costa Rica	10,950	2.35
India	2,960	2.05
Pakistan	2,770	1.53
Nigeria	1,940	1.11
Zambia	1,230	–0.60

SOURCES: *World Bank Development Indicators* (2010) and Alan Heston, Robert Summers, and Bettina Aten, *Penn World Table* Version 6.3, Center for International Comparisons at the University of Pennsylvania (CICUP), October 2010.

APPLICATION 1

GLOBAL WARMING, RICH COUNTRIES, AND POOR COUNTRIES

APPLYING THE CONCEPTS #1: How may global warming affect economic growth?

Many people believe that global warming will hurt economic development, but research shows that the effects are more complex. Recent research by economists Melissa Dell, Benjamin Jones, and Benjamin Olken provides some useful insights. First, the effects of increases in temperature seem to be confined to poor countries. Rich countries do not suffer from increases in temperature. In a study of municipalities within Latin and South America, the economists found that a one-degree Celsius rise in temperature was associated with between a 1.2 and 1.9 percentage decline in municipal per capita income. Over time, as economies adapt to higher temperatures approximately half of this effect disappears. Second, some of the adverse effects from higher temperatures seem to work through international trade. A one-degree Celsius increase in temperatures reduces poor countries' exports between 2.0 and 5.7 percentage points. The effect appears to be concentrated within the agricultural and light manufacturing goods sectors.

The fact that poor countries are affected but not rich countries suggests that the timing of global warming may matter. If global warming can be deferred sufficiently far into the future, poorer countries will have opportunities to develop and perhaps be less subject to global warming trends. However, if global warming occurs relatively soon, then poor countries are likely to be adversely affected.   **Related to Exercise 1.9.**

SOURCES: Based on Melissa Dell, Benjamin Jones, and Benjamin Olken, "Temperature and Income: Reconciling Cross-Sectional and Panel Estimates," *American Economic Review Papers & Proceedings* (May 2009): 199–204 and Benjamin Jones and Benjamin Olken, "Climate Shocks and Exports," forthcoming *American Economic Review Papers & Proceedings* (May 2010).

---

countries are Mexico and Costa Rica, with GNIs per capita in 2008 of $14,270 and $10,950, respectively. Costa Rica's GNI per capita is less than 25 percent of per capita GNI in the United States. Very poor countries have extremely low GNI per capita. Pakistan, for example, had a GNI per capita of $2,770—less than 6 percent of the GNI per capita of the United States.

In the third column of Table 8.1, notice the differences in growth rates. Consider Japan. In 1960, Japan had a GNI per capita that was only one-half that of France and one-fourth that of the United States. But notice from the third column that Japan's GNI per capita grew on average 4.09 percent per year during the period, compared to 2.38 percent for the United States and 2.91 percent for France. To place Japan's growth rate for this period into perspective, recall the rule of 70. If an economy grows at an average annual rate of x percent a year, it takes $70/x$ years for output to double. In Japan's case, per capita output was doubling every $70/4.09$ years, or approximately every 17 years. At this rate, from the time someone was born to the time he or she reached the age of 34, living standards would have increased by a factor of four—an extraordinary rate of growth. The rule of 70 reinforces the importance of small differences in economic growth rates. A per capita GDP growth rate of 5 percent per year means that the living standard doubles in 14 years. With only 1 percent growth, doubling would take 70 years.

The differences in per capita incomes between the developed and developing countries are very large and are also reflected in many different aspects of society. Take, for example, child labor. In the developed world, we disapprove of child labor and wonder how we can work toward its elimination. The answer is relatively simple—more economic growth has been shown to lead to less child labor.

Are Poor Countries Catching Up?

One question economists ask is whether poorer countries can close the gap between their level of GDP per capita and the GDP per capita of richer countries. Closing this gap is called **convergence**. To converge, poorer countries have to grow at more rapid rates than richer countries. Since 1960, Japan, Italy, and France all have grown more rapidly than the United States and have narrowed the gap in per capita incomes.

Let's look at some evidence provided by two distinguished international economists, Maurice Obstfeld of the University of California, Berkeley, and Kenneth Rogoff of Harvard University. Figure 8.2 plots the average growth rate for 16 currently developed countries from 1870 to 1979 against the level of per capita income in 1870. Each point represents a different country. Notice that the countries with the lowest initial per capita incomes are plotted higher on the graph. That is, they had higher growth rates than the countries with more income per capita. The downward-sloping line plotted through the points indicates that the countries with higher levels of per capita income in 1870 grew more slowly than countries with lower levels. In other words, the tendency was for countries with lower levels of initial income to grow faster and catch up. The graph shows that among the currently developed countries—for example, the United States, France, and the United Kingdom—there was a tendency for convergence over the last century.

Now let's compare the countries that are currently less developed to the advanced industrial countries using the data in Table 8.1. Here, the picture is not so clear in recent times. While India grew at a faster rate than the United States, Pakistan grew only 1.53 percent per year and fell farther behind advanced economies. In Africa, Zambian GNI per capita grew less than 1 percent. In general, economists who have studied the process of economic growth in detail find weak evidence that poorer countries are currently closing the gap in per capita income with richer countries.

Indeed, in the last 20 years there has been little convergence. Economist Stanley Fischer, governor of the Bank of Israel and formerly with the IMF and the Massachusetts Institute of Technology, found that, on average, countries with higher GDP per capita in 1980 grew slightly faster from 1980 to 2000 than countries with lower GDP per capita.[2] African countries, which were among the poorest, grew most slowly. However, there were some important exceptions: The two most populous countries, China and India, grew very rapidly. Because these countries contain approximately

convergence

The process by which poorer countries close the gap with richer countries in terms of real GDP per capita.

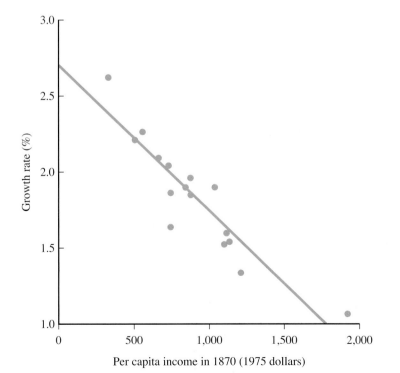

◀ **FIGURE 8.2**
Growth Rates versus Per Capita Income, 1870–1979
Each point on the graph represents a different currently developed country. Notice that the countries with the lowest per capita incomes in 1870 (shown along the horizontal axis) are plotted higher on the graph. In other words, the tendency was for countries with lower levels of initial income to grow faster.
SOURCE: M. Obstfeld and K. Rogoff, Foundations of International Macroeconomics (Cambridge, MA: MIT Press, 1996), Table 7.1.

APPLICATION 2

GROWTH NEED NOT CAUSE INCREASED INEQUALITY

APPLYING THE CONCEPTS #2: Does economic growth necessarily cause more inequality?

For many years, following the work of Nobel Laureate Simon Kuznets, economists believed that as a country developed, inequality within it followed an inverted "U" pattern—it initially increased and then narrowed over time. However, recent research by economists Emmanuel Saez of Harvard and Thomas Piketty, a French economist, challenges the assumption that this phenomenon is solely the result of growth.

Piketty and Saez looked carefully at data in the United States over the twentieth century. Inequality—as measured by the income share of the top 10 percent of families—increased from 40 percent at the beginning of the 1920s to 45 percent through the end of the Great Depression, consistent with Kuznets's theory. But things changed during World War II. During that time, the share fell to 32 percent by 1944 and remained at that level until the early 1970s, at which time inequality began to again increase.

Piketty and Saez suggest that wage and price controls during World War II reduced differentials in wages and salaries and thereby reduced inequality. Moreover, even after the war these patterns persisted until the 1970s, because society perceived them to be fair. After the 1970s, salaries at the top of the income distribution increased sharply. (Think of the vast sums paid to some major league baseball players or corporate executives.) These findings, as well as related results from other countries, suggest that inequality does not naturally accompany economic development. Social norms and other factors, such as perceived fairness of compensation and the nature of the tax system, also play a role in generating inequality. Moreover, the U.S. experience suggests these norms can change over time, even within the same country, regardless of growth rates. **Related to Exercise 1.10.**

SOURCE: Based on Thomas Piketty and Emmanuel Saez, "Income Inequality in the United States, 1913–1998," *Quarterly Journal of Economics* 118, no. 1 (2003): 1–39.

---

35 percent of the world's population, the good news is that living conditions for many people around the globe have therefore improved substantially in the last 20 years.

Other commentators are less sanguine. Professor Brad DeLong at UC Berkeley wrote, "Those nations and economies that were relatively rich at the start of the twentieth century have by and large seen their material wealth and prosperity explode. Those nations and economies that were relatively poor have grown richer, but for the most part slowly. And the relative gulf between rich and poor economies has grown steadily. Today this relative gulf is larger than at any time in humanity's previous experience, or at least larger than at any time since there were some tribes that had discovered how to use fire and other tribes that had not."[3]

What about the distribution of income *within* countries as they develop? Many economists thought that as countries developed, inequality would increase among their populations. But recent research challenges this finding.

8.2 CAPITAL DEEPENING

One of the most important mechanisms of economic growth economists have identified is increases in the amount of capital per worker due to capital deepening.

In Chapter 7, we studied the effects of an increase in capital in a full-employment economy. Figure 8.3 shows the effects on output and real wages. For simplicity, we assume the supply of labor is not affected by real wages and therefore draw a vertical line (see Panel B). In Panel A, an increase in capital shifts the production function upward because more output can be produced from the same amount of labor. In

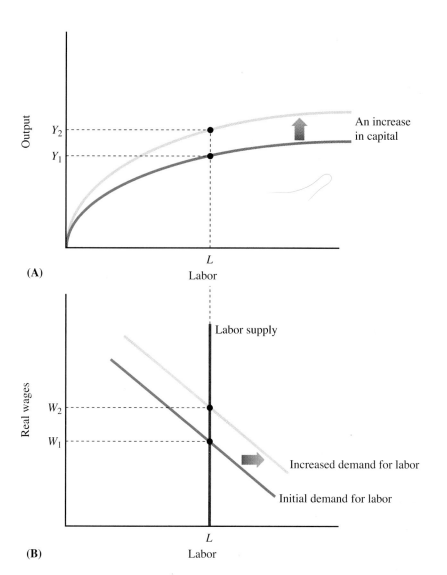

◀ FIGURE 8.3
Increase in the Supply of Capital
An increase in the supply of capital will shift the production function upward, as shown in Panel A, and increase the demand for labor, as shown in Panel B. Real wages will increase from W_1 to W_2, and potential output will increase from Y_1 to Y_2.

addition, firms increase their demand for labor because the marginal benefit from employing labor will increase. Panel B shows how the increase in capital raises the demand for labor and increases real wages. That is, as firms increase their demand and compete for a fixed supply of labor, they will bid up real wages in the economy.

An economy is better off with an increase in the stock of capital. With additions to the stock of capital, workers will enjoy higher wages, and total GDP in the economy will increase. Workers are more productive because each worker has more capital at his or her disposal. But how does an economy increase its stock of capital per worker? The answer is with saving and investment, which we'll discuss next.

Saving and Investment

Let's begin with the simplest case: an economy with a constant population, producing at full employment. This particular economy has no government or foreign sector. Its output can be purchased only by consumers or by firms. In other words, output consists solely of consumption (C) and investment (I). At the same time, output generates an amount of income equivalent to the amount of output. That is, output (Y) equals income. Any income that is not consumed we call **saving**.

In this economy, saving must equal investment. Here's why: By definition, consumption plus saving equals income:

$$C + S = Y$$

saving

Income that is not consumed.

but at the same time income—which is equivalent to output—also equals consumption plus investment:

$$C + I = Y$$

Thus, saving must equal investment:

$$S = I$$

This means that whatever consumers decide to save goes directly into investment. Here is a simple way to remember this idea: A farmer produces corn (Y) and can either consume it directly (C) or set it aside as "seed corn" (I) for next year. The part the farmer sets aside and does not consume is also the farmer's saving (S).

Next, we need to link the level of investment in the economy to the stock of capital in the economy. The stock of capital depends on two factors: investment and depreciation. The stock of capital increases with any gross investment spending but decreases with depreciation. Why does depreciation decrease the stock of capital? The answer is simple: As capital stock items such as buildings and equipment get older (depreciate), they wear out and become less productive. New investment is needed to replace the buildings and equipment that become obsolete.

Suppose, for example, the stock of capital at the beginning of the year is $10,000. During the year, if there were $1,000 in gross investment and $400 in depreciation, the capital stock at the end of the year would be $10,600 (= $10,000 + $1000 − $400).

It may be helpful to picture a bathtub. The level of water in the bathtub (the stock of capital) depends on the flow of water into the bathtub through the input faucet (gross investment) minus the flow of water out of the bathtub down the drain (depreciation). As long as the flow in exceeds the flow out, the water level in the bathtub (the stock of capital) will increase.

Higher saving, which leads to higher gross investment, will therefore tend to increase the stock of capital available for production. As the stock of capital grows, however, there typically will be more depreciation, because there is more capital (building and equipment) to depreciate. It is the difference between gross investment and depreciation—*net investment*—that ultimately determines the change in the stock of capital for the economy, the level of real wages, and output. In our example, net investment is $1,000 − $400 = $600.

How Do Population Growth, Government, and Trade Affect Capital Deepening?

So far, we've considered the simplest economy. Let's consider a more realistic economy that includes population growth, a government, and trade.

First, consider the effects of population growth: A larger labor force will allow the economy to produce more total output. However, with a fixed amount of capital and an increasing labor force, the amount of capital per worker will be less. With less capital per worker, output per worker will also be less, because each worker has fewer machines to use. This is an illustration of the principle of diminishing returns.

PRINCIPLE OF DIMINISHING RETURNS

Suppose that output is produced with two or more inputs and that we increase one input while holding the other inputs fixed. Beyond some point—called the *point of diminishing returns*—output will increase at a decreasing rate.

Consider India, the world's second most populous country, with over a billion people. Although India has a large labor force, its amount of capital per worker is low. With sharp diminishing returns to labor, per capita output in India is low, only $2,960 per person.

The government can affect the process of capital deepening in several ways through its policies of spending and taxation. Suppose the government taxed its citizens so that it could fight a war, pay its legislators higher salaries, or give foreign aid to needy countries—in other words, to engage in government consumption spending. The higher taxes will reduce total income. If consumers save a fixed fraction of their income, total private savings (savings from the nongovernmental sector) will fall. This taxation drains the private sector of savings that would have been used for capital deepening.

Now suppose the government took all the extra tax revenues and invested them in valuable infrastructure, such as roads, buildings, and airports. These infrastructure investments add to the capital stock. We illustrate this idea in Figure 8.4. If consumers were saving 20 percent of their incomes and the government collected $100 in taxes from each taxpayer, private saving and investment would fall by $20 per taxpayer, but government investment in the infrastructure would increase by a full $100 per taxpayer. In other words, the government "forces" consumers (by taxing them) to invest an additional $80 in infrastructure that they otherwise wouldn't invest. The net result is an increase in total social investment (private plus government) of $80 per taxpayer.

Finally, the foreign sector can affect capital deepening. The United States, Canada, and Australia built their vast railroad systems in the nineteenth century by running *trade deficits*—selling fewer goods and services to the rest of the world than they were buying—and financing this gap by borrowing. This enabled them to purchase the large amount of capital needed to build their rail networks and grow at more rapid rates by deepening capital. Eventually, these economies had to pay back the funds they had borrowed from abroad by running *trade surpluses*—selling more goods and services to the rest of the world than they were buying from abroad. But because economic growth had increased their GDP and wealth, the three countries were able to afford to pay back the borrowed funds. Therefore, this approach to financing deepening capital was a reasonable strategy for them to pursue.

Not all trade deficits promote capital deepening, however. Suppose a country runs a trade deficit because it wants to buy more consumer goods. The country would be borrowing from abroad, but there would be no additional capital deepening—just additional consumption spending. When the country is forced to pay back the funds, there will be no additional GDP to help foot the bill. In order to fund current consumption, the country will be poorer in the future.

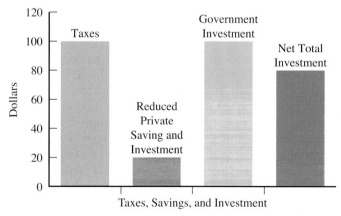

▲ FIGURE 8.4

Taxes and Government Investment

If the government raises taxes by $100 and the people tend to save 20 percent of changes in income, then private savings and investment will fall by $20. However, if the government invests the funds, total investment—private and public—will increase by $80.

8.3 THE KEY ROLE OF TECHNOLOGICAL PROGRESS

The other mechanism affecting economic growth is technological progress. Economists use the term *technological progress* in a very specific way: It means an economy operates more efficiently by producing more output without using any more inputs.

In practice, technological progress can take many forms. The invention of the lightbulb made it possible to read and work indoors at night, the invention of the thermometer assisted doctors and nurses in their diagnoses, and the invention of disposable diapers made life easier at home. All these examples—and you could provide many more—enable society to produce more output without more labor or more capital. With higher output per person, we enjoy a higher standard of living.

We can think of technological progress as the birth of new ideas. These new ideas enable us to rearrange our economic affairs and become more productive. Not all technological innovations are necessarily major scientific breakthroughs; some are much more basic. An employee of a soft-drink company who discovers a new and popular flavor for a soft drink is engaged in technological progress, just like scientists and engineers. Even simple, commonsense ideas from workers or managers can help a business use its capital and labor more efficiently to deliver a better product to consumers at a lower price. For example, a store manager may decide that rearranging the layout of merchandise and location of cash registers helps customers find products and pay for them more quickly and easily. This change is also technological progress. As long as there are new ideas, inventions, and new ways of doing things, the economy can become more productive and per capita output can increase.

How Do We Measure Technological Progress?

If someone asked you how much of the increase in your standard of living was due to technological progress, how would you answer? Robert Solow, a Nobel Laureate in economics from the Massachusetts Institute of Technology, developed a method for measuring technological progress in an economy. Like most good ideas, his theory was simple. It was based on the idea of a production function.

You know from Chapter 7 that the production function links inputs to outputs:

$$Y = F(K,L)$$

where output (Y) is produced from capital (K) and labor (L), which are linked through the production function (F). What Solow did was include in the production function some measure of technological progress, A:

$$Y = F(K,L,A)$$

Increases in A represent technological progress. Higher values of A mean that more output is produced from the same level of inputs K and L. If we could find some way to measure A, we could estimate how much technological progress affects output.

Solow noted that over any period we can observe increases in capital, labor and output. Using these we can measure technological progress indirectly. We first ask how much of the change in output can be explained by contributions from increases in the amount of capital and labor used. Whatever growth we cannot explain in this way must therefore be caused by technological progress. The method Solow developed to measure the contributions to economic growth from capital, labor, and technological progress is called **growth accounting**.

Figure 8.5 illustrates the relative contributions of these growth sources for the U.S. economy from 1929 to 1982 using growth accounting, based on a classic study by the economist Edward Denison. During this period, total output grew at a rate of nearly 3 percent. Because capital and labor growth are measured at 0.56 and 1.34 percent per year, respectively, the remaining portion of output growth, 1.02 percent per

growth accounting

A method to determine the contribution to economic growth from increased capital, labor, and technological progress.

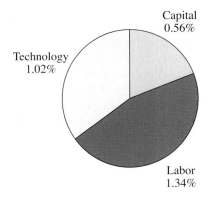

Technology
1.02%
Capital
0.56%
Labor
1.34%

◄ FIGURE 8.5
Contributions to Real GDP Growth, 1929–1982 (average annual percentage rates)
SOURCE: Edward F. Denison, Trends in American Economic Growth 1929–1982 *(Washington, D.C.: The Brookings Institution, 1985).*

year, must be due to technological progress. That means approximately 35 percent of output growth came directly from technological progress.

Other recent estimates give a similar picture of the contribution of technological progress to economic growth. For example, the Bureau of Labor Statistics estimates that between 1987 and 2007 technological progress accounted for 1.0 percentage points of economic growth in the private nonfarm business sector, very similar to Denison's estimates.

APPLICATION 3

SOURCES OF GROWTH IN CHINA AND INDIA

APPLYING THE CONCEPTS #3: How can we use economic analysis to understand the sources of growth in different countries?

China and India are the two most populous countries in the world and have also grown very rapidly in recent years. From 1978 to 2004, GDP in China grew at the astounding rate of 9.3 percent per year while India's GDP grew at a lower but still robust rate of 5.4 percent per year. What were the sources of this growth? Economists Barry Bosworth from the Brookings Institution and Susan Collins from the University of Michigan used growth accounting to answer this question.

Employment in China and India both grew at 2 percent per year over the period, so the remaining differences must be attributed to capital deepening and technological progress. Bosworth and Collins in turn broke capital deepening into two parts: increases in physical capital (buildings, machines, and equipment) and increases in human capital (the knowledge of workers, as measured by their educational attainment). Their analysis revealed that China's more rapid growth was primarily caused by more rapid accumulation of physical capital and more rapid technological progress. The contributions from human capital for each country were similar. Why did China grow faster than India over this 26-year period? Simply put, China invested much more than India in physical capital and was able to increase its technological progress at a more rapid rate.

Looking ahead, Bosworth and Collins find no evidence that growth in China and India is slowing. Capital formation and technological progress is still rapid in both countries and India has even improved its rate of technological advance in recent years. Despite this rapid growth and pockets of wealth in major cities, both countries are still poor: Chinese GNP per capita is only 15 percent and India's GDP is only 8 percent of U.S. GNP per capita. But at these growth rates, the gap will diminish in the coming decades.   **Related to Exercises 3.3 and 3.6.**

SOURCE: Based on Barry Bosworth and Susan M. Collins, "Accounting for Growth: Comparing China and India," *Journal of Economic Perspectives* (Winter 2008): 45–66.

Using Growth Accounting

Growth accounting is a useful tool for understanding different aspects of economic growth. As an example, economic growth slowed throughout the entire world during the 1970s. Using growth accounting methods, economists typically found the slowdown could not be attributed to changes in the quality or quantity of labor inputs or to capital deepening. Either a slowdown in technological progress or other factors not directly included in the analysis, such as higher worldwide energy prices, must have been responsible. This led economists to suspect that higher energy prices were the primary explanation for the reduction in economic growth.

APPLICATION 4

GROWTH ACCOUNTING AND INFORMATION TECHNOLOGY

APPLYING THE CONCEPTS #4: How much did the information revolution contribute to U.S. productivity growth?

In analyses of the sources of economic growth, a common statistic reported about the U.S. economy is **labor productivity**. Defined as output per hour of work, labor productivity is a simple measure of how much a typical worker can produce given the amount of capital in the economy and the state of technological progress. From 1973 to 1993, the growth of labor productivity slowed in the United States. Figure 8.6 shows U.S. productivity growth for different periods since 1959.

The figure shows that productivity growth was extremely high during the 1960s. It slowed a bit in the late 1960s, and then slowed dramatically after the oil shocks in the 1970s. In recent years, productivity growth has increased, reaching 2.5 percent from 1994 to 2007.

As the figure shows, U.S. productivity growth did climb in the last half of the 1990s. Some observers believe the computer and Internet revolution are responsible for the increase in productivity growth. Skeptics wonder, however, whether this increase in productivity growth is truly permanent or just temporary. Higher investment in computer technology began in the mid-1980s, but until recently there was little sign of increased productivity growth. Had the investment in information technology finally paid off? And would it continue?

Robert J. Gordon of Northwestern University used growth accounting methods to shed light on this issue. After making adjustments for the low unemployment rate and high GDP growth rate in the late 1990s, he found there *had* been increases in technological progress. In earlier work, Gordon had found these increases were largely confined to the durable goods manufacturing industry, including the production of computers themselves. Because the increase in technological progress was confined to a relatively small portion of the economy, Gordon was originally skeptical that we were

labor productivity
Output produced per hour of work.

▶ FIGURE 8.6

U.S. Annual Productivity Growth, 1959–2007

In recent years, there has been a resurgence of productivity growth in part caused by the information technology revolution.

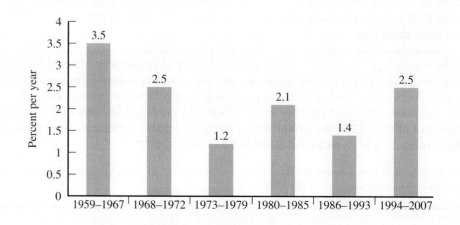

now operating in a "new economy" with permanently higher productivity growth. However, in subsequent studies he found that productivity growth had spread to other sectors of the economy, such as retail sales and financial institutions.

But will this contribution from information technology to labor productivity growth last? Professor Dale Jorgenson of Harvard University and his co-authors looked carefully at the contributions of information technology to labor productivity in recent years. They examined the effects of information technology on labor productivity growth, both through increased investment or capital deepening in that sector and also through its impact on technological progress. They found that from 2000 to 2006, labor productivity had continued to grow at rates like those in the late 1990s, but the contribution the information technology sector made to this growth had decreased. This naturally raises questions as to whether productivity growth will continue to be robust in future decades.   **Related to Exercises 3.7 and 3.8.**

SOURCES: Based on Robert J. Gordon, "Exploding Productivity Growth: Contexts, Causes, Implications," *Brookings Papers on Economic Activity* 2 (2003): 207–298 and Dale W. Jorgenson et. al., "A Retrospective Look at the U.S. Productivity Growth Resurgence," *Journal of Economic Perspectives* (Winter 2008): 3–24.

Review the two other applications of how economists use growth accounting. The first compares growth in China and India, the second explores how the Internet and information technology have affected U.S. GDP.

8.4   WHAT CAUSES TECHNOLOGICAL PROGRESS?

Because technological progress is an important source of growth, we want to know how it occurs and what government policies can do to promote it. Economists have identified a variety of factors that may influence the pace of technological progress in an economy.

Research and Development Funding

One way for a country to induce more technological progress in its economy is to pay for it. If the government or large firms employ workers and scientists to advance the frontiers of knowledge in basic sciences, their work can lead to technological progress in the long run. Figure 8.7 presents data on the spending on research and development as a percent of GDP for seven major countries for 1999. The United States has the highest number of scientists and engineers in the world. However, although it spends the most money overall, as a percent of GDP the United States

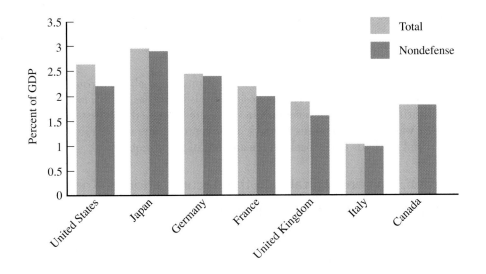

◄ FIGURE 8.7
Research and Development as a Percent of GDP, 1999
The United States spends more total money than any other country on research and development. However, when the spending is measured as a percentage of each nation's GDP, Japan spends more. A big part of U.S. spending on research and development is in defense-related areas.
SOURCE: National Science Foundation, National Patterns of R&D Resources, 2002, Washington D.C.

spends less than Japan. Moreover, a big part of U.S. spending on research and development is in defense-related areas, unlike in Japan. Some economists believe defense-related research and development is less likely to lead to long-run technological change than nondefense spending; however, many important technological developments, including the Internet, partly resulted from military-sponsored research and development.

Monopolies That Spur Innovation

The radical notion that monopolies spur innovation was put forth by economist Joseph Schumpeter. In Schumpeter's view, a firm will try to innovate—that is, come up with new products and more efficient ways to produce existing products—only if it reaps a reward. The reward a firm seeks from its innovations is high profit, and it can obtain a high profit if it is the sole seller, or monopolist, for the product. Other firms will try to break the firm's monopoly through more innovation, a process Schumpeter called **creative destruction**. Schumpeter believed that by allowing firms to compete to become monopolies, society benefits from increased innovation.

Governments do allow temporary monopolies for new ideas by issuing patents. A *patent* allows the inventor of a product to have a monopoly until the term of the patent expires, which in the United States is now 20 years. With a patent, we tolerate some monopoly power (the power to raise prices that comes with limited competition) in the hope of spurring innovation.

An idea related to patents that is becoming increasingly important is the need to protect intellectual property rights. Information technology has made possible the free flow of products and ideas around the world. Publishers of both books and computer software face problems of unauthorized copying, particularly in some developing countries. While residents of those countries clearly benefit from inexpensively copied books or software, producers in the developed countries then face reduced incentives to enter the market. Even in the United States, pirated music and movies pose a threat to the viability of the entertainment industry. Large and profitable firms may continue to produce despite unauthorized copying, but other firms may be discouraged. The United States has put piracy and unauthorized reproduction among its top agenda items in recent trade talks with several countries.

The Scale of the Market

Adam Smith stressed that the size of a market was important for economic development. In larger markets, firms have more incentives to come up with new products and new methods of production. Just as Schumpeter suggested, the lure of profits guides the activities of firms, and larger markets provide firms the opportunity to make larger profits. This supplies another rationale for free trade. With free trade, markets are larger, and there is more incentive to engage in technological progress.

Induced Innovations

Some economists have emphasized that innovations come about through inventive activity designed specifically to reduce costs. This is known as *induced innovation*. For example, during the nineteenth century in the United States, the largest single cost in agriculture was wages. Ingenious farmers and inventors came up with many different machines and methods to cut back on the amount of labor required.

Education, Human Capital, and the Accumulation of Knowledge

Education can contribute to economic growth in two ways. First, the increased knowledge and skills of people complement our current investments in physical capital. Second, education can enable the workforce in an economy to use its skills to develop new ideas or to copy ideas or import them from abroad. Consider a developing country

creative destruction
The view that a firm will try to come up with new products and more efficient ways to produce products to earn monopoly profits.

today. In principle, it has at its disposal the vast accumulated knowledge of the developed economies. But using this knowledge probably requires a skilled workforce—one reason why many developing countries send their best students to educational institutions in developed countries.

Increasing knowledge and skills are part of human capital—an investment in human beings. Human capital is as important, maybe even more important, than physical capital. Many economists, including Nobel Laureate Gary Becker of the University of Chicago, have studied human capital in detail.

A classic example of human capital is the investment a student makes to attend college. The costs of attending college consist of the direct out-of-pocket costs (tuition and fees) plus the opportunity costs of forgone earnings while at school. The benefits of attending college are the higher wages and more interesting jobs offered to college graduates compared to high-school graduates. Individuals decide to attend college when these benefits exceed the costs, and it is a rational economic decision. A similar calculation faces a newly graduated doctor who must decide whether to pursue a specialty. Will the forgone earnings of a general physician (which are quite substantial) be worth the time spent learning a specialty that will eventually result in extra income? We can analyze investments in health and nutrition within the same framework. The benefits of regular exercise and watching your weight are a healthier lifestyle and higher energy level.

Human capital theory has two implications for understanding economic growth. First, not all labor is equal. When economists measure the labor input in a country, they must adjust for differing levels of education. These levels of education reflect past investments in education and skills; individuals with higher educational levels will, on average, be more productive. Second, health and fitness also affect productivity. In developing countries, economists have found a strong correlation between the height of individuals (reflecting their health) and the wages they can earn in the farming sector.

APPLICATION 5

THE ROLE OF POLITICAL FACTORS IN ECONOMIC GROWTH

APPLYING THE CONCEPTS #5: How do varying political institutions affect economic growth?

Economist Daron Acemoglu of the Massachusetts Institute of Technology has written extensively about the role of political institutions and economic growth. Acemoglu distinguishes broadly between two types of political institutions: *authoritarian* institutions, such as monarchies, dictatorships, or tightly controlled oligarchies, and *participatory* institutions, such as constitutionally limited monarchies and democracies. History has witnessed growth under both types of regimes. At various points in time, China, Spain, Turkey and ancient Greece and Rome all exhibited technological innovation and economic growth.

But transformative economic growth, such as the world witnessed with the Industrial Revolution that began in western Europe in the late 1700s, typically requires more participatory institutions. The key reason is that sustained technological progress is disruptive and authoritarian regimes have difficulty coping with all the subsequent changes. Acemoglu highlights the fall in the old, authoritarian regimes in Europe and the rise of constitutional or limited monarchies that set the preconditions for the birth of the Industrial Revolution.

Acemoglu's theory does raise important questions for today. Can China, with its authoritarian political culture, continue to grow without eventual political transformation? If that does eventually come, can it be absorbed peacefully within the society?
Related to Exercise 4.6.

SOURCE: Based on Daron Acemoglu, epilogue to *Introduction to Modern Economic Growth* (University Press, 2009).

APPLICATION 6

CULTURE, EVOLUTION, AND ECONOMIC GROWTH

APPLYING THE CONCEPT #6: Did culture or evolution spark the Industrial Revolution?

In studying the economic history of England before the Industrial Revolution, Professor Gregory Clark discovered an interesting fact. Examining archival data on wills and estates, he found that children of the more affluent members of English society were more likely to survive than those of the less affluent. Coupled with the slow growth of population over several centuries, this differential survival of the wealthy had the effect of creating downward mobility for the rich, as their sons and daughters increasingly populated the society.

According to Professor Clark, this change had profound effects on English society. The cultural habits of the rich filtered through the entire society. Social virtues such as thrift, prudence, and hard work became more commonplace, while impulsive and violent behaviors were reduced. Eventually, these changes in culture became sufficiently pronounced that a qualitative change took place in society. Individuals now were able to take advantage of new developments in science and technology and embrace new technologies and social change.

Economists Oded Galor and Omer Moav suggest that development can be viewed in more traditional evolutionary terms. They argue that at some point during the human evolutionary process, families that had fewer children but invested more in them, gained a competitive advantage in the evolutionary cycle. The offspring of these families had more human capital and more easily adapted to technological progress and the other changes that were taking place in societies. Human genetic evolution, in their view, set the stage for the Industrial Revolution. Both views share some similarities. According to Clark, the evolution was primarily cultural, whereas for Galor and Moav it was genetic. In both cases, however, humans transformed themselves as the Industrial Revolution began.   **Related to Exercise 4.10.**

SOURCES: Based on Gregory Clark, *A Farewell to Alms* (Princeton: Princeton University Press, 2007) and Oded Galor and Omer Moav, "Natural Selection and the Origin of Economic Growth," *Quarterly Journal of Economics* (November 2002): 1133–1191.

Human capital theory can also serve as a basis for important public policy decisions. Should a developing country invest in capital (either public or private) or in education? The poorest developing countries lack good sanitation systems, effective transportation, and capital investment for agriculture and industry. However, the best use of investment funds may not be for bridges, sewer systems, and roads, but for human capital and education. Studies demonstrate that the returns from investing in education are extremely high in developing countries. The gains from elementary and secondary education, in particular, often exceed the gains from more conventional investments. In developing countries, an extra year in school can often raise individuals' wages by 15 to 20 percent a year.

New Growth Theory

For many years, economists who studied technological progress typically did so independently of economists who studied models of economic growth. But starting in the mid-1980s, several economists, including Nobel Laureate Robert E. Lucas of the University of Chicago and Paul Romer of Stanford University, began to develop models of growth that contained technological progress as essential features. Their work helped to initiate what is known as **new growth theory**, which accounts for technological progress within a model of economic growth.

In this field, economists study, for example, how incentives for research and development, new product development, or international trade interact with the accumulation of

new growth theory

Modern theories of growth that try to explain the origins of technological progress.

physical capital. New growth theory enables economists to address policy issues, such as whether subsidies for research and development are socially justified and whether policies that place fewer taxes on income earned from investment will spur economic growth or increase economic welfare. Current research in economic growth now takes place within a broad framework that includes explanations of technological progress. As an example, new growth theory suggests that investment in comprehensive education in a developing country will lead to permanent increases in the rate of technological progress as the workforce will be better able to incorporate new ideas and technologies into the workplace.

Some researchers also suggest the type of education might also matter for technological innovation. Phillipe Aghion of Harvard University and Peter Howitt of Brown University make the case that when a country is far behind the world's technological frontier, it is best for that country to invest in relatively basic education so that the workforce can essentially copy the changes that are occurring in the more advanced economies. But once an economy reaches the world's technological frontier, investment in the most advanced higher education might be most advantageous.[4]

New growth theory suggests that any social factor influencing the willingness of individuals to pursue technological advancement will be a key to understanding economic growth. Can cultural factors also play a role? The historical sociologist Max Weber argued that changes in religious beliefs could help us understand growth, as he emphasized how the rise of Protestantism, with its emphasis on the individual, set the stage for the Industrial Revolution in Europe. This thesis has always been controversial because the links between changes in religious beliefs and changes in economic or other behaviors are not well understood. More recently, Professor Gregory Clark has emphasized how the growth of middle-class values in England could possibly explain why the Industrial Revolution began there.

8.5   A KEY GOVERNMENTAL ROLE: PROVIDING THE CORRECT INCENTIVES AND PROPERTY RIGHTS

As we discussed in Chapter 3, governments play a critical role in a market economy. They must enforce the rules of the market economy, using police powers to ensure that contracts are upheld, individual property rights are enforced, and firms can enter safely into economic transactions. Although we may take these features of our economy for granted, not all countries enjoy the benefits of clear enforcement of property rights.

What is the connection between property rights and economic growth? Without clear property rights, there are no proper incentives to invest in the future—the essence of economic growth. Suppose, for example, that you lived on land that needed costly improvements in order to be made valuable. You might be willing to make the investment in these improvements if you were sure you would gain the economic benefits from making them. But suppose there was a risk someone else would reap the benefits—in that case, you would not have incentive to invest.

Clear property rights are, unfortunately, lacking in many developing countries throughout the world. As many economists have argued, their absence has severely impeded the growth of these economies.

Governments also have a broader role in designing the institutions in which individuals and firms work, save, and invest. Economists have increasingly recognized the importance of these institutions in determining economic growth. For example, the residents of Hong Kong link their rapid economic growth to free and open institutions that provide the right incentives for technological innovations. They wanted to preserve these institutions after they officially became part of China in 1997 and have indeed been successful in maintaining an open society.

But for many countries, growth has been more elusive. For many years, international organizations such as the World Bank—a consortium of countries created to promote development—have tried a variety of diverse methods to assist developing countries. These have included increases in foreign aid, infusions of new machinery, promotion of universal education, and efforts to stem population growth. Despite these efforts, some areas of the world, such as sub-Saharan Africa, have failed to grow at all.

William Easterly, a former World Bank economist, believes the World Bank and other international organizations have failed to take into account one of the basic laws of economics: Individuals and firms respond to incentives. According to Easterly, governments in developing countries have failed to provide the proper economic environment that would motivate individuals and firms to take actions that promote economic development.[5] As an example, providing free schooling is not enough—individuals need to know their investments in education will pay off in the future in terms of higher incomes or better jobs. Without the prospect that it will lead to an improvement in their lives, individuals will not make the effort to obtain an education.

What else can go wrong? Governments in developing countries often adopt policies that effectively tax exports, pursue policies that lead to rampant inflation, and enforce laws that inhibit the growth of the banking and financial sectors. The results are predictable: fewer exports, an uncertain financial environment, and reduced saving and investment. All these outcomes can cripple an economy's growth prospects. Sometimes they are based on bad economic advice. Other times, racial or ethnic groups in polarized societies use the economic system to take advantage of their rivals.

What can be done? In Easterly's view, the World Bank and other international organizations need to stop searching for the magic bullet for development. Instead, they should hold governments responsible for creating the proper economic environment. With the right incentives, Easterly believes individuals and firms in developing countries will take actions that promote economic growth.

APPLICATION 7

LACK OF PROPERTY RIGHTS HINDERS GROWTH IN PERU

APPLYING THE CONCEPTS #7: Why are clear property rights important for economic growth in developing countries?

On the hills surrounding Lima, Peru, and many other South American cities, large numbers of residents live in urban slums, many having taken over these lands through "urban invasions." Many families have resided in these dwellings for a long time, and most have basic water, sewage, and electricity. But what they don't have is clear titles to their properties.

Hernando DeSoto, a Peruvian economist and author of *The Mystery of Capital*, has studied the consequences of "informal ownership" in detail. He argues that throughout the developing world, property is often held without clear title. Without this evidence of ownership, people are not willing to make long-term investments to improve their lives. But there are other important consequences as well.

Economists recognize that strong credit systems—the ability to borrow and lend easily—are critical to the health of developing economies. But without clear title, people cannot use property as collateral (or security) for loans. As a consequence, the poor may in fact be living on very valuable land, but are unable to borrow against that land to start a new business. Also, the types of investments made will depend on the availability of credit. DeSoto observed that producing palm oil in Peru is very profitable, but it takes time and depends upon the ability to borrow funds. Production of coca paste—an ingredient of cocaine—does not take as much time and does not depend on finance. It is also a plague on the developed world. Switching farmers away from production of coca paste to palm oil requires improvements in finance, which are very difficult without clear property rights. **Related to Exercise 5.7.**

SOURCE: Based on Hernando DeSoto, *The Mystery of Capital: Why Capitalism Triumphs in the West and Fails Everywhere Else* (New York: Basic Books, 2000).

SUMMARY

In this chapter, we explored the mechanisms of economic growth. Although economists do not have a complete understanding of what leads to growth, they regard increases in capital per worker, technological progress, human capital, and governmental institutions as key factors. Here are the main points to remember:

1 *Per capita GDP* varies greatly throughout the world. There is debate about whether poorer countries in the world are converging in per capita incomes to richer countries.

2 Economies grow through two basic mechanisms: *capital deepening* and *technological progress*. Capital deepening is an increase in capital per worker. Technological progress is an increase in output with no additional increases in inputs.

3 Ongoing technological progress will lead to sustained economic growth.

4 Various theories try to explain the origins of technological progress and determine how we can promote it. They include spending on research and development, *creative destruction*, the scale of the market, induced inventions, and education and the accumulation of knowledge, including investments in human capital.

5 Governments can play a key role in designing institutions that promote economic growth, including providing secure property rights.

KEY TERMS

capital deepening, p. 159

convergence, p. 163

creative destruction, p. 172

growth accounting, p. 168

growth rate, p. 160

human capital, p. 159

labor productivity, p. 170

new growth theory, p. 174

real GDP per capita, p. 160

rule of 70, p. 160

saving, p. 165

technological progress, p. 159

EXERCISES

Visit www.myeconlab.com to complete these exercises online and get instant feedback.

8.1 Economic Growth Rates

1.1 To gauge living standards across countries with populations of different sizes, economists use _____ .

1.2 In poor countries, the relative prices for nontraded goods (such as household services) to traded goods (such as jewelry) are _____ than in rich countries.

1.3 Economists who have studied economic growth find strong evidence for convergence among European counties since 1890. _____ (True/False)

1.4 At a 2 percent annual growth rate in GDP per capita, it will take _____ years for GDP per capita to double.

1.5 **Future Generations.** Some economists say that economic growth involves a trade-off between current generations and future generations. If a current generation raises its saving rate, what does it sacrifice? What will be gained for future generations?

1.6 **Will the Poorer Country Catch Up?** Suppose one country has a GDP that is one-eighth the GDP of its richer neighbor. But the poorer country grows at 10 percent a year, while the richer country grows at 2 percent a year. In 35 years, which country will have a higher GDP? (*Hint:* Use the rule of 70.)

1.7 **Understanding Convergence in a Figure.** Suppose the line in Figure 8.2 was horizontal. What would that tell us about economic convergence?

1.8 **Growth in Per Capita GDP.** The growth rate of real GDP per capita equals the growth rate of real GDP minus the growth rate of the population. If the growth rate of the population is 1 percent per year, how fast must real GDP grow for real GDP per capita to double in 14 years?

1.9 **Economic Growth and Global Warning.** Basing your answer on the research reported in the text, is it likely that India is more vulnerable now to increases in temperatures than it will be in 20 years? (Related to Application 1 on page 162.)

1.10 **Economic Growth, World Markets for Entertainment, and Inequality.** With worldwide economic growth, markets are much larger, so movies and music have much larger audiences. Could this lead to increased inequality for entertainers? Discuss. (Related to Application 2 on page 164.)

1.11 **Comparing Economic Performance Using International GDP Data.** The Web site for the Penn World Tables (http://pwt.econ.upenn.edu) contains historical economic data. Using this link, compare the relative growth performance for real GDP per capita of France and Japan from 1950 to 2000. Do the data support the theory of convergence for these two countries?

8.2 Capital Deepening

2.1 In an economy with no government sector or foreign sector, saving must equal investment because

    a. total demand is equal to consumption and investment.

    b. total income is equal to consumption and saving.

    c. total income is equal to total demand.

    d. All of the above

    e. None of the above

2.2 If everything else is held equal, a decrease in the size of the population will _____ total output and _____ per capita output.

2.3 If the private sector saves 10 percent of its income and the government raises taxes by $200 to finance public investments, total investment—private and public investment—will increase by _____.

2.4 If a country runs a trade surplus to finance increased current consumption, it will have to reduce consumption in the future to pay back its borrowings. _____ (True/False)

2.5 **Policies That Promote Capital Deepening.** Which of the following will promote economic growth through capital deepening?

    a. Higher taxes used to finance universal health care

    b. Increased imports to purchase new DVD players for consumers

    c. Increased imports to purchase supercomputers for industry

2.6 **Diminishing Returns to Capital and Real Wages.** Explain why this statement is wrong: "Since capital is subject to diminishing returns, an increase in the supply of capital will reduce real wages."

2.7 **Government Spending, Taxes, and Investment.** Suppose a government places a 10 percent tax on incomes and spends half the money from taxes on investment and half on public consumption goods, such as military parades. Individuals save 20 percent of their income and consume the rest. Does total investment (public and private) increase or decrease in this case?

2.8 **Trade Deficits and Capital Deepening.** The United States ran large trade deficits during the 1980s and 1990s. What data would you want if you were to investigate whether these trade deficits led to increased or decreased capital deepening?

8.3 The Key Role of Technological Progress

3.1 Robert Solow added _____ to the conventional production function to account for technological change.

3.2 Once we account for changes in the labor force, _____ is the next biggest source of the growth of GDP in the United States.

3.3 China has a higher rate of technological progress than India. _____ (True/False) (Related to Application 3 on page 169.)

3.4 According to growth accounting studies, which of the following is a possible reason for the slowdown in growth in the 1970s?

    a. Reduced rates of capital deepening

    b. Changes in the quality or experience of the labor force

    c. A slowdown in technological progress or other factors

    d. All of the above are possible factors according to growth accounting studies.

3.5 **Technological Progress in Banking.** Computers have revolutionized banking for consumers through the growth of ATMs and electronic bill paying capabilities. Why might not all of these improvements for consumers be counted as technological progress?

3.6 **Foreign Investment and Technological Progress.** Many economists believe countries that open themselves to foreign investment of plant and equipment will benefit in terms of increased technological change because local companies will learn from the foreign companies. In the last several decades, China has been more open to foreign investment than India. Explain how this is consistent with the two countries' patterns of economic growth. (Related to Application 3 on page 169.)

3.7 **Technological Progress in Health Care.** The introduction of electronic health records is currently viewed as an important innovation in the delivery of health care. Explain how this innovation may increase the supply of capital or labor used in health-care delivery and provide additional benefits to the consumer. (Related to Application 4 on page 170.)

3.8 **Information Technology Spillovers and Economic Growth.** Why would it matter if the productivity gains associated with information technology spill over into other sectors of the economy besides information technology itself? Give a few examples of changes in information technology improving productivity in other sectors of the economy. (Related to Application 4 on page 170.)

3.9 **Health Insurance, Wages, and Compensation.** In recent years, total compensation of employees—including benefits—has grown, but wages, not including benefits, have not. Explain why this may have occurred, taking into account that many employers provide health insurance to their employees and health-care costs have grown more rapidly than GDP. Is health insurance "free" to employees?

8.4
8.4 What Causes Technological Progress?

4.1 Who developed the theory of scale of the market?
   a. Joseph Schumpeter
   b. Milton Friedman
   c. Adam Smith
   d. John Maynard Keynes

4.2 Investment in human capital includes purchases of computers used by professors. _____ (True/False)

4.3 Which of the following may influence technological progress?
   a. The scale of the market
   b. Monopolies
   c. Research and development spending
   d. All of the above

4.4 A policy of not enforcing patents or copyrights would _____ the incentive to be innovative.

4.5 **Cutting the Length of Patents.** Suppose a group of consumer activists claims drug companies earn excessive profits because of the patents they have on drugs. The activists advocate cutting the length of time that a drug company can hold a patent to five years. They argue that this will lead to lower prices for drugs because competitors will enter the market after the five-year period. Do you see any drawbacks to this proposal?

4.6 **Dictatorships and Economic Growth.** Discuss this quote: "With a strong economy, dictators could raise more money for armies and police to help keep themselves in power. Therefore, dictators should welcome rapid economic growth." (Related to Application 5 on page 173.)

4.7 **How Do We Measure Technological Progress?** If we cannot measure every invention or new idea, how can we possibly measure the contribution to growth of technological progress?

4.8 **Height and Weight during Rapid Industrialization.** Economic historians have found that the average height of individuals in both the United States and the United Kingdom fell during the mid-nineteenth century before rising again. This was a period of rapid industrialization as well as migration into urban areas. What factors do you think might account for this fall in height and how would it affect your evaluation of economic welfare during the period?

4.9 **Going to Medical School at the Age of 50.** While we might admire someone who decides to attend medical school at the age of 50, explain using human capital theory why this is so rare.

4.10 **Timing and Cultural Explanations of Economic Growth.** Some critics of cultural theories of economic growth note that some societies can suddenly start to grow very rapidly with no obvious accompanying cultural changes. How well does Professor Gregory Clark's theory fit the rapid growth in some East Asian economies in recent years? (Related to Application 6 on page 174.)

8.5 A Key Governmental Role: Providing the Correct Incentives and Property Rights

5.1 Clear property rights reduce growth in an economy because producers are not able to freely use innovations. _____ (True/False)

5.2 Which of the following methods has the World Bank *not* tried to assist developing countries?
   a. Increases in foreign aid
   b. Infusions of new machinery
   c. Promotion of universal education
   d. Promotion of population growth

5.3 The return from education in developing countries is often higher than in developed countries. _____ (True/False)

5.4 New growth theory suggests that consumption spending will lead to permanent increases in the rate of technological progress. _____ (True/False)

5.5 **Diversity and Economic Growth.** Some economists and political scientists have suggested that when communities are more racially or ethnically diverse, they invest less in education and spend more on private goods. Assuming this theory is true, what are the consequences for economic growth?

5.6 **The "Brain Drain" and Incentives for Education.** Some economists are concerned about the "brain drain," the phenomenon in which highly educated workers leave developing countries to work in developed countries. Other economists have argued that "brain drain" could create incentives for others in the country to secure increased education, and many of the newly educated might not emigrate. Explain why the "brain drain" could lead to increased education among the remaining residents. How would you test this theory?

5.7 **Secure Property Rights and Work outside the Home.** With secure land titles, parents can work outside the home (rather than guarding their property) and earn higher incomes. Explain why this might reduce child labor. (Related to Application 7 on page 176.)

A MODEL OF CAPITAL DEEPENING

Here's a simple model showing the links among saving, depreciation, and capital deepening. Developed by Nobel Laureate Robert Solow of the Massachusetts Institute of Technology, the Solow model will help us understand more fully the critical role technological progress must play in economic growth. We rely on one of our basic principles of economics to help explain the model as well as make a few simplifying assumptions. We assume constant population and no government or foreign sector. In the chapter, we discussed the qualitative effects of population growth, government, and the foreign sector on capital deepening. Here we focus solely on the relationships among saving, depreciation, and capital deepening.

Figure 8A.1 plots the relationship in the economy between output and the stock of capital, holding the labor force constant. Notice that output increases as the stock of capital increases, but at a decreasing rate. This is an illustration of the principle of diminishing returns.

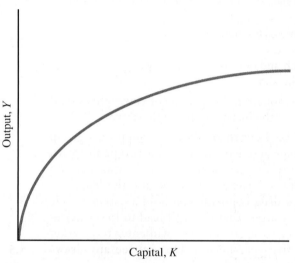

▲ **FIGURE 8A.1**
Diminishing Returns to Capital
Holding labor constant, increases in the stock of capital increase output, but at a decreasing rate.

PRINCIPLE OF DIMINISHING RETURNS

Suppose output is produced with two or more inputs and we increase one input while holding the other inputs fixed. Beyond some point—called the *point of diminishing returns*—output will increase at a decreasing rate.

Increasing the stock of capital while holding the labor force constant will increase output, but at a decreasing rate.

As Figure 8A.1 indicates, output increases with the stock of capital. But what causes the stock of capital to increase? The capital stock will increase as long as gross investment exceeds depreciation. Therefore, we need to determine the level of gross investment and the level of depreciation to see how the capital stock changes over time.

Recall that without government or a foreign sector, saving equals gross investment. Thus, to determine the level of investment, we need to specify how much of output is saved and how much is consumed. We will assume that a fraction s of total output (Y) is saved. For example, if $s = 0.20$, then 20 percent of GDP would be saved and 80 percent would be consumed. Total saving will be sY, the product of the saving rate and total output.

In Panel A of Figure 8A.2, the top curve is total output as a function of the stock of capital. The curve below it represents saving as a function of the stock of capital. Because saving is a fixed fraction of total output, the saving curve is a constant fraction of the output curve. If the saving rate is 0.2, saving will always be 20 percent of output for any level of the capital stock. Total saving increases in the economy with the stock of capital, but at a decreasing rate.

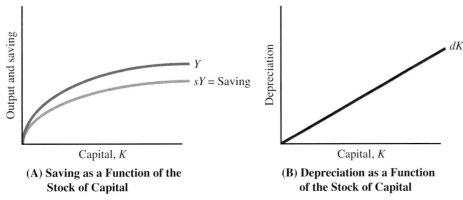

(A) Saving as a Function of the
Stock of Capital

(B) Depreciation as a Function
of the Stock of Capital

▲ FIGURE 8A.2
Saving and Depreciation as Functions of the Stock of Capital

To complete our model, we need to determine depreciation. Let's say the capital stock depreciates at a constant rate of d per year. If $d = 0.03$, the capital stock would depreciate at 3 percent per year. If the capital stock were 100 at the beginning of the year, depreciation would equal 3. Total depreciation can be written as dK, where K is the stock of capital.

Panel B of Figure 8A.2 plots total depreciation as a function of the stock of capital. The larger the stock of capital, the more total depreciation there will be. Because the depreciation rate is assumed to be constant, total depreciation as a function of the stock of capital will be a straight line through the origin. Then if there is no capital, there will be no depreciation, no matter what the depreciation rate.

If the depreciation rate is 3 percent and the stock of capital is 100, depreciation will be 3; if the stock of capital is 200, the depreciation rate will be 6. Plotting these points will give a straight line through the origin.

We are now ready to see how the stock of capital changes:

$$\text{change in the stock of capital} = \text{saving} - \text{depreciation} = sY - dK$$

The stock of capital will increase—the change will be positive—as long as total saving in the economy exceeds depreciation.

Figure 8A.3 shows how the Solow model works by plotting output, saving, and depreciation all on one graph. Suppose the economy starts with a capital stock K_0. Then total saving will be given by point a on the saving schedule. Depreciation at the capital stock K_0 is given by point b. Because a lies above b, total saving exceeds depreciation, and the capital stock will increase. As the capital stock increases, there will be economic growth through capital deepening. With more capital per worker in the economy, output is higher and real wages increase. The economy benefits from the additional stock of capital.

Using the graph, we can trace the future for this economy. As the stock of capital increases, we move to the right. When the economy reaches K_1, total saving is at point c and total depreciation is at point d. Because c is still higher than d, saving exceeds depreciation and the capital stock continues to increase. Economic growth continues. Eventually, after many years, the economy reaches capital stock K^*. The level of output in the economy now is Y^*, and the saving and depreciation schedules intersect at

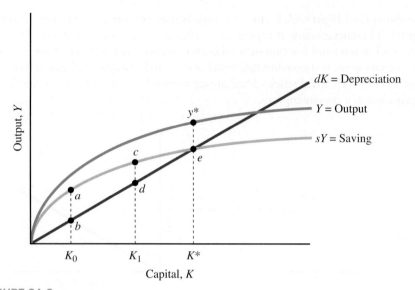

▲ FIGURE 8A.3
Basic Growth Model
Starting at K_0, saving exceeds depreciation. The stock of capital increases. This process continues until the stock of capital reaches its long-run equilibrium at K^*.

point e. Because total saving equals depreciation, the stock of capital no longer increases. The process of economic growth through capital deepening has stopped.

In this simple model, the process of capital deepening must eventually come to an end. As the stock of capital increases, output increases, but at a decreasing rate because of diminishing returns. Because saving is a fixed fraction of output, it will also increase but at a diminishing rate. On the other hand, total depreciation is proportional to the stock of capital. As the stock of capital increases, depreciation will always catch up with total saving in the economy. It may take decades for the process of capital deepening to come to an end. But as long as total saving exceeds depreciation, the process of economic growth through capital deepening will continue.

What would happen if a society saved a higher fraction of its output? Figure 8A.4 shows the consequences of a higher saving rate. Suppose the economy were originally saving at a rate s_1. Eventually, the economy would reach e_1, where saving and depreciation meet. If the economy had started to save at the higher rate s_2, saving would exceed depreciation at K_1, and the capital stock would increase until the economy reached K_2. At K_2, the saving line again crosses the line representing depreciation.

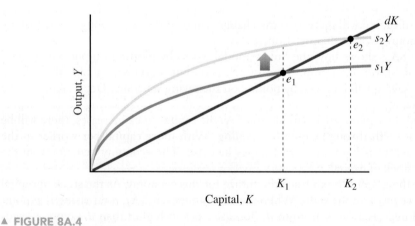

▲ FIGURE 8A.4
Increase in the Saving Rate
A higher saving rate will lead to a higher stock of capital in the long run. Starting from an initial capital stock of K_1, the increase in the saving rate leads the economy to K_2.

Output is higher than it was initially, but the process of capital deepening stops at this higher level of output.

If there is ongoing technological progress, economic growth can continue. If technological progress raises GDP, saving will increase as well, because saving increases with GDP. This will lead to a higher stock of capital. In Figure 8A.5, technological progress is depicted as an upward shift of the saving function. The saving function shifts up because saving is a fixed fraction of output, and we have assumed that technological progress has raised the level of output.

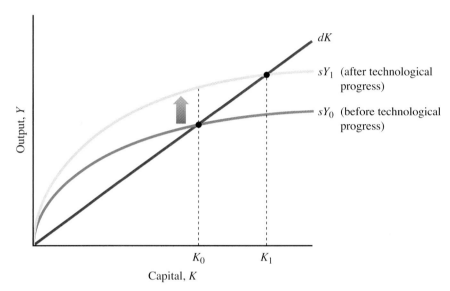

▲ FIGURE 8A.5
Technological Progress and Growth
Technological progress shifts up the saving function and promotes capital deepening.

With a higher level of saving, the stock of capital will increase. If the stock of capital were originally at K_0, the upward shift in the saving schedule will lead to increases in the stock of capital to K_1. If there is further technological progress, capital deepening will continue.

Technological progress conveys a double benefit to a society. Not only does the increased efficiency directly raise per capita output, it also leads to additional capital deepening. Therefore, output increases for two reasons.

Let's summarize the basic points of the Solow model:

1 Capital deepening, an increase in the stock of capital per worker, will occur as long as total saving exceeds depreciation. As capital deepening occurs, there will be economic growth and increased real wages.

2 Eventually, the process of capital deepening will come to a halt as depreciation catches up with total saving.

3 A higher saving rate will promote capital deepening. If a country saves more, it will have a higher output. But eventually, the process of economic growth through capital deepening alone comes to an end, even though this may take decades to occur.

4 Technological progress not only directly raises output, but also it allows capital deepening to continue.

It is possible to relax our assumptions and allow for population growth, government taxes and spending, and the foreign sector. In more advanced courses, these issues are treated in detail, but the underlying message is the same. There is a natural limit to economic growth through capital deepening. Technological progress is required to ensure that per capita incomes grow over time.

A.1 _____ and _____ are the two factors that determine how the stock of capital changes over time.

A.2 Which of the following causes capital deepening to come to an end?

   a. The marginal principle
   b. The principle of diminishing returns
   c. The principle of opportunity cost
   d. The reality principle

A.3 A higher saving rate leads to a permanently higher rate of growth. _____ (True/False)

A.4 **Germany and Japan after World War II.** Much of the stock of capital in the economies of Japan and Germany was destroyed during World War II. Use the Solow model graph to show and explain why growth in these economies after the war was higher than that in the United States.

A.5 **Faster Depreciation.** Suppose a society switches to equipment that depreciates rapidly. Use the Solow model graph to show what will happen to the stock of capital and output if the rate of depreciation increases.

NOTES

1. Xavier Sala-i-Martin and Martin Pinkovskiy, "African Poverty is Falling: Much Faster Than You Think," NBER Working Paper Series, Working Paper No. 15775, February 2010.

2. Stanley Fischer, "Globalization and Its Challenges," *American Economic Review Papers and Proceedings* 93, no.2 (May 2003): 1–32.

3. Bradford DeLong, "Slouching Toward Utopia," http://www.j-bradford-delong.net/TCEH/Slouch_divergence5.html (accessed June 27, 2008).

4. Phillipe Aghion and Peter Howitt, "Appropriate Growth Theory: A Unifying Framework," December 2005, http://www.economics.harvard.edu/faculty/aghion/papers.html (accessed February 2006).

5. William Easterly, *The Elusive Quest for Growth: Economists' Adventures and Misadventures in the Tropics* (Cambridge, MA: MIT Press, 2002).

Aggregate Demand and Aggregate Supply

As we explained in previous chapters, recessions occur when output fails to grow and unemployment rises. But *why* do recessions occur?

In a sense, recessions are massive failures in economic coordination. For example, during the Great Depression in the 1930s, nearly one-fourth of the U.S. labor force was unemployed. Unemployed workers could not afford to buy goods and services. Factories that manufactured those goods and services had to be shut down because there was little or no demand. As these factories closed, even more workers became unemployed, fueling additional factory shutdowns. This vicious cycle caused the U.S. economy to spiral downward. Similar failures in coordination were happening throughout the world. The worldwide depression continued through the 1930s. How could this destructive chain of events have been halted?

This failure of coordination is not just a historical phenomenon. In December 2007 the economy also entered a very steep downturn—although not nearly as severe as the Great Depression. Business activity slowed and many workers lost their jobs. What was the cause of this slowdown of economic activity?

APPLYING THE CONCEPTS

1 What does the behavior of prices in consumer markets demonstrate about how quickly prices adjust in the U.S. economy?
   Measuring Price Stickiness in Consumer Markets

2 How can we determine what factors cause recessions?
   Two Approaches to Determining the Causes of Recessions

3 Do changes in oil prices always hurt the U.S. economy?
   How the U.S. Economy Has Coped with Oil Price Fluctuations

conomies do not always operate at full employment, nor do they always grow smoothly. At times, real GDP grows below its potential or falls steeply, as it did in the Great Depression. Recessions and excess unemployment occur when real GDP falls. At other times, GDP grows too rapidly, and unemployment falls below its natural rate.

"Too slow" or "too fast" real GDP growth are examples of *economic fluctuations*—movements of GDP away from potential output. We now turn our attention to understanding these economic fluctuations, which are also called *business cycles*.

During the Great Depression, there was a failure in coordination. Factories would have produced more output and hired more workers if there had been more demand for their products. In his 1936 book, *The General Theory of Employment, Interest, and Money*, British economist John Maynard Keynes explained that insufficient demand for goods and services was a key problem of the Great Depression. Following the publication of Keynes's work, economists began to distinguish between real GDP in the long run, when prices have time to fully adjust to changes in demand, and real GDP in the short run, when prices don't yet have time to fully adjust to changes in demand. During the short run, economic coordination problems are most pronounced. In the long run, however, economists believe the economy will return to full employment, although economic policy may assist it in getting there more quickly.

In the previous two chapters, we analyzed the economy at full employment and studied economic growth. Those chapters provided the framework for analyzing the behavior of the economy in the long run, but not in the short run, when there can be sharp fluctuations in output. We therefore need to develop an additional set of tools to analyze both short- and long-run changes and the relationship between the two.

9.1   STICKY PRICES AND THEIR MACROECONOMIC CONSEQUENCES

Why do recessions occur? In Chapter 7 we discussed how real, adverse shocks to the economy could cause economic downturns. We also outlined the theory of real business cycles, which focuses on how shocks to technology cause economic fluctuations. Now we examine another approach to understanding economic fluctuations.

Led by Keynes, many economists have focused attention on economic coordination problems. Normally, the price system efficiently coordinates what goes on in an economy—even in a complex economy. The price system provides signals to firms as to who buys what, how much to produce, what resources to use, and from whom to buy. For example, if consumers decide to buy fresh fruit rather than chocolate, the price of fresh fruit will rise and the price of chocolate will fall. More fresh fruit and less chocolate will be produced on the basis of these price signals. On a day-to-day basis, the price system works silently in the background, matching the desires of consumers with the output from producers.

Flexible and Sticky Prices

But the price system does not always work instantaneously. If prices are slow to adjust, then they do not give the proper signals to producers and consumers quickly enough to bring them together. Demands and supplies will not be brought immediately into equilibrium, and coordination can break down. In modern economies, some prices are very flexible, whereas others are not. In the 1970s, U.S. economist Arthur Okun distinguished between *auction prices*, prices that adjust on a nearly daily basis, and *custom prices*, prices that adjust slowly. Prices for fresh fish, vegetables, and other food products are examples of auction prices—they typically are very flexible and adjust rapidly. Prices for industrial commodities, such as steel rods or machine tools, are custom prices and tend to adjust slowly to changes in demand. As shorthand, economists often refer to slowly adjusting prices as "sticky prices" (just like a door that won't open immediately but sometimes gets stuck).

Steel rods and machine tools are input prices. Like other input prices, the price of labor also adjusts very slowly. Workers often have long-term contracts that do not allow employers to change wages at all during a given year. Union workers, university professors, high-school teachers, and employees of state and local governments are all groups whose wages adjust very slowly. As a general rule, there are very few workers in the economy whose wages change quickly. Perhaps movie stars, athletes, and rock stars are the exceptions, because their wages rise and fall with their popularity. But they are far from the typical worker in the economy. Even unskilled, low-wage workers are often protected from a decrease in their wages by minimum-wage laws.

For most firms, the biggest cost of doing business is wages. If wages are sticky, firms' overall costs will be sticky as well. This means that firms' product prices will remain sticky, too. Sticky wages cause sticky prices and hamper the economy's ability to bring demand and supply into balance in the short run.

How Demand Determines Output in the Short Run

Typically, firms that supply intermediate goods such as steel rods or other inputs let demand—not price—determine the level of output in the short run. To understand this idea, consider an automobile firm that buys material from a steelmaker on a regular basis. Because the auto firm and the steel producer have been in business with one another for a long time and have an ongoing relationship, they have negotiated a contract that keeps steel prices fixed in the short run.

But suppose the automobile company's cars suddenly become very popular. The firm needs to expand production, so it needs more steel. Under the agreement made earlier by the two firms, the steel company would meet this higher demand and sell more steel—without raising its price—to the automobile company. As a result, the production of steel is totally determined in the short run by the demand from automobile producers, not by price.

But what if the firm discovered that it had produced an unpopular car and needed to cut back on its planned production? The firm would require less steel. Under the agreement, the steelmaker would supply less steel but not reduce its price. Again, demand—not price—determines steel production in the short run.

Similar agreements between firms, both formal and informal, exist throughout the economy. Typically, in the short run, firms will meet changes in the demand for their products by adjusting production with only small changes in the prices they charge their customers.

What we have just illustrated for an input such as steel applies to workers, too, who are also "inputs" to production. Suppose the automobile firm hires union workers under a contract that fixes their wages for a specific period. If the economy suddenly thrives at some point during that period, the automobile company will employ all the workers and perhaps require some to work overtime. If the economy stagnates at some point during that period, the firm will lay off some workers, using only part of the union labor force. In either case, wages are sticky—they will not change during the period of the contract.

Retail prices to consumers, like input prices to producers, are also subject to some "stickiness." Economists have used information from mail-order catalogues to document this stickiness. Retail price stickiness is further evidence that many prices in the economy are simply slow to adjust.

Over longer periods of time, prices do change. Suppose the automobile company's car remains popular for a long time. The steel company and the automobile company will adjust the price of steel on their contract to reflect this increased demand. These price adjustments occur only over long periods. In the short run, demand, not prices, determines output, and prices are slow to adjust.

To summarize, the **short run in macroeconomics** is the period in which prices do not change or do not change very much. In the macroeconomic short run, both

short run in macroeconomics
The period of time in which prices do not change or do not change very much.

APPLICATION 1

MEASURING PRICE STICKINESS IN CONSUMER MARKETS

APPLYING THE CONCEPTS #1: What does the behavior of prices in consumer markets demonstrate about how quickly prices adjust in the U.S. economy?

Economists have taken a number of different approaches to analyze the behavior of retail prices. Anil Kashyap of the University of Chicago examined prices in consumer catalogs. In particular, he looked at the prices of 12 selected goods from L.L. Bean, Recreational Equipment, Inc. (REI), and The Orvis Company, Inc. Kashyap tracked several goods over time, including several varieties of shoes, blankets, chamois shirts, binoculars, and a fishing rod and fly. He found considerable price stickiness. Prices of the goods he tracked were typically fixed for a year or more (even though the catalogs came out every six months). When prices did eventually change, Kashyap observed a mixture of both large and small changes. During periods of high inflation, prices tended to change more frequently, as we might expect.

Mark Bils of the University of Rochester and Peter Klenow of Stanford University examined the frequency of price changes for 350 categories of goods and services covering about 70 percent of consumer spending, based on unpublished data from the BLS for 1995 to 1997. Compared with previous studies they found more frequent price changes, with half of goods' prices lasting less than 4.3 months. Some categories of prices changed much more frequently. Price changes for tomatoes occurred about every three weeks. And some, like coin-operated laundries, changed prices on average only every $6\frac{1}{2}$ years or so.   **Related to Exercises 1.5, 1.7, and 1.8.**

SOURCES: Based on Anil Kashyap, "Sticky Prices: New Evidence from Retail Catalogs," *Quarterly Journal of Economics* 110, no. 1 (1995): 245–274 and Mark Bils and Peter Klenow, "Some Evidence on the Importance of Sticky Prices," *Journal of Political Economy* 112, no. 5 (2004): 987–985.

formal and informal contracts between firms mean that changes in demand will be reflected primarily in changes in output, not prices.

9.2 UNDERSTANDING AGGREGATE DEMAND

In this section, we develop a graphical tool known as the *aggregate demand curve*. Later in the chapter, we will develop the *aggregate supply curve*. Together the aggregate demand and aggregate supply curves form an economic model that will enable us to study how output and prices are determined in both the short run and the long run. This economic model will also provide a framework in which we can study the role the government can play in stabilizing the economy through its spending, tax, and money-creation policies.

What Is the Aggregate Demand Curve?

Aggregate demand is the total demand for goods and services in an entire economy. In other words, it is the demand for currently produced GDP by consumers, firms, the government, and the foreign sector. Aggregate demand is a macroeconomic concept, because it refers to the economy as a whole, not to individual goods or markets.

aggregate demand curve (AD)

A curve that shows the relationship between the level of prices and the quantity of real GDP demanded.

The **aggregate demand curve (AD)** shows the relationship between the level of prices and the quantity of real GDP demanded. An aggregate demand curve, AD, is shown in Figure 9.1. It plots the total demand for GDP as a function of the price level. (Recall that the price level is the average level of prices in the economy, as measured by

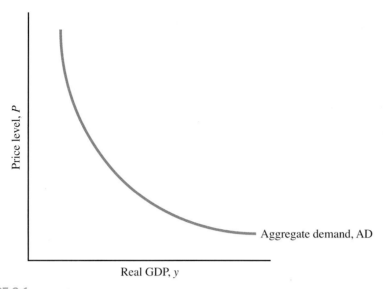

▲ **FIGURE 9.1**

Aggregate Demand

The aggregate demand curve plots the total demand for real GDP as a function of the price level. The aggregate demand curve slopes downward, indicating that the quantity of aggregate demand increases as the price level in the economy falls.

a price index.) At each price level, shown on the y axis, we ask what the total quantity demanded will be for all goods and services in the economy, shown on the x axis. In Figure 9.1, the aggregate demand curve is downward sloping. As the price level falls, the total quantity demanded for goods and services increases. To understand what the aggregate demand curve represents, we must first learn the components of aggregate demand, why the aggregate demand curve slopes downward, and the factors that can shift the curve.

The Components of Aggregate Demand

In our study of GDP accounting, we divided GDP into four components: consumption spending (C), investment spending (I), government purchases (G), and net exports (NX). These four components are also the four parts of aggregate demand because the aggregate demand curve really just describes the demand for total GDP at different price levels. As we will see, changes in demand coming from any of these four sources—C, I, G, or NX—will shift the aggregate demand curve.

Why the Aggregate Demand Curve Slopes Downward

To understand the slope of the aggregate demand curve, we need to consider the effects of a change in the overall price level in the economy. First, let's consider the supply of money in the economy. We discuss the supply of money in detail in later chapters, but for now, just think of the supply of money as being the total amount of currency (cash plus coins) held by the public and the value of all deposits in savings and checking accounts. As the price level or average level of prices in the economy changes, so does the purchasing power of your money. This is an example of the real-nominal principle.

REAL-NOMINAL PRINCIPLE

What matters to people is the real value or purchasing power of money or income, not the face value of money or income.

As the purchasing power of money changes, the aggregate demand curve is affected in three different ways:

- The wealth effect
- The interest rate effect
- The international trade effect

Let's take a closer look at each.

wealth effect

The increase in spending that occurs because the real value of money increases when the price level falls.

THE WEALTH EFFECT   The increase in spending that occurs because the real value of money increases when the price level falls is known as the **wealth effect**. Lower prices lead to higher levels of wealth, and higher levels of wealth increase spending on total goods and services. Conversely, when the price level rises, the real value of money decreases, which reduces people's wealth and their total demand for goods and services in the economy. When the price level rises, consumers can't simply substitute one good for another that's cheaper, because at a higher price level *everything* is more expensive.

THE INTEREST RATE EFFECT   With a given supply of money in the economy, a lower price level will lead to lower interest rates. With lower interest rates, both consumers and firms will find it cheaper to borrow money to make purchases. As a consequence, the demand for goods in the economy (consumer durables purchased by households and investment goods purchased by firms) will increase. (We'll explain the effects of interest rates in more detail in later chapters.)

THE INTERNATIONAL TRADE EFFECT   In an open economy, a lower price level will mean that domestic goods (goods produced in the home country) become cheaper relative to foreign goods, so the demand for domestic goods will increase. For example, if the price level in the United States falls, it will make U.S. goods cheaper relative to foreign goods. If U.S. goods become cheaper than foreign goods, exports from the United States will increase and imports will decrease. Thus, net exports—a component of aggregate demand—will increase.

Shifts in the Aggregate Demand Curve

A fall in price causes the aggregate demand curve to slope downward because of three factors: the wealth effect, the interest rate effect, and the international trade effect. What happens to the aggregate demand curve if a variable *other* than the price level changes? An increase in aggregate demand means that total demand for all the goods and services contained in real GDP has increased—even though the price level hasn't changed. In other words, increases in aggregate demand shift the curve to the right. Conversely, factors that decrease aggregate demand shift the curve to the left—even though the price level hasn't changed.

Let's look at the key factors that cause these shifts. We will discuss each factor in detail in later chapters:

- Changes in the supply of money
- Changes in taxes
- Changes in government spending
- All other changes in demand

CHANGES IN THE SUPPLY OF MONEY   An increase in the supply of money in the economy will increase aggregate demand and shift the aggregate demand curve to the right. We know that an increase in the supply of money will lead to higher demand by both consumers and firms. At any given price level, a higher supply of money will mean more consumer wealth and an increased demand for goods and services. A decrease in the supply of money will decrease aggregate demand and shift the aggregate demand curve to the left.

CHANGES IN TAXES   A decrease in taxes will increase aggregate demand and shift the aggregate demand curve to the right. Lower taxes will increase the income available to households and increase their spending on goods and services—even though the price level in the economy hasn't changed. An increase in taxes will decrease aggregate demand and shift the aggregate demand curve to the left. Higher taxes will decrease the income available to households and decrease their spending.

CHANGES IN GOVERNMENT SPENDING   At any given price level, an increase in government spending will increase aggregate demand and shift the aggregate demand curve to the right. For example, the government could spend more on national defense or on interstate highways. Because the government is a source of demand for goods and services, higher government spending naturally leads to an increase in total demand for goods and services. Similarly, decreases in government spending will decrease aggregate demand and shift the curve to the left.

ALL OTHER CHANGES IN DEMAND   Any change in demand from households, firms, or the foreign sector will also change aggregate demand. For example, if the Chinese economy expands very rapidly and Chinese citizens buy more U.S. goods, U.S. aggregate demand will increase. Or, if U.S. households decide they want to spend more, consumption will increase and aggregate demand will increase. Expectations about the future also matter. For example, if firms become optimistic about the future and increase their investment spending, aggregate demand will also increase. However, if firms become pessimistic, they will cut their investment spending and aggregate demand will fall.

When we discuss factors that shift aggregate demand, we must *not* include any changes in the demand for goods and services that arise from movements in the price level. Changes in aggregate demand that accompany changes in the price level are already included in the curve and do not shift the curve. The increase in consumer spending that occurs when the price level falls from the wealth effect, the interest rate effect, and the international trade effect is already *in* the curve and does not shift it.

Figure 9.2 and Table 9.1 summarize our discussion. Decreases in taxes, increases in government spending, and increases in the supply of money all shift the aggregate demand curve to the right. Increases in taxes, decreases in government spending, and decreases in the supply of money shift it to the left. In general, any increase in demand

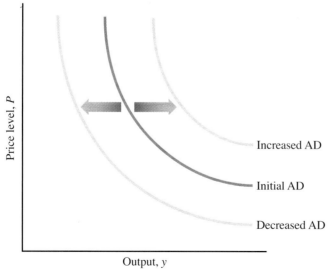

▲ FIGURE 9.2
Shifting Aggregate Demand
Decreases in taxes, increases in government spending, and an increase in the supply of money all shift the aggregate demand curve to the right. Higher taxes, lower government spending, and a lower supply of money shift the curve to the left.

TABLE 9.1 FACTORS THAT SHIFT AGGREGATE DEMAND	
Factors That Increase Aggregate Demand	Factors That Decrease Aggregate Demand
Decrease in taxes	Increase in taxes
Increase in government spending	Decrease in government spending
Increase in the money supply	Decrease in the money supply

(not brought about by a change in the price level) will shift the curve to the right. Decreases in demand shift the curve to the left.

How the Multiplier Makes the Shift Bigger

Let's take a closer look at the shift in the aggregate demand curve and see how far changes really make the curve shift. Suppose the government increases its spending on goods and services by $10 billion. You might think the aggregate demand curve would shift to the right by $10 billion, reflecting the increase in demand for these goods and services. Initially, the shift will be precisely $10 billion. In Figure 9.3, this is depicted by the shift (at a given price level) from *a* to *b*. But after a brief period of time, total aggregate demand will increase by *more* than $10 billion. In Figure 9.3, the total shift in the aggregate demand curve is shown by the larger movement from *a* to *c*. The ratio of the total shift in aggregate demand to the initial shift in aggregate demand is known as the **multiplier**.

Why does the aggregate demand curve shift more than the initial increase in desired spending? The logic goes back to the ideas of economist John Maynard Keynes. Here's how it works: Keynes believed that as government spending increases and the aggregate demand curve shifts to the right, output will subsequently increase, too. As we saw with the circular flow in Chapter 5, increased output also means increased income for households, as firms pay households for their labor and for supplying other factors of production. Typically, households will wish to spend, or consume, part of that income, which will further increase aggregate demand. It is this additional spending by consumers, over and above what the government has already spent, that causes the further shift in the aggregate demand curve.

The basic idea of how the multiplier works in an economy is simple. Let's say the government invests $10 million to renovate a federal court building. Initially, total spending in the economy increases by this $10 million paid to a private construction firm. The construction workers and owners are paid $10 million for their work. Suppose the owners and workers spend $6 million of their income on new cars

multiplier

The ratio of the total shift in aggregate demand to the initial shift in aggregate demand.

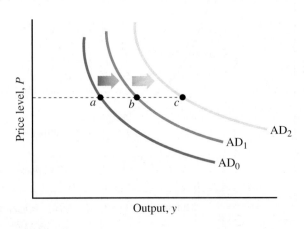

▲ **FIGURE 9.3**

The Multiplier

Initially, an increase in desired spending will shift the aggregate demand curve horizontally to the right from *a* to *b*. The total shift from *a* to *c* will be larger. The ratio of the total shift to the initial shift is known as the multiplier.

(although, as we will see, it does not really matter what they spend it on). To meet the increased demand for new cars, automobile producers will expand their production and earn an additional $6 million in wages and profits. They, in turn, will spend part of this additional income—let's say, $3.6 million—on televisions. The workers and owners who produce televisions will then spend part of the $3.6 million they earn, and so on.

To take a closer look at this process, we first need to look more carefully at the behavior of consumers and how their behavior helps to determine the level of aggregate demand. Economists have found that consumer spending depends on the level of income in the economy. When consumers have more income, they want to purchase more goods and services. The relationship between the level of income and consumer spending is known as the **consumption function**:

$$C = C_a + by$$

where consumption spending, C, has two parts. The first part, C_a, is a constant and is independent of income. Economists call this **autonomous consumption spending**.

Autonomous spending is spending that does not depend on the level of income. For example, all consumers, regardless of their current income, will have to purchase some food. The second part, by, represents the part of consumption that is dependent on income. It is the product of a fraction, b, called the **marginal propensity to consume (MPC)**, and the level of income, or y, in the economy. The MPC (or b in our formula) tells us how much consumption spending will increase for every dollar that income increases. For example, if b is 0.6, then for every $1.00 that income increases, consumption increases by $0.60.

Here is another way to think of the MPC: If a household receives some additional income, it will increase its consumption by some additional amount. The MPC is defined as the ratio of additional consumption to additional income, or

$$\text{MPC} = \frac{\text{additional consumption}}{\text{additional income}}$$

For example, if the household receives an additional $100 and consumes an additional $70, the MPC will be

$$\frac{\$70}{\$100} = 0.7$$

You may wonder what happens to the other $30. Whatever the household does not spend out of income, it saves. Therefore, the **marginal propensity to save (MPS)** is defined as the ratio of additional savings to additional income

$$\text{MPS} = \frac{\text{additional savings}}{\text{additional income}}$$

The sum of the MPC and the MPS always equals one. By definition, additional income is either spent or saved.

Now we are in a better position to understand the multiplier. Suppose the government increases its purchases of goods and services by $10 million. This will initially raise aggregate demand and income by $10 million. But because income has risen by $10 million, consumers will now wish to increase their spending by an amount equal to the marginal propensity to consume multiplied by the $10 million. (Remember that the MPC tells us how much consumption spending will increase for every dollar that income increases.) If the MPC were 0.6, then consumer spending would increase by $6 million when the government spends $10 million. Thus, the aggregate demand curve would continue to shift to the right by another $6 million in addition to the original $10 million, for a total of $16 million.

But the process does not end there. As aggregate demand increases by $6 million, income will also increase by $6 million. Consumers will then wish to increase their

consumption function
The relationship between consumption spending and the level of income.

autonomous consumption spending
The part of consumption spending that does not depend on income.

marginal propensity to consume (MPC)
The fraction of additional income that is spent.

marginal propensity to save (MPS)
The fraction of additional income that is saved.

spending by the MPC × $6 million or, in our example, by $3.6 million (0.6 × $6 million). The aggregate demand curve will continue to shift to the right, now by *another* $3.6 million. Adding $3.6 million to $16 million gives us a new aggregate demand total of $19.6 million. As you can see, this process will continue, as consumers now have an additional $3.6 million in income, part of which they will spend again. Where will it end?

Table 9.2 shows how the multiplier works in detail. In the first round, there is an initial increase in government spending of $10 million. This additional demand leads to an initial increase in GDP and income of $10 million. Assuming that the MPC is 0.6, the $10 million of additional income will increase consumer spending by $6 million. The second round begins with this $6 million increase in consumer spending. Because of this increase in demand, GDP and income increase by $6 million. At the end of the second round, consumers will have an additional $6 million; with an MPC of 0.6, consumer spending will therefore increase by 0.6 × $6 million, or $3.6 million. The process continues in the third round with an increase in consumer spending of $2.16 million. It continues, in diminishing amounts, through subsequent rounds. If we add up the spending in all the (infinite) rounds, we will find that the initial $10 million of spending leads to a $25 million increase in GDP and income. That's 2.5 times what the government initially spent. So in this case, the multiplier is 2.5.

TABLE 9.2 THE MULTIPLIER IN ACTION
The initial $10 million increase in aggregate demand will, through all the rounds of spending, eventually lead to a $25 million increase.

Round of Spending	Increase in Aggregate Demand (millions)	Increase in GDP and Income (millions)	Increase in Consumption (millions)
1	$10.00	$10.00	$6.00
2	6.00	6.00	3.60
3	3.60	3.60	2.16
4	2.16	2.16	1.30
.	.	.	.
Total	**$25.00**	**$25.00**	**$15.00**

Instead of calculating spending round by round, we can use a simple formula to figure out what the multiplier is:

$$\text{multiplier} = \frac{1}{(1 - \text{MPC})}$$

Thus, in the preceding example, when the MPC is 0.6, the multiplier would be

$$\frac{1}{(1 - 0.6)} = 2.5$$

Now you should clearly understand why the total shift in the aggregate demand curve from *a* to *c* in Figure 9.3 is greater than the initial shift in the curve from *a* to *b*. This is the multiplier in action. The multiplier is important because it means that relatively small changes in spending could lead to relatively large changes in output. For example, if firms cut back on their investment spending, the effects on output would be "multiplied," and this decrease in spending could have a large, adverse impact on the economy.

In practice, once we take into account other realistic factors such as taxes and indirect effects through financial markets, the multipliers are smaller than our previous examples, typically near 1.5 for the U.S economy. This means that a $10 million increase in one component of spending will shift the U.S. aggregate demand curve by approximately $15 million. Some economists believe the multiplier is even closer to one. Knowing the value of the multiplier is important for two reasons. First, it tells us how much shocks to aggregate demand are "amplified." Second, to design effective economic policies to shift the aggregate demand curve, we need to know the value of the multiplier to measure the proper "dose" for policy. In the next chapter, we present a more detailed model of aggregate demand and see how policymakers use the real-world multipliers.

9.3 UNDERSTANDING AGGREGATE SUPPLY

Now we turn to the supply side of our model. The **aggregate supply curve (AS)** shows the relationship between the level of prices and the total quantity of final goods and output that firms are willing and able to supply. The aggregate supply curve will complete our macroeconomic picture, uniting the economy's demand for real output with firms' willingness to supply output. To determine both the price level and real GDP, we need to combine *both* aggregate demand and aggregate supply. One slight complication is that because prices are "sticky" in the short run, we need to develop two different aggregate supply curves, one corresponding to the long run and one to the short run.

aggregate supply curve (AS)
A curve that shows the relationship between the level of prices and the quantity of output supplied.

The Long-Run Aggregate Supply Curve

First we'll consider the aggregate supply curve for the long run, that is, when the economy is at full employment. This curve is also called the **long-run aggregate supply curve**. In previous chapters, we saw that the level of full-employment output, y_p (the "p" stands for potential), depends solely on the supply of factors—capital, labor—and the state of technology. These are the fundamental factors that determine output in the long run, that is, when the economy operates at full employment.

In the long run, the economy operates at full employment and changes in the price level do not affect employment. To illustrate why this is so, imagine that the price level in the economy increases by 50 percent. That means firms' prices, on average, will also increase by 50 percent. However, so will their input costs. Their profits will be the same and, consequently, so will their output. Because the level of full-employment output does not depend on the price level, we can plot the long-run aggregate supply curve as a vertical line (unaffected by the price level), as shown in Figure 9.4.

long-run aggregate supply curve
A vertical aggregate supply curve that reflects the idea that in the long run, output is determined solely by the factors of production and technology.

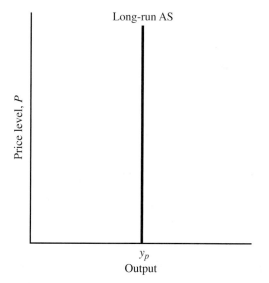

▲ **FIGURE 9.4**
Long-Run Aggregate Supply
In the long run, the level of output, y_p, is independent of the price level.

DETERMINING OUTPUT AND THE PRICE LEVEL   We combine the aggregate demand curve and the long-run aggregate supply curve in Figure 9.5. Together, the curves show us the price level and output in the long run when the economy returns to full employment. Combining the two curves will enable us to understand how changes in aggregate demand affect prices in the long run.

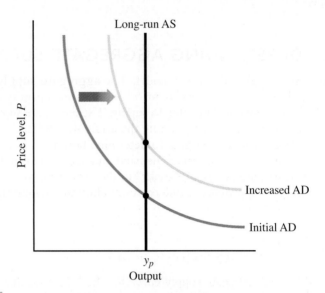

▲ **FIGURE 9.5**
Aggregate Demand and the Long-Run Aggregate Supply
Output and prices are determined at the intersection of AD and AS. An increase in aggregate demand leads to a higher price level.

The intersection of an aggregate demand curve and an aggregate supply curve determines the price level and equilibrium level of output. At that intersection point, the total amount of output demanded will just equal the total amount supplied by producers—the economy will be in macroeconomic equilibrium. The exact position of the aggregate demand curve will depend on the level of taxes, government spending, and the supply of money, although it will always slope downward. The level of full-employment output determines the long-run aggregate supply curve.

An increase in aggregate demand (perhaps brought about by a tax cut or an increase in the supply of money) will shift the aggregate demand curve to the right, as shown in Figure 9.5. In the long run, the increase in aggregate demand will raise prices but leave the level of output unchanged. In general, shifts in the aggregate demand curve in the long run do not change the level of output in the economy, but only change the level of prices. Here is an important example to illustrate this idea: If the money supply is increased by 5 percent a year, the aggregate demand curve will also shift by 5 percent a year. In the long run, this means that prices will increase by 5 percent a year—that is, there will be 5 percent inflation. An important lesson: In the long run, increases in the supply of money do not increase real GDP—they only lead to inflation.

This is the key point about the long run: In the long run, output is determined solely by the supply of human and physical capital and the supply of labor, not the price level. As our model of the aggregate demand curve with the long-run aggregate supply curve indicates, changes in demand will affect only prices, not the level of output.

The Short-Run Aggregate Supply Curve

short-run aggregate supply curve
A relatively flat aggregate supply curve that represents the idea that prices do not change very much in the short run and that firms adjust production to meet demand.

In the short run, prices are sticky (slow to adjust) and output is determined primarily by demand. This is what Keynes thought happened during the Great Depression. We can use the aggregate demand curve combined with a **short-run aggregate supply curve** to illustrate this idea. Figure 9.6 shows a relatively flat short-run aggregate

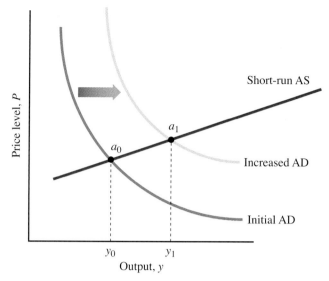

▲ **FIGURE 9.6**
Aggregate Demand and Short-Run Aggregate Supply
With a short-run aggregate supply curve, shifts in aggregate demand lead to large changes in output but small changes in price.

supply curve (AS). The short-run aggregate supply curve shows the short-run relationship between the price level and the willingness of firms to supply output to the economy. Let's look first at its slope and then the factors that shift the curve.

The short-run aggregate supply curve has a relatively flat slope because we assume that in the short run firms supply all the output demanded, with small changes in prices. We've said that with formal and informal contracts firms will supply all the output demanded with only relatively small changes in prices. The short-run aggregate supply curve has a small upward slope. As firms supply more output, they may have to increase prices somewhat if, for example, they have to pay higher wages to obtain more overtime from workers or pay a premium to obtain some raw materials. Our description of the short-run aggregate supply curve is consistent with evidence about the behavior of prices in the economy. Most studies find that changes in demand have relatively little effect on prices within a few quarters. Thus, we can think of the aggregate supply curve as relatively flat over a limited time.

The position of the short-run supply curve will be determined by the costs of production that firms face. Higher costs will shift up the short-run aggregate supply curve, while lower costs will shift it down. Higher costs will shift up the curve because, faced with higher costs, firms will need to raise their prices to continue to make a profit. What factors determine the costs firms must incur to produce output? The key factors are

• input prices (wages and materials),

• the state of technology, and

• taxes, subsidies, or economic regulations.

Increases in input prices (for example, from higher wages or oil prices) will increase firms' costs. This will shift up the short-run aggregate supply curve. Improvement in technology will shift the curve down. Higher taxes or more onerous regulations raise costs and shift the curve up, while subsidies to production shift the curve down. As we shall see later in this chapter, when the economy is not at full employment, wages and other costs will change. These changes in costs will shift the entire short-run supply curve upward or downward as costs rise or fall.

The intersection of the AD and AS curves at point a_0 determines the price level and the level of output. Because the aggregate supply curve is flat, aggregate demand primarily determines the level of output. In Figure 9.6, as aggregate demand increases, the new equilibrium will be at a slightly higher price, and output will increase from y_0 to y_1.

If the aggregate demand curve moved to the left, output would decrease. If the leftward shift in aggregate demand were sufficiently large, it could push the economy into a recession. Sudden decreases in aggregate demand have been important causes of recessions in the United States. However, the precise factors that shift the aggregate demand curve in each recession will typically differ.

Note that the level of output where the aggregate demand curve intersects the short-run aggregate supply curve need not correspond to full-employment output. Firms will produce whatever is demanded. If demand is very high and the economy is "overheated," output may exceed full-employment output. If demand is very low and the economy is in a slump, output will fall short of full-employment output. Because prices do not adjust fully over short periods of time, the economy need not always remain at full employment

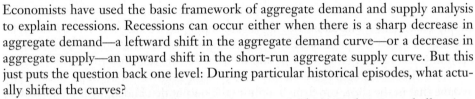

APPLICATION 2

TWO APPROACHES TO DETERMINING THE CAUSES OF RECESSIONS

APPLYING THE CONCEPTS #2: How can we determine what factors cause recessions?

Economists have used the basic framework of aggregate demand and supply analysis to explain recessions. Recessions can occur either when there is a sharp decrease in aggregate demand—a leftward shift in the aggregate demand curve—or a decrease in aggregate supply—an upward shift in the short-run aggregate supply curve. But this just puts the question back one level: During particular historical episodes, what actually shifted the curves?

Figuring out what caused a recession in any particular episode is very challenging. Here is one complication. Policymakers typically respond to shocks that hit the economy. So, for example, when worldwide oil prices rose in 1973 causing U.S. prices to increase, policymakers also reduced aggregate demand to prevent further price increases. Was the recession that resulted due to (1) the increase in oil prices that shifted the short-run aggregate supply curve or (2) the decrease in aggregate demand engineered by policymakers? It is very difficult to know.

One approach is to use economic models to address this question. Economists James Fackler and Douglas McMillin built a small model of the economy to address this issue. To distinguish between demand and supply shocks, they used an idea that we discuss in this chapter. Shocks to aggregate demand only affect prices in the long run but do not affect output. On the other hand, shocks to aggregate supply can affect potential output in the long run. Using this approach, they find that a mixture of demand and supply shocks were responsible for fluctuations in output in the United States.

Using more traditional historical methods, economic historian Peter Temin looked back at all recessionary episodes from 1893 to 1990 in the United States to try to determine their ultimate causes. According to his analysis, recessions were caused by many different factors. Sometimes, as in 1929, they were caused by shifts in aggregate demand from the private sector, as consumers cut back their spending. Other times, as in 1981, the government cut back on aggregate demand to reduce inflation. Supply shocks were the cause of the recessions in 1973 and 1979.

Based on both economic models and traditional economic history, it does appear that both supply and demand shocks have been important in understanding recessions.
Related to Exercises 3.6 and 3.9.

SOURCE: Based on Peter Temin, "The Causes of American Business Cycles: An Essay in Economic Historiography," in Federal Reserve Bank of Boston Conference Series 42, *Beyond Shocks: What Causes Business Cycles*, http://www.bos.frb.org/economic/conf/conf42 (accessed April 12, 2010) and James Fackler and Douglas McMillin, "Historical Decomposition of Aggregate Demand and Supply Shocks in a Small Macro Model," *Southern Economic Journal* 64, no. 3 (1998): 648–684.

APPLICATION 3

HOW THE U.S. ECONOMY HAS COPED WITH OIL PRICE FLUCTUATIONS

APPLYING THE CONCEPTS #3: Do changes in oil prices always hurt the U.S. economy?

During the 1970s, the world economy was hit with a series of unfavorable supply shocks that raised prices and lowered output, including spikes in oil prices and the prices of many agricultural commodities due to hurricanes, droughts, and floods that destroyed crops or land. As we have discussed, increases in oil prices shift the aggregate supply curve. However, they also have an adverse effect on aggregate demand. Because the United States is a net importer of foreign oil, an increase in oil prices is just like a tax that decreases the income of consumers. As we have seen, an increase in taxes will shift the aggregate demand curve to the left.

However, in the 1990s, things were different—pleasantly different. Between 1997 and 1998, the price of oil on the world market fell from $22 a barrel to less than $13 a barrel. The result was that gasoline prices, adjusted for inflation, were lower than they had been in over 50 years. This not only meant cheaper vacations and commuting and an increase in SUV purchases, it also had positive macroeconomic effects. Favorable supply shocks allowed output to rise and prices to fall simultaneously—the best of all worlds.

In 2008, oil prices shot up to $145 a barrel, largely because of increased demand throughout the world, particularly in fast-growing countries such as China and India. Gasoline prices in the United States exceeded $4.00 a gallon. The economy had been weak prior to these increases, and policymakers feared the negative effects this major supply disturbance would have both on inflation and GDP. Indeed, although the price of gasoline fell in 2009 and 2010, the price increases in 2008 helped exacerbate the recession brought on by the difficulties experienced in the financial system.   **Related to Exercises 3.4 and 3.7.**

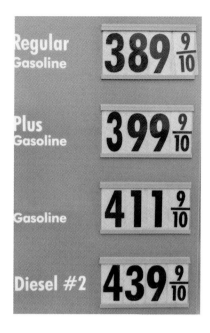

or potential output. With sticky prices, changes in demand in the short run will lead to economic fluctuations and over- and underemployment. Only in the long run, when prices fully adjust, will the economy operate at full employment.

Supply Shocks

Up to this point, we have been exploring how changes in aggregate demand affect output and prices in the short run and in the long run. However, even in the short run, it is possible for external disturbances to hit the economy and cause the short-run aggregate supply curve to move. **Supply shocks** are external events that shift the aggregate supply curve.

The most notable supply shocks for the world economy occurred in 1973 and again in 1979 when oil prices increased sharply. Oil is a vital input for many companies because it is used to both manufacture and transport their products to warehouses and stores around the country. The higher oil prices raised firms' costs and reduced their profits. To maintain their profit levels, firms raised their product prices. As we have seen, increases in firms' costs will shift up the short-run aggregate supply curve—increases in oil prices are a good example.

Figure 9.7 illustrates a supply shock that raises prices. The short-run aggregate supply curve shifts up with the supply shock because, as their costs rise, firms will supply their output only at a higher price. The AS curve shifts up, raising the price level and lowering the level of output from y_0 to y_1. Adverse supply shocks can therefore cause a recession (a fall in real output) with increasing prices. This phenomenon is known as **stagflation**, and it is precisely what happened in 1973 and 1979. The U.S. economy suffered on two

supply shocks
External events that shift the aggregate supply curve.

stagflation
A decrease in real output with increasing prices.

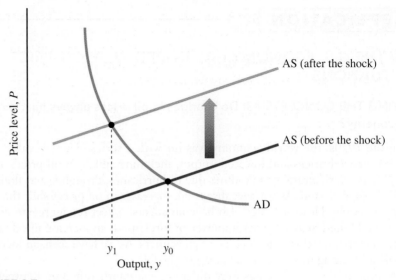

▲ **FIGURE 9.7**
Supply Shock
An adverse supply shock, such as an increase in the price of oil, will cause the AS curve to shift upward. The result will be higher prices and a lower level of output.

grounds: rising prices and falling output. Favorable supply shocks, such as falling prices, are also possible, and changes in oil prices can affect aggregate demand.

9.4 FROM THE SHORT RUN TO THE LONG RUN

Up to this point, we have examined how aggregate demand and aggregate supply determine output and prices both in the short run and in the long run. You may be wondering how long it takes before the short run becomes the long run. Here is a preview of how the short run and the long run are connected.

In Figure 9.8, we show the aggregate demand curve intersecting the short-run aggregate supply curve at a_0 at an output level y_0. We also depict the long-run aggregate supply curve in this figure. The level of output in the economy, y_0, exceeds the level of potential output, y_p. In other words, this is a boom economy: Output exceeds potential.

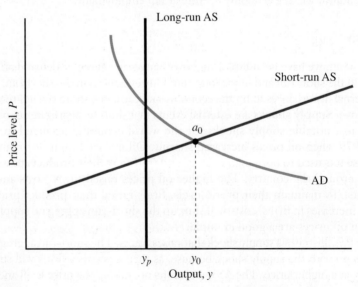

▲ **FIGURE 9.8**
The Economy in the Short Run
In the short run, the economy produces at y_0, which exceeds potential output y_p.

What happens during a boom? Because the economy is producing at a level beyond its long-run potential, the level of unemployment will be very low. This will make it difficult for firms to recruit and retain workers. Firms will also find it more difficult to purchase needed raw materials and other inputs for production. As firms compete for labor and raw materials, the tendency will be for both wages and prices to increase over time.

Increasing wages and prices will shift the short-run aggregate supply curve upward as the costs of inputs rise in the economy. Figure 9.9 shows how the short-run aggregate supply curve shifts upward over time. As long as the economy is producing at a level of output that exceeds potential output, there will be continuing competition for labor and raw materials that will lead to continuing increases in wages and prices. In the long run, the short-run aggregate supply curve will keep rising until it intersects the aggregate demand curve at a_1. At this point, the economy reaches the long-run equilibrium—precisely the point where the aggregate demand curve intersects the long-run aggregate supply curve.

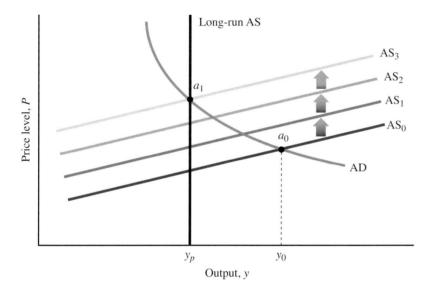

◄ **FIGURE 9.9**
Adjusting to the Long Run
With output exceeding potential, the short-run AS curve shifts upward over time. The economy adjusts to the long-run equilibrium at a_1.

When the economy is producing below full employment or potential output, the process works in reverse. Unemployment will exceed the natural rate, and there will be excess unemployment. Firms will find it easy to hire and retain workers, and they will offer workers less wages. As firms cut wages, the average wage level in the economy falls. Because wages are the largest component of costs and costs are decreasing, the short-run aggregate supply curve shifts down, causing prices to fall as well.

The lesson here is that adjustments in wages and prices take the economy from the short-run equilibrium to the long-run equilibrium. In later chapters, we will explain in detail how this adjustment occurs, and we will show how changes in wages and prices can steer the economy back to full employment in the long run.

Looking Ahead

The aggregate demand and aggregate supply model in this chapter provides an overview of how demand affects output and prices in both the short run and the long run. The next several chapters explore more closely how aggregate demand determines output in the short run. We expand our discussion of aggregate demand to see in detail how such realistic and important factors as spending by consumers and firms, government policies on taxation and spending, and foreign trade affect the demand for goods and services. We will also study the critical role that the financial system and monetary policy play in determining demand. Finally, in later chapters we will study in more depth how the aggregate supply curve shifts over time, enabling the economy to recover both from recessions and the inflationary pressures generated by economic booms.

SUMMARY

In this chapter we discussed how sticky prices—or lack of full-wage and price flexibility—cause output to be determined by demand in the short run. We developed a model of aggregate demand and supply to help us analyze what is happening or has happened in the economy. Here are the main points in this chapter:

1 Because prices are sticky in the short run, economists think of GDP as being determined primarily by demand factors in the short run.

2 The *aggregate demand curve* depicts the relationship between the price level and total demand for real output in the economy. The aggregate demand curve is downward sloping because of the wealth effect, the interest rate effect, and the international trade effect.

3 Decreases in taxes, increases in government spending, and increases in the supply of money all increase aggregate demand and shift the aggregate demand curve to the right. Increases in taxes, decreases in government spending, and decreases in the supply of money all decrease aggregate demand and shift the aggregate demand curve to

the left. In general, anything (other than price movements) that increases the demand for total goods and services will increase aggregate demand.

4 The total shift in the aggregate demand curve is greater than the initial shift. The ratio of the total shift in aggregate demand to the initial shift in aggregate demand is known as the *multiplier*.

5 The *aggregate supply curve* depicts the relationship between the price level and the level of output that firms supply in the economy. Output and prices are determined at the intersection of the aggregate demand and aggregate supply curves.

6 The *long-run aggregate supply curve* is vertical because, in the long run, output is determined by the supply of factors of production. The *short-run aggregate supply curve* is fairly flat because, in the short run, prices are largely fixed, and output is determined by demand. The costs of production determine the position of the short-run aggregate supply curve.

7 *Supply shocks* can shift the short-run aggregate supply curve.

8 As costs change, the short-run aggregate supply curve shifts in the long run, restoring the economy to the full-employment equilibrium.

KEY TERMS

aggregate demand curve (AD), p. 188

aggregate supply curve (AS), p. 195

autonomous consumption spending, p. 193

consumption function, p. 193

long-run aggregate supply curve, p. 195

marginal propensity to consume (MPC), p. 193

marginal propensity to save (MPS), p. 193

multiplier, p. 192

short run in macroeconomics, p. 187

short-run aggregate supply curve, p. 196

stagflation, p. 199

supply shocks, p. 199

wealth effect, p. 190

EXERCISES   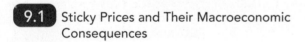   Visit www.myeconlab.com to complete these exercises online and get instant feedback.

9.1 Sticky Prices and Their Macroeconomic Consequences

1.1 Arthur Okun distinguished between _____ prices, which changed rapidly, and custom prices, which are slow to change.

1.2 For most firms, the biggest cost of doing business is _____.

1.3 The price system always coordinates economic activity, even when prices are slow to adjust to changes in demand and supply. _____ (True/False)

1.4 Determine whether the wages of each of the following adjust slowly or quickly to changes in demand and supply.
   a. Union workers
   b. Internationally known movie stars or rock stars
   c. University professors
   d. Athletes

1.5 **The Internet and Price Flexibility.** The Internet enables consumers to search for the lowest prices of various goods, such as books, music CDs, and airline tickets. Prices for these goods are likely to become more flexible as consumers shop around quickly and easily on the Internet. What types of goods and services do you think may not become more flexible because of the Internet? Give an example of a good or service for which you have searched the Internet for price information and one for which you have not. (Related to Application 1 on page 188.)

1.6 Airlines and Stable Fuel Prices. Southwest Airlines made it a company policy to engage in complex financial transactions to keep the cost of fuel constant. Why would the airline want to have stable fuel prices?

1.7 Supermarket Prices. In a supermarket, prices for tomatoes change quickly, but prices for mops tend to not change as rapidly. Can you offer an explanation why? (Related to Application 1 on page 188.)

1.8 Retail Price Stickiness in Catalogs. During periods of high inflation, retail prices in catalogs changed more frequently. Explain why this occurred. (Related to Application 1 on page 188.)

9.2 Understanding Aggregate Demand

2.1 Which of the following is *not* a component of aggregate demand?
a. Consumption
b. Investment
c. Government expenditures
d. The supply of money
e. Net exports

2.2 In the Great Depression, prices in the United States fell by 33 percent. *Ceteris paribus*, this led to an increase in aggregate demand through three channels: the _____ effect, the interest rate effect, and the international trade effect.

2.3 President George W. Bush and Congress lowered taxes in 2001, 2003, and 2008. *Ceteris paribus*, these decreases in taxes shifted the aggregate demand curve to the _____.

2.4 If the MPC is 0.9, the simple multiplier will be _____.

2.5 Because of other economic factors, such as taxes, the multiplier in the United States is _____ (larger/smaller) than 2.5.

2.6 Opening Export Markets. Suppose a foreign country, which originally prevented the United States from exporting to it, opens its market and U.S. firms start to make a considerable volume of sales. What happens to aggregate demand?

2.7 Calculating the MPC. In one year, a consumer's income increases by $200 and her savings increases by $40. What is her marginal propensity to *consume*?

2.8 Saving Behavior and Multipliers in Two Countries. Consumers in Country A have an MPS of 0.5 while consumers in Country B have an MPS of 0.4. Which country has the higher value for the multiplier?

2.9 State and Local Governments and Aggregate Demand. If state governments cut back their spending to balance their budgets, what will happen to aggregate demand?

9.3 Understanding Aggregate Supply

3.1 The long-run aggregate supply curve is _____ (vertical/horizontal).

3.2 A decrease in material costs will shift the short-run aggregate supply _____.

3.3 Using the long-run aggregate supply curve, a decrease in aggregate demand will _____ prices and _____ output.

3.4 A negative supply shock, such as higher oil prices, will _____ output and _____ prices in the short run. (Related to Application 3 on page 199.)

3.5 Higher Gas Prices, Frugal Consumers, and Economic Fluctuations. Suppose gasoline prices increased sharply and consumers became fearful of owning too many expensive cars. As a consequence, they cut back on their purchases of new cars and decided to increase their savings. How would this behavior shift the aggregate demand curve? Using the short-run aggregate supply curve, what will happen to prices and output in the short run?

3.6 What Caused This Recession? Suppose the economy goes into a recession. The political party in power blames it on an increase in the price of world oil and food. Opposing politicians blame a tax increase that the party in power had enacted. On the basis of aggregate demand and aggregate supply analysis, what evidence should you look at to try to determine what, or who, caused the recession? (*Hint*: look at the behavior of both prices and output in each case.) (Related to Application 2 on page 198.)

3.7 Understanding Stagflation. In 1974, oil prices suddenly increased dramatically and the economy experienced an adverse supply shock. *Ceteris paribus*, what happened to the price level and real GDP? Why is this sometimes called stagflation? (Related to Application 3 on page 199.)

3.8 China Comes Roaring Back. In the 2008 recession, China was one of the first economies to recover and its GDP growth quickly returned to its pre-recession levels. How did this affect aggregate demand in the rest of the world?

3.9 Long-Run Effects of a Shock to Demand. Suppose consumption spending rose quickly and then fell back to its normal level. What do you think would be the long-run effect on real GDP of this temporary shock? (Related to Application 2 on page 198.)

9.4 From the Short Run to the Long Run

4.1 Suppose the supply of money increases, causing output to exceed full employment. Prices will _____ and real GDP will _____ in the short run, and prices will _____ and real GDP will _____ in the long run.

4.2 Consider a decrease in the supply of money that causes output to fall short of full employment. Prices will _____ and real GDP will _____ in the short run, and prices will _____ and real GDP will _____ in the long run.

4.3 In a recession, real GDP is _____ potential GDP. This implies that unemployment is _____, driving wages _____. This results in a(n) _____ shift of the short-run aggregate supply curve.

4.4 A negative supply shock temporarily lowers output below full employment and raises prices. After the negative supply shock, real GDP is _____ potential GDP. This implies that unemployment is _____, driving wages. This results in a(n) _____ shift of the short-run aggregate supply curve.

4.5 **Lack of Credit and Aggregate Demand and Supply.** In the 2008 recession, both firms and households had limited access to credit. Explain how this could be *both* a negative shock to aggregate demand and a negative shock to aggregate supply.

4.6 **Shifts in Aggregate Demand and Cost-Push Inflation.** When wages rise and the short-run aggregate supply curve shifts up, the result is "cost-push" inflation. If the economy was initially at full-employment and the aggregate demand curve was shifted to the right, explain how "cost-push" inflation would result as the economy adjusts back to full employment.

4.7 **Exports and Real GDP.** Are increases in exports associated with increases in real GDP? A good place to start to find out is the Web site of the Federal Reserve Bank of St. Louis (http://research.stlouisfed.org/fred2).

Fiscal Policy

As President Obama's administration began in January 2009, the economy was in the midst of a very severe recession. Most observers believed that some fiscal stimulus was needed, but the size and composition came under fierce debate. Should the stimulus primarily take the form of tax cuts, as many Republicans advocated, or should it be primarily concentrated in increased government spending, as Democrats generally supported? And how large should the entire stimulus package be relative to the size of the gross domestic product?

After very contentious political negotiations, President Obama signed into law a $787 billion stimulus package, which was approximately 5.5 percent of GDP, the largest fiscal policy in U.S. history. Approximately one-third of the package was devoted to tax cuts, the remaining two-thirds to spending increases. Included in the spending increases were a large number of infrastructure projects as well as aid to state governments for assistance in meeting their health-care obligations.

As the bill was being passed, White House advisers claimed that with the stimulus unemployment would not rise above 8 percent; however, by later in the summer unemployment was near 10 percent. It also proved difficult to spend so much money. By August of 2009, only 20 percent of the stimulus funds had gone into effect. Did the biggest fiscal stimulus work as expected?

APPLYING THE CONCEPTS

1 Why are the United States and many other countries facing dramatically increasing costs for their government programs?
   Increasing Life Expectancy and Aging Populations Spur Costs of Entitlement Programs

2 How are tax rates and tax revenues related?
   The Confucius Curve?

3 Did President Obama's fiscal stimulus work as expected?
   Evaluating the Obama Fiscal Stimulus

fiscal policy

Changes in government taxes and spending that affect the level of GDP.

When the U.S. economy began to slow in late 2007 and early 2008, it was not long before policymakers and politicians from both major parties were calling for government action to combat the downturn. Common prescriptions included increasing government spending or reducing taxes, although specific recommendations differed sharply among those making them. As the economy was mired in a deep recession in 2008, even louder calls for action were heard.

In this chapter, we study how governments can use **fiscal policy**—changes in taxes and spending that affect the level of GDP—to stabilize the economy. We explore the logic of fiscal policy and explain why changes in government spending and taxation can, in principle, stabilize the economy. However, stabilizing the economy is much easier in theory than in actual practice, as we will see.

The chapter also provides an overview of spending and taxation by the federal government. These are essentially the tools the government uses to implement its fiscal policies. We will examine the federal deficit and begin to explore the controversies surrounding deficit spending.

One of the best ways to really understand fiscal policy is to see it in action. In the last part of the chapter, we trace the history of U.S. fiscal policy from the Great Depression in the 1930s to the present. As you will see, the public's attitude toward government fiscal policy has not been constant but has instead changed over time.

10.1 THE ROLE OF FISCAL POLICY

In the last chapter, we discussed how output and prices are determined where the aggregate demand curve intersects the short-run aggregate supply curve. We also saw that over time the short-run aggregate supply curve will shift to bring the economy back to full employment. In this section, we will explore how the government can shift the aggregate demand curve.

Fiscal Policy and Aggregate Demand

As we discussed in the last chapter, government spending and taxes can affect the level of aggregate demand. Increases in government spending or decreases in taxes will increase aggregate demand and shift the aggregate demand curve to the right. Decreases in government spending or increases in taxes will decrease aggregate demand and shift the aggregate demand curve to the left.

Why do changes in government spending or taxes shift the aggregate demand curve? Recall from our discussion in the last chapter that aggregate demand consists of four components: consumption spending, investment spending, government purchases, and net exports. These four components are the four parts of aggregate demand. Thus, increases in government purchases directly increase aggregate demand because they are a component of aggregate demand. Decreases in government purchases directly decrease aggregate demand.

Changes in taxes affect aggregate demand indirectly. For example, if the government lowers taxes consumers pay, consumers will have more income at their disposal and will increase their consumption spending. Because consumption spending is a component of aggregate demand, aggregate demand will increase as well. Increases in taxes will have the opposite effect. Consumers will have less income at their disposal and will decrease their consumption spending. As a result, aggregate demand will decrease. Changes in taxes can also affect businesses and lead to changes in investment spending. Suppose, for example, that the government cuts taxes in such a way as to provide incentives for new investment spending by businesses. Because investment spending is a component of aggregate demand, the increase in investment spending will increase aggregate demand.

In Panel A of Figure 10.1 we show a simple example of fiscal policy in action. The economy is initially operating at a level of GDP, y_0, where the aggregate demand curve AD_0 intersects the short-run aggregate supply curve AS. This level of output is below

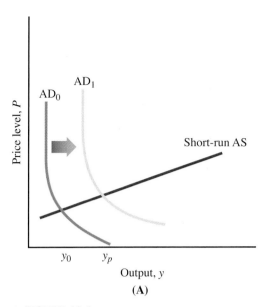
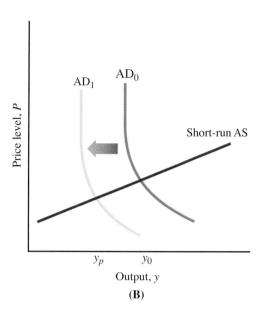

▲ FIGURE 10.1

Fiscal Policy in Action

Panel A shows that an increase in government spending shifts the aggregate demand curve from AD_0 to AD_1, restoring the economy to full employment. This is an example of expansionary policy. Panel B shows that an increase in taxes shifts the aggregate demand curve to the left, from AD_0 to AD_1, restoring the economy to full employment. This is an example of contractionary policy.

the level of full employment or potential output, y_p. To increase the level of output, the government can increase government spending—say, on military goods—which will shift the aggregate demand curve to the right, to AD_1. Now the new aggregate demand curve intersects the aggregate supply curve at the full-employment level of output. Alternatively, instead of increasing its spending, the government could reduce taxes on consumers and businesses. This would also shift the aggregate demand curve to the right. Government policies that increase aggregate demand are called **expansionary policies**. Increasing government spending and cutting taxes are examples of expansionary policies.

The government can also use fiscal policy to decrease GDP if the economy is operating at too high a level of output, which would lead to an overheating economy and rising prices. In Panel B of Figure 10.1, the economy is initially operating at a level of output, y_0, that exceeds full-employment output, y_p. An increase in taxes can shift the aggregate demand curve from AD_0 to AD_1. This shift will bring the economy back to full employment. Alternatively, the government could cut its spending to move the aggregate demand curve to the left. Government policies that decrease aggregate demand are called **contractionary policies**. Decreasing government spending and increasing taxes are examples of contractionary policies.

Both examples illustrate how policymakers use fiscal policy to stabilize the economy. In these two simple examples, fiscal policy seems very straightforward. But as we will soon see, in practice it is more difficult to implement effective policy.

expansionary policies
Government policy actions that lead to increases in aggregate demand.

contractionary policies
Government policy actions that lead to decreases in aggregate demand.

The Fiscal Multiplier

Let's recall the multiplier we developed in the last chapter. The basic idea is that the final shift in the aggregate demand curve will be larger than the initial increase. For example, if government purchases increased by $10 billion, that would initially shift the aggregate demand curve to the right by $10 billion. However, the total shift in the aggregate demand curve will be larger, say, $15 billion. Conversely, a decrease in purchases by $10 billion may cause a total shift of the aggregate demand curve to the left by $15 billion.

This multiplier effect occurs because an initial change in output will affect the income of households and thus change consumer spending. For example, an increase in government spending of $10 billion will initially raise household incomes by $10 billion and lead to increases in consumer spending. As we discussed in the last chapter, the precise amount of the increase will depend on the marginal propensity to consume and other factors. In turn, the increase in consumer spending will raise output and income further, leading to further increases in consumer spending. The multiplier takes all these effects into account.

As the government develops policies to stabilize the economy, it needs to take the multiplier into account. The total shift in aggregate demand will be larger than the initial shift. As we will see later in this chapter, U.S. policymakers have taken the multiplier into account as they have developed policies for the economy.

The Limits to Stabilization Policy

We've seen that the government can use fiscal policy—changes in the level of taxes or government spending—to alter the level of GDP. If the current level of GDP is below full employment or potential output, the government can use expansionary policies, such as tax cuts and increased spending, to raise the level of GDP and reduce unemployment.

Both expansionary and contractionary policies are examples of **stabilization policies**, actions to move the economy closer to full employment or potential output.

It is very difficult to implement stabilization policies for two big reasons. First, there are lags, or delays, in stabilization policy. Lags arise because decision makers are often slow to recognize and respond to changes in the economy, and fiscal policies and other stabilization policies take time to operate. Second, economists simply do not know enough about all aspects of the economy to be completely accurate in all their forecasts. Although economists have made great progress in understanding the economy, the difficulties of forecasting the precise behavior of human beings, who can change their minds or sometimes act irrationally, place limits on our forecasting ability.

LAGS   Poorly timed policies can magnify economic fluctuations. Suppose that (1) GDP is currently below full employment but will return to full employment on its own within one year, and that (2) stabilization policies take a full year to become effective. If policymakers tried to expand the economy today, their actions would not take effect until a year from now. One year from now, the economy would normally be back at full employment by itself. But if stabilization policies were enacted, one year from now the economy would be stimulated unnecessarily, and output would exceed full employment.

Figure 10.2 illustrates the problem caused by lags. Panel A shows an example of successful stabilization policy. The solid line represents the behavior of GDP in the absence of policies. Successful stabilization policies can dampen, that is, reduce in magnitude, economic fluctuations, lowering output when it exceeds full employment and raising output when it falls below full employment. This would be easy to accomplish if there were no lags in policy. The dashed curve shows how successful policies can reduce economic fluctuations.

Panel B shows the consequences of ill-timed policies. Again, assume that policies take a year before they are effective. At the start of year 0, the economy is below potential. If policymakers engaged in expansionary policies at the start of year 1, the change would not take effect until the end of year 1. This would raise output even higher above full employment. Ill-timed stabilization policies can magnify economic fluctuations.

Where do the lags in policy come from? Economists recognize two broad classes of lags: *inside lags* and *outside lags*. **Inside lags** refer to the time it takes to formulate a policy. **Outside lags** refer to the time it takes for the policy to actually work. To help you understand inside and outside lags, imagine that you are steering a large ocean liner and you are looking out for possible collisions with hidden icebergs. The time it takes you to spot an iceberg, communicate this information to the crew, and initiate the process of changing course is the inside lag. Because ocean liners are large and

stabilization policies
Policy actions taken to move the economy closer to full employment or potential output.

inside lags
The time it takes to formulate a policy.

outside lags
The time it takes for the policy to actually work.

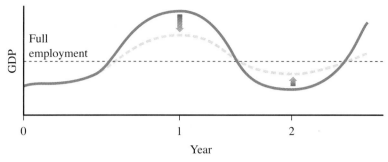

(A) Successful stabilization policy can dampen fluctuations.

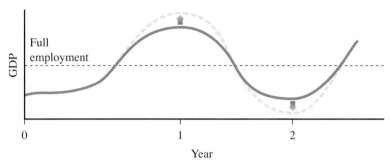

(B) Ill-timed policies can magnify fluctuations.

▲ FIGURE 10.2

Possible Pitfalls in Stabilization Policy

Panel A shows an example of successful stabilization policy. The solid line represents the behavior of GDP in the absence of policies. The dashed line shows the behavior of GDP when policies are in place. Successfully timed policies help smooth out economic fluctuations. Panel B shows the consequences of ill-timed policies. Again, the solid line shows GDP in the absence of policies and the dashed line shows GDP with policies in place. Notice how ill-timed policies make economic fluctuations greater.

have lots of momentum, it will take a long time before your ocean liner begins to turn; this time is the outside lag.

Inside lags occur for two basic reasons. One is that it takes time to identify and recognize a problem. For example, the data available to policymakers may be poor and conflicting. Some economic indicators may look fine, but others may cause concern. It often takes several months to a year before it is clear that there is a serious problem with the economy.

A good example of an inside lag occurred at the beginning of the Great Depression. Although the stock market crashed in October 1929, we know from newspaper and magazine accounts that business leaders were not particularly worried about the economy for some time. Not until late in 1930 did the public begin to recognize the severity of the depression.

The other reason for inside lags is that once a problem has been diagnosed, it still takes time before the government can take action. This delay is most severe for fiscal policy because any changes in taxes or spending must be approved by both houses of Congress and by the president. In recent years, political opponents have been preoccupied with disagreements about the size of the government and the role it should play in the economy, making it difficult to reach a consensus on action in a timely manner.

For example, soon after he was inaugurated in 1993, President Bill Clinton proposed an expansionary stimulus package as part of his overall budget plan. The package contained a variety of spending programs designed to increase the level of GDP and avert a recession. However, the plan was attacked as wasteful and unnecessary, and it did not survive. As it turned out, the stimulus package was not necessary—the economy grew rapidly in the next several years. Nonetheless, this episode illustrates how difficult it is to develop expansionary fiscal policies in time to have the effect we want them to.

Policies are also subject to outside lags—the time it takes for them to become effective. For example, if taxes are cut, it takes time for individuals and businesses to change their spending plans to take advantage of the tax cuts. Therefore, it will be a while before increases in spending raise GDP. Outside lags in fiscal policy are relatively short. Moreover, the multiplier effects tend to work through the economy rather quickly.

Economists use *econometric models* to replicate the behavior of the economy mathematically and statistically, and to assist them in developing economic forecasts. They can also use models to estimate the length of outside lags. One such model predicts that an increase in government spending will increase GDP by its maximum effect after just six months.

FORECASTING UNCERTAINTIES   What makes the problem of lags even worse is that economists are not very accurate in forecasting what will happen in the economy. For example, a classic problem policymakers face when the economy appears to be slowing down is knowing whether the slowdown is temporary or will persist. Unfortunately, stabilization policy cannot be effective without accurate forecasting. If economic forecasters predict an overheated economy and the government adopts a contractionary policy, the result could be disastrous if the economy weakened before the policy took effect. Today, most economic policymakers understand these limitations and are cautious in using activist policies.

10.2   THE FEDERAL BUDGET

The federal budget—the document that describes what the federal government spends and how it pays for that spending—provides the framework for fiscal policy. In this section, we will take a closer look at federal spending and taxation and what happens when one exceeds the other. The federal budget is extremely large, and the programs that the federal government supports are very complex. To give you a sense of the magnitude of the budget, in 2009 total federal spending was approximately 24.7 percent of GDP, or $3.52 trillion. Federal taxes were 14.8 percent of GDP. With a U.S. population of about 300 million, total federal spending amounted to approximately $11,722 per person.

Probably the best way to begin to grasp the scope and complexities of the U.S. federal budget is to look at recent data to see where we spend money and how we raise it. As we explore the budgetary data, keep in mind that the government runs its budget on a *fiscal-year basis*, not a calendar-year basis. Fiscal year 2009, for example, began on October 1, 2008, and ended on September 30, 2009.

States and local governments also provide government services and collect taxes. Some important services (for example, education) are primarily funded by state and local governments, and others, such as welfare and health care for the poor, are funded jointly by the federal government and state governments. However, because our focus in this chapter is on federal fiscal policy, we will concentrate our discussion on federal spending and taxation.

Federal Spending

Federal spending, spending by the U.S. government, consists of two broad components: federal government purchases of goods and services and transfer payments. As you should recall from our discussion of GDP accounting, only federal government purchases of goods and services are included in GDP. Transfer payments, although an important part of the federal budget, are not a component of GDP because they do not represent any currently produced goods or services.

To study the components of federal spending, we will look at the final data from fiscal year 2007 provided by the Congressional Budget Office, a nonpartisan agency of Congress that provides both budgetary forecasts and historical data on the budget.

Table 10.1 provides key data on federal expenditures for fiscal year 2009, both in absolute dollar terms and as a percent of GDP.

TABLE 10.1 FEDERAL SPENDING FOR FISCAL YEAR 2009

Category	Outlays (billions)	Percent of GDP
Total outlays	$3,518	24.7%
Discretionary spending	1,237	8.7
Defense	656	4.6
Nondefense	581	4.1
Entitlements and mandatory spending	2,094	14.7
Social Security	678	4.8
Medicare and Medicaid	750	5.3
Other programs	666	4.6
Net interest	187	1.3

SOURCE: Congressional Budget Office, January 2010.

Let's begin with the broad categories of the budget. Total spending, or outlays, in fiscal year 2009 were $3,518 billion or approximately 24.7 percent of GDP. Three components of the budget comprise this total: discretionary spending, entitlements and mandatory spending, and net interest.

Discretionary spending constitutes all the programs that Congress authorizes on an annual basis that are not automatically funded by prior laws. It includes defense spending and all nondefense domestic spending. When people commonly discuss federal spending, they often focus on this category, which includes the Defense Department, the Environmental Protection Agency, the State Department, the Interior Department, and other agencies. However, discretionary spending is less than 40 percent of total federal spending. Total nondefense spending is about 4 percent of GDP.

Congress and the president can use discretionary funds directly for activist fiscal policy. To stimulate the economy, they can authorize additional spending by government agencies, or they can urge agencies to accelerate their current spending plans. However, it does take time for bureaucracies to act, and just because Congress authorizes new spending does not mean the agencies will spend the funds immediately.

Entitlement and mandatory spending constitutes all spending that Congress has authorized by prior law. These expenditures must be made by the federal government unless Congress changes the laws. The terms *entitlement* and *mandatory* spending are not totally accurate, however. Individuals are "entitled" to benefits only to the extent they meet the requirements passed by Congress. Congress can always change the rules. Similarly, this category of spending is "mandatory" only to the extent Congress maintains the current programs in place.

Entitlements and mandatory spending are the single largest component of the federal budget. One of the most familiar programs is **Social Security**, which provides retirement payments to retirees as well as a host of other benefits to widows and families of disabled workers. **Medicare** provides health care to all individuals once they reach the age of 65. **Medicaid** provides health care to the poor, in conjunction with the states. Spending on these two health programs by the federal government now exceeds spending on Social Security. The government provides a range of other programs as well, including additional retirement and disability programs (aside from Social Security) and farm price supports to provide income to farmers. Some of these programs are *means tested*. That is, the amount of benefit is partly based on the income of the recipient. Medicaid, for example, is a means-tested program.

Net interest is the interest the government pays on the government debt held by the public, for example, U.S. Treasury bonds, bills, and U.S. savings bonds. We will discuss how the government borrows money later in the chapter. In fiscal year 2009, total net interest payments to the public were $187 billion, or approximately 1.3 percent of

discretionary spending

The spending programs that Congress authorizes on an annual basis.

entitlement and mandatory spending

Spending that Congress has authorized by prior law, primarily providing support for individuals.

Social Security

A federal government program to provide retirement support and a host of other benefits.

Medicare

A federal government health program for the elderly.

Medicaid

A federal and state government health program for the poor.

APPLICATION 1

INCREASING LIFE EXPECTANCY AND AGING POPULATIONS SPUR COSTS OF ENTITLEMENT PROGRAMS

APPLYING THE CONCEPTS #1: Why are the United States and many other countries facing dramatically increasing costs for their government programs?

As life expectancies increase, the population ages, and new medical technologies become available to help people live longer, economists and budget analysts predict that spending on federal retirement and health programs will grow extremely rapidly. Today, Social Security, Medicare, and Medicaid constitute approximately 10 percent of GDP. Experts estimate that in 2075—when children born today are in their retirement years—spending on these programs will be approximately 22 percent of GDP. This is a larger share of GDP than *all* federal government spending today! How will our society cope with increased demands for these services?

One possibility is to leave the existing programs in place and just raise taxes to pay for them. This strategy would have two implications. First, if we maintained the federal share of GDP of all other programs, it would mean a large expansion of federal government spending, from 20 percent of GDP to 32 percent of GDP. Second, it would mean a very large increase in the tax burden on future workers and businesses.

Some economists suggest the government should save and invest now to increase GDP in the future, reducing the burden on future generations. However, the saving and investment would increase GDP, and entitlement payments would grow right along with it. As a result, the relative burden of taking care of the elderly would not change dramatically.

Another strategy is to try to reform the entitlement systems, placing more responsibility on individuals and families for their retirement and well-being. For example, we could increase the age at which retirement benefits begin to be paid, and thereby encourage individuals to spend more years in the labor force. Or we could try to reform the health-care system to encourage more competition to reduce health-care expenditures.

All these changes would be very difficult to make, however. Other countries, including Japan and many nations in Europe, which have even older populations and low birth rates, will face more severe challenges and face them earlier than the United States will. Perhaps we can learn from them. Nonetheless, pressures on the federal budget will begin to escalate in the next decade, and policymakers will need to take steps soon to cope with the challenge.   **Related to Exercise 2.8.**

GDP. Total expenditures on net interest are directly related to the total government debt held by the public and the level of interest rates. Increased government debt and higher interest rates will lead to higher net interest payments by the government.

As the population ages, entitlements and net interest are becoming the fastest-growing component of the federal budget.

Federal Revenues

The federal government receives its revenue from taxes levied on both individuals and businesses. Table 10.2 shows the revenues the federal government received in fiscal year 2009 in both dollar terms and as a percent of GDP.

Let's review the categories that comprise total federal revenue. The single largest component of federal revenue is the familiar *individual income tax*. Tax returns calculating the tax individuals or couples owed during the prior year must be filed by April 15 of every year. During the year, the federal government collects in advance some of the

TABLE 10.2 SOURCES OF FEDERAL GOVERNMENT REVENUE, FISCAL YEAR 2009		
Category	Receipts (billions)	Percent of GDP
Total revenue	$2,105	14.8%
Individual income taxes	915	6.4
Social insurance taxes	891	6.3
Corporate taxes	138	1.0
Estate, excise, and others	160	1.1

SOURCE: Congressional Budget Office, January 2010.

taxes due by *withholding* a portion of workers' paychecks. Taxpayers not subject to withholding or who earn income through investments must make estimated tax payments each quarter, so the tax due the federal government is paid evenly over the year in which it is earned.

The second-largest component of federal revenue is *social insurance taxes*, which are taxes levied on earnings to pay for Social Security and Medicare. Today, social insurance taxes are almost as large as individual income taxes, and together they comprise nearly 80 percent of total federal revenue. Unlike individual income taxes, social insurance taxes are paid only on wages and not on income from investments.

Other taxes paid directly by individuals and families include *estate and gift taxes*, *excise taxes*, and *custom duties*. Estate and gift taxes, sometimes known as the "death tax," are levied on the estates and previous gifts of individuals when they pass away. In 2009 estates were taxed only if they exceeded a threshold of $3.5 million—so small estates did not pay this tax. In 2010 the estate tax was allowed to expire but it was expected to be revived and changed in 2010—otherwise the law dictated that much lower thresholds would be in place in 2011. The estate and gift tax was expected to raise only 0.2 percent of total federal revenue in fiscal year 2009, but it generated a great deal of controversy. Opponents of the tax argue that it destroys family-held businesses, such as family farms passed down from one generation to the next. Proponents claim the tax is necessary to prevent what they see as unfair accumulation of wealth across generations.

The corporate tax is a tax levied on the earnings of corporations. This tax raised less than 7 percent of total federal revenues during fiscal year 2009. The tax was a more important source of revenue in past decades but has declined to today's relatively low level. This decline has been attributed to many factors, including falling corporate profits as a share of GDP, the growth of opportunities for tax shelters, incentives provided by Congress to stimulate business investment and research and development, and complex rules for taxing multinational corporations that operate on a global basis. It was especially low in 2009 because corporate profits fell sharply during the recession.

The other sources of government revenue are relatively minor. *Federal excise taxes* are taxes levied on the sale of certain products, for example, gasoline, tires, firearms, alcohol, and tobacco. *Custom duties* are taxes levied on goods imported to the United States, such as foreign cars or wines.

SUPPLY-SIDE ECONOMICS AND THE LAFFER CURVE   Is it possible for a government to cut tax rates yet still raise more revenue? That's a politician's dream. People would face lower tax rates, yet there would be more money for politicians to spend. Economist Arthur Laffer argued in the late 1970s that there was a strong possibility we could do this in the U.S. economy. Laffer's views influenced many politicians at the time and became the basis for supply-side economics. **Supply-side economics** is a school of thought that emphasizes the role taxes play in the supply of output in the economy. Supply-side economists look at the effects of taxes not just on aggregate demand, as we did earlier in this chapter, but also on aggregate supply. As we saw in Chapter 7, a decrease in tax rates will typically tend to increase labor supply and output. Thus, changes in taxes can also shift the aggregate supply curve.

supply-side economics

A school of thought that emphasizes the role that taxes play in the supply of output in the economy.

APPLICATION 2

THE CONFUCIUS CURVE?

APPLYING THE CONCEPTS #2: How are tax rates and tax revenues related?

While the idea that cutting tax rates might actually increase tax revenue is often attributed to economist Arthur Laffer, in fact, it is actually a much older idea than that. Yu Juo, one of the 12 wise men who succeeded Confucius in ancient China, had a very similar idea. He was asked by Duke Ai, "It has been a year of famine and there are not enough revenues to run the state. What should I do?"

> Juo said, "Why can't you use a 10 percent tax?"
>
> The Duke answered, "I can't even get by on a 20 percent tax; how am I going to do it on 10 percent?"
>
> Juo said, "If the people have enough what prince can be in want? If the people are in want how can the Prince be satisfied?"

Clearly, Yu Juo was skeptical that raising rates would raise revenues and advocated for lower tax rates.

Today, revenue estimators in Washington, D.C., do not share entirely in Yu Juo's wisdom. But they do recognize that cutting tax rates will stimulate economic activity, which will offset some of the loss in potential revenues to the government.   **Related to Exercise 2.9.**

SOURCE: Based on The Analects of Confucius, 12.9, http://www.ibiblio.org/chinesehistory/contents/08fea/c02files.02lib/text001.html (accessed April 13, 2010).

Laffer curve

A relationship between the tax rates and tax revenues that illustrates that high tax rates could lead to lower tax revenues if economic activity is severely discouraged.

Laffer also developed a model known today as the **Laffer curve**. Suppose a government imposed extremely high tariffs (taxes) on imported goods—tariffs so high that no one could afford to import any goods whatsoever. If this were the case, the government would not collect any revenue from the tariffs. But if the government cut the rates and individuals began to buy imported goods, the government would start to collect at least some tariff revenue. This was Laffer's point: Lower taxes (tariffs) could actually lead to higher government revenues.

Virtually all economists today believe Laffer's tax revenue idea won't work when it comes to broad-based income taxes or payroll taxes. For these types of taxes, cutting rates from their current levels would simply reduce the revenues the government collects, because most economists believe the supply of labor is not as sensitive to changes in tax rates as Laffer believed it was. But there are some taxes, such as tariffs or taxes on the gains investors earn by holding stocks and bonds, for which Laffer's claim is plausible.

The Federal Deficit and Fiscal Policy

budget deficit

The amount by which government spending exceeds revenues in a given year.

The federal government runs a **budget deficit** when it spends more than it receives in tax revenues in a given year. Here is how it works. Suppose a government wishes to spend $100 billion but receives only $95 billion in tax revenue. To actually spend the $100 billion, the government must obtain funds from some source. Facing a $5 billion shortfall, it will borrow that money from the public by selling the public government bonds. A *government bond* is an IOU in which the government promises to later pay back the money lent to it, with interest. Thus, when the public purchases $5 billion of these bonds, it transfers $5 billion to the government. Later the public will receive its $5 billion back with interest.

If the government collects more in taxes than it wishes to spend in a given year, it is running a **budget surplus**. In this case, the government has excess funds and can buy back bonds it previously sold to the public, eliminating some of its debt.

Many political and economic considerations enter into the decisions to change government spending or taxes or raise or lower deficits. In the last part of this chapter we will see how fiscal policy has been used historically in the United States. In later chapters, we will look in more depth at other political considerations that influence fiscal policy.

budget surplus
The amount by which government revenues exceed government expenditures in a given year.

Automatic Stabilizers

Both government spending and tax revenues are very sensitive to the state of the economy. Because tax collections are based largely on individual and corporate income, tax revenues will fall sharply during a recession as national income falls. At the same time, government transfer payments for programs such as unemployment insurance and food stamps will also tend to increase during a recession. The result is higher government spending and lower tax collections and the increased likelihood that the government will run a budget deficit. Similarly, when the economy grows rapidly, tax collections increase and government expenditures on transfer payments decrease, and the likelihood of the federal government running a surplus is greater.

Now suppose an economy had a balanced federal budget—neither deficit nor surplus. An external shock (such as a dramatic increase in oil prices or drought) then plunged the economy into a recession. Tax revenues fall and expenditures on transfer payments increase, resulting in a budget deficit. Believe it or not, the deficit actually serves a valuable role in stabilizing the economy. It works through three channels:

1 Increased transfer payments such as unemployment insurance, food stamps, and other welfare payments increase the income of some households, partly offsetting the fall in household income.

2 Other households whose incomes are falling pay less in taxes, which partly offsets the decline in their household income. Because incomes do not fall as much as they would have in the absence of the deficit, consumption spending does not decline as much.

3 Because the corporation tax depends on corporate profits and profits fall in a recession, taxes on businesses also fall. Lower corporate taxes help to prevent businesses from cutting spending as much as they would otherwise during a recession.

The government deficit itself, in effect, offsets part of the adverse effect of the recession and thus helps stabilize the economy.

Similarly, during an economic boom, transfer payments fall and tax revenues increase. This dampens the increase in household income and also the increase in consumption and investment spending that would accompany higher household income and higher corporate profits. Taxes and transfer payments that stabilize GDP without requiring explicit actions by policymakers are called **automatic stabilizers**.

The great virtue of automatic stabilizers is that they do not require explicit action from the president and Congress to change the law. Given the long inside lags caused by ideological battles in Washington, D.C., over spending, taxes, and the deficit, it is fortunate that we have mechanisms in place to dampen economic fluctuations without requiring explicit and deliberative action.

automatic stabilizers
Taxes and transfer payments that stabilize GDP without requiring policymakers to take explicit action.

Are Deficits Bad?

Let's take a closer look at fiscal policy designed to stabilize the economy. If the budget were initially balanced and the economy plunged into a recession, a budget deficit would emerge as tax revenues fell and expenditures increased. To combat the recession, policymakers could then either increase government spending or cut taxes. Both actions, however, would increase the deficit—an important point to remember.

Despite concerns about increasing the deficit, this is precisely the right policy. If policymakers tried to avoid running a deficit by raising taxes or cutting spending, that would actually make the recession worse. The key lesson here is that during a recession, we should focus on what our fiscal policy actions do to the economy, not what they do to the deficit.

Does that mean concerns about the federal budget deficit are misplaced? No, because in the long run, large budget deficits can have an adverse effect on the economy. We explore these issues in more detail in a later chapter, but we can easily understand the basic problem. We have seen that when an economy is operating at full employment, output must be divided between consumption, investment, government spending, and net exports. Suppose, then, the government cuts taxes for households and runs a deficit. The reduced taxes will tend to increase consumer spending. Consumers may save some of the tax cut but will consume the rest. However, because output is fixed at full employment, some other component of output must be reduced, or crowded out, which we first discussed in Chapter 7. Crowding out is an example of the principle of opportunity cost.

PRINCIPLE OF OPPORTUNITY COST
The opportunity cost of something is what you sacrifice to get it.

In this case, we normally expect that the increased consumption spending will come at the sacrifice of reduced investment spending. As we have seen, with reduced investment spending the economy will grow more slowly in the future. Thus, the budget deficit will increase current consumption but slow the growth of the economy in the future. This is the real concern with prolonged budget deficits.

Another way to understand the concern about long-run deficits is to think of what happens in the financial markets when the government runs large deficits. As the government runs large deficits, it will have to borrow increasing amounts of money from the public by selling U.S. government bonds. In the financial markets, the government will be in increased competition with businesses that are trying to raise funds from the public to finance their investment plans, too. This increased competition from the government will make it more difficult and costly for businesses to raise funds and, as a result, investment spending will decrease.

10.3 FISCAL POLICY IN U.S. HISTORY

The fiscal policies that Congress and the president use have evolved over many years. In this section, we review the historical events that helped create today's U.S. fiscal policies.

The Depression Era

The basic principles of fiscal policy—using government spending and taxation to stabilize the economy—have been known for many years and, indeed, were discussed in the 1920s. However, it took a long time before economic policy decisions were based on these principles. Many people associate active fiscal policy in the United States with actions taken by President Franklin Roosevelt during the Great Depression of the 1930s. But this view is misleading, according to E. Cary Brown, a former economics professor at the Massachusetts Institute of Technology.[1]

During the 1930s, politicians did not believe in modern fiscal policy, largely because they feared the consequences of government budget deficits. According to

Brown, fiscal policy was expansionary only during two years of the Great Depression, 1931 and 1936. In those years, Congress voted for substantial payments to veterans, over objections of presidents Herbert Hoover and Franklin Roosevelt. Although government spending increased during the 1930s, taxes increased sufficiently during that same period, with the result that there was no net fiscal expansion.

The Kennedy Administration

Although modern fiscal policy was not deliberately used during the 1930s, the growth in military spending at the onset of World War II in 1941 increased total demand in the economy and helped pull the economy out of its long decade of poor performance. But to see fiscal policy in action, we need to turn to the 1960s. It was not until the presidency of John F. Kennedy during the early 1960s that modern fiscal policy came to be accepted.

Walter Heller, the chairman of the president's Council of Economic Advisers under John F. Kennedy, was a forceful advocate of active fiscal policy. From his perspective, the economy was operating far below its potential, and a tax cut was the perfect medicine to bring it back to full employment. When Kennedy entered office, the unemployment rate was 6.7 percent. Heller believed the unemployment rate at full employment—the "natural rate" of unemployment, that is—was really only about 4 percent. He convinced Kennedy of the need for a tax cut to stimulate the economy, and Kennedy put forth an economic program based largely on modern fiscal policy principles.

Two other factors led the Kennedy administration to support the tax cut. First, tax rates were extremely high at the time. The top individual tax rate was 91 percent, compared to about 40 percent today. The corporate tax rate was 52 percent, compared to 35 percent today. Second, Heller convinced Kennedy that even if a tax cut led to a federal budget deficit, it was not a problem. In 1961, the federal deficit was less than 1 percent of GDP, and future projections indicated it would disappear as the economy grew because of higher tax revenues.

The tax cuts were enacted in February 1964, after Lyndon Johnson became president following Kennedy's assassination. They included permanent cuts in rates for both individuals and corporations. Estimating the actual effects these tax cuts had on the economy is difficult. To make a valid comparison, we need to estimate how the economy would have behaved without them. What we do know is that the economy grew at a rapid rate following the tax cuts. From 1963 to 1966, both real GDP and consumption grew at rates exceeding 4 percent per year. We cannot rule out the possibility that the economy could have grown just as rapidly without the tax cuts. Nonetheless, the rapid growth during this period suggests the tax cuts had the effect, predicted by Heller's theory, of stimulating economic growth.

The Vietnam War Era

The next major use of modern fiscal policy occurred in 1968. As the Vietnam War began and military spending increased, unemployment fell to very low levels. From 1966 to 1969, the overall unemployment rate fell below 4 percent. Policymakers became concerned that the economy was overheating and this would lead to a higher inflation rate. In 1968, a temporary tax surcharge of 10 percent was enacted to reduce total demand for goods and services. The 10 percent surcharge was a "tax on a tax," so it raised the taxes paid by households by 10 percent. Essentially, the surcharge was specifically designed to be temporary and expired within a year.

The surcharge did not decrease consumer spending as much as economists had initially estimated, however. Part of the reason was that it was temporary. Economists who have studied consumption behavior have noticed that consumers often base their

permanent income

An estimate of a household's long-run average level of income.

spending on an estimate of their long-run average income, or **permanent income**, not on their current income.

For example, consider a salesperson who usually earns $50,000 a year, although her income in any single year might be slightly higher or lower. Knowing her permanent income is $50,000, she consumes $45,000. If her income in one year is higher than average, say $55,000, she is still likely to consume $45,000 (as if she earned just her normal $50,000) and save the rest.

The one-year tax surcharge during the Vietnam War had a similar effect. Because consumers knew the surcharge was not permanent, they didn't alter their spending habits very much. The surtax reduced households' savings, not their consumption. The result was a smaller decrease in demand for goods and services than economists anticipated.

During the 1970s, there were many changes in taxes and spending but no major changes in overall fiscal policy. A recession in 1973 led to a tax rebate and other incentives in 1975, but, by and large, changes to fiscal policy were mild.

The Reagan Administration

The tax cuts enacted during 1981 at the beginning of the first term of President Ronald Reagan were significant. However, they were not proposed to increase aggregate demand. Instead, the tax cuts were justified on the basis of improving economic incentives and increasing the supply of output. In other words, they were supply-side motivated. Taxes can have important effects on the supply of labor, saving, and economic growth. Proponents of the 1981 tax cuts emphasized these particular effects and not increases in aggregate demand. Nonetheless, the tax cuts did appear to increase consumer demand and helped the economy recover from the back-to-back recessions in the early 1980s.

By the mid-1980s, large government budget deficits began to emerge, and policymakers became concerned. As the deficits grew and became the focus of attention, interest in using fiscal policy to manage the economy waned because policymakers placed primary concern on deficit reduction, not stabilization policy. Although there were government spending and tax changes in the 1980s and 1990s, few were justified solely as policies to change aggregate demand.

The Clinton and George W. Bush Administrations

At the beginning of his administration, President Bill Clinton proposed a "stimulus package" that would increase aggregate demand, but it was defeated in Congress. Clinton later successfully passed a major tax increase that brought the budget into balance. A Republican-controlled Congress that had different priorities than the Clinton administration limited government spending. By 1998, the federal budget actually began to show surpluses rather than deficits, setting the stage for tax cuts.

During his first year in office in 2001, President George W. Bush passed a 10-year tax cut plan that decreased tax rates, in part to eliminate the government surpluses and return revenues to households, but also to stimulate the economy that was slowing down as the high-tech investment boom was ending.

The first year of the tax cut featured tax rebates or refunds of up to $600 per married couple. The refunds were intended to increase aggregate demand.

After the September 11, 2001, terrorist attacks, President Bush and Congress became less concerned with balancing the federal budget and authorized new spending programs to provide relief to victims and to stimulate the economy, which had entered into a recession prior to September 11.

In May 2003, President Bush signed another tax bill to stimulate the sluggish economy and, in particular, to increase investment spending. This bill had many distinct features, including moving up some of the previously scheduled cuts in tax rates

APPLICATION 3

EVALUATING THE OBAMA FISCAL STIMULUS

APPLYING THE CONCEPTS #3: Did President Obama's fiscal stimulus work as expected?

As part of President Obama's fiscal stimulus package, the Council of Economic Advisers was required to make quarterly reports to the Congress on the role that the stimulus package played in economic recovery. The chairperson of the council, Christina Romer from U.C., Berkeley, was charged with the difficult task of assessing the efficacy of the stimulus package and the council delivered its first report to the Congress in September 2009.

The council examined the effects of the stimulus project in several ways. First, it used statistical methods to suggest that both employment and economic growth were higher in the second and third quarters of 2009 then would have been predicted by statistical models. This method, however, does not distinguish between the effects of the stimulus package and other economic interventions such as monetary policy. Second, the council used conventional economic models to estimate the effects of the stimulus—essentially assuming conventional multipliers for government spending and taxes. Third, the council compared international experiences of countries that used different stimulus strategies and argued that those countries that had the most ambitious programs of fiscal stimulus improved the most.

The council estimated that the stimulus package avoided a loss of about 1 million jobs by August 2009. But critics pointed out that unemployment was near 10 percent and most forecasters were still projecting high unemployment for several years. Even if the stimulus package did have a positive effect, the lingering effects of the recession would still be painful.   **Related to Exercise 3.7.**

SOURCE: Based on Executive Office of the President, Council of Economic Advisers, *The Economic Impact of the American Recovery and Reinvestment Act of 2009, First Quarterly Report.* September 10, 2009, http://www.whitehouse.gov/assets/documents/CEA_ARRA_Report_Final.pdf

---

that were part of the 2001 tax bill, increasing the child tax credit, and lowering taxes on dividends and capital gains.

In 2008, a slowing economy led President Bush and Congress to adopt tax rebates and some investment incentives in early 2008. The tax cuts were relatively large, approximately 1 percent of GDP, and the rebates, some as large as $1,800, were designed to reach 128 million households. As we noted in the chapter opener, President Obama and Congress enacted the largest stimulus package in history in February 2009. Although it was likely to have some positive impact on employment and GDP growth, its size and composition proved to be controversial.

The combination of the 2001 and 2007 recessions, the financial crisis of 2008 and its aftermath, the various tax cuts, the large stimulus package of 2009, and the increased expenses associated with the wars in Afghanistan and Iraq sharply changed the fiscal landscape from the beginning of the decade. Although the deficit temporarily became smaller in 2006 and 2007, the situation changed radically. By fiscal year 2009 the deficit had soared to 9.9 percent of GDP, far above usual historical levels. Future projections indicated that the deficit would likely fall, but still remain high for future years.

Figure 10.3 plots the course of spending, taxes, and the deficit since 1996 and shows the recent reemergence of deficits from the surpluses of the late 1990s and the dramatic deficits in 2009. The prospect of future deficits may limit the ability of the U.S. government to conduct expansionary fiscal policy in the near future and will set the background for the political debates in Washington, D.C., for many years to come.

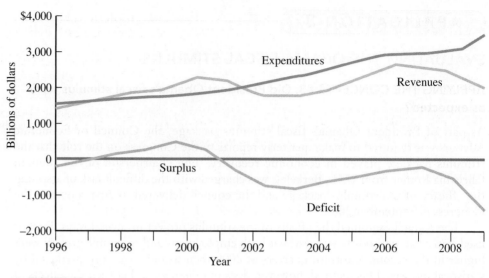

▲ FIGURE 10.3
Federal Taxes, Spending, and Deficits, 1996–2009

SUMMARY

This chapter explored the role of government fiscal policy. Using the AD–AS model, we showed how fiscal policy can stabilize the economy. We also discussed the multiplier and the limits to stabilization policy. In addition, the chapter gave us an overview of the federal budget, including spending, revenues, deficits, and surpluses. Finally, we explored how fiscal policy in the United States has changed over time. Here are the key points:

1 Increases in government spending or decreases in taxes will increase aggregate demand.

2 Decreases in government spending or increases in taxes will decrease aggregate demand.

3 Because of the multiplier, the total shift in the aggregate demand curve will be larger than the initial shift. Policymakers need to take the multiplier into account as they formulate policy.

4 Both *inside lags* (the time it takes to formulate policy) and *outside lags* (the time it takes the policy to work) limit the effectiveness of active fiscal policy.

5 The largest component of federal spending is *entitlements and mandatory programs.*

6 The largest components of federal revenues are income taxes and social insurance taxes collected from individuals.

7 Government deficits act as an *automatic stabilizer* that helps to stabilize the economy in the short run.

8 In the short run, fiscal policy actions taken to combat a recession will increase the deficit; in the long run, deficits are a concern because they may lead to the crowding out of investment spending.

9 Active fiscal policy has been periodically used in the United States to stimulate the economy; at other times, concerns about deficits have limited the use of fiscal policy.

KEY TERMS

automatic stabilizers, p. 215
budget deficit, p. 214
budget surplus, p. 215
contractionary policies, p. 207
discretionary spending, p. 211
entitlement and mandatory
  spending, p. 211

expansionary policies, p. 207
fiscal policy, p. 206
inside lags, p. 208
Laffer curve, p. 214
Medicaid, p. 211
Medicare, p. 211

outside lags, p. 208
permanent income, p. 218
Social Security, p. 211
stabilization policies, p. 208
supply-side economics, p. 213

10.1 The Role of Fiscal Policy

1.1 To decrease aggregate demand, a government can either decrease spending or _____ taxes.

1.2 Contractionary fiscal policy shifts the aggregate demand curve to the _____, _____ prices, and _____ real GDP.

1.3 If the multiplier for taxation is –1.10, then a $110 billion increase in taxes will ultimately shift the demand curve by _____.

1.4 _____ lags refer to the time it takes for policymakers to recognize an economic problem and take appropriate actions.

1.5 **A Chinese Experiment.** In 2000 the Chinese government mandated three one-week holidays throughout the year to stimulate consumer spending. The idea was that these extended vacations would induce the Chinese to spend more of their earnings while on vacation.

a. Using the AD–AS framework, show the mechanism through which the Chinese government believed that the mandated holidays would stimulate the economy.

b. Although consumption spending rose during the vacation period, the data show that consumption fell before and after the vacation. Did the policy work?

1.6 **Time-Dated Certificates as Fiscal Policies.** When Japan faced a decade-long recession in the 1990s, many ideas were offered to combat the recession. Here is one unusual fiscal policy: The government would issue time-dated certificates to each person that had to be spent on goods and services within a fixed period (say, three months) or become worthless. Suppose the government was considering whether to issue $400 in time-dated certificates to each household or give each household $400 in cash instead.

a. Which plan would lead to the greatest economic stimulus?

b. Which plan do you think the government would find easier to administer?

c. Suppose a household had large credit card debt, which it wished to reduce. Which of the two plans would that household prefer?

1.7 **Political Systems and the Inside Lag for Fiscal Policy.** Under a parliamentary system like in Britain, there are fewer checks and balances on the government than in the United States. In a parliamentary system, the party that controls the legislature also runs the executive branch. How do you think the inside lag for fiscal policy in England compares to that in the United States?

1.8 **Looking Backward.** Some critics of stabilization policy say that policymakers are always looking backward—through a rear view mirror at past data—and thus cannot conduct stabilization policy. Can you give a defense for policymakers despite the fact that they must look at past data?

1.9 **Airplane Wings and Forecasting.** When an airplane wing falls off, a pilot cannot use his normal controls to navigate the plane. How does this analogy apply to economic policy making?

10.2 The Federal Budget

2.1 Fiscal year 2009 began on October 1, _____.

2.2 Discretionary spending is the largest component of federal spending. _____ (True/False)

2.3 Two examples of entitlement spending are _____ and _____.

2.4 The two primary sources of federal government revenue are _____ and _____.

2.5 **The States and Balanced Budgets.** Unlike the U.S. federal government, virtually all states have requirements that they must either plan for or maintain a balanced budget.

a. Suppose the national economy experiences a recession. How will this affect the budgets of the states?

b. What actions must the states then take to balance the budget?

c. Graphically show how these actions, taken together, may destabilize the national economy.

2.6 **Automatic Stabilizers and Fluctuations in Output.** Because of automatic stabilizers, states with more generous unemployment insurance programs will experience _____ fluctuations in output.

2.7 **A Temporary End to the Estate Tax.** The estate tax was eliminated for one year in 2010 and then was scheduled to be restored in 2011. In an attempt at humor, some commentators referred to the movie "Throw Momma from the Train." What was the basis of this comparison?

2.8 **Mandatory Spending and Entitlements.** Is "mandatory spending" really mandatory? _____. (yes/no) Explain how mandatory spending differs from discretionary spending. In the face of the coming crisis in entitlement spending, do you believe that mandatory spending will be harder to change than discretionary spending? (Related to Application 1 on page 212.)

2.9 **High Tax Rates and Summer Employment.** Suppose you were considering taking a summer job to earn additional spending money for school. The job pays $12 an hour but you have to pay both income and social insurance taxes on your earnings. If you faced a 50 percent rate of taxation on your earnings (so you could keep only $6), would you keep working? How about a 70 percent rate? (Related to Application 2 on page 214.)

10.3 Fiscal Policy in U.S. History

3.1 _____ was the first president to consciously use fiscal policy to stabilize the economy.

3.2 Walter Heller was President Lyndon Johnson's chief economic adviser. _____ (True/False)

3.3 The U.S. economy witnessed federal budget surpluses in _____.

3.4 Long-run average income is known as _____ income.

3.5 Tax Refunds and Consumer Spending. In 1999, the Internal Revenue Service began to mail out refund checks because of changes in the tax law in 1998. Economic forecasters predicted that consumption and GDP would increase because of higher refunds on income taxes. Using each of the following assumptions, do you think the forecasters were correct? Answer yes or no.

  a. Taxpayers were not aware they would receive refunds until they had completed their income tax statements.

  b. Taxpayers did know they would receive refunds but, as consumers, based their spending decisions solely on their current levels of income.

  c. Taxpayers did know they would receive refunds and, as consumers, based their consumption decisions on their permanent incomes.

NOTES

1. E. Cary Brown, "Fiscal Policy in the 1930s: A Reappraisal," *American Economic Review* 46 (December 1956): 857–879.

3.6 The Rise and Fall of Fiscal Surpluses. What factors led the United States from federal surpluses at the end of the 1990s to deficits in the first decade of the twenty-first century? What factors led to the demise of surpluses?

3.7 The Most Effective Part of the Stimulus Package. President Obama's stimulus package contained several different components: tax cuts for individuals, infrastructure projects, and other government spending and aid to the states to pay for health and other services. Many economists believed that the component that was most effective was the aid to the states. Explain why this component might be particularly effective and give reasons why the others may not be. (Related to Application 3 on page 219.)

3.8 College Students and Tax Rebates. If a college student with a low credit card limit received a tax rebate, do you think he or she would be more likely to save it or spend it? How about a middle-aged married man that does not have a low credit card limit? Explain your reasoning.

3.9 A Dramatic Drop in the Corporate Tax. Go to the Web site for the Congressional Budget Office (www.cbo.gov) and find the data for corporate tax revenue between 2007 and 2009. What was the decrease and how can you explain it?

3.10 Long-Run Deficit Projections. The Congressional Budget Office makes long-run deficit budget projections, extending far into the twenty-first century. What are the main causes of the long-run deficits projected by the CBO?

The Income-Expenditure Model

Heading into the global recession in 2007, the Chinese economy was growing at the extraordinary rate of 11 percent per year. As Chinese policymakers began to see the severity of the oncoming global recession, they became concerned that real GDP growth would fall below the 7 percent level they needed to incorporate the influx of new entrants into the labor force. As a consequence, they embarked on a massive stimulus package, more in the spirit of Keynes than Mao.

In late 2008 the Chinese government announced it was undertaking a stimulus plan equivalent to $586 billion in U.S. dollars. This was a massive program, approximately 13 percent of GDP. Public infrastructure was the largest single component of the plan, with investments for new railways, roads, irrigation, and transportation. Another major component of the plan was funds to restore the damage caused by the severe earthquakes that had hit Sichuan province earlier in the year. Additional funds in the package were allocated for housing, social programs, and human capital.

Since China was already embarking on a state-run, large-scale investment program, it was able to put these programs into effect rather quickly. That was in sharp contrast to the United States, which needed to gear up new programs to spend funds on infrastructure. As a result, China managed to avoid the worst of the global recession, with real GDP growth around 9 percent for both 2008 and 2009. A robust Chinese economy also helped the other economies in the world to recover as well.[1]

APPLYING THE CONCEPTS

1 How do changes in the value of homes affect consumer spending?
Falling Home Prices, the Wealth Effect, and Decreased Consumer Spending

2 What evidence does the long historical record provide about multipliers?
Using Long-Term Macro Data to Measure Multipliers

3 How influential a figure was John Maynard Keynes?
John Maynard Keynes: A World Intellectual

4 How do countries benefit from growth in their trading partners?
The Locomotive Effect: How Foreign Demand Affects a Country's Output

Newspaper and television stories about the economy tend to focus on what causes changes in short-term real GDP. For example, we often read about how changes in economic conditions in Europe or Asia or changes in government spending or taxation will affect near-term economic growth. To understand these stories, we need to understand the behavior of the economy in the short run.

As we have seen, in the short run changes in aggregate demand play the key role in determining the level of output. In the short run, prices are slow to change, and therefore fluctuations in aggregate demand translate directly into fluctuations in GDP and income. In this chapter, we take a more detailed look at short-run fluctuations in GDP.

The model we develop in this chapter is called the *income-expenditure model*, sometimes referred to as the *Keynesian cross*. The model was developed by the economist John Maynard Keynes in the 1930s and later extended and refined by many economists. When Keynes developed his approach to macroeconomics, the world economy was in the midst of a severe depression. Unlike many other economists at the time, Keynes did not believe the economy would return to full employment by itself. An economy could get "trapped" in a depression and not recover.

Keynes provided both a diagnosis of an economic depression and a cure. He argued that the fundamental problem causing the world depression was insufficient demand for goods and services. Here was the problem: Firms would not increase their production and put the unemployed back to work unless there was sufficient demand for the goods and services they produced. But consumers and firms would not demand enough goods and services unless the economy improved and their incomes were higher. Keynes argued that active fiscal policy—increasing government spending or cutting taxes—could increase total demand for goods and services and bring the economy back to full employment. This income-expenditure model is based on the idea that higher *expenditures* were necessary to generate higher levels of *income* in the economy.

The income-expenditure model focuses on changes in the level of output or real GDP. However, it does not take into account changes in prices. The model is thus very useful for understanding economic fluctuations in the short run when prices do not change very much. It is less useful in the intermediate or longer run, when prices do adjust to economic conditions. For intermediate or longer-run analysis, we need to use the aggregate demand and aggregate supply curves to understand movements in both output and prices.

In this chapter, we focus on the short run. In the last part of this chapter, we show how Keynes's income-expenditure model also provides an important building block for our model of aggregate demand. In later chapters, we will incorporate financial markets into our discussion of aggregate demand.

This chapter will primarily use graphical tools to explain the income-expenditure model. An appendix to the chapter provides an algebraic treatment of the model and shows how some of the key formulas are derived.

11.1 A SIMPLE INCOME-EXPENDITURE MODEL

First, we will develop a very simple income-expenditure model to illustrate the ideas of Keynes. Later in the chapter, we will expand the income-expenditure model to make it more realistic.

Equilibrium Output

Let's begin with the simplest income-expenditure model. It uses a graph like Figure 11.1, with total expenditures for goods and services represented on the vertical axis, output (*y*) represented on the horizontal axis, and a 45° line. The 45° line marks all the points on the graph at which the value of the variable measured on the horizontal axis (output) equals the value of the variable measured on the vertical axis (total expenditures). In our most basic model, we temporarily omit the government and the foreign sector. Only consumers

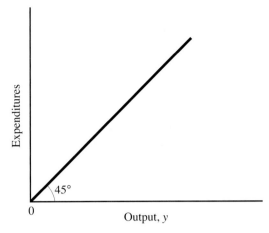

▲ **FIGURE 11.1**
The 45° Line
At any point on the 45° line, the distance to the horizontal axis is the same as the distance to the vertical axis.

and firms can demand output: Consumers demand consumption goods, and firms demand investment goods. We make things even simpler by assuming that consumers and firms each demand a fixed amount of goods. Let consumption demand be an amount C, and let investment demand be an amount I. Total demand will be $C + I$. Total demand for goods and services is also called **planned expenditures**. Thus, planned expenditures in this simple economy are equal to $C + I$.

planned expenditures
Another term for total demand for goods and services.

In the income-expenditure model, we assume firms supply all the output that is demanded. This means the short-run aggregate supply curve is flat, so firms will produce whatever is demanded without changing their prices. This assumption is reasonable in the short run.

Because firms are willing to supply whatever is demanded, demand is the key factor in determining the level of output, or GDP. In the income-expenditure model, the level of output will adjust to equal the level of planned expenditures. We call the level of output the **equilibrium output**.

Let's denote the level of equilibrium output as y^*. Then the level of equilibrium output will be

equilibrium output
The level of GDP at which planned expenditure equals the amount that is produced.

$$\text{equilibrium output} = y^* = C + I = \text{planned expenditures}$$

At equilibrium output, planned expenditures for goods and services equal the level of output or GDP.

Figure 11.2 can help us understand how the level of equilibrium output, or GDP, in the economy is determined. On the expenditure-output graph, we superimpose the line representing planned expenditures, $C + I$, which is a horizontal line because both C and I are fixed amounts. Because planned expenditures are fixed at $C + I$, they do not depend on the level of output. Equilibrium output is at y^*, the level of output at which the planned expenditure line crosses the 45° line. The two lines cross at point a, where output measured on the horizontal axis equals planned expenditures by consumers and firms measured on the vertical axis. Recall that on a 45° line the value on the horizontal axis equals the value on the vertical axis.

Adjusting to Equilibrium Output

What would happen if the economy were producing at a higher level of output, such as y_1 in Figure 11.3? At that level of output, more goods and services are being produced than consumers and firms are demanding. Goods that are produced but not purchased will pile up on the shelves of stores. Firms will react to these piles of goods

▶ **FIGURE 11.2**
Determining Equilibrium Output
At equilibrium output y*, total expenditures demand y* equals output y*.

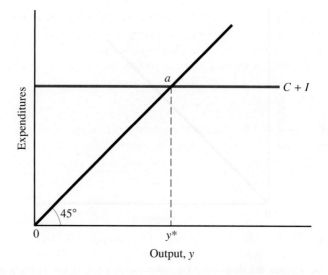

by cutting back on production. The level of output will fall until the economy reaches y*, as indicated by the leftward arrow in Figure 11.3.

If the economy were producing at a lower level of output, y_2, planned expenditures would exceed total output. Firms would find that the demand for consumption and investment goods is greater than their current production. Inventories now disappear from the shelves of stores, and firms face increasing backlogs of orders for their products. They respond by stepping up production, so GDP increases back to y*, as indicated by the rightward arrow in Figure 11.3.

▶ **FIGURE 11.3**
Equilibrium Output
Equilibrium output (y*) is determined at a, where demand intersects the 45° line. If output were higher (y_1), it would exceed demand and production would fall. If output were lower (y_2), it would fall short of demand and production would rise.

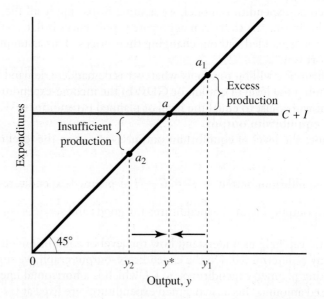

Table 11.1 also helps to illustrate the process that determines equilibrium output. The table shows, with a numerical example, what happens to production when planned expenditures do not equal output. Planned expenditures, consumption (C) plus investment (I), equal $100 billion. In the first row, we see that if current production is only

TABLE 11.1 ADJUSTMENTS TO EQUILIBRIUM OUTPUT (IN BILLIONS OF DOLLARS)			
C + I	Production	Inventories	Direction of Output
$100	$ 80	Depletion of inventories of $20	Output increases
100	100	No change	Output stays constant
100	120	Excess of inventories of $20	Output decreases

$80 billion, stocks of inventories will be depleted by $20 billion, so firms will increase output to restore their inventory levels. In the third row, production is at $120 billion, creating an excess of inventories of $20 billion, and firms will cut back production. In the second row, planned expenditures equal output, so neither inventories nor production changes.

Be sure you remember that the equilibrium level of output occurs where planned expenditures equal production. If the economy were not producing at that level, we would find either that the demand for goods was too great relative to production, or that there was insufficient demand relative to production. In either case, the economy would rapidly adjust to reach the equilibrium level of output.

11.2 THE CONSUMPTION FUNCTION

To make the income-expenditure model more realistic, we will need to introduce other components of demand, including the government and the foreign sector. But first we need to recognize that consumers' planned expenditures will depend on their level of income.

Consumer Spending and Income

Let's begin by reviewing the **consumption function** we first introduced in Chapter 9. The consumption function describes the relationship between desired spending by consumers and the level of income. When consumers have more income, they will want to purchase more goods and services.

As we have seen, a simple consumption function can be described by the equation

$$C = C_a + by$$

in which total consumption spending, C, has two parts. The first part, C_a, is called **autonomous consumption**, and it does not directly depend on the level of income. The second part, by, represents the part of consumption that does depend on income. It is the product of the fraction b, called the **marginal propensity to consume (MPC)**, and level of income in the economy, y. The MPC, which has a value of b in our formula, tells us how much consumption spending will increase for every dollar that income increases. If b equals 0.7, then for every $1 that income increases, consumption would increase by $0.7 \times \$1$, or $0.70.

In our simple income-expenditure model, *output is also equal to the income that flows to households*. As firms produce output, they pay households income in the form of wages, interest, profits, and rents. We can therefore use y to represent both output and income.

We plot a consumption function in Figure 11.4. The consumption function is a line that intersects the vertical axis at C_a, the level of autonomous consumption spending, which is typically greater than zero (therefore, it has a positive intercept). The slope of the consumption function equals b, the marginal propensity to consume. Although output is plotted on the horizontal axis, remember that it is also equal to income, so income rises dollar for dollar with output. That is why we can plot the consumption function, which depends on income, on the same graph that determines output.

Changes in the Consumption Function

The consumption function is determined by the level of autonomous consumption and by the MPC. The level of autonomous consumption can change, and so can the MPC. Changes in either shift the consumption function to another position on the graph. A higher level of autonomous consumption but no change in MPC will shift the entire consumption function upward and parallel to its original position. More

consumption function
The relationship between consumption spending and the level of income.

autonomous consumption
The part of consumption that does not depend on income.

marginal propensity to consume (MPC)
The fraction of additional income that is spent.

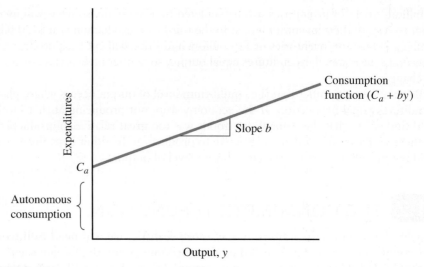

▲ **FIGURE 11.4**

Consumption Function

The consumption function relates desired consumer spending to the level of income.

consumption occurs at every level of income. We show an increase in autonomous consumption in Panel A of Figure 11.5.

A number of factors can cause autonomous consumption to change. Here are two:

- **Increases in consumer wealth will cause an increase in autonomous consumption.** Wealth consists of the value of stocks, bonds, and consumer durables (consumer goods that last a long time, such as automobiles and refrigerators). Note that a person's wealth is not the same as income. *Income* is the amount of money someone earns during a period, such as in a given year, whereas *wealth* represents the person's total net worth. Nobel Laureate Franco Modigliani found that increases in stock prices, which raise consumer wealth, will lead to increases in autonomous consumption. Conversely, a sharp fall in stock prices will lead to a decrease in autonomous consumption.

- **Increases in consumer confidence will increase autonomous consumption.** Forecasters pay attention to consumer confidence, a measure based on household surveys of how positive consumers are feeling about the future, because it

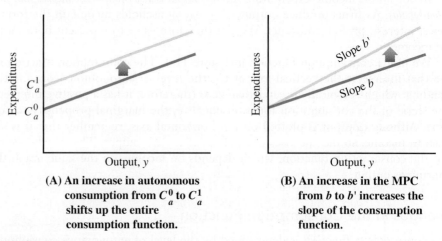

(A) An increase in autonomous consumption from C^0_a to C^1_a shifts up the entire consumption function.

(B) An increase in the MPC from b to b' increases the slope of the consumption function.

▲ **FIGURE 11.5**

Movements of the Consumption Function

Panel A shows that an increase in autonomous consumption from C^0_a to C^1_a shifts the entire consumption function upward. Panel B shows that an increase in the MPC from b to b' increases the slope of the consumption function.

APPLICATION 1

FALLING HOME PRICES, THE WEALTH EFFECT, AND DECREASED CONSUMER SPENDING

APPLYING THE CONCEPTS #1: How do changes in the value of homes affect consumer spending?

The value of homes in excess of what people borrow with a mortgage is known as their home equity. Home equity is the single largest component of net wealth for most families in the United States. Compared to wealth holdings in the stock market, which tend to be concentrated in the highest income brackets, home-equity wealth is more widely dispersed across the income spectrum. Changes in the value of home equity—like other forms of wealth—affect consumer spending.

The period from 1997 to mid-2006 was paradise for consumers. Housing prices rose nationally by approximately 90 percent and consumer wealth grew by $6.5 trillion dollars over that period. The party ended in the summer of 2006 as housing prices began to fall. In some regions of the country, where housing prices had risen most sharply, they fell from their peak by about 30 percent. No longer were households refinancing their mortgages and pulling out money to buy new cars, boats, or other consumer durables. Instead, many recent home purchasers actually owed more than their homes were worth—and, as a result, some defaulted on their loans and turned their property over to lenders. How do these changes affect consumer spending?

In its review of the literature, the Congressional Budget Office found most studies estimated a decrease of consumer wealth of $1 would lower consumption spending by somewhere between $0.02 and $0.07. Based on forecasts for housing prices, the Congressional Budget Office estimated the declines in housing prices would reduce consumer wealth and ultimately consumer spending between $21 and $72 billion or subtract 0.1 to 0.5 percentage points from economic growth during 2007. This partly explains the reduced rate of economic growth that occurred during that year.   **Related to Exercises 2.5 and 2.7.**

SOURCE: Based on Congressional Budget Office, *Housing Wealth and Consumer Spending*, January 2007, http://www.cbo.gov/ftpdocs/77xx/doc7719/01-05-Housing.pdf (accessed April 11, 2010).

---

helps them to predict consumption spending. The Conference Board, a non-profit organization devoted to disseminating economic analysis, publishes an index of consumer confidence each month that many forecasters rely on.

A change in the marginal propensity to consume will cause a change in the slope of the consumption function. We show an increase in the MPC in Panel B of Figure 11.5, where we assume autonomous consumption is fixed. As the MPC increases, the consumption function rotates upward, counterclockwise. This rotation means the consumption function line gets steeper.

11.3 EQUILIBRIUM OUTPUT AND THE CONSUMPTION FUNCTION

Using the consumption function, we can now begin to look at more complex versions of the income-expenditure model. We continue to assume investment spending, *I*, does not depend on the level of income. The only difference between what we did in the preceding section and what we are about to do here is that we now recognize consumption increases with the level of income. Figure 11.6 shows how GDP is

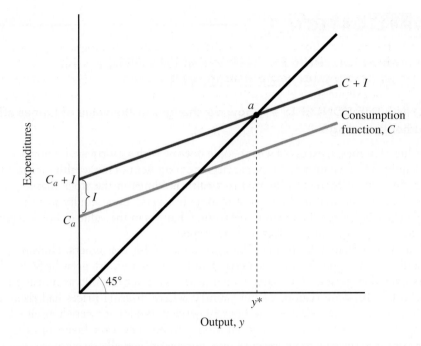

determined. We first plot the consumption function, C, as before: A sloping line graphically representing that consumption spending is a function of income. Because we are assuming investment is constant at all levels of income, to get the C + I line, we can simply vertically add the constant level of investment I to the consumption function. Adding vertically gives us the C + I line, which represents total planned expenditures in the economy. This line is upward sloping because consumption spending increases with income. At any level of income, we now know the level of total planned expenditures, C + I.

The level of equilibrium output, y*, occurs where the planned expenditure line C + I crosses the 45° line. At this level of output, planned expenditures equal output. At any other level of production, planned expenditures will not equal output, and the economy will adjust back to y* for the same reasons and in the same way as in the corresponding example in the preceding section.

In the appendix to this chapter, we show that the equilibrium output in this simple economy is

$$\text{equilibrium output} = \frac{(\text{autonomous consumption} + \text{investment})}{(1 - \text{MPC})}$$

or, in the mathematical terms representing those words,

$$y^* = \frac{(C_a + I)}{(1 - b)}$$

From this relationship and the numerical values for C_a, b, and I, we can calculate equilibrium output. Suppose

$$C_a = 100$$
$$b = 0.6$$
$$I = 40$$

This means the consumption function is C = 100 + 0.6y. Then, using our formula for equilibrium output, we have

$$y^* = \frac{100 + 40}{1 - 0.6} = \frac{140}{0.40} = 350$$

Saving and Investment

We can determine equilibrium output another way, which highlights the relationship between saving and investment. To understand this relationship, recall that in an economy without taxation or government, the value of output, or production (y), equals the value of income. Households receive this income and either consume it (C), save it (S), or a combination of both. We can therefore say that saving equals output minus consumption or, in mathematical terms,

$$S = y - C$$

In our simple economy, output is determined by planned expenditures, $C + I$, or

$$y = C + I$$

If we subtract consumption from both sides of this equation, we have

$$y - C = I$$

But we just saw that the left side, $y - C$, equals saving, S, so we have

$$S = I$$

Thus, equilibrium output is determined at the level of income where savings equal investment.

However, the level of savings in the economy is not fixed. A **savings function** describes the relationship between savings and the level of income. Total savings will increase with the level of GDP. Recall from Chapter 9 the concept of the marginal propensity to save (MPS): It is the ratio of additional savings to additional income. Since households will increase their total savings as their income increases, total savings will increase with GDP.

Figure 11.7 illustrates how equilibrium income is determined where savings equals investment. The horizontal line is a fixed level of investment in the economy. The upward-sloping line is the savings function. The two lines intersect at the equilibrium level of output, y^*.

savings function
The relationship between the level of saving and the level of income.

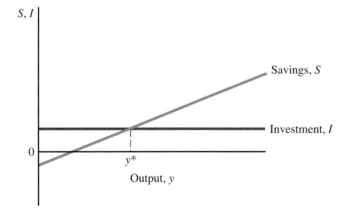

◄ **FIGURE 11.7**
Savings, Investment, and Equilibrium Output
Equilibrium output is determined at the level of output, y^*, where savings equals investment.

To illustrate these ideas with a numerical example, let's return to the previous case in which the consumption function is $C = 100 + 0.6y$. Because $S = y - C$, saving is

$$S = y - (100 + 0.6\,y)$$
$$S = -100 + 0.4\,y$$

This equation is the savings function for this example. The marginal propensity to save (MPS) is 0.4. That means that for every dollar y increases, saving increases by $0.40. Notice the slope of the savings function is the MPS.

In our previous example, investment was 40 and equilibrium output was 350. Let's check that saving does equal that level of investment. Plugging in the value of equilibrium output, or income, into the savings function, we get

$$S = -100 + 0.4(350)$$
$$S = -100 + 140$$
$$S = 40$$

So saving equals investment at the level of equilibrium output.

Understanding the Multiplier

In all economies, investment spending fluctuates. We can use the model we developed that determines output in the short run, the income-expenditure model, to see what happens if there are changes in investment spending. Suppose investment spending originally was I_0 and increased to I_1—an increase we will call ΔI (the symbol Δ, the Greek capital letter delta, is universally used to represent change). What happens to equilibrium output?

Figure 11.8 shows how equilibrium output is determined at the original level of investment and at the new level of investment. The increase in investment spending shifts the $C + I$ curve upward by ΔI. The intersection of the $C + I$ curve with the 45° line shifts from a_0 to a_1. GDP increases from y_0 to y_1 by the amount Δy. The figure shows that the increase in GDP—that is, the amount Δy—is greater than the increase in investment—the amount ΔI—or $\Delta y > \Delta I$. This is a general result: The increase in output always exceeds the increase in investment because of the multiplier effect we discussed in the last chapter.

Let's review the logic of the multiplier. Suppose there is an initial increase of investment spending by $20 million. This additional demand will initially increase output, income, and aggregate demand by $20 million. Assuming the MPC is 0.8, the $20 million in additional income will lead to $16 million in increased consumer spending (the MPC of 0.8 × $20 million). With an increase in consumer demand of $16 million, output, income, and aggregate demand will therefore increase by another $16 million. In

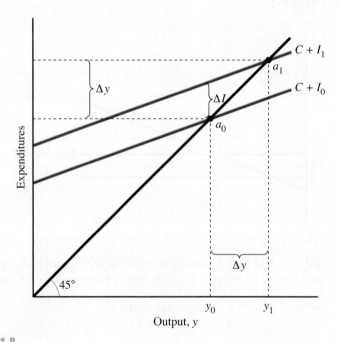

▲ **FIGURE 11.8**
The Multiplier
When investment increases from I_0 to I_1, equilibrium output increases from y_0 to y_1. The change in output (Δy) is greater than the change in investment (ΔI).

APPLICATION 2

USING LONG-TERM MACRO DATA TO MEASURE MULTIPLIERS

APPLYING THE CONCEPTS #2: What evidence does the long historical record provide about multipliers?

One of the difficulties in estimating multipliers is that during normal times, government spending and taxes do not change too much so it is difficult to isolate their effects on the economy. Economists Robert Barro and Charles Redlick went back in the historical record to look at times when government expenditures and taxes did change substantially: during the buildups and aftermaths of major wars.

In their work, they typically found much smaller multipliers for defense expenditures, typically less than one. This means that increases in government spending did increase the economy, but less than the amount of government spending itself. It also implies that there must have been crowding out of other components of spending. They found that multipliers were larger when there was more unemployment in the economy. Barro and Redlick also suggest that other researchers found larger associations between government spending and GDP because they had the causality backward—nondefense spending often rises when GDP grows rapidly. Untangling these issues is a difficult task for social scientists.   **Related to Exercise 3.9.**

SOURCE: Based on Robert J. Barro and Charles Redlick, "Stimulus Spending Doesn't Work," *Wall Street Journal*, October 1, 2009.

turn, this will increase consumer spending by another $12.8 million (the MPC of 0.8 × $16 million). This increased demand will therefore increase output, income, and aggregate demand by $12.8 million, generating further increases in consumer spending of $10.24 million. As this process continues over time, total spending will continue to increase, but in diminishing amounts. If we add up all the spending in the (infinite) rounds, we find the initial increase in investment spending will generate a total increase in equilibrium income of $100 million, far more than the initial $20 million with which we began. In this case, the multiplier is 5 (5 × $20 million = $100 million).

We show how to derive the formula for a simple multiplier in the appendix to this chapter:

$$\text{multiplier} = \frac{1}{(1 - \text{MPC})}$$

Suppose the MPC equals 0.8. Then the multiplier would be

$$\text{multiplier} = \frac{1}{(1 - 0.8)} = 5$$

Notice that the multiplier increases as the MPC increases. If MPC equals 0.4, the multiplier is 1.67; if the MPC equals 0.6, the multiplier is 2.5. To see why the multiplier increases as the marginal propensity to consume increases, think back to our examples of the multiplier. The multiplier occurs because the initial increase in investment spending increases income, which leads to higher consumer spending. With a higher MPC, the increase in consumer spending will be greater, because consumers will spend a higher fraction of the additional income they receive as the multiplier increases. For example, if the MPC is 0.8, they will spend an additional $0.80, whereas if the multiplier was 0.6, they would spend only an additional $0.60. With a higher MPC, the eventual increase in output will be greater, and therefore so will the multiplier.

One implication of the multiplier is that the effect of any change in investment "multiplies" throughout the economy. This explains why economies can often recover quickly after natural disasters.

11.4 GOVERNMENT SPENDING AND TAXATION

We now make our income-expenditure model more realistic by bringing in government spending and taxation, which makes the model useful for understanding economic policy debates. In those debates, we often hear recommendations for either increasing government spending or cutting taxes to increase GDP. As we will explain, both the level of government spending and the level of taxation, through their influence on the demand for goods and services, affect the level of GDP in the short run.

Using taxes and spending to influence the level of GDP in the short run is known as *Keynesian fiscal policy*. As we discussed in Chapter 7, changes in taxes can also affect the supply of output in the long run through the way taxes can change incentives to work or invest. However, in this chapter we concentrate on the role of taxes and spending in determining demand for goods and services, and therefore output, in the short run.

Fiscal Multipliers

Let's look first at the role government spending plays in determining GDP. Government purchases of goods and services are a component of total spending:

$$\text{planned expenditures including government} = C + I + G$$

Increases in government purchases, G, shift the $C + I + G$ line upward, just as increases in investment, I, or autonomous consumption do. If government spending increases by \$1, the $C + I + G$ line will shift upward by \$1.

Panel A of Figure 11.9 shows how increases in government spending affect GDP. The increase in government spending from G_0 to G_1 shifts the $C + I + G$ line upward and increases the level of GDP from y_0 to y_1.

As you can see, changes in government purchases have exactly the same effects as changes in investment or changes in autonomous consumption. The multiplier for government spending is also the same as for changes in investment or autonomous consumption:

$$\text{multiplier for government spending} = \frac{1}{(1 - \text{MPC})}$$

▶ **FIGURE 11.9**
Government Spending, Taxes, and GDP
Panel A shows that an increase in government spending leads to an increase in output. Panel B shows that an increase in taxes leads to a decrease in output.

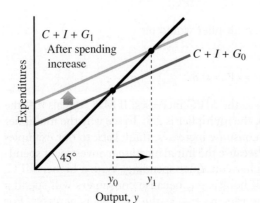

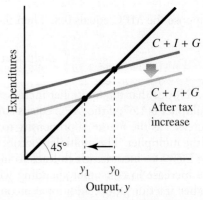

(A) An increase in government spending leads to an increase in output.

(B) An increase in taxes leads to a decrease in output.

For example, if the MPC is 0.6, the multiplier is 2.5:

$$\frac{1}{(1 - 0.6)} = 2.5$$

Therefore, a $10 billion increase in government spending will increase GDP by $25 billion. The multiplier for government spending works just like the multiplier for investment or consumption. An initial increase in government spending raises GDP and income. The increase in income, however, generates further increases in demand as consumers increase their spending.

Now let's consider taxes. We need to take into account that government programs affect households' disposable personal income—income that ultimately flows back to households (and thus consumption) after subtraction from their income of any taxes paid and after addition to their income of any transfer payments they receive, such as Social Security, unemployment insurance, or welfare. If the government takes $10 net of every $100 you make, your income after taxes and transfer payments is only $90.

Here's how we include taxes and transfers into the model: We make consumption spending depend on income after taxes and transfers, or $y - T$, where T is net taxes (taxes paid to government minus transfers received by households). For simplicity, we'll just refer to T as taxes, but remember that it is taxes less transfer payments. The consumption function with taxes is

$$C = C_a + b(y - T)$$

If taxes increase by $1, after-tax income will decrease by $1. Because the marginal propensity to consume is b, this means consumption will fall by $b \times$ $1, and the $C + I + G$ line will shift downward by $b \times$ $1. For example, if b is 0.6, a $1 increase in taxes will mean that consumers will have a dollar less of income and will therefore decrease consumption spending by $0.60.

Panel B of Figure 11.9 shows how an increase in taxes will decrease the level of GDP. As the level of taxes increases, the demand line will shift downward by b (the increase in taxes). Equilibrium income will fall from y_0 to y_1. The multiplier for taxes is slightly different than the multiplier for government spending. If we cut government spending by $1, the $C + I + G$ line will shift downward by $1. However, if we increase taxes by $1, consumers will cut back their consumption by only $b \times$ $1. Thus, the $C + I + G$ line will shift downward by slightly less than $1, or $b \times$ $1. For example, if b is 0.6, the demand line would shift down vertically by $0.60.

Because the demand line does not shift by the same amount with taxes as it does with government spending, the formula for the tax multiplier is slightly different. Here's the formula for the tax multiplier; we show how to derive it in the appendix:

$$\text{tax multiplier} = \frac{-\text{MPC}}{(1 - \text{MPC})}$$

The tax multiplier is negative because increases in taxes decrease disposable personal income and lead to a reduction in consumption spending. If the MPC is 0.6, the tax multiplier will be

$$\frac{-0.6}{(1 - 0.6)} = -1.5$$

Notice that the tax multiplier is smaller (in absolute value) than the government spending multiplier, which for the same MPC is 2.5. The reason the tax multiplier is smaller is that an increase in taxes first reduces income of households by the amount of the tax. However, because the MPC is less than one (0.6), the decrease in consumer spending is less than the increase in taxes.

Finally, you may wonder what would happen if we increased both government spending and taxes by an equal amount at the same time. Because the multiplier for government spending is larger than the multiplier for taxes, equal increases in both government spending and taxes will increase GDP. Economists call the multiplier for equal increases in government spending and taxes the *balanced-budget multiplier* because equal changes in government spending and taxes will not unbalance the budget. In the appendix we show that the balanced-budget multiplier in our simple model is always equal to one. For example, if spending and taxes are both increased by $10 billion, then GDP will also increase by $10 billion.

Using Fiscal Multipliers

Let's look at several examples of how we can use fiscal policy, altering taxes, and government spending to affect GDP. In all these examples, suppose GDP is $6,000 billion and the marginal propensity to consume is 0.6. The government-spending multiplier is

$$\frac{1}{(1 - 0.6)} = 2.5$$

The tax multiplier is

$$\frac{-0.6}{(1 - 0.6)} = -1.5$$

1 *Suppose policymakers want to increase GDP by 1 percent, or $60 billion.* By how much do policymakers have to increase government spending to meet this target? Because the multiplier for government spending is 2.5, we need to increase government spending by only $24 billion. With a multiplier of 2.5, the $24 billion increase in government spending leads to an increase in GDP of $60 billion ($24 billion × 2.5 = $60 billion).

2 *Suppose policymakers wanted to use tax cuts rather than government-spending increases to increase GDP by $60 billion.* How large a tax cut would be necessary? Because the tax multiplier is –1.5, we need to cut taxes by $40 billion. The $40 billion tax cut times the multiplier will lead to the objective, a $60 billion increase in GDP (–$40 billion × (–1.5) = $60 billion).

3 *If policymakers wanted to change taxes and government spending by equal amounts, so as to not affect the federal budget, how large a change would be needed to increase GDP by $60 billion?* Because the balanced-budget multiplier is one, both government spending and taxes must be increased by $60 billion.

The models we are using are very simple and leave out important factors. Nonetheless, the same basic principles apply in real situations. Here are five examples of activist Keynesian fiscal policy from recent times:

1 In 1993, the three members of the President's Council of Economic Advisers wrote a letter to President Clinton stating they thought the cuts in government spending being proposed at the time were $20 billion too large. The economic model the council members used had a multiplier for government spending of approximately 1.5. With this multiplier, the decrease in GDP from the $20 billion spending cut would be $30 billion ($20 billion × 1.5). This was approximately 0.5 percent of GDP. If GDP was expected to grow at 3 percent a year without the cuts, the president's advisers estimated that with the cuts, GDP would grow at only 2.5 percent a year. However, their advice came too late to influence the policy decisions.

2 During 1994, the U.S. government urged the Japanese to increase public spending and cut taxes to stimulate their economy. The Japanese came up with a plan and presented it to U.S. policymakers, who evaluated it using multiplier analysis. They thought the plan did not provide enough fiscal stimulus and urged the

Japanese to take more aggressive actions. Several years later, the Japanese did adopt a more aggressive plan. Unfortunately, as our chapter-opening story describes, the Japanese government raised taxes in 1997, actually sending the country further into a recession.

3 During the late 1990s, the Chinese economy came under pressure from the economic downturn in Asia and its own attempts to reform and restructure its economy. To prevent a severe economic slowdown, the Chinese successively engaged in active fiscal policy, increasing spending on domestic infrastructure, including roads, rails, and urban facilities.

4 After the September 11, 2001, terrorist attack on the United States, the government increased spending for disaster relief in New York and provided subsidies and loan guarantees to the airlines. In addition, President Bush and Congress immediately began to work on additional spending programs and tax-relief programs to stimulate the economy.

5 President Obama's economic advisors used multiplier analysis to gauge the size of their stimulus package. The multipliers they used ranged between 1 and 2 for different components of spending. Although some observers suggested the stimulus package should be even larger than $787 billion, or 5.5 percent of GDP, the economic advisors argued that this size stimulus would be sufficient to offset the worst of the recession.

Though it is very simple, our income-expenditure model illustrates some important lessons:

- An increase in government spending will increase total planned expenditures for goods and services.
- Cutting taxes will increase the after-tax income of consumers and will also lead to an increase in planned expenditures for goods and services.
- Policymakers need to take into account the multipliers for government spending and taxes as they develop policies.

The idea that governments should use active fiscal policy to combat recessions was argued forcibly by John Maynard Keynes in the 1930s. His book *The General Theory of Employment, Interest, and Money* provided the intellectual foundation for the income-expenditure model in this chapter and explained why economies could become mired in recessions and fail to recover on their own. As a consequence, Keynes strongly advocated aggressive fiscal policymaking as the best option policymakers have for bringing economies out of recessions. Keynes was a very public figure and took a major role in policy debates throughout his life.

One of Keynes's controversial ideas was that governments could stimulate the economy even if they spent money on wasteful projects. In the *General Theory*, he even remarked (tongue-in-cheek) how lucky the Egyptians were, because the death of the pharaohs would lead to new pyramids being built. Pyramids do not add to the stock of capital to produce regular goods and services. But Keynes's point was that building pyramids (or antisatellite missiles today) does add to planned expenditures and stimulates GDP in the short run.

In the long run, of course, we are better off if government spends the money wisely, such as on needed infrastructure like roads and bridges. This is an example of the principle of opportunity cost.

PRINCIPLE OF OPPORTUNITY COST

The opportunity cost of something is what you sacrifice to get it.

But even here, we can carry things too far. Japan is notorious for its excessive public spending on infrastructure, driven in part by the central government's doing favors

APPLICATION 3

JOHN MAYNARD KEYNES: A WORLD INTELLECTUAL

APPLYING THE CONCEPTS #3: How influential a figure was John Maynard Keynes?

John Maynard Keynes was born into an academic family in Cambridge, England, in 1883. His father, John Neville Keynes, was an economist and later an academic administrator at King's College in Cambridge. His mother was one of the first female graduates of the same university, which Keynes entered in 1902. At King's College, Keynes began a lifetime association with an important group of writers and artists, the Bloomsbury group, which included the well-regarded writer Virginia Woolf. Members of the group were known both for their progressive views and their controversial lifestyles. In 1925, Keynes married the Russian ballerina Lydia Lopokova and was very active in promoting the arts.

After earning his degrees, Keynes became a civil servant, taking a job with the India Office in Whitehall England. He then returned to Cambridge, where he taught economics. With the onset of World War I, Keynes returned to government employment, this time in the Treasury. After World War I, he attended the Versailles Peace Conference and wrote a book, *The Economic Consequences of the Peace*, which condemned the peace treaty and its negotiators for what he believed were the unfair and devastating burdens of the reparations, payments for causing the war, that Germany was required to make to the Allies. This book established Keynes as both a first-rate economic analyst and a brilliant writer, with a keen wit and shrewd political insights. Indeed, the reparation burdens on Germany partly led to its disastrous postwar economy and the rise of Nazism and Hitler.

Between the wars, Keynes wrote his most famous work, *The General Theory of Employment, Interest, and Money*, which challenged the conventional wisdom that economies would automatically recover from economic downturns. It was a bold and controversial work, probably the most famous economics book written in the twentieth century. Because he believed economies would not necessarily recover by themselves and monetary policies could be ineffective during deep recessions, Keynes argued that governments needed to adopt active policies, such as increased public works, in order to stimulate the economy. His work influenced an entire generation of economists, especially in the United States and Great Britain, and provided the rationale for activist fiscal policy today.

The *General Theory* was Keynes's last major written work. Near the end of World War II, he played a prominent role at the Bretton Woods Conference in 1944, which established the postwar world monetary system and led to the creation of the International Monetary Fund and the World Bank. His last major public service was his negotiation in 1945 of a multibillion-dollar loan the United States granted to Britain for post–World War II rebuilding efforts. Keynes died in 1946.   **Related to Exercise 4.9.**

SOURCE: Based on Robert Skidelsky, *John Maynard Keynes: 1883–1946: Economist, Philosopher, Statesman* (London: Penguin Books Ltd., 2003).

---

for local politicians by creating jobs in their districts. Economists have even compared spending on bridges and roads in Japan to Keynes's famous pyramids.

Understanding Automatic Stabilizers

With a slight addition to our basic model, we can explain one of the important facts in U.S. economic history. Figure 11.10 plots the rate of growth of U.S. real GDP from 1871 to 2009. It is apparent from the graph that the U.S. economy has been much more stable after World War II than before. A major reason is that government taxes and transfer payments, such as unemployment insurance and welfare payments, grew

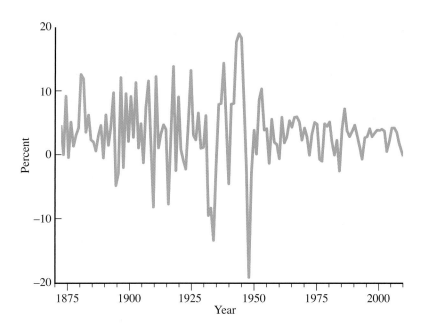

◄ **FIGURE 11.10**
**Growth Rates of U.S. GDP,
1871–2009**
After World War II, fluctuations in GDP
growth became considerably smaller.
SOURCE: Angus Maddison, Dynamic Forces
in Capitalist Development *(New York: Oxford
University Press, 1991); U.S. Department of
Commerce.*

sharply after the war. These taxes and transfer payments can automatically reduce fluctuations in real GDP and thereby stabilize the economy. As we saw in the last chapter, taxes and transfers act as automatic stabilizers for the economy.

Again, here is how the automatic stabilizers work. On the one hand, when income is high the government collects more taxes and pays out less in transfer payments. Because the government is taking funds out of the hands of consumers, there will be reduced consumer spending. On the other hand, when output is low (such as during recessions), the government collects less in taxes and pays out more in transfer payments, increasing consumer spending because the government is putting funds into the hands of consumers. The automatic stabilizers prevent consumption from falling as much in bad times and from rising as much in good times. This stabilizes the economy without any need for decisions from Congress or the White House.

To see how automatic stabilizers work in our model, we must take into account that the government levies income taxes by applying a tax rate to the level of income. To simplify, suppose there is a single tax rate of 0.2 (or 20 percent) and income is $100. The government would then collect $20 in taxes (0.2 × $100).

If consumption depends on after-tax income, we have the following consumption function:

$$C = C_a + b(1 - t)y$$

This is the consumption function with income taxes. The only difference between the consumption function with income taxes and the consumption function without income taxes is that the marginal propensity to consume is adjusted for taxes, and so

$$\text{adjusted MPC} = b(1 - t)$$

The reason for this adjustment is that consumers keep only a fraction $(1 - t)$ of their income; the rest, t, goes to the government. When income increases by $1, consumers' after-tax incomes increase by only $1 × $(1 - t)$, and of that $(1 - t)$ they spend a fraction, b.

Raising the tax rate therefore lowers the MPC adjusted for taxes. Figure 11.11 shows the consequences of raising tax rates. With a higher tax rate, the government takes a higher fraction of income, and less is left over for consumers. Recall that the slope of the $C + I + G$ line is the marginal propensity to consume. Raising the tax rate lowers the adjusted MPC and reduces the slope of this line. The $C + I + G$ line with taxes intersects the 45° line at a lower level of income. Output falls from y_0 to y_1.

▶ **FIGURE 11.11**
Increase in Tax Rates
An increase in tax rates decreases the slope of the $C + I + G$ line. This lowers output and reduces the multiplier.

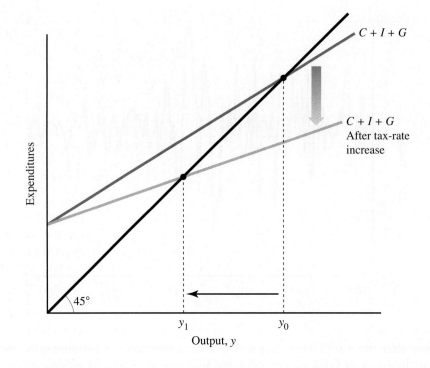

Note that as we raise tax rates, the $C + I + G$ schedule rotates and does not just move down vertically as in our previous examples. The reason for this difference is that as we change the tax rate, we change the adjusted MPC, and thus the slope of the line.

Remember that a smaller marginal propensity to consume also leads to a lower value for the multiplier. As tax rates increase and the adjusted MPC falls, the multiplier will decrease. A smaller multiplier means that any shocks, such as shocks to investment, will have less of an impact on the economy.

Now that we have introduced income taxes into our model, we can see how automatic stabilizers work. Since World War II, taxes and transfer payments in the United States have increased sharply. As we have seen, higher tax rates will lower the multiplier and make the economy less susceptible to shocks. With higher taxes and transfer payments, the link between fluctuations in disposable personal income and fluctuations in GDP is much looser. Because disposable personal income is more stable, consumption spending is also more stable. Thus, the multiplier is smaller, and the economy is more stable.

As we have said, automatic stabilizers work silently in the background, doing their job without requiring explicit action by policymakers. Total tax collections rise and fall with GDP without requiring that policymakers change tax rates. The fact that the automatic stabilizers work without any laws being enacted is particularly important at times when it is difficult to obtain a political consensus for taking any action, and policymakers are reluctant to use Keynesian fiscal policy as a deliberate policy tool.

Other factors contribute to the stability of the economy as depicted in Figure 11.10. As we explained in the last chapter, many consumers base their spending decisions in part on their long-run average income or permanent income, not just their current level of income. If households base their consumption on their long-run income, they will not be very sensitive to changes in their current income. For example, if their income temporarily rises, they are likely to save, not spend, the additional income. Similarly, if their income temporarily falls, they are likely to maintain their consumption and reduce their current savings. In effect, when consumers base their consumption on their long-run average income, their MPC out of current income (which could be higher or lower than their long-run income) will be small. And because the MPC out of current income is small, the multiplier will be small as well.

Another important factor in promoting the stability of the economy is firms' knowledge that the federal government will be taking actions to stabilize the economy. Firms are less likely to decrease their investment spending in the face of a possible recession if they believe the government is likely to intervene to offset the severity of recessions. Because investment spending tends to be a very volatile component of spending, any factor that helps stabilize investment spending will also stabilize the economy. The same logic also applies to consumers. If they believe the government will offset the severity of economic fluctuations, they are less likely to change their consumption spending in the face of shocks to their income.

Finally, in recent decades changes in firms' inventory management practices have also contributed to the stability of the economy. In the past, manufacturing firms often kept large inventories at their factories. If an unexpected shock slowed the economy, the demand for firms' products would decrease and inventories would pile up. Firms would be forced to cut production even further to reduce their stock of inventories, adding additional downward pressure on the economy. This additional decrease in demand was known as the *inventory cycle* and was a significant component of earlier recessions. In recent times, U.S. firms have paid more attention to forecasting changes in the demand for their products and have adopted sophisticated computer management techniques to reduce the size of inventories they normally hold. With less inventory on hand, firms do not have to change their production as much to adjust their inventories. The result is that the inventory cycle has become a less important factor for economic instability.

11.5 EXPORTS AND IMPORTS

With international trade becoming increasingly important economically and politically, it is critical to understand how exports and imports affect the level of GDP. Two simple modifications of our income-expenditure model will enable us to understand how exports and imports affect GDP in the short run.

Exports affect GDP through their influence on how other countries demand goods and services produced in the United States. An increase in exports means there's an increase in the demand for goods produced in the United States. An increase in imports means there's an increase in foreign goods purchased by U.S. residents. Importing goods rather than purchasing them from our domestic producers reduces the demand for U.S. goods. For example, if we in the United States spend a total of $10 billion on all automobiles but we import $3 billion of them, then we've spent only $7 billion on U.S. automobiles.

To get a clearer picture of the effects on GDP from exports and imports, let's for the moment ignore government spending and taxes. In the appendix, we present a complete model with both a domestic government and foreign countries to whom we sell our exports and from whom we buy our imports. To modify our model to include the effects of world spending on exports and U.S. spending on imports, we need to take two steps:

1 Add exports, X, as another source of demand for U.S. goods and services.

2 Subtract imports, M, from total spending by U.S. residents. We will assume that imports, like consumption, increase with the level of income.

Consumers will import more goods as their income rises. We can write this as

$$M = my$$

where m is a fraction known as the **marginal propensity to import**. We subtract this fraction from b, the overall marginal propensity to consume, to obtain the MPC for spending on domestic goods, $b - m$. For example, if b is 0.8 and m is 0.2, then for every $1 that GDP increases, total consumption increases by $0.80, but spending on domestic goods increases by only $0.60 because $0.20 is spent on imports. The MPC in this example, adjusted for imports, is 0.8 − 0.2, or 0.6.

Figure 11.12 shows how equilibrium output is determined in an open economy, that is, an economy that engages in trade with the rest of the world. We plot planned expenditures for U.S. goods and services on our graph and find the level of equilibrium

marginal propensity to import
The fraction of additional income that is spent on imports.

▶ FIGURE 11.12
U.S. Equilibrium Output in an
Open Economy
Output is determined when the demand
for domestic goods equals output.

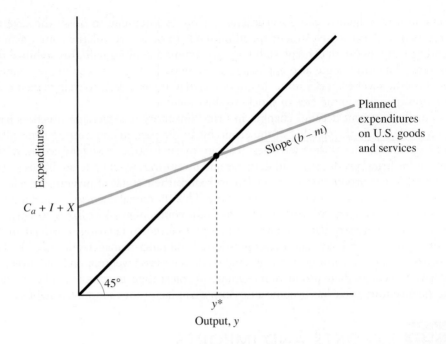

income where it intersects the 45° line. The planned expenditure line has an intercept on the vertical axis of $C_a + I + X$, which is the sum of autonomous consumption, investment, and exports. The slope of the line is $b - m$, which is the MPC adjusted for imports. Equilibrium output is the value of output where planned expenditures for U.S. goods cross the 45° line.

APPLICATION 4

THE LOCOMOTIVE EFFECT: HOW FOREIGN DEMAND AFFECTS A COUNTRY'S OUTPUT

APPLYING THE CONCEPTS #4: How do countries benefit from growth in their trading partners?

From the early 1990s until quite recently, the United States was what economists term the "locomotive" for global growth, growing faster than the rest of the world and increasing its demand for foreign products. As a share of the world economy, the United States grew from approximately 26 percent in 1992 to over 32 percent in 2001. Imports increase as an economy grows, and U.S. imports also increased along with output during this period. Because the U.S. economy is such an important part of the world economy, its demands for foreign goods—U.S. imports—fueled exports in foreign countries and promoted their growth. Studies have shown that the increase in demand for foreign goods was actually more pronounced for developing countries than for developed countries. The United States was truly a locomotive, pulling the developing countries along.

When the U.S. economy began to slow in 2007 because of our housing and financial difficulties, growth in other parts of the world, including China and India, was still robust. Their demand for U.S. goods spurred our exports and helped prevent U.S. GDP from falling any further. In this case, foreign countries were the true locomotives. As our chapter opening story describes, China remained a locomotive during the downturn. **Related to Exercise 5.7.**

SOURCE: Based on William R. Cline, *The United States As a Debtor Nation* (Washington, D.C.: Institute for International Economics, 2005), chap. 6.

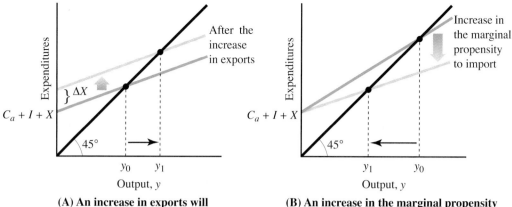

(A) An increase in exports will increase the level of GDP.

(B) An increase in the marginal propensity to import will decrease the level of GDP.

▲ **FIGURE 11.13**
How Increases in Exports and Imports Affect U.S. GDP
Panel A shows that an increase in exports will increase the level of GDP. Panel B shows that an increase in the marginal propensity to import will decrease the level of GDP.

Let's examine an application of the model we just developed. Suppose Japan decides to buy another $5 billion worth of goods from the United States. What will happen to U.S. domestic output? Panel A of Figure 11.13 shows the effect of an increase in exports. The demand line will shift vertically upward by the increase in exports (ΔX). This will increase equilibrium income from y_0 to y_1.

The increase in income will be larger than the increase in exports because of the multiplier effect. This multiplier is based on the MPC adjusted for trade. For example, if b is 0.8 and m is 0.2, the adjusted MPC ($b - m$) is 0.6, and the multiplier will be

$$\frac{1}{(1 - 0.6)} = 2.5$$

Therefore, a $5 billion increase in exports will lead to a $12.5 billion increase in GDP.

Now, suppose U.S. residents become more attracted to foreign goods, and as a result our marginal propensity to import increases. What happens to GDP? Panel B of Figure 11.13 depicts the effect of an increase in imported foreign goods. The adjusted MPC ($b - m$) will fall as the marginal propensity to import increases. This reduces the slope of the planned expenditure line, and output will fall from y_0 to y_1. The reason the line rotates rather than shifting down vertically is that an increase in the propensity to import changes the *slope* of the planned expenditure line.

We can now understand why our domestic political leaders are eager to sell our goods abroad. Whether it is electronics or weapons, increased U.S. exports will increase U.S. GDP and reduce unemployment in the short run. We can also understand how a recession abroad that led to a decrease in imports of U.S. goods could cause a recession here. At the same time, we can further understand why politicians will find "buy American" policies attractive in the short run. To the extent that U.S. residents buy U.S. goods rather than imports, output will be higher. This reasoning is also why other countries like to see the United States grow rapidly.

11.6 THE INCOME-EXPENDITURE MODEL AND THE AGGREGATE DEMAND CURVE

We used the income-expenditure model in this chapter to understand more fully short-term economic fluctuations. The income-expenditure model is based on the assumption that prices do not change. In Figure 11.14, we see how the model provides

▶ **FIGURE 11.14**
Deriving the Aggregate Demand Curve
As the price level falls from P_0 to P_1, planned expenditures increase, which increases the level of output from y_0 to y_1. The aggregate demand curve shows the combination of prices and equilibrium output.

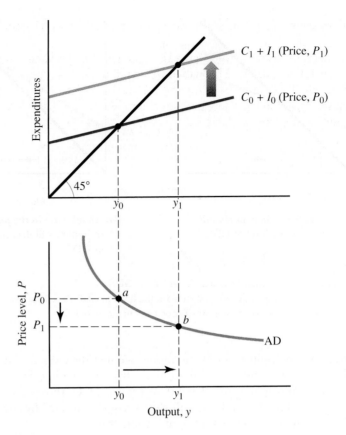

the foundation for the aggregate demand curve, which will enable us to analyze changes both in output and prices.

Suppose the price level in the economy is P_0 and, at that level of prices, planned expenditures are $C_0 + I_0$. At the top of the figure, we show how equilibrium output is determined at level of output, y_0. In the bottom part of the figure, we plot the price level, P_0, and corresponding level of output, y_0. In the graph, this is point a.

Now let's lower the price level to P_1. Recall from our discussion in Chapter 9 that a lower price level will increase the demand for goods and services through wealth effects, the interest rate effect, and the international trade effect. (You may want to go back and review this discussion.) As a consequence of the increased demand for goods and services arising from a lower price level, we show a higher level of planned expenditure, $C_1 + I_1$, and a higher level of equilibrium output, y_1, in the top part of the figure. In the bottom part, we again plot the price level, P_1, and the corresponding level of output, y_1. In the graph, this is point b.

Both point a and point b are on the aggregate demand curve. By the same logic, we can create all the other points on the aggregate demand curve by either raising or lowering the aggregate price level. For any price level, the income-expenditure model can be used to determine the level of output and the corresponding point on the aggregate demand curve. Thus, the income-expenditure model provides the basic foundation for the aggregate demand curve.

At any price level, the income-expenditure model determines the level of equilibrium output and the corresponding point on the aggregate demand curve. What would happen if we kept the price level at P_0 but increased planned expenditures, let's say through an increase in government expenditures from G_0 to G_1? We depict this case in Figure 11.15. The increase in government expenditure will raise the equilibrium output, from y_0 to y_1. Because the price level has not changed, we have a higher level of output at the same level of price. This means the aggregate demand curve would shift to the right, from AD_0 to AD_1. In general, increases in planned expenditures that are not directly caused by changes in prices will shift the aggregate demand curve to the right; decreases in planned expenditures will shift the curve to the left.

In the remaining chapters, we will use the aggregate demand and supply curves to analyze economic fluctuations. This will enable us to understand movements in both prices and output in the intermediate and longer runs. But, as we have seen, the income-expenditure model developed in this chapter provides the underlying foundation for the aggregate demand curve.

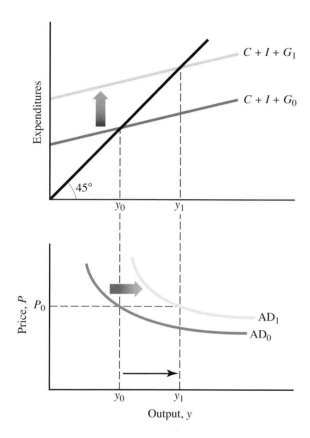

◀ **FIGURE 11.15**
Shifts in Aggregate Demand
As government spending increases from G_0 to G_1, planned expenditures increase, which raises output from y_0 to y_1. At the price level P_0, this shifts the aggregate demand curve to the right, from AD_0 to AD_1.

SUMMARY

This chapter developed the income-expenditure model, which is useful for understanding short-run fluctuations. We developed the graphical and algebraic tools to study the effects of consumer behavior, government spending and taxation, and exports and imports in determining GDP in the short run. Here are the chapter's main points:

1 In the *income-expenditure model*, the level of output in the economy will adjust to equal the level of planned expenditures. This level of output is called *equilibrium output*.

2 Consumption spending consists of two parts. One part is independent of income, but it can be influenced by changes in wealth or consumer sentiment. The other part depends on the level of income.

3 Increases in planned expenditures by households, the government, or the foreign sector lead to increases in equilibrium output.

4 Because of the multiplier, the final increase in equilibrium output is larger than the initial increase. The formula for the simple multiplier is

$$\text{multiplier} = \frac{1}{(1 - \text{MPC})}$$

5 Policymakers can use *multipliers* to calculate the appropriate size of economic policies.

6 Higher tax rates, by reducing the multiplier, can reduce fluctuations in GDP.

7 Increases in exports lead to increases in equilibrium output; increases in imports lead to decreases in equilibrium output.

8 The income-expenditure model can be used to derive the aggregate demand curve.

KEY TERMS

autonomous consumption, p. 227

consumption function, p. 227

equilibrium output, p. 225

marginal propensity to consume (MPC), p. 227

marginal propensity to import, p. 241

planned expenditures, p. 225

savings function, p. 231

EXERCISES

Visit www.myeconlab.com to complete these exercises online and get instant feedback.

11.1 A Simple Income-Expenditure Model

1.1 The income-expenditure model is most appropriate for long-run analysis. _____ (True/False)

1.2 Equilibrium output occurs when real output equals planned expenditures. _____ (True/False)

1.3 If output is currently higher than planned expenditures, inventories are _____ (increasing/decreasing).

1.4 At any point on the 45° line, planned expenditures equal _____.

1.5 **Understanding Inventory Behavior.** Use the simple income-expenditure model to analyze the following scenarios.

    a. Suppose clothing stores anticipate a good fashion season and add substantially to inventories in their stores. What will happen to GDP?

    b. Suppose economists see inventories suddenly increasing. Does this necessarily mean that there are increases in demand for final goods and services?

1.6 **Understanding the 45° Line.** Use the simple income-expenditure diagram depicted in Figure 11.3 on page 226 to answer the following questions.

    a. If output equals y_1, what is the level of expenditures?

    b. At output equal to y_1, does the level of expenditures fall above, below, or on the 45° line?

    c. What does this say about the relationship between output and expenditures?

11.2 The Consumption Function

2.1 The slope of the consumption function is called _____.

2.2 A decrease in consumer confidence will shift the consumption function _____ (upward/downward).

2.3 If housing prices fall, you would expect the consumption function to shift _____ (upward/downward).

2.4 If the MPC increases, the slope of the consumption function will _____ (increase/decrease).

2.5 **Housing Price Increases and Falling Savings.** Explain why some economists believed the increase in housing prices after 2002 was related to the fall in household savings that was also observed during that period. (Related to Application 1 on page 229.)

2.6 **Retirement Savings and the Decline in the Stock Market.** When the stock market fell sharply in 2007 and 2008, many people near retirement found that their savings for retirement were dramatically reduced. What would be their logical response in this situation? Is this consistent with the wealth effect?

2.7 **Is the Wealth Effect on Consumption from Housing Symmetrical?** When housing prices rose, some households took out a larger loan on their homes and used the additional funds they borrowed to finance purchases of consumer durables. This option is not available when housing prices fall. Explain how this difference might lead to a larger wealth effect for increases in housing prices than decreases in prices. (Related to Application 1 on page 229.)

11.3 Equilibrium Output and the Consumption Function

3.1 In our simple model, if $C = 100 + 0.8y$, and $I = 50$, equilibrium output will be _____.

3.2 If in Exercise 3.1 I increases to 100,

    a. the equilibrium income will be _____.

    b. the multiplier is _____.

3.3 If the marginal propensity to save is 0.3, the MPC must be _____.

3.4 If the MPC decreases, the multiplier will _____.

3.5 **Estimating Changes in Aggregate Demand.**

    a. Suppose $C = C_a + 0.6y$ and that a shock decreases C_a by $10 billion. By how much will equilibrium income decrease?

    b. An economy has an MPC of 0.6. By how much will a $10 billion increase in government purchases increase equilibrium income? By how much will a $10 billion increase in taxes decrease equilibrium income?

3.6 **The Paradox of Thrift.** The United States has instituted many policies to attempt to increase savings rates in the United States. One such policy was the creation of individual retirement accounts and other incentives for savings. An implication of the income-expenditure model is that an increase in the desire of consumers to save will not necessarily lead to higher savings. In fact, total savings will either remain the same or perhaps fall. This is known as the paradox of thrift. Let's see why this is true with an example.

   a. Suppose I equals 40 and the savings function is $S = -100 + 0.4y$. Equilibrium income, y, in the economy is 350. Now suppose consumers wish to increase their savings; the new savings function becomes $S = -80 + 0.4y$. Calculate the new level of equilibrium output and savings after the change in the savings function.

   b. Explain why equilibrium savings are unchanged.

   c. Now suppose that with a decline in equilibrium income, investment also falls. What would be the effect on equilibrium output and total savings if households now wished to increase their desired savings?

   d. What does this suggest about the ability of policymakers to increase aggregate savings by affecting citizens' savings rates?

3.7 Solving a Simple Model. Consider an economy in which $C = 200 + 0.5y$ and $I = 200$.

   a. Determine the equilibrium income algebraically.

   b. What is the multiplier for investment spending for this economy?

   c. What is the savings function?

   d. Draw the savings function on a graph with the investment level and indicate how equilibrium income is determined.

   e. What is the level of saving at the level of equilibrium income? Show it is equal to investment.

3.8 Earthquakes and Subsequent GDP Growth. Massive earthquakes, such as the one that afflicted Sichuan province in China in 2008 are terrible events. Yet, economists believe that GDP typically rises after an earthquake. Explain why this happens and whether that means that earthquakes are really "good things."

3.9 A Difficulty in Estimating Government Spending Multipliers. Tax revenues typically rise along with GDP. Governments may typically spend some of this additional revenue on discretionary items in the budget. Assuming this is true, how does this complicate the work of analysts trying to determine the multiplier effects of discretionary spending on GDP? (Related to Application 2 on page 233.)

11.4 Government Spending and Taxation

4.1 The multiplier for taxes is greater than the multiplier for government spending. _____ (True/False)

4.2 A decrease in the tax rate will _____ the government spending multiplier.

4.3 Economic fluctuations have _____ since World War II.

4.4 An increase in both government spending and taxes by the same amount _____ GDP.

4.5 Using Fiscal Multipliers. Suppose that during a recession a country wishes to increase its GDP by 100. The MPC is 0.8.

   a. Using the government spending multiplier, by how much should government spending be increased?

   b. Using the tax multiplier, by how much should taxes be decreased?

4.6 The Broken Window Fallacy. Critics of Keynes pointed out that not all spending is really productive. If vandals break windows and you replace them, GDP will certainly rise. Yet, you are probably worse off than before because you had to use resources to repair the windows. Discuss.

4.7 President Ford's Theory. During the 1970s, President Gerald Ford proposed that taxes be decreased but that, to avoid increasing the government budget deficit, government spending should be decreased by the same amount.

   a. What happens to GDP if taxes and government spending are both decreased by the same amount?

   b. Should President Ford have been worried about his tax-reduction plan? Why or why not?

4.8 Inventory Policies and Economic Stability. In recent years, many companies have adopted Japanese-style "just-in-time" inventory management. For example, when your cashier at Walmart records your purchase of a new toaster, it automatically triggers a process to re-order a toaster for the store. In the past, store managers had to forecast their inventory needs. Why might this method of inventory management lead to more economic stability?

4.9 Keynes's Other Contributions. Although John Maynard Keynes is best known today for his book *The General Theory of Employment, Interest, and Money*, he made other important contributions as well. Search the Web to find out (1) Keynes's main criticism of the Treaty of Versailles, which ended World War I and (2) his contribution to the post–World War II monetary system. (Related to Application 3 on page 238.)

11.5 Exports and Imports

5.1 An increase in the marginal propensity to import will _____ the multiplier for investment spending.

5.2 An increase in exports will lead to a(n) _____ in GDP.

5.3 Use the income-expenditure graph to illustrate how an increase in exports will affect GDP.

5.4 As a country's income increases imports will also increase. _____ (True/False)

5.5 Trade Wars. During the 1930s, many countries in the world—including the United States—tried to help their own economies by restricting imported goods.

But because one country's imports are another country's exports, such actions cause international repercussions. Let's look at the worldwide consequences of such policies using the income-expenditure model.

a. Suppose the United States adopted policies to reduce imports from Europe. This means European exports to the United States would be reduced. What would happen to European equilibrium income?

b. Suppose, in response to U.S. policies, Europe decides to restrict imports from the United States. What then happens to U.S equilibrium income?

c. What do you think happened to the volume of world trade during the 1930s?

5.6 **Using Open-Economy Multipliers.** In an open economy, the marginal propensity to consume is 0.9, and the marginal propensity to import is 0.3. How much of an increase in investment would be necessary to raise GDP by 200? What would be your answer if this was a closed economy?

5.7 **U.S. Export Growth.** In 2007, several components of GDP grew much more slowly than in prior years but exports increased sharply. The rest of the world was growing rapidly during this period. Based on this information, what is the most natural explanation for the growth in U.S. exports? (Related to Application 4 on page 242.)

11.6 The Income-Expenditure Model and the Aggregate Demand Curve

6.1 An increase in the price level will _____ GDP and thereby move the economy _____ the aggregate demand curve.

6.2 At any price level, the income-expenditure model determines the level of equilibrium output and the corresponding point on the _____ curve.

6.3 A decrease in the price level will not shift the aggregate demand curve. _____ (True/False)

6.4 A rightward shift in the aggregate demand curve corresponds to a(n) _____ in equilibrium income.

6.5 **Using Multipliers to Determine the Shift of the Aggregate Demand Curve.**

a. Suppose the MPC is equal to 0.8. Government spending increases by $20 billion. How far does the aggregate demand curve shift to the right?

b. Now suppose that the MPC is 0.8 and the marginal propensity to import is 0.2. How far to the right will the $20 billion in government spending shift the aggregate demand curve?

6.6 **Increasing Exports and Aggregate Demand.** Suppose foreign countries grow more rapidly than anticipated and U.S. exports also grow.

a. Using the income-expenditure model, first show how the increase in exports will increase U.S. GDP.

b. Using your results in part (a), explain how the aggregate demand curve shifts with the increase in exports.

6.7 **The Size of the Wealth Effect and the Slope of the Aggregate Demand Curve.** Suppose the wealth effect is very small; that is, a large fall in prices will not increase consumption by very much. Explain carefully why this will imply that the aggregate demand curve will have a steep slope.

ECONOMIC EXPERIMENT

Estimating the Marginal Propensity to Consume

For this experiment, each class member is asked to fill out the following table. Given a certain monthly income, how would you spend it and how much would you save? The top row of each column gives you the monthly disposable income. How would you allocate it each month among the various categories of spending in the table and savings? Complete each column in the table. The sum of your entries should equal your disposable income at the top of each column.

After you have filled out the chart, compute the changes in your savings and total consumption as your income goes up. What is your marginal propensity to save (MPS)? What is your marginal propensity to consume (MPC) over your total expenditures? Graph your consumption function.

Monthly Disposable Income	$1,250	$1,500	$1,750	$2,000
Expenditures and Savings				
Food				
Housing				
Transportation				
Medical				
Entertainment				
Other expenses				
Savings				

 For additional economic experiments, please visit www.myeconlab.com.

APPENDIX

FORMULAS FOR EQUILIBRIUM INCOME AND THE MULTIPLIER

In the chapter, we developed the logic of the income-expenditure model and generally relied on graphical analysis. However, we also referred to a few formulas. In this appendix, we explain where these formulas, both for equilibrium income and the multiplier, come from.

Specifically, in this appendix, we do three things:

- Derive a simple formula for calculating equilibrium output for the simplest economy in which there is no government spending or taxes.
- Derive the multipliers for the economy with the government.
- Derive equilibrium output with both government and the foreign sector.

To derive the formula for equilibrium output, we use simple algebra in the following steps:

1   We know that equilibrium output occurs where output equals planned expenditures, and we know that planned expenditures equal $C + I$; therefore,

$$\text{output} = \text{planned expenditures} = C + I$$
$$\text{output} = C + I$$

2   Next, we substitute the symbol y for output; more importantly, we substitute for the consumption function, $C = (C_a + by)$:

$$y = (C_a + by) + I$$

3   Collect all terms in y on the left side of the equation:

$$y - by = C_a + I$$

4   Factor the left side:

$$y(1 - b) = C_a + I$$

5   Divide both sides by $(1 - b)$:

$$y^* = \frac{(C_a + I)}{(1 - b)}$$

where y^* means the equilibrium level of output. This is the formula for equilibrium output in the text.

Now let's find the multiplier for investment in this simple economy. To do that, we use the formula we just derived and calculate the equilibrium income at one level of investment, which we call the *original level*, and then calculate the equilibrium income at some other level of investment, which we call the *new level*. (We will "calculate" in general terms, not in specific numerical quantities.) What we will get is a formula for the change in output that results from the changes in investment.

For the original level of investment at I_0, we have

$$y_0 = \frac{(C_a + I_0)}{(1 - b)}$$

For a new level of investment at I_1, we have

$$y_1 = \frac{(C_a + I_1)}{(1 - b)}$$

The change in output, Δy, is the difference between the two levels of output that occur at each level of investment:

$$\Delta y = y_1 - y_0$$

Substituting for the levels of output, we have

$$\Delta y = \frac{(C_a + I_1)}{(1 - b)} - \frac{(C_a + I_0)}{(1 - b)}$$

Because the denominator in both expressions is the same $(1 - b)$, we can put the numerators over that common denominator:

$$\Delta y = \frac{(C_a + I_1) - (C_a + I_0)}{(1 - b)}$$

$$\Delta y = \frac{(I_1 - I_0)}{(1 - b)}$$

Finally, because $(I_1 - I_0)$ is the change in investment, ΔI, we can write

$$\Delta y = \frac{\Delta I}{(1 - b)}$$

or

$$\frac{\Delta y}{\Delta I} = \frac{1}{(1 - b)}$$

Therefore, because the multiplier is the ratio of the change in income to the change in investment spending, we have

$$\text{the multiplier} = \frac{\Delta y}{\Delta I} = \frac{1}{(1 - b)}$$

Here is another way to derive the formula for the multiplier. This way helps to illustrate its underlying logic. Suppose investment spending increases by $1. Because spending determines output, output will rise by $1. However, because consumption depends on income, consumption will increase by the marginal propensity to consume times the change in income. This means that as output rises by $1, consumption will increase by $(b \times \$1)$. Because spending determines output, this additional increase in consumer demand will cause output to rise further $(b \times \$1)$. But again, as output and income increase, consumption will increase by MPC times the change in income, which in this case will be $b \times (b \times \$1)$ or $b^2 \times \$1$. As we allow this process to continue, the total change in output will be

$$\Delta y = \$1 + (\$1 \times b) + (\$1 \times b^2) + (\$1 \times b^3) \cdots$$

or

$$\Delta y = \$1 \times (1 + b + b^2 + b^3 + \cdots)$$

The term in parentheses is an infinite series whose value is equal to

$$\frac{1}{(1 - b)}$$

Substituting this value for the infinite series, we have the expression for the multiplier:

$$\Delta y = \$1 \times \frac{1}{(1 - b)}$$

Now we introduce government spending and taxes. Government spending is another determinant of planned expenditures, and consumption spending depends on after-tax income, so consumption equals $C_a + b(y - T)$. Following the same steps we used for equilibrium output without government, we do the same, but now with government:

$$\text{output} = \text{planned expenditures} = (C + I + G)$$
$$y = C_a + b(y - T) + I + G$$

We first collect all terms in y on the left and leave the other terms on the right:

$$y - by = C_a - bT + I + G$$

We then factor the left side:

$$y(1 - b) = C_a - bT + I + G$$

We then divide both sides by $(1 - b)$:

$$y^* = \frac{(C_a - bT + I + G)}{(1 - b)}$$

Using this formula and the method just outlined, we can find the multiplier for changes in government spending and the multiplier for changes in taxes:

$$\text{government spending multiplier} = \frac{1}{(1 - b)}$$

$$\text{tax multiplier} = \frac{-b}{(1 - b)}$$

The multiplier for an increase in government spending is larger than the tax multiplier for a reduction in taxes in the same amount as an increase in government spending. Government spending increases total demand directly. Reductions in taxes first affect consumer's incomes. Because consumers will save a part of their income increase from the tax cut, not all of the tax cut is spent. Therefore, the tax multiplier is smaller (in absolute value) than the government spending multiplier.

As we explained in the text, because government spending has a larger multiplier than taxes, equal increases in government spending and taxes, called balanced-budget increases, will increase total output. For equal dollar increases in both taxes and government spending, the positive effects from the spending increase will outweigh the negative effects from the tax increase. To find the balanced-budget multiplier, just add the government spending and tax multipliers:

$$\text{balanced-budget multiplier} = \text{government spending multiplier} + \text{tax multiplier}$$
$$= \frac{1}{(1 - b)} + \frac{-b}{(1 - b)}$$
$$= \frac{(1 - b)}{(1 - b)}$$
$$= 1$$

The balanced-budget multiplier equals 1; a \$10 billion increase in both taxes and government spending will increase GDP by \$10 billion.

Finally, we derive equilibrium output with government spending, taxes, and the foreign sector. First, recall that equilibrium output occurs where output equals demand. We now must include planned expenditures from both the government sector and the foreign sector. Planned expenditures from the foreign sector are exports minus imports:

$$\text{output} = \text{planned expenditures} = (C + I + G + X - M)$$

Consumption depends on disposable income:

$$C = C_a + b(y - T)$$

and imports depend on the level of output:

$$M = my$$

Substitute the equations for consumption and imports into the equation where output equals demand:

$$y = C_a + b(y - T) + I + G + X - my$$

Collect all terms in y on the left and leave the other terms on the right:

$$y - (b - m)y = C_a - bT + I + G + X$$

Factor the left side:

$$y\big[1 - (b - m)\big] = C_a - bT + I + G + X$$

Divide both sides by $[1 - (b - m)]$:

$$y^* = \frac{(C_a - bT + I + G + X)}{\big[1 - (b - m)\big]}$$

This is the expression for equilibrium income with government in an open economy. It can be used, following the method we outlined, to calculate multipliers in the open economy.

EXERCISES

Visit www.myeconlab.com to complete these exercises online and get instant feedback.

A.1 Find the Multiplier. An economy has a marginal propensity to consume (b) of 0.6 and a marginal propensity to import (m) of 0.2. What is the multiplier for government spending for this economy?

A.2 The Effects of Taxes and Spending. Suppose the economy has a marginal propensity to consume (b) of 0.6 and a marginal propensity to import (m) of 0.2. The government increases its spending by $2 billion and raises taxes by $1 billion. What happens to equilibrium income?

A.3 Savings and Taxes. When there are taxes, savings is defined as disposable income minus consumption, or $S = (y - T) - C$. In an economy with government but no foreign sector—a closed economy—equilibrium income is determined where output equals demand, or $y = C + I + G$. Show that we can also determine equilibrium income using the relationship $S + T = I + G$.

A.4 Working with a Model. An economy has the following dimensions:

$$C = 100 + 0.5(y - T)$$
$$I = 50$$
$$G = 50$$
$$T = 20$$

a. Draw the income-expenditure graph for this economy.

b. Find the equilibrium income and plot it on the graph.

c. What is the multiplier for government spending?

d. Find the savings function.

e. What is the level of savings when the economy is in equilibrium?

f. Show that at equilibrium $S + T = I + G$.

NOTES

1. "GDP Growth in China 1952–2009," Chinability, http://www.chinability.com/GDP.htm

Investment and Financial Markets

The housing market is a perfect example of the close links between investment and finance. With the stock market falling sharply in 2000, housing looked like an alternative and attractive investment. Interest rates were low and homeowners and potential investors found that it was easy to borrow money to purchase new or larger homes. Wall Street and government agencies developed ever more complex ways to pour money into the housing market, and banks and finance companies did not seem to be asking too many questions about their borrowers. As housing prices continued to rise, the building industry responded to the general euphoria. Investment in residential housing increased 40 percent in real terms from 2000 to 2006.

It was too good to last. With all the new construction, the increased supply of housing stopped the rise in prices. Some buyers made foolish decisions and took on loans that were too large for their incomes. As financial markets became nervous, lenders became more cautious and sharply cut back on funds available to the market. With increased supply and reduced demand, housing prices began to fall. The building industry recognized it had too many new houses in the pipeline and began to cut back. From its peak in the first quarter of 2006 to the fourth quarter of 2009, new housing construction fell by 53 percent. The fall in residential housing alone brought down real GDP by 3 percent and devastated many state economies.

APPLYING THE CONCEPTS

1 How do fluctuations in energy prices affect investment decisions by firms?
Energy Price Uncertainty Reduces Investment Spending

2 How can understanding the concept of present value help a lucky lottery winner?
Options for a Lottery Winner

3 Why did many homeowners in 2010 owe more to banks than their home was worth?
Underwater Homes: Bets Gone Wrong

4 How have recent financial innovations created new risks for the economy?
Securitization: The Good, the Bad, and the Ugly

Investment spending plays a number of critical roles in the economy. As we have seen, economic growth depends on whether the stock of capital—plant and equipment—increases in the economy. Moreover, investment is also a key component of aggregate demand, so fluctuations in investment spending can cause recessions and booms. In this chapter, we will study the factors that determine investment spending by firms. We also will examine the role that institutions such as banks, savings and loans, and other new and evolving financial institutions play in facilitating that investment.

An *investment*, broadly defined, is an action that creates a cost today but provides benefits in the future. A firm builds a new plant today to earn more revenue in the future. College students pay money to attend school now so they can earn higher salaries later. A government spends money today to construct a dam that will provide hydroelectric power for years to come. These are examples of investments. Notice that we're using the term *investment* in a broader sense than we did in Chapter 5 when we discussed GDP. In that chapter when we talked about investment, we were talking about expenditures by firms on currently produced goods and services. In this chapter, we broaden the definition to include actions taken by anyone—individuals, firms, and governments—to improve well-being later.

12.1 AN INVESTMENT: A PLUNGE INTO THE UNKNOWN

When individuals, firms, or governments make an investment, they incur costs today in the hope of future gains. The phrase "hope of" is an important aspect of investment decisions. That simply means that payoffs occurring in the future cannot be known with certainty. Investments are a plunge into the unknown.

Firms and individuals frequently revise their outlook on the future precisely because it is uncertain. These revisions can occur suddenly and lead to sharp swings in investment spending. Sometimes investors are optimistic and decide to increase their investment spending; at other times, they may quickly become pessimistic and cut back on their investment spending. To estimate future events, firms pay careful attention to the current pace of the economy. If economic growth is sluggish, they are likely to forecast that it will be sluggish in the future and cut back on investment spending. If economic growth is strong, they are likely to forecast that it will remain so and increase their investment spending. In other words, investment spending tends to be closely related to the current pace of economic growth.

accelerator theory

The theory of investment that says that current investment spending depends positively on the expected future growth of real GDP.

This phenomenon is known as the **accelerator theory** of investment spending. It postulates that when real GDP growth is expected to be high, firms anticipate that investing in plants and equipment will pay off later, so they increase their total investment spending. However, John Maynard Keynes had another theory. Keynes said the sharp swings in optimism and pessimism related to investment spending were often irrational, reflecting, perhaps, our most basic, primal instincts. He often referred to them as "the animal spirits" of investors. It was, in part, animal spirits that led to the rise and fall in residential investment that we discussed in the chapter-opening story.

It is likely that *both* projections for the future *and* Keynes's animal spirits are closely associated with current investment. If this is the case, we would expect investment spending to be a very volatile component of GDP. As Figure 12.1 indicates, this is indeed the case.

Figure 12.1 plots total investment spending as a share of U.S. GDP from 1970 to 2009. Notice two things about Figure 12.1:

- From 1970 to 2009, the share of investment as a component of GDP ranged from a low of about 10 percent in 1975 to a high of over 18 percent in 2000—a dramatic 8-percentage-point difference.
- Swings in investment spending often occurred over short periods of time. For example, during recessions (noted by the shaded areas in the figure), investment spending fell sharply. During booms, investment spending rose sharply. In other words, investment spending is highly **procyclical**; it increases during booms and falls during recessions.

procyclical

Moving in the same direction as real GDP.

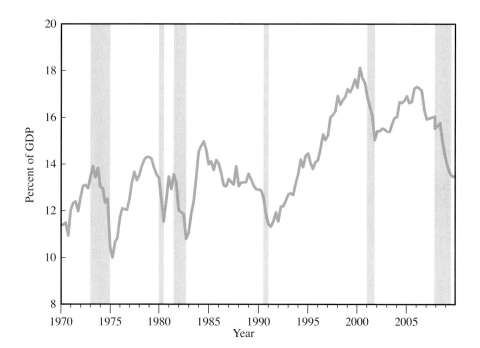

Investment Spending as a Share of U.S. GDP, 1970–2009
The share of investment as a component of GDP ranged from a low of about 10 percent in 1975 to a high of over 18 percent in 2000. The shaded areas represent U.S. recessions.

Many different factors can contribute to uncertainty in the economy. Volatile energy prices are one. In general, when the future is uncertain, firms become cautious in their behavior and may postpone making investment decisions.

Although investment spending is a much smaller component of GDP than consumption (70 versus 16 percent), it is much more volatile than consumption. Recall that changes in the components of GDP—C, I, G, or NX—are amplified by the multiplier. For example, if the multiplier is 1.5, and investment spending initially falls by 1 percent of GDP, then GDP will fall by 1.5 percent. However, if the fall in GDP makes firms more pessimistic, they may cut investment even further. This further cut

APPLICATION 1

ENERGY PRICE UNCERTAINTY REDUCES INVESTMENT SPENDING

APPLYING THE CONCEPTS #1: How Do Fluctuations in Energy Prices Affect Investment Decisions By Firms?

As we have seen in previous chapters, increases in oil prices can lead to a drop in GDP. However, uncertainty about oil prices is also an important factor. Economists Hui Guo and Kevin Kliesen found evidence that volatility in oil prices adversely affects GDP growth.

One important way volatility of oil prices can hurt the economy is by creating uncertainty for firms making investment decisions. For example, consider whether a firm should invest in an energy-saving technology for a new plant. If energy prices remain high, it may be profitable to invest in energy-saving technology, but if energy prices fall, these investments would be unwise. If firms are faced with an increasingly uncertain future, they will delay their investment decisions until the uncertainty is resolved. In 2008, oil prices reached $145 a barrel, but later in the year fell below $50. On what number should firms base their investment decisions?   **Related to Exercise 1.8.**

SOURCE: Based on Hui Guo and Kevin Kliesen, "Oil Price Volatility and Macroeconomic Activity," *Federal Reserve Bank of St. Louis Review* (November–December 2005): 669–684.

in investment will decrease GDP even more. That is, a small initial fall in investment can trigger a much larger fall in GDP. Nobel Laureate Paul Samuelson described this phenomenon of investment volatility by developing the multiplier-accelerator model. The **multiplier-accelerator** model showed that a downturn in real GDP leads to an even sharper fall in investment, which further reduces GDP via the multiplier.

multiplier-accelerator model
A model in which a downturn in real GDP leads to a sharp fall in investment, which triggers further reductions in GDP through the multiplier.

Psychology and expectations about future real GDP growth are not the only factors that affect investment. Because investments are really trade-offs—something in the present traded for something in the future—the "terms" affecting the trade-off are also important. These terms are interest rates, which we discuss next.

12.2 EVALUATING THE FUTURE

A dollar paid today does not have the same value as a dollar paid next year. Because investments yield future payoffs, we need to be able to compare costs and benefits at different points in time. As we will see, we can use interest rates to do this.

Understanding Present Value

Suppose a good friend comes to you and says, "I need some cash, badly. If you give me $100 today, I can give you back $105 next year. Do we have a deal?" How would you decide whether to accept this deal? Somehow, you need a tool to be able to compare dollars today with dollars received in the future. That tool is present value. The **present value** of a payment to be received in the future is the maximum amount a person is willing to pay today to receive the future payment. Recall the principle of opportunity cost.

present value
The maximum amount a person is willing to pay today to receive a payment in the future.

PRINCIPLE OF OPPORTUNITY COST
The opportunity cost of something is what you sacrifice to get it.

Let's think about how much you are willing to pay for the right to receive $105 in one year. Suppose you can earn 5 percent per year in a savings account or money market account. A moment of thought will show you that you would be willing to lend your friend $100. Here is why: If you kept your $100 in the bank at 5 percent interest, you would have $105 at the end of the year—just the amount your friend would repay you. While you would have sacrificed $5 in interest, you would have earned $5 on the loan ($105 – $100).

However, you would not want to lend your friend more than $100. If you lent more—say $102—then your loss in interest of $5.10 (5 percent of $102) would be greater than your $3 gain on the loan ($105 – $102). In this case, the amount you sacrifice will be greater than what you get in return.

Of course, you would like to lend your friend less than $100 and make even more profit. But the *maximum amount* you would be willing to pay today to receive $105 next year, when the interest rate is 5 percent, is $100. Thus, the present value of $105 in this example is $100.

PRESENT VALUE AND INTEREST RATES   Here is another useful way to think of present value. Suppose you want to buy a new car in five years for $20,000. You want to know how much you need to have in your bank account today, so that after five years you have the $20,000 to make the payment for the car. A simple formula can answer this and similar questions. If K is an amount of money at some point in the future; t is the amount of time, or years, in the future until you need the money; and i is the interest rate you earn on your account, then the amount you need today is just the present value of the K dollars, which is

$$\text{present value} = \frac{K}{(1 + i)^t}$$

In the example of your friend, her payment (K) is $105, the interval of time (t) in which she's going to pay it is one year, and the interest rate (i) is 0.05. Using the present value formula, the present value of $105 in one year is $100:

$$\text{present value} = \frac{\$105}{(1 + 0.05)^1} = \$100$$

This is the maximum amount you are willing to lend her today to receive $105 from her in one year.

Let's consider another example. Suppose the interest rate were 10 percent and you were offered $1,000 to be paid to you in 20 years. How much is that $1,000 worth today? That is, how much of your money today would you be willing to "tie up" (loan out) to get $1,000 in 20 years? At an interest rate of 10 percent, this is how much:

$$\text{present value} = \frac{\$1,000}{(1 + 0.10)^{20}} = \$148.64$$

You would be willing to pay only $148.64 today to receive $1,000 in 20 years. The reason you would be willing to pay so much less than $1,000 is that money earning interest grows over time. At a 10 percent interest rate, after 20 years you would have received exactly $1,000 by initially investing just $148.64.

Returning to our original example with your friend, what happens if the interest rate is 10 percent instead of 5 percent? If your friend still promises you $105 after one year but the interest rate is double, how much would you be willing to loan her today? Using the formula, you would loan only $95.45 today:

$$\text{present value} = \frac{\$105}{(1 + 0.10)^1} = \$95.45$$

What this means is that if the interest rate is higher, you will be willing to pay *less* for the same payment in the future. This is an important result. *The present value of a given payment in the future decreases as the interest rate increases.* Here is why: With a higher interest rate, the opportunity cost of lending out your money is higher. Because you can earn more on your money with a higher rate, you will not be willing to pay as much now to get the same $105 dollars in the future. Similarly, *when interest rates fall, the present value of a given payment in the future increases.* For example, if interest rates fell to 2 percent, the present value (the value today) of $105 in one year would be higher—$102.94:

$$\text{present value} = \frac{\$105}{(1 + 0.02)^1} = \$102.94$$

With a lower interest rate, the opportunity cost of keeping your money in the bank or loaning it to a friend is less. That means you will be willing to pay more money now for the same $105 payment in the future.

Let's summarize our discussion of present value:

1 The present value—the value today—of a given payment in the future is the maximum amount a person is willing to pay today for that payment.

2 As the interest rate increases, the opportunity cost of your funds also increases, so the present value of a given payment in the future falls. In other words, you need *less* money today to get to your future "money goal."

3 As the interest rate decreases, the opportunity cost of your funds also decreases, so the present value of a given payment in the future rises. In other words, you need *more* money today to get to your money goal.

Individuals, firms, and the government all use interest rates to make decisions that involve the future. For example, individuals take interest rates into account when they decide how much to save for the future or even when to retire. And, as we will see, firms and the government use interest rates to decide whether to undertake important investments.

(**APPLICATION 2**)

OPTIONS FOR A LOTTERY WINNER

APPLYING THE CONCEPTS #2: How Can Understanding The Concept of Present Value Help a Lucky Lottery Winner?

The lucky winner of a lottery was given an option. She could either receive $1 million a year for 20 years, for a total of $20 million, or simply receive $10 million today. Why would anyone take the $10 million today?

To answer this question, we need to use the concept of present value. A dollar paid today is not the same as a dollar paid next year. Depending on the interest rate, the $10 million today might be more valuable than the $20 million paid over 20 years. Indeed, if interest rates were 10 percent, you could take the $10 million today, put it in the bank, and earn $1 million in interest (10 percent of $10 million) forever—not just for 20 years! To determine which payment option is best, our lottery winner would first need to calculate the present value of $1 million for each of the 20 years, add up the results, and compare the sum to the $10 million being offered to her today. With an 8 percent interest rate, the present value of an annual payment of $1 million every year for 20 years is $9.8 million. So if interest rates exceed 8 percent, it is better to take the $10 million dollars. (The actual calculation—adding up the present value at an 8 percent interest rate for all 20 years—is a bit tedious. In the problems at the end of the chapter, we show you how to make this calculation using an Excel spreadsheet.) **Related to Exercise 2.7.**

Real and Nominal Interest Rates

Even if you deposit $100 in a bank account and get $105 at the end of the year, if the economy's annual rate of inflation amounts to 5 percent or more, your purchasing power would not have increased at all. In other words, the 5 percent inflation will eat up all your 5 percent earnings. This is an example of the real-nominal principle.

REAL-NOMINAL PRINCIPLE

What matters to people is the real value of money or income—the purchasing power—not the face value of money.

nominal interest rate
Interest rates quoted in the market.

real interest rate
The nominal interest rate minus the inflation rate.

When there is inflation, economists make a distinction between the interest rate quoted in the market, which is called the **nominal interest rate**, and the **real interest rate**, which is what you actually earn after taking account of inflation. The real interest rate is defined as the nominal interest rate minus the inflation rate:

$$\text{real rate} = \text{nominal rate} - \text{inflation rate}$$

If the nominal rate of interest is 6 percent per year and the inflation rate is 4 percent during the year, the real rate of interest is 2 percent (6 – 4).

To understand what the real rate of interest means, suppose you have $100 and annual inflation is 4 percent. It's not hard to figure out that next year you will need $104 to have the same purchasing power you do today. Let's say you deposit today $100 at a 6 percent annual interest rate. At the end of the year, you will have $106 ($100 × 1.06).

Now let's calculate your real gain. After one year, you will have increased your holdings by $6, but taking into account the $4 you needed to keep up with inflation, your gain is only $2. The real rate of interest you earned, the nominal rate adjusted for inflation, is 2 percent, or $2.

Let's see what happens when you borrow money. Suppose you borrow $100 at a 10 percent annual interest rate, but inflation is 6 percent during the year. At the end of the year, you must pay back $110 ($100 × 1.10). But with an inflation rate of 6 percent, the lender would need 6 of the 10 dollars you paid in interest just to keep up with inflation. That means the lender would effectively get just a $4 gain ($10 – $6), instead of the full $10 gain. Thus, when corrected for the effects of inflation, the real rate of interest you will have to pay is just 4 percent, or $4, on the original $100 loan.

As an example, in 2002 if seniors invested their money in three-month U.S. government Treasury bills, they would have earned an average interest rate of 1.6 percent. However, inflation, as measured by the Consumer Price Index, was 2.4 percent. In real terms, these seniors would have actually lost money during the year, earning a negative real rate of interest of –0.8 percent.

We defined the real interest rate as the nominal interest rate minus the actual inflation rate. When firms or individuals borrow or lend money, they do not know what the rate of inflation will actually be in the future. Instead, they must form an expectation—an estimate—of what they believe the inflation rate will be in the future. For a given nominal interest rate, we can define the **expected real interest rate** as the nominal interest rate minus the expected inflation rate. The expected real interest rate is the rate at which borrowers or lenders *expect* to make transactions.

expected real interest rate
The nominal interest rate minus the expected inflation rate.

It is difficult to precisely determine expected real rates of interest because we never know exactly what inflation rates people really anticipate. One approach is to rely on the judgments of professional forecasters. Here is an example. In April 2010 nominal interest rates on three-month U.S. government securities was 0.22 percent. The nominal rate was very low, but positive. However, inflation forecasts for the remainder of that year were about 2 percent. This meant that the expected real rate was –1.78 percent. To determine real returns, we need to know both the nominal rate of interest and forecasts for inflation.

Up to this point, we have discussed "the" interest rate. However, at any point in time, there are really many different interest rates. One reason is that loans vary by their riskiness and by their maturity (the length of the loan). Riskier loans and loans for longer maturities typically have higher interest rates.

Figure 12.2 depicts the movement in three interest rates from 2002 to 2008 for three types of investments: corporate AAA bonds (loans investors make to corporations that are good credit risks), 10-year U.S. Treasury bonds (loans to the government for 10 years), and six-month treasuries (loans to the U.S. government for six months).

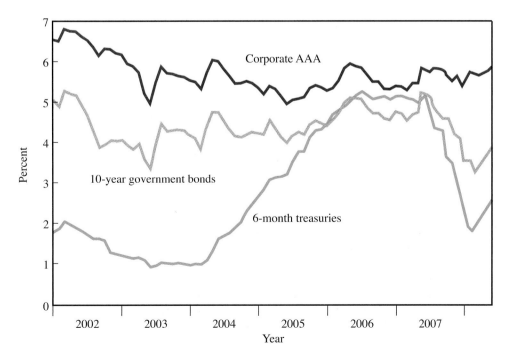

◄ **FIGURE 12.2**
Interest Rates on Corporate and Government Investments, 2002–2008

Notice that rates for corporate bonds are higher than rates for 10-year Treasury bonds. The reason is that corporations are less likely to pay back their loans than the U.S. government. Notice, too, that for most of this time period, the U.S. government typically paid a lower rate when it borrowed for shorter periods of time (6 months) than for longer periods of time (10 years). That is the normal pattern. However, in 2006 and 2007, it became cheaper for the government to borrow for the longer period. In later chapters we'll look more carefully at the factors that determine interest rates.

12.3 UNDERSTANDING INVESTMENT DECISIONS

Now that we understand the concept of present value and interest rates, we can use these tools to understand investment decisions. Consider a project we have to pay for today in order to benefit in the future. Here is the simple investment rule for such a project: *Invest in a project if the cost you incur today is less than or equal to the present value of the future payments from the project.*

In our first present-value example, the "project" (the loan to your friend) pays $105 in one year, and the present value (with an interest rate of 5 percent) is $100. Because the cost of the project is also $100, the project is worthwhile.

Consider a more complicated project that pays $110 in year 1 and in year 2. The interest rate is 10 percent. The present value of the benefits from this project is

$$\text{present value} = \frac{\$110}{(1 + 0.10)} + \frac{\$110}{(1.10)^2} = \$191$$

As long as the cost of the project today is less than $191, it pays to invest in it.

We can use our theory to develop the relationship between investment spending and the real rate of interest in the economy. In the economy as a whole, millions of different investment projects can be undertaken, nearly all providing different returns. Consider the array of investments A through E in Table 12.1. Each project costs $100 in the current period and provides a return one period later. The returns are expressed in real terms; that is, they have been adjusted for inflation.

TABLE 12.1 RETURN ON INVESTMENT BY PROJECT

Project	Cost	Return
A	$100	$101
B	100	103
C	100	105
D	100	107
E	100	109

Let's look at the present value of these investments at various interest rates. At an interest rate of 2 percent per year, only investment A is unprofitable. For the other investments, the present value of the return exceeds the cost. If the interest rate in the market increases to 4 percent, both A and B will be unprofitable. At an interest rate of 6 percent, A, B, and C will be unprofitable; D will be unprofitable as well if the market interest rate increases to 8 percent. If the interest rate exceeds 9 percent, all the investments will be unprofitable.

As interest rates rise, there will be fewer profitable investments in which firms are willing to invest, and the total level of investment spending in the economy will decline. Figure 12.3 depicts the negative relationship, graphically represented as the downward-sloping line, between real interest rates and investment. As the graph indicates, high real interest rates will deter investment spending. As an

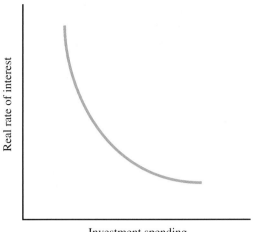

◄ **FIGURE 12.3**
The Relationship between Real Interest Rates and Investment Spending
As the real interest rate declines, investment spending in the economy increases.

example, during the early 1980s when real interest rates rose, business investment dropped sharply.

In practice, firms need to take into account other factors besides interest rates in making their investment decisions. In the **neoclassical theory of investment**, pioneered by Dale Jorgenson of Harvard University, taxes along with real interest rates play a key role in determining investment spending. Jorgenson used his theory to analyze how investors respond to a variety of tax incentives, including investment tax credits.

Should we use a real or nominal interest rate to determine whether to invest? The answer is that it doesn't really matter, as long as we are consistent. If the future benefits of the project are not adjusted for inflation, then we should use the nominal interest rate because it takes into account overall inflation—inflation is built into the nominal rate, so to speak. But if we first express the future benefits of the investment in current dollars—that is, if we reduce their nominal value by the amount that prices in the economy are expected to increase—then we should use the real rate of interest in our calculations.

Keep this distinction between real and nominal interest rates in mind. If nominal interest rates are 10 percent but inflation is 9 percent, the real rate of interest is only 1 percent. A firm makes its investment decisions by comparing its expected real net return from investment projects to the real rate of interest. Just because nominal interest rates are high does not mean the real interest rate is also high.

During the 1970s, homeowners in California understood this. They purchased homes in record numbers, even though it meant borrowing money at interest rates exceeding 10 percent. Buyers were willing to borrow at such high rates because housing prices in California had been rising by more than 10 percent annually, and they believed the trend would continue. They realized, for example, that if housing prices rose by 12 percent per year, they were essentially earning a 2 percent annual return because their mortgage loans were just 10 percent. (They would earn the returns only when they sold their homes.) That would make the real interest rate of the money borrowed –2 percent. This caused a housing boom in California that lasted until housing prices stopped rising at such high rates.

Investment and the Stock Market

Economists have long noticed a correlation between the stock market and investment spending. All other things being equal, when the level of the stock market is high, investment spending also tends to be high. It makes sense that the two are related. Consider a firm's options when it wants to finance a new project. The firm really has three choices: First, it can rely on its **retained earnings**—the earnings the firm hasn't paid out in dividends to its owners. Second, it can borrow funds

neoclassical theory of investment
A theory of investment that says both real interest rates and taxes are important determinants of investment.

retained earnings
Corporate earnings that are not paid out as dividends to their owners.

corporate bond

A bond sold by a corporation to the public in order to borrow money.

Q-theory of investment

The theory of investment that links investment spending to stock prices.

from a bank or sell **corporate bonds** to the public. Third, it can issue and sell new shares, or stock. When a firm's stock price is high, it can issue shares at a premium and use the proceeds from their sale to finance new investments. The higher the share price, the fewer shares the firm needs to sell to raise capital. This means, essentially, that the cost of the project the firm wants to undertake falls as the company's stock price climbs. In other words, high stock prices lead to high investment. This is known as the **Q-theory of investment**, and it was originally developed by the late Nobel Laureate James Tobin of Yale University. In the boom of the late 1990s when the level of the stock market was high along with share prices, many firms financed large investments by selling their shares.

During roughly this same time period, the stock market and investment spending appeared to be even more tightly linked than in the past. Figure 12.4 plots the Standard and Poor's index of stock prices on the same graph as the share of investment spending as a component of GDP from 1997 to 2003. As you can see, both the stock market and investment spending rose sharply from 1997, peaking in mid-2000. They then both fell sharply—the stock market plunged, investment spending fell, and the economy entered a recession.

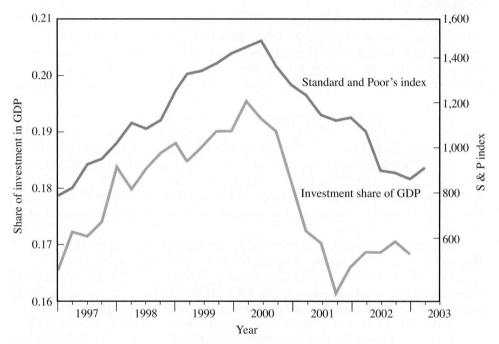

▲ **FIGURE 12.4**

The Stock Market and Investment Levels, 1997–2003

Both the stock market and investment spending rose sharply from 1997, peaking in mid-2000.

The reason the two were so tightly linked was that investors were overly optimistic about the future. They believed that, driven by new technology, the newfound economic prosperity would last forever (or at least certainly longer than it did). With optimistic expectations about the future, stock prices should have been high because stock prices are based on the present value of the dividends people expect firms to pay in the future:

price of a stock = present value of expected future dividend payments

Because investors' expectations about future dividends were high, stock prices were high. Firms, like individual investors, rushed to make massive, long-term investments, particularly in the fiber-optics and telecommunications industries. Some observers questioned whether the expectations were rational. Still, there were enough optimistic investors to sufficiently drive up prices.

As we saw in Figure 12.1 on page 255, investment spending during this period in the United States reached new highs. In many cases, stock prices for companies that had never turned a profit nonetheless soared to astronomical heights. Unfortunately, both investors and firms may have been subject to what former Federal Reserve chairman Alan Greenspan famously dubbed "irrational exuberance"—something similar to Keynes's "animal spirits." Although the economy had performed very well in the late 1990s, it could not grow at those rates forever. Many investors and firms believed it could, though. When they began to realize it couldn't, the stock market plunged and investment plans were curtailed. What linked the stock market and investment in both their rise and their fall were first optimistic and then pessimistic expectations about the economy. Rather than causing the rise and fall of investment spending, the stock market mirrored expectations about the economy held by firms and individual investors.

12.4 HOW FINANCIAL INTERMEDIARIES FACILITATE INVESTMENT

Households save and invest their funds for different reasons than firms. A typical couple might be saving money for their retirement or for their children's education, and they generally won't like the idea of their savings being subject to risk. They do, however, want their savings to be readily accessible and convertible to money—what economists call **liquid**—in case they have a financial emergency. Funds deposited in a bank account, for example, provide a source of liquidity for households because they can be withdrawn at any time.

Unlike households, firms and business managers are typically risk-takers. They are gambling that their vision of the future will come true and make them vast profits. These investors need funds they can tie up for long periods of time. For example, an entrepreneur who wants to build a skyscraper or casino may need financing for several years before beginning construction and for years afterward until the business begins to produce profits.

Suppose individual entrepreneurs had to obtain funds directly from individual savers. First, they would have to negotiate with thousands of people to obtain sufficient funds. This would take a lot of time and be costly. Second, the savers would face extraordinarily high risks if they loaned all their money to a single entrepreneur who had a risky project to undertake. Not only would all their funds be tied up in a single project, it would not be easy to monitor the investor's decisions. How could they be certain the entrepreneur wouldn't run off with their money? Additionally, their investments would not be liquid. To compensate these savers for the risk they would be taking and the lack of liquidity they would face, entrepreneurs would have to pay them extremely high interest rates, but higher interest rates would make it harder, perhaps impossible, for the entrepreneur to make a profit. No prospect of profits would mean no one would invest in the project in the first place. In other words, society would not be able to turn its savings into profitable investment projects. Figure 12.5 depicts this dilemma. How can the problem be solved?

liquid
Easily convertible into money on short notice.

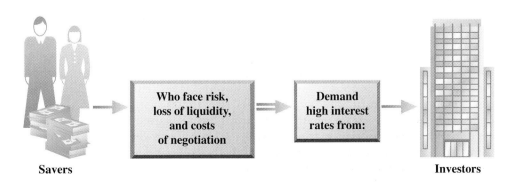

◀ **FIGURE 12.5**
Savers and Investors

Savers

Who face risk, loss of liquidity, and costs of negotiation

Demand high interest rates from:

Investors

financial intermediaries
Organizations that receive funds from savers and channel them to investors.

The answer is through financial intermediaries. **Financial intermediaries** include banks, savings and loans, insurance companies, brokerage firms, companies that run mutual funds, and other types of financial institutions. These institutions accept funds from savers and make loans to businesses and individuals. For example, a local bank accepts deposits from savers and uses the funds to make loans to local businesses. Savings and loan institutions will accept deposits in savings accounts and use these funds to make loans, often for housing. Insurance companies accept premium payments from individuals in exchange for the protection provided by the insurance payments. Then insurance companies lend the premiums received to earn returns from investments so they can pay off the insurance claims of individuals. Figure 12.6 shows how financial intermediaries create a valuable link between savers and investors. Pooling the funds of savers to make loans to individual borrowers reduces the costs of negotiation. Financial institutions also have more expertise to evaluate and monitor investments than most individual investors.

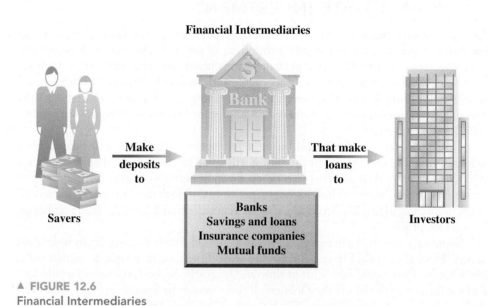

▲ **FIGURE 12.6**
Financial Intermediaries

To some degree, these financial intermediaries also provide liquidity. In normal circumstances, not all households withdraw their money at the same time, so financial intermediaries can lend out most of the money and still have enough on hand to meet withdrawals by depositors.

But how do financial intermediaries reduce risk? They do this by diversifying investors' assets—by not putting "all the eggs in one basket," so to speak. Intermediaries invest (that is, make loans) in a large number of projects whose returns, although uncertain, are independent of one another. By *independent*, we mean the return from one investment is unrelated to the return on another investment. Consider a bank investing in a large number of projects that all together produce an average return of 8 percent annually. Each project alone is risky and could pay a return either higher or lower than 8 percent. However, as long as the returns on all these projects are independent of one another, those with higher returns will likely offset those with lower returns. By investing in a large number of projects, the bank increases the odds that as a group the projects will earn 8 percent.

Other financial intermediaries reduce risks in related ways. A fire insurance company accepts premiums from many individuals in communities throughout the country and uses the funds to make investments. Because not all houses will

APPLICATION 3

UNDERWATER HOMES: BETS GONE WRONG

APPLYING THE CONCEPTS #3: Why Did Many Homeowners in 2010 Owe More to Banks Than Their Home Was Worth?

In early 2010, one quarter of all U.S. homes were "underwater." No, there was not massive flooding across the entire country. The term *underwater* means that homeowners owed more on their mortgages than their home was worth. How did this happen?

Consider someone who purchased a $600,000 home in 2007 and borrowed $540,000 to make this purchase. Although the homeowner had invested $60,000, it was still a highly levered investment. If the price of the home fell by 20 percent to $480,000, the homeowner would still owe the bank the original $540,000 and be $60,000 "underwater."

In states where the housing boom was strongest—Nevada, Florida, Arizona, and parts of California—this phenomenon was most pronounced. In the Las Vegas area, for example, approximately 70 percent of all homeowners were underwater! This is a striking example of the down-side from leverage.   **Related to Exercise 4.6.**

SOURCE: Based on "Quarter of U.S. Homes Underwater," *Chicago Sun Times*, http://www.suntimes.com/news/nation/2125780,CST-NWS-underwater27.article

burn down in the same year, the insurance company knows it will have a stable source of funds for its investments. Insurance diversification works well only when companies insure events that are independent of one another, however. Some situations are not independent and therefore can't easily be insured by the same company. For example, an insurance company would be unwise to provide earthquake insurance for just the Los Angeles area. If an earthquake did occur, the firm would be faced with making payments to many clients who suffered loss without anyone else's payments to offset them. In somewhat the same way, even bank loans are not fully independent. During a recession, many more firms will experience financial difficulties and have trouble meeting their loan obligations to their banks.

In recent years, we have seen an innovation in financial intermediation. In the past, if a savings and loan company made a loan to a home purchaser, it would hold onto the loan until it was paid off. That meant the savings and loan could make new loans or mortgages only if it was able to attract new deposits to provide the funds.

Two large government-sponsored financial intermediaries, Fannie Mae and Freddie Mac, changed the way mortgage markets operated. They purchased mortgages from savings and loans and banks throughout the country, packaged them, and sold them to investors in the financial market. This enabled savings and loans to offer additional mortgages with the funds they received from Fannie Mae or Freddie Mac, and it allowed investors to own a part of a diversified collection of mortgages from around the country. The private sector quickly adopted these practices as well.

The practice of purchasing loans, re-packaging them, and selling them to the financial markets is known as **securitization**. Although it started with home mortgages, securitization now applies to other types of financial obligations, such as credit card and consumer debt. Financial intermediaries will often borrow money from financial markets to purchase loans in order to re-package and sell them. Using borrowed funds to purchase assets is known as **leverage**. Increases in leverage increase the risk that financial intermediaries undertake because they are obligated to pay off

securitization

The practice of purchasing loans, re-packaging them, and selling them to the financial markets.

leverage

Using borrowed funds to purchase assets.

the funds they have borrowed, regardless of the actual performance of the assets they have purchased.

When Financial Intermediaries Malfunction

Financial intermediation can sometimes go wrong. When it does, the economy suffers. Important examples of the failure of financial intermediation include commercial bank failures during the Great Depression, the U.S. savings and loan crisis of the 1980s, a similar crisis in Japan in the 1990s, and the U.S. housing credit and securitization crisis of 2007 and 2008.

In the early days of the Great Depression, many banks in the United States, particularly in rural areas, provided farmers and local businesses with loans that turned out to be unprofitable. This worried depositors, and rumors circulated that banks would fail. Depositors panicked, and many tried to withdraw their money simultaneously in what is called a **bank run**. During the Great Depression, bank runs occurred throughout the world. In 1931, a panic broke out after the collapse of Creditanstalt, Austria's largest bank. Banking panics occurred throughout other countries in Europe, including Belgium, France, Germany, Italy, and Poland.

bank run

Panicky investors simultaneously trying to withdraw their funds from a bank they believe may fail.

Few banks, profitable or unprofitable, can survive a run, because not all deposits are kept on hand. The result of the bank runs was that thousands of healthy U.S. banks shut down, leaving large parts of the United States without a banking system. Many farms and businesses could no longer find a source of loans, and the severity of the Great Depression worsened. Studies have shown that the countries with the most severe banking panics were hardest hit by the Depression.

To prevent banking panics from happening again, in 1933 the U.S. government began providing **deposit insurance** on money placed in banks and savings and loans. Today deposit insurance guarantees the government will reimburse depositors for amounts up to $250,000 in each account at each bank should their banks fail. Because everyone knows their deposits are secure, bank runs no longer regularly occur. Today, most countries have some form of deposit insurance intended to prevent panics.

deposit insurance

Federal government insurance on deposits in banks and savings and loans.

Ironically, deposit insurance indirectly led to the U.S. savings and loan crisis, which occurred during the 1980s. In the early 1970s, savings and loan institutions (S&Ls) made mortgage loans to households at low interest rates. However, later in the decade nominal interest rates rose sharply as inflation increased. The savings and loans were in trouble: They had to pay high interest rates to attract deposits, but they were earning interest at low rates from the money they had loaned out previously. Many of the S&Ls failed.

The government tried to assist the savings and loan industry by broadening the range of investments the industry could make. Some S&Ls soon began aggressively investing in speculative real estate and other risky projects to earn higher returns. Depositors weren't worried, though, because they knew their savings were insured by the government. Unfortunately, many of these risky projects failed, and the government was forced to bail out the S&Ls at a cost of nearly $100 billion to taxpayers. Because depositors' savings were insured, most people didn't suffer directly from the collapse of their savings and loan institutions. As taxpayers they suffered, though, because they had to foot the bill.

Japan suffered similar problems in the 1990s. By 1995, seven of the eight largest Japanese mortgage lenders had gone bankrupt following a crash in real estate prices. Like the U.S. government, the Japanese government also used taxpayers' funds to bail these lenders out.

The decline in housing prices that we described in the chapter opening story triggered a severe crisis in the newly developed securitization markets. Although the actual details are complex, the basic story is simple. Lenders had made loans to borrowers who had limited ability to repay, and when borrowers began to miss payments or default on their loans, it caused major disruptions in the market for securitized loans, which, in turn, disrupted credit to other sectors in the economy,

APPLICATION 4

SECURITIZATION: THE GOOD, THE BAD, AND THE UGLY

APPLYING THE CONCEPTS #4: How have recent financial innovations created new risks for the economy?

As securitization developed, it allowed financial intermediaries to provide new funds for borrowers to enter the housing market. This led to a rise in the rate of homeownership and was hailed as a positive development. But there was a dark side to this process as well.

As the housing boom began in 2002, lenders and home purchasers began to take increasing risks. Lenders made "subprime" loans to borrowers with limited ability to actually repay their mortgages and did not exercise full diligence in making loans. Some households were willing to take on considerable debt because they were confident they could make money in a rising housing market. Lenders securitized the subprime loans and financial firms offered exotic investment securities to investors based on these loans. Many financial institutions purchased these securities without really knowing what was inside them. Because the securities were so new, the agencies that traditionally evaluated the riskiness of these investments did not post sufficient warning.

When the housing boom stopped and borrowers stopped making payments on subprime loans, it created panic in the financial market. Not only did investors and financial firms now realize their investments were extremely risky, they began to worry about the creditworthiness of banks and other financial intermediaries that held these securities as assets. Many were highly leveraged and exposed to great risk. Effectively, through securitization the damage from the subprime loans spread to the entire financial market, causing a major crisis.   **Related to Exercise 4.7.**

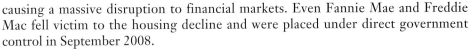

causing a massive disruption to financial markets. Even Fannie Mae and Freddie Mac fell victim to the housing decline and were placed under direct government control in September 2008.

As the housing-generated financial crisis spread to the rest of the financial markets, the credit markets essentially "froze" and banks worldwide would no longer lend to each other. Customers scrambled to withdraw their funds in financial institutions that they perceived were weak, leading to a "run" on these institutions. As a result, financial institutions such as Bear Stearns and Lehman Brothers were forced to close and institutions such as Merrill Lynch and Wachovia Bank were taken over by other financial institutions. When the financial institution Lehman Brothers failed it set off a panic in the markets that spread to other international banks and financial institutions. The stock market plunged dramatically worldwide, reflecting the severity of the crisis and fear that it would lead to a total worldwide financial collapse. As credit became unavailable, businesses began to suffer as well, as they were not able to borrow funds to run their enterprises on a day-to-day basis. State and local government also found it nearly impossible to borrow at the height of the crisis.

Governments around the world took a number of steps to alleviate this crisis. Central banks, whose activities during the crisis are described in more detail in the next chapter, provided loans and credit through a wide variety of channels. After considerable turmoil, the U.S. Congress passed a bailout package, called the Troubled Asset Relief Program, or TARP, that enabled the Treasury to use up to $700 billion to shore up the financial system. Following the lead of Great Britain, the U.S. Treasury used some of these proceeds to provide funds to large banks in order to restore confidence in the financial system and took limited ownership in these banks. As previously noted, the government took control of Fannie Mae and Freddie Mac and also provided funding to some large financial firms, such as the American International Group (AIG), which provided financial insurance to other firms and was deemed essential to keep afloat during the crisis. The United States and other countries around the world also increased the limits on the amounts eligible for deposit insurance to bolster consumer confidence in banking institutions. The goals of all these actions were to restore confidence in a system of financial intermediation that was under considerable stress.

From these examples you can see why financial intermediation does not always work. There is a continual debate on the role government should play in investment decisions for the economy and its role in regulating financial intermediaries. Today, some economists and policymakers are carefully reassessing the risks in our complex financial markets.

SUMMARY

In this chapter we discussed investment spending, present value, interest rates, and financial intermediaries. We saw that investment spending is volatile, rising and falling sharply with real GDP, and depends on expectations about the future. By developing the concept of present value, we saw how firms can make investment decisions when the costs and benefits of an investment occur at different times. We also explained why investment spending also depends inversely on real interest rates and explained the distinction between real and nominal interest rates. Finally, we examined how financial intermediaries channel funds from savers to investors, reduce interest rates, and promote investment—and sometimes malfunction. Here are the main points to keep in mind:

1 Investments incur costs today but provide benefits in the future.

2 Investment spending is a volatile component of GDP because expectations about the future are uncertain and ever changing.

3 We use the concept of *present value* to compare the costs and benefits of investments that occur at different points in time. The present value of a payment K, t years in the future, at an interest rate of i is

$$\text{present value} = \frac{K}{(1 + i)^t}$$

4 The *real interest rate* equals the *nominal interest rate* minus inflation.

5 Investment spending depends inversely on real interest rates.

6 *Financial intermediaries* reduce the risk and costs of making investments by pooling the funds of savers and monitoring the projects of borrowers. Financial intermediaries can package loans for sale to the broader financial markets through *securitization*.

7 While financial intermediaries do make the economy more efficient, they can break down at times, causing severe economic disruptions.

KEY TERMS

12.1 An Investment: A Plunge into the Unknown

1.1 Investment is a larger component of GDP than consumption, but it is much more volatile. _____ (True/False)

1.2 Investment spending is very _____, since it moves in conjunction with GDP.

1.3 The economist who developed the multiplier-accelerator model was _____.

1.4 Since investment spending rises and falls with GDP, it is _____.

1.5 **Animal Spirits.** Use an aggregate demand and supply graph to show the effects on GDP of a burst or spurt of "animal spirits" that leads to higher investment in the economy.

1.6 **Index of Consumer Confidence and Investment in Durable Goods.** Using the ideas of "animal spirits," explain why changes in measures of consumer confidence would be correlated to consumer spending on durable goods.

1.7 **Residential Housing Investment, the 1990 Recession, and the Most Recent Downturn.** Use the Web site for the Federal Reserve Bank of St. Louis (www.research.stlouisfed.org/fred2) to find out how investment in residential housing behaved over the 1990–1991 recession and compare it to the period from 2006 to 2009.

1.8 **Oil Price Floor and Investment Spending.** Suppose the government said that it would not let the U.S. price for a barrel of oil fall below $50. It could do this by raising taxes on oil if the price fell below $50. What incentives do you think this would provide for investment in energy-saving technologies? (Related to Application 1 on page 255.)

12.2 Evaluating the Future

2.1 If the interest rate is 10 percent, the present value of $200 paid one year from now equals _____.

2.2 If the interest rate is 5 percent, the present value of $200 paid one year from now equals _____. If the $200 is received in two years, the present value will equal _____.

2.3 If interest rates increase, the present value of a fixed payment in the future _____.

2.4 The present value of lottery winnings paid over a 20-year period will _____ (rise/fall) with a rise in interest rates.

2.5 **Investments in Solar Energy.** Proponents of solar energy point to the vast savings that come in the long run from using a free source of energy (the sun) rather than paying high prices for electricity. Unfortunately, solar energy systems typically have large up-front expenses to install the system. Use the concept of present value to show that solar energy systems are more likely to be profitable when interest rates are low.

2.6 **Real Interest Rates and Opportunity Cost.** "When real interest rates are high, so is the opportunity cost of funds." What does this statement mean?

2.7 **Present Value.** A lottery pays a winner $1 million a year for 20 years (starting in year 1). What is the present value of this sum at an interest rate of 8 percent? You can do this by hand (not recommended) or in an Excel spreadsheet. Here is how: Enter "1" in cells A1 through A20. In cell C3, enter @NPV(.08, A1:A20) and press enter. This will give you the result. What happens to the present value of the lottery if the interest rate falls to 5 percent? (Related to Application 2 on page 258.)

2.8 **Pension Funds and Interest Rates.** Many firms have pension funds that have fixed dollar obligations to their retirees. For financial purposes, firms must estimate the present value of these obligations to determine how much they truly owe their retirees. What happens to the value of these obligations as interest rates fall? Why?

12.3 Understanding Investment Decisions

3.1 If a project costs $100 and pays $107 next year, the maximum interest rate at which the present value of the investment exceeds its cost is _____.

3.2 As real interest rates rise, investment spending in the economy _____.

3.3 Corporate bonds, retained earnings, and tax deductions are the three sources of funds that firms have for investments. _____ (True/False)

3.4 The Q-theory of investment was developed by _____.

3.5 The price of a stock can be thought of as the present value of future _____.

3.6 **Low Interest Rates but No Takers.** In 2010, interest rates on home mortgages were in the neighborhood of 5 percent—very low by historical standards—but many individuals did not wish to buy homes. Using the concept of the real interest rate, can you explain why low interest rates did not entice new buyers?

3.7 The Implications of Zero Real Interest Rates. "If the real interest rate were zero, it would be a financially sound decision to level the Rocky Mountains so that automobiles and cars would save on gas mileage." Putting aside ecological concerns, why is this statement true?

3.8 Hydroelectric Dams. Hydroelectric dams are very costly to build and construct, but there are considerable savings in operating costs compared to other energy alternatives. Explain why hydroelectric dams are more likely to be profitable when interest rates are low.

3.9 Stock Prices, Interest Rates, and Corporate Earnings. Holding other factors constant, explain why stock prices tend to rise when

a. interest rates fall.

b. expected corporate earnings rise.

12.4 How Financial Intermediaries Facilitate Investment

4.1 An illiquid financial asset is one that can easily be used to buy goods and services. _____ (True/False)

4.2 Creation of _____ following the Great Depression has greatly reduced the likelihood of runs on banks today.

4.3 Financial intermediaries reduce the risk of assets through _____.

4.4 If a financial intermediary buys loans from a mortgage company and then packages them to sell in the financial markets, this is known as _____.

4.5 Understanding Banks. How can a bank invest in illiquid loans (say, lend depositors' savings to home buyers over 25 years) and still provide liquid deposits (give depositors their savings when they ask for it)?

4.6 A Leverage Example. Suppose you purchased an asset for $1000. The asset is risky and can either increase in value to $1,200 or fall in value to $900. Let's look at the effects of leverage on your returns to this investment.

a. Suppose you did not borrow any money, but put in your own $1000 to purchase the asset. What percent gain would you make if the asset increased and what percent loss would you experience if the asset fell in value?

b. Now, suppose you borrowed $950 to purchase the asset. What is your percentage gain or loss on your investment now?

(Related to Application 3 on page 265.)

4.7 "Ninja" Loans. During the housing boom, overeager lenders were said to have made "ninja" loans—that is, loans to individuals with "no income, job, or assets." How did ninja loans contribute to the securitization crisis in financial markets in 2007 and 2008? (Related to Application 4 on page 267.)

4.8 Savings and Loans and Risk. Traditionally, savings and loan institutions made loans only for home mortgages and held on to those mortgages. At one point, this was viewed as a safe way of doing business. However, it became a risky way of doing business for U.S. savings and loans in the 1970s. Explain why making loans only for housing and holding on to the mortgages may be very risky. Why does this risk provide a rationale for securitization?

4.9 Mutual Funds. Why does it make sense for individual investors to invest in mutual funds (which invest in a wide range of stocks), rather than in just a few individual companies?

ECONOMIC EXPERIMENT

Diversification

This classroom exercise illustrates the power of diversification. Your instructor will describe the game and how to participate. To take part in this exercise, you need to recall a simple lesson from basic statistics: If you flip a coin many times, the fraction of heads that results approaches one-half as you increase the number of flips.

You are offered a chance to play this game in which you receive a payoff according to the following formula:

$$\text{Payoff} = \$10$$
$$+ \$100 \,[(\text{number of heads}/$$
$$\text{number of tosses}) - 0.5]$$

In this game, you first get $10, but you win or lose additional funds, depending on whether the fraction of heads that comes up exceeds one-half.

To help you understand what's going on in this game, suppose you toss the coin only once. Here, the outcome depends only on whether the coin comes up either heads or tails:

Heads: $10 + $100(1/1 − 0.5) = $60

Tails: $10 + $100(0/1 − 0.5) = −$40

The game does have a positive expected payoff. The expected or average payoff for this game is the probability of getting a head (one-half) times $60 plus the probability of getting a tail (one-half) times –$40. This is

$$\text{Expected payoff} = (0.5)\$60 + (0.5)(-\$40) = \$10$$

On average, if you toss the coin many times, this game would pay $10. But this game is risky if you are allowed to toss the coin only once. Now that you understand the game, answer the following question: Would you play this game if limited to only one toss?

Now suppose you were free to toss the coin 1,000 times and received 450 heads. If that happened, your payoff would be

$$\$10 + \$100(450/1000 - 0.5) = \$5$$

Would you play if you could toss the coin 1,000 times?

Questions for Discussion

1. Did a higher percentage of the class agree to play the game with 1,000 tosses? How does this illustrate the principle of diversification?

2. If you toss the coin 1,000 times, what is the expected payoff?

3. If you toss the coin 1,000 times and receive heads fewer than 400 times, you will lose money. What do you think is the probability of this occurring?

CHAPTER

13   Money and the Banking System

As long as there has been paper money, there have been counterfeiters. To combat these counterfeiters (many of whom now just use high-quality photocopiers to recreate money), the U.S. Treasury has introduced one cutting-edge printing technique after another. For example, if you hold a real $5 dollar bill up to the light, you'll notice a faint hologram of Lincoln directly to the right of his printed image. The hologram can't be reproduced easily with a photocopier but is easily visible to cashiers and bank personnel (and anyone else willing to look).

The government must keep innovating to stay ahead. In 2008 the Federal Reserve Banks issued a redesigned $5 bill with two new watermarks and a security thread that glows blue under ultraviolet light, with numbers and letters running alongside. These may all seem like technological marvels, but the institution of money is an even greater miracle.

APPLYING THE CONCEPTS

1 What types of money did cities issue during the Great Depression?
  City-Issued Money in the Great Depression

2 Why have banks recently started to hold vast amounts of excess reserves?
  The Growth in Excess Reserves

3 How did the Fed manage to keep the financial system in operation immediately following the attacks on September 11, 2001?
  The Financial System under Stress: September 11, 2001

4 How did the Fed respond to the collapse of major financial institutions in 2008?
  Coping with the Financial Chaos Caused by the Mortgage Crisis

The term *money* has a special meaning for economists, so in this chapter we'll look carefully at how money is defined and the role it plays in the economy. The overall level of money affects the performance of an economy. In Chapter 9, we learned that increases in the money supply increase aggregate demand. In the short run, when prices are largely fixed, this increase will raise total demand and output. But in the long run, continuing money growth leads to inflation.

Our nation's central bank, the Federal Reserve (commonly called the "Fed"), is responsible for controlling the money supply. In this chapter, we'll see how the Federal Reserve is structured, how it operates, and why it's so powerful.

13.1 WHAT *IS* MONEY?

Economists define **money** as any items that are regularly used in economic transactions or exchanges and accepted by buyers and sellers. Let's consider some examples of money used in that way.

We use money regularly every day. In a coffee shop, we hand the person behind the counter some dollar bills and coins, and we receive a cup of coffee. This is an example of an economic exchange: One party hands over currency—the dollar bills and the coins—and the other party hands over goods and services—the coffee. Why do the owners of coffee shops accept dollar bills and coins in payment for coffee? The reason is that they will be making other economic exchanges with the dollar bills and coins they accept. Suppose a cup of coffee costs $1.50 and 100 cups are sold in a day. The seller then has $150 in currency. If the coffee costs the seller $100, the seller pays $100 of the currency received and keeps $50 for other expenses and profits. Money makes that possible.

In the real world, transactions are somewhat more complicated. The coffee shop owners take the currency they receive each day, deposit it in bank accounts, and then pay suppliers with checks drawn on those accounts. Clearly, currency is money because it is used to purchase coffee. Checks also function as money because they are used to pay suppliers. In some ancient cultures, precious stones were used in exchanges. In more recent times, gold bars have served as money. During World War II, prisoners of war did not have currency, but they did have rations of cigarettes, so they used them like money, trading them for what they wanted.

Three Properties of Money

Regardless of what money is used in a particular society, it serves several functions, all related to making economic exchanges easier. Here we discuss three key properties of money.

MONEY SERVES AS A MEDIUM OF EXCHANGE   As our examples illustrate, money is given by buyers to sellers in economic exchanges; therefore, it serves as a **medium of exchange**. Suppose you had a car you wanted to sell in order to buy a boat and money did not exist. You could look for a person who had a boat and wanted to buy a car and then trade your car directly for a boat. This is an example of **barter**: the exchange of one good or service for another.

But there are obvious problems with barter. Suppose local boat owners were interested in selling boats but not interested in buying your car. Unless there were a **double coincidence of wants**—that is, unless you wanted to trade a car for a boat, and the boat owner wanted to trade a boat for your car—this economic exchange wouldn't occur. The probability of a double coincidence of wants occurring is very, very tiny. Even if a boat owner wanted a car, he or she might want a different type of car than yours.

By serving as a medium of exchange, money solves this bartering problem. The car owner can sell the car to anyone who wants it and receive money in return. With that money, the car owner can then find someone who owns a boat and purchase the

money
Any items that are regularly used in economic transactions or exchanges and accepted by buyers and sellers.

medium of exchange
Any item that buyers give to sellers when they purchase goods and services.

barter
The exchange of one good or service for another.

double coincidence of wants
The problem in a system of barter that one person may not have what the other desires.

boat for money. The boat owner can use the money in any way he or she pleases. With money, there is no need for a double coincidence of wants. This is why money exists in all societies: It makes economic transactions much easier.

Here is another way to think about this. One of our key principles of economics is that individuals are better off through voluntary exchange.

PRINCIPLE OF VOLUNTARY EXCHANGE

A voluntary exchange between two people makes both people better off.

Money allows individuals to actually *make* these exchanges. Without money, we would be left with a barter system, and most transactions that make both people better off would not be possible.

MONEY SERVES AS A UNIT OF ACCOUNT   Money also provides a convenient measuring rod when prices for all goods are quoted in money terms. A boat may be listed for sale at $5,000 in money terms, a car at $10,000, and a movie ticket at $5. We could, in principle, quote everything in terms of movie tickets. The boat would be worth 1,000 tickets, and the car would be worth 2,000 tickets. But because we are using money and not movie tickets as a medium of exchange, it is much easier to express all prices in terms of money. A **unit of account** is a standard unit in which we can state prices and compare the value of goods and services. In our economy, money is the unit of account because we quote all prices in terms of money. It is convenient to use the medium of exchange as the unit of account, so we can quote prices for all goods and services in terms of the same units we use in transactions—in our case, money.

MONEY SERVES AS A STORE OF VALUE   If you sell your car to purchase a boat, you may not be able to purchase the boat immediately. In the meantime, you will be holding the money you received from the sale. Ideally, during that period, the value of the money will not fall. What we are referring to here is the function of money as a **store of value**.

Money is actually a somewhat imperfect store of value because of inflation. Suppose inflation is 10 percent a year, which means average prices rise 10 percent each year. Let's say you sold a tennis racket for $100 in order to buy 10 CDs worth $100, but you waited a year to buy them. Unfortunately, because of inflation, at the end of the year the 10 CDs cost $110 (%100 × 1.10), or $11 each. With your $100, you can now buy only 9 CDs and get $1 in change. Your money has lost some of its stored value.

As long as inflation is low and you do not hold the money for a long time, the loss in its purchasing power won't be a big problem. But as inflation rates increase, money becomes less useful as a store of value.

Different Types of Monetary Systems

Through history, the world has witnessed different types of monetary systems. In one system a commodity serves as money, such as gold or silver in bars or coins. This is an example of **commodity money**. At some point, governments began issuing paper money. However, the paper money was backed by an underlying commodity, for example, so many ounces of gold per unit of paper currency. Under a traditional **gold standard**, an individual could present paper money to the government and receive its stated value in gold. In other words, paper money could be exchanged for gold. Until 1933 in the United States, individuals could exchange their dollars for gold. However, President Franklin Roosevelt banned private possession of gold in 1933, although foreign governments could still exchange dollars for gold until 1971. The next step in the evolution of monetary systems was to break the tie between paper money and gold and create a system of *fiat money*. **Fiat money** has no intrinsic value like gold or silver—it is simply created by a government decree and becomes the official legal

---

unit of account

A standard unit in which prices can be stated and the value of goods and services can be compared.

store of value

The property of money that holds that money preserves value until it is used in an exchange.

commodity money

A monetary system in which the actual money is a commodity, such as gold or silver.

gold standard

A monetary system in which gold backs up paper money.

fiat money

A monetary system in which money has no intrinsic value but is backed by the government.

tender of the society. In the United States today, if you take a $100 bill to the government you will not receive any gold or silver—just another $100 bill in return.

You may wonder what gives money value under a fiat system if it has no intrinsic value. The answer is that the government controls the value of fiat money by controlling its supply in the economy. That is why it is important to prevent counterfeiting, as our chapter-opening story described. In the next chapter, we will see precisely how the government controls the supply of money.

Measuring Money in the U.S. Economy

In the United States and other modern economies, people can carry out economic transactions in several different ways. In practice, this leads to different measures of money. The most basic measure of money in the United States is called **M1**. It is the sum of currency in the hands of the public, demand deposits, other checkable deposits, and traveler's checks. M1 totaled $1,712 billion in March 2010. Table 13.1 contains the components of M1 and their size; Figure 13.1 shows their relative percentages.

M1

The sum of currency in the hands of the public, demand deposits, other checkable deposits, and traveler's checks.

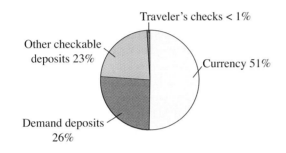

◄ **FIGURE 13.1**
Components of M1 for the United States
Currency is the largest component of M1, the most basic measure of money. Demand and other checkable deposits are the next largest components.
SOURCE: Board of Governors of the Federal Reserve.

TABLE 13.1 COMPONENTS OF M1, MARCH 2010	
Currency held by the public	$ 871 billion
Demand deposits	446 billion
Other checkable deposits	390 billion
Traveler's checks	6 billion
Total of M1	1,712 billion

SOURCE: Board of Governors of the Federal Reserve.

The first part of M1 is currency held by the public, that is, all currency held outside bank vaults. The second component is deposits in checking accounts, called *demand deposits*. Until the 1980s, checking accounts did not pay interest. The third component, other checkable deposits, was introduced in the early 1980s and did pay interest. Today, the distinction between the two types of deposit accounts is not as meaningful as it used to be because many checking accounts earn interest if the balances are sufficiently high. Finally, traveler's checks are included in M1 because they are regularly used in economic exchanges.

Let's take a closer look at the amount of currency in the economy. Because there are approximately 300 million people in the United States, the $871 billion of currency amounts to over $2,903 in currency for every man, woman, and child in the United States. Do you and your friends each have $2,903 of currency?

Most of the currency in the official statistics is not used in ordinary commerce in the United States. Who is using and holding this currency? Some is used in illegal transactions such as the drug trade. Few drug dealers open bank accounts to deposit currency. In addition, a substantial fraction of U.S. currency is held abroad.

M1 does not include all the assets we use to make economic exchanges. **M2** is a somewhat broader definition of money that includes M1 plus deposits in saving accounts, deposits in money market mutual funds, and time deposits of less than $100,000. These investment-type assets often can't readily be used for exchanges

M2

M1 plus other assets, including deposits in savings and loans accounts and money market mutual funds.

without first being converted to M1. In March 2010 M2 totaled $8,512 billion. That's about five times the total of M1. Figure 13.2 shows the relative sizes of the components of M2.

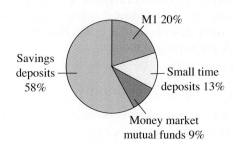

▶ **FIGURE 13.2**
Components of M2 in the United States
Savings deposits are the largest component of M2, followed by M1, small time deposits, and money market mutual funds.
SOURCE: Board of Governors of Federal Reserve.

Economists use different definitions of money because it is not always clear which assets are used primarily as money—that is, which assets are used for economic exchanges and which are used primarily for saving and investing. Money market mutual funds came into existence only in the late 1970s. Some people temporarily "park" their assets in these funds, anticipating they will move them into riskier, higher-earning stock market investments later. Others may use them to earn interest while avoiding the risks of the stock market or bond market. Sometimes, people use money market mutual funds like regular checking accounts or like savings accounts. If money market mutual funds are used like checking accounts, they should be considered part of M1. If they are used like savings accounts, however, they should be part of M2. Economists keep an eye on both M1 and M2 because they don't know precisely how people are using all these money market accounts.

Although consumers commonly use credit cards to make transactions in our economy, they are not part of the money supply. Here's why: Suppose you have a credit card from the First Union Bank and purchase a new television from an electronics store. As you use your credit card, you are effectively borrowing the amount

APPLICATION 1

CITY-ISSUED MONEY IN THE GREAT DEPRESSION

APPLYING THE CONCEPTS #1: What types of money did cities issue during the Great Depression?

As banks failed during the Great Depression, residents in many cities and towns faced a shortage of money to make transactions. Both individuals and businesses lost funds in failed banks or had their funds frozen during banking closure. While some businesses and individuals resorted to barter, this strategy naturally had its limitations.

A number of cities around the country began issuing their own currencies and perhaps, at its peak in the 1930s, a total of $1 billion was in circulation. Some corporation and school boards also issued their own scrip. Some of it looked like regular government-issued money, but there were some unusual creations. Two California towns issued their money on clamshells and Hal's Tire Service in Oregon created $1 bills on old tires.

Whatever party issued the money obtained goods in exchange for this scrip and thus directly benefited from issuing new money. These benefits would last until they were forced to return real U.S. money in exchange for their privately-issued scrip. **Related to Exercise 1.9.**

SOURCE: Based on Stephanie Simon, "Cash-Strapped California's IOUs: Just the Latest Subs for Dollars," *Wall Street Journal*, July 25, 2009, p. A1.

you charge from the First Union Bank, which, in turn, will pay the electronics store on your behalf. When you receive your credit card bill from the bank, you must begin to pay off the loan. Credit cards enable you to purchase goods now but pay for them at a later date. Unlike money, a credit card is not a medium of exchange, a unit of account, or a store of value. Credit cards do make it easier to conduct business, but they are not an official part of the money supply.

What about debit cards? If you own a debit card, you can use it to access the funds you have in your checking account when you make the transaction. When you use your debit card to make a purchase—say at a supermarket—it is exactly the same thing as writing a check. Thus, a debit card is not an independent source of money. The money supply consists of the balances in checking accounts plus currency held by the public.

13.2 HOW BANKS CREATE MONEY

In this section, we will learn the role that banks play in the creation of money in a modern economy. To understand this role, we first have to look more carefully at the behavior of banks.

A Bank's Balance Sheet: Where the Money Comes from and Where It Goes

In Chapter 12 we learned that a typical commercial bank accepts funds from savers in the form of deposits, for example, in checking accounts. The bank does not leave all these funds idle, because if it did it would never make a profit. Instead, the bank turns the money around and loans it out to borrowers. It will be easier to understand how banks create money if we first look at a simplified **balance sheet** for a commercial bank. The balance sheet will show us how the bank raises money and what it does with it.

Balance sheets have two sides: one for assets and one for liabilities. **Liabilities** are the source of funds for the bank. If you open a checking account and deposit your funds in it, the bank is liable for returning the funds to you when you want them. The bank must also pay you interest on the account if you keep enough money in it. Your deposits are therefore the bank's liabilities. **Assets**, in contrast, generate income for the bank. Loans made by the bank are examples of its assets, because borrowers must pay interest on the loans the bank collects.

When a bank is initially opened, its owners must place their own funds into it so it has some startup funds. We call these funds **owners' equity**. If the bank subsequently makes a profit, owners' equity increases; if it loses money, owners' equity decreases.

In Figure 13.3, we show the assets and liabilities of a hypothetical bank. On the liability side, the bank has $2,000 of deposits, and owners' equity is $200. Owners' equity is entered on the liability side of the balance sheet because it is a source of the bank's funds. The total source of funds is therefore $2,200—the deposits in the bank plus owners' equity.

balance sheet
An account statement for a bank that shows the sources of its funds (liabilities) as well as the uses of its funds (assets).

liabilities
The sources of funds for a bank, including deposits and owners' equity.

assets
The uses of the funds of a bank, including loans and reserves.

owners' equity
The funds provided to a bank by its owners.

Assets	Liabilities
$ 200 Reserves	$2,000 Deposits
$2,000 Loans	$ 200 Owners' equity
Total: $2,200	Total: $2,200

▲ **FIGURE 13.3**
A Balance Sheet for a Bank
The figure shows a hypothetical balance sheet for a bank holding 10 percent in required reserves, $200. Banks don't earn interest on their reserves, so they will usually want to loan out any excess of the amounts they are required to hold. This bank has loaned out all of its excess reserves, $2,000.

reserves

The portion of banks' deposits set aside in either vault cash or as deposits at the Federal Reserve.

required reserves

The specific fraction of their deposits that banks are required by law to hold as reserves.

excess reserves

Any additional reserves that a bank holds above required reserves.

reserve ratio

The ratio of reserves to deposits.

On the asset side, the bank holds $200 in **reserves**. These are assets that are not lent out. Reserves can be either cash kept in a bank's vaults or deposits in the nation's central bank, the Federal Reserve. Banks are required by law to hold a specific fraction of their deposits as reserves, called **required reserves**. If a bank chooses to hold additional reserves beyond what is required, these are called **excess reserves**. A bank's reserves are the sum of its required and excess reserves.

In our example, the bank is holding 10 percent of its deposits, or $200, as reserves. The remainder of the bank's assets, $2,000, consists of the loans it has made. By construction, total assets will always equal liabilities, including owners' equity. Balance sheets must therefore always balance.

How Banks Create Money

To understand the role banks play in determining the supply of money, let's suppose someone walks into the First Bank of Hollywood and deposits $1,000 in cash to open a checking account. Because currency held by the public and checking deposits are both included in the supply of money, the total money supply has not changed with this transaction. The cash deposited into the checking account reduced the currency held by the public by precisely the amount the checking account increased it.

Now let's assume banks keep 10 percent of their deposits as reserves. That means the **reserve ratio**—the ratio of reserves to deposits—will be 0.1. The First Bank of Hollywood will keep $100 in reserves and make loans totaling $900. The top panel in Figure 13.4 shows the change in the First Bank of Hollywood's balance sheet after it has made its loan.

Suppose the First Bank of Hollywood loans the funds to an aspiring movie producer. The producer opens a checking account at the First Bank of Hollywood with the $900 he borrowed. He then buys film equipment from a supplier, who accepts his $900 check and deposits it in the Second Bank of Burbank. The next panel in Figure 13.4 shows what happens to the balance sheet of the Second Bank of Burbank. Liabilities increase by the

▶ **FIGURE 13.4**

Process of Deposit Creation: Changes in Balance Sheets

The figure shows how an initial deposit of $1,000 can expand the money supply. The first three banks in the figure loaned out all their excess reserves and the borrowers deposited the full sum of their loans. In the real world, though, people hold part of their loans as cash and banks don't necessarily loan out all their excess reserves. Consequently, a smaller amount of money will be created than what's shown here.

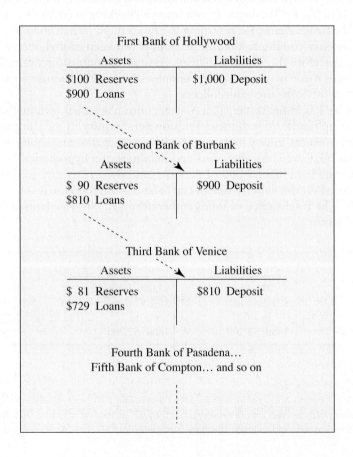

deposit of $900. The bank holds $90 in reserves (10 percent of the $900 deposit) and can lend out $810.

Suppose the Second Bank of Burbank lends the $810 to the owner of a coffeehouse and she opens a checking account there with the $810 as her balance. She then purchases $810 worth of coffee with a check made out to a coffee supplier, who deposits it into the Third Bank of Venice.

The Third Bank of Venice receives a deposit of $810. It keeps $81 in reserves and can lend out $729. This process continues throughout the Los Angeles area with new loans and deposits. The Fourth Bank of Pasadena will receive a deposit of $729, hold $72.90 in reserves, and lend out $656.10. The Fifth Bank of Compton will receive a deposit of $656.10, and the process goes on.

How the Money Multiplier Works

The original $1,000 cash deposit has created checking account balances throughout Los Angeles. What's the total amount? Adding up the new accounts in all the banks (even the ones we have not named), we have

$$\$1,000 + \$900 + \$810 + \$729 + 656.10 + \cdots = \$10,000$$

How did we come up with this sum? It's from the following simple formula, which we derive in the appendix to this chapter:

total increase in checking account balance throughout all banks

$$= \text{(initial cash deposit)} \times \frac{1}{\text{(reserve ratio)}}$$

In our example, the reserve ratio is 0.1, so the increase in checking account balances is 1/0.1, or 10 times the initial cash deposit. The initial $1,000 deposit led to a total increase in checking account balances of $10,000 throughout all of the banks.

Recall that the money supply, M1, is the sum of deposits at commercial banks plus currency held by the public. Therefore, the change in the money supply, M1, will be the change in deposits in checking accounts plus the change in currency held by the public. Notice that we referred to "change," meaning an increase or decrease. Here's why: In our example, the public, represented by the person who initially made the $1,000 deposit at the First Bank of Hollywood, holds $1,000 less in currency. However, deposits increased by $10,000. Therefore, the money supply, M1, increased by $9,000 ($10,000 − $1,000). No single bank lent out more than it had in deposits. Yet for the banking system as a whole, the money supply expanded by a multiple of the initial cash deposit.

The term 1/reserve ratio in the formula is called the **money multiplier**. It tells us what the total increase in checking account deposits would be for any initial cash deposit. Recall the multiplier for government spending in our demand-side models: An increase in government spending led to larger increases in output through the multiplier. The government-spending multiplier arose because additional rounds of consumption spending were triggered by an initial increase in government spending. In the banking system, an initial cash deposit triggers additional rounds of deposits and lending by banks. This leads to a multiple expansion of deposits.

As of 2010 in the United States, banks were required to hold 3 percent in reserves against checkable deposits between $10.7 million and $55.2 million and 10 percent on all checkable deposits exceeding $55.2 million. Because large banks would face a 10 percent reserve requirement on any new deposits, you might think, on the basis of our formula, that the money multiplier would be approximately 10.

However, the money multiplier for the United States has typically been between two and three—much smaller than the value of 10 implied by our simple formula. There are two reasons for this. First, our formula assumed all loans made their way directly into checking accounts. In reality, people hold part of their loans as cash. That cash is

money multiplier
The ratio of the increase in total checking account deposits to an initial cash deposit.

APPLICATION 2

THE GROWTH IN EXCESS RESERVES

APPLYING THE CONCEPTS #2: Why have banks recently started to hold vast amounts of excess reserves?

During the height of the financial crisis in September 2008, the Fed injected large amounts of reserves into banks, and in the next month, it started paying interest to banks on these reserves. Prior to this time, banks earned no interest on either required or excess reserves. This created an incentive for banks to keep minimal excess reserves and lend any extra funds they had. However, once banks began to earn interest on excess reserves, they did not have to lend their funds out to earn interest. If lending opportunities were not very attractive, the bank could safely keep their funds on hand.

As Figure 13.5 indicates, banks have responded to the new incentives. Prior to the change in law, banks held few excess reserves. After the change in the law, excess reserves increased sharply and total reserves now far exceed required reserves. In the long run, the Federal Reserve will need to make sure that banks do not lend out too many reserves or the result will be higher inflation.   **Related to Exercises 2.2 and 2.10.**

▶ **FIGURE 13.5**

Required and Total Reserves of Banks

Until September of 2008, banks held few excess reserves so total reserves (in red) were very close to required reserves (in purple). In response to the financial crisis of 2008, the Fed injected large amounts of reserves into the system and began paying interest on reserves in October. As a result, excess reserves rose and total reserves now exceed excess reserves.

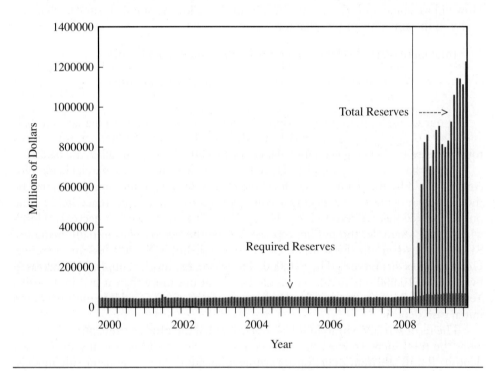

not available for the banking system to lend out. The more money people hold in cash, the less they have on deposit that can be loaned out again. This decreases the money multiplier. Second, the money multiplier will also be less if banks held excess reserves. Until recently, this was not an important factor, but a recent change to pay interest on excess reserves has sharply increased their levels. We can represent these factors in a money multiplier ratio, but it will not be as simple as the one we introduced here.

How the Money Multiplier Works in Reverse

The money-creation process also works in reverse. Suppose you go to your bank and ask for $1,000 in cash from your checking account. The bank must pay you the $1,000. The bank's liabilities fall by $1,000, but its assets must also fall by $1,000.

Withdrawing your $1,000 means two things at the bank. First, if the reserve ratio is 0.1, the bank will reduce its reserves by $100. Second, your $1,000 withdrawal minus the $100 reduction in reserves means the bank has $900 less to lend out. The bank will therefore reduce its loans by $900. With fewer loans, there will be fewer deposits in other banks. The money multiplier working in reverse decreases the money supply.

You may wonder how a bank goes about reducing its outstanding loans. If you had borrowed from a bank to invest in a project for your business, you would not want the bank phoning you to ask for its funds, which are not lying idle but are invested in your business. So banks do not typically call in outstanding loans from borrowers. Instead, if banks cannot tap into their excess reserves when their customers want to withdraw cash, they have to make fewer new loans. In these circumstances, a new potential borrower would find it harder to obtain a loan from the bank.

Up to this point, our examples have always started with an initial cash deposit. However, suppose Paul receives a check from Freda and deposits it into his bank. Paul's bank will eventually receive payment from Freda's bank. When it does, it will initially have an increase in both deposits and reserves—just as if a cash deposit were made. Because Paul's bank has to hold only a fraction of the deposits as reserves, it will be able to make loans with the remainder.

However, there is one crucial difference between this example, in which one individual writes a check to another, and our earlier example, in which an individual makes a cash deposit: When Paul receives the check from Freda, the money supply will not be changed in the long run. Here's why: When Freda's check is deposited in Paul's bank, the money supply will begin to expand, but when Freda's bank loses its deposit, the money supply will start to contract. The expansions and contractions offset each other when private citizens and firms write checks to one another.

In the next chapter, we will see how the Federal Reserve can *change* the money supply to stabilize the economy. In the remainder of this chapter, we'll look at the structure of the Federal Reserve and the critical role that it plays as a central bank stabilizing the financial system.

13.3 A BANKER'S BANK: THE FEDERAL RESERVE

The Federal Reserve System was created in 1913 after a series of financial panics in the United States. Financial panics can occur when there is bad news about the economy or the stability of financial institutions. During these panics, numerous bank runs occurred, depleting the funds on hand that banks could loan out. Severe economic downturns followed.

Congress created the Federal Reserve System to be a **central bank**, or "a banker's bank." One of the Fed's primary jobs is thus to serve as a **lender of last resort**. When banks need to borrow money during a financial crisis, they can turn to the central bank as "a last resort" for these funds. If a bank experienced a run, the Federal Reserve could lend it the funds it needed.

Functions of the Federal Reserve

The Federal Reserve has several key functions. Let's briefly describe them.

THE FED SUPPLIES CURRENCY TO THE ECONOMY   Working through the banking system, the Federal Reserve is responsible for supplying currency to the economy. Although currency is only one component of the money supply, if individuals prefer to hold currency rather than demand deposits, the Federal Reserve and the banking system will facilitate the public's preferences.

THE FED PROVIDES A SYSTEM OF CHECK COLLECTION AND CLEARING   The Federal Reserve is responsible for making our system of complex financial transactions "work." This means that when Paul writes Freda a check, the Federal Reserve oversees the banks to ensure Freda's bank receives the funds from Paul's bank. This is

central bank
A banker's bank: an official bank that controls the supply of money in a country.

lender of last resort
A central bank is the lender of last resort, the last place, all others having failed, from which banks in emergency situations can obtain loans.

known as *check clearing*. As our economy moves to more electronic transactions, the Federal Reserve provides oversight over these transactions as well.

THE FED HOLDS RESERVES FROM BANKS AND OTHER DEPOSITORY INSTITUTIONS AND REGULATES BANKS As we have seen, banks are required to hold reserves with the Federal Reserve System. The Federal Reserve also serves as a regulator to banks to ensure they are complying with rules and regulations. Ultimately, the Federal Reserve wants to ensure the financial system is safe.

THE FED CONDUCTS MONETARY POLICY One of the important responsibilities of the Federal Reserve is to conduct **monetary policy**, the range of actions that influence the level of real GDP or inflation.

> **monetary policy**
> The range of actions taken by the Federal Reserve to influence the level of GDP or inflation.

Virtually all countries have central banks. The Indian central bank is known as the Reserve Bank of India. In the United Kingdom, the central bank is the Bank of England. Central banks serve as lenders of last resort to the banks in their countries and also help to control the level of economic activity. If the economy is operating at a level that's "too hot" or "too cold," they can manipulate the money supply to fend off economic problems. We'll see how central banks use monetary policy to influence real GDP or inflation and fend off economic problems in the next chapter.

The Structure of the Federal Reserve

When members of Congress created the Federal Reserve System, they were aware the institution would be very powerful. Consequently, they deliberately created a structure that attempted to disperse the power, moving it away from major U.S. financial centers (such as New York) to other parts of the country. They divided the United States into 12 Federal Reserve districts, each of which has a **Federal Reserve Bank**. These district banks provide advice on monetary policy, take part in decision making on monetary policy, and act as a liaison between the Fed and the banks in their districts.

> **Federal Reserve Bank**
> One of 12 regional banks that are an official part of the Federal Reserve System.

Figure 13.6 shows where each of the 12 Federal Reserve Banks is located. At the time the Fed was created, economic and financial power in the United States was concentrated

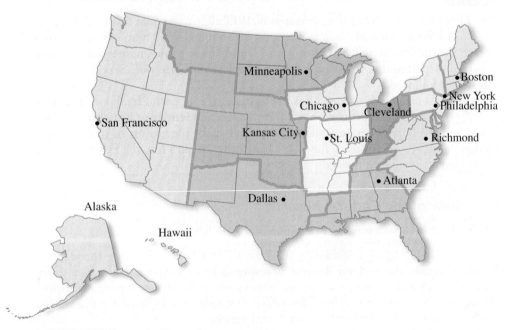

▲ **FIGURE 13.6**
Locations of the 12 Federal Reserve Banks
The 12 Federal Reserve Banks are scattered across the United States. These district banks serve as a liaison between the Fed and the banks in their districts. Hawaii and Alaska are in the 12th district, which is headquartered in San Francisco.

in the East and the Midwest. Although this is no longer the case, the locations of the Federal Reserve Banks still reflect the Fed's historical roots. Which major western city does not have a Federal Reserve Bank? It is, of course, Los Angeles.

There are two other subgroups of the Fed in addition to the Federal Reserve Banks. The **Board of Governors of the Federal Reserve** is the true seat of power in the Federal Reserve System. Headquartered in Washington, D.C., the seven members of the board are appointed for 14-year terms by the president and confirmed by the Senate. The chairperson serves a 4-year term as the principal spokesperson for monetary policy in the United States. Financial markets throughout the world anticipate and carefully observe what the chairperson says.

The third subgroup of the Fed is the **Federal Open Market Committee (FOMC)**, which makes decisions about monetary policy. The FOMC is a 12-person board consisting of the 7 members of the Board of Governors, the president of the New York Federal Reserve Bank, and the presidents of four other regional Federal Reserve Banks. (The presidents of the regional banks other than New York serve on a rotating basis; the 7 nonvoting bank presidents attend the meetings and offer their opinions.) The chairperson of the Board of Governors also serves as the chairperson of the FOMC. The FOMC makes the actual decisions on changes in the money supply. Its members are assisted by vast teams of professionals at the Board of Governors and at the regional Federal Reserve Banks. The structure of the Federal Reserve System is depicted in Figure 13.7.

Board of Governors of the Federal Reserve
The seven-person governing body of the Federal Reserve System in Washington, D.C.

Federal Open Market Committee (FOMC)
The group that decides on monetary policy: It consists of the 7 members of the Board of Governors plus 5 of 12 regional bank presidents on a rotating basis.

◄ **FIGURE 13.7**
The Structure of the Federal Reserve System
The Federal Reserve System in the United States consists of the Federal Reserve Banks, the Board of Governors, and the Federal Open Market Committee (FOMC). The FOMC is responsible for making monetary policy decisions.

On paper, monetary policymaking power appears to be spread throughout the government and the country. In practice, however, the Board of Governors, and especially the chairperson, has the real control. The Board of Governors operates with considerable independence. Presidents and members of Congress can bring political pressures on the Board of Governors, but their 14-year terms tend to insulate the members from external pressures. The current chairman of the Federal Reserve is Ben S. Bernanke, who began his term on February 1, 2006.

The Independence of the Federal Reserve

Countries differ in the degree to which their central banks are independent of political authorities. In the United States, the chairperson of the Board of Governors is required to report to Congress on a regular basis, but in practice the Fed makes its own decisions and later informs Congress what it did. The Fed chairperson also often meets with members of the executive branch to discuss economic affairs. Following the Fed's interventions during the financial crisis, there is increasing interest in Congress to make the Fed disclose additional information.

The central banks in both the United States and the United Kingdom currently operate with considerable independence of elected officials. In other countries, the central bank is part of the treasury department of the government and is potentially subject to more direct political control. There has been a lively debate among economists and political scientists as to whether countries with more independent central banks (banks with less external political pressure) experience less inflation. Central banks that are not independent will always be under pressure to help finance their country's government deficits by creating money. We'll see in a later chapter that when central banks succumb to this pressure, the result is inflation. Independence, on the other hand, typically means less inflation.

13.4 WHAT THE FEDERAL RESERVE DOES DURING A FINANCIAL CRISIS

As the lender of last resort, the Fed can quell disturbances in the financial markets. Let's look at a historical example and the Fed's action in the midst of the 2008 financial crisis.

APPLICATION 3

THE FINANCIAL SYSTEM UNDER STRESS: SEPTEMBER 11, 2001

APPLYING THE CONCEPTS #3: How did the Fed manage to keep the financial system in operation immediately following the attacks on September 11, 2001?

The Fed was tested on September 11, 2001, following the terrorist attacks against the United States. Many financial firms keep little cash on hand and expect to borrow on a daily basis to pay their ongoing bills and obligations. When the financial markets closed after September 11, many of these firms were in trouble. Unless some actions were taken quickly, they would default on their debts, leading to payment problems for other firms and further defaults. To prevent a default avalanche, the Federal Reserve immediately took a number of steps to provide additional funds to the financial system.

The first tool the Federal Reserve used was to allow banks to borrow more. Ordinarily the volume of these direct loans from the Federal Reserve is not very large. On Wednesday, September 12, total lending to banks rose to $45.5 *billion*, up from just $99 million the week before.

The Federal Reserve System also serves as a clearinghouse for checks. A bank will bring checks it receives from customers to the Federal Reserve and receive immediate credit on its accounts. The Federal Reserve then debits the account of the bank upon which the check was written. The difference between the credits and the debits extended by the Federal Reserve is called the "Federal Reserve float." Immediately following September 11, the Federal Reserve allowed this float to increase sharply from $2.9 billion to $22.9 billion. These actions effectively put an additional $20 billion into the banking system.

The Federal Reserve also purchased government securities in the marketplace and as a result put $30 billion into the hands of private citizens and their banks. It arranged to provide dollars to foreign central banks such as the Bank of England so they could meet their needs and the needs of their banks to facilitate any dollar transactions they had during the crisis. Taken together, these actions increased the credit extended by the Federal Reserve by over $90 billion. This massive response prevented a financial panic that could have had devastating effects on the world economy. **Related to Exercises 4.3 and 4.7.**

APPLICATION 4

COPING WITH THE FINANCIAL CHAOS CAUSED BY THE MORTGAGE CRISIS

APPLYING THE CONCEPTS #4: How did the Fed successfully respond to the collapse of major financial institutions in 2008?

Sunday, March 16, 2008, was not a peaceful day for the Board of Governors. Over the prior week, one of Wall Street's most famous investment houses, Bear Stearns, had gone into full collapse. Although Bears Stearns had roughly $17 billion in readily available assets, it appeared this was not enough to satisfy the market. Other investment firms believed Bear Stearns had made so many poor investments that it was not financially viable. They rapidly began pulling out their funds from the firm.

The Fed feared that a complete collapse of Bear Stearns would devastate the financial system and cause a global panic as investors would want to pull out their funds from all financial institutions, effectively causing a "run" in the financial markets. During the week the Fed began to search for ways to deal with this crisis. One solution was to try to convince another financial institution to take over Bear Stearns and keep the financial markets open. The problem, however, was that no one had a clear idea precisely what quality of assets Bears Stearns had on its balance sheet, and thus no firm wanted to be exposed to the risk of purchasing them. Finally, the Fed convinced the investment firm JPMorgan Chase & Co. to buy Bear Stearns—but only after the Fed agreed to loan Chase $30 billion. The Fed had successfully averted a major financial crisis but had put U.S. taxpayers at risk by lending such a large amount to a private investment house.

Unfortunately, Bear Stearns was only an early symptom of a problem that increased in severity over the coming months. As we discussed in Chapter 12, by September and October of 2008 the mortgage crisis had effectively spilled over into the world's financial markets. Banks and other financial institutions were afraid to lend to one another because they were not sure whether or not their loans would be repaid. The world's financial markets were freezing up, stock markets were in sharp decline, and there was growing panic.

The panic was brought to a head when the Fed and Treasury decided not to arrange a bailout for Lehman Brothers, another major financial institution, as they had done for Bear Stearns. The markets worldwide reacted adversely to this decision. The Fed and Treasury quickly changed tactics, however, and authorized an $85 billion loan to the American International Group (AIG) and took an 80 percent ownership stake in the company. The Fed had thought that the failure of AIG would trigger massive failures of other institutions whose assets were insured by AIG. As the crisis continued, the Fed continued to develop new programs, such as purchasing the short-term debt of corporations—commercial paper—so that it effectively spread its lender of last resort function beyond financial institutions. It also began a program to extend loans to money market funds, some of which had come under financial pressure, and it started to make purchases of securities backed by mortgages in order to keep funds flowing to the housing sector. Finally, it began to pay interest on deposits held at the Fed, a move designed to induce banks to hold more reserves and increase the Fed's own ability to make critical loans.

Taken together, these were sweeping changes to the Fed's role in the financial system. The Fed has now abandoned its efforts to support the commercial paper market and money market funds, but has maintained the other programs. Only time will tell whether the remaining changes, adopted during a two-month period, will become permanent tools of the Fed or will fade away when the economy eventually recovers.

Related to Exercises 4.1, 4.6, and 4.8.

SUMMARY

We began this chapter by examining the role money plays in the economy and how economists define money. We then looked at the flow of money in and out of banks and saw how banks can create money with deposits and loans. Finally, we examined the structure of the Federal Reserve and the key roles that central banks can play during financial crises. Here are the main points you should remember from this chapter:

1 *Money* consists of anything we regularly use to make exchanges. In modern economies, money consists primarily of currency and deposits in checking accounts.

2 Banks are financial intermediaries that earn profits by accepting deposits and making loans. Deposits, which are liabilities of banks, are included in the money supply.

3 Banks are required by law to hold a fraction of their deposits as reserves, either in cash or in deposits with the Federal Reserve. Total reserves consist of *required reserves* plus *excess reserves.*

4 If there is an increase in reserves in the banking system, the supply of money will expand by a multiple of the initial deposit. This multiple is known as the *money multiplier.*

5 Decisions about the supply of money are made at the *Federal Open Market Committee* (FOMC), which includes the 7 members on the Board of Governors and the president of the New York Federal Reserve Bank, as well as 4 of the 11 other regional bank presidents, who serve on a rotating basis.

6 In a financial crisis like those that occurred in 2001 and 2008, the Fed can help stabilize the economy. Current and recent Fed chairmen have been powerful figures in the national economy.

KEY TERMS

assets, p. 277

balance sheet, p. 277

barter, p. 273

Board of Governors of the Federal Reserve, p. 283

central bank, p. 281

commodity money, p. 274

double coincidence of wants, p. 273

excess reserves, p. 278

Federal Open Market Committee (FOMC), p. 283

Federal Reserve Bank, p. 282

fiat money, p. 274

gold standard, p. 274

lender of last resort, p. 281

liabilities, p. 277

M1, p. 275

M2, p. 275

medium of exchange, p. 273

monetary policy, p. 282

money, p. 273

money multiplier, p. 279

owners' equity, p. 277

required reserves, p. 278

reserve ratio, p. 278

reserves, p. 278

store of value, p. 274

unit of account, p. 274

EXERCISES

Visit www.myeconlab.com to complete these exercises online and get instant feedback.

13.1 What *Is* Money?

1.1 Money solves the problem of double coincidence of wants that would regularly occur under a system of _____.

1.2 Gold is a good example of fiat money. _____ (True/False)

1.3 Deposits in checking accounts are included in the definition of money because they are a very liquid asset. _____ (True/False)

1.4 The largest component of M2 is deposits in _____.

1.5 Money market mutual funds are hard to classify in a definition of money because they are only held to facilitate transactions. _____ (True/False)

1.6 So much U.S. currency is in global circulation because it is a safe asset compared to assets denominated in foreign currency. _____ (True/False)

1.7 **Debit Cards.** In recent years, debit cards have become popular. Debit cards allow the holder of the card to pay a merchant for goods and services directly from a checking account. How do you think the introduction of debit cards affected the amount of currency in the economy? How about the amount of checking account deposits?

1.8 **Gift Cards.** Gifts cards have grown in popularity as a mechanism to give gifts. Cards are available for popular book stores and for coffee shops. Should these gift cards be considered part of the money supply? How do they differ from traveler's checks?

1.9 **California Money?** In 1992, the state of California ran out of funds and could not pay its bills. It issued IOUs, called *warrants*, to its workers and suppliers. Only large banks and credit unions accepted the warrants. Should these warrants be viewed as money? (Related to Application 1 on page 276.)

1.10 **Credit Cards.** Why aren't traditional credit cards part of the money supply?

1.11 **Inflation and Currency Held Abroad.** Suppose inflation in the United States rose to around 7 percent a year. How do you think this would affect the demand for U.S. currency by foreigners?

1.12 **Currency and Underground Economy.** Search the Web for articles on "currency and the underground economy." How have various authors used estimates of currency to measure the underground economy?

13.2 How Banks Create Money

2.1 Banks are required by law to keep a fraction of their deposits as _____.

2.2 When reserves do not pay interest, banks prefer to keep reserves rather than make loans. _____ (True/False) (Related to Application 2 on page 280.)

2.3 If the reserve ratio is 0.2 and a deposit of $100 is made into a bank, the bank can lend out _____.

2.4 If the reserve ratio is 0.2, the simplified money multiplier will be _____.

2.5 **Bad Loans to South America.** During the 1980s, U.S. banks made loans to South American countries. Many of these loans turned out to be worthless. How did this affect the assets, liabilities, and owners' equity of these banks?

2.6 **Banks versus Insurance Companies.** Both insurance companies and banks are financial intermediaries. Why do macroeconomists study banks more intensively than insurance companies?

2.7 **Understanding M1 and M2.** If you write a check from your checking account to your money market account, what happens to M1 and M2?

2.8 **Cash Withdrawals and Changes in the Money Supply.** If a customer withdrew $2,000 in cash from a bank and the reserve ratio was 0.2, by how much could the supply of money eventually be reduced?

2.9 **Money Market Mutual Funds, Banks, and Reserves.** Money market mutual funds typically invest in government securities and other financial instruments that can be easily bought and sold. They are not subject to reserve requirements and, in fact, hold minimal reserves. Banks, on the other hand, make loans to businesses for investment purposes. If there were no reserve requirements for banks, how do you think their reserve holdings would compare to money market mutual funds?

2.10 **Setting the Interest Rate on Reserves.** What would be the danger if the Fed set an interest rate on reserves close to the market interest rate on loans? (Related to Application 2 on page 280.)

13.3 A Banker's Bank: The Federal Reserve

3.1 The Federal Reserve is the "_____ of last resort."

3.2 The San Francisco Federal Reserve Bank is the only one in the West because San Francisco outbid Los Angeles to be its host. _____ (True/False)

3.3 The _____ votes on monetary policy.

3.4 _____ -year terms help ensure the political independence of the Board of Governors.

3.5 The Fed provides a system of check collection and _____.

3.6 **The Treasury Secretary and the Fed.** Occasionally, some economists or politicians suggest that the secretary of the Treasury become a member of the Federal Open Market Committee. How do you think this would affect the operation of the Federal Reserve?

3.7 **Where Should Regional Banks Be Located Today?** Given the changes in the location of economic activity that have occurred since the founding of the Federal Reserve, how would the location of the regional banks change if they were allocated by economic activity?

3.8 **The President of the New York Federal Reserve Bank.** The president of the New York Federal Reserve Bank is always a voting member of the Federal Open Market Committee. Given your understanding of the conduct of monetary policy, why is this true?

3.9 **How Much Oversight?** After the financial crisis in 2008, Congress wanted to have more oversight of the Fed and some suggested that the Government Accountability Office even audit the decisions of the Fed. What are the risks of this increased oversight?

13.4 What the Federal Reserve Does During a Financial Crisis

4.1 The Federal Reserve arranged for JPMorgan Chase & Co. to _____ Bears Stearns during the financial crisis in 2008. (Related to Application 4 on page 285.)

4.2 The "float" in the banking system is the difference between the Federal Reserve's _____ and _____ when clearing checks.

4.3 Two actions the Fed took after September 11, 2001, to ensure the financial system operated smoothly were _____ and _____. (Related to Application 3 on page 284.)

4.4 **Required Reserves during the Great Depression.** During the Great Depression, banks held excess reserves because they were concerned depositors might be more inclined to withdraw funds from their accounts. At one point, the Fed became concerned that excess reserves were too high and raised the reserve requirements for banks.

    a. Assuming banks were holding excess reserves for precautionary purposes, do you think they would continue to want to hold them even after reserve requirements were raised? Explain.

    b. What do you think happened to the money supply after the Fed raised reserve requirements?

4.5 **Crisis in the Short-Term Credit Market.** In 1973, several major companies went bankrupt and were not going to be able to pay interest on their short-term loans. This caused a crisis in the market. There was concern that the short-term credit market would collapse, and that even healthy corporations would not be able to borrow. How do you think the Fed should have handled that situation?

4.6 **The Federal Reserve Loan to JPMorgan Chase & Co.** When the Federal Reserve makes a loan to a bank or financial institution, it requires the institution to specify certain assets the Federal Reserve can take possession of if the loan is not repaid. These assets are known as collateral. When the Federal Reserve made its $30 billion loan to JPMorgan, it allowed JPMorgan to use some of the assets of Bears Stearns as collateral. Why was this risky for the Federal Reserve and a good deal for JPMorgan? (Related to Application 4 on page 285.)

4.7 **Check Clearing and September 11.** How did the Federal Reserve manipulate the check-clearing process to increase liquidity in response to the potential financial crisis following the terrorist attacks of September 11, 2001? (Related to Application 3 on page 284.)

4.8 **Bailouts?** Some critics of the Fed's actions with AIG and Bear Stearns said that the government was just bailing out failing financial firms that should have been allowed to fail. It is true that owners of both firms did benefit from these actions. Nonetheless, can you defend the Fed? (Related to Application 4 on page 285.)

ECONOMIC EXPERIMENT

Money Creation

This experiment demonstrates the money-creation process. Students act like bankers and investors. Bankers loan money to investors, who then buy machines that produce output. The experiment is divided into several separate days. On each day, all loans are executed in the morning, all deposits happen over the lunch hour, and all machines are purchased in the afternoon. Each bank can receive only one deposit and issue only one loan. The interest rate paid to depositors and the interest rate paid by borrowers are negotiable. The experiment starts when the instructor deposits $625 from the sale of a government bond into a bank.

Bank Actions

The sequence of possible bank actions on a given day is as follows:

1. Early morning: Count money. Check for excess reserves, including deposits from the previous noon.

2. Middle morning: Loan out any excess reserves in a single loan to a borrower and negotiate an interest rate for the loan. The loan is executed by writing a bank check to the borrower.

3. Noon: Receive a deposit (bank check deposited into a checking account).

4. Afternoon: Relax, golf.

Rules for Banks

The rules for banks are as follows:

1. For each $1 deposited, you must hold $0.20 in reserve.

2. If you don't issue a loan, you can earn 3 percent by investing overseas.

Investor Actions

The sequence of possible investor actions on a given day is as follows:

1. Early morning: Sleep in while bankers count their money.

2. Middle morning: Borrow money from a bank and negotiate an interest rate for the loan.

3. Noon: Deposit the loan at the bank of your choice and negotiate an interest rate for the deposit.

4. Afternoon: Buy machines from Machine, Inc., paying with a personal check.

Investor Payoffs

Each machine costs $1, generates $1.10 worth of output, and then expires.

As the students play, the instructor keeps track of the model economy on a tally sheet, which shows the money-creation process in action, round by round.

What role do the return on overseas investment (3 percent) and the return from owning a machine ($1.10 on a $1.00 investment) play in this experiment?

MONEY-CREATION EXPERIMENT: TALLY SHEET

Bank Receiving Deposit	Amount Deposited	Interest Rate on Deposit	Amount Loaned	Interest Rate on Loan	Amount Added to Reserves	Change in Money Supply

 For additional economic experiments, please visit *www.myeconlab.com*.

APPENDIX
FORMULA FOR DEPOSIT CREATION

To show how to derive the formula for deposit creation, let's use the example in the text. We showed that with 10 percent held as reserves, a $1,000 deposit led to total deposits of

$$\$1,000 + \$900 + \$810 + \$729 + \$656.10 + \ldots$$

Let's find the total sum of all these deposits. Because each bank successively had to hold 10 percent in its reserves, each successive bank received only 0.9 of the deposits of the prior bank. Therefore, we can write the total for the deposits in all the banks as

$$\$1,000 \times (1 + 0.9 + 0.9^2 + 0.9^3 + 0.9^4 + \ldots)$$

We need to find the sum of the terms in parentheses. Using a formula for an infinite sum,

$$1 + b + b^2 + b^3 + b^4 + \cdots = \frac{1}{(1 - b)}$$

the expression becomes

$$1 + 0.9 + 0.9^2 + 0.9^3 + 0.9^4 + \cdots = \frac{1}{(1 - 0.9)} = 10$$

Therefore, the total increase in deposits will be

$$\$1,000 \times 10 = \$10,000$$

To derive the general formula, note that if the reserve ratio is r, the bank will lend out $(1 - r)$ per dollar of deposits. Following the steps we just outlined, we find the infinite sum will be $1/[1 - (1 - r)] = 1/r$, or 1/reserve ratio. Therefore, in general, we have the formula

$$\text{Increase in checking account balances} = (\text{initial deposit}) \times \frac{1}{\text{reserve ratio}}$$

The Federal Reserve and Monetary Policy

Little did Ben S. Bernanke know when he took over the reins as chairman of the Federal Reserve on February 1, 2006, that he would face a novel and complex crisis brought on by the fall in housing prices and its reverberations throughout the entire financial system in 2007 and 2008. Unlike his immediate predecessors, Alan Greenspan and Paul Volcker, who had gained their experience and expertise working on Wall Street and in banking, Bernanke had primarily an academic career. As a former chairman of the Economics Department at Princeton University, he was known for his scholarly work focused on the Great Depression and the role of monetary policy in controlling inflation. Although he had little direct experience in financial markets, he did have some experience in economic policy and monetary policy in Washington.

Bernanke used his academic and policy experience to his advantage in meeting the challenges of the financial crisis. He convened brainstorming sessions with the president of the New York Federal Reserve Bank and leading financiers on Wall Street to further develop his own understanding of rapidly changing financial structures and the risks the mortgage crisis posed to them. As a scholar of the Great Depression, he also understood that the Federal Reserve had to take bold action to avert major crises. This background helped him to devise new and daring strategies for the Fed to deal with an unforeseen financial crisis. After a career in academia, his job as chairman provided Bernanke with a new education—by fire.

APPLYING THE CONCEPTS

1 How has the Fed recently expanded its role in financial markets?
Beyond Purchasing Treasury Securities

2 What happens to interest rates when the economy recovers from a recession?
Rising Interest Rates during an Economic Recovery

3 Is it better for decisions about monetary policy to be made by a single individual or by a committee?
The Effectiveness of Committees

In this chapter, we will learn why everyone is so interested in what the Federal Reserve is about to do. In the short run, when prices don't have enough time to change and we consider them temporarily fixed, the Federal Reserve can influence interest rate levels in the economy. When the Federal Reserve lowers interest rates, investment spending and GDP increase because the cost of funds is cheaper. Conversely, when the Fed increases interest rates, investment spending and GDP decrease because the cost of funds is higher. It is this power of the Fed to affect interest rates in the short run that will influence firms' decisions to invest. Individuals who want to invest in or purchase homes also want to know what the Fed will do about interest rates in the near future.

14.1 THE MONEY MARKET

money market

The market for money in which the amount supplied and the amount demanded meet to determine the nominal interest rate.

The **money market** is the market for money where the amount supplied and the amount demanded meet to determine the nominal interest rate. Recall that the nominal interest rate is the stated or quoted interest rate before adjusting for inflation. We begin by learning the factors that determine the public's demand for money. Once we understand what affects the demand for money, we can see how the actions of the Federal Reserve determine the supply of money. Then we'll see how the demand and supply of money together determine interest rates.

The Demand for Money

Let's think of money as simply one part of wealth. Suppose your total wealth is valued at $1,000. In what form will you hold your wealth? Should you put all your wealth into the stock market? Or perhaps into the bond market? Or should you hold some of your wealth in money, that is, currency and deposits in checking accounts?

INTEREST RATES AFFECT MONEY DEMAND   If you invest in assets such as stocks or bonds, you will generally earn income on them. *Stocks* are shares in the ownership of a corporation. There are two sources of income from stocks: dividends paid to their owners out of the profits of the corporation, and the typical increase in their value over time. *Bonds* are loans that are repaid with interest. Thus, both stocks and bonds provide returns to investors. If you hold your wealth in currency or in a checking account, however, you will receive either no interest or very low interest. And if inflation rises sharply, you might even lose money. Holding your wealth as money in currency or a checking account means you sacrifice some potential income.

Money does, however, provide a valuable service. It facilitates transactions. If you go to a grocery store to purchase cereal, the store will accept currency or a check, but you won't be able to pay for cereal with your stocks and bonds. People hold money primarily for this basic reason: Money makes it easier to conduct everyday transactions. Economists call this reason for holding money the **transaction demand for money**.

transaction demand for money

The demand for money based on the desire to facilitate transactions.

To understand the demand for money, we rely on the principle of opportunity cost.

PRINCIPLE OF OPPORTUNITY COST
The opportunity cost of something is what you sacrifice to get it.

The opportunity cost of holding money is the return you could have earned by holding your wealth in other assets. We measure the opportunity cost of holding money by the interest rate. Suppose the interest rate available to you on a long-term bond is 6 percent per year. If you hold $100 of your wealth in the form of this bond, you'll earn $6 a year. If you hold currency instead, you'll earn no interest. So the opportunity cost of holding $100 in currency is $6 per year, or 6 percent per year.

As interest rates increase in the economy, the opportunity cost of holding money also increases. Economists have found that as the opportunity cost of holding money increases, the public demands less money. The quantity demanded of money will decrease with an increase in interest rates.

In Figure 14.1, we draw a demand for money curve, M^d, as a function of the interest rate. At higher interest rates, individuals will want to hold less money than they will at lower interest rates because the opportunity cost of holding money is higher. As interest rates rise from r_0 to r_1, the quantity of money demanded falls from M_0 to M_1.

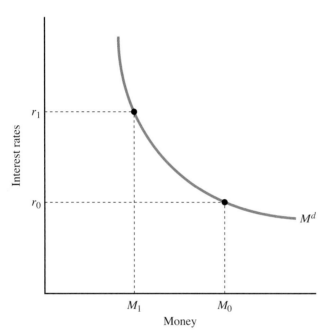

▲ **FIGURE 14.1**
Demand for Money
As interest rates increase from r_0 to r_1, the quantity of money demanded falls from M_0 to M_1.

THE PRICE LEVEL AND GDP AFFECT MONEY DEMAND   The demand for money also depends on two other factors. One is the overall price level in the economy. The demand for money will increase as the level of prices increases. If prices for your groceries are twice as high, you will need twice as much money to purchase them. The amount of money people typically hold during any time period will be closely related to the dollar value of the transactions they make. This is an example of the real-nominal principle in action.

REAL-NOMINAL PRINCIPLE

What matters to people is the real value of money or income—its purchasing power—not the face value of money or income.

The other factor that influences the demand for money is the level of real GDP or real income. It seems obvious that as income increases, individuals and businesses will make more purchases. Similarly, as real GDP increases, individuals and businesses will make more transactions. To facilitate these transactions, they will want to hold more money.

Figure 14.2 shows how changes in prices and GDP affect the demand for money. Panel A shows how the demand for money shifts to the right as the price level increases. At any interest rate, people will want to hold more money as prices increase. Panel B shows how the demand for money shifts to the right as real GDP increases. At any interest rate, people will want to hold more money as real GDP increases. These graphs both show the same result. An increase in prices or an increase in real GDP will increase money demand.

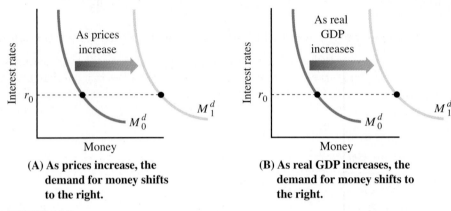

(A) As prices increase, the demand for money shifts to the right.

(B) As real GDP increases, the demand for money shifts to the right.

▲ FIGURE 14.2
Shifting the Demand for Money
Changes in prices and real GDP shift the demand for money.

OTHER COMPONENTS OF MONEY DEMAND   Traditionally, economists have identified other motives besides transactions for individuals or firms to hold money. If you hold your wealth in the form of property, such as a house or a boat, it is costly to sell it on short notice if you need to obtain funds. These forms of wealth are **illiquid**, meaning that they are not easily transferable into money. If you hold your wealth in currency or checking accounts, you do not have this problem. Economists recognize that people have a **liquidity demand for money**; they want to hold money so they can make transactions on quick notice.

During periods of economic volatility, investors might not want to hold stocks and bonds because their prices might fall. Instead, they might convert them into holdings that fall into the M2 category, such as savings accounts and money market funds. These investments earn lower interest rates on average, but are less risky than stocks and bonds, whose prices can fluctuate. This demand for safer assets is called the **speculative demand for money**. For example, after the stock market began to fall in 2000, individuals became very uncertain about the future and shifted their funds from the stock market to money market mutual funds. This shift of assets from stocks to money temporarily increased M2. When the market started to recover, some investors shifted funds back into the stock market.

In summary, individuals hold money for three motives: to facilitate transactions, to provide liquidity, and to reduce risk. The amount of money they want to hold will depend on interest rates, the level of real GDP, and the price level.

illiquid
Not easily transferable to money.

liquidity demand for money
The demand for money that represents the needs and desires individuals and firms have to make transactions on short notice without incurring excessive costs.

speculative demand for money
The demand for money that arises because holding money over short periods is less risky than holding stocks or bonds.

14.2 HOW THE FEDERAL RESERVE CAN CHANGE THE MONEY SUPPLY

As we discussed in the last chapter, the banking system as a whole can expand the money supply only if new reserves come into the system. As we saw, when private citizens and firms write checks to one another, there will be no net change in the supply of money. Because the total amount of reserves in the system is unchanged, the money supply cannot expand. There is one organization, however, that has the power to change the total amount of reserves in the banking system: the Federal Reserve.

Open Market Operations

The Fed can increase or decrease the total amount of reserves in the banking system through **open market operations**, which are the purchase or sale of U.S. government securities by the Fed. There are two types of open market operations:

- In **open market purchases**, the Fed buys government bonds from the private sector.
- In **open market sales**, the Fed sells government bonds to the private sector.

To understand how the Fed can increase the supply of money, let's trace what happens after an open market purchase. Suppose the Federal Reserve purchases $1 million worth of government bonds currently owned by the private sector. The Fed writes a check for $1 million and presents it to the party who sold the bonds. The Federal Reserve now owns those bonds. The party who sold the bonds then deposits the $1 million in its bank.

Here is the key to how the supply of money increases when the Fed purchases government bonds: As we explained in the last chapter, each bank must keep an account with the Fed containing both its required and excess reserves. The check written against the Federal Reserve increases the bank's total reserves, essentially giving it more money to loan out. In this case, the bank's account balance increases by $1 million. If the reserve requirement is 10 percent, the bank must keep $100,000 in reserves, but it can now loan out $900,000 from its excess reserves. Basically, when the Fed buys bonds, the proceeds go out into the economy. Open market purchases of bonds therefore increase the money supply.

The Federal Reserve has powers that ordinary citizens and even banks do not have. The Fed can write checks against itself to purchase government bonds without having any explicit "funds" in its account for the purchase. Banks accept these checks because they count as part of their total reserves.

As you might expect, open market sales will, conversely, decrease the supply of money. Suppose the Federal Reserve sells $1 million worth of government bonds to a Wall Street firm. The firm will pay for the bonds with a check for $1 million drawn on its bank and give this check to the Federal Reserve. The bank must either hand over $1 million in cash or, more likely, reduce its total reserves with the Federal Reserve by $1 million. When the Fed sells bonds, it is basically taking the money exchanged for them out of the hands of the public. Open market sales therefore decrease the money freely available in the economy.

In summary, if the Federal Reserve wishes to increase the money supply to stimulate the economy (perhaps it is operating too sluggishly), it buys government bonds from the private sector in open market purchases. If the Fed wishes to decrease the money supply to slow the economy down (perhaps it is growing too quickly and inflation is occurring), it sells government bonds to the private sector in open market sales.

Other Tools of the Fed

Open market operations are by far the most important way in which the Federal Reserve changes the supply of money. There are two other ways in which the Fed can change the supply of money, which we'll discuss next.

CHANGING RESERVE REQUIREMENTS   Another way the Fed can change the money supply is by changing the reserve requirements for banks. If the Fed wishes to increase the supply of money, it can reduce banks' reserve requirements so they have

open market operations
The purchase or sale of U.S. government securities by the Fed.

open market purchases
The Fed's purchase of government bonds from the private sector.

open market sales
The Fed's sale of government bonds to the private sector.

APPLICATION 1

BEYOND PURCHASING TREASURY SECURITIES

APPLYING THE CONCEPTS #1: How has the Fed recently expanded its role in financial markets?

Traditionally, to conduct monetary policy and to expand the money supply, the Fed purchased—either outright or on a temporary basis—Treasury securities. When it purchased these securities for the public, it credited the reserve accounts in banks and the amount of these reserves in banks would, in part, determine the amount of money and credit in the economy. The Fed did not intervene directly in particular security or credit markets, instead leaving those decisions to be made by the private market.

After the financial crisis of 2008, the Fed sharply changed its policies. It greatly expanded its involvement in the economy both in size and scope. The first way to see this is to note that the Fed's total assets increased during 2008 from less than $1 trillion to over $2 trillion. The second way is to note the change in composition of its assets. Prior to the financial crisis, the Fed primarily held Treasury securities as its assets. In 2010 the Fed held over $1 trillion in mortgage-backed securities. During the financial crisis, the Fed designed a wide variety of new programs to channel funds to particular credit markets.

The Fed's support of the mortgage market and other specific credit markets was designed to make these markets work more smoothly and prevent disruptions during the crisis. Critics of the Fed's policies suggest that through its support of specific markets, the Fed crossed a political threshold that may pose risks to its long-term independence. During 2009 the Fed did wind down its investments in many specific markets, but increased the size of its mortgage-backed securities. Through these financial holdings, the Fed is still playing a direct role in the housing market. **Related to Exercise 2.7.**

---

more money to loan out. This would expand the money supply. To decrease the supply of money, the Federal Reserve can raise reserve requirements.

Changing reserve requirements is a powerful tool, but the Federal Reserve doesn't use it very often, because it disrupts the banking system. Suppose a bank is required to hold exactly 10 percent of its deposits as reserves and has loaned the other 90 percent out. If the Federal Reserve suddenly increases its reserve requirement to 20 percent, the bank would be forced to call in or cancel many of its loans. Its customers would not like this! Today, the Fed doesn't make sharp changes in reserve requirements. It did in the past, including during the Great Depression, because it mistakenly believed that the banks were holding too much in excess reserves. Banks, however, were holding additional reserves because they wanted to protect themselves from bank runs. As a result, after the increase in required reserves, banks increased their reserves even more, further reducing the supply of money to the economy.

CHANGING THE DISCOUNT RATE Another way the Fed can change the money supply is by changing the *discount rate*. The **discount rate** is the interest rate at which banks can borrow directly from the Fed. Suppose a major customer asks for a large loan from a bank that has no excess reserves. Unless the bank can find an additional source of funds, it will not be able to make the loan. Banks are reluctant to turn away major customers. They first try to borrow reserves from other banks through the **federal funds market**, a market in which banks borrow and lend

discount rate
The interest rate at which banks can borrow from the Fed.

federal funds market
The market in which banks borrow and lend reserves to and from one another.

reserves to and from one another. If the rate—called the **federal funds rate**—seems too high to the bank, it could borrow directly from the Federal Reserve at the discount rate. By changing the discount rate, the Federal Reserve can influence the amount of borrowing by banks. If the Fed raises the discount rate, banks will be discouraged from borrowing reserves because it has become more costly. Lowering the discount rate will induce banks to borrow additional reserves. Recently, the Fed has developed new methods to allow banks and other institutions to borrow from it.

federal funds rate
The interest rate on reserves that banks lend each other.

14.3 HOW INTEREST RATES ARE DETERMINED: COMBINING THE DEMAND AND SUPPLY OF MONEY

Combining the demand for money, determined by the public, with the supply of money, determined by the Fed, we can see how interest rates are determined in the short run in a demand-and-supply model of the money market.

Figure 14.3 depicts a model of the money market. The supply of money is determined by the Federal Reserve, and we assume for simplicity that it is independent of interest rates. We represent this independence by a vertical supply curve for money, M^s. In the same graph, we draw the demand for money M^d. Market equilibrium occurs where the demand for money equals the supply of money, at an interest rate of r^*.

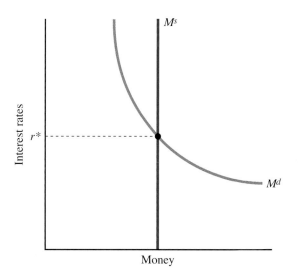

▲ **FIGURE 14.3**
Equilibrium in the Money Market
Equilibrium in the money market occurs at an interest rate of r^*, at which the quantity of money demanded equals the quantity of money supplied.

At this equilibrium interest rate r^*, the quantity of money demanded by the private sector equals the quantity of money supplied by the Federal Reserve. What happens if the interest rate is higher than r^*? At a higher interest rate, the quantity of money demanded will be less than the fixed quantity supplied, so there will be an excess supply of money. In other markets, excess supplies cause the price to fall. The same result happens here. The "price of money" in the market for money is the interest rate. If the interest rate were below r^*, the demand for money would exceed the fixed supply: There would be an excess demand for money. As in other markets when there are excess demands, the price rises. Here, the price of money or the interest rate would rise until it reached r^*. As you can see, money-market equilibrium follows the same logic as any other economic equilibrium.

We can use this simple model of the money market to understand the power of the Federal Reserve. Suppose the Federal Reserve increases the money supply through an open market purchase of bonds. In Panel A of Figure 14.4, an increase in the supply of money shifts the money supply curve to the right, leading to lower interest rates. A decrease in the money supply through the Fed's open market sale of bonds, as depicted in Panel B of Figure 14.4, decreases the supply of money, shifting the money supply curve to the left and increasing interest rates.

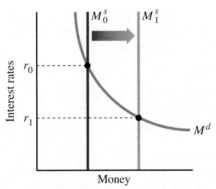 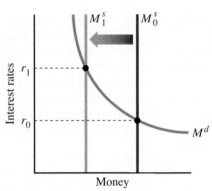

(A) An open market purchase shifts the supply of money to the right and leads to lower interest rates.

(B) An open market sale shifts the supply of money to the left and leads to higher interest rates.

▲ FIGURE 14.4
Federal Reserve and Interest Rates
Changes in the supply of money will change interest rates.

We can also think of the process from the perspective of banks. Recall our discussion of money creation through the banking system. After the Fed's open market purchase of bonds, some of the money the Fed paid for the bonds gets deposited into banks. Banks will want to make loans to consumers and businesses with that money, because holding it in their reserves with the Fed earns them no interest. To entice people to borrow, banks will lower the interest rates they charge on their loans. After an open-market purchase of bonds by the Fed, interest rates will fall throughout the entire economy.

Now we understand why businesspeople and politicians all want to know what the Federal Reserve is likely to do in the near future. The Fed exerts direct control over interest rates in the short run. If the Fed decides interest rates should be lower, it buys bonds in the open market to increase the supply of money. If the Fed wants higher interest rates, it sells bonds in the open market to decrease the money supply.

Interest Rates and Bond Prices

Sometimes you see in the financial section of the newspaper a statement like, "Today, interest rates rose as bond prices fell." You may wonder whether these two actions are connected. Indeed they are. When the Fed raises interest rates, bond prices fall.

To see why, recall that bonds represent a promise to pay money in the future. If you own a bond, you are entitled to receive payments on it at a later time. But why do the prices of bonds move in the opposite direction of interest rates?

Because a bond payment occurs in the future, we need to use the concept of present value from Chapter 12 to determine the value of this payment today. The price of a bond is simply the present value of its future payments. Consider a bond that makes a payment one period in the future. The price of the bond—the present value of the payment—is equal to

$$\text{price of bond} = \frac{\text{promised payment}}{(1 + \text{interest rate})}$$

That is, the price of a bond is the payment promised, divided by one plus the interest rate.

Suppose the promised payment next year is $106 and the interest rate is 6 percent per year. The price of the bond will be

$$\text{price of bond} = \frac{\$106}{1.06} = \$100$$

In this case, the bond would cost $100 if it were issued today. But what happens if interest rates in the economy change later? What if rates rise higher than 6 percent or fall lower than 6 percent? What will the bond you are holding be worth then, if you decided, for example, you needed the money and had to sell it to someone else? This is an important question because most of the bonds for sale on the market are not newly issued bonds—they are bonds that have already been issued with specific promised payments that people are buying and selling from one another.

Let's consider two examples:

- Suppose the promised payment is still $106, but the interest rate falls from 6 to 4 percent per year. Using the formula, the price of the bond will rise to $106/1.04, or $101.92—$1.92 more than it was with an interest rate of 6 percent. The price of the bond rose because, at the lower interest rate of 4 percent, a buyer will need more money—$101.92 versus $100—to get the same $106 the bond will pay next year. In other words, at a lower interest rate the value today of a future payment (its present value) is higher.

- Now suppose interest rates rise from 6 to 8 percent per year. In this case, the price you could sell your bond for will fall to $106/1.08, or $98.15. The reason the price falls is that a buyer would need only $98.15 to get the $106 next year. As interest rates rose, the price of the bond fell. In other words, at a higher interest rate, the value today of a future payment (its present value) is lower.

In financial markets, many types of complex bonds pay different sums of money at different times in the future. However, all bonds, no matter how complex or simple, promise to pay some money in the future. The same logic that applies to simple one-period bonds, like the one just described, applies to more complex bonds. As interest rates rise, investors need less money to meet the promised payments in the future, so the price of all these bonds falls. As interest rates fall, investors need more money to meet the promised payments. Therefore, as the Fed changes interest rates, bond prices will move in the opposite direction of interest rates.

RISING INTEREST RATES DURING AN ECONOMIC RECOVERY

APPLYING THE CONCEPTS #2: What happens to interest rates when the economy recovers from a recession?

Economists have often noticed that as an economy recovers from a recession, interest rates start to rise. And, in general, interest rates tend to rise as the economy grows quickly. An example occurred during 2005, when interest rates on three-month Treasury bills rose from 2.3 percent at the beginning of the year to 3.9 percent at the end of the year, as real GDP grew very rapidly.

Some observers think this is puzzling because they associate higher interest rates with lower output. Why should a recovery be associated with higher interest rates?

The simple model of the money market helps explain why interest rates can rise during an economic recovery. One key to understanding this phenomenon is that the extra income being generated by firms and individuals during the recovery will increase the demand for money. Because the demand for money increases while the supply of money remains fixed, interest rates rise.

Another factor is that the Federal Reserve itself may want to raise interest rates as the economy grows rapidly to avoid overheating the economy. In this case, the Fed cuts back on the supply of money to raise interest rates. In both cases, however, the public should expect rising interest rates during a period of economic recovery and rapid GDP growth. **Related to Exercise 3.7.**

HOW OPEN MARKET OPERATIONS DIRECTLY AFFECT BOND PRICES   There is another way to understand why when bond prices change in one direction, interest rates will change in opposite directions. We know that when the Federal Reserve buys bonds in the open market, interest rates fall. But think about what the Federal Reserve is doing when it conducts the open market purchase. The Federal Reserve is buying bonds from the public. As the Fed buys bonds, it increases the demand for bonds and raises their price. This is another reason bond prices rise as interest rates fall.

Similarly, interest rates rise following an open market sale of bonds by the Fed. When the Fed conducts an open market sale, it is selling bonds, increasing the supply of bonds in the market. With an increase in the supply of bonds, the price of bonds will fall.

Because the Federal Reserve can change interest rates with open-market purchases and sales and thereby affect the price of bonds, you can now see why Wall Street firms typically hire Fed watchers (often former officials of the Federal Reserve) to try to predict what the Fed will do. If a Wall Street firm correctly predicts the Fed will surprise the market and lower interest rates, the firm could buy millions of dollars of bonds for itself or its clients prior to the Fed's announcement and make vast profits as the prices of the bonds inevitably rise.

GOOD NEWS FOR THE ECONOMY IS BAD NEWS FOR BOND PRICES   You may have heard on television or read in the newspaper that prices in the bond market often fall in the face of good economic news, such as an increase in real output. Are the markets perverse? Why is good news for the economy bad news for the bond market?

We can understand the behavior of the bond market by thinking about the demand for money. When real GDP increases, the demand for money will increase.

As the demand for money increases, the money demand curve will shift to the right. From our model of the money market, we know that increased money demand will increase interest rates. Bond prices move in the opposite direction from interest rates. Therefore, good news for the economy is bad for the bond market.

14.4 INTEREST RATES AND HOW THEY CHANGE INVESTMENT AND OUTPUT (GDP)

Higher or lower interest rates are just a means to an end, though, for the Fed. The Fed's ultimate goal is to change output—either to slow or speed the economy by influencing aggregate demand.

To show how the Fed affects the interest rate, which in turn affects investment (a component of GDP), and finally GDP itself, we combine our demand and supply for money with the curve that shows how investment spending is related to interest rates. This appears in Figure 14.5. Panel A in Figure 14.5 shows how interest rates are determined by the demand and supply for money. It is identical to Figure 14.3 on page 297, which we studied earlier. The graph shows us the equilibrium interest rate for money. Now let's move to Panel B in Figure 14.5. We can see that at the equilibrium interest rate r^* the level of investment in the economy will be given by I^*.

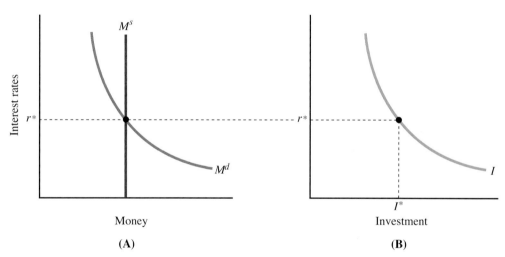

▲ **FIGURE 14.5**
The Money Market and Investment Spending
The equilibrium interest rate r^* is determined in the money market. At that interest rate, investment spending is given by I^*.

We should note that consumption as well as investment can depend on interest rates. That is, spending on consumer durables, such as automobiles and refrigerators, will also depend negatively on the rate of interest. Consumer durables are really investment goods for the household: If you buy an automobile, you incur the cost today and receive benefits, such as the ability to use the car, in the future. As interest rates rise, the opportunity costs of investing in an automobile will rise. Consumers will respond to the increase in opportunity cost by purchasing fewer cars. In this chapter, we discuss how changes in interest rates affect investment, but keep in mind that the purchases of consumer durables are affected too.

In Figure 14.6, we show the effects of an increase in the money supply using our money market and investment graphs. As the supply of money increases, interest rates fall from r_0 to r_1. With lower interest rates, investment spending will increase from I_0 to I_1. This increase in investment spending will then increase aggregate demand—the total demand for goods and services in the economy—and shift the aggregate demand curve to the right.

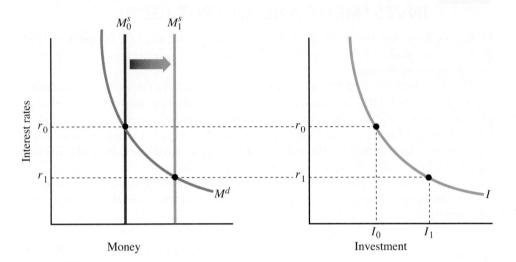

▲ FIGURE 14.6
Monetary Policy and Interest Rates
As the money supply increases, interest rates fall from r_0 to r_1. Investment spending increases from I_0 to I_1.

We show the shift of the aggregate demand curve in Figure 14.7. With the increase in aggregate demand, both output (y) and the price level (P) in the economy as a whole will increase in the short run. Thus, by reducing interest rates, the Fed affects output and prices in the economy.

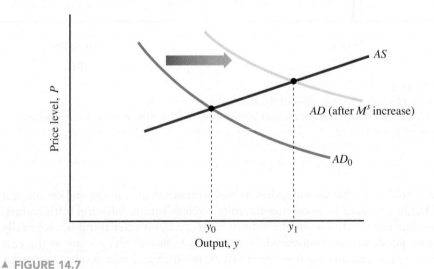

▲ FIGURE 14.7
Money Supply and Aggregate Demand
When the money supply is increased, investment spending increases, shifting the AD curve to the right. Output increases and prices increase in the short run.

In summary, when the Fed increases the money supply, it leads to lower interest rates and increased investment spending. In turn, a higher level of investment spending will ultimately lead to a higher level of GDP.

open market bond purchases $\rightarrow$ increase in money supply $\rightarrow$ fall in interest rates $\rightarrow$ rise in investment spending $\rightarrow$ increase in GDP

The Fed can also use its influence to increase interest rates, which will have the exact opposite effect. Investment spending will fall, along with aggregate demand. The aggregate demand curve will shift to the left, and the price level and output in the economy will fall, too. We can again represent this entire sequence of events:

open market bond sale $\rightarrow$ decrease in money supply $\rightarrow$ rise in interest rates $\rightarrow$ fall in investment spending $\rightarrow$ decrease in GDP

Monetary Policy and International Trade

We have been discussing monetary policy without taking into account international trade or international movements of financial funds across countries. Once we bring in these considerations, we will see that monetary policy operates through an additional route.

Suppose the Federal Reserve lowers U.S. interest rates through an open market purchase of bonds. As a result, investors in the United States will be earning lower interest rates and will seek to invest some of their funds abroad. To invest abroad, they will need to sell their U.S. dollars and buy the foreign currency of the country where they intend to invest. This will affect the **exchange rate**—the rate at which one currency trades for another currency in the market. As more investors sell their dollars to buy foreign currency, the exchange rate will fall. A fall in the exchange rate or a decrease in the value of a currency is called **depreciation of a currency**. Lower U.S. interest rates brought on by the Fed will cause the dollar to depreciate. This will ultimately change the demand and supply of goods and services around the globe because it will make U.S. goods cheaper than foreign goods. Let's see why.

In this case, the lower value of the dollar will mean that U.S. goods become relatively cheaper on world markets. Suppose the exchange rate is two Swiss francs to the dollar, meaning you will receive two Swiss francs for every dollar you exchange. If a U.S. machine sells for $100,000, it will cost 200,000 Swiss francs. Now suppose the value of the dollar depreciates so that one dollar now buys only one Swiss franc. The same U.S. machine will now cost Swiss residents half of what they used to pay for it—just 100,000 francs instead of 200,000. In other words, the lower value of the dollar makes U.S. goods cheaper for foreigners. As a result, foreign residents will want to buy more U.S. goods, and U.S. companies will want to export more goods to meet the higher foreign demand.

That's the good news about the lower value of the U.S. dollar. The bad news is that the lower value of the dollar will make it more expensive for U.S. residents to buy foreign goods. If the exchange rate were still two Swiss francs to the dollar as it originally was at the outset of our example, Swiss chemicals with a price tag of 60,000 francs would cost a U.S. resident $30,000. If the exchange rate of the dollar depreciates to one franc per dollar, however, the same chemicals will cost twice as much—$60,000. As the dollar depreciates, imports become more expensive, and U.S. residents tend to import fewer of them.

exchange rate
The price at which currencies trade for one another in the market.

depreciation of a currency
A decrease in the value of a currency.

Let's recap this: As the exchange rate for the U.S. dollar falls, U.S. goods become cheaper and foreign goods become more expensive. The United States then exports more goods and imports fewer goods. *Net* exports increase, in other words. This increase in net exports increases the demand for U.S. goods and increases GDP. Remember that this all began with an open market purchase of bonds by the Fed that increased the money supply. Here is the sequence of events:

open market bond purchase	→	increase in money supply	→	fall in interest rates	→	fall in exchange rate	→	increase in net exports	→	increase in GDP

The three new links in the sequence are from interest rates to exchange rates, from exchange rates to net exports, and from net exports to GDP.

This sequence also works in reverse. If the Fed conducts an open market sale of bonds, U.S. interest rates rise. As a result, foreign investors earning lower interest rates elsewhere will want to move their money to the United States where they can earn a higher return. As they buy more U.S. dollars, the exchange rate for the dollar will increase, and the dollar will increase in value. An increase in the value of a currency is called **appreciation of a currency**. The appreciation of the dollar will make U.S. goods more expensive for foreigners and imports cheaper for U.S. residents. Suppose the U.S. dollar appreciates, and each dollar can now be exchanged for three Swiss francs instead of two. The same machine the Swiss had to pay 200,000 francs for when the exchange rate was one dollar to two francs now costs 300,000 francs. The Swiss chemicals U.S. residents bought for $30,000 will now cost them less—just $20,000.

When U.S. interest rates rise as a result of an open market sale by the Fed, we expect exports to decrease and imports to increase, decreasing net exports. The decrease in net exports will reduce the demand for U.S. goods and lead to a fall in output. Here is the sequence of events:

open market bond sale	→	decrease in money supply	→	rise in interest rates	→	rise in exchange rate	→	decrease in net exports	→	decrease in GDP

appreciation of a currency
An increase in the value of a currency.

To summarize, an increase in interest rates will reduce both investment spending (including consumer durables) and net exports. A decrease in interest rates will increase investment spending and net exports. As you can see, monetary policy in an open economy is even more powerful than monetary policy used in a closed economy.

The Fed and other central banks are well aware of the power they have to influence exchange rates and international trade. Countries that depend extensively on international trade—such as Canada and Switzerland—find that the effects of monetary policy on exchange rates are critical to their economic well-being. We'll study these issues in more depth in Chapter 19.

14.5 MONETARY POLICY CHALLENGES FOR THE FED

Now that we have seen how changes in the money supply affect aggregate demand, we can see that the government has two different types of tools to change the level of GDP in the short run: The government can use either fiscal policy—changes in the level of taxes or government spending—or monetary policy—changes in the supply of money and interest rates—to alter the level of GDP.

If the current level of GDP is below full employment or potential output, the government can use expansionary policies such as tax cuts, increased spending, or

APPLICATION 3

THE EFFECTIVENESS OF COMMITTEES

APPLYING THE CONCEPTS #3: Is it better for decisions about monetary policy to be made by a single individual or by a committee?

When Professor Alan Blinder returned to teaching after serving as vice-chairman of the Federal Reserve from 1994 to 1996, he was convinced that committees were not effective for making decisions about monetary policy. With another researcher, Blinder developed an experiment to determine whether individuals or groups make better decisions.

The experiment Blinder and his colleague developed was designed to explore how quickly individuals and groups could distinguish between changes in underlying trends and random events. For example, if unemployment were to rise in one month, it could be a temporary aberration or it could be the beginning of a recession. Changing monetary policy would be a mistake if the rise were temporary, but waiting too long to change policy would be costly if the change were permanent. Who is better at making these sorts of determinations?

The results of the experiment showed that committees make decisions as quickly as, and more accurately than, individuals making decisions by themselves. Moreover, it was not the performance of the individual committee members that contributed to the superiority of committee decisions—the actual *process* of having meetings and discussions appears to have improved the group's overall performance.

In later research, Blinder also found that it did not really matter whether the committee had a strong leader. His findings suggest it is the wisdom of the group, not its leader, that really matters. Also, to the extent the leader has too much power—and the committee functions more like an individual than a group—monetary policy will actually be worse!   **Related to Exercise 5.9.**

SOURCES: Based on Alan Krueger, "Economic Scene: A Study Shows Committees Can Be More Than the Sum of Their Members," *New York Times*, December 7, 2000, and Alan Blinder and John Morgan, "Leadership in Groups: A Monetary Experiment," (working paper no. 13391, National Bureau of Economic Research, September 2007).

---

increases in the money supply to raise the level of GDP and reduce unemployment. If the current level of GDP exceeds full employment or potential output, the economy will overheat, and the rate of inflation will increase. To avoid this overheating, the government can use contractionary policies to reduce the level of GDP back to full employment or potential output.

In Chapter 10, we explored some of the limitations of stabilization policy. We saw that fiscal policy is subject to lags and fraught with complications because political parties have different ideas about what the government should or should not do, and it takes them time to reach agreement. Monetary policy also has its complications.

Lags in Monetary Policy

Recall that there are two types of lags in policy. *Inside lags* are the time it takes for policymakers to recognize and implement policy changes. *Outside lags* are the time it takes for policy to actually work.

The inside lags for monetary policy are relatively short compared to those for fiscal policy. The FOMC meets eight times a year and can decide on major policy changes at any time and very quickly. It can even give the chairperson of the Board of Governors some discretion to make changes between meetings.

Of course, it does take time for the people working at the Fed to recognize that problems are beginning to occur in the economy. A good example is the 1990 recession. In 1990, Iraq invaded Kuwait. After the invasion, there was some concern that higher oil prices and the uncertainty of the political situation in Kuwait would trigger a recession in the United States, which, of course, is heavily dependent on oil. However, Alan Greenspan, then chairman of the Federal Reserve, testified before Congress as late as October 1990 that the economy had not yet slipped into a recession. Not until December did Greenspan declare that the economy had entered into a recession. Yet, looking back, we now know the recession had actually started five months earlier, in July.

The outside lags related to monetary policy, however, are quite long. Most econometric models predict it will take at least two years for most of the effects of an interest rate cut to be felt. This delay means that for the Fed to conduct successful monetary policy, it must be able to accurately forecast two years in the future! However, the Fed has difficulty predicting when recessions are about to occur. As an example, in May 2000 the Fed—fearing a rise in inflation—raised the federal funds rate from 6.00 to 6.50 percent. Yet, on January 3, 2001, the Fed reversed itself and restored the rate to 6.00 percent, because it feared a recession. It was too little—and too late—to prevent the 2001 recession.

Because of the lags for monetary policy and the difficulties of forecasting the economy, many economists believe the Fed should not take a very active role in trying to stabilize the economy. Instead, they recommend the Fed concentrate on keeping the inflation rate low and stable.

Decisions about monetary policy are made by a committee. How does this affect the effectiveness of monetary policy?

Influencing Market Expectations: From the Federal Funds Rate to Interest Rates on Long-Term Bonds

It is important to recognize that the Fed directly controls only very short-term interest rates in the economy, not long-term interest rates. In fact, when the Fed makes its decisions on monetary policy, it really decides what the rate should be in the federal funds market—the market in which banks trade reserves *overnight*. Once the Fed decides what rate it wants in the market, it conducts open-market operations—buying and selling short-term government bonds—to achieve this rate. Thus, when the Federal Reserve decides the course of monetary policy, it is really just setting a very short-term interest rate for the economy.

However, when a firm is deciding on a long-term investment or a household is deciding whether to purchase a new home, it will base its decisions on the interest rate at which it can borrow money, and this will typically be a long-term interest rate—not a short-term rate. For example, a household might take out a 30-year mortgage to purchase a home. If the rate is too high, it might not take out the loan. So for the Fed to control investment spending it must also somehow influence long-term rates. It can do this indirectly by influencing short-term rates. Here's how.

Long-term interest rates can be thought of as averages of current and expected future short-term interest rates. To see why future short-term interest rates are important, consider putting $100 of your money in the bank for two years. If the interest rate is 5 percent for the first year, you would have $105 at the end of that year. If the interest rate for the following year were 10 percent, you would then have $115.50 ($105 × 1.10) at the end of the second year. *Both* the current short-term interest rate (5 percent) and next year's short-term interest rate (10 percent) would determine the value of your bank account. Similarly, both the current short-term interest rate and future short-term rates determine the present value of payments in the future on a bond or loan. Long-term interest rates are an average of the current short-term interest rate and expected future short-term rates.

The Fed can directly control the federal funds rate and other short-term interest rates. Its actions also provide information to the market about the likely course for future short-term rates. If the Fed wishes to stimulate long-term investment by cutting the short-term interest rate, it must also convince the public that it will keep future short-term rates low as well in order to reduce long-term interest rates. Influencing expectations of the financial markets is an important part of the Fed's job.

The Fed does try to communicate its general intentions for future policy actions to the public to help make those policies more effective. However, the public ultimately must form its own expectations of what the Fed is going to do. Coping with financial market expectations complicates the Fed's task in developing monetary policy. The Fed itself has debated how best to communicate with the financial markets.

To further complicate matters, the Fed can also monitor the public's expectations of its future policies in the financial markets. There are now "futures" markets for the federal funds rates in which market participants essentially place bets on future federal funds rates. Thus, before the Fed takes any actions on interest rates or even makes any statements about its future intentions, it can see what the market is thinking. The Fed has to decide whether to take actions consistent with market expectations of Fed actions or to surprise the market in some way.

To cope with this trend, the Fed has gradually become more open in its deliberations. For many years, the Fed would not even say whether it had changed interest rates. These policies began to change slowly in the 1990s. Starting in 2000, after each FOMC meeting the Fed has announced its target for the federal funds rate and made a brief statement explaining its actions.

Looking Ahead: From the Short Run to the Long Run

The model for monetary policy we developed in this chapter can help you understand the behavior of the economy only in the short run, when prices do not change very much. Monetary policy can affect output in the short run when prices are largely fixed, but in the long run changes in the money supply affect only the price level and inflation. In the long run, the Federal Reserve can only indirectly control nominal interest rates, and it can't control *real* interest rates—the rate after inflation is figured in. In the next part of the book, we will explain how output and prices change over time, and how the economy makes the transition by itself from the short to the long run regardless of what the Fed does.

SUMMARY

This chapter showed how monetary policy affects aggregate demand and the economy in the short run. Together, the demand for money by the public and the supply of money determined by the Federal Reserve determine interest rates. Changes in interest rates will in turn affect investment and output. In the international economy, interest rates also affect exchange rates and

net exports. Still, there are limits to what effective monetary policies can do. Here are the main points of the chapter:

1 The demand for money depends negatively on the interest rate and positively on the level of prices and real GDP.

2 The Fed can determine the supply of money through *open market purchases and sales,* changing reserve requirements, changing the discount rate, or increasing lending to banks and other institutions. Open market operations are the primary tool the Fed uses to implement monetary policy.

3 The level of interest rates is determined in the *money market* by the demand for money and the supply of money.

4 To increase the level of GDP, the Federal Reserve buys bonds on the open market. To decrease the level of GDP, the Federal Reserve sells bonds on the open market.

5 An increase in the money supply will decrease interest rates, increase investment spending, and increase output. A decrease in the money supply will increase interest rates, decrease investment spending, and decrease output.

6 In an open economy, a decrease in interest rates will depreciate the local currency and lead to an increase in net exports. Conversely, an increase in interest rates will appreciate the local currency and lead to a decrease in net exports.

7 Both lags in economic policies and the need to influence market expectations make successful monetary policy difficult in practice.

KEY TERMS

appreciation of a currency, p. 304

depreciation of a currency, p. 303

discount rate, p. 296

exchange rate, p. 303

federal funds market, p. 296

federal funds rate, p. 297

illiquid, p. 294

liquidity demand for money, p. 294

money market, p. 292

open market operations, p. 295

open market purchases, p. 295

open market sales, p. 295

speculative demand for money, p. 294

transaction demand for money, p. 292

EXERCISES

Visit www.myeconlab.com to complete these exercises online and get instant feedback.

14.1 The Money Market

1.1 We measure the opportunity cost of holding money with _____.

1.2 Money demand will _____ (increase/decrease) as prices fall.

1.3 The principle of _____ suggests that the demand for money should increase as prices increase.

1.4 The _____ demand for money arises because individuals and businesses use money in ordinary business.

1.5 **Checking Account Interest Rates.** During the 1980s, banks started to pay interest (at low rates) on checking accounts for the first time. Given what you know about opportunity costs, how would interest paid on checking affect the demand for money?

1.6 **Pegging Interest Rates.** Suppose the Federal Reserve wanted to fix, or "peg," the level of interest rates at 6 percent per year. Using a simple demand-and-supply graph, show how increases in money demand would change the supply of money if the Federal Reserve pursued the policy of this fixed interest rate. Use your answer to explain this statement: "If the Federal Reserve pegs interest rates, it loses control of the money supply."

1.7 **An ATM Next to Your Apartment Building.** Suppose an ATM connected to your own bank is installed right next to your apartment building.

a. How will this affect the average amount of currency you carry around with you?

b. If you withdraw funds at your ATM only from your checking account, will your action have any effect on total money demand?

1.8 **Flea Markets and the Demand for Money.** People often like to visit flea markets to look for unexpected opportunities. Flea markets also typically use cash. Explain why this is an example of the liquidity demand for money.

14.2 How the Federal Reserve Can Change the Money Supply

2.1 To increase the supply of money, the Fed should _____ bonds.

2.2 Increasing reserve requirements _____ the supply of money.

2.3 Banks trade reserves with one another in the _____ market.

2.4 Banks borrow from the Fed at the _____ rate.

2.5 **Purchasing Foreign Currency.** What would happen to the supply of money if a central bank purchased foreign currency held by the public?

2.6 **China's Increase in Reserve Requirements.** The Chinese government purchased U.S. dollars in the foreign exchange market with Chinese currency. During the same period, the Chinese sharply raised the reserve requirement on banks because they wanted to prevent the money supply from expanding too rapidly. Explain carefully how these two actions, taken together, could keep the supply of money in China from increasing.

2.7 **Other Channels of Monetary Policy.** Consider this quote: "Monetary policy does not work simply through lowering interest rates. Sometimes it can directly affect particular credit markets in the economy." Can you give an example of actions that the Fed has taken that fit this quotation? (Related to Application 1 on page 296.)

14.3 How Interest Rates Are Determined: Combining the Demand and Supply of Money

3.1 Interest rates typically fall in a recession because the demand for money depends _____ on changes in real income.

3.2 If interest rates are 9 percent per year, the price of a bond that promises to pay $109 next year will be equal to _____.

3.3 Through its effect on money demand, an increase in prices will _____ interest rates.

3.4 Open market purchases lead to rising bond prices and _____ interest rates.

3.5 **Pricing a Bond.** If a bond promises to pay $110 next year and the interest rate is 5 percent per year:
a. What will the price of the bond be?
b. What will the new price of the bond be if the interest rate falls to 3 percent?

3.6 **Buy or Sell Bonds?** If you strongly believed the Federal Reserve was going to surprise the markets and raise interest rates, would you want to buy bonds or sell bonds?

3.7 **Recessions and Interest Rates.** The economy starts to head into a recession. Using a graph of the money market, show what happens to interest rates. What happens to bond prices? (Related to Application 2 on page 300.)

3.8 **A Decrease in the Riskiness of the Stock Market.** If investors began to think the stock market is becoming less risky, how will this belief affect the demand for money? Would this more likely affect M1 or M2?

3.9 **Rising Prices and the Money Market.** Draw a graph of the money market to show the effects of an increase in prices on interest rates.

14.4 Interest Rates and How They Change Investment and Output (GDP)

4.1 When the Federal Reserve sells bonds on the open market, it leads to _____ (higher/lower) levels of investment and output in the economy.

4.2 To decrease the level of output, the Fed should conduct an open market _____ (sale/purchase) of bonds.

4.3 An open market purchase _____ the supply of money, which _____ interest rates, which _____ investment, and finally results in a(n) _____ in output.

4.4 An increase in the supply of money will _____ (appreciate/depreciate) a country's currency.

4.5 **Interest Rates, Durable Goods, and Nondurable Goods.** Refrigerators and clothing are to some extent durable. Explain why the decision to purchase a refrigerator is likely to be more sensitive to interest rates than the decision to buy clothing.

4.6 **Where Is Monetary Policy Stronger?** In an open economy, changes in monetary policy affect both interest rates and exchange rates. Comparing the United States and Switzerland, in which country would monetary policy have a more significant effect on GDP through changes in exchange rates?

4.7 **Side Effects of Supporting a Currency.** Suppose a country's currency came under attack by speculators, and to prevent the value of its currency from falling, the central bank needed to raise interest rates. What would be the side effect of such a policy?

14.5 Monetary Policy Challenges for the Fed

5.1 _____ (Inside/Outside) lags are longer for the Fed.

5.2 Experimental evidence shows us that individuals perform _____ than committees in making monetary policy decisions.

5.3 Long-term interest rates can be thought of as _____ of short-term rates.

5.4 The Fed directly controls long-term interest rates. _____ (True/False)

5.5 **Open Economies and Outside Lags in Monetary Policy.** Research suggests that the effects of monetary policy through interest rates, exchange rates, and net exports are more rapid than the effects of monetary policy on investment. As an economy becomes more open, how will this change affect the outside lag in monetary policy?

5.6 **Asset Prices as a Guide to Monetary Policy?** Some central bankers have looked at asset prices, such as prices of stocks, to guide monetary policy. The idea is that if stock prices begin to rise, it might signal future inflation or an overheated economy. Are there any dangers to using the stock market as a guide to monetary policy?

5.7 Rates on Two-Year Bonds and One-Year Bonds. Suppose the interest rate on a two-year bond was higher than the interest rate on a one-year bond. What does the market believe will happen next year to one-year interest rates?

5.8 International Influences on Fed Policy. As international trade becomes more important, monetary policy becomes more heavily influenced by developments in the foreign exchange markets. Go to the Web page of the Federal Reserve (www.federalreserve.gov) and read some recent speeches given by Fed officials. Do international considerations seem to affect policymakers in the United States today?

5.9 Are Federal Reserve Chairmen Too Powerful? Economic research has shown that the chairman of the Federal Reserve is more powerful, relative to other committee members, than the head of the central bank in other countries. Fed chairpersons have much more influence over actual decisions than other members. Recall Professor Blinder's findings that committees make better decisions than individuals and that leaders of groups, per se, do not matter for the quality of decision making. Make an argument that the tradition of a strong chairman in the United States reduces the effectiveness of monetary policy. (Related to Application 3 on page 305.)

5.10 Should the Fed Adopt a Fixed Formula for Monetary Policy? Some economists suggest that the Fed should follow an explicit rule or formula for monetary policy. For example, the rule would specify how interest rates would change based on changes in real GDP and inflation. Only with a fixed rule, these economists argue, would the public really understand the Fed's future intentions for policy. What are some of the disadvantages of adopting an explicit rule or formula?

Modern Macroeconomics: From the Short Run to the Long Run

Just prior to the start of the December 2007 recession, unemployment stood at 4.7 percent. It rose to over 10 percent in 2009. In 2010 both the Federal Reserve Board and the Congressional Budget Office projected that unemployment would still remain above 7 percent in 2012. Thus, looking ahead to five years after the recession started, unemployment was still forecast to be stubbornly high.

This path for prolonged unemployment raises a number of questions. What forces bring the economy back to full employment? How fast do these forces work by themselves? What policies, if any, can speed this process along?

These questions are not new. They were tackled by John Maynard Keynes in the 1930s and, in modern times, by leading economists like Milton Friedman and Paul Samuelson. Some economists advocate aggressive government action, but others feel that such actions may impede the recovery. The debate continues today.

APPLYING THE CONCEPTS

1 What steps can policymakers take to deal with a possible liquidity trap?
Avoiding a Liquidity Trap

2 What are the links between presidential elections and macroeconomic performance?
Elections, Political Parties, and Voter Expectations

3 Will increases in health-care expenditures crowd out consumption or investment spending?
Increasing Health-Care Expenditures and Crowding Out

One of the great debates surrounding macroeconomic policymaking centers on the short run versus the long run. Up to this point in the book, we have discussed the short and long run separately. Now, however, we'll explain how the economy evolves *from* the short run *to* the long run. The relationship between the two is one of the most important dimensions of modern macroeconomics, which carefully distinguishes between them.

15.1 LINKING THE SHORT RUN AND THE LONG RUN

To begin to understand how the short run and the long run are related, let's return to what we mean by each in macroeconomics.

The Difference between the Short and Long Run

short run in macroeconomics
The period of time in which prices do not change or do not change very much.

long run in macroeconomics
The period of time in which prices have fully adjusted to any economic changes.

In Chapter 9, we explained how in the short run, wages and prices are sticky and do not change immediately in response to changes in demand. The **short run in macroeconomics** is the period of time over which prices do not change or do not change very much. Over time, though, wages and prices adjust, and the economy reaches its long-run equilibrium. Short-run analysis applies to the period when wages and prices do not change—at least not substantially. Long-run, full-employment economics applies after wages and prices have largely adjusted to changes in demand. The **long run in macroeconomics** is the period of time in which prices have fully adjusted to any economic changes.

In the short run, GDP is determined by the current demand for goods and services in the economy, so fiscal policy—such as tax cuts or increased government spending—and monetary policy—such as adjusting the money supply—can affect demand and GDP. However, in the long run, GDP is determined by the supply of labor, the stock of capital, and technological progress—in other words, the willingness of people to work and the overall resources the economy has to work with. Full employment is another characteristic of the long run. Because the economy is operating at full employment in the long run, output can't be increased in response to changes in demand. So, for example, an increase in government spending won't increase GDP in the long run because spending on one good or service has to come at the expense of another good or service. Similarly, increasing the supply of money won't increase GDP in the long run either. It will only cause the price level in the economy to rise.

Should economic policy be guided by what we expect to happen in the short run or what we expect to happen in the long run? To answer this question, we need to know two things:

1 How does what happens in the short run determine what happens in the long run?
2 How long is the short run?

Wages and Prices and Their Adjustment over Time

Wages and prices change every day. If the demand for scooters rises at the same time that demand for tennis rackets falls, we would expect to see a rise in the price of scooters and a fall in the price of tennis rackets. Wages in the scooter industry would tend to increase, and wages in the tennis racket industry would tend to fall.

Sometimes, we see wages and prices in all industries rising or falling together. For example, prices for steel, automobiles, food, and fuel may all rise together. Why? Wages and prices will all tend to increase together during booms when GDP exceeds its full-employment level or potential output. Wages and prices will fall together during periods of recessions when GDP falls below full employment or potential output.

If the economy is producing at a level above full employment, firms will find it increasingly difficult to hire and retain workers, and unemployment will be below its natural rate. Workers will find it easy to get and change jobs. To attract workers and prevent them from leaving, firms will raise their wages. As one firm raises its wage, other firms will have to raise their wages even higher to attract the workers that remain.

Wages are the largest cost of production for most firms. Consequently, as labor costs increase, firms have no choice but to increase the prices of their products. However, as prices rise, workers need higher nominal wages to maintain their real wages. This is an illustration of the real-nominal principle.

REAL-NOMINAL PRINCIPLE

What matters to people is the real value of money or income—its purchasing power—not the face value of money or income.

This process by which rising wages cause higher prices and higher prices feed higher wages is known as a **wage–price spiral**. It occurs when the economy is producing at a level of output that exceeds its potential.

wage–price spiral
The process by which changes in wages and prices cause further changes in wages and prices.

When the economy is producing below full employment or potential output, the process works in reverse. Unemployment will exceed the natural rate. Firms will find it easy to hire and retain workers, and they can offer workers less. As all firms cut wages, the average level of wages in the economy falls. As we have said, wages are the largest component of firms' costs. So, when wages fall, prices start to fall, too. In this case, the wage–price spiral works in reverse.

Table 15.1 summarizes our discussion of unemployment, output, and changes in wages. Let's emphasize one point: In addition to the changes in wages and prices that occur when the economy is producing at more or less than full employment, there is also typically ongoing inflation in the economy. For example, suppose an economy that has been operating at full employment has been experiencing 4 percent annual inflation. If output later exceeds full employment, prices will begin to rise at a rate faster than 4 percent. Conversely, if output falls to a level less than full employment, prices will then rise at a slower rate than 4 percent.

TABLE 15.1 UNEMPLOYMENT, OUTPUT, AND WAGE AND PRICE CHANGES	
When unemployment is below the natural rate . . .	When unemployment is above the natural rate . . .
• output is above potential. • wages and prices rise.	• output is below potential. • wages and prices fall.

In summary, when output exceeds potential output, wages and prices throughout the economy will rise above previous inflation rates. If output is less than potential output, wages and prices will fall relative to previous inflation rates. (We will explore ongoing inflation more in Chapter 16.)

15.2 HOW WAGE AND PRICE CHANGES MOVE THE ECONOMY NATURALLY BACK TO FULL EMPLOYMENT

The transition between the short run and the long run is easy to understand. If GDP is higher than potential output, the economy starts to overheat and wages and prices increase. This increase in wages and prices will then push the economy back to full employment.

Using aggregate demand and aggregate supply, we can illustrate graphically how changing prices and wages help move the economy from the short to the long run. First, let's review the graphical representations of aggregate demand and aggregate supply:

aggregate demand curve

A curve that shows the relationship between the level of prices and the quantity of real GDP demanded.

1 *Aggregate demand.* Recall from Chapter 9 that the **aggregate demand curve** shows the relationship between the level of prices and the quantity of real GDP demanded.

2 *Aggregate supply.* Also recall from Chapter 9 that there are two aggregate supply curves: one for the short run and one for the long run. The **short-run aggregate supply curve** is represented as a relatively flat curve. The shape of the curve reflects the idea that prices do not change very much in the short run and that firms adjust production to meet demand. The **long-run aggregate supply curve**, however, is represented by a perfectly vertical line. The vertical line means that at any given price level, firms in the long run are producing all that they can, given the amount of labor, capital, and technology available to them in the economy. The line represents what firms can supply in the long run at a state of full employment or potential output.

short-run aggregate supply curve

A relatively flat aggregate supply curve that represents the idea that prices do not change very much in the short run and that firms adjust production to meet demand.

long-run aggregate supply curve

A vertical aggregate supply curve that reflects the idea that in the long run, output is determined solely by the factors of production and technology.

Returning to Full Employment from a Recession

In Chapter 9, we looked at the adjustment process for an economy producing at a level of output exceeding full employment or potential output. Now let's look at what happens if the economy is in a slump, producing below full employment or potential output. Panel A of Figure 15.1 shows an aggregate demand curve and the two aggregate supply curves. In the short run, output and prices are determined where the aggregate demand curve intersects the short-run aggregate supply curve—point *a*. This point corresponds to the level of output y_0 and a price level P_0. Notice that y_0 is a level less than full employment or potential output, y_p. In the long run, the level of prices and output is given by the intersection of the aggregate demand curve and the long-run aggregate supply curve—point *c*. Output is at full employment, y_p, and prices are at P_F. How does the economy move from point *a* in the short run to point *c* in the long run? Panel B shows us how.

At point *a*, the current level of output, y_0, falls short of the full-employment level of output, y_p. With output less than full employment, the unemployment rate is above the natural rate. Firms find it relatively easy to hire and retain workers, and wages and then prices begin to fall. As the level of prices decreases, the short-run aggregate supply curve shifts downward over time, as shown in Panel B. This downward shift occurs because decreases in wages lower costs for firms. Competition between firms will lead to lower prices for their products.

As shown in Panel B, this shift in the short-run aggregate supply curve will bring the economy to long-run equilibrium. The economy initially starts at point *a*,

▶ **FIGURE 15.1**

How the Economy Recovers from a Downturn

If the economy is operating below full employment, as shown in Panel A, prices will fall, shifting down the short-run aggregate supply curve, as shown in Panel B. This will return output to its full-employment level.

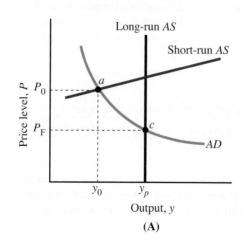

(A)

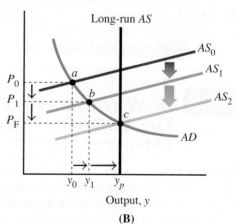

(B)

where output falls short of full employment. As prices fall from P_0 to P_1, the aggregate supply curve shifts downward from AS_0 to AS_1. The aggregate demand curve and the new aggregate supply curve intersect at point b. This point corresponds to a lower level of prices and a higher level of real output. However, the higher level of output still is less than full employment. Wages and prices will continue to fall, shifting the short-run aggregate supply curve downward.

Eventually, the aggregate supply curve will shift to AS_2, and the economy will reach point c, the intersection of the aggregate demand curve and the long-run aggregate supply curve. At this point, the adjustment stops because the economy is at full employment and the unemployment rate is at the natural rate. With unemployment at the natural rate, the downward wage–price spiral ends. The economy has made the transition to the long run. Prices are lower and output returns to full employment. This is how an economy recovers from a recession or a downturn.

Returning to Full Employment from a Boom

But what if the economy is "too hot" instead of sluggish? What will then happen is the process we just described, only in reverse, as we show in Figure 15.2. When output exceeds potential, unemployment will be below the natural rate. As firms bid for labor, the wage–price spiral will begin, but this time in an upward direction instead of downward as in Panel B. The short-run aggregate supply curve will shift upward until the economy returns to full employment. That is, wages and prices will rise to return the economy to its long-run equilibrium at full employment.

In summary:

- If output is less than full employment, prices will fall as the economy returns to full employment, as shown in Figure 15.1.

- If output exceeds full employment, prices will rise and output will fall back to full employment, as shown in Figure 15.2.

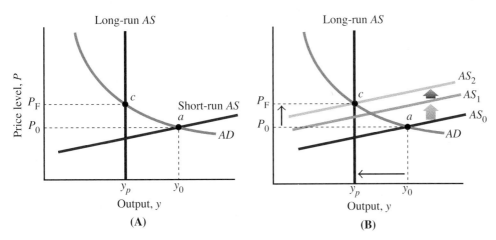

▲ **FIGURE 15.2**
How the Economy Returns from a Boom
If the economy is operating above full employment, as shown in Panel A, prices will rise, shifting the short-run aggregate supply curve upward, as shown in Panel B. This will return output to its full-employment level.

Economic Policy and the Speed of Adjustment

How long does it take to move from the short run to the long run? Economists disagree on the answer. Some economists estimate it takes the U.S. economy two years or less, some say six years, and others say somewhere in between. Because the adjustment process is slow, there is room, in principle, for policymakers to step in and guide the economy back to full employment.

Suppose the economy is operating below full employment at point *a* in Figure 15.3. One alternative for policymakers is to do nothing, allowing the economy to adjust itself with falling wages and prices until it returns by itself to full employment, point *b*. This may take several years. During that time, the economy will experience excess unemployment and a level of real output below potential.

▶ **FIGURE 15.3**

Using Economic Policy to Fight a Recession

Rather than letting the economy naturally return to full employment at point *b*, economic policies could be implemented to increase aggregate demand from AD_0 to AD_1 to bring the economy to full employment at point *c*. The price level within the economy, however, would be higher.

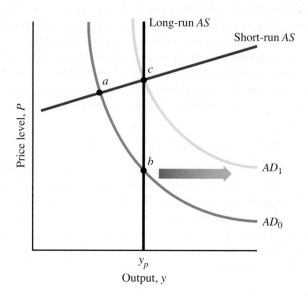

Another alternative is to use expansionary policies, such as open market purchases by the Fed or increases in government spending and tax cuts, to shift the aggregate demand curve to the right. In Figure 15.3, we show how expansionary policies could shift the aggregate demand curve from AD_0 to AD_1 and move the economy to full employment, point *c*. Notice here that the price level is higher at point *c* than it would be at point *b*.

Demand policies can also prevent a wage–price spiral from emerging if the economy is producing at a level of output above full employment. Rather than letting an increase in wages and prices bring the economy back to full employment, we can reduce aggregate demand. Either contractionary monetary policy—open market sales—or contractionary fiscal policy—cuts in government spending or tax increases—can be used to reduce aggregate demand and the level of GDP until it reaches potential output.

Expansionary policies and demand policies are stabilization policies, which look simple on paper or on graphs. In practice, the lags and uncertainties we discussed for both fiscal and monetary policy make economic stabilization difficult to achieve. For example, suppose we are in a recession and the Fed decides to increase aggregate demand using expansionary monetary policy. There will be a lag in the time it takes for the aggregate demand curve to shift to the right. In the meantime, the adjustment that occurs during a recession—falling wages and prices—has begun to shift the short-run aggregate supply curve downward. It is conceivable that if the adjustment were fast enough, the economy would be restored to full employment before the effects of the expansionary monetary policy were actually felt. When the expansionary monetary policy kicks in and the aggregate demand curve finally shifts to the right, the additional aggregate demand would increase the level of output so it exceeded the full-employment level, leading to a wage–price spiral. In this case, monetary policy would have destabilized the economy.

Active economic policies are more likely to destabilize the economy if the adjustment is quick enough. Economists like Milton Friedman of the University of Chicago (1912–2006) believed the economy adjusts rapidly to full employment and generally opposed using monetary or fiscal policy to try to stabilize the economy. Economists

APPLICATION 1

AVOIDING A LIQUIDITY TRAP

APPLYING THE CONCEPTS #1: What steps can policymakers take to deal with a possible liquidity trap?

As a keen student of the Great Depression, Federal Reserve Chairman Ben Bernanke became concerned when short term interest rates—such as the federal funds rate—fell below 0.5 percent in late 2008 as the Fed responded to the financial crisis. Bernanke recognized that with interest rates already so low, there was little room for the Fed to decrease them further. What steps could the Fed take to deal with what appeared to be a looming liquidity trap?

A number of academic economists suggested that the Fed commit to increasing inflation in the future by promising to create new money far into the future. Then, even if nominal rates could not fall below zero, real rates of interest (nominal minus expected inflation) could be negative. However, since the Fed is responsible for maintaining a low inflation rate, this was not an ideal policy.

The Fed decided to begin paying interest on bank reserves. Although there were several reasons for this policy, one reason that the Fed advanced was that this would put a floor on market interest rates. After all, if banks could earn, for example, 0.5 percent on their reserves, they would not lend those reserves out at lower rates to other banks or make loans at lower rates. The Fed had found a new tool to manage an economy with low interest rates.   **Related to Exercises 2.7 and 2.8.**

---

like John Maynard Keynes believed that the economy adjusted slowly and were more sympathetic to using monetary or fiscal policy to stabilize the economy.

It is possible that the speed of adjustment can vary over time, making decisions about policy even more difficult. As an example, economic advisers for President George H. W. Bush had to decide whether the economy needed any additional stimulus after the recession of 1990. Based on the view that the economy would recover quickly on its own, they took only some minor steps. The economy did largely recover by the very end of the Bush administration, but too late for his reelection prospects.

Liquidity Traps

Up to this point, we have assumed the economy could always recover from a recession without active policy, although it may take a long time. As our chapter-opening story mentioned, Keynes expressed doubts about whether a country could recover from a major recession without active policy. He had two distinct reasons for these doubts. First, as we will discuss later in the chapter, the adjustment process requires interest rates to fall and thereby increase investment spending. But suppose nominal interest rates become so low that they could not fall any further. Keynes called this situation a **liquidity trap**. When the economy is experiencing a liquidity trap, the adjustment process no longer works. Second, Keynes feared falling prices could hurt businesses. Japan seems to have suffered from both these problems in the 1990s.

liquidity trap
A situation in which nominal interest rates are so low, they can no longer fall.

Political Business Cycles

Up to now, we have assumed policymakers are motivated to use policy to try to improve the economy. But suppose they are more interested in promoting their personal well-being and the fortunes of their political parties? Using monetary or fiscal

APPLICATION 2

ELECTIONS, POLITICAL PARTIES, AND VOTER EXPECTATIONS

APPLYING THE CONCEPTS #2: What are the links between presidential elections and macroeconomic performance?

The original political business cycle theories focused on incumbent presidents trying to manipulate the economy in their favor to gain reelection. Subsequent research began to incorporate other, more realistic factors.

The first innovation was to recognize that political parties could have different goals or preferences. In particular, in the United States, Republicans historically have been more concerned about fighting inflation, whereas Democrats have placed more weight on reducing unemployment. Economists and political scientists began to incorporate these *partisan* effects into their analyses.

The second major innovation was to recognize that the public would anticipate that politicians will try to manipulate the economy. Suppose that, if elected, Republicans will contract the economy to fight inflation, whereas Democrats will stimulate the economy to lower unemployment. If the public is not sure who will win the election, the outcome will be a surprise to them—a contractionary surprise if Republicans win and an expansionary surprise if Democrats win. As Professor Alberto Alesina of Harvard University first pointed out, this suggests that economic growth should be less if Republicans win and greater if Democrats win. The postwar U.S. evidence is generally supportive of this theory.   **Related to Exercise 2.9.**

SOURCE: Based on Steven M. Sheffrin, *The Making of Economic Policy* (New York: Basil Blackwell, 1989), chap. 6.

---

political business cycle

The effects on the economy of using monetary or fiscal policy to stimulate the economy before an election to improve reelection prospects.

policy in the short run to improve a politician's reelection prospects may generate what is known as a **political business cycle**.

Here is how a political business cycle might work. About a year or so before an election, a politician might use expansionary monetary policy or fiscal policy to stimulate the economy and lower unemployment. If voters respond favorably to lower unemployment, the incumbent politician may be reelected. After reelection, the politician faces the prospect of higher prices or crowding out. To avoid this, the politician may engage in contractionary policies. The result is a classic political business cycle: Because of actions taken by politicians for reelection, the economy booms before an election but contracts afterwards. Good news comes before the election, and bad news comes later.

It is clear the classic political business cycle does not always occur; however, a number of episodes fit the scenario. President Nixon used expansionary policies during a reelection campaign in 1972, which resulted in inflation. However, counterexamples also exist, such as President Carter's deliberate attempt to reduce inflation with contractionary policies just before his reelection bid in the late 1970s. Although the evidence on the classic political business cycle is mixed, there may be links between elections and economic outcomes. More recent research has investigated the systematic differences that may exist between political parties and economic outcomes. All this research takes into account both the short- and long-run effects of economic policies.

15.3 UNDERSTANDING THE ECONOMICS OF THE ADJUSTMENT PROCESS

Earlier in the chapter we explained that changes in wages and prices restore the economy to full employment in the long run, and that the government and the Fed can get it there more quickly with fiscal and monetary policy. But what is happening behind the scenes? What do changes in wages and the price level mean for the economy in terms of money demand, interest rates, and investment spending? Let's go back and take a closer look at the adjustment process in terms of these factors so we can better understand how the adjustment process actually works.

First, recall that when an economy is producing below full employment, the tendency will be for wages and prices to fall. Similarly, when an economy is producing at a level exceeding full employment or potential output, the tendency will be for wages and prices to rise.

The adjustment process first begins to work as changes in prices affect the demand for money. Recall the real-nominal principle.

REAL-NOMINAL PRINCIPLE

What matters to people is the real value of money or income—its purchasing power—not the face value of money or income.

According to this principle, the amount of money people want to hold depends on the price level in the economy. If prices are cut in half, you need to hold only half as much money to purchase the same goods and services. Decreases in the price level will cause the money demand curve to shift to the left; increases in the price level will shift it to the right. Now let's put this idea to use.

Suppose the economy is initially in a recession. With output below full employment, actual unemployment will exceed the natural rate of unemployment, so there will be excess unemployment. Wages and prices will start to fall. Figure 15.4 shows how the fall in the price level can restore the economy to full employment via money demand, interest rates, and investment without active fiscal or monetary policy. First, we show with the *AD–AS* diagram in Panel A of Figure 15.4 how prices fall when the economy is operating below full employment. Second, in Panel B, the fall in the price level decreases the demand for holding money. As the price level decreases from P_0 to P_1, the demand for money shifts to the left from M_0^d to M_1^d. Interest rates fall from r_0 to r_1, and the falling interest rates increase investment spending from I_0 to I_1. As the level of investment spending in the economy increases, total demand for goods and

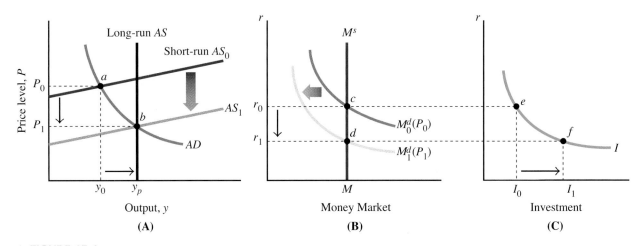

▲ **FIGURE 15.4**

How the Changing Price Level Restores the Economy to Full Employment
With the economy initially below full employment, the price level falls, as shown in Panel A, stimulating output. In Panel B, the lower price level decreases the demand for money and leads to lower interest rates at point *d*. In Panel C, lower interest rates lead to higher investment spending at point *f*. As the economy moves down the aggregate demand curve from point *a* toward full employment at point *b* in Panel A, investment spending increases along the aggregate demand curve.

services also increases, and the economy moves down along the aggregate demand curve as it returns to full employment.

Now you can also understand why the aggregate demand curve is downward-sloping through the interest rate effect. As we move down the aggregate demand curve, lower prices lead to lower interest rates, higher investment spending, and a higher level of aggregate demand. Thus, aggregate demand increases as the price level falls, which explains why the curve slopes downward.

What we have just described continues until the economy reaches full employment. As long as actual output is below the economy's full-employment level, prices will continue to fall. A fall in the price level reduces money demand and interest rates.

Lower interest rates stimulate investment spending and push the economy back toward full employment. All this works in reverse if output exceeds the economy's potential output. In this case, the economy is overheating and wages and prices rise. A higher price level will increase the demand for money and raise interest rates. Higher interest rates will decrease investment spending and reduce the level of output. The process continues until the economy "cools off" and returns to full employment.

Now you should understand why changes in wages and prices restore the economy to full employment. The key is that (1) changes in wages and prices change the demand for money, and (2) this changes interest rates, which then affect aggregate demand for goods and services and ultimately GDP.

We can also use the model we just developed to understand the liquidity trap. If an economy is in a recession, interest rates will fall, restoring the economy to full employment. But at some point, interest rates may become so low they equal zero. Nominal interest rates cannot go far below zero, because investors would rather hold money (which pays a zero rate) than hold a bond that promises a negative return. Suppose, however, that as interest rates approach zero, the economy is still in a slump. The adjustment process then has nowhere to go. This appears to be what happened in Japan in the 1990s. Interest rates on government bonds were zero, but prices continued to fall. At this point, the fall in prices by itself could not restore the economy to full employment. Policymakers in the United States also became concerned by this possibility. When interest rates on three-month U.S. government bills fell below 1 percent from June 2003 to May 2004, Fed officials openly discussed their limited options if further monetary stimulus became necessary.

What can policymakers do if an economy is in a recession but nominal rates become so close to zero that the natural adjustment process ceases to work? Economists have suggested several solutions to this problem. First, expansionary fiscal policy—cutting taxes or raising government spending—still remains a viable option to increase aggregate demand. Second, the Fed could become extremely aggressive and try to expand the money supply so rapidly that the public begins to anticipate future inflation. If the public expects inflation, the expected real rate of interest (the nominal rate minus the expected inflation rate) can become negative, even if the nominal rate cannot fall below zero. A negative expected real interest rate will tempt firms to invest, and this will increase aggregate demand. Finally, as we described in Application 1, the Fed began to pay interest on reserves to give itself more leverage for monetary policy. Even though a liquidity trap may make it more difficult for an economy to recover on its own, there is still room for proper economic policy to have an impact.

The Long-Run Neutrality of Money

An increase in the money supply has a different effect on the economy in the short run than it does in the long run. In Figure 15.5, we show the effects of expansionary monetary policy in both the short run and the long run. In the short run, as the supply of money increases, the economy moves from the original equilibrium to point *a*, with output above potential. But in the long run, the economy returns to point *b* at full employment, but at a higher price level than at the original equilibrium. How can the Federal Reserve change the level of output in the short run but affect prices only in

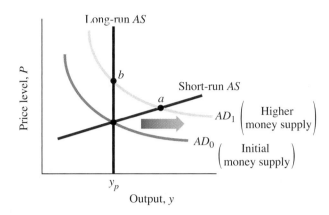

◄ **FIGURE 15.5**
Monetary Policy in the Short Run and the Long Run
As the Fed increases the supply of money, the aggregate demand curve shifts from AD_0 to AD_1 and the economy moves to point a. In the long run, the economy moves to point b.

the long run? Why is the short run different from the long run? We can use our model of the demand for money and investment to understand this issue.

Assume the economy starts at full employment. In Figure 15.6, interest rates are at r_F, and investment spending is at I_F. Now, suppose the Federal Reserve increases the money supply from M_0^s to M_1^s. We show this as a rightward movement in the money-supply curve. In the short run, the increase in the supply of money will reduce interest rates to r_0, and the level of investment spending will increase to I_0. Increased investment will stimulate the economy and increase output above full employment. All this occurs in the short run. The red arrows show the movements in interest rates and investment in the short run.

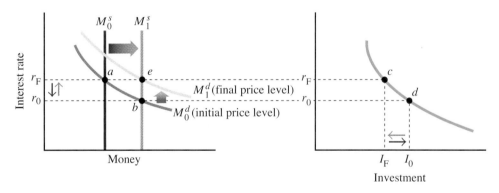

▲ **FIGURE 15.6**
The Neutrality of Money
Starting at full employment, an increase in the supply of money from M^s_0 to M^s_1 will initially reduce interest rates from r_F to r_0 (from point a to point b) and raise investment spending from I_F to I_0 (point c to point d). We show these changes with the red arrows. The blue arrows show that as the price level increases, the demand for money increases, restoring interest rates and investment to their prior levels—r_F and I_F, respectively. Both money supplied and money demanded will remain at a higher level, though, at point e.

However, once output exceeds full employment, wages and prices will start to increase. As the price level increases, the demand for money will increase. This will shift the money-demand curve upward and will start to increase interest rates. Investment will start to fall as interest rates increase, leading to a fall in output. The blue arrows in Figure 15.6 show the transition as prices increase. As long as output exceeds full employment, prices will continue to rise, money demand will continue to increase, and interest rates will continue to rise. Where does this process end? It ends only when interest rates return to their original level of r_F. At an interest rate of r_F, investment spending will have returned to I_F. This is the level of investment that meets the total level of demand for goods and services and keeps the economy at full employment.

long-run neutrality of money

A change in the supply of money has no effect on real interest rates, investment, or output in the long run.

When the economy returns to full employment, the levels of real interest rates, investment, and output are precisely the same as they were before the Fed increased the supply of money. The increase in the supply of money had no effect on real interest rates, investment, or output in the long run. Economists call this the **long-run neutrality of money**. In other words, in the long run, changes in the supply of money are neutral with respect to real variables in the economy. For example, if the price of everything in the economy doubles, including your paycheck, you are no better or worse off than you were before. In the long run, increases in the supply of money have no effect on real variables, only on prices.

This example points out how, in the long run, it really does not matter how much money is in circulation, because prices will adjust to the amount of nominal money available. In the short run, however, money is not neutral. In the short run, changes in the supply of money do affect interest rates, investment spending, and output. The Fed does have strong powers over real GDP, but those powers are ultimately temporary. In the long run, all the Fed can do is determine the level of prices in the economy.

Now we can understand why the job of the Federal Reserve has been described by William McChesney Martin, Jr., a former Federal Reserve chairman, as "taking the punch bowl away at the party." The punch bowl is money: If the Fed sets out the punch bowl, this will temporarily increase output or give the economy a brief high. But if the Federal Reserve is worried about increases in prices in the long run, it must take the punch bowl away and everyone must sober up. If not, the result will be continuing increases in prices, or inflation.

Crowding Out in the Long Run

Some economists are strong proponents of increasing government spending on defense or other programs to stimulate the economy. Critics, however, say increases in spending provide only temporary relief and ultimately harm the economy because government spending "crowds out" investment spending. In Chapter 7, we discussed the idea of *crowding out*. We can now understand the idea in more detail.

Suppose the economy starts out at full employment and then the government increases its spending. This will shift the aggregate demand curve to the right, causing output to increase beyond full employment. As we have seen, the result of this boom will be that wages and prices increase.

Now let's turn to our model of money demand and investment. Figure 15.7 shows that as prices increase, the demand for money shifts upward in Panel A, raising interest rates from r_0 to r_1 and reducing investment from I_0 to I_1, as shown in

▶ **FIGURE 15.7**

Crowding Out in the Long Run
Starting at full employment, an increase in government spending raises output above full employment. As wages and prices increase, the demand for money increases, as shown in Panel A, raising interest rates from r_0 to r_1 (point a to point b) and reducing investment from I_0 to I_1 (point c to point d). The economy returns to full employment, but at a higher level of interest rates and a lower level of investment spending.

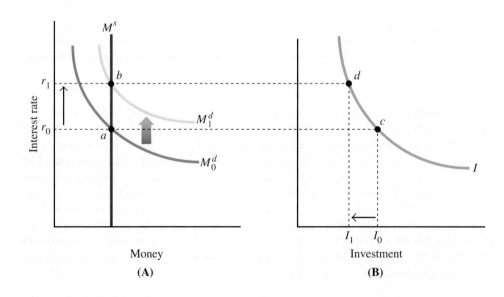

Money	Investment
(A)	(B)

Panel B. Higher interest rates are the mechanism through which crowding out of public investment occurs. As investment spending by the public then falls (gets crowded out), we know that aggregate demand decreases. This process will continue until the economy returns to full employment. Once the economy returns to full employment, the decrease in investment spending by the public will exactly match the increase in government spending. However, when the economy does return to full employment, it will be at a higher interest rate level and lower level of investment spending by the public.

Thus, the increase in government spending has no long-run effect on the level of output—just on the interest rate. Instead, the increase in government spending displaced, or crowded out, private investment spending. If the government spending went toward government investment projects—such as bridges or roads—then it will have just replaced an equivalent amount of private investment. If the increased government spending did not go toward providing investment but, for example, went for military spending, then the reduction in private investment will have reduced total investment in the economy, private and public. This decrease in total investment would have further negative effects on the economy over time. As we saw in earlier chapters, a reduction in investment spending reduces capital deepening and leads to lower levels of real income and wages in the future.

Economists make similar arguments when it comes to tax cuts. Tax cuts initially will increase consumer spending and lead to a higher level of GDP. In the

APPLICATION 3

INCREASING HEALTH-CARE EXPENDITURES AND CROWDING OUT

APPLYING THE CONCEPTS #3: Will increases in health-care expenditures crowd out consumption or investment spending?

In 1950 health-care expenditures in the United States were 5.2 percent of GDP; by 2000 this share had risen to 15.4 percent. Driving these increases were several factors: increasing relative prices of health care compared to other goods, a larger population of the elderly, and increased longevity. Since 1950 the average life span has increased by 1.7 years per decade.

Many observers think these trends will continue. Health-care costs have continued to rise rapidly in recent years. Two economists, Charles I. Jones and Robert E. Hall, go further and suggest normal increases in economic growth will propel health-care expenditures to approximately 30 percent of GDP by mid-century. Their argument is that as societies grow wealthier, individuals face the tradeoff of buying more goods (automobiles or cars) to enjoy their current life span or spending more on health care to extend their lives. At some point, the extra years of life become more valuable than consumer durables, with the result that spending on health care rises rapidly.

Assuming this argument is correct and health-care expenditures increase, what other component of GDP will fall? If investment is crowded out, living standards would fall in the long run, reducing the ability to consume both health and non-health goods. Perhaps it is more likely that other types of consumption spending will fall. Spending on health would then come at the expense of spending on consumer durables or larger houses. That would be the preferred outcome.   **Related to Exercise 3.7.**

SOURCE: Based on Robert E. Hall and Charles I. Jones, "The Value of Life and the Rise in Health Spending," *Quarterly Journal of Economics* (February 2007): 39–72.

long run, however, adjustments in wages and prices restore the economy to full employment. However, interest rates will rise during the adjustment process and this increase in interest rates will crowd out private investment. In the long run, the increase in consumption spending will come at the expense of lower investment spending, decreased capital deepening, and lower levels of real income and wages in the future.

Crowding out can occur from sources other than the government. Expected increases in U.S. health-care expenditures will pose similar challenges to crowding out in the coming decades as well.

What about decreases in government spending or increases in taxes? Decreases in government spending, such as cuts in military spending, will lead to increases in investment in the long run, which we call *crowding in*. Initially, a decrease in government spending will cause a decrease in real GDP. But as prices fall, the demand for money will decrease, and interest rates will fall. Lower interest rates will crowd in investment as the economy returns to full employment. In the longer run, the higher investment spending will raise living standards through capital deepening. Increased taxes, to the extent they reduce consumption spending, will crowd in investment through precisely the same mechanism.

15.4 CLASSICAL ECONOMICS IN HISTORICAL PERSPECTIVE

The term *classical economics* refers to the work of the originators of modern economic thought. Adam Smith was the first so-called classical economist. Other classical economists—Jean-Baptiste Say, David Ricardo, John Stuart Mill, and Thomas Malthus—developed their work during the late eighteenth and nineteenth centuries. Keynes first used the term *classical model* in the 1930s to contrast it with his Keynesian model, which emphasized the difficulties the economy could face in the short run. The ideas developed in this chapter can shed some light on a historical debate in economics about the role of full employment in modern Keynesian and classical thought.

Say's Law

Classical economics is often associated with *Say's law*, the doctrine that "supply creates its own demand." To understand Say's law, recall from our discussion of GDP accounting in Chapter 5 that production in an economy creates an equivalent amount of income. For example, if GDP is $10 trillion, then production is $10 trillion, and $10 trillion in income is generated. The classical economists argued that the $10 trillion of production also created $10 trillion in demand for current goods and services. This meant there could never be a shortage of demand for total goods and services in the economy, nor any excess.

But suppose consumers, who earned the income, decided to save rather than spend it. Wouldn't this increase in saving lead to a shortfall in the total demand for goods and services? Wouldn't, say, inventories of goods pile up in warehouses? Classical economists argued no, that the increase in savings would *eventually* find its way to an equivalent increase in investment spending by firms, because the savings by households would eventually get channeled to firms via financial markets. As a result spending on consumption and investment together would be sufficient so that all the goods and services produced in the economy would be purchased.

Keynes, on the other hand, argued that there could be situations in which total demand fell short of total production in the economy for extended periods of time. In particular, if consumers increased their savings, there was no guarantee that investment spending would rise to offset the decrease in consumption. And if total spending did fall short of total demand, goods and services would go unsold. When producers could not sell their goods, they would cut back on production, and output in the economy would consequently fall, leading to a recession or depression.

Keynesian and Classical Debates

The debates between Keynesian and classical economists continued for several decades after Keynes developed his theories. In the 1940s, Professor Don Patinkin and Nobel Laureate Franco Modigliani clarified the conditions for which the classical model would hold true. In particular, they studied the conditions under which there would be sufficient demand for goods and services when the economy was at full employment. Both economists emphasized that one of the necessary conditions for the classical model to work was that wages and prices must be fully flexible—that is, they must adjust rapidly to changes in demand and supply.

If wages and prices are not fully flexible, then Keynes's view that demand could fall short of production is more likely to hold true. We've seen that over short periods of time, wages and prices, indeed, are not fully flexible, so Keynes's insights are important. However, over longer periods of time, wages and prices do adjust and the insights of the classical model are restored.

To help clarify the conditions under which the economy will return to full employment in the long run on its own, Patinkin and Modigliani developed the adjustment-process model we used in this chapter. They highlighted many of the key points we emphasized, including the speed of the adjustment process and possible pitfalls, such as liquidity traps.

In the chapter-opening story, we noted that some economists advocate aggressive government action during recessions, while others feel that such actions may impede recovery. We now have a better understanding of why economists differ on these issues. Economists who feel the adjustment process is slow typically recommend activist policies, while those who believe that adjustment is more rapid will tend to be skeptical of activist policies. In addition, economists will differ in their judgments about the ability of the government to act quickly and make effective decisions. That will also determine whether they believe policy will make the economy perform better or worse.

SUMMARY

This chapter explained how the economy makes the transition from the short run to the long run. It also highlighted why monetary and fiscal policies have different effects in the short run and in the long run. Understanding the distinction between the short run and the long run is critical to evaluating economic policy. Here are the main points to remember from this chapter:

1 *The short run in macroeconomics* refers to the period of time in which prices do not change very much. The *long run in macroeconomics* is the period over which prices have time to change in response to economic changes.

2 When output exceeds full employment, wages and prices rise faster than their past trends. If output is less than full employment, wages and prices fall relative to past trends.

3 The price changes that occur when the economy is away from full employment push the economy back to full employment. Economists disagree on the length of time this adjustment process takes; estimates range from less than two years to six years.

4 Economic policies are most effective when the adjustment process is slow. However, to improve their chances of being reelected, politicians can take advantage of the difference between the short-run and long-run effects of economic policies.

5 If the economy is operating below full employment, falling wages and prices will reduce money demand and lower interest rates. The fall in interest rates will stimulate investment and lead the economy back to full employment.

6 The reverse occurs when output exceeds full employment. Increases in wages and prices will increase money demand and interest rates. As investment spending falls, the economy returns to full employment.

7 In the long run, increases in the supply of money are neutral. That is, increases in the money supply do not affect real interest rates, investment, or output. This characteristic is known as the *long-run neutrality of money*.

8 Increases in government spending will raise real interest rates and *crowd out* investment in the long run. Decreases in government spending will lower real interest rates and crowd in investment in the long run.

9 The adjustment model in this chapter helps us to understand the debate between Keynes and the classical economists.

KEY TERMS

aggregate demand curve, p. 314

liquidity trap, p. 317

long-run aggregate supply curve, p. 314

long run in macroeconomics, p. 312

long-run neutrality of money, p. 322

political business cycle, p. 318

short-run aggregate supply curve, p. 314

short run in macroeconomics, p. 312

wage–price spiral, p. 313

EXERCISES  Visit www.myeconlab.com to complete these exercises online and get instant feedback.

15.1 Linking the Short Run and the Long Run

1.1 Wages and prices will increase when actual output exceeds potential. _____ (True/False)

1.2 The short run in macroeconomics is the time period over which _____ do not adjust to economic conditions.

1.3 According to the logic of the wage–price spiral, an increase in wages leads to a(n) _____ in _____, which in turn leads to a(n) _____ in _____.

1.4 In the long run, the level of GDP is determined by demand. _____ (True/False)

1.5 **Cost of Living Adjustments and the Wage–Price Spiral.** Suppose organized labor has successfully bargained for cost of living increases for its workers. That is, when prices rise—as measured by the CPI—wages are automatically adjusted by the same percentage. Would this make the economy more or less likely to experience a wage–price spiral?

1.6 **Unemployment and Wage Price Changes.** If the natural rate of unemployment is 6 percent and the actual rate of unemployment is 7 percent, how will wages and prices change? Suppose the natural rate was 7 percent?

15.2 How Wage and Price Changes Move the Economy Naturally Back to Full Employment

2.1 The short-run aggregate supply curve will move _____ if the economy's actual output is below full-employment output.

2.2 If the adjustment process works slowly, then economic policy is less necessary. _____ (True/False)

2.3 A political business cycle may occur because policymakers are willing to trade off a current reduction in unemployment for future increases in inflation. _____ (True/False)

2.4 **Supply Shocks and Policy Choices.** In Chapter 9, we discussed supply shocks, sudden increases in the prices of commodities such as oil or food. These shocks shift the short-run aggregate supply curve. For example, the increase in oil prices in 2006 will shift the short-run aggregate supply curve upward, because firms' costs have risen and firms must charge higher prices to avoid losing money.

a. Suppose the economy is operating at full employment and foreign countries raise the world price of oil. Assuming policymakers do not take any action, describe what will happen to prices and output in the short run and in the long run. Show these situations graphically.

b. Suppose the Federal Reserve decided it wanted to offset any adverse effects on output due to a supply shock. What actions could it take? What would happen to the price level if the Fed used monetary policy to fight unemployment in this situation?

c. Economists say supply shocks create a dilemma for the Federal Reserve that shocks to demand (for example, from sudden increases in investment spending by optimistic firms) do not create. Using your answer to part (b) and the aggregate demand and aggregate supply graph, explain why economists say this.

2.5 **Foreign Firms Opening Their Markets in the Long Run.** Suppose the economy is at full employment and foreign firms open their markets and U.S. firms start to produce more for export. Everything else remains the same.

a. In the short run, what happens to GDP?

b. Assuming that exchange rates do not change, what happens to U.S. prices in the long run? How might this affect the export market?

2.6 Stabilization Policy and the Speed of Adjustment. Economists who believe the transition from the short run to the long run occurs rapidly do not generally favor using active stabilization policy. Use the aggregate demand and aggregate supply graphs to illustrate how active policy, with a rapid adjustment process, could destabilize the economy.

2.7 Understanding the Liquidity Trap. The adjustment process can run into problems during a liquidity trap when interest rates are driven close to zero and the economy remains below full employment. Both Japan in the 1990s and the United States during the Great Depression in the 1930s are possible examples of liquidity traps. (Related to Application 1 on page 317.)

    a. Draw a money-demand curve and an investment schedule to illustrate this possibility.

    b. During the Great Depression in the United States, some interest rates dropped close to zero. Search the historical database at the Web site of the National Bureau of Economic Research (www.nber.org) to find out how low interest rates actually dropped and when they were at their lowest.

    c. Use the Web to find data on a variety of Japanese interest rates from 1985 through 2006. Over what period do you think low interest rates may have become a policy problem? You might wish to start with the Economagic Web site (www.economagic .com/bjap.htm).

2.8 Analyzing a Bernanke Speech on Deflation and Liquidity Traps. While he was a member of the Board of Governors of the Federal Reserve but before he became its chairman, Ben S. Bernanke delivered a speech to the National Economists Club in Washington, D.C., on the risks of deflation, liquidity traps, and how to prevent them. Read Bernanke's speech and discuss how he recommends preventing deflation and combating liquidity traps. The speech from November 21, 2002, is available at http://www .federalreserve.gov/boarddocs/speeches/2002/ 20021121/default.htm (accessed April 21, 2010). (Related to Application 1 on page 317.)

2.9 Investigating Political Business Cycles. Use the Web site for the Federal Reserve Bank of St. Louis (www.research.stlouisfed.org/fred2) to find historical data on unemployment rates. Use these data to explore whether unemployment behaves differently in the first two years of a presidential term than in the final two years. Are there any systematic differences in unemployment between Democratic and Republican presidencies? (Related to Application 2 on page 318.)

15.3 Understanding the Economics of the Adjustment Process

3.1 As the price level increases, the demand for money _____ and interest rates _____.

3.2 If output is above full employment, we expect wages and prices to rise, money demand to increase, and interest rates to fall. _____ (True/False)

3.3 An increase in the money supply will have no effect on the real rate of interest in the long run. _____ (True/False)

3.4 An increase in government spending will _____ interest rates in the long run.

3.5 Understanding Japanese Fiscal Policy. Japan's finance ministry agreed to income tax cuts to combat a decade-long recession in the 1990s—but only if national sales taxes were increased several years later.

    a. What would you expect to be the short-run effect of the income tax cuts? Draw a graph to show this effect.

    b. What would you expect to be the long-run effect of the income tax cuts? Draw a graph to show this effect.

    c. Why did the Finance Ministry require an increase in sales taxes several years later?

    d. What was the Finance Ministry trying to prevent?

3.6 Can Monetary Policy Prevent Crowding Out? Explain what is wrong with this quote: "In the long run, we do not have to worry about increased government spending causing crowding out, because the Fed can always increase the money supply to lower interest rates to prevent this."

3.7 Increasing Health Spending and Economic Growth. Analyze how the following factors associated with increased spending on health care might affect economic growth. (Related to Application 3 on page 323.)

    a. With increased longevity, workers will need to postpone their retirement in order to save more for old age.

    b. Households may cut down on purchases of consumer durables to spend more on health.

    c. Households may reduce their savings in order to spend more on health care.

    d. New and expensive technologies allow people to live longer.

3.8 Money and Output Growth in the Long Run. Countries that have high money growth for long periods do not grow more rapidly than countries with low money growth. Why?

3.9 Economic Policy and the Housing Industry. Explain why advocates for the housing industry (an industry very sensitive to interest rates) might want to advocate lower government spending for the long term.

3.10 Tax Increases and Crowding In. Using an aggregate demand and aggregate supply graph, show how tax increases for consumers today will eventually lead to lower interest rates and crowd in investment spending in the long run.

15.4 Classical Economics in Historical Perspective

4.1 Professors Don _____ and Franco _____ developed the adjustment-process model used in this chapter.

4.2 Keynes's objection to Say's law was that it is possible for demand to create its own supply. _____ (True/False)

4.3 Today, some economists might claim that Say's law holds in the _____ run, but not the _____ run.

4.4 David Ricardo and John Stuart Mill are known as _____ economists.

4.5 Milton Friedman and the Great Depression. Economist Milton Friedman was an opponent to activist stabilization policy. His views on economic policy were greatly influenced by his interpretation of the Great Depression. Search the Web for discussions of Friedman's views on the Great Depression and discuss how they may have affected his attitudes toward stabilization policy. You may want to start with the entry at http://www.econlib.org/library/Enc/bios/Friedman.html (accessed April 21, 2010).

The Dynamics of Inflation and Unemployment

As the financial crisis spread in 2008, central banks around the world increased the supply of money and liquidity, and governments borrowed extensively and incurred increasing amounts of government debt. Increases in the supply of money and debt are often precursors for inflation. Although a slack economy limited any inflationary pressures and, in some cases, led to mild deflation, there were concerns by some that inflation would inevitably follow in the not-too-distant future.

One traditional indicator of a fear of inflation was the price of gold. From 2005 to 2010, the price of an ounce of gold rose from approximately $400 to $1200, an increase by a factor of three! This was precisely during the same period when stock markets worldwide first rose and then sharply fell. Commercials for investing in gold products appeared on cable television and radio stations throughout the country.

Gold, however, is a very risky investment and not suitable for most people. An alternative strategy some investors use is to buy Treasury Inflation Protected Securities—or TIPS. These securities provide investors with guaranteed purchasing power, but typically with a lower return. Buying insurance against inflation is costly—it is much better if central banks do not let inflation develop in the first place.

APPLYING THE CONCEPTS

1 How can data on vacancies and unemployment be used to measure shifts in the natural rate?
   Shifts in the Natural Rate of Unemployment

2 Can changes in the way central banks are governed affect inflation expectations?
   Increased Political Independence for the Bank of England Lowered Inflation Expectations

3 What caused a severe hyperinflation to emerge recently in Zimbabwe?
   Hyperinflation in Zimbabwe

In this chapter, we integrate two themes we've been stressing separately:

- In the short run, changes in money growth affect real output and real GDP.
- In the long run, the rate of money growth determines the rate of inflation, not real GDP.

Economic policy debates often concern inflation and unemployment because they affect us all so directly. We will look at the relationships between inflation and unemployment, examining macroeconomic developments in the United States in the last several decades. We also explore why heads of central banks typically appear to be strong enemies of inflation.

Although the United States had serious difficulties fighting inflation in the 1970s and 1980s, other countries have, at times, had much more severe problems with inflation. In this chapter, we'll study the origins of extremely high inflationary periods and their links to government budget deficits.

16.1 MONEY GROWTH, INFLATION, AND INTEREST RATES

An economy can, in principle, produce at full employment with any inflation rate. No "magic" inflation rate is necessary to sustain full employment. To understand this point, consider the long run when the economy operates at full employment. As we have seen, in the long run, money is neutral. If the Federal Reserve increases the money supply at 5 percent a year, annual inflation will be 5 percent. That is, prices in the economy will rise by 5 percent a year.

Inflation in a Steady State

nominal wages
Wages expressed in current dollars.

real wage
The wage rate paid to employees adjusted for changes in the price level.

money illusion
Confusion of real and nominal magnitudes.

expectations of inflation
The beliefs held by the public about the likely path of inflation in the future.

Let's think about how this economy looks in this "steady state" of constant inflation. The **nominal wages**—wages in dollars—of workers are all rising at 5 percent a year. However, because prices are also rising at 5 percent a year, **real wages**—wages adjusted for changes in purchasing power—remain constant.

Some workers may feel cheated by the inflation. They might believe that without inflation, they would experience real-wage increases, because their nominal wages are rising 5 percent a year. Unfortunately, these workers are wrong. They suffer from what economists call **money illusion**, a confusion of real and nominal magnitudes. Here's the source of the illusion: Because real wages are constant, the only reason nominal wages are rising by 5 percent a year is the general 5 percent inflation. If there were no inflation, nominal wages would not increase at all.

After a time, everyone in the economy would begin to expect the 5 percent annual inflation that had occurred in the past to continue in the future. Economists call this belief **expectations of inflation**. People's expectations of inflation affect all aspects of economic life. For example, in the steady-state economy we just described, automobile producers will expect to increase the price of their products by 5 percent every year. They will also expect their costs—of labor and steel, for example—to increase by 5 percent a year. Workers will begin to believe the 5 percent increase in their wages will be matched by a 5 percent increase in the prices of the goods they buy. Continued inflation becomes the normal state of affairs, and people build it into their daily decision making. For example, they expect the price of a car to be 5 percent higher next year and will take that into consideration when they go shopping for a new car.

INFLATION EXPECTATIONS AND INTEREST RATES   When the public expects inflation, real and nominal rates of interest will differ because we need to account for inflation in calculating the real return from lending and borrowing. Recall that the nominal interest rate—the rate quoted in the market—is equal to the real rate of interest plus the expected inflation rate. If the real rate of interest is 2 percent and inflation is 5 percent a year, the nominal interest rate will be 7 percent. Although lenders receive 7 percent a year on their loans, their real return after inflation is just 2 percent.

In Chapter 15 you saw that in the long run, the *real* rate of interest does not depend on monetary policy because money is neutral. That is, even though the money supply may be higher or lower, the price level will be higher or lower. However, *nominal* rates of interest do depend on monetary policy, because whether the Fed expands or contracts the money supply affects the rate of inflation, which in the long run is determined by the growth of the money supply. As Nobel Laureate Milton Friedman pointed out, countries with higher money growth typically have higher nominal interest rates than countries with lower money growth rates because they have higher inflation. If Country A and Country B have the same real rate of interest, but Country A has a higher inflation rate, Country A will also have a higher nominal interest rate.

INFLATION EXPECTATIONS AND MONEY DEMAND   Money demand—the amount of money people want to hold—will also be affected by expectations about inflation. If people expect 5 percent inflation a year, then their demand for money will also increase by 5 percent a year. The reason, of course, is that people know everything will cost 5 percent more, so they'll need more money in their pockets to pay for the same goods and services. This is an example of the real-nominal principle.

REAL-NOMINAL PRINCIPLE

What matters to people is the real value of money or income—its purchasing power—not the face value of money or income.

As long as the Fed allows the supply of money to increase by 5 percent—the same amount as inflation—the demand for money and its supply will both grow at the same rate. Because money demand and supply are both growing at the same rate, real interest rates and nominal interest rates will not change.

How Changes in the Growth Rate of Money Affect the Steady State

If the growth rate of money changes, however, there will be short-run effects on real interest rates. To continue with our example, suppose the public expects 5 percent annual inflation and both the money supply and money demand grow at 5 percent a year. Now suppose the Fed suddenly decreases the annual growth rate of money to 4 percent, while the public continues to expect 5 percent annual inflation. Because money demand grows at 5 percent but the money supply grows at only 4 percent, growth in the demand for money will exceed growth in the supply of money. The result will be an increase in both real interest rates and nominal interest rates.

We have seen that higher real rates of interest will reduce investment spending by firms and reduce consumer durable goods spending by households. With reduced firm and consumer demand for goods and services, real GDP will fall and unemployment will rise. The reduction in the growth rate of the money supply is contractionary. In the long run, however, output will return to full employment through the adjustment process described in Chapter 15. The economy will eventually adjust to the lower rate of money growth, and inflation will eventually fall from 5 percent to 4 percent per year to match it. In the long run, the *real* rate of interest will eventually fall and return to its previous value. *Nominal* interest rates, which reflect expectations of ongoing inflation, will be 1 percent lower, because inflation has fallen from 5 percent to 4 percent per year. Table 16.1 depicts the long-run relationships between money growth, inflation, increases in money demand, and real and nominal interest rates in this example.

TABLE 16.1 MONEY, INFLATION, AND INTEREST RATES IN A STEADY-STATE ECONOMY				
Money Growth Rate	Inflation	Growth in Money Demand	Real Interest Rate	Nominal Interest
4%	4%	4%	2%	6%
5%	5%	5%	2%	7%

This basic pattern fits U.S. history in the late 1970s and early 1980s. At that time, the Federal Reserve sharply decreased the growth rate of the money supply, so interest rates rose temporarily. By 1981, interest rates on three-month Treasury bills rose to over 14 percent from 7 percent in 1978. The economy went into a severe recession, with unemployment exceeding 10 percent. By the mid-1980s, however, the economy returned to full employment with lower interest rates and lower inflation rates. By 1986, Treasury bill rates were below 6 percent.

This is another example in which the long-run effects of policy actions differ from their short-run effects. In the short run, a policy of tight money leads to slower money growth, higher interest rates, and lower output. But in the long run, reduced money growth results in lower interest rates, lower inflation, and no effect on the level of output.

16.2 UNDERSTANDING THE EXPECTATIONS PHILLIPS CURVE: THE RELATIONSHIP BETWEEN UNEMPLOYMENT AND INFLATION

In the late 1950s, A.W. Phillips was studying British economic data and noticed that lower unemployment was associated with higher inflation. That is, the inflation rate rises when economic activity booms and unemployment is low. Phillips also noticed that the inflation rate falls when the economy is in a recession and unemployment is high. This inverse relationship between unemployment and inflation became known as the *Phillips curve*.

In the early 1960s, Nobel Laureates Paul Samuelson and Robert Solow found a similar relationship between unemployment and the inflation rate in the United States. However, these early studies examined periods when there was no significant underlying inflation, and they did not take into account people's expectations of inflation. The relationship between unemployment and inflation when we take into account expectations of inflation is known as the **expectations Phillips curve**.

expectations Phillips curve
The relationship between unemployment and inflation when taking into account expectations of inflation.

The expectations Phillips curve was introduced into the economics profession in the late 1960s by Edmund Phelps of Columbia University and Milton Friedman, then at the University of Chicago. The expectations Phillips curve included the notion that unemployment varies with *unanticipated inflation*. Friedman argued, for example, that when the inflation rate suddenly increases, it is likely that workers did not fully anticipate some of this sudden increase. Actual inflation will then exceed expected inflation. Workers will see their nominal wages increase, but because they do not fully expect this sudden inflation, they will think their real wages have risen. With higher perceived real wages being offered, potential workers will be inclined to accept the jobs firms offer them. As a result, unemployment will fall below the natural rate. That's why we often see an association between increases in the inflation rate and a decrease in the unemployment rate.

After workers recognize that the inflation rate is higher, though, they will incorporate this higher inflation rate into their expectations of inflation. They will no longer confuse the higher nominal wages firms offer with higher real wages. Unemployment will then return to its natural rate. So there is no permanent relationship between the level of unemployment and the level of inflation.

Similarly, if the inflation rate falls, workers may not expect some of this fall. Because inflation is less than expected, workers will believe their real wages aren't rising as fast as they actually are. With lower perceived real wages being offered, potential workers will be less inclined to accept the jobs firms offer them. The unemployment rate will increase as a result. However, once they recognize that inflation is lower than they realized, and that the wages firms offered them really aren't that low, workers will be more inclined to accept work. Unemployment will then again return to the natural rate. So a decrease in the inflation rate is likely to be associated with temporary increases in unemployment.

Later in this chapter we'll see an example of this relationship between inflation and unemployment in the late 1980s and early 1990s. A "disconnect" between what people expect and what ultimately occurs can adversely affect the economy, as we'll see next. Table 16.2 summarizes the key points about the expectations Phillips curve.

TABLE 16.2 EXPECTATIONS AND BUSINESS FLUCTUATIONS

When the economy experiences a . . .	Unemployment is . . .	Inflation is . . .
boom	below the natural rate.	higher than expected.
recession	above the natural rate.	lower than expected.

Are the Public's Expectations about Inflation Rational?

As we just saw, expectations about inflation affect actual inflation because workers and firms build their inflation forecasts into their wage- and price-setting decisions. Mistakes in predicting inflation therefore have consequences. But *how* do workers and firms form inflation expectations in the first place? And, second, *when* do they form their inflation expectations?

Two broad classes of theories attempt to explain how the public forms its expectations of inflation. Some economists and psychologists, including Nobel Laureate Herbert Simon, believe the public uses simple *rules of thumb* to predict future inflation. One such rule of thumb might be to assume next year's inflation rate will be the same as this year's. According to this view, it is unreasonable to expect too much sophistication from the public because of the complexity of the economy and the difficulty of forecasting it.

In the 1970s, a group of economists led by Nobel Laureate Robert E. Lucas, Jr., from the University of Chicago developed an alternative view, called the theory of **rational expectations**. The rational expectations theory portrayed workers and firms as much more sophisticated, basing their expectations on all the information available to them. According to the theory, the public, on average, anticipates the future correctly. Although the public may make mistakes in specific instances, on average, people's expectations are rational or correct.

The two approaches—rules of thumb versus rational expectations—tend to deliver similar predictions when the economy is very stable and there are no major policy changes. However, when there are major policy changes—for example, when the government introduces new policies to fight inflation or reduce federal deficits—the two approaches predict different outcomes. The rational expectations theory predicts the public will anticipate the consequences of these policies and change its expectations about inflation accordingly; the rule-of-thumb theory says it won't. Which view is correct? The truth lies somewhere in the middle. On the one hand, sophisticated firms, such as Microsoft and Walmart, do appear to take advantage of available information. On the other hand, a considerable amount of inertia and non-rationality appears to enter into the general public's decision-making process. And sometimes the public may be rational about small signals but miss the big picture. For

rational expectations

The economic theory that analyzes how the public forms expectations in such a manner that, on average, it forecasts the future correctly.

example, during the stock-market boom in the late 1990s, investors may have had an accurate assessment of *which* tech stocks were relatively more promising but failed to recognize that *all* tech stocks were overvalued.

The other major issue is the question of *when* inflation expectations are formed. As we discussed in Chapter 9, both workers and firms often make explicit long-term contracts or enter into implicit long-term agreements. With long-term contracts, workers and firms must make forecasts far into the future. For example, if a union is negotiating wages for three years, it will need to forecast inflation three years into the future and negotiate current and future wages today based on that forecast. Making decisions this far in advance is clearly very difficult, so it is understandable that mistakes can occur. Indeed, workers and firms can be quite rational but still make mistakes when predicting inflation simply because of the long time frames involved. Wage contracts set in the early 1980s, for example, would have "rationally" anticipated continued high inflation, although changes in monetary policy brought inflation below what was predicted.

U.S. Inflation and Unemployment in the 1980s

We can use the expectations Phillips curve to help understand the patterns of inflation and unemployment that occurred in the 1980s. For the sake of this discussion, we will assume workers and firms follow relatively simple rules of thumb and that sudden increases in inflation are partly unanticipated and thus accompanied by lower unemployment. Conversely, sudden decreases in inflation are accompanied by temporarily higher unemployment.

When President Jimmy Carter took office at the beginning of 1977, the inflation rate was approximately 6.5 percent per year and unemployment exceeded 7 percent of the labor force. By 1980, inflation had risen to 9.4 percent. There were two reasons for this increase. First, utilizing expansionary policy, the Carter administration had steadily reduced unemployment to under 6 percent by 1979. Because the natural rate of unemployment was close to 6 percent of the labor force at that time, reducing unemployment below this rate led to an increase in the annual inflation rate. Second, there was an oil shock in 1979, which also contributed to higher inflation.

Fears of even higher inflation led President Carter to appoint a well-known inflation fighter, Paul Volcker, as chairman of the Federal Reserve. Volcker immediately began to institute a tight money policy, and interest rates rose sharply by 1980. When President Ronald Reagan took office, he supported Volcker's policy. Eventually, high real-interest rates took their toll, and unemployment rose to over 10 percent by 1983. As actual unemployment exceeded the natural rate of unemployment, the inflation rate fell, just as the expectations Phillips curve predicted. By 1986, the inflation rate fell to approximately 2.7 percent per year with unemployment at 7 percent of the labor force. The severe recession had done its job in reducing the inflation rate.

However, as we can see in Figure 16.1, after 1986 the unemployment rate began to fall again, from about 7 percent to a little over 6 percent in 1987. Notice that as actual unemployment fell below the natural rate (which, at that time, was about 6.5 percent), inflation began to rise, increasing from about 2.75 to 3 percent. By 1989, as unemployment continued to fall, annual inflation had risen to 4.5 percent, and the Fed then raised interest rates to combat it. The Fed's action reduced output and increased unemployment to over 7 percent. Notice that by 1992, inflation had fallen dramatically because unemployment exceeded the natural rate.

By the time President George H. W. Bush took office in 1989, actual unemployment was below the natural rate of unemployment, inflation had been rising, and the Fed started slowing down the economy. The rate of inflation was eventually reduced, but the recovery back to full employment in 1992–1993 came too late in Bush's term for the voters to fully appreciate, and he lost his bid for reelection.

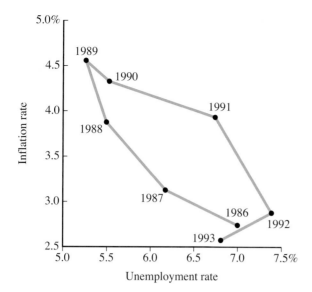

▲ FIGURE 16.1

The Dynamics of Inflation and Unemployment, 1986–1993

Inflation rose and the unemployment rate fell below the natural rate. Inflation later fell as unemployment exceeded the natural rate.

SOURCE: Economic Report of the President (Washington, D.C.: U.S. Government Printing Office, yearly).

Shifts in the Natural Rate of Unemployment in the 1990s

Up to this point, our analysis assumes that the natural rate of unemployment is a constant—say, for example, 5 percent of the labor force. If actual unemployment falls below this constant rate (the economy is hot, in other words), inflation will tend to increase. Similarly, if the actual unemployment exceeds 5 percent (the economy is sluggish), inflation will fall.

But the natural rate of unemployment can shift over time. At the beginning of the 1980s in the United States, most economists believed that the natural rate of unemployment was between 6 or 7 percent. By the late 1990s, many economists had begun to believe the natural rate of unemployment had fallen to about 5 percent. What can shift the natural rate of unemployment? Economists have identified a number of factors:

- **Demographics.** The composition of the workforce can change, decreasing the natural rate. For example, we know teenagers have higher unemployment rates than adults. If changes in population lead to a lower percentage of teenagers in the labor force, we would expect the natural rate of unemployment to decrease. In the 1990s, the share of teenagers in the labor force fell. This change in demographics appears to have been what caused the natural rate of unemployment to decline in the United States.

- **Institutional changes.** Changes in laws, regulations, and economic institutions can influence the natural rate of unemployment. Suppose the government shortens the length of time unemployed workers can collect benefits. We would then expect the unemployed to return to work more rapidly and the natural rate of unemployment to fall. Some economists have argued that the rise of temporary employment agencies in the United States during the 1990s made the labor market more efficient. Workers were matched more quickly with jobs, and this contributed to the decline of the natural rate. In Europe, a very different set of institutional factors had the opposite result: Generous benefits for the unemployed increased the time they spent unemployed. Restrictions on employers making it difficult to fire workers led them to hire fewer people in the first place. Both these factors raised the natural rate of employment.

- **The recent history of the economy.** Some economists believe the economic performance of the economy itself may influence the natural rate of unemployment. Suppose the economy goes into a long recession. During that time, many young people may not be able to find jobs and will fail to develop a strong work ethic. Other workers may lose some of their skills during a prolonged period of unemployment. Both factors could lead to longer-term unemployment and an increase in the natural rate of unemployment.

- **Changes in growth of labor productivity.** If the growth rate in labor productivity falls, wages must also rise more slowly because they are tied to productivity increases in the long run. However, if workers don't realize this, they might continue to push for higher nominal wage increases and be less inclined to accept lower nominal wages. This will increase the natural rate of unemployment. Similarly, if productivity growth is higher than anticipated, wages will rise more quickly because firms will be willing to pay more to retain their workers and recruit new ones. As a result of this unexpected productivity growth, workers may not be as aggressive in asking for additional nominal wage increases because they are pleased with what they are already getting. They will be more inclined to accept these wages, and this will effectively lower the natural rate of unemployment. Some economists believe this in fact happened in the late 1990s when productivity growth soared and the natural rate of unemployment temporarily fell. Actual unemployment fell to near 4 percent without any visible signs of increasing inflation. Of course, once workers in the economy understand that a shift in productivity growth has occurred, the natural rate will return to its original value, closer to, say, 5 percent.

APPLICATION 1

SHIFTS IN THE NATURAL RATE OF UNEMPLOYMENT

APPLYING THE CONCEPTS #1: How can data on vacancies and unemployment be used to measure shifts in the natural rate?

Economists believe that the natural rate of unemployment changes over time, although they often have difficulty pinning down an exact estimate. Policymakers need to have an accurate assessment of the natural rate to avoid any unnecessary unemployment or prevent inflation from emerging. But how can we estimate changes in the natural rate?

One way to estimate the shifts in the natural rate of unemployment is to look at the relationships between job vacancies and unemployment. Normally, the higher the unemployment rate, the fewer job vacancies there will be. This relationship is known as the Beveridge curve. But if the labor market matches individuals with jobs more efficiently, resulting in a decline in the natural rate of unemployment—for example, through the use of Internet searches or new technology—there will be fewer job vacancies corresponding to any level of unemployment. Using a variety of vacancy measures, economist William Dickens found that shifts in the relationship between vacancies and unemployment allowed him to make new estimates of the natural rate. He found that the natural rate was approximately 5 percent in the mid 1960s, but then rose in the late 1960s and peaked near 7 percent in the late 1970s and early 1980s. The natural rate began to drift down in the late 1980s and through the 1990s, again reaching the 5 percent level in 2000. It has since remained at this level. **Related to Exercise 2.8.**

SOURCE: Based on William Dickens, "A New Approach to Estimating the Natural Rate of Unemployment," July 2009, paper available at http://www.brookings.edu/papers/2009/07_unemployment_dickens.aspx

16.3 HOW THE CREDIBILITY OF A NATION'S CENTRAL BANK AFFECTS INFLATION

Why are the heads of central banks, such as the chair of the Federal Reserve Board of Governors, typically very conservative and constantly warning about the dangers of inflation? The basic reason is that these monetary policymakers can influence expectations of inflation, and expectations of inflation will influence actual behavior of workers and firms. For example, when workers anticipate inflation, they will push for higher nominal wages. When firms anticipate inflation, they will set their prices accordingly. If policymakers are not careful in the way they respond to expectations of inflation, they can actually make it difficult for a society to fight inflation.

Consider an example. A large union is negotiating wages for workers in the auto and steel industries. If the union negotiates a very high nominal wage, other unions will likely follow, negotiating for and winning higher wages. Prices of autos and steel will inevitably rise as a result, and the Fed will begin to see higher inflation emerge. Suppose the Fed has been keeping the money supply constant. What are its options?

We depict the Fed's dilemma in Figure 16.2. By setting a higher nominal wage, the union shifts the aggregate supply curve from AS_0 to AS_1. The Fed then has a choice:

- Keep the money supply and aggregate demand at AD_0. The economy will initially fall into a recession.

- Increase the money supply and raise aggregate demand from AD_0 to AD_1. This will keep the economy at full employment but lead to higher prices.

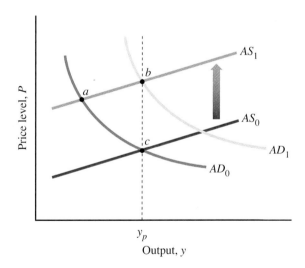

◄ **FIGURE 16.2**

Choices of the Fed: Recession or Inflation

If workers push up their nominal wages, the aggregate supply curve will shift from AS_0 to AS_1. If the Fed keeps aggregate demand constant at AD_0, a recession will occur at point *a*, and the economy will eventually return to full employment at point *c*. If the Fed increases aggregate demand, the economy remains at full employment at *b*, but with a higher price level.

The actions of the union will depend on what its leaders expect the Fed to do. On the one hand, if they believe the Fed will not increase aggregate demand, their actions will trigger a recession. Union leaders know this and might be reluctant to negotiate a high wage because of it. If they don't negotiate an increase in nominal wages, the economy will remain at full employment and there will be no increase in prices. On the other hand, if union leaders believe the Fed will increase aggregate demand, they have nothing to lose and will push for higher nominal wages. The result will be higher prices in the economy.

As this example illustrates, expectations about the Fed's determination to fight inflation will affect behavior in the private sector. If the Fed is credible or believable in its desire to fight inflation, it can deter the private sector from taking aggressive actions that drive up prices. This is the reason the heads of central banks are conservative, preferring to risk increasing unemployment rather than inflation. For example, having a conservative chair of the Fed, someone who strongly detests inflation, sends a signal to everyone in the economy that the Fed will be unlikely to increase the money supply, regardless of what actions are taken in the private sector.

After experiencing relatively high average inflation from 1955 to 1988, New Zealand took a different approach to ensure the credibility of its central bank. Since 1989, the central bank has been operating under a law that specifies its only goal is to attempt to maintain stable prices, which, in practice, requires it to keep inflation between 0 and 2 percent a year. This policy sharply limits the central bank's ability to stabilize real GDP, but it does signal to the private sector that the central bank will not be increasing the money supply, regardless of the actions taken by wage setters or unions.

Our example suggests that with a credible central bank, a country can have lower inflation without experiencing extra unemployment. Some political scientists and economists have suggested that central banks that have true independence from the rest of the government, and are therefore less subject to political influence, will be more credible in their commitment to fighting inflation.

There is evidence to support this conjecture. Figure 16.3 plots an index of independence against average inflation rates from 1955 to 1988 for 16 countries. The points appear to lie along a downward-sloping line, meaning more independence is associated with lower inflation. Germany and Switzerland, the countries with the most-independent central banks during that time period, had the lowest inflation rates. Another piece of evidence that credible banks can lower inflation safely is provided by the changes that occurred in the United Kingdom in the late 1990s.

As our discussion illustrates, how a central bank influences expectations is important for understanding the behavior of prices and output in an economy. Understanding how the private sector forms its inflation expectations in the first place is also important. Economists have used the theory of rational expectations we discussed earlier to explain the credibility of central banks. In our example, the theory of rational expectations implies the union will, on average, anticipate whether the Fed will expand the money supply in the face of wage increases. A credible Fed will tend to deter wage increases by not expanding the money supply. Many economists believed Fed Chairman Alan Greenspan was very credible in his determination to fight inflation. This in itself helped reduce inflation during the 1990s. People expected that Greenspan would refuse to set out the "punch bowl" of money (see Chapter 15), and they were right.

But suppose someone does *not* believe the central bank will control inflation. Does that person have any recourse? In the United States and some other countries, he or she does. As we mentioned in the chapter opening story, the U.S. government now sells bonds—TIPS—that protect an investor from inflation. Investors can protect themselves from unexpected inflation by buying TIPS.

▶ **FIGURE 16.3**

How Central Bank Independence Affects Inflation

Countries in which central banks are more independent from the rest of the government have, on average, lower inflation rates.

SOURCE: A. Alesina and L. Summers, "Central Bank Independence and Macroeconomic Performance," Journal of Money, Credit, and Banking *(May 1993).*

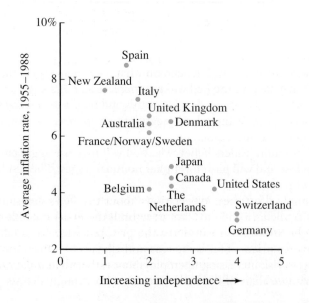

APPLICATION 2

INCREASED POLITICAL INDEPENDENCE FOR THE BANK OF ENGLAND LOWERED INFLATION EXPECTATIONS

APPLYING THE CONCEPTS #2: Can changes in the way central banks are governed affect inflation expectations?

On May 6, 1997, the then-chancellor of the exchequer in Great Britain, Gordon Brown, announced a major change in monetary policy. From that time forward, the Bank of England would be more independent from the government. Although the government would still retain the authority to set the overall goals for policy, the Bank of England would be free to pursue its policy goals without direct political control.

Mark Spiegel, an economist with the Federal Reserve Bank of San Francisco, studied how the British bond market reacted to the policy change. He compared the interest rate changes on two types of long-term bonds: British bonds that are automatically adjusted (or indexed) for inflation (such as TIPS in the United States) and bonds that are not. The difference between the two interest rates primarily reflects expectations of inflation. Thus, if the gap narrowed following the policy announcement, this would be evidence that the new policy reduced expectations of inflation. If it did not, the announced policy would have had no effect on inflation expectations.

After the announcement, the gap narrowed, and Spiegel concluded the announcement did, indeed, cause expectations about inflation to fall by about half a percentage. **Related to Exercise 3.5.**

SOURCE: Based on "British Central Bank Independence and Inflation Expectations," *Federal Reserve Bank of San Francisco Economic Letter*, November 28, 1997.

16.4 INFLATION AND THE VELOCITY OF MONEY

Countries sometimes experience stunning inflation rates. For example, in 15 months from August 1922 to November 1923, the price level in Germany rose by a factor of 10 billion! To explain these extremely high inflation rates and their relationship to money growth, we now introduce a concept that is closely related to money demand: the *velocity of money*. The **velocity of money** is defined as the ratio of nominal GDP to the money supply:

$$\text{velocity of money} = \frac{\text{nominal GDP}}{\text{money supply}}$$

velocity of money
The rate at which money turns over during the year. It is calculated as nominal GDP divided by the money supply.

One useful way to think of velocity is that it is the number of times money must change hands, or turn over, in economic transactions during a given year for an economy to reach its GDP level. To understand this, consider a simple example. Suppose nominal GDP is $5 trillion per year and the money supply is $1 trillion. The velocity of money in this economy will then be as follows:

$$\text{velocity} = \frac{\$5 \text{ trillion per year}}{\$1 \text{ trillion}} = 5 \text{ per year}$$

In this economy, the $1 trillion money supply has to change hands, or turn over, five times a year to purchase the $5 trillion of nominal GDP. If the money supply turns over five times in one year, this means people are holding each dollar of money for 365 days/5, or 73 days. If velocity is very high, people turn money over very quickly on average and do not hold it for a long time. If velocity is low, people turn over money slowly and hold onto it longer.

To further understand the role of money and velocity, let's rewrite the definition of velocity as

$$\text{money supply} \times \text{velocity} = \text{nominal GDP}$$

or

$$M \times V = P \times y$$

where M is the money supply, V is the velocity of money, P is a price index for GDP, and y is real GDP. This equation is known as the equation of exchange, or the **quantity equation**. On the right side, $P \times y$ is nominal GDP. It is the product of the price index and real GDP. It also represents total nominal spending. On the left side, the money supply, M, is multiplied by V, the velocity, or turnover rate, of money.

As you can see, the quantity equation links the money supply and velocity to nominal GDP. If velocity is predictable, we can use the quantity equation and the supply of money to predict nominal GDP. But it's not quite that easy; the velocity of money does vary over time. Figure 16.4 plots the velocity of M2 (the measure of the money supply that includes currency, demand deposits, savings accounts, time deposits, and deposits in money market mutual funds) in the United States between 1959 and 2009. During this period, velocity reached a low of around 1.6 in the 1960s and a high of 2.1 in the late 1990s. In other words, the total amount of M2 held by the public turned over between 1.6 and 2.1 times a year for the U.S. economy to reach nominal GDP.

quantity equation

The equation that links money, velocity, prices, and real output. In symbols, we have $M \times V = P \times y$.

▶ **FIGURE 16.4**
The Velocity of M2, 1959–2009
SOURCE: Federal Reserve Bank of St. Louis.

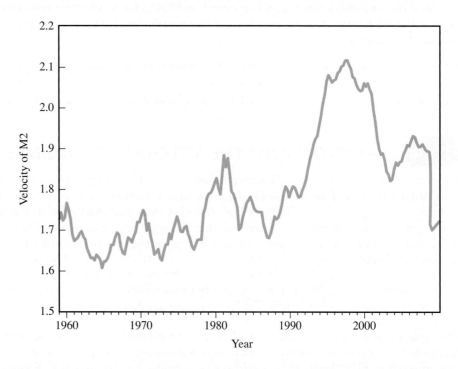

We can use the basic quantity equation to derive a closely related formula for understanding inflation in the long run:

growth rate of money + growth rate of velocity

= growth rate of prices + growth rate of real output

growth version of the quantity equation

An equation that links the growth rates of money, velocity, prices, and real output.

We will call this the **growth version of the quantity equation**. Here is how to use this formula: Suppose money growth is 10 percent a year, the growth of real output is 3 percent a year, and velocity has zero growth (it is constant). Then the rate of growth of prices—the inflation rate, in other words—is

10 percent + 0 percent = growth rate of prices + 3 percent

7 percent = growth rate of prices (inflation)

Inflation will be 7 percent a year. The formula allows for real economic growth and for growth in velocity. For example, if velocity grew during this period at the rate of 1 percent a year instead of zero, the annual inflation rate would be 8 percent (10 + 1 − 3). Economists use this formula to provide quick estimates of the inflation rate.

As we've learned, there is a definite link between increases in the growth of money and the rate of inflation. Inflation was lowest in the 1950s, when money growth was lowest. It was also highest in the 1970s, when money growth was highest. The link is not perfect, because real GDP and velocity grew at different rates during these two decades. However, years of economic research have revealed that sustained increases in money growth will, indeed, lead to inflation.

The links between money growth and inflation are particularly dramatic when money growth is extremely high. But what leads countries to vast increases in their money supply? We'll explore that next.

16.5 HYPERINFLATION

The inflation rates observed in the United States in the last 40 years are insignificant compared to some of the inflation rates around the world throughout history. Economists call very high inflation rates—over 50 percent per month, which is approximately 13,000 percent per year—**hyperinflation**. One of the first hyperinflation studies was conducted by Phillip Cagan of Columbia University in the 1950s. Table 16.3 presents selected data from his study.

hyperinflation
An inflation rate exceeding 50 percent per month.

TABLE 16.3 HYPERINFLATIONS AND VELOCITY

Country	Dates	Monthly Rate of Inflation	Monthly Rate of Money Growth	Approximate Increase in Velocity
Greece	November 1943 to November 1944	365%	220%	14.00
Hungary	August 1945 to July 1946	19,800%	12,200%	333.00
Russia	December 1921 to January 1924	57%	49%	3.70

SOURCE: Adapted from Phillip Cagan, "The Monetary Dynamics of Hyperinflation," in *Studies in the Quantity Theory of Money*, ed. Milton Friedman (Chicago: University of Chicago Press, 1956), 26.

Greece, Hungary, and Russia are three countries that have experienced hyperinflation. According to the data in Table 16.3, for a period of one year, Greece had a monthly inflation rate of 365 percent. A monthly inflation rate of 365 percent means the price level rises by a factor of 4.65 each month. If the price level rises by 4.65, its percent increase is

$$\frac{4.65 - 1}{1} = 3.65 = 365 \text{ percent}$$

To get a sense of what a 365 percent inflation rate means, suppose we had inflation of this magnitude in the United States. At the beginning of the month, $1 could buy a large order of french fries. Because prices are rising by a factor of 4.65 each month, by the end of the month it would take $4.65 to buy the same order of french fries, and $1 by the end of the month would be worth only 21.5 cents (1/4.65 = 0.215, or 21.5 cents). After two months, a dollar would be worth only 4.6 cents (0.215 × 0.215 = 0.046). Suppose this inflation continues month after month. After one year, a dollar bill would be worth only 1 millionth of 1 cent! In hyperinflations, money doesn't hold its value very long.

In Hungary after World War II prices rose by 19,800 percent each month. The hyperinflation in Russia in the early 1920s seems moderate by comparison: Prices there rose by only 57 percent per month. However, hyperinflations have also occurred in recent times. Table 16.4 presents data on three hyperinflations during the 1980s—in Bolivia, Argentina, and Nicaragua, all averaging about 100 percent per month.

TABLE 16.4 HYPERINFLATIONS IN THE 1980S				
Country	Year	Yearly Rate of Inflation	Monthly Rate of Inflation	Monthly Money Growth Rate
Bolivia	1985	1,152,200%	118%	91%
Argentina	1989	302,200	95	93
Nicaragua	1988	975,500	115	66

SOURCE: International Financial Statistics, International Monetary Fund.

On the basis of the quantity theory, we suspect these hyperinflations must have all been caused by money growth. You can see this in the data. For example, in Greece, the monthly inflation of 365 percent was accompanied by money growth of 220 percent. In Hungary, the monthly inflation of 19,800 percent was accompanied by money growth of 12,200 percent.

The value of money deteriorates sharply during hyperinflations and no longer serves as a good store of value. In these extreme circumstances, we would expect people wouldn't want to hold money very long but would immediately try to spend it. In other words, the velocity of money should increase sharply during hyperinflations. This is precisely what happens. The last column of Table 16.3 shows how velocity increases during hyperinflations. In the hyperinflation in Greece, velocity increased by a factor of 14. In the hyperinflation in Hungary, velocity increased by a factor of 333.

During hyperinflations, money doesn't facilitate exchange well. Because prices are changing so fast and unpredictably, there is typically massive confusion about the true value of commodities. Different stores may be raising prices at different rates, so the same commodities may sell for radically different prices. People spend all their time hunting for bargains and the lowest prices, a process that becomes very costly in human terms. Hyperinflation also means people have less time to produce goods and services. No country can easily live very long with a hyperinflation. The government must take swift measures to end a hyperinflation before it completely destroys the economy.

How Budget Deficits Lead to Hyperinflation

If the cause of hyperinflations is excessive money growth, why do governments allow the money supply to grow so fast, risking economic catastrophe? The answer lies in the way some governments finance their deficits—the gap between government spending and revenues.

A government must cover its deficit in some way. If a government wants to spend $1,000 but is collecting only $800 in taxes, where can it get the needed $200? One option is to borrow the $200 by selling government bonds—IOUs—to the public. In the future, the government will have to repay the $200 in bonds plus the interest the public earns on them. Another alternative is to create $200 of new money. All governments have the ability to run the printing presses and come up with $200 in new currency. The revenue raised from money creation is called **seignorage**. In principle, governments can do a combination of both—selling bonds and printing money—as long as the deficit is covered:

seignorage
Revenue raised from money creation.

government deficit = new borrowing from the public + new money created

APPLICATION 3

HYPERINFLATION IN ZIMBABWE

APPLYING THE CONCEPTS #3: What caused a severe hyperinflation to emerge recently in Zimbabwe?

In June 2008 the consumer price index in Zimbabwe was 8 million percent higher than it was a year before. A $12 lunch in local currency cost 1.1 trillion Zimbabwe dollars. What caused Zimbabwe to suffer from this crippling hyperinflation?

The simple answer is that the political and economic system began to self-destruct. Zimbabwe has been ruled since 1980 by the dictator Robert Mugabe, whose policies to intervene militarily in African conflicts and expropriate white-owned farms had the cumulative effect of crippling the economy. As the economy deteriorated, tax revenues declined, as well as export revenues necessary to purchase imported fuel. To pay soldiers to help keep him in power, to bribe his supporters, and to keep the government functioning, Mugabe and his central bank simply resorted to printing new banknotes. The result was hyperinflation and further deterioration of the economy as the financial system collapsed. **Related to Exercise 5.5.**

SOURCES: Based on Roger Bate, "How Inflation May Topple Mugabe, *Wall Street Journal*, July 7, 2008, and Andrew Wiggins, "Zimbabwe Central Banker Answers to Mugabe, Bible," *Wall Street Journal*, July 8, 2008.

Now we are in a position to understand how hyperinflations originate. Consider Hungary after World War II. The country's economy was destroyed by the war, and its citizens were demanding government services. The government had limited ability to collect taxes because of the poor state of the economy, but it gave in to the demands from its citizens for spending at levels that far exceeded what it could collect. The result was a large deficit. Then the government faced a problem: How would it finance this large deficit? No individuals or governments wanted to buy bonds or IOUs from Hungary (lend it money) because the country's economy was in such bad shape that prospects for repayment in the near future were grim. Unable to borrow, Hungary resorted to printing money at a massive rate. The result was hyperinflation.

A more recent example of a devastating hyperinflation occurred in Zimbabwe, beginning in 2007. What were the causes of this hyperinflation?

To end hyperinflation, governments must eliminate their budget deficits by either increasing taxes, cutting spending, or both. This, of course, will cause some economic pain, but there is no other remedy. Once the deficit has been cut and the government stops printing money, the hyperinflation will end. Without money growth to feed it, hyperinflation will quickly die of starvation.

Economists who emphasize the role the supply of money plays in determining nominal income and inflation are called **monetarists**. The most famous monetarist was Milton Friedman, who studied complex versions of the quantity equation and explored the role of money in all aspects of economic life. Friedman had many influential students, such as Phillip Cagan, who is best known for his work on hyperinflations (see Table 16.3). Friedman and Cagan, along with other monetarist economists, pioneered research on the link between money, nominal income, and inflation. During the 1960s, little attention was being paid to the role of money in determining aggregate demand. The work of Friedman and other monetarists was extremely influential in changing the opinions of economic thinkers at that time. Moreover, the monetarists were also insistent that, in the long run, inflation was a monetary problem. Today, most economists agree with them that, in the long run, inflation is caused by growth in the money supply.

monetarists

Economists who emphasize the role that the supply of money plays in determining nominal income and inflation.

SUMMARY

In this chapter, we explored the role expectations of inflation play in the economy and how societies deal with inflation. Interest rates, as well as changes in wages and prices, both reflect expectations of inflation. These expectations depend on the past history of inflation and on expectations about central bank behavior. To reduce inflation, policymakers must increase actual unemployment above the natural rate of unemployment. We also looked at the ultimate causes of hyperinflations. Here are the key points to remember from this chapter:

1. In the long run, higher money growth leads to higher inflation and higher nominal interest rates.

2. A decrease in the growth rate of money will initially lead to higher real-interest rates and higher nominal-interest rates. In the long run, real rates return to their original level; nominal rates are permanently lower because of reduced inflation.

3. The rate of inflation increases when actual unemployment falls below the natural rate of unemployment; the rate of inflation decreases when actual unemployment exceeds the natural rate of unemployment. Economists explain this relationship using the *expectations Phillips curve*.

4. How the public forms expectations of inflation and the time frame in which it must form them are important factors in understanding the behavior of inflation and unemployment. Sometimes the public uses rules of thumb to form expectations; other times it may use *rational expectations*.

5. Monetary policymakers need to be cautious about the statements and pronouncements they make because what they say can influence inflation expectations. Conservative central bankers can dampen expectations of inflation.

6. The *quantity equation* and the *growth version of the quantity equation* show how money, velocity, and nominal income are related. The simple quantity equation is

$$M \times V = P \times y$$

7. Governments sometimes create new money to finance large portions of their budget deficits. Raising funds through printing money is known as *seignorage*. When governments do this excessively, the result is *hyperinflation*. Stopping hyperinflation requires closing the government deficit and reducing money creation.

KEY TERMS

expectations of inflation, p. 330

expectations Phillips curve, p. 332

growth version of the quantity equation, p. 340

hyperinflation, p. 341

monetarists, p. 343

money illusion, p. 330

nominal wages, p. 330

quantity equation, p. 340

rational expectations, p. 333

real wages, p. 330

seignorage, p. 342

velocity of money, p. 339

EXERCISES

Visit www.myeconlab.com to complete these exercises online and get instant feedback.

16.1 Money Growth, Inflation, and Interest Rates

1.1 The expected real rate of interest is the nominal interest rate minus the expected inflation rate. _____ (True/False)

1.2 Countries with higher rates of money growth have _____ interest rates.

1.3 If the growth rate of money increases from 3 to 5 percent, initially interest rates will _____.

1.4 A firm that expects higher profits from higher prices but does not recognize its costs are increasing is suffering from _____.

1.5 **Inflation: A Recipe for Japan?** In the late 1990s, Japan's economy was still in a prolonged slump. Nominal interest rates were approximately zero, which many economists believed limited the scope for monetary policy. Professor Paul Krugman of Princeton University, and a Nobel Laureate, disagreed. He argued that Japan's central bank should increase the money supply rapidly with the intention of causing inflation. Moreover, it should credibly promise to continue this inflation policy into the future. The result, he predicted, would be increased investment and higher GDP growth. Krugman's recommendation was based on the distinction between real and nominal interest rates. Can you explain his logic?

1.6 **Money Neutrality, Long Run Inflation, and the Natural Rate.** Explain carefully the relationship between the concept of monetary neutrality and the idea that the natural rate is independent of the long run inflation rate.

1.7 **Taxes, Inflation, and Interest Rates.** If a business borrows funds at 10 percent per year, the business has a 40 percent tax rate, and the annual inflation rate is 5 percent, what are the real after-tax costs of funds to the business? Similarly, if an investor receives a nominal return of 8 percent on a savings deposit, the tax rate is 30 percent, and the inflation rate is 6 percent, what is the after-tax rate of return?

1.8 Examples of Money Illusion. What do the following two quotes have in common?
  a. "My wages are going up 5 percent a year. If only inflation weren't 5 percent a year, I would be rich."
  b. "My bank is paying 10 percent a year, but the 8 percent inflation rate is just eating up all my real investment gains."

16.2 Understanding the Expectations Phillips Curve: The Relationship between Unemployment and Inflation

2.1 If inflation increases less than expected, the actual unemployment rate will be _____ (above/below) the natural rate.

2.2 Robert E, Lucas, Jr., explained business cycles by rules of thumb. _____ (True/False)

2.3 The increase in the fraction of young people in the labor force that occurred when the baby-boom generation came of working age tended to _____ (raise/lower) the natural rate of unemployment.

2.4 In the late 1980s, as unemployment fell below the natural rate, inflation _____.

2.5 Targeting the Natural Rate? Because the natural rate of unemployment is the economists' notion of what constitutes "full employment," it might seem logical for the Fed to use monetary policy to move unemployment toward its natural rate. However, many economists believe such a policy would be unwise because the natural rate may shift over time and policymakers may misjudge the correct rate. What would happen if the Fed targeted a 5 percent unemployment rate but the true natural rate were 6 percent?

2.6 Explaining a Movement in the Inflation Rate. In Figure 16.1 you can see that inflation rose between 1988 and 1989 with little change in the unemployment rate. Can you explain why?

2.7 Hysteresis and the Natural Rate of Unemployment. In economics the term "hysteresis" means that the history of the economy has a lingering effect on current economic performance. Using this idea, explain why a deep recession could lead to an increase in the natural rate of unemployment. Which demographic groups do you think would be affected the most?

2.8 Oil Price Changes, Vacancies, and the Natural Rate. During the mid-1970s, changes in oil prices required products to be produced by different types of firms in different locations. This raised the number of vacancies relative to the unemployment rate. According

to the theory of William Dickens, how did this affect the natural rate of unemployment? (Related to Application 1 on page 336.)

16.3 How the Credibility of a Nation's Central Bank Affects Inflation

3.1 An aggressive union will shift the aggregate supply curve _____, causing prices to _____ and real GDP to _____.

3.2 In the face of an upward shift in the aggregate supply curve, the Fed can increase the supply of money. This will prevent a recession, but will cause an increase in _____.

3.3 The evidence shows that lower inflation rates are associated with central bank _____.

3.4 When the Bank of England became independent, inflation expectations _____.

3.5 Public Pronouncements and Fed Officials. In addition to political and institutional factors, public pronouncements also affect the credibility of the Fed. When Alan Blinder, a Princeton University professor of economics, was appointed vice-chair of the Federal Reserve in 1994, he gave a speech to a group of central bankers and monetary policy specialists. In that speech, he repeated one of the lessons in this chapter: In the long run, the rate of inflation is independent of unemployment and depends only on money growth; in the short run, lower unemployment can raise the inflation rate. Blinder's speech caused an uproar in the financial press. Some commentators attacked him as not being sufficiently vigilant against inflation. Use the idea of credibility to explain why an apparently innocent speech would create such a reaction. (Related to Application 2 on page 339.)

3.6 Pay Incentives for Fed Officials? In the private sector, the pay of executives is typically tied to the performance of their company. Could this work in the public sector as well? Suppose pay for the chairman of the Federal Reserve is tied to the price of long-term bonds. That is, if bond prices rise, the chairman receives a bonus, but if they fall, the chairman's salary will decrease. Would this provide a credible incentive for the chairman to keep inflation low? (*Hint*: Think of the links between inflation, interest rates, and bond prices.) Do you see any disadvantages to this proposal?

3.7 Buying Gold to Protect Against Inflation. Consider the following statement: "Since gold is a commodity and prices of commodities by definition increase with inflation, buying gold will protect me from any inflationary increases." Can you point out a possible problem with buying gold to protect yourself against inflation?

16.4 Inflation and the Velocity of Money

4.1 The velocity of money is defined as _____ income divided by the supply of money.

4.2 The quantity equation links money, velocity, real income, and _____.

4.3 If we know the growth of velocity, income, and the money supply, we can explain the _____ rate.

4.4 If the growth of the money supply is 4 percent a year, velocity decreases by 1 percent, and there is no growth in real output, the inflation rate equals _____.

4.5 **Velocity and ATMs.** Suppose the introduction of ATMs led households to hold less of their wealth as deposits in banks or savings and loans. How would this affect measured velocity?

4.6 **Using the Quantity Equation.** If the growth rate of money is 10 percent per year, annual inflation is 7 percent, and the growth rate of velocity is 1 percent per year, what is the growth rate of real output?

4.7 **Velocity of Money in the United States.** Using the Federal Reserve Bank of St. Louis Web site (www.research.stlouisfed.org/fred2), calculate the velocity of M1 and M2 in 1960 and 2000. How have they changed?

16.5 Hyperinflation

5.1 To finance a budget deficit, a government can either borrow from the public or create _____.

5.2 During hyperinflations the velocity of money tends to _____ sharply.

5.3 Economists call inflation "hyperinflation" when the inflation rate exceeds _____ percent per month.

5.4 Hyperinflations cannot occur unless the growth rate of _____ is very high.

5.5 **Hyperinflation and Barter.** Some economists and journalists noticed that during Zimbabwe's hyperinflation, the economy was turning to a barter economy. Why do you think this would occur? (Related to Application 3 on page 343.)

5.6 **Losing Wars and Hyperinflation.** Why do hyperinflations occur more frequently after countries lose wars than when they win them?

5.7 **Unprofitable Government Enterprises and Inflation.** In some developing countries, governments are forced to support large enterprises that persistently lose substantial sums of money. Why might this cause inflation?

ECONOMIC EXPERIMENT

Money Illusion

Economists say that people suffer from money illusion if their behavior is influenced by nominal changes that are also not real changes. Consider the following scenarios and be prepared to discuss them in class.

a. Erin bought an antique clock for $100. Two years later, Betsy bought an identical clock for $121. Meanwhile, there had been inflation each year of 10 percent. Both Erin and Betsy sold their clocks to other collectors. Erin sold hers for $130, and Betsy sold hers for $133. Who profited more from her transaction?

b. Bob and Pete are traders in classic comic books. A year ago, Bob and Pete each bought the same comic book for $10. Bob sold his a couple of days later for $20. Pete waited a year and sold his for $21. If inflation last year was 6 percent, who made the better deal?

 For additional economic experiments, please visit *www.myeconlab.com*.

Macroeconomic Policy Debates

Economists are often cautious and try to warn policymakers that carrying out effective economic policy is difficult. But politicians must ultimately make decisions. As we learned in Chapter 1, President Harry S. Truman made the following observation about his cautious economists: "All my economists say, 'On the one hand, . . . ; On the other hand, . . .' Give me a one-handed economist!"

Decisions about government spending, taxes, deficits, interest rates, and exchange rates may seem very abstract, but they directly affect our lives. Poor economic policies can lead to the virtual collapse of countries. Policymaking therefore requires prudence. Of course, it is always very easy to criticize politicians in power when something goes wrong. In another famous quote, Truman recognized that decision making is not easy. Before air conditioning was commonplace, he was known to have remarked, "If you can't stand the heat, get out of the kitchen."

APPLYING THE CONCEPTS

1 What are the long-term fiscal imbalances for the United States?
   New Methods to Measure the Long-Term Fiscal Imbalances for the United States

2 Did the Federal Reserve cause the housing boom through excessively loose monetary policy?
   Would a Policy Rule Have Prevented the Housing Boom?

3 Can the United States adopt a European-style value-added tax?
   Is a VAT in Our Future?

As a student and citizen, you are inevitably drawn into economic debates. In most cases, the debates are complex because they involve a mixture of facts, theories, and opinions. Value judgments play a large role in economic debates. Your views on the proper role of tax policy, for example, will depend on whether you believe low-income earners should receive a higher share of national income. Your views on the size of government will depend on whether you believe individuals or the government should play a larger role in economic affairs.

In previous chapters, you learned the basic vocabulary of economics and studied different theories of the economy. Now you are ready to examine some of the key policy issues in macroeconomics. In this chapter, we will focus on three macroeconomics issues that are the subject of much debate:

- Should we balance the federal budget?
- Should the Fed target inflation or pursue other objectives?
- Should we tax consumption rather than income?

17.1 SHOULD WE BALANCE THE FEDERAL BUDGET?

Before we begin to consider answers to the question "Should we balance the federal budget?" let's review some terms from Chapter 10: *Government expenditures* include goods and services purchased by the government and transfer payments, such as Social Security and welfare, made to citizens. A *surplus* occurs when the government's revenues exceed its expenditures in a given year. The government runs a *deficit* when it spends more than it receives in revenues from either taxes or fees in a given year.

The *government debt* is the *total* of all its yearly deficits. For example, if a government initially had a debt of $100 billion and then ran deficits of $20 billion the next year, $30 billion the year after that, and $50 billion during the third year, its total debt at the end of the third year would be $200 billion: the initial $100 billion debt plus the successive yearly deficits of $20 billion, $30 billion, and $50 billion. If a government ran a surplus, it would decrease its total debt. For example, suppose the debt were $100 billion and the government ran a surplus of $10 billion. With the surplus, the government would buy back $10 billion of debt from the private sector, thereby reducing the remaining debt to $90 billion.

In this chapter, we focus on the government debt held by the public, not the total federal debt, which includes debt held by other governmental agencies. Sometimes popular accounts in the press or on the Web highlight the total federal debt. However, the debt held by the public is the best measure to assess the burden the federal debt can have on the economy.

The Budget in Recent Decades

The fiscal picture for the United States has changed substantially over the last 30 years. Beginning in the 1980s and through most of the 1990s, the federal budget ran large deficits—"deficits as far as the eye can see," as David Stockman, the director of the Office of Management and Budget in President Reagan's administration, put it. What Stockman could not see at that point, however, was what would occur in the late 1990s. In fiscal year 1998, during President Clinton's administration, the federal government ran a budget surplus of $69 billion—its first surplus in 30 years. It continued to run surpluses for the next 3 fiscal years as well.

The surplus emerged for two key reasons. First, economic growth was very rapid and tax revenues—including tax revenues from the sales of stocks and bonds—grew more quickly than anticipated. Second, federal budget rules were in place that limited total spending.

When President George W. Bush took office in January 2001, the large surplus led him to propose substantial tax cuts. Bush and Congress then passed a 10-year tax cut amounting to $1.35 trillion over the course of the decade. Although the tax cuts were large, the Congressional Budget Office (CBO) estimated at that time that the federal government would nonetheless continue to run surpluses through 2010.

The CBO noted that, as a result of these federal government surpluses, the outstanding stock of federal debt held by the public would be reduced. Because GDP would be growing over this period, the stock of debt relative to GDP, which is the standard way to measure the effect of debt in an economy, would also decline. The CBO estimated that in 2011, the ratio of debt to GDP would fall despite Bush's tax cuts, in part because the tax cuts were set to expire in 2010. Figure 17.1 depicts the debt/GDP ratio from 1791 to 2009. As you can see, except for a period in the 1980s typically the ratio rises sharply during wars and the Great Depression and falls during peacetime. With neither a war nor a recession looming on the horizon in early 2001, the CBO predicted that the debt/GDP ratio would be relatively low by the end of the decade.

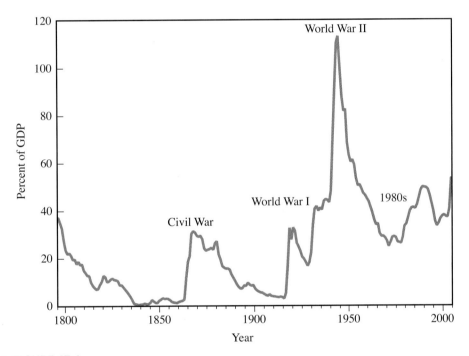

▲ FIGURE 17.1

Debt as a Percent of GDP, 1791–2009

The nation's debt/GDP ratio tends to rise sharply during wars because more spending is needed to finance them. However, the ratio also can rise during peacetime, as it did during the Reagan presidency in the 1980s.

SOURCES: Congressional Budget Office, "The Long-Term Budget Outlook," December 2003, and yearly updates.

Unfortunately, a series of events intervened to bring deficits back into the picture and prevent the debt/GDP ratio from falling. The fight against terrorism led to higher spending on homeland security and military spending as wars were launched in Afghanistan and Iraq. The Bush tax cuts, the collapse of the stock market twice during the decade, the recessions that began in 2001 and 2007, and the housing bust mid-decade all sharply reduced tax revenues. President Obama's stimulus package in 2009 added new tax cuts and additional spending, which fueled the deficit. The federal government ran a budget deficit of approximately $1.3 trillion in fiscal year 2010, a far cry from the surpluses in the late 1990s. You can see from the last few years of Figure 17.1 that the debt-to-GDP ratio has recently risen. Current projections by the CBO suggest that the debt-to-GDP ratio will increase even when the economy resumes a normal level of economic growth.

Five Debates about Deficits

As we have seen, federal budgets are affected by a wide range of factors, including wars, demographic pressures, recessions, and the choices our politicians make on spending and taxes. But what principles should guide policymakers? Should they cut spending and raise taxes to reduce the national debt over time? Or does the level of the national debt really matter? Let's take a look at the debates over the national debt.

DEBATE 1: DO DEFICITS LEAD TO INFLATION? If a government is spending $2,000 but collecting only $1,600 in taxes, where does it get the $400 needed to fill the gap? One option is to borrow $400 from the public in return for government bonds, which are, in effect, IOUs. In the future the government would have to pay back the $400 plus any interest on the bonds. Another way to cover the gap is simply to create $400 worth of new money. In principle, governments could use a mix of borrowing money and creating money, as long as the total covers its deficits:

government deficit = new borrowing from the public + new money created

monetizing the deficit
Purchases by a central bank of newly issued government bonds.

In the United States, the Treasury Department issues government bonds to finance the deficit. The Federal Reserve has the option of buying existing government bonds, including those newly issued by the Treasury Department. If the Federal Reserve does purchase the government's bonds, the purchase creates money by taking debt out of the hands of the public in exchange for money. Economists call the purchase by a central bank of newly issued government debt **monetizing the deficit**. If governments finance deficits by creating new money, the result will be inflation. In the United States, we normally finance only a very small portion of our deficits by creating money. For example, between 2005 and 2006 the Federal Reserve purchased only $34 billion in government bonds of approximately $330 billion issued by the Treasury during that period. The Fed sold the remainder to the public. However, during the financial crisis, the Fed engaged in massive purchases in securities, adding over a trillion dollars to its balance sheet. However, by paying interest on reserves, it induced banks to hold matching excess reserves and thus prevented the money supply held by the public from increasing. This prevented inflation from emerging.

If a country has no options other than creating money to finance its deficits—in other words, if the public is unwilling to buy its bonds, as was the case in Hungary following World War II—those deficits will inevitably cause inflation. As we discussed in Chapter 16, hyperinflations occur when economies run large deficits and monetize them. Germany and Russia after World War I, Bolivia and Argentina in the 1980s, Russia in the 1990s, and most recently Zimbabwe are just some of the countries that, in addition to Hungary, have endured massive inflations because they monetized their deficits. However, large, stable countries like the United Kingdom, the United States, and Japan don't monetize much of their debt because they are able to borrow from the public. In these countries, deficits do not lead inevitably to inflation.

DEBATE 2: IS GOVERNMENT DEBT A BURDEN ON FUTURE GENERATIONS? The national debt, another commonly used term for total government debt, can impose two different burdens on society, both of which fall on the shoulders of future generations. First, a large debt can reduce the amount of capital in the economy and thereby reduce future income and real wages for its citizens. Here's how.

The savings of individuals and institutions flow into capital formation and increase an economy's capital stock. For example, when savers purchase new stocks and bonds, the companies issuing them use the proceeds to invest in plants and equipment.

When the government runs a deficit and increases its national debt, it also finances its spending by selling bonds to these same savers, who might hold both types of assets in, say, their retirement portfolios. Further, let's say that the total amount that the public can save is fixed at $1,000. If the government needs to finance a $200 deficit and does so by selling new bonds, then only $800 in savings is available to invest in private companies. The selling of $200 in government bonds to finance the deficit therefore "crowds out" $200 that could have been raised by private companies.

The result of government deficits is that less savings are available to firms for investment. This illustrates one of our basic principles in economics.

PRINCIPLE OF OPPORTUNITY COST

The opportunity cost of something is what you sacrifice to get it.

As we discussed in earlier chapters, reduced saving and investment will ultimately reduce the stock of private capital, the building of new factories, and the purchasing of equipment to expand production and raise GDP. As a result, there will be less capital deepening. With lower capital per worker, real incomes and real wages will be lower than they otherwise might have been. The government deficit (caused by increased spending or decreased taxes) comes at a cost in the future.

Governments can spend the proceeds of borrowing on investments, such as productive infrastructure—in this case, future real wages and incomes will not be adversely affected. With productive investment, government deficits will not be a burden on society.

Second, a large national debt will mean that higher taxes will be imposed on future generations to pay the interest that accumulates on the debt. Just like your college loans, the bill eventually comes due—even for the national debt.

Sometimes you hear that these interest payments are not a real burden because "we owe the national debt to ourselves." This is a misleading argument for several reasons. First, we don't owe the interest payments only to ourselves. In 2009, approximately 52 percent of U.S. public debt was held by foreigners. Second, a high proportion of the debt is held by older, wealthy individuals or by institutions, but the taxes levied to service it will be paid by everyone in the United States.

Some economists do not believe that government deficits, resulting in government debt, impose a burden on a society. These economists believe in **Ricardian equivalence**, the proposition that it does not matter whether government expenditure is financed by taxes or financed by issuing debt. This idea is named after David Ricardo, a nineteenth-century classical economist. To understand the case for Ricardian equivalence, consider the following example. A government initially has a balanced budget. It then cuts taxes and issues new debt to finance the deficit left by the reduction in taxes. Everyone understands the government will have to raise taxes in the future to service the debt, so everyone increases savings to pay for the taxes that will be increased in the future. If saving rises sufficiently, the public—everyone—will be able to purchase the new debt without reducing the funds they invest in the private sector. Because net investment doesn't decline, there will be no debt burden.

As you can see, Ricardian equivalence requires that savings by the private sector increase when the deficit increases. Do savers behave this way? It is actually difficult to provide a definite answer, because we must take many other factors into account in any empirical studies of savings. It appears, however, that during the early 1980s, savings decreased somewhat when government deficits increased. This is precisely the opposite of what Ricardian equivalence predicts. As long as Ricardian equivalence

Ricardian equivalence

The proposition that it does not matter whether government expenditure is financed by taxes or debt.

does not fully hold true, it's reasonable to assume the government debt imposes a burden on society. Nonetheless, many economists believe using the deficit as the sole measure of a society's future burdens doesn't tell the whole story. These economists believe we should look at broader measures that take into account long run promises of the federal government.

From an international perspective, the United States does not have the largest government debt measured relative to GDP. Figure 17.2 depicts the percentage of debt to GDP for several developed countries. By this measure, Japan has the most serious public debt problem.

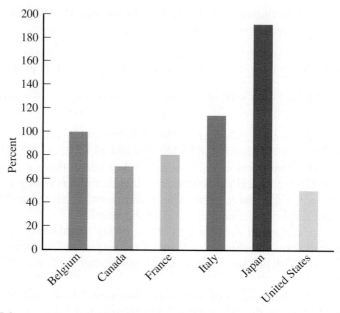

▲ **FIGURE 17.2**

International Comparisons of Government Debt as Percentage of GDP, 2009
Among developed countries, the United States has a relatively small percentage of debt to GDP. Japan has the highest percentage of debt of the countries depicted.
SOURCE: Central Intelligence Agency, The World Factbook, *https://www.cia.gov/library/publications/the-world-factbook/rankorder/2186rank.html (accessed April 26, 2010).*

DEBATE 3: HOW DO DEFICITS AFFECT THE SIZE OF GOVERNMENT? Nobel Laureate James Buchanan has argued that people are less aware of government deficits than of the taxes they're forced to pay. Therefore, financing government expenditures through deficits, rather than through higher taxes, will inevitably lead to higher government spending and bigger government. Although this argument may seem plausible, it presents two problems. First, in recent U.S. history, spending by state and local governments has grown much faster than federal spending. However, state and local governments face many more restrictions when it comes to borrowing money than the federal government faces. For example, many states require legislators to run a balanced budget. Deficit spending isn't allowed. Second, if politicians trying to get reelected really prefer higher government spending and deficits to higher taxes and surpluses, why did the federal government run surpluses in the late 1990s?

Some research suggests politicians can use deficits strategically to actually reduce the growth of government. During the 1980s, for example, the government ran large deficits caused by a combination of a deep recession and major tax cuts. The deficits subsequently made it difficult for other politicians to propose new spending programs. Proponents of smaller government, therefore, may wish to cut taxes to reduce surpluses or increase deficits in order to make it more difficult for other politicians to increase government spending. These deficit proponents want to create deficits to

APPLICATION 1

NEW METHODS TO MEASURE THE LONG-TERM FISCAL IMBALANCES FOR THE UNITED STATES

APPLYING THE CONCEPTS #1: What are the long-term fiscal imbalances for the United States?

Even though federal budget-deficit projections have increased sharply in recent years, they still don't accurately portray the long-run fiscal problems facing the United States. As the population ages, life expectancies increase, and health-care costs continue to grow, expenditures on Social Security and Medicare are expected to increase significantly, too. Although payroll taxes today exceed expenditures, in the not-too-distant future these taxes will fall far short of anticipated expenditures. Over time, there will be an escalating gap between revenues and expenditures, which will have to be met by outright borrowing.

How can we measure the size of the gap? Economists Jagadeesh Gokhale of the Cato Institute and Kent Smetters of the University of Pennsylvania have developed a more comprehensive measure of a nation's indebtedness. The method includes estimating the present value of the gap between the government's revenues and expenditures and adding it to the current national debt.

In 2005 Gokhale and Smetters calculated this new total measure, which they call the "fiscal imbalance," as approximately $63 trillion, or 5 times GDP. This is a huge number. Even during World War II, government debt was only 1.2 times GDP. In the long run, a fiscal imbalance of this size is not sustainable—no one will lend the U.S. government that amount of money. Eliminating these imbalances will require dramatic increases in taxes or reduced expenditures. To maintain the current level of benefits, workers and firms would have to pay nearly 30 percent in payroll taxes—about double what they pay today—or income taxes would have to nearly double. Alternatively, benefits programs could be scaled back.

Gokhale and Smetters estimate that about 80 percent of the fiscal imbalance will stem from Medicare—which pays the rising health-care costs for the elderly. What these numbers suggest is that our current health-care system for retirees will need to undergo fundamental reform to make it more sustainable. Otherwise, the United States will need to radically increase taxes to meet the shortfall.   **Related to Exercise 1.7.**

SOURCE: Based on Jagadeesh Gokhale and Kent Smetters, "Fiscal and Generational Imbalances: An Update," August 2005, http://www.philadelphiafed.org/research-and-data/events/2005/fed-policy-forum/papers/Smetters-Assessing_the_Federal_Government.pdf (accessed April 27, 2010).

---

prevent Congress from having too much money to be able to spend. Some congressmen supported President Bush's tax cut in 2001, which reduced the surplus over a 10-year period, precisely for this reason.

DEBATE 4: CAN DEFICITS BE GOOD FOR AN ECONOMY?   Recall from the fiscal policy chapter that during a downturn, running a deficit helps stimulate private-sector spending. Consequently, the government may deliberately run a deficit to pull the economy out of a recession. The deficit the government creates puts additional income into the hands of the public. With more money, people don't have to drastically cut their consumption spending. Because total spending in the economy does not fall as much, the severity of the recession is lessened.

Deficits automatically emerge during recessions, which also stabilize the economy. Recall how automatic stabilizers work. As incomes fall during a recession, so do tax payments. Moreover, transfer payments such as welfare and food stamps rise. Because government spending increases while tax revenues fall, the deficit must, of course, rise. However, a rising deficit may be what it takes to steer the economy back to full employment. Automatic stabilizers were clearly in evidence in the recession that began in late 2007, as tax revenues fell sharply for the next several years.

The existence of automatic stabilizers and the use of expansionary fiscal policy during recessions suggest that we should not worry about short-run government deficits. Over short time periods, deficits can help the economy to cope with shocks, such as oil price increases or a collapse in the stock market. They give the government some room to maneuver out of a recession. Most economists believe automatic stabilizers reduced economic fluctuations during the twentieth century.

Deficits can also play a role in tax smoothing. Suppose there is a large, temporary increase in government spending, as might occur during a war. The government could either finance the war by running a deficit and issuing debt or by increasing tax rates to keep the budget in balance. Professor Robert Barro of Harvard University has argued that it is more efficient to keep tax rates relatively constant than to raise them sharply and then lower them later. Temporarily raising tax rates to very high levels could cause distortions in economic behavior that we would like to avoid. Thus, by running deficits and only gradually raising taxes later to service the debt, we avoid creating excess distortions in the economy.

DEBATE 5: WOULD A BALANCED-BUDGET AMENDMENT REALLY WORK?

For many years, there were strong efforts to enact a Constitutional amendment to balance the federal budget. As recently as 1995, Congress came very close to passing a balanced-budget amendment, sending it back to the states for ratification. The amendment passed in the House of Representatives but failed by a single vote in the Senate. How would a balanced-budget amendment actually work?

Many different budgetary constitutional amendments have been proposed. They all require that, after a phase-in period, Congress propose in each fiscal year a budget in which total revenues (excluding borrowing) cover total expenditures. The amendments also have various escape clauses—for example, to allow borrowing during wartime. Some amendments also allow Congress to suspend the requirement to balance the budget for other reasons, such as during a recession when deficits naturally emerge. Finally, some versions would limit the rate of spending increases to the rate at which GDP is growing.

Proponents of the balanced-budget amendment say it will finally exert discipline on the federal government, preventing large deficits in peacetime, such as those that occurred in the 1980s. With a balanced budget we could be sure to avoid the negative effects of deficits: reduced capital formation and tax burdens that are shifted onto future generations.

Critics of a balanced-budget amendment point to many different problems, such as the following:

- A balanced budget may not allow enough flexibility, or room, for the government to effectively deal with recessions. Under some versions of the amendment, unless three-fifths of Congress votes to suspend requirements, the government would have to cut expenditures or raise taxes during a recession. This would make the recession worse and limit the ability of the government to use fiscal policy to stabilize the economy.

- The Constitution is not the right mechanism to try to enforce complicated budget rules. As various interested parties challenge the actions of Congress, the courts would become heavily engaged in federal budget matters.

- Congress could devise special budgets to get around the requirement, for example, by taking some types of spending "off budget," which means simply not counting them as part of the official budget.

- Congress could also find nonbudgetary ways to carry out the policies that it desires. For example, it could issue more regulations or impose mandates or requirements on businesses or other governments to carry out its will. These regulations or mandates could be even more costly to the economy than added deficits.

17.2 SHOULD THE FED TARGET INFLATION OR PURSUE OTHER OBJECTIVES?

In previous chapters we looked at the various roles that the Federal Reserve can play. Monetary policy can be used to stabilize the real economy, preventing unemployment from exceeding the natural rate or falling too far below the natural rate. As we saw in Chapters 13 and 14, the Fed also plays a critical role as a lender of last resort and a unique resource to combat financial crises.

On the other hand, we also learned that, in the long run, money was neutral and monetary policy cannot affect the real level of output or unemployment. We also saw that the natural rate can shift over time, making it difficult to target the appropriate unemployment rate. In these circumstances, what should the Fed do? Should it just focus on inflation or try to follow some other rule or procedure to balance concerns of inflation and unemployment?

In the early years of the first decade of the twenty-first century, the rate of inflation had fallen to between 1 and 2 percent. Some economists thought the time was right for the Fed to concentrate on simply keeping the inflation rate low and stable. In other words, they thought the Fed should use monetary policy to "target" an appropriate inflation rate and make its primary objective keeping inflation in check. Following the expansion of the Fed's activities during the financial crisis of 2008 and its aftermath, there is continuing concern about long-run inflation.

In recent years, various inflation-targeting methods have been adopted in a number of developed countries, including Canada, the United Kingdom, New Zealand, Sweden, Australia, and Spain. In addition, many developing countries have found that inflation targeting increased the autonomy of their central banks, helping them fight inflation.

Two Debates about Inflation Targeting

Inflation targeting has had many strong proponents. Let's take a close look at two key debates about this topic.

DEBATE 1: SHOULD THE FED FOCUS ON ONLY INFLATION?   We have learned that in the long run monetary policy can influence only the level of prices, not the level of employment. Proponents of inflation targeting argue that the Fed should have only one primary goal: controlling inflation. Having it worry about other factors—unemployment or the exchange rate—will, they say, distract it from its mission and lead to long-run inflationary pressures building in the economy. Moreover, if the Fed were committed to the single goal of controlling inflation, its credibility would be enhanced. As we have seen, if the Fed is credible, the private sector will become more responsive to changes in monetary policy. For example, long-term interest rates will become more responsive to changes in short-term rates if the public understands what the Fed's motives are and what it is doing. And credible policies may actually decrease the need for active monetary policies. Having a single goal would also help to keep the Fed free of political pressures. Such political pressures might include attempts by one political party or the other to stimulate the economy or give financial markets a temporary boost before an election.

Other proponents of inflation targeting hold a somewhat less rigid view. Although they believe fighting inflation should be the primary objective of the Fed, or of a central bank, they believe an inflation-targeting regimen could be designed to give the central bank some flexibility. For example, the central bank could be required to target a broader range of inflation—say, between 1 and 3 percent—and meet the target several years in the future. Under either of these alternatives, central banks would have some room to meet employment or other policy objectives besides just inflation. In practice, many countries do allow some "wiggle room" in their inflation targeting regimens by using broad inflation bands or distant targets.

APPLICATION 2

WOULD A POLICY RULE HAVE PREVENTED THE HOUSING BOOM?

APPLYING THE CONCEPTS #2: Did the Federal Reserve cause the housing boom through excessively loose monetary policy?

John Taylor from Stanford University has argued that the Fed's "easy money" policy from mid-2001 through 2004 was largely responsible for the housing boom in the decade that ultimately caused so much financial damage. Taylor used his own model of monetary policy—the "Taylor rule"—to analyze the Fed's behavior. In his prior work, he demonstrated that the Fed's behavior could be closely described by a model that allowed for some monetary policy tightening and easing in response to output movements. Applying this model to the decade of 2000, however, Taylor found that, compared to past experience, the Fed was much too aggressive in lowering interest rates. Interest rates fell from 2 percent in mid-2001 to 1 percent by 2004. Past experience, however, would have suggested that the Fed would have raised interest rates to 4 percent by 2004—a very significant deviation.

Taylor then showed that housing starts—which are very sensitive to interest rates—would have been much lower if the Fed had not followed its easy money policy. The boom and bust would have been avoided. Finally, as an additional piece of evidence, Taylor looked at the experiences of European countries. There the same phenomenon occurred. Countries that deviated most from the Taylor rule—for example, Spain—experienced the worst boom and bust cycles for housing. **Related to Exercise 2.7.**

SOURCE: Based on John B. Taylor, "The Financial Crisis and Policy Responses: An Empirical Analysis of What Went Wrong," http://www.stanford.edu/~johntayl/FCPR.pdf (accessed April 27, 2010).

Before he took over as chairman of the Federal Reserve in 2006, Ben Bernanke was an advocate for inflation targeting. While he was a member of the Board of Governors in 2003, Bernanke gave a speech outlining his own views on the merits of inflation targeting. For Bernanke, inflation targeting increased the effectiveness of monetary policy because it provided a long-term anchor for inflation expectations. As long as the private sector—individuals and firms—understood the Fed was holding firm to long-run inflation targets, it would have added flexibility to use aggressive monetary policy in the short run to offset adverse shocks to the economy—without upsetting long-run inflation expectations. Bernanke called inflation targeting a policy of *constrained discretion*. Under inflation targeting, the Fed could take actions to offset shocks to real output or to the financial system, but it had to keep its long-run inflation targets in clear view. After the financial crisis of 2008, Bernanke stopped speaking about inflation targeting and devoted his speeches to explaining the Fed's actions during the crisis and designing an "exit strategy" for the Fed's massive interventions.

Even prior to the recent recession, many economists disagreed with the idea of inflation targeting because they strongly objected to the Fed concentrating solely on controlling inflation. In the United States, Congress and the president are frequently incapable of quickly agreeing on a fiscal policy to stave off or end a recession. Of course, automatic fiscal stabilizers exist, but they are often not sufficient to cushion the economy when a shock hits. Practically speaking, only monetary policy is available to stabilize output and prevent deep recessions from emerging. If monetary policy is geared solely toward controlling inflation, as inflation-targeting proponents would like, and if fiscal policies are difficult for Congress and the president to pass, that leaves the government no other tools to fight a recession.

Economists also debate the level for an inflation target. Suppose there were general agreement that the ultimate goal should be total price stability—that is, zero inflation. There would still be legitimate questions about what constitutes "stable" prices. It is very difficult to measure changes in prices accurately when there is a great deal of technological change occurring in the economy, because technological improvements change the quality of goods so rapidly that government statisticians can't easily catch up with them. If, as many economists believe, our price indexes overstate the true inflation rate, annual inflation of 2 percent may in reality be true price stability. Indeed, many proponents of inflation targeting agree with this point and recommend a 2 percent inflation rate as "price stability."

Critics of stabilization policy, of course, believe that not using monetary policy to try to stabilize the economy would actually improve our economic performance. In their view, attempts to stabilize the economy have done more harm than good over the years by making fluctuations worse. In previous chapters, we discussed the difficulties in conducting stabilization policy. These include lags, uncertainties about the strength and timing of policies, and difficulties in estimating the natural rate of unemployment. If you believe these difficulties are insurmountable, you will likely think the Fed should target just inflation. If you think they can be overcome, you will likely believe the Fed should be allowed to stabilize output and employment, too.

Some economists like the idea of the Fed having to meet targets, but they have suggested alternatives to inflation targeting. One approach that has wide appeal was developed by economist John Taylor of Stanford University. Taylor suggested that the Fed follow a rule that keeps a long-run inflation target but allows the Fed to raise or lower interest rates depending on whether output is above or below potential. His own analysis suggests that the performance of the Fed would be superior if it followed a rule of this type, rather than making ad hoc decisions. The advantage of a rule of this nature is that it allows the Fed to offset shocks to the economy, but requires the Fed to meet long run inflation targets.

DEBATE 2: IF THERE WERE AN INFLATION TARGET, WHO WOULD SET IT?   Even if the United States decided to adopt inflation targeting as a policy, several important questions would remain. Perhaps the most important is "Who would set the target?"

In the United Kingdom, which adopted targeting in 1992, the elected government decides on the inflation target for the central bank. These elected officials typically specify a range for the inflation rate that the bank must meet. The central bank participates in the discussions and has an opportunity to present its views to the public through its publications and published minutes of its meetings. But ultimately it is the elected government that makes the final decision.

In other countries, the central bank has even more influence in setting the inflation target. In New Zealand, for example, the central bank has the responsibility of "achieving and maintaining stability in the general level of prices" without any competing goals, such as stabilizing employment or output. The law also requires the head of the central bank and the finance minister to negotiate inflation goals and make them public.

What would be an appropriate arrangement for the United States? Under current law, the Fed chairman reports regularly to Congress, but the Fed has considerable power to use monetary policy to stabilize output as well as to fight inflation as it pleases. Would our Congress and president be willing to cede power to the Fed and allow it to focus only on fighting inflation? And, if they did, would Congress or the president want to determine the target range for inflation and instruct the Fed how quickly to meet these targets?

As you can see, changing our current system would require major decisions about who has authority and control over our economic system. Currently, the Fed has considerable power and autonomy. Although inflation targeting might make the Fed more independent, another phenomenon could occur, too: Congress and the president might end up with more power over monetary policy. And that might lead to more inflation, not less.

17.3 SHOULD WE TAX CONSUMPTION RATHER THAN INCOME?

As we discussed in earlier chapters, the United States is a country with a low saving rate. This hurts our long-run growth prospects because our investment spending is determined by our own savings and savings from abroad. Many factors—not purely economic ones—contribute to our low saving rate. For example, colleges generally give less financial aid to students whose families have saved for their education. Many of our welfare programs cut the benefits of families who have saved in the past and still have some funds left in their accounts. The U.S. tax system also discourages savings. Here's how.

In the United States, you must pay taxes on both the wages you earn and the earnings you make on your savings. Suppose you earn $100 at your job and you have a tax rate of 20 percent. That means you keep $80 after taxes. Now suppose you save $50 of that money and invest it at 10 percent. At the end of one year, you will have earned an additional $5 on the $50 you saved (10% × $50), but you will get to keep only $4 of it because the government will take $1 in taxes (20% × $5). So, you will have to pay the government $21 in total: $20 on the $100 you earned in wages, plus $1 on the $5 you earned on your savings. If you did not save at all, you would pay only $20 in taxes, not $21.

Not all tax systems work this way. Tax systems based on consumption do not penalize individuals who save. Sales taxes in the United States and value-added taxes abroad are familiar examples of **consumption taxes**. It is also possible to create a consumption tax from an income tax by not taxing the earnings on savings—just as we do with tax-exempt bonds issued by state and municipal governments. Or, as an alternative, the government could allow savings to be deducted from gross income before the calculation for total taxes owed is made. The key feature of consumption taxation is that you do not face any additional taxes if you decide to save more of your income.

There are, however, ways in the United States to save money and still limit your taxes. In addition to buying tax-exempt bonds, you can invest in an IRA (individual retirement account) or 401(k), 403(b), and Keogh plans, which are also types of retirement accounts. The money in pension funds is treated similarly. It isn't taxed until the person who contributed it retires and withdraws it. During retirement, most people earn less money than when they were working, so the tax rate they pay on the money they withdraw from these accounts is lower than when they saved it. Also, the money accumulates more quickly because it grows tax-free while it's in these accounts. In practice, the U.S. tax system is a hybrid system, part way between an income tax and a consumption tax.

consumption taxes
Taxes based on the consumption, not the income, of individuals.

Two Debates about Consumption Taxation

Proponents claim that taxes based on consumption will increase total savings and may even be more equitable. Let's explore these claims.

DEBATE 1: WILL CONSUMPTION TAXES LEAD TO MORE SAVINGS? There is no question that taxing consumption instead of savings creates an incentive to save. However, there's no guarantee the incentive will actually result in more money saved in the economy. Suppose the tax burden is shifted to consumption by reducing the tax rate on savings. People will want to take advantage of this incentive and reduce their consumption and increase their saving. On the other hand, people will also want to spend more because, with the tax cut, they are wealthier.

Although there has been much research done on how a consumption tax would affect savings, the results are far from conclusive. It is true that individuals will allocate their savings to tax-favored investments over investments that are not favored. For example, they will put money into their IRAs. What is not clear is whether the funds they will put there are literally new savings—meaning reduced consumption—or merely transfers from other accounts, such as conventional savings accounts, which do not have the same tax advantages. Untangling these effects is a difficult issue, and it remains an active area of ongoing research.

The tax system imposed on corporations in the United States also creates disincentives to save and invest. Suppose you purchase a share of stock in a corporation. When the corporation earns a profit, it pays taxes on the profit at the corporate tax rate. When the corporation pays you a dividend on the stock out of the profits it earns, you must pay taxes on the dividend income that you receive. Corporate income is taxed twice, in other words—first when it is earned by the corporation and again when it is paid out to shareholders.

Some economists have argued that the corporate taxes lead to less-efficient investment because they result in capital flowing into other sectors of the economy (into real estate, for example) that do not suffer from double taxation. For this reason, in 2003 Congress passed a bill introduced by President Bush that lowered—but did not eliminate—taxes on corporate dividends.

DEBATE 2: ARE CONSUMPTION TAXES FAIR? The basic idea behind a consumption tax seems fair. Individuals should be taxed on what they take away from the economy's total production—that is, what they consume—not on what they actually produce. If an individual produces a lot but does not consume the proceeds from what was produced and instead plows it back into the economy for investment, that individual is contributing to the growth of total output and should be rewarded, not punished. Individual A earns $50 and consumes it all; individual B earns $100 but consumes only $40. Who should pay more?

In practice, moving to a consumption-tax system could have a major impact on the distribution of income in the economy. Suppose we simply exempted the returns from savings from the income tax. This exception would clearly favor wealthy and high-income individuals who save the most and earn a lot of income in interest, dividends, rents, and capital gains. Table 17.1 shows estimates based on the capital gains received by different income classes for the year 2009 and dividends paid by corporations. **Capital gains** are the profits investors earn when they sell stocks, bonds, real estate, or other assets. As you can see, taxpayers with annual incomes exceeding $1,000,000 earned over half of the economy's capital gains over this period. Obviously, capital assets are highly concentrated among the wealthy.

capital gains
Profits investors earn when they sell stocks, bonds, real estate, or other assets.

TABLE 17.1 DISTRIBUTION OF CAPITAL GAINS AND DIVIDENDS BY INCOME CLASS, 2009	
Cash Income Level	Share of Capital Gains and Dividends
Less than $40,000	0%
$40,000 to $50,000	0.1
$50,000 to $75,000	0.9
$75,000 to $100,000	1.4
$100,000 to $200,000	8.2
$200,000 to $500,000	19.5
$500,000 to $1,000,000	13.8
Greater than $1,000,000	55.9

SOURCE: Estimates from the Urban-Brookings Tax Policy Center Microsimulation Model, http://www.taxpolicycenter.org/index.cfm (Accessed April 27, 2010).

(**APPLICATION 3**)

IS A VAT IN OUR FUTURE?

APPLYING THE CONCEPTS #3: Can the United States adopt a European-style value-added tax?

Virtually all developed countries and many developing countries have a value-added tax, commonly known as a VAT. The United States is a prominent exception. The VAT is essentially a sales tax that is levied on each stage of production. Firms pay the VAT on their sales and then receive a credit for VAT paid on their purchases. Unlike a sales tax, the VAT is embedded in the price of goods. It is rebated when goods are exported but imports are required to pay the VAT. Rates on the VAT can be high—for example, the basic rate in the United Kingdom is 17.5 percent.

The VAT has some important advantages. It is relatively easy to collect and, as a consumption tax, does not penalize savings. There are some potential difficulties. Since U.S. states already levy retail sales taxes, incorporating a VAT at the state level could be difficult and be seen to impinge on state taxing authority. In addition, some conservatives worry that it is too efficient and consumers will not notice all the taxes they pay. Liberals worry that the VAT, like all consumption taxes, could be regressive. An old joke goes that the time will come for the VAT when liberals recognize it is a money machine and conservatives recognize it is regressive. **Related to Exercise 3.7.**

If capital gains and other types of capital income were not taxed, total tax revenue would fall, and the government would have to raise tax rates on everyone to maintain the same level of spending. Excluding capital income from taxation does have its costs.

Some economists believe it is important that high-income individuals continue to pay a significant share of total taxes. In the last several decades, the distribution of income has become more unequal, as superstar athletes, famous actors and musicians, CEOs, and successful entrepreneurs and investors have all earned large fortunes. The tax system is one way we have to at least partially reduce inequalities in income. Critics of consumption taxes worry that moving our tax system in that direction will take away this important tool for social equality. However, other economists believe that high-income individuals already shoulder a very high share of the total tax burden and that we need to focus on designing an efficient system to promote economic growth.

Proponents of consumption taxes have tried to meet the challenge of fairness in different ways. The "flat tax" designed by Robert E. Hall of Stanford University and Alvin Rabushka of the Hoover Institute brings the personal income tax and corporate income tax into a single, unified tax system. Under the flat tax, one low, single tax rate applies to both businesses and individuals. Businesses deduct their wage payments before they pay taxes. In addition, they can deduct any investment spending they make from their income before the tax is calculated. Recall that in a simple economy, without government or the foreign sector, saving equals investment, $S = I$. Allowing a deduction for investment has generally the same effect as allowing a deduction for savings. So this flat tax is a type of consumption tax.

This version of the flat tax has an important feature that ensures that wealthy individuals (and other owners of corporations) still pay taxes. Suppose the corporation or business makes an extraordinary return on its investment. Consider, for example, the tremendous profit generated by Apple's iPod. Over 14 million iPods were shipped in fiscal year 2006. If the profit for each iPod were $100, Apple's total profit from iPods would be $1.4 billion. Under this version of the flat tax, these extraordinary gains would be taxed in full. Owners of a corporation or business may earn extraordinary gains, but if they do, they will pay taxes on them.

The projected federal deficit has led many policymakers to consider whether a European-style value-added tax (VAT) would make sense for the United States. Grafting a VAT on to the U.S. fiscal system would pose many challenges.

SUMMARY

In this chapter we explored three topics that are the center of macroeconomic policy debates today. Here are the key points to remember:

1 A *deficit* is the difference between the government's current expenditures and revenue. The government debt is the sum of all past yearly deficits.

2 Deficits can be financed through either borrowing or money creation. Financing deficits through money creation is called *monetizing the deficit*. It leads to inflation.

3 Deficits can be good for the country. Automatic stabilizers and expansionary fiscal policy both work through the creation of deficits.

4 The national debt incurs two burdens on citizens: It can reduce the amount of capital in an economy, leading to lower levels of income; it can also result in higher taxes that future generations will have to pay.

5 A number of developed countries have recently changed their monetary policy to emphasize targeting the inflation rate or a range for the inflation rate.

6 Although targeting inflation can increase the credibility of a central bank, it does limit the tools left for active stabilization policy.

7 A *consumption tax* would increase the incentives for private saving. However, it is not clear that total savings would necessarily increase, and there would be concerns about the fairness of this form of taxation.

KEY TERMS

capital gains, p. 359

consumption taxes, p. 358

monetizing the deficit, p. 350

Ricardian equivalence, p. 351

EXERCISES  Visit www.myeconlab.com to complete these exercises online and get instant feedback.

17.1 Should We Balance the Federal Budget?

1.1 If a government runs a deficit, it will _____ its outstanding debt.

1.2 Proponents of Ricardian equivalence are primarily concerned about deficits crowding out the stock of capital. _____ (True/False)

1.3 When a central bank purchases new government bonds, it is _____ the deficit.

1.4 Historically, debt/GDP ratios increase during periods of _____.

1.5 **Debt and Deficits in Belgium.** Here are some data for Belgium in 1989:

GDP: 6,160 billion Belgian francs
Debt: 6,500 billion Belgian francs

Deficit: 380 billion Belgian francs
Interest Rate on Bonds: 8.5 percent

Use the data to answer the following questions:

a. What are the deficit/GDP ratio and debt/GDP ratio? How do these ratios compare to the same ratios in the United States today? To what period in U.S. history does the debt/GDP ratio in Belgium correspond?

b. Approximately how much of the budget in Belgium is devoted to interest payments on its debt? If Belgium could wipe out its debt overnight, what would happen to its current budget deficit?

1.6 **Interest Rates, Primary Surpluses, and Government Debt.** The gap between taxes and spending, *excluding* interest on the debt, is known as the *primary surplus*. Suppose there is $100 million of outstanding public debt. Show that a primary surplus of $10 million with an interest rate of 10 percent has the same consequence for next year's debt level as a primary surplus of $5 million and an interest rate of 5 percent.

1.7 The Effects of Changing Entitlement Rules. How is a decrease in the age at which workers are eligible for Social Security similar to an increase in the government deficit? (Related to Application 1 on page 353.)

1.8 Tax Smoothing or Strategic Tax Policy? Assume the pressures of an aging population and increases in health-care costs will increase total federal spending in the future significantly.

a. Under the theory of tax smoothing, what should happen to the current level of taxes if future spending is scheduled to rise?

b. Now suppose future spending increases are not inevitable and that, as a practical matter, you believe Congress will spend whatever revenue it collects. Would you still recommend tax smoothing?

1.9 Policy Options for the Federal Budget. The Web site for the Congressional Budget Office (www.cbo.gov) contains its projections for future budget surpluses and deficits as well as options for increasing the surplus. Using this site, find some options you think are desirable and that would have a significant effect on increasing the budget surplus.

17.2 Should the Fed Target Inflation or Pursue Other Objectives?

2.1 Proponents of inflation targeting argue that it would make central banks more _____ if they were committed to a long-run inflation target.

2.2 In _____, inflation targeting was adopted in 1992, and elected officials determine the precise inflation targets that the central bank must meet.

2.3 Economist _____ developed a rule for monetary policy that maintains a low rate of inflation but allows the Fed to adjust interest rates when output deviates from potential.

2.4 If the Federal Reserve is more credible, long-term interest rates will be more responsive to changes in short term rates. _____ (True/False)

2.5 Targeting the Price Level with Supply Shocks. Suppose the Fed has brought the inflation rate down to zero to stabilize the price level. An adverse supply shock (such as an increase in the world price of oil) now hits the economy.

a. Using the aggregate demand-and-supply model, show how targeting the price level would make the

fall in output from the shock greater as compared to no policy at all.

b. Some proponents of price-level or inflation targeting recommend that the Fed target "core inflation," which is based on a price index that excludes supply shocks. What is their rationale?

2.6 What Rate for Inflation Targeting? An economist suggests that what matters for financial markets is a stable inflation rate, not a zero inflation rate. As long as inflation is stable, all individuals can take this into account in their actions.

a. What are the costs associated with a stable inflation rate of 2 percent?

b. Is it easier or more difficult to stabilize inflation at 2 percent rather than at zero?

2.7 The Fed on Autopilot. Some economists believe that the Federal Reserve should follow strict rules for the conduct of monetary policy. These rules would require the Fed to make adjustments to interest rates based on information that is fully available to the public, information such as the current unemployment rate and the current inflation rate. Essentially, they would put the Fed on autopilot and remove its discretion. What are the pros and cons of such an approach? Would it work in a financial crisis? (Related to Application 2 on page 356.)

2.8 What Difference Would Focusing on Asset Prices Make? Suppose you believed the Fed should make its decisions by focusing partly on asset prices, such as stocks or prices of housing, and should have used monetary policy to offset both the stock market increase in the late 1990s and the housing price increases after 2002. How would your policy have affected interest rates and real output during the period in question? What would be the benefit of your policies?

17.3 Should We Tax Consumption Rather than Income?

3.1 Suppose there is a consumption tax of 20 percent. An individual earns $100 and saves $30. Her tax will be equal to _____.

3.2 A sales tax that is levied at all stages of production is known as a(n) _____ tax.

3.3 Most capital gains accrue to low-income individuals because there are more of them. _____ (True/False)

3.4 Under our current corporate tax system, earnings from corporations that are paid out as dividends are taxed _____ times.

3.5 Traditional and Roth IRAs. With a traditional IRA, you get to deduct the amount you contribute from your current taxable income, invest the funds free from tax, but then pay taxes on the full amount you withdraw when you retire. Suppose your tax rate is 50 percent and you initially deposit $2,000 in an IRA. The proceeds double in seven years to $4,000. You then retire and pay taxes on the $4,000 at your 50 percent rate.

a. Taking into account your tax deduction for the IRA, how much did your investment in the IRA really cost you? What is your return after seven years?

b. With a Roth IRA, you do not get a deduction for your savings but the interest you earn is tax free. Is the outcome for a Roth IRA the same as for the traditional IRA if you invest $1,000 for seven years and double your initial investment?

c. Suppose you believed that in seven years tax rates would be higher. Are the traditional and Roth IRAs still equivalent? If not, which would you prefer?

3.6 **Tax Policy and National Savings.** Suppose the government launches a new program that allows individuals to place funds of up to $2,000 in a tax-free account. Do you believe that this will have a significant effect on national savings? (Recall that federal deficits reduce national savings.) What are the arguments on both sides of this debate?

3.7 **Why Has the United States Not Instituted a VAT?** The United States differs from virtually all developed countries in that it does not have a VAT. What important aspect of the U.S. political system might account for this difference with other countries? (Related to Application 3 on page 360.)

18 International Trade and Public Policy

Countries always want to have foreign markets open for their exporters. But if a country limits access to its own markets, foreign countries may take action to limit access to their own markets. The United States, despite an overall strong record in trade, is no exception. Here are a few examples.

As part of the North American Free Trade Agreement, the United States was required to open its borders to trucks from Mexico, although it resisted allowing this. As a result, in 2009 Mexico imposed tariffs on over $2 billion of U.S. goods, reducing employment in U.S. export industries.

In 2010 the United States accused China of selling aluminum products below their fair market value and imposed sanctions on the Chinese. In turn, China decided that the United States was doing precisely the same thing with nylon products and imposed its own tariffs on these products.

Trade agreements can help lower barriers to international commerce, but countries still have to believe that other countries are "playing fair." Otherwise, two can tango.

◁ APPLYING THE CONCEPTS ▷

1 Do tariffs (taxes) on imported goods hurt the poor disproportionately?
   The Impact of Tariffs on the Poor

2 Does the concept of "unfair" competition make sense?
   Protection for Candle Makers

3 How does the Commerce Department try to determine whether countries are dumping their products?
   Are They Really Dumping?

4 Why might international trade reduce measured inequality in the United States?
   Trade, Consumption, and Inequality

As the world economy grows, U.S. policies toward international trade become ever more important. Many people view trade as a "zero-sum game." They believe that if one country gains from international trade, another must lose. Based on this belief, they advocate restricting trade with other countries. The United States does restrict trade to protect U.S. jobs in many sectors, such as those in the apparel and steel industries. One lesson from this chapter is that free trade could make all countries better off. The challenge for government officials is to create policies that accomplish, or come close to accomplishing, this goal.

In this chapter, we discuss the benefits of international trade and the effects of policies that restrict trade.

18.1 BENEFITS FROM SPECIALIZATION AND TRADE

What if you lived in a nation that could produce everything it consumed and didn't depend on any other country for its economic livelihood? If you were put in charge of your nation, would you pursue a policy of national self-sufficiency? Although self-sufficiency might sound appealing, it would actually be better for your country to specialize in the production of some products and then trade some of those products to other countries. You saw in Chapter 3 that specialization and exchange can make both parties better off. In this chapter, we use a simple example to explain the benefits of specialization and international trade between two nations.

Let's say there are two nations, Shirtland and Chipland. Each nation produces computer chips and shirts, and each consumes computer chips and shirts. Table 18.1 shows the daily output of the two goods for the two nations. In a single day, Shirtland can produce a maximum of either 108 shirts or 36 computer chips, whereas Chipland can produce a maximum of either 120 shirts or 120 computer chips. The last two rows of the table show the opportunity costs of the two goods. Recall the principle of opportunity cost.

PRINCIPLE OF OPPORTUNITY COST

The opportunity cost of something is what you sacrifice to get it.

In Chipland, the trade-off between shirts and chips is one to one: The opportunity cost of one shirt is one chip, and the opportunity cost of one chip is one shirt. In Shirtland, people can produce three times as many shirts as chips in a given amount of time: The opportunity cost of one chip is three shirts. Conversely, the opportunity cost of one shirt is one-third of a chip.

TABLE 18.1 OUTPUT AND OPPORTUNITY COST			
	Quantity Produced Per Day	Opportunity Cost of Shirts	Opportunity Cost of Chips
Shirtland	108 shirts 36 chips	1/3 chip	3 shirts
Chipland	120 shirts 120 chips	1 chip	1 shirt

Production Possibilities Curve

Let's start by seeing what happens if Shirtland and Chipland are each self-sufficient. Each nation can use its resources (labor, land, buildings, machinery, and equipment) to produce its own shirts and chips. The *production possibilities curve* shows all the possible combinations of products that an economy can produce, given that its productive resources are fully employed and efficiently used. This curve, which we discussed in Chapter 2, provides a menu of production options. To keep things simple, we assume the curve is a straight line, indicating a constant trade-off between the two goods. As shown by Shirtland's production possibilities curve in Figure 18.1, the following combinations of chips and shirts are possible:

1 *All shirts and no chips*: point *a*. If Shirtland uses all its resources to produce shirts, it will produce 108 shirts per day.

2 *All chips and no shirts*: point *d*. If Shirtland uses all its resources to produce chips, it will produce 36 chips per day.

3 *Equal division of resources*: point *b*. Shirtland could divide its resources between shirts and chips to produce 54 shirts and 18 chips each day.

All the other points on the line connecting points *a* and *d* are also feasible. One option is point *c*, with 28 chips and 24 shirts. The steepness of the curve's slope—negative 3.0—shows the opportunity cost of computer chips: 1 chip per 3 shirts. Figure 18.1 also shows the production possibilities curve for Chipland. Chipland can daily produce 120 shirts and no chips (point *e*), 120 chips and no shirts (point *g*), or any combination of chips and shirts between these two points. In Chipland, the trade-off is 1 shirt per computer chip: The opportunity cost of 1 chip is 1 shirt, so the slope of the production possibilities curve is negative 1.0.

Each nation could decide to be self-sufficient, picking a point on its production possibilities curve and producing everything it wants to consume. For example,

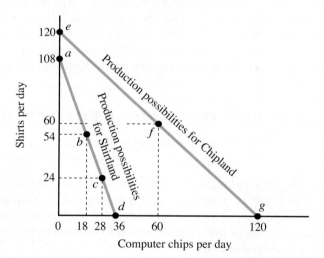

Point	Shirts	Chips
a	108	0
b	54	18
c	24	28
d	0	36

Shirtland Possibilities

Point	Shirts	Chips
e	120	0
f	60	60
g	0	120

Chipland Possibilities

▲ FIGURE 18.1

Production Possibilities Curve

The production possibilities curve shows the combination of two goods that can be produced with a nation's resources. For Chipland, the trade-off between the two goods is one to one. For Shirtland, the trade-off is 3 shirts for every computer chip. In the absence of trade, Shirtland can pick point *c*—28 chips and 24 shirts—and Chipland can pick point *f*—60 chips and 60 shirts.

Shirtland could pick point *c*, daily producing 28 chips and 24 shirts, and Chipland could pick point *f*, daily producing 60 chips and 60 shirts. In the language of international trade, this is a case of *autarky*, or self-sufficiency (in Greek, *aut* means "self" and *arke* means "to suffice").

Comparative Advantage and the Terms of Trade

Would the two nations be better off if each specialized in the production of one good and traded with the other nation? To decide which nation should produce a particular good, we need to look at each good and figure out which nation has the lower opportunity cost of producing it. As you saw in Chapter 3, the nation with the lower opportunity cost has a *comparative advantage* in producing that good. As we emphasized in Chapter 3, it is comparative advantage that matters for trade—not *absolute advantage*, the ability of a nation to produce a particular good at a lower absolute cost than that of another nation. Let's see how it works.

1 *Chips produced in Chipland.*   The opportunity cost of one chip is one shirt in Chipland, and the opportunity cost of one chip is three shirts in Shirtland. Chipland has a comparative advantage in the production of chips. Because Chipland sacrifices fewer shirts to produce one chip, Chipland should produce chips.

2 *Shirts produced in Shirtland.*   The opportunity cost of one shirt is one chip in Chipland, and the opportunity cost of one shirt is one-third of a chip in Shirtland. When it comes to producing shirts, Shirtland has a comparative advantage because it sacrifices fewer chips to produce one shirt. Shirtland should therefore produce shirts.

Trade will make it possible for people in each specialized nation to consume both goods. At what rate will the two nations exchange shirts and chips? To determine the **terms of trade**, the rate at which units of one product can be exchanged for units of another product, let's look at how much Shirtland is willing to pay to get one chip and how much Chipland is willing to accept to give up one chip.

terms of trade
The rate at which units of one product can be exchanged for units of another product.

1 To get one chip, Shirtland is willing to pay up to three shirts. That's how many shirts it would sacrifice if it produced its own chip. For example, if the nations agree to exchange two shirts per chip, Shirtland could rearrange its production, producing one fewer chip but three more shirts. After exchanging two of the newly produced shirts for one chip, Shirtland will have the same number of chips but one additional shirt.

2 To give up one chip, Chipland is willing to accept any amount greater than one shirt. For example, if the nations agree to exchange two shirts per chip, Chipland could rearrange its production, producing one more chip and one fewer shirt. After it exchanges the newly produced chip for two shirts, Chipland will have the same number of chips but one additional shirt.

The potential for mutually beneficial trade between the two countries is possible because the willingness to pay—three shirts by Shirtland—exceeds the willingness to accept—one shirt by Chipland. It's possible for Shirtland and Chipland to split the difference between the willingness to pay and the willingness to accept, exchanging two shirts per chip. This will actually make both countries better off in terms of the total amount of goods they can consume. We'll see why next.

The Consumption Possibilities Curve

A nation that decides to specialize and trade is no longer limited to the options shown by its own production possibilities curve. The **consumption possibilities curve** shows the combinations of two goods (computer chips and shirts in our

consumption possibilities curve
A curve showing the combinations of two goods that can be consumed when a nation specializes in a particular good and trades with another nation.

example) that a nation can consume when it specializes in one good and trades with another nation.

Figure 18.2 shows the consumption possibilities curve for our two nations, assuming that they exchange two shirts per chip:

- In Panel A, Chipland specializes in chip production, the good for which it has a comparative advantage. It produces 120 chips and no shirts (point *g*). Given the terms of trade, Chipland can exchange 40 of its 120 chips for 80 shirts, leading to point *h*. At point *h*, Chipland can consume 80 chips and 80 shirts.

- In Panel B, Shirtland specializes in shirt production. It produces 108 shirts and no chips (point *a*). Given the terms of trade, it can exchange 80 of its 108 shirts for 40 chips, leading to point *k* on its consumption possibilities curve. Shirtland can consume 28 shirts and 40 chips.

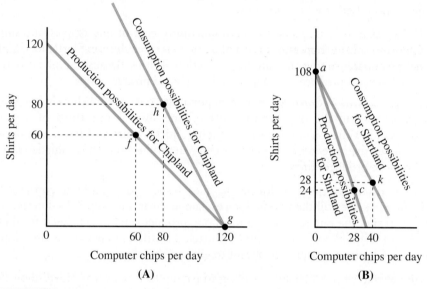

▲ **FIGURE 18.2**

Consumption Possibilities Curve

The consumption possibilities curve shows the combinations of computer chips and shirts that can be consumed if each country specializes and trades. In Panel A, Chipland produces 120 chips and trades 40 of these chips to Shirtland for 80 shirts. In Panel B, Shirtland produces 108 shirts and trades 80 of these shirts to Chipland for 40 chips. The trade allows each nation to consume more.

How do the outcomes with specialization and trade compare to the autarky outcomes? Chipland moves from point *f* (autarky) to point *h*, so trade increases the consumption of each good by 20 units. Shirtland moves from point *c* to point *k*, so this nation consumes 12 additional chips and 4 additional shirts.

In Figure 18.2, each consumption possibilities curve lies above the nation's production possibilities curves, meaning each nation has more options about how much to consume under specialization and trade. In most cases, a nation picks a point on the consumption possibilities curve that provides more of each good. Of course, this is a very simple example. In the actual world market, many countries produce and trade many goods. The marketplace determines what the terms of those trades will be, depending upon supply, demand, and pricing.

How Free Trade Affects Employment

You've now seen that trade allows each nation to consume more of each good. But we haven't yet discussed the effects of trade on employment. Under free trade, each nation will begin to specialize in a single good, causing considerable changes in the country's employment in different industries. In Chipland, the chip industry doubles in size—output increases from 60 to 120 chips per day—while the shirt industry disappears. Workers and other resources will leave the shirt industry and move to the chip industry. In Shirtland, the flow is in the opposite direction: Workers and other resources move from the chip industry to the shirt industry.

Is free trade good for everyone? Switching from self-sufficiency to specialization and trade increases consumption in both nations, so on average, people in each nation benefit from free trade. But some people in both nations will be harmed by free trade. In Chipland, for example, people in the shirt industry will lose their jobs when the shirt industry disappears. Some workers can easily move into the expanding computer chip industry. For these workers, free trade is likely to be beneficial. However, other shirt workers will be unable to make the move to the chip industry and will be forced to accept lower-paying jobs or face unemployment. Free trade is likely to make these displaced workers worse off. There is a saying, "Where you stand on an issue depends on where you sit." In our example, a worker sitting at a sewing machine in Chipland is likely to oppose free trade because that worker is likely to lose a job. A worker sitting at a workstation in a computer chip fabrication facility is likely to support free trade because the resulting increase in computer chip exports will generate more employment opportunities in that industry.

18.2 PROTECTIONIST POLICIES

Now that you know the basic rationale for specialization and trade, we can explore the effects of public policies that restrict it. All the restrictions we explore limit the gains from specialization and trade. We will consider four common import-restriction policies: an outright ban on imports, an import quota, voluntary export restraints, and a tariff.

Import Bans

To show how an import ban affects the market, let's start with an unrestricted market—no import ban. Figure 18.3 shows the market for shirts in Chipland, a nation with a comparative advantage in producing computer chips, not shirts. The domestic supply

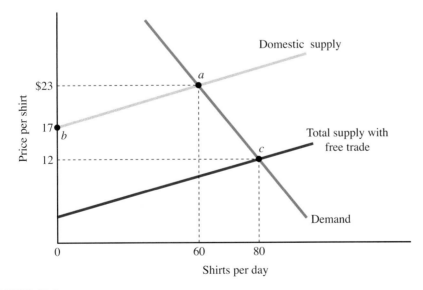

▲ **FIGURE 18.3**
Effects of an Import Ban
In the free-trade equilibrium, demand intersects the total supply curve at point c, with a price of $12 and a quantity of 80 shirts. If shirt imports are banned, the equilibrium is shown by the intersection of the demand curve and the domestic supply curve (point a). The price increases to $23.

curve shows the quantity of shirts supplied by firms in Chipland. Looking at point *b*, we see that Chipland firms will not supply any shirts unless the price is at least $17 per shirt. The total supply curve for shirts, which shows the quantity supplied by both domestic firms and foreign firms (in Shirtland), lies to the right of the domestic supply curve. At each price, the total supply of shirts exceeds the domestic supply because foreign firms supply shirts, too. Point *c* shows the free-trade equilibrium. The demand curve from domestic residents intersects the total supply curve at a price of $12 per shirt and a quantity of 80 shirts. Because this price is below the minimum price for domestic firms, domestic firms produce no shirts, and all the shirts in Chipland are imported from Shirtland.

What will happen if Chipland bans imported shirts? Foreign suppliers will disappear from the shirt market, so the total supply of shirts will be the domestic supply. In Figure 18.3, point *a* shows the equilibrium when Chipland bans imported shirts: The domestic demand curve intersects the domestic supply curve at a price of $23 per shirt and a quantity of 60 shirts. In other words, the decrease in supply resulting from the import ban increases the price consumers have to pay for shirts and decreases the quantity available for them to buy.

Quotas and Voluntary Export Restraints

import quota

A government-imposed limit on the quantity of a good that can be imported.

An alternative to an import ban is an **import quota**—a government-imposed limit on the quantity of a good that can be imported. An import quota is a restrictive policy that falls between free trade and an outright ban: Imports are cut, but not eliminated. For example, if a quota were put on shirts, the price consumers would have to pay would fall somewhere between the price they would pay with free trade ($12 per shirt, as in our example) and the price they would pay if imported shirts were banned ($23 per shirt). Where exactly the price would fall would depend on how high or low the quotas are.

voluntary export restraint (VER)

A scheme under which an exporting country voluntarily decreases its exports.

Import quotas are illegal under international trading rules. To get around these rules, an exporting country will sometimes agree to a **voluntary export restraint (VER)**. VERs are similar to import bans. When an exporting nation adopts a VER, it decreases its exports to avoid having to face even more restrictive trade policies importing countries might be tempted to impose on them. Although VERs are legal under global-trade rules, they violate the spirit of international free-trade agreements. In any case, quotas and VERs have the same effect. Like a quota, a VER increases the price of the restricted good, making it more feasible for domestic firms to participate in the market.

Figure 18.4 shows the effect of an import quota or VER. Starting from the free-trade equilibrium at point *c*, an import quota will shift the total supply curve to the left: At each price there will be a smaller quantity of shirts supplied because foreign suppliers aren't allowed to supply as many. The total supply curve when there is an import quota or VER will lie between the domestic supply curve and the total supply curve under free trade. The equilibrium under an import quota or VER occurs at point *d*, where the demand curve intersects the total supply curve under an import limitation. The $20 price per shirt with the import quota exceeds the $17 minimum price of domestic firms, so domestic firms supply 22 shirts (point *e*). Under a free-trade policy, they would have supplied no shirts.

import licenses

Rights, issued by a government, to import goods.

A quota or a VER produces winners and losers. The winners include foreign and domestic shirt producers. In our example, foreign firms can sell shirts at a price of $20 instead of $12 each, and the price is high enough for domestic firms to participate in the market. This generates benefits for the firms and their workers. The losers are consumers, who pay a higher price for shirts. In some cases, the government issues **import licenses** to some citizens, who can then buy shirts from foreign firms at a low price, such as $12, and sell the shirts at the higher domestic price, $20. Because import licenses provide profits to the holder, they are often awarded to politically powerful

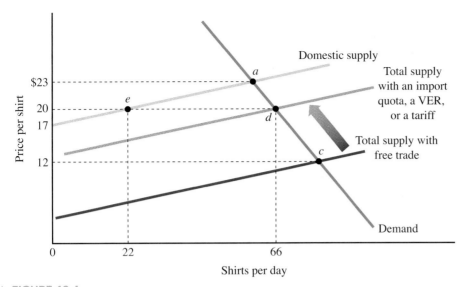

▲ FIGURE 18.4
Market Effects of a Quota, a VER, or a Tariff
An import quota shifts the supply curve to the left. The market moves upward along the demand curve to point *d*, which is between point *c* (free trade) and *a* (an import ban). We can reach the same point with a tariff that shifts the total supply curve to the same position.

firms or individuals. Moreover, because they are so valuable, some people may bribe government officials to obtain them.

We know consumers pay higher prices for goods that are subject to protectionist policies, but how much more? Here is one example. In the United States, voluntary export restraints on Japanese automobiles in 1984 increased the price of a Japanese car by about $1,300 and the price of a domestic car by about $660.[1]

APPLICATION 1

THE IMPACT OF TARIFFS ON THE POOR

APPLYING THE CONCEPTS #1: Do tariffs (taxes) on imported goods hurt the poor disproportionately?

Economists have found that tariffs in the United States fall most heavily on lower-income consumers. In the United States, tariffs are very high on textiles, apparel items, and footwear. These goods represent a higher fraction of the consumption of lower-income households than higher-income households. For example, footwear accounts for 1.3 percent of the expenditure of lower-income households, as compared to 0.5 percent for higher-income households.

Moreover, even within these categories of goods for which tariffs are high, the highest tariffs fall on the cheapest products—precisely those that will be purchased by lower-income consumers. For example, low-price sneakers face a 32 percent tariff whereas expensive track shoes face only a 20 percent tariff. In general, to protect U.S. industries, tariffs are highest on labor-intensive goods; goods that use relatively more labor than capital. But these goods tend to be lower priced. That is why tariffs do fall disproportionately on the poor.   **Related to Exercise 2.7.**

SOURCE: Based on *Economic Report of the President 2006*, February 2006 (Washington, D.C.: Government Printing Office), chap. 7.

tariff
A tax on imported goods.

An alternative to a quota or a VER is an import **tariff**, which is a tax on an imported good. Tariffs have the same effect as quotas and VERs. We know from our earlier discussions that a tax shifts the supply curve to the left and increases the equilibrium price. In Figure 18.4, suppose the tariff shifts the total supply curve with free trade so that it intersects the domestic demand curve at point *d*. In other words, we reach the same point we reached with the quota: Consumers pay the same $20 price per shirt, and domestic firms produce the same quantity (22 shirts).

There is one fundamental difference between a quota and a tariff. An import quota allows importers to buy shirts from foreign suppliers at a low price—say, $12 per shirt—and sell them for $20 each, the artificially high price. In other words, importers make money from the quota. Under a tariff, the government gets the money, collecting $8 per shirt from foreign suppliers. Citizens in Chipland will prefer the tariff to the quota because the government can use the revenue from the tariff to cut other taxes or expand public programs.

In the real world, tariffs can have major effects. One trade expert estimated that cutting industrial tariffs by 50 percent would increase the output of the world's economy by $270 billion per year. Similar easing of tariffs on agricultural products would cut the world's food bill by $100 billion.[2]

Tariffs also appear to disproportionately affect the poor.

Responses to Protectionist Policies

A restriction on imports is likely to lead to further restrictions on trade. For example, if Chipland bans shirt imports, Shirtland might retaliate by banning computer chips from Chipland. A trade war of this sort could escalate to the point where the two nations return to self-sufficiency. If this happens, the two countries would be forced to scale back their consumption. We can see that by looking back at Figure 18.2: Chipland will move from point *h* to point *f*, and Shirtland will move from point *k* to point *c*. This sort of retaliatory response is common. Because it is, we know that protecting one industry in a nation is likely to harm that nation's other exports. Chipland's shirt industry, if protected from imports, may grow, but it will be at the expense of its computer-chip industry.

Many import restrictions have led to retaliatory policies and substantially lessened trade. The most famous was the Smoot-Hawley Tariff Act of 1930. When the United States increased its average tariff on imports to 59 percent, its trading partners retaliated with higher tariffs on U.S. products. The resulting trade war reduced international trade and deepened the worldwide depression of the 1930s.

The threat of retaliatory policies may persuade a nation to loosen its protectionist policies. For example, in 1995 the United States announced it would impose 100 percent tariffs on Japanese luxury cars if Japan didn't ease its restrictions on imported auto parts. Just hours before the tariffs were to take effect, the two nations reached an agreement that was expected to increase the sales of U.S. auto parts to Japanese firms. In 2002, President Bush imposed tariffs on steel. However, when faced with the threat of retaliatory policies in Europe, he ended the sanctions in 2003.

Import restrictions also create an incentive to smuggle goods. The restrictions create a gap between the cost of purchasing the restricted goods abroad and the price goods can be sold for in the protected economy, so there is a profit to be made.

18.3 WHAT ARE THE RATIONALES FOR PROTECTIONIST POLICIES?

Why would a government impose protectionist policies such as an import ban, quota, VER, or tariff? We'll look at three possible reasons:

1 To shield workers from foreign competition

2 To nurture infant industries until they mature

3 To help domestic firms establish monopolies in world markets

To Shield Workers from Foreign Competition

One of the most basic arguments for protectionism is that it shields workers in industries that would be hurt by trade. Suppose, relative to the United States, nations in the Far East have a comparative advantage in producing textiles. If the United States were to reduce existing tariffs on textiles, domestic manufacturers could not compete. They would have to close their factories and lay off workers. In an ideal world, the laid-off workers would take new jobs in other sectors of the economy. In practice, this is difficult. Many workers don't immediately have the skills to go to work in other sectors, and obtaining those skills takes time. Moreover, the textile industry is heavily concentrated in the southeastern part of the United States. Politicians from that region will try to keep tariffs in place to prevent temporary unemployment and changes in employment patterns in their areas—they have an incentive to protect their own constituents, even though it may cause major economic losses for the economy. The result of this protection will be less-efficient production, higher prices, and lower consumption for the United States. How much does it cost to protect a job?

To Nurture Infant Industries until They Mature

During World War II the United States built hundreds of boats, called Liberty ships, for the navy. As more and more of these ships were built, each required fewer hours to complete because workers acquired knowledge during the production process and got better at it. Engineers and economists call this phenomenon **learning by doing**. To learn a new game, such as Ping-Pong, you learn by doing. At first, you may find it difficult to play, but your skills improve as you go along.

Tariffs and other protectionist policies are often defended on the grounds that they protect new or **infant industries** that are in the early stages of development and can benefit from learning by doing. A tariff shields a young industry from the competition of its more mature rivals. After the infant industry "grows up," the tariff can eventually be eliminated because the industry is able to compete. In practice, infant industries rarely become competitive with their foreign rivals. During the 1950s and 1960s, many Latin American countries used tariffs and other policies to protect their young manufacturing industries from foreign competition. Unfortunately, the domestic industries never became as efficient as foreign suppliers, and the Latin American countries that tried this policy suffered. Another problem with protecting an infant industry is that once a government gives an industry tariff protection, it is difficult to take that protection away. More generally, even some established companies also complain about "unfair competition," but this concept does not always make sense.

learning by doing
Knowledge and skills workers gain during production that increase productivity and lower cost.

infant industries
Industries that are at an early stage of development.

To Help Domestic Firms Establish Monopolies in World Markets

If the production of a particular good requires extremely large economies of scale, the world market will support only a few, or perhaps just one, firm. In this case, a nation might be tempted to adopt policies to ensure a company within its borders will end up being the world monopolist. Suppose the commercial aircraft industry can support only one large firm. If two firms enter the industry, both will lose money. A nation could agree to provide financial support to a domestic firm to guarantee the firm will make a profit. With such a guarantee, the domestic firm will enter the industry. Knowing this, a foreign firm will be reluctant to enter, so the domestic firm will capture the monopoly profit. The country where the successful firm is located will benefit from higher production and more jobs for its citizens.

APPLICATION 2

PROTECTION FOR CANDLE MAKERS

APPLYING THE CONCEPTS #2: Does the concept of "unfair" competition make sense?

In response to the spread of protectionism, the French economist Frédéric Bastiat (1801–1850) wrote the following fictitious petition, in which French candle makers asked for protection from "unfair" competition:

> We are suffering from the intolerable competition of a foreign rival, placed, it would seem, in a condition so far superior to ours for the production of light, that he absolutely inundates our national market at a price fabulously reduced. The moment he shows himself, our trade leaves us—all of our customers apply to him; and a branch of native industry, having countless ramifications, is all at once rendered completely stagnant. This rival … is none other than the sun.

> What we pray for is, that it may please you to pass a law ordering the shutting up of all windows, sky-lights, dormer windows, curtains, blinds, bull's eyes; in a word all openings, holes, chinks, clefts, and fissures, by or through which the light of the sun has been in use to enter houses, to the prejudice of the meritorious manufactures with which we … have accommodated our country—a country which, in gratitude, ought not to abandon us now.

> Does it not argue to the greatest inconsistency to check as you do the importation of coal, iron, cheese, and goods of foreign manufacture, merely because … their price approaches zero, while at the same time you freely admit, and without limitation, the light of the sun, whose price is during the whole day at zero?   **Related to Exercise 3.7.**

SOURCE: Based on Frédéric Bastiat, *Economics Sophisms* (Edinburgh: Oliver & Boyd, 1873), 49–53.

One famous example is Airbus, an airplane-manufacturing consortium in Europe that competes with the U.S. firm Boeing. Several European countries provided large subsidies for the firms producing the Airbus line of planes. These subsidies allowed the consortium firms to underprice their rivals in the United States, and at least one U.S. manufacturer of commercial airplanes was forced out of business.

What could go wrong with these monopoly creation policies? First, if both nations subsidize their domestic firms, both firms will enter the market and lose money. The taxpayers in both countries will then have to pay for the subsidies. Second, a nation may pick the wrong industry to subsidize. Together, the British and French subsidized an airplane known as the Concorde, which flew at supersonic speeds, rapidly shuttling passengers between Europe and the United States. Although the Concorde captured the market, the market was not worth capturing. The venture lost money because the Concorde was very costly to develop and fly, and few people were willing to pay a large premium for supersonic travel. The Concorde stopped flying in 2003. Finally, the subsidized firm may not perform well. As an example, in 2006, Airbus was facing severe problems with its planes and losing business to its competitor, Boeing.

18.4 A BRIEF HISTORY OF INTERNATIONAL TARIFF AND TRADE AGREEMENTS

Today, the average U.S. tariff is 4.6 percent of the value of imported goods, a rate close to the average tariffs in Japan and most European nations but very low by historical standards. When the Smoot-Hawley tariffs were implemented in the

1930s, the average U.S. tariff was a whopping 59 percent of a product's price. Tariffs are lower today because several international agreements subsequently reduced them.

The first major international trade agreement following World War II was the **General Agreement on Tariffs and Trade (GATT)**. This agreement was initiated in 1947 by the United States and 23 other nations and now has over 149 members. Nine rounds of GATT negotiations over tariffs and trade regulations have taken place, resulting in progressively lower tariffs for the member nations. The last completed set of negotiations, the Uruguay round (1994), decreased tariffs by about one-third of the previous level. In 1995, the **World Trade Organization (WTO)** was formed to enforce GATT and other international trade agreements. Under GATT's "most favored nation" provision, a country that reduces tariffs for one nation must do so for all members of GATT. This provision helps reduce tariffs throughout the world.

The most recent round of trade negotiations began in Doha, Qatar, in 2001 but collapsed in 2008. This round was billed as an attempt to benefit developing countries that exported agricultural goods. The idea was that reductions in subsidies and tariffs on agriculture goods in developed countries would promote exports of agriculture goods for developing countries. In turn, developed countries wanted lower tariffs for industrial goods in developing countries. Why did the negotiations fail? One reason was that China and India, rapidly growing countries each with populations over a billion, were more interested in promoting their industrial bases than their agricultural exports. Perhaps a second reason was that previous trade negotiations had been successful, leaving less room for "grand bargains" that would motivate all countries to embrace new agreements.

If global negotiations do no work, what alternatives are there? In addition to the large group of nations in the WTO, other groups of nations have formed trade associations to lower trade barriers and promote international trade. Here are some of the best-known agreements:

- The North American Free Trade Agreement (NAFTA) took effect in 1994 and was implemented over a 15-year period. It eliminates all tariffs and other trade barriers between Canada, Mexico, and the United States.

- The European Union (EU) was designed to remove all trade barriers within Europe and create a single market. Initially, the EU consisted of just six countries: Belgium, Germany, France, Italy, Luxembourg, and the Netherlands. Denmark, Ireland, and the United Kingdom joined in 1973; Greece in 1981; Spain and Portugal in 1986; and Austria, Finland, and Sweden in 1995. In 2004, the biggest ever enlargement took place with 10 new countries joining the EU.

- The leaders of 18 Asian nations have formed an organization called Asian Pacific Economic Cooperation (APEC). In 1994, APEC signed a nonbinding agreement to reduce trade barriers among these nations.

- The Dominican Republic–Central America Free Trade Agreement (DR-CAFTA) promotes trade liberalization between the United States, the Dominican Republic, and five Central American countries: Costa Rica, El Salvador, Guatemala, Honduras, and Nicaragua. DR-CAFTA is modeled after NAFTA.

Some economists are concerned that these regional trade agreements may stand in the way of broader international trade agreements under GATT. Although regional agreements may lead to reduced tariffs for neighboring or member countries, they do little to promote efficiency across the globe. For example, a Belgian firm may find it easier to sell goods in France than does a firm from South America that has a lower cost of production.

General Agreement on Tariffs and Trade (GATT)

An international agreement established in 1947 that has lowered trade barriers between the United States and other nations.

World Trade Organization (WTO)

An organization established in 1995 that oversees GATT and other international trade agreements, resolves trade disputes, and holds forums for further rounds of trade negotiations.

18.5 RECENT POLICY DEBATES AND TRADE AGREEMENTS

We're now ready to discuss three recent policy debates concerning international trade:

1 Are foreign producers dumping their products?
2 Do trade laws inhibit environmental protection?
3 Do outsourcing and trade cause income inequality?

Are Foreign Producers Dumping Their Products?

dumping
A situation in which the price a firm charges in a foreign market is lower than either the price it charges in its home markets or the production cost.

Although tariff rates have been reduced in recent years, a number of controversies surrounding free trade remain. One of these relates to *dumping*. A firm is **dumping** when the price it charges in a foreign market is either lower than the price it charges in its home market or lower than its production cost. Dumping is illegal under international trade agreements. Hundreds of cases of alleged dumping are presented to WTO authorities each year. Here are some cases in which the WTO concluded that dumping had indeed occurred: Hong Kong VCRs sold in Europe; Chinese bicycles sold in the United States; Asian TV sets sold in Europe; steel from Brazil, India, Japan, and Spain sold in the United States; U.S. beef sold in Mexico; and Chinese computer disks sold in Japan and the United States. Under the current provisions of the WTO, a

---

APPLICATION 3

ARE THEY REALLY DUMPING?

APPLYING THE CONCEPTS #3: How does the Commerce Department try to determine whether countries are dumping their products?

Dumping is selling a product in a foreign market at a lower price than a firm's own domestic market. You might think that this would require a comparison of *actual* prices charged in home markets compared to foreign markets. But that is rarely the case in the United States. For example, from 1995 to 1998, only 4 out of 141 cases of dumping used actual prices.

Instead, the U.S. Department of Commerce typically uses a "constructed value" method where it makes its own estimates of what prices in countries' own markets *would be* based on available data on production costs, transportation, and other expenses and also a margin for profit and administration. In many cases, these are very crude and dated estimates. In other cases, they rely solely on the information provided by the parties who filed the complaint, who clearly have a vested interest in the outcome.

Perhaps this is why the Commerce Department virtually always finds that foreign countries are in fact guilty of dumping their products. Chinese companies have been accused of dumping for a wide array of products including crawfish, paint brushes, sodium nitrate, and plastic shopping bags. Critics of dumping believe that "constructed values" calculations overstate prices in domestic markets and inevitably lead to the conclusion that firms are in fact guilty of dumping their products.   **Related to Exercise 5.7.**

SOURCE: Based on Douglas A. Irwin, *Free Trade Under Fire* (Princeton, New Jersey: Princeton University Press, 2009), chap. 5.

nation can impose antidumping duties, a tax, on products that are being dumped within its borders.

Why would a firm dump—charge a low price in the foreign market? The first reason is price discrimination. **Price discrimination** occurs when a firm charges a different price to different customers buying the same product. If a firm has a monopoly in its home market but faces strong competition in a foreign market, it will naturally charge a higher price in the home market. What the firm is doing is using its monopoly power to charge higher prices to consumers at home and charge lower prices to consumers abroad where it faces competition. This strategy maximizes the firm's profits.

price discrimination
The practice of selling a good at different prices to different consumers.

To illustrate how international price discrimination works, let's look at the case of Korean VCRs.[3]

In the 1980s there were only three firms, all Korean, selling VCRs in Korea, but there were dozens of firms selling VCRs in Europe. The lack of competition in Korea generated very high prices for Korean consumers, who paid much more than European consumers paid for identical Korean VCRs and VCRs produced by firms in other countries. Essentially, Korean firms used their market power to discriminate against consumers in their own country. When international trade authorities concluded these companies were, indeed, dumping VCRs in Europe, the Korean firms responded by cutting prices in their home market. However, they didn't increase their prices in Europe—much to the delight of European consumers and the dismay of European producers, who had sought relief from the dumping in the first place.

The Korean VCR example brings up a second reason for dumping: **predatory pricing**—cutting prices in an attempt to drive rival firms out of business. The predatory firm sets its price below its production cost, low enough that both the predator and its prey (a firm in the foreign market) lose money. After the prey goes out of business, the predator increases its price to earn a monopoly profit.

predatory pricing
A firm sells a product at a price below its production cost to drive a rival out of business and then increases the price.

Although the rationale for antidumping laws is to prevent predatory pricing, it is difficult to determine whether low prices are the result of this or price discrimination. Many economists are skeptical about how frequently predatory pricing actually occurs, as opposed to price discrimination. They suspect many nations use their antidumping laws as protectionist policies in disguise. Because WTO rules limit tariffs and quotas, some nations may be tempted to substitute antidumping duties for these protectionist policies.

Until the 1990s, antidumping cases were brought almost exclusively by Australia, New Zealand, Europe, Canada, and the United States. However, starting in the 1990s, the number of antidumping cases alleged by developing countries began to rise. Today, approximately half the cases are brought by developing countries. Professor Thomas Prusa of Rutgers University has studied antidumping and has found it is a potent weapon for protecting domestic industries. If an antidumping case is settled and a tariff is imposed as a result, imports typically fall by 50 to 70 percent during the first three years of the protection period. Even if a country loses a claim, imports still fall by 15 to 20 percent.[4]

Do Trade Laws Inhibit Environmental Protection?

In recent trade negotiations, a new player—environmental groups—appeared on the scene. Starting in the early 1990s, environmentalists began to question whether policies that liberalized trade could harm the environment. They were concerned that increased trade would lead to worldwide environmental degradation. An important issue that attracted their attention was the killing of dolphins by tuna fishers.

Anyone who catches tuna with a large net will also catch the dolphins that swim with the tuna, and most of the dolphins will die. In 1972, the United States outlawed the use of tuna nets by U.S. ships. However, ships from other nations, including Mexico, were still catching tuna with nets and selling that tuna in the United States. The United States responded with a ban of Mexican tuna caught with nets. The Mexican government complained to an international trade authority that the tuna boycott was an unfair trade barrier. The trade authority agreed with Mexico and forced the United States to remove the boycott.

Under current WTO rules, a country can adopt any environmental standard it chooses, as long as it does not discriminate against foreign producers. For example, the United States can limit the exhaust emissions of all cars that operate in the United States. As long as emissions rules apply equally to all cars, domestic and imports, the rules are legal according to the WTO. An international panel upheld U.S. fuel efficiency rules for automobiles on this principle.

The tuna boycott was a violation of WTO rules because killing dolphins does not harm the U.S. environment directly. For the same reason, the United States cannot ban imported goods produced by factories that generate air or water pollution in other countries. It is easy to understand why WTO rules do not allow countries to restrict trade on the basis of the methods that are used to produce goods and services. Countries differ in the value they place on the environment. For example, a poor nation may be willing to tolerate more pollution if it means attaining a higher standard of living for its citizens.

If trade restrictions cannot be used to protect the dolphins and deal with other global environmental problems, what else can we do? Shouldn't we have the right to protect dolphins? International agreements have been used for a variety of different environmental goals, from limiting the harvest of whales to reducing the chemicals that deplete the ozone layer. These agreements are difficult to reach, however, so some nations will be tempted to use trade restrictions to pursue environmental goals. If they do, they will encounter resistance because WTO rules mean that a nation can pursue its environmental goals only within its own borders. In recent years, environmentalists have lobbied Congress not to approve bilateral trade deals unless sufficient environmental standards are in place. This trend is likely to continue.

Trade disputes about environmental issues are part of a larger phenomenon that occurs when trade issues and national regulations collide. At one time, most trade disputes were simply matters of protecting domestic industries from foreign competition. Agriculture, textile, and steel industries around the world frequently benefited from various forms of protection. But in recent years, a new breed of trade disputes has erupted revolving around social problems and the role that government regulation should play in solving them.

The EU, for example, has banned imports of hormone-treated beef. The United States and Canada successfully challenged this ban with the WTO. They argued there was no scientific evidence that hormone-treated beef adversely affected human health. The EU refused to rescind the ban and, as a consequence, the United States and Canada were permitted to impose retaliatory tariffs on a wide range of European products that affected many EU industries.

The EU's ban on hormone-treated beef was intended to protect European farmers from imports, but it also reflected Europeans' nervousness about technology. After all, Europe banned all hormone-treated beef, not just imported beef. Shouldn't a country have a right to pursue this policy, even if it is not based on the best science of the day? Although the costs of the policy are straightforward in terms of higher beef prices, the benefits, in terms of potential safety and peace of mind, are much more difficult to assess. Similar issues have arisen as genetically modified crops have become more commonplace. As a world trading community, we will have to decide at what point we allow national policy concerns to override principles of free trade.

APPLICATION 4

TRADE, CONSUMPTION, AND INEQUALITY

APPLYING THE CONCEPTS #4: Why might international trade reduce measured inequality in the United States?

While it is conventional wisdom now that inequality in the United States has increased in the last several decades, until recently no one had taken a careful look at the actual living standards of different income groups, taking into account the goods they purchase. Two economists from the University of Chicago, Christian Broda and John Romalis, discovered that the prices low-income groups paid for goods and services increased substantially less than for high-income groups. As a result, living standards have not become more unequal.

The key to understanding this result is that consumption patterns of the rich and poor differ. The poor consume a higher ratio of nondurable goods (such as cosmetics, toys, and sporting goods) to services than the rich, while prices for nondurable goods have risen less than prices for services. Prices for the nondurable goods purchased by the poor, which are typically sold in grocery, drug, and mass merchandise stores, also increased less than the prices of nondurable goods purchased by the rich. And the poor typically consume a higher fraction of new goods, whose prices have often fallen.

Trade with China is an important part of this story. About one-third of the change in relative prices that has helped the poor can be accounted for by an increase in imports from China. These are the goods that stock the shelves of Walmart and other lower-end stores where the poor shop. Sam Walton and his successors effectively ran their own antipoverty program.

The moral of the story: Trade does not just affect employment patterns—it also changes prices. We must take both factors into account to understand how living standards have changed for the rich and poor.   **Related to Exercise 5.8.**

SOURCE: Based on Christian Broda and John Romalis, "Inequality and Prices: Does China Benefit the Poor in America?" March 26, 2008, http://siteresources.worldbank.org/INTMACRO/Resources/June5&62008MGConferencePAPER-BRODA.pdf (accessed April 29, 2010).

Do Outsourcing and Trade Cause Income Inequality?

Inequality in wages has been growing in the United States since 1973. The wages of skilled workers have risen faster than the wages of unskilled workers. World trade has also boomed since 1973. Could there be a connection between the two?

Trade theory suggests a link between increased trade and increased wage inequality. Here is how they might be linked. Suppose the United States produces two types of goods: one using skilled labor (say, airplanes) and one using unskilled labor (say, textiles). The United States is likely to have a comparative advantage in products that use skilled labor, and developing countries are likely to have a comparative advantage in products that use unskilled labor. An increase in world trade will increase both exports and imports. An increase in U.S. exports means we'll need to produce more goods requiring skilled labor, so the domestic demand for skilled labor will increase, and so will the wages of these workers. At the same time, an increase in U.S. imports means we'll be buying more goods produced by unskilled laborers abroad, so the demand for unskilled workers here will decrease, and these people's wages will fall. As

outsourcing

Firms producing components of their goods and services in other countries.

a result, the gap between the wages of the two types of workers in the United States will grow.

In addition, U.S. firms will produce some components of their goods and services overseas, which is known as **outsourcing**. If a firm outsources products that use unskilled labor, the demand for unskilled labor in the United States will decline, and this will also increase the gap between wages for the skilled and the unskilled.

Economists have tried to determine how much trade has contributed to growing wage inequality in the United States. As usual, other factors make such a determination difficult. It is difficult, for example, to distinguish between the effects of trade and the effects of technical progress. Technical change, such as the rapid introduction and use of computers, will also tend to increase the demand for skilled workers and decrease the demand for unskilled workers. Economists have noted, however, that the exports of goods using skilled labor and the imports of goods using unskilled labor have both increased, just as the theory predicts. Nonetheless, at least some of the increased wage inequality is caused by international trade. Trade, however, may also reduce the prices of goods and services purchased by consumers in different income classes. We must take this factor into account in assessing trade and inequality.

One response to this undesirable side effect of trade is to use trade restrictions to protect industries that use unskilled workers. Another approach is to make the transition to an economy with more skilled than unskilled jobs less traumatic. In the long run, of course, workers will move to industries that require skilled labor, and they will eventually earn higher wages. However, in the short run the government could facilitate the transition by providing assistance for the education and training of unskilled workers.

More recently, there has been another concern. In recent years, jobs in call centers for airlines and credit card companies, customer service and technical support for computers, and the work of writing computer code have been relocated overseas. Some of these jobs require considerable skill, and therefore not all jobs that are outsourced will be low-skilled jobs. Nor can all services be outsourced, particularly those that are less routine. In the coming years, we will gain better insights into how international trade and outsourcing affect the wages of skilled workers.

Why Do People Protest Free Trade?

We have seen some of the important policy issues surrounding trade. Under current international trade rules, a country cannot dictate the terms under which another country actually produces the goods and services it sells—even if production harms the environment. It is also possible that free trade can contribute to inequality within the United States, although lower prices for goods consumed partially offset this effect. But do these reasons explain the passion we sometimes see in protests against free trade, such as the riots in 1999 in Seattle at a WTO meeting or the protestors dressed in death masks gathering at world trade meetings? Possibly, but protestors are more likely driven by something very basic. As we have seen in this chapter, trade and specialization provide important opportunities to raise living standards throughout the globe. But they also mean individuals and nations surrender some of their independence and sovereignty. By not producing precisely what we consume, we become dependent on others to trade with us. By cooperating with other nations, we need to develop agreed-upon rules that, at times, limit our own actions.

The protestors may simply not understand the principles of trade, but they also may fear loss of cultural identity and independence. In today's world, "no man is an island." Nations have become increasingly dependent on one another. Multinational corporations are the ultimate symbol of this interdependence, producing and distributing goods on a global scale. Thus companies such as McDonald's, Starbucks, or Nike can come under attack by protestors. The benefits of trade, however, are so vast that countries will need to find ways to address issues of sovereignty and control while retaining an open and prosperous trading system.

SUMMARY

In this chapter, we discussed the benefits of specialization and trade, and we explored the trade-offs associated with protectionist policies. There is a basic conflict between consumers who prefer free trade because free trade decreases prices and workers in the protected industries who want to keep their jobs. Here are the main points of the chapter:

1 If one country has a *comparative advantage* vis-à-vis another country in producing a particular good (a lower opportunity cost), specialization and trade will benefit both countries.

2 An import ban or an *import quota* increases prices, protecting domestic industries, but domestic consumers pay the price.

3 Because the victims of protectionist policies often retaliate, the protection of a domestic industry can harm an exporting industry.

4 A *tariff*, a tax on imports, generates revenue for the government, whereas an *import quota*—a limit on imports—generates revenue for foreigners or importers.

5 In principle, the laws against *dumping* are designed to prevent *predatory pricing*. In practice, predatory pricing laws are often used to shield domestic industries from competition. Allegations of it are hard to prove.

6 Under *World Trade Organization (WTO)* rules, each country may pursue its environmental goals only within its own borders.

7 International trade has contributed to the widening gap between the wages of low-skilled and high-skilled labor. However, it also has reduced the relative prices facing the poor, offsetting some of the effects on inequality.

KEY TERMS

consumption possibilities curve, p. 367

dumping, p. 376

General Agreement on Tariffs and Trade (GATT), p. 375

import licenses, p. 370

import quota, p. 370

infant industries, p. 373

learning by doing, p. 373

outsourcing, p. 380

predatory pricing, p. 377

price discrimination, p. 377

tariff, p. 372

terms of trade, p. 367

voluntary export restraint (VER), p. 370

World Trade Organization (WTO), p. 375

EXERCISES

Visit www.myeconlab.com to complete these exercises online and get instant feedback.

18.1 Benefits from Specialization and Trade

1.1 A country has a comparative advantage if it has a lower _____ cost of producing a good.

1.2 The terms of trade is the rate at which two goods can be _____ for one another.

1.3 Suppose a country has a comparative advantage in shirts but not computer chips. Workers in the chip industry will be _____ with trade.

1.4 Trade requires absolute advantage to make both parties better off. _____ (True/False)

1.5 **Finding Comparative Advantage.** In one minute, Country B can produce either 1,000 TVs and no computers or 500 computers and no TVs. Similarly, in one minute Country C can produce either 2,400 TVs or 600 computers.

   a. Compute the opportunity costs of TVs and computers for each country. Which country has a comparative advantage in producing TVs? Which country has a comparative advantage in producing computers?

   b. Draw the production possibilities curves for the two countries.

1.6 **Benefits from Trade.** In Country U, the opportunity cost of a computer is 10 pairs of shoes. In Country C, the opportunity cost of a computer is 100 pairs of shoes.

   a. Suppose the two countries split the difference between the willingness to pay for computers and the willingness to accept computers. Compute the terms of trade, that is, the rate at which the two countries will exchange computers and shoes.

   b. Suppose the two countries exchange one computer for the number of shoes dictated by the terms of trade you computed in part (a). Compute the net benefit from trade for each country.

1.7 **Measuring the Gains from Trade.** Consider two countries, Tableland and Chairland, each capable of producing tables and chairs. Chairland can produce the following combinations of chairs and tables:

All chairs and no tables: 36 chairs per day

All tables and no chairs: 18 tables per day

Tableland can produce the following combinations of chairs and tables:

All chairs and no tables: 40 chairs per day

All tables and no chairs: 40 tables per day

In each country, there is a fixed trade-off of tables for chairs.

a. Draw the two production possibilities curves, with chairs on the vertical axis and tables on the horizontal axis.

b. Suppose each country is initially self-sufficient and divides its resources equally between the two goods. How much does each country produce and consume?

c. Which country has a comparative advantage in producing tables? Which country has a comparative advantage in producing chairs?

d. If the two countries split the difference between the buyer's willingness to pay for chairs and the seller's willingness to accept, in terms of chairs per table, what are the terms of trade?

e. Draw the consumption possibilities curves.

f. Suppose each country specializes in the good for which it has a comparative advantage, and it exchanges 14 tables for some quantity of chairs. Compute the consumption bundles—*bundles* mean the consumption of tables and chairs—for each country.

1.8 Short-Term Employment Effects. Explain how trade can adversely affect employment in a sector of the economy that is suddenly opened to trade. What is likely to happen in the long run?

18.2 Protectionist Policies

2.1 If a country bans the importation of a particular good, the market equilibrium is shown by the intersection of the _____ curve and the _____ curve.

2.2 The equilibrium price under an import quota is _____ (above/below) the price that occurs with an import ban and _____ (above/below) the price that occurs with free trade.

2.3 From the perspective of the government, a _____ (tariff/quota) is better.

2.4 Threatening to impose a tariff on a country's exports if it doesn't open up its markets to trade is an example of a _____ policy.

2.5 Incentives for Smuggling. If a country bans imports, smugglers may try to penetrate its markets.

Suppose Chipland bans shirt imports, causing some importers to bribe customs officials who "look the other way" as smugglers bring shirts into the country. Your job is to combat shirt smuggling. Use the information in Figure 18.3 on page 369 to answer the following questions:

a. Suppose importers can sell their shirts on the world market at a price of $12 per shirt. How much is an importer willing to pay to get customs officials to look the other way?

b. What sort of change in trade policy would make your job easier?

2.6 Tariffs on Computer Chips. Suppose a country imposed tariffs on computer chips to protect its chip-making industries. What other types of firms in that economy might object to this policy?

2.7 Tariffs and the Poor. Historically, apparel and textiles were subject to high tariffs. Explain why this might hurt low-income consumers more than high-income consumers. (Related to Application 1 on page 371.)

2.8 Auctioning Import Licenses. In the text we explained that tariffs can be set to have the same effects as import quotas. However, if the government gives import licenses to producers, it will not collect any revenues. Suppose the government auctions the import licenses to the highest bidders. How will the revenue from the auction compare to the revenue raised by tariffs?

18.3 What Are the Rationales for Protectionist Policies?

3.1 The _____-industry argument is often given to provide a rationale for tariffs for new firms.

3.2 Knowledge gained during production is known as _____ by doing.

3.3 If only one firm can exist in a market, a government may try to subsidize the firm so that the country can share in the _____ profits.

3.4 In the 1950s and 1960s, countries in _____ used tariffs and other policies to nurture domestic industries.

3.5 Learning By Doing? An industry has been operating for 10 years under protection. The government wants to remove the trade protection, but the industry claims that it needs the protection because of learning by doing. Evaluate its claim. Can you think of a circumstance where it could be true?

3.6 Two Countries Fighting Over Airplane Production. Suppose there are monopoly profits in the production of airplanes, but two countries are each determined to capture the industry. When one country subsidizes its domestic firm, the other country matches the tactic. As a result, both firms stay in business. Who gains and who loses? Consider the effects on the firms, consumers, and taxpayers.

3.7 Unfair Competition. We are amused by candle makers asking for protection from the sun under the guise of unfair competition. How does this differ from U.S. producers of clothing claiming there is unfair competition from low-wage countries? (Related to Application 2 on page 374.)

18.4 A Brief History of International Tariff and Trade Agreements

4.1 The latest trade round is called the _____ round.

4.2 The _____ was formed in 1995 to oversee GATT.

4.3 NAFTA is a free-trade agreement between the United States, Mexico, and _____.

4.4 The average tariff rate in the United States is roughly _____ percent.

4.5 A Major Change in U.S. Trade Policy? In Chapter 7 of the 2006 *Economic Report of the President* (www.gpoaccess.gov/eop/download.html), the authors of the report discuss the important changes that occurred in 1934 under the Reciprocal Trade Agreements Act. They contend that it began to move the United States to a policy of more open trade after the Smoot-Hawley tariffs. Identify the key changes enacted in 1934.

4.6 Expansion in the European Union. When the EU originated, member countries generally had similar standards of living. However, with the most recent expansion of the EU, countries that were less developed joined the developed countries. What implications might the entry of the new countries have for wage inequality within the more established European countries?

4.7 Trade in Intellectual Property. Trade in international property (for example, patents, licenses, royalty agreements) has been particularly controversial. Go to the intellectual property section of the WTO's Web site (http://www.wto.org/english/tratop_e/trips_e/trips_e.htm) and explore some of its case studies. Do developing countries, as well as developed countries, have an interest in protecting intellectual property?

18.5 Recent Policy Debates and Trade Agreements

5.1 Pricing below production cost or selling at prices in foreign markets less than those in domestic markets is known as _____.

5.2 Under global trade rules, the United States was allowed to ban Mexican tuna because Mexico used fishing nets that killed dolphins. _____ (True/False)

5.3 Suppose the United States has a comparative advantage in goods that use skilled labor. If we trade with a country that has a comparative advantage in goods using unskilled labor, the wage differences between skilled and unskilled labor in the United States will _____.

5.4 Under a scheme of _____ pricing, a firm cuts its price to drive out rivals and then raises its price later.

5.5 Trade in Genetically Modified Crops. Suppose the residents of a country become fearful of using genetically modified crops in their food supply. Consider the following two possible scenarios:

a. Aware of consumer sentiment, the largest supermarket chains in the country vow they will not purchase food products that use genetically modified crops.

b. The government, aware of voter sentiment during an election year, bans the import of the food products that use genetically modified crops.

In both cases, no genetically modified crops enter the country. Does either of these cases run afoul of WTO policies?

5.6 Blinder versus Bhagwati on Outsourcing of Services. In an essay in the journal *Foreign Affairs*, Princeton economist Alan Blinder warned that the United States potentially faces great dangers from outsourcing of services. Columbia economist Jagdish Bhagwati was highly skeptical of this argument. Read both articles and come to your own assessment. The Blinder article, "Offshoring: The Next Industrial Revolution," *Foreign Affairs*, March/April 2006, is available at www.foreignaffairs.org/20060301faessay85209/alan-s-blinder/offshoring-the-next-industrial-revolution.html (accessed April 29, 2010).

The Bhagwati article, "Don't Cry for Free Trade," New York: Council of Foreign Relations, October 15, 2007, is available at www.cfr.org/publication/14526/dont_cry_for_free_trade.html (accessed April 29, 2010).

5.7 A Dumping Calculation. To produce 100 units of a good, a firm needs $40,000 in labor, $60,000 in material and capital cost, and requires a 10 percent profit rate. What would be the hypothetical price calculated for this firm? Suppose the profit rate was 20 percent—how would the price change? (Related to Application 3 on page 376.)

5.8 What Do the Poor and the Rich Buy? In Application 4, we highlighted research showing that the nondurable goods the poor buy have gone up in price less than those purchased by the rich and that the poor buy a higher percentage of newer goods than the rich. Can you give some examples of these price differences from your experience at normal and upscale supermarkets? Visit a couple of same-industry stores such as Walmart and Whole Foods to collect data if necessary. (Related to Application 4 on page 379.)

NOTES

1. *A Review of Recent Developments in the U.S. Automobile Industry, Including an Assessment of the Japanese Voluntary Restraint Agreements* (Washington, D.C.: U.S. International Trade Commission, February 1985).

2. Gary C. Hufbauer, "The Benefits of Open Markets and the Costs of Trade Protection and Economic Sanction," ACCF Center for Policy Research, www.accf.org/publications/reports/sr-benefits-openmarkets1997.html (accessed June 2006).

3. Taeho Bark, "The Korean Consumer Electronics Industry: Reaction to Antidumping Actions," in *Antidumping: How It Works and Who Gets Hurt*, ed. J. Michael Finger (Ann Arbor, MI: University of Michigan Press, 1993), chap. 7.

4. Virginia Postrel, "Curb Demonstrates Faults of Courting Special Interests," *New York Times*, June 14, 2001.

The World of International Finance

Today, the world currency markets are always open. When foreign-exchange traders in New York City are sound asleep at 3:00 A.M., their counterparts in London are already on their phones and computers at 8:00 A.M. In Tokyo, it's 6:00 P.M., and the day is just ending. By the time Tokyo traders return home after their long commutes, the New York traders are back at work. The currency markets keep working even when the labor market rests.

On any given day, trillions of dollars of value are exchanged in currency markets. The fortunes of industries, and sometimes countries, are determined by the ups and downs of currencies. Controversies have always swirled around exchange markets. Are they dominated by large speculators, or are they driven by the necessities of doing business around the world? Most importantly, do these markets work efficiently and effectively?

APPLYING THE CONCEPTS

1 How can the price of a Big Mac in China shed light on U.S.-Chinese currency tensions?
The Chinese Yuan and Big Macs

2 What factors may allow the United States to continue running large trade deficits with the rest of the world?
World Savings and U.S. Current Account Deficits

3 How did the 2008 financial crisis lead to problems for some countries in the Euro-zone?
A Downside to the Euro

4 What are the causes of financial collapses that occur throughout the globe?
The Argentine Financial Crisis

All currencies are traded 24 hours a day. The value of every currency depends on news and late-breaking developments throughout the world. Rising gas prices, a new terrorist attack, or a change in the leadership of a foreign government can easily affect the price at which currencies trade with one another. If the U.S. secretary of the Treasury utters a casual remark about the dollar or the value of the Chinese currency, it reverberates instantly throughout the world. Modern communications—e-mail, instant messaging, smart phones, videoconferencing, and satellite transmissions—accelerate the process.

How do changes in the value of currencies affect the U.S. economy? In Chapter 14, we explored the role of monetary policy in an open economy and its effects on exchange rates. In this chapter, we take a more comprehensive and in-depth look at exchange rates as well as other aspects of the international financial system. Understanding our international financial system will help you to interpret the often complex financial news from abroad. For example, if the value of the dollar starts to fall against the Japanese yen, what does it mean? Is this good news or bad news?

19.1 HOW EXCHANGE RATES ARE DETERMINED

In this section, we examine how the value of a currency is determined in world markets. We then look at the factors that can change the value of a currency.

What Are Exchange Rates?

exchange rate
The price at which currencies trade for one another in the market.

To conduct international transactions between countries with different currencies, it is necessary to exchange one currency for another. The **exchange rate** is defined as the price at which we can exchange one currency for another.

Suppose a U.S. songwriter sells the rights of a hit song to a Japanese producer. The U.S. songwriter agrees to accept $50,000. If the exchange rate between the U.S. dollar and Japanese yen is 100 yen per dollar, it will cost the Japanese producer 5,000,000 yen to purchase the rights to the song. Because international trade occurs between nations with different currencies, the exchange rate—the price at which one currency trades for another currency—is a crucial determinant of trade. Fluctuations in the exchange rate can have a huge impact on what goods countries import or export and the overall trade balance.

Throughout this chapter, we will measure the exchange rate in units of foreign currency per U.S. dollar, that is, as 100 Japanese yen per dollar or 0.8 euro per dollar. The **euro** is the common currency in Europe. With these exchange rates, you would receive 100 yen for each dollar, but only 0.8 euro for each dollar.

euro
The common currency in Europe.

We can think of the exchange rate as the price of dollars in terms of foreign currency. Recall from Chapter 14 that an increase in the value of a currency relative to the currency of another nation is called an *appreciation of a currency*. If the exchange rate between the dollar and the yen increases from 100 yen per dollar to 110 yen per dollar, one dollar will purchase more yen. Say, for instance, you've taken a trip to Japan for spring break. Because the dollar has appreciated, your dollar will exchange for more yen. You will now have more yen to spend on Japanese goods—say, MP3 players, DVD players, or entertainment—than you had before the dollar appreciated. The dollar has become more expensive in terms of yen. Its price has risen, in other words. Because the dollar has increased in value, we say the dollar has appreciated against the yen.

A *depreciation of a currency* is a decrease in the value of a currency relative to the currency of another nation. If the exchange rate falls from 100 to 90 yen per dollar, you'll get fewer yen for each dollar you exchange. Japanese goods—whose prices remain the same in Japanese yen—will become more expensive to U.S. residents. You'll have to use more dollars to obtain the yen to purchase the same MP3 and DVD players. The price of dollars in terms of yen has fallen, in other words, so we say the dollar has depreciated against the yen.

Be sure you understand that if one currency appreciates, the other must depreciate. If the dollar appreciates against the yen, for example, the yen must depreciate against the dollar. You'll get more yen in exchange for the dollar, but now when you trade your yen back, you'll get fewer dollars. For example, if the dollar appreciates from 100 to 110 yen per dollar, when you trade 100 yen back into U.S. currency, no longer will you get $1.00—you'll get just $0.91. Conversely, if the dollar depreciates against the yen, the yen must appreciate against the dollar. If the dollar depreciates from 100 yen to 90 yen per dollar, when you trade back 100 yen, you'll get $1.11, rather than just $1.00.

The exchange rate enables us to convert prices in one country to values in another country. A simple example illustrates how an exchange rate works. If you want to buy a watch from France, you need to know what it would cost. You e-mail the store in France and are told the watch sells for 240 euros. The store owners live in France and want to be paid in euros. To figure out what it will cost you in dollars, you need to know the exchange rate between euros and dollars. If the exchange rate is 0.8 euro per dollar, the watch will cost you $300:

$$\frac{240 \text{ euros}}{0.8 \text{ euro per dollar}} = \$300$$

If the exchange rate is one euro per dollar, the watch will cost only $240. As you can see, changes in the exchange rate will affect the prices of goods purchased on world markets and partly determine the pattern of imports and exports throughout the world.

How Demand and Supply Determine Exchange Rates

How are exchange rates determined? The exchange rate between U.S. dollars and euros is determined in the foreign-exchange market, the market in which dollars trade for euros. To understand this market, we can use demand and supply. In Figure 19.1, we plot the demand and supply curves for dollars in exchange for euros.

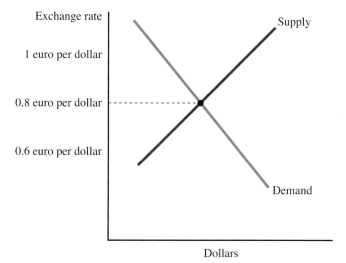

▲ **FIGURE 19.1**
The Demand for and Supply of U.S. Dollars
Market equilibrium occurs where the demand for U.S. dollars equals the supply.

The supply curve is the quantity supplied of dollars in exchange for euros. Individuals or firms that want to buy European goods or assets will need to exchange dollars for euros. The supply curve is drawn under the assumption that as euros become cheaper, total spending on European goods and assets will increase. Therefore, the supply curve slopes upward: As the value of the dollar increases, more dollars will be supplied to the currency market in exchange for euros.

The demand curve represents the quantity demanded of dollars in exchange for euros. Individuals or firms in Europe that want to buy U.S. goods or assets must trade euros for dollars. For example, to visit Disney World in Florida, a German or French family must exchange euros for dollars. As the exchange rate for the U.S. dollar falls, dollars become cheaper in terms of euros. This makes U.S. goods and assets less expensive for European residents, because each euro buys more U.S. dollars. As U.S. goods and assets become cheaper, we assume more European residents will want to trade euros for dollars. Therefore, the demand curve for dollars in exchange for euros slopes downward: Total demand for dollars will increase as the price of the dollar falls, or depreciates, against the euro.

Equilibrium in the market for foreign exchange occurs where the demand curve intersects the supply curve. In Figure 19.1, equilibrium occurs at an exchange rate of 0.8 euro per dollar. At this price, the willingness to trade dollars for euros just matches the willingness to trade euros for dollars. The foreign exchange market is in balance, and the price of euros in terms of a dollar is $1.25.

Price of euros per dollar in equilibrium:

$$0.8 \text{ euro per dollar} = \frac{1 \text{ dollar}}{0.8 \text{ euro}} = 1.25 \text{ dollars per euro, or } \$1.25 \text{ per euro}$$

Now, however, suppose the demand and supply forces between dollars and euros change. If the exchange rate, e, increases, the dollar buys *more* euros—the price of dollars in terms of euros increases, in other words. For example, if e increases from 0.8 euro per dollar to 1 euro per dollar, the dollar has become more valuable—meaning it has appreciated against the euro. Be sure you see both sides of the same exchange coin: If the dollar appreciates against the euro, then the euro must depreciate against the dollar. So, if the exchange rate increases from 0.8 to 1 euro per dollar, what will the price of a single euro be now?

When the dollar appreciates, each euro is worth less. In this case, the price of the euro will fall from $1.25 per euro to $1.00 per euro.

Dollar appreciates:

$$1.0 \text{ euro per dollar} = \frac{1 \text{ dollar}}{1 \text{ euro}} = 1.0 \text{ dollar per euro, or } \$1.00 \text{ per euro}$$

If the exchange rate falls from 0.8 euro to 0.6 euro per dollar, the dollar has depreciated in value against the euro—the price of dollars in terms of euros has decreased, in other words. When the dollar depreciates, each euro is worth more. In this case, the price of the euro will rise from $1.25 to $1.67.

Dollar depreciates:

$$0.6 \text{ euro per dollar} = \frac{1 \text{ dollar}}{0.6 \text{ euro}} = 1.67 \text{ dollars per euro, or } \$1.67 \text{ per euro}$$

Changes in Demand or Supply

Changes in demand or changes in supply will change equilibrium exchange rates. In Figure 19.2, we show how an increase in demand, a shift of the demand curve to the right, will increase, or appreciate, the exchange rate. U.S. dollars will become more expensive relative to euros as the price of U.S. dollars in terms of euros increases.

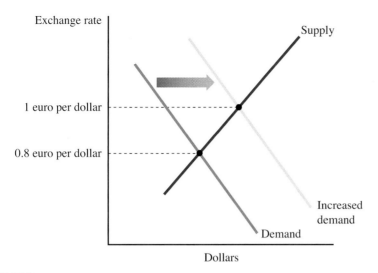

▲ FIGURE 19.2
Shifts in the Demand for U.S. Dollars
An increase in the demand for dollars will increase (appreciate) the dollar's exchange rate. Higher
U.S. interest rates or lower U.S. prices will increase the demand for dollars.

Two factors are the main causes of shifts of the demand curve for dollars: First, higher U.S. interest rates will lead to an increased demand for dollars. With higher returns in U.S. markets, investors throughout the world will want to buy dollars to invest in U.S. assets. The other factor, lower U.S. prices, will also lead to an increased demand for dollars. For example, if prices at Disney World fell, there would be an overall increase in the demand for dollars, because more tourists would want to visit Disney World.

Figure 19.3 shows the effects of an increase in the supply of dollars, a shift in the supply curve to the right. An increase in the supply of dollars will lead to a fall, or depreciation, of the value of the dollar against the euro. What are the main causes of and increase in the supply of dollars? Again, the same two factors: interest rates and prices. Higher European interest rates will lead U.S. investors to purchase European

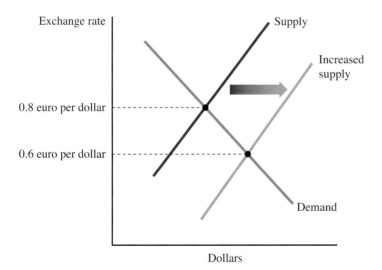

▲ FIGURE 19.3
Shifts in the Supply of U.S. Dollars
An increase in the supply of dollars will decrease (depreciate) the dollar exchange rate. Higher
European interest rates or lower European prices will increase the supply of dollars.

bonds or other interest-paying assets. Purchasing European bonds will require U.S. investors to supply dollars for euros, which will drive down the exchange rate for dollars. Lower European prices will also lead to an increase in the supply of dollars for euros.

Let's summarize the key facts about the foreign exchange market, using euros as our example:

1 The demand curve for dollars represents the demand for dollars in exchange for euros. The curve slopes downward. As the dollar depreciates, there will be an increase in the quantity of dollars demanded in exchange for euros.

2 The supply curve for dollars is the supply of dollars in exchange for euros. The curve slopes upward. As the dollar appreciates, there will be an increase in the quantity of dollars supplied in exchange for euros.

3 Increases in U.S. interest rates and decreases in U.S. prices will increase the demand for dollars, leading to an appreciation of the dollar.

4 Increases in European interest rates and decreases in European prices will increase the supply of dollars in exchange for euros, leading to a depreciation of the dollar.

19.2 REAL EXCHANGE RATES AND PURCHASING POWER PARITY

As our examples of Disney World and watches from France indicate, changes in market exchange rates can affect the demand for a country's goods and services. However, we have been assuming that the prices of watches and trips to Disney World do not change. In general, prices do change over time, so we need to adjust the exchange rate determined in the foreign exchange market to take into account changes in prices. This adjustment is an application of the real-nominal principle.

 ## REAL-NOMINAL PRINCIPLE

What matters to people is the real value of money or income—its purchasing power—not the face value of money or income.

real exchange rate
The price of U.S. goods and services relative to foreign goods and services, expressed in a common currency.

Economists have developed a concept called the *real exchange rate* that adjusts the market exchange rates for changes in prices. The **real exchange rate** is defined as the price of U.S. goods and services relative to foreign goods and services, expressed in a common currency. We measure it by expressing U.S. prices for goods and services in foreign currency and comparing them to foreign prices. Here is the formula for the real exchange rate:

$$\text{real exchange rate} = \frac{\text{exchange rate} \ \times \ \text{U.S. price index}}{\text{foreign price index}}$$

We can use this formula to help us understand the factors that change the real exchange rate. First, an increase in U.S. prices will raise the real exchange rate. When foreign prices and the exchange rate are held constant, an increase in U.S. prices will raise the relative price of U.S. goods. Second, an appreciation of the dollar when prices are held constant will also increase the price of U.S. goods relative to foreign goods. And if foreign prices fall, U.S. goods will become relatively more expensive as well.

Notice that the real exchange rate takes into account changes in a country's prices over time because of inflation. Suppose Country A had an inflation rate of

20 percent, and Country B had no inflation. Suppose, too, the exchange rate of Country A's currency depreciated 20 percent against the currency of Country B. In this case, there would be no change in the real exchange rate between the two countries. Although prices in Country A would have increased by 20 percent, its currency would be 20 percent cheaper. From the point of view of residents of Country B, nothing has changed at all—they pay the same price in their currency to buy goods in Country A.

Economists have found that a country's net exports (exports minus its imports) will fall when its real exchange rate increases. For example, if the U.S. real exchange rate increases, the prices of U.S. goods will increase relative to foreign goods. This will reduce U.S. exports because our goods will have become more expensive; it will also increase imports to the United States because foreign goods will have become cheaper. As a result of the decrease in U.S. exports and the increase in U.S. imports, net exports will decline.

Figure 19.4 plots an index of the real exchange rate for the United States against net exports as a share of GDP from 1980 to 2009, a period in which there were large changes in the real exchange rate and net exports. The index, called a *multilateral real exchange rate*, is based on an average of real exchange rates with all U.S. trading partners. Notice that when the multilateral real exchange rate increased, U.S. net exports fell. As you can see in the figure, starting in both 1983 and 1996 the real exchange rate increased sharply. Subsequently, net exports as a share of GDP fell. A decrease in the real exchange rate increases net exports. For example, in 1986 and 2005, the real exchange rate began to decrease and net exports subsequently increased. The relationship between the real exchange rate and net exports is not perfect, however—other factors, such as the growth of GDP, also affect net exports.

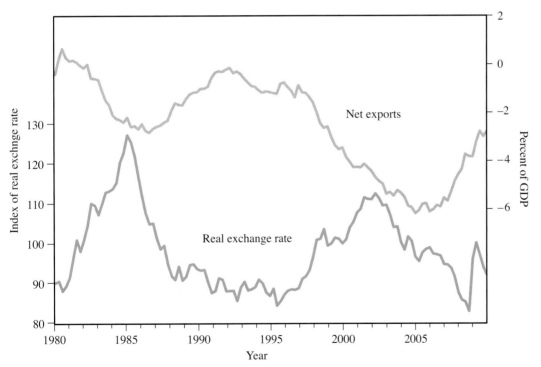

▲ FIGURE 19.4

Real Exchange Rate and Net Exports as Percent of GDP, 1980–2009
The figure shows the real exchange rate for the United States compared to its net exports as a share of GDP. Notice that, in general, when the real (multilateral) exchange rate increased, U.S. net exports fell.
SOURCE: U.S. Department of Commerce and the Federal Reserve.

APPLICATION 1

THE CHINESE YUAN AND BIG MACS

APPLYING THE CONCEPTS #1: How can the price of a Big Mac in China shed light on the U.S.-Chinese currency tensions?

In recent years, the U.S. and Chinese governments have been at odds about the appropriate value of the exchange rate between the Chinese yuan and the U.S. dollar. The United States believes that the Chinese government is holding the yuan below its true value. Can the price of a Big Mac in China shed light on this controversy?

For a number of years, the magazine the *Economist* measured the price of a Big Mac throughout the world and used these prices to explore whether currency values were too high or too low compared to the law of one price. Table 19.1 contains the results for selected countries, including China.

Big Macs sell for widely different prices around the globe, as measured in dollars compared to the $3.58 price in the United States in March 2010. They are a bargain in China at $1.83, but very expensive in Switzerland at $6.16. Table 19.1 also contains the market-exchange rate predicted by the theory of purchasing power parity. To obtain this exchange rate, divide the price of Big Macs in the foreign country by the dollar price. For example, for China the purchasing power exchange rate is

$$\frac{12.50 \text{ Chinese yuan (the price of a Big Mac in China)}}{\$3.58 \text{ (the price of a Big Mac in the United States)}}$$
$$= 3.49 \text{ Chinese yuan per U.S. dollar}$$

TABLE 19.1 BIG MAC PRICING AROUND THE WORLD VERSUS ACTUAL EXCHANGE RATES

Country	Price of a Big Mac in Local Currency	Price of a Big Mac in Dollars	Predicted Purchasing Power Exchange Rate Based on Big Mac Pricing (Foreign Currency per U.S. Dollar)	Actual Exchange Rate (Foreign Currency per U.S. Dollar)
United States	3.58 dollars	$ 3.58	—	—
United Kingdom	2.30 pounds	3.48	0.64	0.66
China	12.50 yuan	1.83	3.49	6.83
Switzerland	6.52 Swiss francs	6.16	1.82	1.06
Mexico	32.05 pesos	2.56	8.95	12.52
Euro Area	3.37 euros	4.62	0.94	0.73

At this "Big Mac" exchange rate—3.49 Chinese yuan to every U.S. dollar—the Big Mac in China would cost the same as in the United States. However, the actual exchange rate for the Chinese yuan in March 2010 when these prices were computed was 6.83 Chinese yuan per U.S. dollar, so the Big Mac was actually cheaper in China. Relative to the exchange rate implied by the law of one price, the Chinese yuan was 95 percent undervalued. This is a very large difference and cannot easily be attributed to measurement issues. This calculation gives a hint as to the Chinese-U.S. exchange rate controversy.   **Related to Exercises 2.6 and 2.7.**

SOURCE: Based on the data on Big Mac prices from the *Economist* for March, 16, 2010 and market exchange rates.

Real exchange rates vary over time, as shown in Figure 19.4. But for goods traded easily across countries (such as gold bars), we would expect the price to be the same when expressed in a common currency. For example, the price of gold bars sold in France should be nearly identical to the price of gold bars sold in New York. If the price were higher in France, demand would shift to New York, raising the price in New York and lowering the price in France until the prices were equal. The tendency for easily tradable goods to sell at the same price when expressed in a common currency is known as the **law of one price**. Metals, agricultural commodities, computer chips, and other tradable goods follow the law of one price.

If all goods were easily tradable and the law of one price held exactly, exchange rates would reflect no more than the differences in the way the price levels are expressed in the two countries. For example, if a basket of goods in Europe costs 3,000 euros and the identical basket costs $3,750 in the United States, an exchange rate of 0.8 euros to one dollar would make the costs the same in either currency ($3,750 × 0.8 euros/dollar = 3,000 euros).

According to one theory of how market exchange rates are determined, they simply reflect differences in the overall price levels between countries. According to the theory of **purchasing power parity**, a unit of any given currency should be able to buy the same quantity of goods in all countries. In our European-U.S. example, the theory of purchasing power parity predicts a market exchange rate of 0.8 euro per dollar. At that exchange rate, European and U.S. goods would sell for the same price if their products were expressed in a common currency. Research has shown that purchasing power parity does not hold precisely.

Many systematic studies have confirmed that purchasing power parity does not give fully accurate predictions for exchange rates. The reason is that many goods, such as housing and services like haircuts, are not traded across countries. The law of one price does not hold for notraded goods, which make up approximately 50 percent of the value of production in an economy. There is some truth to purchasing power parity, because exchange rates do reflect differences in the price level between countries. But, as the example with the Big Mac shows, purchasing power parity can provide a clue to exchange rates in some circumstances.

law of one price
The theory that goods easily tradable across countries should sell at the same price expressed in a common currency.

purchasing power parity
A theory of exchange rates whereby a unit of any given currency should be able to buy the same quantity of goods in all countries.

19.3 THE CURRENT ACCOUNT, THE FINANCIAL ACCOUNT, AND THE CAPITAL ACCOUNT

In this section, we examine international transactions in more detail. A useful framework for understanding international transactions is the **balance of payments**, a system of accounts that measures transactions of goods, services, income, and financial assets between domestic households, businesses, and governments and residents of the rest of the world during a specific time period.

Economists find it useful to divide international transactions in the balance of payments into three types: the current account, the financial account, and the capital account. These measures provide the most comprehensive picture of a country's balance of trade with the rest of the world and the consequences of that trade for a country's ownership of assets, such as stocks, bonds, and real estate. A country's **current account** is the sum of its

- net exports (exports minus imports),
- net income received from investments abroad, and
- net transfer payments from abroad (such as foreign aid).

If a country has a positive current account, we say that its current account is in surplus. If a country has a negative current account, we say that its current account is in deficit. If the income from investments abroad and net transfer payments is negligible, the current account becomes equivalent to a country's net exports.

balance of payments
A system of accounts that measures transactions of goods, services, income, and financial assets between domestic households, businesses, and governments and residents of the rest of the world during a specific time period.

current account
The sum of net exports (exports minus imports) plus net income received from abroad plus net transfers from abroad.

financial account

The value of a country's net sales (sales minus purchases) of assets.

A country's **financial account** transactions include all the purchases and sales of existing financial and produced assets (stocks, bonds, real estate) by the private sector and the government. The financial account is defined as the value of the country's net sales (sales minus purchases) of assets. If the United States sold $100 billion net in assets, its financial account would be $100 billion. If the value on the financial account is positive, we say the country has a surplus on the financial account. Similarly, if the value on the financial account is negative, we say it has a deficit on the financial account.

capital account

The value of capital transfer and transaction in nonproduced, nonfinancial assets in the international accounts.

A country's **capital account** transactions consist of two components. First, they include the purchase or sale of nonproduced, nonfinancial assets, such as patents, copyrights, trademarks, and leases. Second, they also include transfers of capital, such as debt forgiveness or migrants' transfers (goods or financial assets accompanying migrants as they leave or enter the country). Capital account transactions are much smaller in magnitude than transactions on the current or financial account.

Rules for Calculating the Current, Financial, and Capital Accounts

Here is a simple rule for understanding transactions on the current, financial, and capital accounts: Any action that gives rise to a demand for foreign currency is a deficit item. Any action that gives rise to a supply of foreign currency is a surplus item.

Let's apply this rule to the current account and the financial account, taking the point of view of the United States (a similar logic applies to the capital account):

1 *Current account.* Items imported into the United States show up as a deficit (negative) on the current account because we have to trade U.S. currency for foreign currency to buy them. Items exported from the United States show up as a surplus (positive) in the current account because foreigners have to trade their currency for U.S. dollars to buy those products. Income from investments abroad and net transfers received are treated like exports because they result in a supply of foreign currency for dollars. Summarizing, we have

$$\text{U.S. current account surplus} = \text{U.S. exports} - \text{U.S. imports}$$
$$+ \text{ net income from foreign investments} + \text{net transfers from abroad}$$

2 *Financial account.* The purchase of a foreign asset by a U.S. resident leads to a deficit (negative) item on the financial account because it requires a demand for foreign currency. (You can think of the purchase of a foreign asset as just another import.) A purchase of a U.S. asset by a foreign resident leads to a supply of foreign currency and a surplus (positive) item on the financial account. (Think of this as an export.) Summarizing, we have

$$\text{U.S. financial account surplus} = \text{foreign purchases of U.S. assets}$$
$$- \text{U.S. purchases of foreign assets}$$

The current, financial, and capital accounts of a country are linked by a very important relationship:

$$\text{current account} + \text{financial account} + \text{capital account} = 0$$

The current account plus the financial account, plus the capital account must sum to zero. Why?

To keep things simple, let's ignore the relatively minor capital account transactions. In that case, the current plus financial accounts must sum to zero, because any excess demand for foreign currency that arises from transactions in goods and services—that means we're looking at the current account—must be met by an excess supply of foreign currency arising from asset transactions—the financial account. Suppose the United States has a current account deficit of $50 billion, which means it is importing more than it is exporting. This excess demand of foreign currency by people in the United States can be met only by an excess supply of foreign currency that arises from the financial account—where foreign residents are purchasing $50 billion more in U.S. assets than U.S. residents are purchasing of foreign assets. In other words, the current account deficit is offset by the financial account surplus.

Let's look at this from a slightly different angle. Consider again the case in which the United States is running a current account deficit because imports from abroad exceed exports. (For simplicity, transfers and income earned from investments abroad are both zero.) The current account deficit means that, on net, foreign residents and their governments are the recipients of dollars because they have sold more goods to the United States than they have purchased.

What do foreign residents do with these dollars? They can either hold the dollars or use them to purchase U.S. assets. In either case, foreign residents and their governments have acquired U.S. assets, either dollars or other U.S. assets, such as U.S. Treasury bills. The value of these assets is the U.S. current account deficit. Because a sale of a U.S. asset to a foreign resident is a surplus item on the U.S. financial account, the value of the financial account will be equal to the negative of the value of the current account. So, from this perspective also, the current account and the financial account must sum to zero.

If a country runs a current account surplus—it is exporting more than importing, in other words—the country acquires foreign exchange. The country can either keep the foreign exchange or use it to buy foreign assets. In either case, its purchases of net foreign assets will equal its current account surplus. Because the financial account is the negative of the purchases of net foreign assets, the current account and financial account will again sum to zero.

Table 19.2 shows the balance of payments for the United States for 2008: the current account, the financial account, and the capital account. The current account is made up of the balance in goods, services, net investment income, and net transfers. In 2008, the United States had a negative balance on the goods account and net transfer, but a positive balance on the services and net income category. However, the large negative balance on the goods account made the overall current account balance

TABLE 19.2 U.S. BALANCE OF PAYMENTS: CURRENT, FINANCIAL, AND CAPITAL ACCOUNTS, 2008 (BILLIONS)

Current Account		Financial Account	
Goods	−840	Increases in U.S. holdings abroad	−1
Services	144	Increases in foreign holding in United States	534
Net Transfers	−128	Total on Financial Account (including other minor items)	507
Net Investment Income	118	**Capital Account**	1
Total on Current Account	−706	**Statistical Discrepancy**	−200
		Sum of Current, Financial, Capital Accounts and Statistical Discrepancy	0

SOURCE: *Economic Report of the President* (Washington, D.C.: U.S. Government Printing Office, 2010).

negative. The financial account includes net increases in U.S. holdings abroad (negative entries in the financial account) and foreign holdings of U.S. assets (positive entries in the financial account). Because the government collects the current account, financial account, and capital account data from separate sources, a statistical discrepancy occurs. (In 2008, this was exceptionally large because of the difficulty of understanding all the transactions involved with the financial crisis.) Once we include this statistical discrepancy, the current account, the financial account, and the capital account sum to zero.

Since 1982, the United States has run a current account deficit every year. This means the United States has run a financial plus capital account surplus of equal value for these years as well. Because a financial account surplus means foreign nations acquire a country's assets, the United States has reduced its net holding of foreign assets. In 1986, the U.S. Department of Commerce estimated the United States had a **net international investment position** of $136 billion, meaning U.S. holdings of foreign assets exceeded foreign holdings of U.S. assets by $136 billion.

Because of its current account deficits, the U.S. net international investment position fell every year. By 2008 the U.S. net international investment position was

net international investment position

Domestic holding of foreign assets minus foreign holdings of domestic assets.

(APPLICATION 2)

WORLD SAVINGS AND U.S. CURRENT ACCOUNT DEFICITS

APPLYING THE CONCEPTS #2: What factors may allow the United States to continue running large trade deficits with the rest of the world?

The *2006 Economic Report of the President* directly addressed whether the United States can continue to run large current account deficits and, of course, financial account surpluses. In the report, the government recognized that the current account deficits would eventually be reduced. However, it also highlighted a number of factors suggesting the deficits could continue for a long period of time.

The report explains that the U.S. current account deficit needs to be placed in a global context. For the United States to continue to run a current account deficit, other countries in the world need to continue to purchase U.S. assets. In essence, they must have total savings in excess of their own investment desires. As long as there are countries in this situation, the United States could continue to run a trade deficit.

In recent years, four major countries experienced circumstances that encouraged them to save by purchasing assets from abroad. Both Japan and Germany had high savings rates, but low rates of domestic investment. Slow economic growth in both countries led firms to be very cautious about making domestic investment. With limited domestic investment opportunities, savers in Japan and Germany thus placed their funds abroad. Russia has large reserves of oil and gas, and increasing energy prices in the last several years provided Russians with substantial new revenue. They decided to use this revenue to invest abroad. Finally, China had high investment rates but even higher savings rates. As a result, China as a whole invested abroad. For the United States to continue to run trade deficits in the future, these or other countries must want to continue to save more than they want to invest domestically.   **Related to Exercise 3.7.**

SOURCE: Based on *Economic Report of the President* (Washington, D.C.: United States Government Printing Office, 2006), chap. 6.

negative $3.5 trillion, meaning foreign residents owned $3.5 trillion more U.S. assets than U.S. residents owned foreign assets. You may have heard the United States referred to as a *net debtor*. This is just another way of saying the U.S. net international investment position is negative. As a consequence of the United States being a net debtor, earnings from international assets flow out of the United States to foreign countries. In the future, part of the incomes earned in the United States will be paid to foreigners abroad. This is a natural consequence of the United States being a net debtor.

What are the consequences of the large U.S. trade deficits?

When the United States runs a trade deficit, U.S. residents are spending more on goods and services than they are currently producing. Although the United States does sell many goods and services abroad (such as supercomputers, movies, DVDs, and accounting services), it buys even more goods and services from abroad (such as clothes, electronics, and machine tools).

A trade deficit forces the United States to sell some of its assets to individuals or governments in foreign countries. Here is how it works: When U.S. residents buy more goods abroad than they sell, they give up more dollars for imports than they receive in dollars from the sale of exports. These dollars given up to purchase imports end up in the hands of foreigners, who can then use them to purchase U.S. assets such as stocks, government bonds, or even real estate. In recent years, Asian investors, including foreign governments, have bought a variety of assets in the United States, including U.S. Treasury bonds and even stakes in investment banking firms. Foreign governments have accumulated considerable assets and invested them in private markets abroad through **sovereign investment funds**. Current estimates place the value of assets in these funds at $3.8 trillion.

sovereign investment fund
Assets accumulated by foreign governments that are invested abroad.

The purchase of U.S. assets by foreign investors should not be surprising, because we have been running large trade deficits with many Asian economies, especially China. These countries were willing to sell us more goods than we were selling to them, and therefore they accumulated U.S. dollars with which they could purchase U.S. assets. There is considerable debate about whether the very large U.S. current account deficits can continue.

19.4 FIXED AND FLEXIBLE EXCHANGE RATES

To set the stage for understanding exchange rate systems, let's recall what happens when a country's exchange rate appreciates—increases in value. There are two distinct effects:

1 The increased value of the exchange rate makes imports less expensive for the residents of the country where the exchange rate appreciated. For example, if the U.S. dollar appreciates against the euro, European watches will become less expensive for U.S. consumers. U.S. consumers would like an appreciated dollar, because it would lower their cost of living.

2 The increased value of the exchange rate makes U.S. goods more expensive on world markets. A U.S. exchange appreciation will increase imports, such as European watches, but decrease exports, such as California wine.

Because exports fall and imports rise, net exports (exports minus imports) will decrease. Similarly, when a country's exchange rate depreciates, there are two distinct effects:

1 For example, if the U.S. dollar depreciates against the Japanese yen, Japanese imports will become more expensive in the United States, thereby raising the cost of living in the United States.

2 At the same time, U.S. goods will become cheaper in world markets. U.S. exports will rise and imports will fall, so net U.S. exports will increase.

Fixing the Exchange Rate

Sometimes countries do not want their exchange rate to change. They may want to avoid sharp rises in the cost of living for their citizens when their currency depreciates, or they may want to keep net exports from falling when their currency appreciates. To prevent the value of the currency from changing, governments can enter the foreign exchange market to try to influence the price of foreign exchange. Economists call these efforts to influence the exchange rate **foreign exchange market intervention**.

In the United States, the Treasury Department has the official responsibility for foreign exchange intervention, though it operates in conjunction with the Federal Reserve. In other countries, governments also intervene in the foreign exchange market. To influence the price at which one currency trades for another, governments have to affect the demand or supply for their currency. To increase the value of its currency, a government must increase the currency's demand. To decrease the value of its currency, the government must increase its supply.

In Figure 19.5, we show how governments can fix, or *peg*, the price of a currency. Suppose the U.S. and European governments want the exchange rate to be 0.8 euro per dollar. The price at which demand and supply are currently equal, however, is only 0.6 euro per dollar. To increase the price of the U.S. dollar, the governments will need to increase the dollar's demand. To do this, either government—the United States or European central banks—or both, can sell euros for dollars in the foreign exchange market. This will shift the demand curve for dollars to the right until the price of dollars rises to 0.8 euro per dollar.

foreign exchange market intervention

The purchase or sale of currencies by the government to influence the market exchange rate.

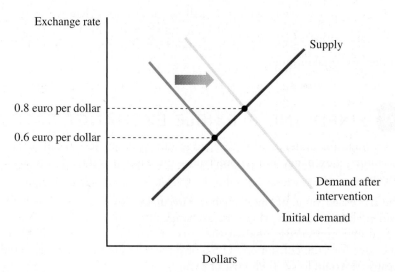

▲ **FIGURE 19.5**
Government Intervention to Raise the Price of the Dollar
To increase the price of dollars, the U.S. government sells euros in exchange for dollars. This shifts the demand curve for dollars to the right.

Conversely, if the governments want to lower the price of the dollar relative to euros, they will buy euros in exchange for dollars. By selling dollars for euros, they increase the supply of dollars. The price of the dollar therefore falls while the price of the euro increases. Note that to affect the price of the euro against the dollar, the U.S. government must exchange euros for dollars. The government will acquire and accumulate euros any time it tries to raise their price. To raise the price of the dollar, which lowers the value of the euro, the U.S. government must sell some of the euros it has accumulated. But what would happen if the United States had no euros to sell? The United States could borrow euros from European governments or persuade them to sell euros for dollars.

Fixed versus Flexible Exchange Rates

Next, we discuss two different types of exchange rate systems. Then we take a brief look at historical U.S exchange rate policy and developments in exchange rates in the world today.

FLEXIBLE EXCHANGE RATE SYSTEM   If exchange rates are determined in free markets, we have a **flexible exchange rate system**. Under a pure flexible exchange rate system, the price of a currency will rise if the demand increases more than supply and will fall if supply increases more than demand. As we have seen, a variety of factors can determine exchange rates, including foreign and domestic interest rates as well as foreign and domestic prices. Other factors, including market psychology, can also affect the value of a nation's currency. Whatever its source, an increase in the demand for currency will raise its price. We have also seen that governments may intervene to prevent currency from changing its value. In the most extreme case, there would be no change in the value of a currency.

flexible exchange rate system
A currency system in which exchange rates are determined by free markets.

FIXED EXCHANGE RATES   Whether you are in California, New York, or Indiana, all prices are quoted in dollars. No one asks whether your dollar came from San Francisco or Miami. Within the United States, a dollar is a dollar. Suppose, though, that every state had its own currency. There might be a California dollar (with a picture of the Golden Gate Bridge), an Oregon dollar (showing pictures of tall trees), and a Florida dollar (showing Disney World, of course). In principle, these dollars might trade at different rates, depending on the demand and supply of one state's dollar relative to the supply and demand for another state's dollar. For example, the Texas dollar might be worth more than the Michigan dollar, trading for 1.2 Michigan dollars.

Think how much more complicated it would be to do business. To buy goods from a mail-order company in Maine, you would have to find out the exchange rate between your state's dollar and the Maine dollar. Any large business operating in all 50 states would be overwhelmed trying to keep track of all the exchange rate movements across the states. The economy would become less efficient because individuals and businesses would have to focus a lot of their attention on exchange rates.

These same ideas apply across nations. Wouldn't it be nice if all countries either used the same currency or fixed their exchange rates against one another so that no one would have to worry about exchange rate movements? Currency systems in which governments try to keep constant the values of their currencies against one another are called **fixed exchange rate systems**. After World War II, the countries of the world operated under a fixed exchange system known as Bretton Woods. The Bretton Woods system was named after the town in New Hampshire where representatives of each nation met in 1944 and agreed to adopt this system. The system centered on the United States: All countries fixed or pegged their currencies against the U.S. dollar.

fixed exchange rate system
A system in which governments peg exchange rates to prevent their currencies from fluctuating.

In a typical fixed exchange rate system, every country that pegs its rate to a central country's exchange rate must intervene in the foreign exchange market when necessary to keep its exchange rate constant. For example, a government would have to intervene if, at the fixed exchange rate, the private demand and supply for its currency were unequal.

BALANCE OF PAYMENTS DEFICITS AND SURPLUSES   Suppose the supply of a country's currency exceeds the demand at the fixed exchange rate. An excess supply of a country's currency at the fixed exchange rate is known as a balance of payments deficit. A **balance of payments deficit** will occur whenever there is a deficit on the current account that is not matched by net sales of assets to foreigners by the private sector. For example, a current account deficit of $100 billion with net sales of assets to foreigners of only $80 billion would mean that there is an excess supply of $20 billion. With an excess supply of a country's currency in the currency market, that currency would fall in value without any intervention. To prevent the currency from depreciating in value and to maintain the fixed exchange rate, the government would have to sell foreign currency and buy its own currency. As you saw from our foreign exchange intervention discussion, if a country sells foreign exchange, its holdings of foreign exchange will fall. So you can see that when a country runs a balance of payments deficit, it has decreased its holdings of foreign exchange.

It's also very possible that the demand for a country's currency will exceed its supply at the fixed exchange rate. An excess demand for a country's currency at the fixed exchange rate is known as a **balance of payments surplus**. A balance of payments surplus arises when there is a current account surplus that is not matched by net purchases of foreign assets by the private sector. With an excess demand for a country's currency, it will rise in value without any intervention. To prevent its currency from appreciating—to maintain the fixed exchange rate, in other words—the government will have to buy foreign currency and sell its own. Because it is buying foreign exchange, its holdings of foreign exchange will increase. From this discussion, you should be able to see that when a country runs a balance of payments surplus, it has increased its holding of foreign exchange.

Under a fixed exchange rate system, countries that run persistent balance of payments deficits or balance of payments surpluses must take corrective actions. If domestic policy actions, such as changing taxes, government spending, or the money supply, do not cure the problem, a country will eventually have to change the level at which the exchange rate is fixed. A country that faces a balance of payments deficit can lower the value at which the currency is pegged to increase its net exports, a process called **devaluation**. Conversely, a country that faces a balance of payments surplus can increase the value at which its currency is pegged and reduce its net exports, a process called **revaluation**.

The U.S. Experience with Fixed and Flexible Exchange Rates

As we discussed earlier, after World War II the countries of the world adopted the Bretton Woods fixed exchange rate system. In the 1970s, the Bretton Woods system was replaced by the current system—a flexible exchange rate system—in which supply and demand primarily determine exchange rates.

If a fixed exchange rate system makes it easier to trade, why did it break down in the early 1970s? Fixed exchange rate systems provide benefits, but they require countries to maintain similar economic policies—especially to maintain similar inflation rates and interest rates. To understand this, suppose the exchange rate between the United States and Germany were fixed, but the United States has an annual inflation rate of 6 percent compared to 0 percent in Germany. Because prices in the United States would be rising by 6 percent per year, the U.S. real exchange rate against Germany would also be increasing at 6 percent per year. This difference in their real exchange rates over time would cause a trade deficit to emerge in the United States as U.S. goods became more expensive on world markets—including in Germany. As long as the differences in inflation continued and the exchange rate remained fixed, the U.S. real exchange rate would continue to appreciate, and the U.S. trade deficit would grow

balance of payments deficit
Under a fixed exchange rate system, a situation in which the supply of a country's currency exceeds the demand for the currency at the current exchange rate.

balance of payments surplus
Under a fixed exchange rate system, a situation in which the demand of a country's currency exceeds the supply for the currency at the current exchange rate.

devaluation
A decrease in the exchange rate to which a currency is pegged under a fixed exchange rate system.

revaluation
An increase in the exchange rate to which a currency is pegged under a fixed exchange rate system.

even worse. Clearly, this course of events would have to be halted under an agreed-upon fixed exchange rate system.

In the late 1960s, inflation in the United States began to exceed inflation in other countries, and a U.S. balance of payments deficit emerged—just as in our example. In 1971, President Nixon surprised the world and devalued the U.S. dollar against the currencies of all the other countries. This was a sharp departure from the rules underlying Bretton Woods. Nixon hoped that a one-time devaluation of the dollar would alleviate the U.S. balance of payments deficit and maintain the underlying system of fixed exchange rates.

However, the U.S. devaluation did not stop the U.S. balance of payments deficit. Germany tried to maintain the mark's fixed exchange rate with the U.S. dollar by purchasing U.S. dollars in the foreign exchange market. What Germany was doing was importing inflation from the United States. With the U.S. balance of payments deficit continuing, Germany was required to buy U.S. dollars to keep the mark from appreciating. Germany bought U.S. dollars with German marks. Those German marks were then put into circulation. The German supply of marks in Germany therefore increased, and this increase in marks raised the inflation rate in Germany.

Private-sector investors knew that Germany did not wish to run persistent trade surpluses and import U.S. inflation. They bet that Germany would revalue the mark against the dollar—that is, raise the value of the mark against the dollar. They bought massive amounts of German assets, trading their dollars for marks to purchase them because they thought the mark's value would eventually sharply increase. Their actions forced the German government to buy even *more* dollars to force the price of the mark upward and keep it pegged to the dollar. The resulting flow of financial capital into Germany was so massive that the German government eventually gave up all attempts to keep its exchange rate fixed to the dollar. Instead, it let the exchange rate be determined in the free market. This was the end of the Bretton Woods system.

Exchange Rate Systems Today

The flexible exchange rate system has worked well enough since the breakdown of Bretton Woods. World trade has grown at a rapid rate. Moreover, the flexible exchange rate system has seamlessly managed many diverse situations, including two major oil shocks in the 1970s, large U.S. budget deficits in the 1980s, and large Japanese and Chinese current account surpluses in the last two decades.

During the Bretton Woods period, many countries placed restrictions on the flows of financial capital by, for example, not allowing their residents to purchase foreign assets or by limiting foreigners' purchases of domestic assets. By the 1970s, these restrictions began to be eliminated, and private-sector transactions in assets grew rapidly. With massive amounts of funds being traded in financial markets, it becomes very difficult to fix, or peg, an exchange rate.

Nonetheless, countries whose economies are closely tied together might want the advantages of fixed exchange rates. One way to avoid some of the difficulties of fixing exchange rates between countries is to abolish individual currencies and establish a single currency. This is precisely what a group of European countries decided to do. They adopted a single currency, the euro, throughout Europe and a single central bank to control the supply of the currency. With a single currency, European countries hope to capture the benefits of serving a large market like the United States does with its single currency.

The United Kingdom, Denmark, and Sweden decided to remain outside this European single currency system. Their currencies, like the U.S. dollar and the Japanese yen, now float against each of the other currencies and the euro. Many other

APPLICATION 3

A DOWNSIDE TO THE EURO

APPLYING THE CONCEPTS #3: How did the 2008 financial crisis lead to problems for some countries in the Euro-zone?

When the euro was launched, countries with typically weaker currencies or fiscal discipline benefited from the discipline of one currency and a strong, single central bank. No longer would investors fear, for example, that Greece or Spain would pursue inflationary monetary polices, as monetary policy was decided by the European Central Bank. As a consequence, the stability created by the euro with the strong influence of Germany—recognized for its monetary and fiscal prudence—benefited the traditionally weaker countries.

As investment picked up worldwide in 2003, funds poured into a wide range of countries in the Euro-zone, fueling real estate and construction booms in Ireland and Spain, and financing a wide range of projects in Italy and Greece. As their economies boomed, prices and wages were driven up substantially. But when the investment boom came to a crashing end, these countries needed to make adjustments as their wage and price structure was out of line. But their options were limited because, as members of the Euro-zone, they could not depreciate their currencies. As a result, they were faced with the prospect of either making major budgetary adjustments, cutting spending or raising taxes, or a prolonged period of unemployment to reduce wages and prices. In 2010 Greece faced a major financial crisis as its budgetary imbalance was particularly severe and investors demanded major readjustments. A currency depreciation would have been a much easier solution for Greece in this situation, but this was no longer possible. This is a downside to a single currency for a collection of countries whose economies and political cultures differ sharply. **Related to Exercise 4.8.**

---

countries have tied their exchange rate to either the dollar or the yen. Some economists believe that the world will eventually settle into three large currency blocs: the euro, the dollar, and the yen.

19.5 MANAGING FINANCIAL CRISES

Hardly a year goes by without some international financial crisis. In 1994 Mexico experienced a severe financial crisis. In 1997 the Asian economic crisis began. The Argentinean economy collapsed in 2002. How do these crises originate? What policies can be followed to prevent or alleviate them?

Let's first consider the Mexican case. During the late 1980s and early 1990s, Mexico decided to fix, or peg, its exchange to the U.S. dollar. Mexico's goal was to signal to investors throughout the world that it was serious about controlling inflation and would take the steps needed to keep its inflation rates in line with that of the United States. Mexico also opened up its markets to let in foreign investors. The country seemed to be on a solid path to development.

However, in some sense, the policies proved to be too successful in encouraging foreign investment. As funds poured into the country, the demand for goods increased, and prices started to rise. This rise in prices caused an increase in Mexico's

APPLICATION 4

THE ARGENTINE FINANCIAL CRISIS

APPLYING THE CONCEPTS #4: What are the causes of financial collapses that occur throughout the globe?

During the late 1980s, Argentina suffered from hyperinflation. As part of its financial reforms, it pegged its currency to the U.S. dollar, making pesos "convertible" into dollars. To issue pesos, the central bank had to have an equal amount of dollars, or its equivalent in other hard currencies, on hand. Some economists believed this reform would bring stability to the financial system. Unfortunately, they were proved wrong.

The financial and other institutional reforms worked well in the early 1990s, but then several problems developed. As the dollar appreciated sharply on world markets after 1995, Argentina began to suffer from a large trade deficit because its currency was pegged to the dollar. Essentially, the United States' rising currency became Argentina's problem. Wage increases also pushed up the real exchange rate, exacerbating the trade deficit. The Argentinean government—including its provincial governments—found it difficult to control spending and had to borrow extensively from abroad in dollar-denominated loans. Then in 1999, Brazil devalued its currency, putting additional pressure on neighboring Argentina. As investors saw the persistent trade and government deficits that were occurring in Argentina, they became doubtful that the country could repay its debts and feared its currency would be devaluated. Local citizens also became fearful of a devaluation and tried to convert their pesos into dollars, further deepening the problem.

Eventually, Argentina was forced to default on its international debt in 2002 and freeze bank accounts. Middle-class Argentineans who still had funds in their banks suffered a sharp decrease in their wealth. A severe economic downturn ensued. The hopes of the reforms in the early 1990s had become a bitter memory. However, the Argentinean economy proved resilient and began a recovery over the next several years.   **Related to Exercise 5.5.**

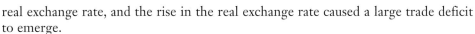

real exchange rate, and the rise in the real exchange rate caused a large trade deficit to emerge.

Initially, the trade deficit did not cause any difficulties for the Mexican government. Because foreign investors were willingly trading foreign currencies for Mexican pesos to buy Mexican securities, the government in Mexico did not have any problem maintaining its pegged exchange rate with the United States. Although the Mexicans were importing more than they were exporting, at this point they could still obtain the dollars they needed to finance the trade imbalance from foreign investors who were purchasing Mexican securities. The government did not have to intervene in the foreign exchange market to keep the price of the peso constant against the dollar. In other words, Mexico did not have a balance of payments deficit.

But then internal political difficulties ensued. Following an assassination of a political candidate and a rural uprising, foreign investors started to pull their funds out of Mexico. At this point, the Mexican government made a crucial mistake. Instead of trying to reduce its trade deficit by taking steps to reduce prices, it allowed the trade deficit to continue. Moreover, both the government and the private sector began to find that they had to borrow in dollars because foreign investors thought

Mexico might be forced to devalue the peso. If a devaluation were to occur, any lender of pesos would suffer a loss because the debt would be repaid at a lower exchange rate. Consequently, Mexican borrowers were forced to borrow in loans denominated in dollars.

Eventually, more political turmoil caused investors to pull out their funds, selling pesos for dollars. The Mexican central bank spent nearly $50 billion buying these pesos in an effort to keep the exchange rate constant. The $50 billion was not enough. Mexico ran out of dollars. Because it could no longer buy pesos to maintain the exchange rate, Mexico had to devalue, putting the peso more in line with its market value. The devaluation created even more turmoil because the government and the private sector had borrowed billions in dollars. When the peso was devalued against the dollar, the burden of these debts measured in pesos increased sharply, so more pesos were needed to pay the dollar-denominated debts. Mexico faced the prospect of massive bankruptcies and the potential collapse of its economy.

To prevent a financial collapse that could easily have spread to many other developing countries, the U.S. government (along with other international financial institutions) arranged for Mexico to borrow dollars with an extended period for repayment. This allowed Mexican banks and corporations to avoid bankruptcies and prevented a major disaster. In 1996, the Mexican government was able to pay off nearly three-fourths of the loan from the United States.

The Asian crisis had a similar flavor. Economic growth had been remarkable in Asia for over 20 years, improving to a great extent the standard of living of millions of people. In the early 1990s, several Asian countries began to open up their capital markets to foreign investors and borrow extensively from abroad. Billions of dollars poured into Asia. In many cases, there was little financial supervision, and many of the investments proved to be unwise. Companies in both Thailand and South Korea began to lose money. Domestic investors and world investors suddenly became pessimistic and pulled their funds out of South Korea and Thailand, among other Asian countries. The withdrawal of funds forced currencies throughout Asia to be devalued. Because many businesses had borrowed in dollars, the devaluations raised the burden of the debt and further deepened the crisis, taking its toll on other countries, including Indonesia, Malaysia, and Hong Kong. The International Monetary Fund attempted to help restore the health of these economies' financial systems, but in many cases, its policies were ineffective. Some economists, such as Nobel Laureate Joseph Stiglitz, believe the entire Asian crisis was an example of market overreaction and could have been avoided by bolder action from world organizations and developed countries.

Even when a country takes strong, institutional steps to peg its currency, a collapse is still possible.

These examples highlight some of the many factors that can bring about financial crises. In vast global capital markets, funds can move quickly from country to country, and economic policies sometimes do not keep pace with changing political and economic developments. It can be extremely difficult to maintain a fixed exchange rate in this environment. The flow of funds, moreover, is often so large that financial failures can rock trade and commerce.

The countries of the world are searching for a reliable set of rules and institutional mechanisms that can avoid and limit the spread of financial crises. Historically, the International Monetary Fund has played a key role in assisting countries that run into financial difficulties. However, in Mexico, the sums were so large that the United States was forced to take the lead in resolving the situation. In Asia, the International Monetary Fund did not have backing from the United States, so the efforts to alleviate the crisis were less successful. In Argentina, rigid adherence to a fixed exchange rate and a government that could not control spending both contributed to a collapse. As world capital markets continue to grow, governments throughout the world will almost surely be tested by new and often unpredictable financial crises, such as they experienced in 2008. They will need to anticipate and react to rapid changes in the economic and political environment to maintain a stable financial environment for world trade.

SUMMARY

In this chapter, we examined the world of international finance. You saw how exchange rates are determined in markets and how governments can influence these markets. You also learned how the real exchange rate affects the trade deficit. Behind the complex world of international financial transactions are these few simple ideas:

1 *Exchange rates* are generally determined in *foreign exchange markets* by supply and demand.

2 The *real exchange rate* is the price of U.S. goods and services relative to foreign goods and services, expressed in a common currency. The equation for the real exchange rate is

$$\text{real exchange rate} = \frac{\text{exchange rate} \times \text{U.S. price index}}{\text{foreign price index}}$$

3 The *balance of payments* consists of three types of international transactions:
- The *current account* is equal to net exports plus net income from existing investments abroad and net transfers from abroad.
- The *financial account* is the value of a country's sales less purchases of assets.
- The *capital account* is the net value of a country's capital transfers and the purchase and sale of non-produced, nonfinancial assets.

The sum of the current account, plus the financial account, plus the capital account is zero.

4 Governments can attempt to change the value of currencies by buying or selling currencies in the foreign exchange market. Purchasing a currency will raise its value; selling a currency will decrease its value.

5 A system of *fixed exchange rates* can provide a better environment for business but requires that countries keep their inflation rates and interest rates within narrow limits.

KEY TERMS

balance of payments, p. 393

balance of payments deficit, p. 400

balance of payments surplus, p. 400

capital account, p. 394

current account, p. 393

devaluation, p. 400

euro, p. 386

exchange rate, p. 386

financial account, p. 394

fixed exchange rate system, p. 399

flexible exchange rate system, p. 399

foreign exchange market intervention, p. 398

law of one price, p. 393

net international investment position, p. 396

purchasing power parity, p. 393

real exchange rate, p. 390

revaluation, p. 400

sovereign investment funds, p. 397

EXERCISES  Visit www.myeconlab.com to complete these exercises online and get instant feedback.

19.1 How Exchange Rates Are Determined

1.1 The dollar _____ against the euro when the European central bank lowers interest rates.

1.2 If the dollar appreciates against the euro, then the euro also _____ against the dollar.

1.3 The dollar _____ against the euro when the inflation rate in the United States increases.

1.4 A shift in the demand for euros and away from dollars will _____ the dollar against the euro.

1.5 **Using Demand and Supply Analysis.** Draw a demand and supply graph for British pounds to determine the effects of the following on the exchange rate between the British pound and the Japanese yen. (The vertical axis will be yen per pound.)

a. An increase in Japanese interest rates
b. An increase in the price of British goods
c. An increase in British interest rates

1.6 **The Effects of Policy Changes in Japan.** Until the early 1980s, Japan required its large insurance companies to invest all of their vast holdings in Japanese securities. At the prompting of the United States, Japan relaxed the restrictions and allowed the companies to invest anywhere in the world. What effect do you think this had on the yen/dollar exchange rate and the trade balance between the two countries?

1.7 **Exchange Rates and Rumors of Default on Government Debt.** Suppose there are rumors that a country undergoing financial difficulties is planning to default on its debt. Explain what you think will happen to that country's exchange rate.

19.2 Real Exchange Rates and Purchasing Power Parity

2.1 When the U.S. price level increases but the nominal exchange rate remains the same, the real exchange rate will _____.

2.2 When the U.S. and foreign price levels remain the same but the dollar appreciates, the real exchange rate will _____.

2.3 The law of one price provides accurate predictions of current exchange rates. _____ (True/False)

2.4 The theory of _____ states that the exchange rate between two countries should be determined by the price levels in those two countries.

2.5 **The Real Exchange Rate between Germany and the United States.** Consider the following data for the United States and Germany:

Year	German GDP Price Deflator	U.S. GDP Price Deflator	Market Exchange Rate
1980	85.7	76.0	2.49 marks per dollar
1990	113.4	119.6	2.12 marks per dollar

a. By what percent did the dollar depreciate against the mark over this period?
b. Using the formula for the real exchange rate,

$$\text{real exchange rate} = \frac{(\text{exchange rate} \times \text{U.S. price index})}{\text{foreign price index}}$$

compute the real exchange rate for 1980 and for 1990.

c. By how much did the real exchange rate change over this period?
d. Compare your answer for part (c) to your answer to part (a).

2.6 **Tall Lattés and the Real Exchange Rate between the Euro and the Dollar.** According to the *Economist*, in early 2004 the average price of a tall latté in Starbucks in the United States was $2.80. In the countries that use the euro, the average price was 2.93 euros. Because the exchange rate at this time was 0.79 euro per dollar, the dollar price of lattés in the euro area was $3.70. (Related to Application 1 on page 392.)

a. At what exchange rate between the dollar and the euro would a latté cost the same in the euro area as it did in the United States?
b. Does this calculation suggest that the euro is "too high" or "too low" relative to the dollar?

2.7 **Big Macs in Switzerland.** Traditionally, the Swiss franc has been a "safe" currency for investors around the world. Explain how this fact might help explain why Big Macs are more expensive in Switzerland than in the United States. (Related to Application 1 on page 392.)

2.8 **Energizer Batteries around the World.** According to the *Wall Street Journal* on August 5, 2008, a pack of four AA batteries sold for $2.33 in Hong Kong, $6.05 in New York, and $8.24 in Paris (prices converted to dollars). At that time, 7.80 Hong Kong dollars were equal to 1 U.S. dollar and the euro (used in Paris) cost $1.54.

a. At what exchange rates would the batteries sell in New York, Hong Kong, and Paris for the same dollar price?
b. Are the actual exchange rates "too high" or "too low" relative to these calculations?
c. The price of the batteries in Brussels was $10.57 and in Rome $6.99. Yet these cities, along with Paris, are in the euro zone. What does this suggest about the "Big Mac" method for calculating ideal exchange rates?

19.3 The Current Account, the Financial Account, and the Capital Account

3.1 Net transfers from abroad are a(n) _____ entry on the current account.

3.2 The current, financial, and capital accounts must sum to _____.

3.3 According to latest data on the U.S. international investment position, the United States is a net _____.

3.4 The United States has a large _____ on the current account but a large _____ on the financial account.

3.5 Calculating the Capital and Current Account. During the year, a country (including its government), acquires an additional $100 billion of foreign assets. At the same time, foreign residents acquire $200 billion of this country's assets. Ignoring minor items, what is the balance on the capital account for this country? What about its current account?

3.6 Understanding Sovereign Investment Funds. China, Kuwait, and other countries that have had large current account surpluses are now investing some of their funds abroad in the private sector through sovereign investment funds. These funds have raised concerns. After reading a report from the Congressional Research Service, "Sovereign Wealth Funds: Background and Policy Issues for Congress," outline what you think are the key issues. This report is available at http://fpc.state .gov/documents/organization/110750.pdf (accessed August 17, 2010).

3.7 A Debt Puzzle for the United States. As we discussed in the chapter, the United States is a net international debtor—that is, U.S. ownership of foreign assets is less than foreign ownership of U.S. assets. Yet, in 2006, net income from abroad was positive. Why is this a puzzle? Can you think of any possible explanations for this puzzle? (*Hint:* Some economists think it has to do with the types of assets that the United States holds abroad versus the types of U.S. assets that foreigners hold.) (Related to Application 2 on page 396.)

19.4 Fixed and Flexible Exchange Rates

4.1 The government _____ foreign currency for dollars if it wants to peg the exchange rate at a higher rate than would normally prevail in the market.

4.2 If there is an excess supply of a country's currency at the fixed exchange rate, there is a balance of payments _____.

4.3 The Bretton Woods agreement broke down during the decade of the _____.

4.4 When European countries joined together to create the euro, they no longer were able to conduct independent fiscal policy. _____ (True/False)

4.5 Expectations of Depreciation and Investing. Individuals wishing to invest in Turkey in 2006 had two choices. They could invest in bonds that would pay returns in 2007 in Turkish lira and earn 14.7 percent, or they could invest in Turkish bonds that would pay returns in U.S. dollars but earn only 5.2 percent. From this data, what do you think the market believes is the expected rate of depreciation of the Turkish lira against the U.S. dollar? Explain.

4.6 Dollarization. Some countries have simply decided to let the U.S. dollar or another foreign currency serve as their local currency. This is called "dollarization." Why would a country decide to abandon its own currency and use a foreign currency?

4.7 Uncovering U.S. Exchange Rate Policy. Suppose the United States reported that the U.S. Treasury had increased its holdings of foreign currencies from last year. What does this tell you about the foreign exchange policies of the United States during the last year?

4.8 Contagion. When investors decided that Greek debt was too risky and Greece could potentially default on its obligations, interest rates on Greek securities rose substantially. At the same time, Spain and Portugal also saw their interest rates rise. Countries outside the Euro-zone were less affected. Can you explain this pattern? (Related to Application 3 on page 402.)

19.5 Managing Financial Crises

5.1 When prices rose in Mexico faster than in the United States and the nominal exchange rate remained constant, the real exchange rate _____.

5.2 If a country borrows in dollars, a depreciation of its own currency against the dollar will _____ the burden of its debt.

5.3 Milton Friedman is the economist who believed that the Asian financial crisis was an example of market overreaction that could have been avoided by bolder actions from world organizations. _____ (True/False)

5.4 In the 1990s, Argentina pegged its currency to the dollar. As the dollar appreciated in world markets, this caused an increase in Argentina's trade _____.

5.5 Argentina after the Crisis. Use the Web to find data on economic growth and well-being for Argentina today. (Try searching for "Argentina and recovery.") How has Argentina fared after its financial crisis in 2002? (Related to Application 4 on page 403.)

5.6 The Dollar and the Financial Crisis. It is generally recognized that the world-wide financial crisis in 2008 originated in the United States, as its financial institutions were most active in fueling the housing boom. However, investors throughout the world had bought U.S. mortgage-related securities and this spread the global crisis. When the crisis hit, the value of the U.S. dollar rose sharply against many other currencies. What might have caused this appreciation?

Determining Exchange Rates

In this experiment, you will see how exchange rates are determined. The class is divided into two groups. One group will be buying a fixed number of Swiss francs. The other group will be selling a fixed number of Swiss francs. Each buyer will have a maximum price that he or she is willing to pay. Each seller will have a minimum price that he or she is willing to accept. Trade will take place in several rounds. In each round, buyers and sellers will meet individually and either negotiate a trade or not. If a trade results, the results will be reported to the instructor and then announced to the class. After each round, the instructor announces the prices at which Swiss francs were traded. After several rounds, what happens to the prices?

 For additional economic experiments, please visit *www.myeconlab.com*.

Glossary

absolute advantage The ability of one person or nation to produce a product at a lower resource cost than another person or nation.

accelerator theory The theory of investment that says that current investment spending depends positively on the expected future growth of real GDP.

aggregate demand curve (AD) A curve that shows the relationship between the level of prices and the quantity of real GDP demanded.

aggregate supply curve (AS) A curve that shows the relationship between the level of prices and the quantity of output supplied.

anticipated inflation Inflation that is expected.

appreciation of a currency An increase in the value of a currency.

assets The uses of the funds of a bank, including loans and reserves.

automatic stabilizers Taxes and transfer payments that stabilize GDP without requiring policymakers to take explicit action.

autonomous consumption The part of consumption that does not depend on income.

autonomous consumption spending The part of consumption spending that does not depend on income.

balance of payments deficit Under a fixed exchange rate system, a situation in which the supply of a country's currency exceeds the demand for the currency at the current exchange rate.

balance of payments A system of accounts that measures transactions of goods, services, income, and financial assets between domestic households, businesses, and governments and residents of the rest of the world during a specific time period.

balance of payments surplus Under a fixed exchange rate system, a situation in which the demand of a country's currency exceeds the supply for the currency at the current exchange rate.

balance sheet An account statement for a bank that shows the sources of its funds (liabilities) as well as the uses of its funds (assets).

bank run Panicky investors simultaneously trying to withdraw their funds from a bank they believe may fail.

barter The exchange of one good or service for another.

Board of Governors of the Federal Reserve The seven-person governing body of the Federal Reserve System in Washington, D.C.

budget deficit The amount by which government spending exceeds revenues in a given year.

budget surplus The amount by which government revenues exceed government expenditures in a given year.

capital account The value of capital transfer and transaction in nonproduced, nonfinancial assets in the international accounts.

capital deepening Increases in the stock of capital per worker.

capital gains Profits investors earn when they sell stocks, bonds, real estate, or other assets.

central bank A banker's bank: an official bank that controls the supply of money in a country.

centrally planned economy An economy in which a government bureaucracy decides how much of each good to produce, how to produce the good, and who gets the good.

ceteris paribus The Latin expression meaning that other variables are held fixed.

chain-weighted index A method for calculating changes in prices that uses an average of base years from neighboring years.

change in demand A shift of the demand curve caused by a change in a variable other than the price of the product.

change in quantity demanded A change in the quantity consumers are willing and able to buy when the price changes; represented graphically by movement along the demand curve.

change in quantity supplied A change in the quantity firms are willing and able to sell when the price changes; represented graphically by movement along the supply curve.

change in supply A shift of the supply curve caused by a change in a variable other than the price of the product.

classical models Economic models that assume wages and prices adjust freely to changes in demand and supply.

closed economy An economy without international trade.

commodity money A monetary system in which the actual money is a commodity, such as gold or silver.

comparative advantage The ability of one person or nation to produce a good at a lower opportunity cost than another person or nation.

complements Two goods for which a decrease in the price of one good increases the demand for the other good.

Consumer Price Index A price index that measures the cost of a fixed basket of goods chosen to represent the consumption pattern of a typical consumer.

consumption expenditures Purchases of newly produced goods and services by households.

consumption function The relationship between consumption spending and the level of income.

consumption possibilities curve A curve showing the combinations of two goods that can be consumed when a nation specializes in a particular good and trades with another nation.

consumption taxes Taxes based on the consumption, not the income, of individuals.

contractionary policies Government policy actions that lead to decreases in aggregate demand.

convergence The process by which poorer countries close the gap with richer countries in terms of real GDP per capita.

corporate bond A bond sold by a corporation to the public in order to borrow money.

cost-of-living adjustments (COLAs) Automatic increases in wages or other payments that are tied to the CPI.

creative destruction The view that a firm will try to come up with new products and more efficient ways to produce products to earn monopoly profits.

crowding in The increase of investment (or other component of GDP) caused by a decrease in government spending.

crowding out The reduction in investment (or other component of GDP) caused by an increase in government spending.

current account The sum of net exports (exports minus imports) plus net income received from abroad plus net transfers from abroad.

cyclical unemployment Unemployment that occurs during fluctuations in real GDP.

deflation Negative inflation or falling prices of goods and services.

demand schedule A table that shows the relationship between the price of a product and the quantity demanded, *ceteris paribus*.

deposit insurance Federal government insurance on deposits in banks and savings and loans.

depreciation Reduction in the value of capital goods over a one-year period due to physical wear and tear and also to obsolescence; also called *capital consumption allowance*.

depreciation of a currency A decrease in the value of a currency.

depression The common name for a severe recession.

devaluation A decrease in the exchange rate to which a currency is pegged under a fixed exchange rate system.

discount rate The interest rate at which banks can borrow from the Fed.

discouraged workers Workers who left the labor force because they could not find jobs.

discretionary spending The spending programs that Congress authorizes on an annual basis.

double coincidence of wants The problem in a system of barter that one person may not have what the other desires.

dumping A situation in which the price a firm charges in a foreign market is lower than either the price it charges in its home markets or the production cost.

economic growth Sustained increases in the real GDP of an economy over a long period of time.

economic model A simplified representation of an economic environment, often employing a graph.

economics The study of choices when there is scarcity.

entitlement and mandatory spending Spending that Congress has authorized by prior law, primarily providing support for individuals.

entrepreneurship The effort used to coordinate the factors of production—natural resources, labor, physical capital, and human capital—to produce and sell products.

equilibrium output The level of GDP at which planned expenditure equals the amount that is produced.

euro The common currency in Europe.

excess demand A situation in which, at the prevailing price, the quantity demanded exceeds the quantity supplied.

excess reserves Any additional reserves that a bank holds above required reserves.

excess supply A situation in which the quantity supplied exceeds the quantity demanded at the prevailing price.

exchange rate The price at which currencies trade for one another in the market.

expansion The period after a trough in the business cycle during which the economy recovers.

expansionary policies Government policy actions that lead to increases in aggregate demand.

expectations of inflation The beliefs held by the public about the likely path of inflation in the future.

expectations Phillips curve The relationship between unemployment and inflation when taking into account expectations of inflation.

expected real interest rate The nominal interest rate minus the expected inflation rate.

export A good or service produced in the home country (for example, the United States) and sold in another country.

factors of production The resources used to produce goods and services; also known as *production inputs* or *resources*.

federal funds market The market in which banks borrow and lend reserves to and from one another.

federal funds rate The interest rate on reserves that banks lend each other.

Federal Open Market Committee (FOMC) The group that decides on monetary policy: It consists of the 7 members of the Board of Governors plus 5 of 12 regional bank presidents on a rotating basis.

Federal Reserve Bank One of 12 regional banks that are an official part of the Federal Reserve System.

fiat money A monetary system in which money has no intrinsic value but is backed by the government.

financial account The value of a country's net sales (sales minus purchases) of assets.

financial intermediaries Organizations that receive funds from savers and channel them to investors.

fiscal policy Changes in government taxes and spending that affect the level of GDP.

fixed exchange rate system A system in which governments peg exchange rates to prevent their currencies from fluctuating.

flexible exchange rate system A currency system in which exchange rates are determined by free markets.

foreign exchange market intervention The purchase or sale of currencies by the government to influence the market exchange rate.

frictional unemployment Unemployment that occurs with the normal workings of the economy, such as workers taking time to search for suitable jobs and firms taking time to search for qualified employees.

full employment The level of unemployment that occurs when the unemployment rate is at the natural rate.

full-employment output The level of output that results when the labor market is in equilibrium and the economy is producing at full employment.

GDP deflator An index that measures how the prices of goods and services included in GDP change over time.

General Agreement on Tariffs and Trade (GATT) An international agreement established in 1947 that has lowered trade barriers between the United States and other nations.

gold standard A monetary system in which gold backs up paper money.

government purchases Purchases of newly produced goods and services by local, state, and federal governments.

gross domestic product (GDP) The total market value of final goods and services produced within an economy in a given year.

gross investment Total new investment expenditures.

gross national product GDP plus net income earned abroad.

growth accounting A method to determine the contribution to economic growth from increased capital, labor, and technological progress.

growth rate The percentage rate of change of a variable from one period to another.

growth version of the quantity equation An equation that links the growth rates of money, velocity, prices, and real output.

human capital The knowledge and skills acquired by a worker through education and experience and used to produce goods and services.

hyperinflation An inflation rate exceeding 50 percent per month.

illiquid Not easily transferable to money.

import A good or service produced in a foreign country and purchased by residents of the home country (for example, the United States).

import licenses Rights, issued by a government, to import goods.

import quota A government-imposed limit on the quantity of a good that can be imported.

individual demand curve A curve that shows the relationship between the price of a good and quantity demanded by an individual consumer, *ceteris paribus*.

individual supply curve A curve showing the relationship between price and quantity supplied by a single firm, *ceteris paribus*.

infant industries Industries that are at an early stage of development.

inferior good A good for which an increase in income decreases demand.

inflation Sustained increases in the average prices of all goods and services.

inflation rate The percentage rate of change in the price level.

inside lags The time it takes to formulate a policy.

intermediate goods Goods used in the production process that are not final goods and services.

labor Human effort, including both physical and mental effort, used to produce goods and services.

labor force The total number of workers, both the employed and the unemployed.

labor force participation rate The percentage of the population over 16 years of age that is in the labor force.

labor productivity Output produced per hour of work.

Laffer curve A relationship between the tax rates and tax revenues that illustrates that high tax rates could lead to lower tax revenues if economic activity is severely discouraged.

law of demand There is a negative relationship between price and quantity demanded, *ceteris paribus*.

law of one price The theory that goods easily tradable across countries should sell at the same price expressed in a common currency.

law of supply There is a positive relationship between price and quantity supplied, *ceteris paribus*.

learning by doing Knowledge and skills workers gain during production that increase productivity and lower cost.

lender of last resort A central bank is the lender of last resort, the last place, all others having failed, from which banks in emergency situations can obtain loans.

leverage Using borrowed funds to purchase assets.

liabilities The sources of funds for a bank, including deposits and owners' equity.

liquid Easily convertible into money on short notice.

liquidity demand for money The demand for money that represents the needs and desires individuals and firms have to make transactions on short notice without incurring excessive costs.

liquidity trap A situation in which nominal interest rates are so low, they can no longer fall.

long-run aggregate supply curve A vertical aggregate supply curve that reflects the idea that in the long run, output is determined solely by the factors of production and technology.

long run in macroeconomics The period of time in which prices have fully adjusted to any economic changes.

long-run neutrality of money A change in the supply of money has no effect on real interest rates, investment, or output in the long run.

M1 The sum of currency in the hands of the public, demand deposits, other checkable deposits, and traveler's checks.

M2 M1 plus other assets, including deposits in savings and loans accounts and money market mutual funds.

macroeconomics The study of the nation's economy as a whole; focuses on the issues of inflation, unemployment, and economic growth.

marginal benefit The additional benefit resulting from a small increase in some activity.

marginal change A small, one-unit change in value.

marginal cost The additional cost resulting from a small increase in some activity.

marginal propensity to consume (MPC) The fraction of additional income that is spent.

marginal propensity to import The fraction of additional income that is spent on imports.

marginal propensity to save (MPS) The fraction of additional income that is saved.

market demand curve A curve showing the relationship between price and quantity demanded by all consumers, *ceteris paribus*.

market economy An economy in which people specialize and exchange goods and services in markets.

market equilibrium A situation in which the quantity demanded equals the quantity supplied at the prevailing market price.

market supply curve A curve showing the relationship between the market price and quantity supplied by all firms, *ceteris paribus*.

Medicaid A federal and state government health program for the poor.

Medicare A federal government health program for the elderly.

medium of exchange Any item that buyers give to sellers when they purchase goods and services.

menu costs The costs associated with changing prices and printing new price lists when there is inflation.

microeconomics The study of the choices made by households, firms, and government and how these choices affect the markets for goods and services.

minimum supply price The lowest price at which a product will be supplied.

monetarists Economists who emphasize the role that the supply of money plays in determining nominal income and inflation.

monetary policy The range of actions taken by the Federal Reserve to influence the level of GDP or inflation.

monetizing the deficit Purchases by a central bank of newly issued government bonds.

money Any items that are regularly used in economic transactions or exchanges and accepted by buyers and sellers.

money illusion Confusion of real and nominal magnitudes.

money market The market for money in which the amount supplied and the amount demanded meet to determine the nominal interest rate.

money multiplier The ratio of the increase in total checking account deposits to an initial cash deposit.

multiplier The ratio of the total shift in aggregate demand to the initial shift in aggregate demand.

multiplier-accelerator model A model in which a downturn in real GDP leads to a sharp fall in investment, which triggers further reductions in GDP through the multiplier.

national income The total income earned by a nation's residents both domestically and abroad in the production of goods and services.

natural rate of unemployment The level of unemployment at which there is no cyclical unemployment. It consists of only frictional and structural unemployment.

natural resources Resources provided by nature and used to produce goods and services.

neoclassical theory of investment A theory of investment that says both real interest rates and taxes are important determinants of investment.

net exports Exports minus imports.

net international investment position Domestic holding of foreign assets minus foreign holdings of domestic assets.

net investment Gross investment minus depreciation.

new growth theory Modern theories of growth that try to explain the origins of technological progress.

nominal GDP The value of GDP in current dollars.

nominal interest rate Interest rates quoted in the market.

nominal value The face value of an amount of money.

nominal wages Wages expressed in current dollars.

normal good A good for which an increase in income increases demand.

normative analysis Answers the question "What *ought to be?*"

open economy An economy with international trade.

open market operations The purchase or sale of U.S. government securities by the Fed.

open market purchases The Fed's purchase of government bonds from the private sector.

open market sales The Fed's sale of government bonds to the private sector.

opportunity cost What you sacrifice to get something.

outside lags The time it takes for the policy to actually work.

outsourcing Firms producing components of their goods and services in other countries.

owners' equity The funds provided to a bank by its owners.

peak The date at which a recession starts.

perfectly competitive market A market with many sellers and buyers of a homogeneous product and no barriers to entry.

permanent income An estimate of a household's long-run average level of income.

personal disposable income Personal income that households retain after paying income taxes.

personal income Income, including transfer payments, received by households.

physical capital The stock of equipment, machines, structures, and infrastructure that is used to produce goods and services.

planned expenditures Another term for total demand for goods and services.

political business cycle The effects on the economy of using monetary or fiscal policy to stimulate the economy before an election to improve reelection prospects.

positive analysis Answers the question "What *is*?" or "What *will be*?"

predatory pricing A firm sells a product at a price below its production cost to drive a rival out of business and then increases the price.

present value The maximum amount a person is willing to pay today to receive a payment in the future.

price discrimination The practice of selling a good at different prices to different consumers.

private investment expenditures Purchases of newly produced goods and services by firms.

procyclical Moving in the same direction as real GDP.

production function The relationship between the level of output of a good and the factors of production that are inputs to production.

production possibilities curve A curve that shows the possible combinations of products that an economy can produce, given that its productive resources are fully employed and efficiently used.

purchasing power parity A theory of exchange rates whereby a unit of any given currency should be able to buy the same quantity of goods in all countries.

Q-theory of investment The theory of investment that links investment spending to stock prices.

quantity demanded The amount of a product that consumers are willing and able to buy.

quantity equation The equation that links money, velocity, prices, and real output. In symbols, we have $M \times V = P \times y$.

quantity supplied The amount of a product that firms are willing and able to sell.

rational expectations The economic theory that analyzes how the public forms expectations in such a manner that, on average, it forecasts the future correctly.

real business cycle theory The economic theory that emphasizes how shocks to technology can cause fluctuations in economic activity.

real exchange rate The price of U.S. goods and services relative to foreign goods and services, expressed in a common currency.

real GDP A measure of GDP that controls for changes in prices.

real GDP per capita Gross domestic product per person adjusted for changes in prices. It is the usual measure of living standards across time and among countries.

real interest rate The nominal interest rate minus the inflation rate.

real value The value of an amount of money in terms of what it can buy.

real wage The wage rate paid to employees adjusted for changes in the price level.

recession Commonly defined as six consecutive months of declining real GDP.

required reserves The specific fraction of their deposits that banks are required by law to hold as reserves.

reserve ratio The ratio of reserves to deposits.

reserves The portion of banks' deposits set aside in either vault cash or as deposits at the Federal Reserve.

retained earnings Corporate earnings that are not paid out as dividends to their owners.

revaluation An increase in the exchange rate to which a currency is pegged under a fixed exchange rate system.

Ricardian equivalence The proposition that it does not matter whether government expenditure is financed by taxes or debt.

rule of 70 A rule of thumb that says output will double in $70/x$ years, where x is the percentage rate of growth.

saving Income that is not consumed.

savings function The relationship between the level of saving and the level of income.

scarcity The resources we use to produce goods and services are limited.

seasonal unemployment The component of unemployment attributed to seasonal factors.

securitization The practice of purchasing loans, re-packaging them, and selling them to the financial markets.

seignorage Revenue raised from money creation.

shoe-leather costs Costs of inflation that arise from trying to reduce holdings of cash.

short-run aggregate supply curve A relatively flat aggregate supply curve that represents the idea that prices do not change very much in the short run and that firms adjust production to meet demand.

short run in macroeconomics The period of time in which prices do not change or do not change very much.

Social Security A federal government program to provide retirement support and a host of other benefits.

sovereign investment fund Assets accumulated by foreign governments that are invested abroad.

speculative demand for money The demand for money that arises because holding money over short periods is less risky than holding stocks or bonds.

stabilization policies Policy actions taken to move the economy closer to full employment or potential output.

stagflation A decrease in real output with increasing prices.

stock of capital The total of all machines, equipment, and buildings in an entire economy.

store of value The property of money that holds that money preserves value until it is used in an exchange.

structural unemployment Unemployment that occurs when there is a mismatch of skills and jobs.

substitutes Two goods for which an increase in the price of one good increases the demand for the other good.

supply schedule A table that shows the relationship between the price of a product and quantity supplied, *ceteris paribus*.

supply shocks External events that shift the aggregate supply curve.

supply-side economics A school of thought that emphasizes the role that taxes play in the supply of output in the economy.

tariff A tax on imported goods.

technological progress More efficient ways of organizing economic affairs that allow an economy to increase output without increasing inputs.

terms of trade The rate at which units of one product can be exchanged for units of another product.

trade deficit The excess of imports over exports.

trade surplus The excess of exports over imports.

transaction demand for money The demand for money based on the desire to facilitate transactions.

transfer payments Payments from governments to individuals that do not correspond to the production of goods and services.

trough The date at which output stops falling in a recession.

unanticipated inflation Inflation that is not expected.

unemployment insurance Payments unemployed people receive from the government.

unemployment rate The percentage of the labor force that is unemployed.

unit of account A standard unit in which prices can be stated and the value of goods and services can be compared.

value added The sum of all the income—wages, interest, profits, and rent—generated by an organization. For a firm, we can measure value added by the dollar value of the firm's sales minus the dollar value of the goods and services purchased from other firms.

variable A measure of something that can take on different values.

velocity of money The rate at which money turns over during the year. It is calculated as nominal GDP divided by the money supply.

voluntary export restraint (VER) A scheme under which an exporting country voluntarily decreases its exports.

wage–price spiral The process by which changes in wages and prices cause further changes in wages and prices.

wealth effect The increase in spending that occurs because the real value of money increases when the price level falls.

World Trade Organization (WTO) An organization established in 1995 that oversees GATT and other international trade agreements, resolves trade disputes, and holds forums for further rounds of trade negotiations.

Photo Credits

Index

Key terms and the page on which they are defined appear in **boldface**.